THE ROUGH GUIDE TO

Punk

by

Al Spicer

ROUGH GUIDES

www.roughguides.com

Credits

The Rough Guide to Punk

Editors: Peter Buckley & Neil Foxlee
Layout & design: Peter Buckley
Picture research: Rufus Silber
Proofreading: David Price
Cover design: Chloe Roberts
Production: Katherine Owers

Rough Guides Reference

Series editor: Mark Ellingham
Editors: Peter Buckley, Duncan Clark,
Tracy Hopkins, Matthew Milton,
Joe Staines, Ruth Tidball
Director: Andrew Lockett

Publishing Information

This first edition published September 2006 by
Rough Guides Ltd, 80 Strand, London WC2R 0RL
345 Hudson St, 4th Floor, New York 10014, USA
Email: mail@roughguides.com

Distributed by the Penguin Group:
Penguin Books Ltd, 80 Strand, London WC2R 0RL
Penguin Putnam, Inc., 375 Hudson Street, NY 10014, USA
Penguin Group (Australia), 250 Camberwell Road, Camberwell, Victoria 3124, Australia
Penguin Books Canada Ltd, 10 Alcorn Avenue, Toronto, Ontario, Canada M4V 1E4
Penguin Group (New Zealand), Cnr Rosedale and Airborne Roads, Albany, Auckland, New Zealand

Printed in LegoPrint S.p.A

Typeset in Minion, Myriad and AG Book Stencil to an original design by Peter Buckley

A catalogue record for this book is available from the British Library

ISBN 13: 978-1-84353-264-4
ISBN 10: 1-843-53473-8

1 3 5 7 9 8 6 4 2

Contents

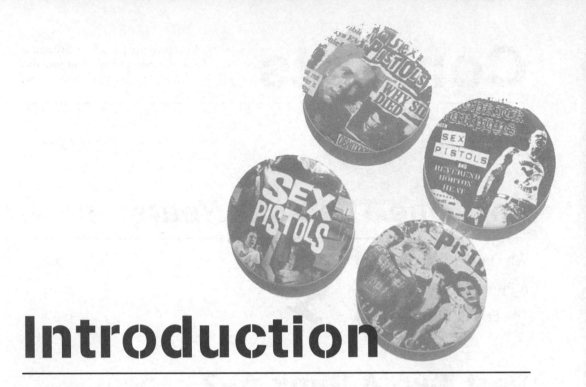

Introduction

Over the years, "punk rock" as a term has become diffused and devalued through being applied to every little gang of snot-nosed rockers to be hailed as the next big thing. It has been overused by journalists, while fans looking for the real deal have been ripped off by the record companies who flood the market with a dozen discs awash with rubbish, but wearing the "punk" tag.

So, with over thirty years of punk history to look back on, that's why I wrote this book, *The Rough Guide To Punk*. I hope it sets the record straight, by attempting to provide all the essential background to the 70s punk rock explosion, as well as biographies of all the major acts and as many of the minor delights as could be crammed in.

It also looks at the most significant of the acts that followed the first explosion, those that would never have existed had it not been for the refreshing experience of 70s punk. Overall, this Rough Guide aims to be the essential accessory for the thirtieth birthday of punk.

As well as a "who's who", this book also tries to be a "where's where". So alongside the bands and iconic figures such as Andy Warhol and even John Otway, you'll find the stories of such legendary venues as NYC's CBGB's and The Roxy,

London – each a place of punk worship and the site of unrepeatable events.

We've not tried for total anthological completeness of every last band ever to appear with a sneer on stage – size and page count constraints mean, for example, that Anti-Pasti went untouched, while both Kleenex & Lilliput remain hidden in their Swiss anonymity. If you find that your favourite punkers are absent from the register, drop us a line.

Equally, the widespread availability of almost everything most of our featured bands ever recorded – with just a few clicks on the web-warehouse of your choice – has allowed us to be ruthless in our recommendations; we suggest the most immediately appealing, punkiest product we can find, and that has generally meant opting for an artist's earliest, rawest and least pretentious records. The Fall's catalogue, for example, is long enough to merit a book in itself, but only the most deranged and obsessive of fans would care to listen to all of them (OK, I'm guilty). We've chosen what we consider to be each act's most representatively young, loud and noisy stuff; material that the performers themselves might prefer not to be reminded of, but which at one time, had them hanging from the P.A. stacks, screaming with sheer excited commitment.

While insisting throughout this book that punk is by no means dead, we do realize that it's not the headline-grabbing craze it used to be: consequently we've concentrated more on the minutiae of old bands' work rather than chasing the latest Internet-driven nine-days-wonder to appear on MySpace (excellent resource and fine website though it may be).

Punk today tends to be small-scale and hard to pin down, and with news of the latest happenings being spread through the web, word of mouth and secret networks of noise enthusiasts worldwide, readers are recommended to get online and get out to a club to experience this music live and at first hand. However much I hope you love this book, punk is something you take part in, not a topic for academic study.

There have, frankly, been more exciting times for punk rock, but it still manages to set termites at the foundations of society's most cherished ideals and it's sure to rock your behind right out of your underwear. Like Patti Smith said: "We created it, let's take it over!".

Al Spicer, Greenwich, May 2006

About This Book

Part one, which follows, highlights the best stories of punk's turbulent past, linking major events in the world outside to concurrent happenings down in the sewers and basement rock'n'roll clubs. Telling the tales in bullet point detail, its chronological layout links together people and bands with the places where they hung out and the kids went berserk. If you need to know whether 999 released "Nasty Nasty" before Skylab fell to Earth, this is where to look, but it will also tell you who they were competing with for ticket-sale income and chart position. The section explores the social upheavals, urban rioting, strikes and economic collapse that surrounded punk's first flowering, follows it into the underground where it lurked for much of the 80s and 90s before re-surfacing to look at its relevance in the world today.

Part two is the bulk of the guide; with the major A–Z listing of bands, people and places. Most entries start with a typical quote from a member of the band, chosen to summarize as pithily as possible the group's attitude to the fans, the biz or the world at large. A lot of these musicians aren't the most eloquent of types, but they make up for what they might lack in verbal elegance in hardcore dues paid.

A lot of the bands we cover extended their careers way past their shelf-life, pressing on through decreasing returns until the message finally sank in: The Ramones, for example, stuck together for twenty years of tour-bus hell, Splodgenessabounds went on and on, and even The Offspring's cerebral post-grad adoption of punk's gleeful dumbness is beginning to grate. Elvis Costello and the brainy team rapidly outgrew the confines of traditional punk, and many moved on to successful un-punk careers in more mainstream musical fields. Here, we cover their time as spikey headed rebels, again as a result of space being tight, bidding them farewell when they hit the mainstream.

Part three, "Punkology", recommends and reminisces at the same time: suggesting books to read, TV show repeats to watch out for, movies to rent and DVD documentaries to fill up your shelf space. There is a phenomenal, and wallet-emptying amount of material categorized as "punk rock" on sale these days; not all of it is worthy of the label and quite a large proportion of it – particularly the "live: in concert" type – is of such rotten quality as to be unlistenable. We've cut the crap and kept to the cream of the crop here, as in the rest of the book, but it's never a bad idea to check the online reviews before you fork out your cash.

Recommendations And Playlists

We've recommended the best of the bands' recordings whenever there's product available. In some cases this has meant suggesting a compilation released long after the demise of the act concerned, in others it has meant listing representative studio albums covering decades of uncompromising output. New editions of classic albums continue to spew forth from the big labels, with previously out of print classics forever re-jacketed and set to battle it out again on the record store shelves, so, again, check online before you buy to be sure you are getting what you want.

This book also recognizes that it is being published at a time when the music industry is still coming to terms with the growth of music download services – such as Apple's iTunes, a huge success partly due to the popularity of the same company's digital music player, the iPod.

Nearly all such services offer a certain amount of punk rock, and more often than not allow you to pay-per-track, rather than buy the whole album. With this in mind, you'll find this book littered with "Playlists" comprising cuts from various sources. And what's more, we managed to squeeze a few **Celebrity Playlists** out of some stars, *Desert Island Discs*-style. So if you wanna know what turned **Billy Bragg** or **Paul Weller** on to punk, or check out **Glen Matlock**'s favourite punk classics, look no further.

Acknowledgements

The book would never have been finished had it not been for the magnificent efforts of Peter Buckley and Neil Foxlee, jointly responsible for turning my grit into the pearl of literature currently adorning your hand.

Thanks to all the friends who helped out with advice and encouragement during the preparation of this book. Massive gratitude and love goes especially to Jane Holly. There's an extra-large side order of respect to Jason Gross of Perfect Sound Forever. I'd like also to mention those who made their own rare, much-loved memorabilia available, particularly John Richardson, and to big up the musicians who helped separate fact from fiction in some of the more convoluted histories and band biographies.

Much backstage magic and aid came from Andrew Lockett, Duncan Clark and Joe Staines, with inspirational guidance coming from Martin Dunford and Mark Ellingham.

Part One

The Punk Years

Part One
Why Punk?
Why Then?

The punk explosion of the late 1970s, which hurtled the Sex Pistols (among others) into the media spotlight, has been labelled many things. On one level it can be seen as an angry and confrontational reaction against the big bad world outside, a rejection of bourgeois conformity and the status quo. But it can also be explained more dynamically – and more straightforwardly – in terms of a meaty combination of teenage rock'n'rollers, art students with a yearning to be noticed and fashion designers hoping to sell a heap of very expensive trousers.

Critics still remain divided about the cultural significance of the punk phenomenon. Was it just another youth craze (with a hairstyle calculated to drive the parents crazy), or did it offer a real challenge to the complacency of the times? A challenge that was more than just musical and sartorial, but political as well? Certainly its unique style was derived from a stew of influences and ideas, which included nihilism, anarchism, Dadaism, and the confrontational aesthetics of the **Situationists** (for their full story, see box on p.6).

1976 and 77 remain the years that most people associate with the "punk" tag – the **Sex Pistols**, the fashion, London, leather, studs, mohawks, and more. And yet England's late-70s rude awakening, though undoubtedly important, is only one piece of the punk story, a

What's In A Word?

Dave Marsh may well get the credit for coining the term "punk rock" in 1971 (see p.12), but the word punk has been around for much longer than that. It first surfaced around 1600 when it meant a whore or prostitute, and was used by **Shakespeare** in his play *Measure for Measure* ("She may be a punk; for many of them are neither maid, widow, nor wife"). A second definition – perhaps related to the first – originated in the US around 1700 and meant a piece of **rotten wood** or fungus which, when dry, could be used as tinder. Different usages then started to proliferate like fungus, usually with the sense of something cheap or rubbishy. In **US prison slang** of the early twentieth century it was the name given to a passive male homosexual (with the verb "to punk" meaning to bugger), from here it came to mean a young hoodlum or petty criminal, cropping up in every other **Hollywood** crime movie from *The Public Enemy* (1931) to *Dirty Harry* (1971). And that's more or less how it remained until the first punk rocker pogoed into sight.

story that extends back into the history of youth culture, and forward to the present day, when many young bands, both corporately manufactured and defiantly underground, still fight the good fight under the punk banner.

State Of The Nations

But to linger for a moment in 1977, the year that *Star Wars* changed the face of popular cinema and Elvis Presley departed this earth, history seems to be shouting that the punk explosion was inevitable. In Britain, political frustration, surging unemployment and a gag-reflex to the patriotic froth generated in celebration of **Queen Elizabeth's Silver Jubilee** gave punk's raw noise a particular spice and vigour.

The UK had been either in decline, recession, stagflation or worse since the end of the swinging 60s. Years of rotten government and industrial decline had turned many inner city areas into brutal wastelands of decay, while the youth – many unemployed – were set at one another's throats often by nothing more than allegiance to this soccer team or that. And as the decade that saw beige, brown, orange and gold recommended as a desirable colour scheme for the home, the 70s had little going for it stylistically either.

Though Britain was in the grip of a mind-set in which everything not specifically permitted was forbidden, in the US, things were even worse. Reeling from the double-whammy of the **Watergate** scandal (1972–74), which led to the collapse of Richard Nixon's presidency, and the end of the **Vietnam War** (1973), America was in shock, denial and a state of deep emotional trauma. Neither

Families around the UK joined in with the celebratory mood of the Silver Jubilee...

Frampton Comes Alive!

the excesses of stadium rock, the nationwide success of *Quaalude* sleeping pills, nor that godawful *Frampton Comes Alive* album (still one of the most successful live LPs of all time) did much to ease the nation's pain.

A New Youth Culture

Teenage culture was well overdue a shave and a haircut. Pre-punk, the wildest youth on the scene were the hippies, long-haired stoner revolutionaries who tended to be happy once they'd confronted a few sexual and clothing taboos, chowed down on the acid and passively watched the world go by in a haze of dope smoke. OK, it's true that in the late 60s – at least in the UK – skinheads and bovver boys offered an aggressive (and sometimes fascistic) alternative to hippy, peace-lovin' idealism. But punks were even more ready to tear down the barriers – sexual, musical, cultural – frequently empowered by, and cranked up to the gills on, speed.

Punk's most obvious cultural marker was the outrageous clothes that the earliest and most extreme fans adopted. Granted, they steered clear of the total public nudity that braver hippies were fond of, but overexposure was common (**Siouxsie Sioux** being the first nipple-parading punkette to make the papers). When set off with Nazi paraphernalia, fluorescent hair, assorted studs and zips, plus the accessories from a dungeon-master's bondage nightmare, punks on the street in their full regalia were a spectacular and provocative sight – which was just what they intended.

"WHAT ARE YOU REBELLING AGAINST, JOHNNY?" "WHADDYA GOT?" MARLON BRANDO IN THE WILD ONE

Spreading The Word

More than just another kids' fad for rock'n'roll, punk came with a philosophy that was influenced by the anti-establishment turmoil still reverberating from the 60s. 1968 was the big year: in the US protests against the war in Vietnam reached their height, while in France a series of student strikes at Paris universities developed into a near-revolutionary confrontation with authority. Two of UK punk's prime movers, art school chums **Jamie Reid** and **Malcolm McLaren**, were caught up in this wave of revolting students. In particular these new futurist babies

Swastika Chic?

By appropriating the symbol of the most viciously destructive political force of the twentieth century, punks were not identifying themselves as Nazis. They weren't even the first counter-cultural group to go there: Hell's Angels regularly sported swastikas, iron crosses and even German helmets.

For punks like **Siouxsie** and **Sid Vicious** it became just one more ingredient in the imagery of offence – not devoid of meaning, but mainly a way of getting up the noses of the straight and the narrow. No more significant than safety pins and S&M bondage wear. When you combined these ingredients together – as in **Vivienne Westwood**'s infamous "Destroy" T-shirt, in which Jesus, the Queen and the swastika all jostled for attention – you got the kind of rule-breaking, confrontational message that the Situationists would have loved.

"I CALLED MY CONGRESSMAN AND HE SAID, QUOTE 'I'D LIKE TO HELP YOU SON, BUT YOU'RE TOO YOUNG TO VOTE'" EDDIE COCHRAN SUMMERTIME BLUES

were grooving to the confrontational, bourgeois-baiting tactics of the Situationists, an international group of political artists (or artistic politicos) with the best postcards, the wittiest slogans and a sharp awareness that the street was the canvas on which to splatter their message.

Eight years later, when the idealism of the 60s had well and truly faded, the strategies and rhetoric of street protest were still going strong. So when mainstream politics wouldn't even listen to what was driving the kids insane, the Sex Pistols' cry of "Anarchy In The UK" seemed like a viable alternative. In the absence of any genuine democratic outlet – much needed in the light of the rise of the right and the accelerating decay of James Callaghan's Labour government – young people found themselves alongside bands such as **The Clash**, **Crass**, **Exploited**, **Dead Kennedys** and **Black Flag**, obliged to pile in with their own opinions and declare which side they were on.

But that's not to say that there was ever a coherent, overarching set of punk beliefs: different bands stood for different things, with the **Sex Pistols** at the head of the nihilist, no future, blank generation tendency (closely followed by **The Fall** and **Siouxsie And The Banshees**). The Clash, on the other hand, espoused a more radical and active political position, regularly playing at Rock Against Racism and Anti-Nazi League gigs. In the US the Ramones were simply the rawest rockers around while the Dead Kennedys came to be the politicized punk band of choice.

What did bind the various strands of punk together was a "fuck you" attitude and a DIY aesthetic that meant any snotty-nosed teenager could

The Situationist Connection

Though many punks on the 1977 scene would have stared at you blankly had you suggested discussing the finer points of the avant-garde, for others Punk derived many of its ideas and strategies from previous movements within left-field twentieth-century art. Some of these are pretty easy to spot: especially when you think of the nihilism of the **Dadaists**, whose anti-art, anti-bourgeoise mentality was, in part, a reaction to the destructive absurdity of World War I. Then there was **Pop Art**, a movement that appropriated and celebrated the cheap and disposable world of comic strips and commercial art, and tried to break down the barrier between art and everyday life.

However, the most significant influence on Punk "ideology" came from the **Situationists**, a movement that began in the late 1950s. The Situationist International, as it was known, was a forum not just for radical artists, but for political activists and philosophers. It provided a playful critique of western consumer capitalism through the creation of "situations" – interventions within cities which would "increase the non-mediocre part of living and reduce null moments as much as possible…". By the 60s, the dominant figure within the SI was the French poet and film-maker **Guy Debord**, who in 1967 published a series of provocative aphorisms entitled *The Society of the Spectacle*. For Debord the developed world had become enslaved by the seductive nature of capitalism and its attendant media, and experience had been replaced by spectacle.

In the UK **Malcolm McLaren**, **Vivienne Westwood** and **Jamie Reid** were all Situ-literate and had a strong sense of how the Situationist concepts fitted in with what was going on around them. In more recent times, the Situationist ideal was again reclaimed by post-punkers such as **Nation Of Ulysses** in The States and the **Manic Street Preachers** in the UK.

join in. **Home-made fanzines** spread like the plague, with cut'n'pasted letters, hand-drawn images and collage all contributing to a weird and wonderful mix. *Sniffin' Glue* (see p.25) was the the UK trailblazer, founded in 1976 by **Mark Perry**, it lasted twelve issues until Perry's band **Alternative TV** started to take off. In the same year another fanzine, *Sideburns*, contained the legendary diagram and instructions "This is a chord. This is another. This is a third. Now Form A Band."

Music In The 70s

It almost goes without saying that when a new musical movement appears from the underground it will take pot shots at the exposed soft underbelly of the established musical form of the day. So it was with punk, which tried hard to kick the support out from under rock's newly created aristocracy. The likes of Bowie, Fleetwood Mac and more notoriously Led Zeppelin, The Rolling Stones and Queen were living a life so far removed from that of the guttersnipe fans who paid for it, that a degree of separation, if not outright hostile envy, was bound to break out sooner or later.

These bands were hiring airliners to wing them from secluded hideaway to gig and back in the same day. The music itself had mutated into etiolated over complex "serious rock" – a baroque parody of its ancestry and, for many, a betrayal of its earthy roots. Punk had the dinosaurs of rock well and truly in its sights, with **Johnny Rotten** famously wearing a Pink Floyd T-shirt with the words "I HATE" scrawled over it.

In contrast to these behemoths, pop music was more brightly coloured, more grotesque and louder than ever; Slade's blend of psychedelic tartans, outrageous mutton-chop whiskers, hair and glitter, for example, sent sensitive youngsters into spasm every time the group stomped onto *Top Of The Pops*. And while others were trying to spread the word about Northern Soul to the rest of the UK, elsewhere, young, otherwise intel-

The Dark Side Of Glitter And Glam Rock

Glam rock took pop music's gender-bending to new and exciting extremes. While everybody knew there were homosexuals in the business, until **David Bowie** made his big "I'm gay" announcement in the *Melody Maker*, nobody had admitted it. And before the silver dust had a chance to settle, glitter (glam's younger pop sibling of indeterminate sex) exploded in a flurry of **Elton John, Gary Glitter, Suzi Quatro** and **The Sweet**. For pop music, these were great times indeed – last week's troglodytic bluesmen were piling on the Max Factor, and dressing up in satin flounces to entertain the teens.

Yet for every glittery Slade pop single there was a darker glam rock act snarling out nasty rock'n'roll. **Alice Cooper** got most of the headlines and painted his horrorshow with the broadest brush. Alice and the band reinvented carnival magic for a gawping audience – impaling baby dolls on the end of a sword, having himself captured, convicted and guillotined for his sins live, twice nightly.

The New York Dolls, on the other hand, along with **Iggy and The Stooges** and **Lou Reed**, now they were several different matters. They took the gender-exploration, consciousness-expansion and S&M fantasies inherent in glam to some serious extremes, losing their looks, their dreams and their health along the way. Iggy famously wanted to "...be your dog" (1969), The Dolls were addicted to the trashiest of aesthetics and Lou, when not dishing out the gossip on the lighter side of spousal abuse in "Caroline Says II" (from the album *Berlin*, 1973), was celebrating an underclass of New York citizens who lived a life of methamphetamine-powered, self-centred drag-queen rambling.

Mud and Showaddywaddy were so clean cut and wholesome by comparison, it's not surprising that the audience for glam moved on to heavy rock, basic rockabilly or punk pretty shortly after the initial rush had worn off. Once everyone was wearing mascara and eyeliner, a guy had to do some real outlandish stuff to get himself noticed.

ligent people swallowed the disco lie – turning themselves into shiny happy groovers, clad in white, good to go strut their funky stuff on a bump of coke and a rockin' beat.

As if that wasn't enough, at roughly the same time during the early 70s, **Adult Oriented Rock** (a phrase to chill the blood) was invented. Bands like Supertramp and 10cc had their brief moments of glory and, as a wave of style overwhelmed any musical substance, the cult of the producer as king began. Every nuance of each moment in the studio was miked, taped, remixed, compressed and boosted until if you listened really hard, you could almost make out the tinkling of razor blade against mirror.

A New Sound

Clearly, a mid-70s return to the simple purity of three chords, a slogan and a sneer was well overdue. In the US the loudest, fiercest, most in-yer-face music was to be found at **CBGB's**, a New York club which from 1973 hosted such cutting edge types as the **Patti Smith Group, Talking Heads, Television** and, of course, **The Ramones**. To celebrate and record the new sounds, a magazine was founded called simply *Punk*. It first hit the streets in December 1975 with an interview with the Ramones in which they claimed to play rock'n'roll "...the way it should be – entertaining, a lot of fun, sexy, dynamic, exciting". Impressed by what he saw, **Malcolm McLaren** briefly – and disastrously – took over the management of The **New York Dolls**, before importing several aspects of New York's burgeoning punk scene back to London, where it mutated into something even more rough'n'ready.

What came next was the birth of an industry. Expressed in a nut-

Punk's Roots In US Garage

Punk rock might have picked up its name in the 70s, but its roots go way back; our brand of young, loud and snotty music started out in the 50s, when motorbikin' hillbilly hellcats such as Gene Vincent were scarring the Eisenhower generation. By the mid 60s those rockabilly rebels had settled down, spawned and now had difficult teenagers of their own to deal with.

Kicking off younger, playing louder and acting defiantly snottier than their parents had ever dared to, this new generation moved into the nation's garages and plugged in some expensive and powerful amplifiers.

Here's a top twelve, most of which can be found on Lenny Kaye's *Nuggets* collection – a massive 4CD trawl through the great lost one-hit wonders of the USA :

🎵 PLAYLIST

1. DIRTY WATER The Standells
(as covered by London's The Inmates in 1979)

2. GLORIA Shadows Of Night
(as covered by Patti Smith)

3. 96 TEARS Question Mark & The Mysterians
(as covered by The Stranglers)

4. LOUIE LOUIE The Kingsmen
(as covered by The Stooges)

5. LET'S TALK ABOUT GIRLS Chocolate Watch Band
(as covered by The Undertones)

6. STRYCHNINE The Sonics
(as covered by The Fall)

7. MR PHARMACIST The Other Half
(as covered by The Fall)

8. YOU'RE GONNA MISS ME
The Thirteenth Floor Elevators

9. FARMER JOHN The Premiers
(as covered by Neil Young)

10. NIGHT TIME The Strangeloves
(also recorded the original of "I Want Candy")

11. PUSHIN' TOO HARD The Seeds
(as covered by Saints and Sinners)

12. PSYCHOTIC REACTION Count Five
(as covered by Tom Petty)

shell, a few freshly minted groups found themselves places where they could play; with the clubs came fanzines, more new bands, independent record labels, publishers, design cooperatives and fiercely capitalist entrepreneurs.

Punk was always an enemy of slickness and virtuosity, whichever side of the pond it was spawned. But from the moment it shook free of the egg, it meant more than just four guys, drums, guitars and a rabble-rousing chorus. It's easy enough to sketch out the music in such terms, but any such outline has to be fuzzy enough to include bands as diverse as **The Lurkers** (the UK's entrant for the "archetypal punk rockers" award, and whose product was the quintessence of back-to-basics rock'n'roll) and **Alternative TV** (who melded dub, tape loops, found sound, slowness and lyrics about sexual impotence). Equally, no workable definition of punk rock would be complete that didn't encompass the sleazy bad-boy US rock of bands such as **The Dead Boys** and fellow Clevelanders **Pere Ubu** (who specialized in unearthly ethereal wailing over a stop/start rhythm).

It's a broad canvas to fill, but then and now, there have always been plenty of engaged musicians to populate every corner. If it's angry, rebellious and proletarian – either by genesis or affiliation – it counts as punk. And against all expectations, **punk has survived**: through the 80s greed-driven "me decade", the globalization of the 90s, and on into this third millennium. Arguably punk is still as bitterly relevant today as when it crystallized out of an oversaturated rock'n'roll stew three decades ago.

Cinema's Proto Punks

Cinema's enduring fascination with moody rebels shrugging their shoulders on the edge of society has provided punk rockers with plenty of characters with which to identify.

Top of the list and holder of the punk archetype award is **Marlon Brando** as Johnny Strabler in *The Wild One* (directed by László Benedek, 1953). Brando plays an outsider's outsider – a biker who wants to quit his gang (The Beetles). The movie drips with resonance for connoisseurs of bad-assed 70s rocking rebels; like many punk legends, this film's reputation had a basis in truth but grew into a scandal when the details were blown out of all recognition in a bid by the studio to stir up a media storm and get bums on seats. The flick, which outraged parents, boasts bunches of leather-clad thugs looking for a good time while small-town girl Kathie Bleeker (played by **Mary Murphy**) dreams of escape from provincial boredom.

> "I WISH I WAS GOING SOMEPLACE. I WISH YOU WERE GOING SOMEPLACE. WE COULD GO TOGETHER."
> KATHY BLEEKER
> THE WILD ONE

Meanwhile, **James Dean**'s ambivalent sexuality, and his legacy as an actor who lived fast and died young had an obvious echo in the brief stardom and gruesome end of Sid Vicious. As Jim Stark in *Rebel Without A Cause* (Nicholas Ray, 1955) – a role originally intended for Brando – Dean wrestles with the same internalized demons that would torment Tom Verlaine, Jim Carroll and Richard Hell in New York twenty years later, demonstrating a similar struggle to communicate an adolescent torrent of feelings to an adult world. Although, this being Hollywood, the movie ends with an implicit reconciliation between the wayward son and his uncomprehending parents.

Closer still to the date of punk's conception, **Robert De Niro** captured the spirit of the age with his portrayal of Travis Bickle, the emotionally scarred Vietnam vet who is the protagonist of the movie *Taxi Driver* (Martin Scorsese, 1976). His view of the city starts out poisoned and grows increasingly bitter as his world collapses. Bickle is the perfect representation of punk's "blank generation" label.

Though British cinema's portrayal of youthful dissent is rather tamer than Hollywood's, it too can claim its share of young alienated outsiders with attitude. In *The Loneliness Of The Long-Distance Runner* (Tony Richardson, 1962) **Tom Courtenay**' plays Colin Smith, a young lad who follows a (still depressingly relevant) path from petty crime to reform school in one of the typical "angry young man" stories of the period.

If... (Lindsay Anderson, 1968) was more subversive still and featured the wonderful **Malcolm McDowell** as the archetypal teenage rebel taking on the establishment in the unlikely setting of one of Britain's exclusive private schools. McDowell reappears in *A Clockwork Orange* (Stanley Kubrick, 1971) as Alex, the leader of the ultraviolent Droogs – a gang with their own subversive visual style and private language. A darkly dystopian vision (which some thought was responsible for inspiring violence in those who saw it), the film's engaging young sociopath is eventually re-programmed by the authorities through a form of aversion therapy – a moment that finds a later echo in The Ramones song "Teenage Lobotomy".

Part One
A Punk
Rock
Timeline

So far we have merely looked at a little of the historic and cultural foundations of what would become punk, and briefly outlined the way the sparks started flying. But to get a true sense of what happened we need to break things down – year by year and month by month. The following pages will take you on a rollercoaster ride through the punk years...

The First Sparks: 1965–1974

In urban centres across the USA, the late 60s and early 70s witnessed a resurgent interest in smaller-scale local scenes, while record companies employed scatter-gun marketing techniques in the hope that something, anything, would eventually make them money. With little to impress being offered by the traditional music suppliers, groups of kids began once more assembling in suburban garages to thrash out Stooges numbers, before writing their own stuff and talking their way into a club gig or two.

1965   The Velvet Underground form in NYC and define a style and attitude that continue to strike a chord to this day.

In New York it was the Velvet Underground (1965–71) who would eventually become important, though their influence (except on Bowie) would remain minuscule until the late 70s when almost everyone on the first wave of punk cited them as masters of decadent, uncaring, blank expression rock'n'roll, and their sales across Europe shot up.

The Velvet Underground never made punk rock as such; despite the absolute punk flavour of some of their best work ("Sister Ray" springs to mind as the consummate punk song with its deadpan, "this happened, then that happened" delivery), their influence was stylistic, attitudinal. This was the band, clad in the leather and the lifestyle, that perfectly bridged the gap between the images of classic silver screen rebels (see box on p.9) and the burgeoning Punk movement.

The Velvet Underground in 1969; from left to right, Doug Yule, Sterling Morrison, 'Moe' Tucker and Lou Reed. And, inset, the cover of 1967's *White Light/White Heat*, which featured the majestic "Sister Ray".

1968 The Stooges form in Detroit.

1969 MC5 release *Kick Out The Jams*, The Stooges release their eponymous classic.

Though it had to be sought out, and despite the hippy leftovers, there was some really fine music being made elsewhere too. Anyone looking for salvation by the redeeming power of overdriven guitar amplifiers set their controls for the heart of Detroit, where the local bands battled

THE PAST IS TO BE TREATED WITH RESPECT, BUT FROM TIME TO TIME IT SHOULD BE AFFRONTED, RAPED. IT SHOULD NEVER BE ALLOWED TO PETRIFY.

ALEXANDER TROCCHI – CAIN'S BOOK, 1959

every week for the ultimate decibel count in front of a sophisticated crowd that knew its rock'n'roll and would cheerily stomp on anyone trying to short-change them.

Bands such as the Amboy Dukes, SRC, Third Power, Frost, and Frijid Pink hit The Grande ballroom, Detroit's premier venue, and swamped the air waves of the city's **WABX radio station**.

Championed by local music rag *Creem* (one of the original and best sources of new music journalism), a few of the Detroit bands managed to break out of Michigan and develop a national or even worldwide following. For most, however, it was too little, too late, and the talent went back to the car factories.

As far as the punks were concerned, it was the MC5 (who formed as early as 1965) that played the role of John The Baptist – foretelling of greater marvels yet to come. The MC5 were older, more experienced, and notwithstanding the craziness that circulated around them, several dimensions wiser than the then-named **Psychedelic Stooges**. The latter bubbled up from the Ann Arbor mud in 1967, soon after the MC5 and, sharing an outlook and illegal interest or two, were kinda "adopted" by **Wayne Kramer**, **Rob Tyner**, **Fred Smith** and the guys. When the MC5 signed to Elektra, The Stooges came along as part of the deal, going on to make two ultra-heavy albums that set the standard high for anyone who would try and follow their path.

Sporting political ideals (see box opposite) and attitudes guaranteed to turn parents against them, these two bands, whose 1969 output – *Kick Out The Jams* and *The Stooges* respectively – still merits a respectful hearing, were merely the loudest, most influential and high-profile of the industrial rustbelt rockers. They propped a door open and a swathe of ever more amplified acts fell through it, turning the Detroit stomp into the first blueprint for Heavy Metal.

1970-72

1970   Stooges release *Fun House*, MC5 release *Back In The USA*; both The New York Dolls and Suicide start making music and noise.

1971   MC5 release *High Time*. Elsewhere, Dave Marsh uses the word "Punk Rock" to describe the music of ? and the Mysterians.

Iggy and the guys kept the faith and stayed true to their offensive roots, pissing off both the suits at the record company and the audience by using free-form jazz as an instrument of torture at the climax of 1970's *Fun House*. The MC5 kept the straightahead beat going with *Back In The USA* and *High Time*, while back in the nation's financial heart The **New York Dolls** and **Suicide** had started making a roughhouse, raw-edged, noisy, funtime music of their own.

MC5 & The White Panthers

Though often worshipped as simply a damn fine proto-punk rock band, the MC5 were also a group with an active and radical political spine. They played a key role within the White Panthers Party, spearheaded in 1968 by, among others, John and Leni Sinclair.

This political collective was founded in Detroit in response to an interview with Huey P. Newton, one of the co-founders of the already established and highly visible Black Panther Party. During the course of the interview Newton was questioned as to what white people could do to support the Black Panthers. He retorted that they could form a White Panther Party. The name would however be a problematic yoke for the collective, with Sinclair frequently finding his outfit mistaken for a white supremacist group.

In 1968 the White Panthers published their manifesto, which included an odd assortment of political and social goals, including the abolition of both money and conscription armies.

Also included in the shopping list of cultural revolution was a demand for a "total assault on the culture by any means necessary, including rock'n'roll, dope and fucking in the streets".

1972 The Saints get noisy down under.

1972 The Strand (soon to become the Sex Pistols) decide to give it a go in London.

1972 Malcolm McLaren in NYC.

In Sydney, Australia, 1972, a bunch of hairy bad boys stumbled upon an explosive mix of drums, guitars and frustration, blew the doors off the studio and emerged as The Saints. Almost simultaneously on the other side of the globe, a gang of thieving little ne'er-do-wells who saw rock as a way to get girls, drunk, and maybe famous had finally "accumulated" enough decent-quality instruments and amps to either form a band or

The MC5, kicking out the jams...

open an equipment hire company. Deciding on **The Strand** as a *nom de rock* (taking inspiration from heroes **Roxy Music** and their track of the same name, as much as reflecting one of London's most congested streets) they worked over a set of cover versions – mainly mod classics but with a few taken from the less-complicated 70s bands it was cool to follow (Thin Lizzy, Bad Company and their hard-stomping ilk).

Then, of course, there was **Malcolm McLaren**. With his first stab at rock'n'roll management, a young McLaren found himself in New York City, trying and failing to cope with **The New York Dolls**, swiping a pose or two from Richard Hell and learning a lot about the superiority of style over substance in the music biz. Returning to London a few months later – and his King's Road shop, *SEX*, which he ran with **Vivienne Westwood** – Malcolm spent the next few years formulating his plan.

1972 The New York Dolls play Wembley.

But we mustn't gallop too far ahead of ourselves; back in 1972 the boys from The Strand joined thousands of other young yobs in a trek out to Wembley Stadium where, in a massive contradiction in styles, **The New York Dolls** were playing support to Rod Stewart. In the triumphant aftermath of wowing London, The Dolls' drummer **Billy Murcia** died of alcohol poisoning at a post-gig party. Management sneaked the remaining members out of the country before the story hit the papers and the spoor was thrown into the whirling blades of the windmill. On the verge of giving it all up, **Johnny Thunders** and **Syl Sylvain** were shaken out of their grief and back onto the stage. **Jerry Nolan**, the hardest hitting drummer in New York, joined the band and a New York Dolls Mk II hit the road.

They Call It Punk...

The first person to put the word "Punk" next to the word "Rock" was **Dave Marsh**, critic and contributor to the classic magazine *Creem*; he used the phrase to describe the music of the US garage bands of the 1960s, specifically that of **? And The Mysterians**, whose "96 Tears" was profitably covered some years later by The Stranglers. The expression caught on immediately, and was adopted in 1972 by **Lenny Kaye** (a critic by trade, but later to become Patti Smith's star-guitar) and used as a catch-all in the liner notes to his famous *Nuggets* garage compilation (since reissued as a must-have 4CD box set).

Lenny Kaye formed a direct link between the 60s garage punks and the New York New Wave mob that sprang up in the 70s, while Patti Smith's spiritual and physical debt to The Velvet Underground (John Cale producing her first album) drew in another stream of influence. With Television and The Dead Boys whipping up a guitar storm of snotty attitude, the enduring influence of the Detroit rockers and a lipstick-full of glam-rock deviant behaviour to draw upon, New York City really had it all – even the magazine...

PUNK magazine (first published in January 1976) rippled with high-voltage rock'n'roll of the sort delivered to mid-70s New York almost exclusively by means of The Dictators, Mink De Ville, Television and the CBGB's crowd. Very much an in-yer-face publication, *PUNK* held no hero sacred (featuring a less-than-flattering cartoon of Lou Reed – an interview with whom was their star feature – on the cover of its first issue), was inspiring in the subjectivity of its reviewers and critics, and a blood-stirring influence on all the worthwhile fanzines that followed it.

Meanwhile, back in the jungle of the rock business, a disillusioned MC5 split up and **The Stooges** lost their recording contract. The band's healthy interest in drugs had turned rotten, with a good percentage of the line-up too heavily addicted to even notice they'd been fired.

1973 CBGB's opens its doors (see box overleaf).

1973 The Neon Boys start to glow.

The USA wallowed in political insecurity and scandal throughout 1973, and while the attention of the teenage nation was diverted by the cavalcade of mid-70s big-assed rock'n'roll, **Television**'s earliest known ancestors, **The Neon Boys**, released their self-titled 7" and **The New York Dolls** released *New York Dolls*. Something wicked is shambling towards the big cities, still unformed, still trying out different styles.

The "bread and circuses" approach of big-business corporate rock and roll was supremely unaware of the termites attacking the foundations. Hugely successful acts splatted ever more tricked-out sets of lighting, smoke and costume into every large stadium, creaming thousands of dollars from thousands of fans every night, and selling shedloads of records the following day. Stadium-size shows in the USA and back in Britain rendered the development of any emotional bond between performer and audience impossible. Rock at this time, was for consuming, not for joining.

1974 Blondie, The Dictators, Pere Ubu, The Ramones, The Stranglers and Talking Heads all make their first appearances.

1974 Heroin finally tears The Stooges apart, Iggy relocates briefly to the UK, introducing his own brand of poison to the local music scene.

In 1974. **Television** talked their way into a residency at the **CBGB's** club down on The Bowery in NYC, while the more successful New York Dolls put out their second album *The New York Dolls In Too Much Too Soon*. **The Stooges** gave it up, while in London, a messed up **Iggy Pop** handed Bowie control of the mixing desk and permited his treble-heavy production job out to the stores. Although many later remixed versions of the album appeared as the years passed, ironically, the resulting original mix of *Raw Power* became the band's best-selling album. The rest of the band having retired to heroin-padded trailerpark comfort, Iggy finally cleaned up his act and set out on a patchy solo career until The Stooges were revived in the 21st century to take *Fun House* on the road and show several younger generations how to kick ass.

1974 The first of 1974's two UK general elections results in a hung parliment.

Trying desperately to keep its guard up in the world arena, Britain spent the mid-70s staggering round the ring, too often on the ropes as a result

CBGB's, New York City

The place where it all started ... 315 Bowery, near the junction with Bleeker Street.

Hilly Kristal, may he live forever, was the guy behind the bar when **Tom Verlaine** sidled in one night in the mid 70s trying to find a place for **Television** to play. Hilly decided that, what with Mondays being a quiet night and this Verlaine feller obviously being a classy, privately educated kinda guy, he'd take the risk, and kiddies, this is where our story begins.

As a bar on the Bowery in Manhattan, when the city was convulsed by a heroin epidemic and where final-stage alkies woke, drank, slept and died without leaving their cardboard mattresses, CBGB's (as it was soon known) had little if no reputation to be sullied. Kristal had been doing little more than polish the glasses and count the bottles since opening in 1973. A long, narrow alleyway of a place with far more bar length than stage area, it had previously struggled to flourish – like a starved weed attempting to bloom in a bombsite – as The Palace bar but with far more space than custom, it had "Music Club" written all over it.

As for its full title, "CBGB & OMFUG", it stands for **C**ountry, **B**lue**G**rass, and **B**lues and **O**ther **M**usic **F**or **U**plifting **G**ormandizers.

Hilly had hoped homespun hillbilly hordes would head in droves to his Bowery heaven, but times were tough and hard-drinking bluegrass fans were thin on the ground when Tom Verlaine made his approach.

After a first gig, which sounded so terrible to Hilly's crystal-clear folk-trained ear that he assumed the band wouldn't want to appear before him again, he was surprised at the persistence of Television's manager in begging for a regular slot, and dumbfounded when he saw the support act they brought along – **The Ramones**.

At this stage in their career, da brudders were much better experienced for their on-stage cabaret of chaos – all false starts, missed intros and different opinions as to the running order – than for their musical offerings, and this legendary appearance struggled to last the twenty minutes the band had anticipated but, with Television and The Ramones on the same bill, both the cerebral arty side and the mental, glue-sniffing wings of **New York's New Wave** found themselves united.

As time passed, CBGB's finally began to develop a reputation, becoming known as the home of late-night rockers, especially those with an aversion to conventional opinions regarding day and night. **Patti Smith** and her group gravitated to the venue as they grew too big and too rock'n'roll for their previous poetry hangouts. By 1975 the New York scene had grown sufficiently to merit attention from the UK music press. **Charles Shaar Murray** blagged an air fare from his masters at the *NME* and hit the streets of Manhattan. The article he produced on his return was a crucial element in the evolution of UK punk, bringing the mythical bored teenagers of this country all the hot news of the New York sound of '75. His analysis and over enthusiastic trumpeting of The Ramones, **Blondie**, Patti Smith, Television, **The Heartbreakers** and **Talking Heads** softened up an audience already slavering for something raw, fresh and vitamin-enriched after half a decade of processed pap from the likes of Genesis, Yes and Jethro Tull; by the time the records began to arrive, the kids were like a pack of wolves, ripping entire boxes of product out of the hands of terrified shop assistants in their hunger for "Beat On The Brat" or "X-Offender".

Regarded as the birthplace of punk rock (along with half a dozen other venues with equally valid claims), CBGB's boomed with the New Wave and managed to maintain its new-found reputation as a respectable place to play. Punk bands from the UK considered it an essential stop on their tour schedules in their (usually doomed) attempts to "break" America and, unlike London's **Roxy** or **Vortex** clubs, it kept the standard of acts booked high enough to weather the rest of the decade and take advantage of the area's gentrification in the 80s.

It remained a cheerfully sordid, grubby-looking place until the end of summer 2005 when, despite benefit gigs a-plenty and countless musical notables and New York aristocrats adding their voices to the protest, Hilly and CBGB's were uprooted, evicted to make way for a tenant able to pay the hugely increased rents the area can now command. Rumours of a move to Hoboken across the river in New Jersey, to Los Angeles or, worse, Las Vegas continue to circulate but at time of writing, things look bad for the future of the venue.

of a multiple whammy of oil-price surges, over-confident domestic policies, International Monetary Fund rules and time-expired national pomposity. The 1974 general election resulted in a hung parliament, in which no party had an overall majority and all policies were diluted by compromise. In the vacuum of traditional politics, the right-wing was becoming more active; 54 National Front candidates stood and although none was elected, their share of the vote rose ominously. Now read on…

The Ramones: Setting The Scene 1974–75

Recalling his first visit to the legendary CBGB's venue (see opposite), **Leee Black Childers** – celebrity punk manager and scenster – wrote "There were literally six people in the audience … and the The Ramones went on stage and I went 'Oh… my… God!' And I knew it, in a minute. The first song. The first song. I knew that I was home and happy and secure and free and rock and roll. I knew it from that first song that first time I went to see them."

Escaping from Forest Hills, Queens, New York, the same dull suburb that had yielded up Simon and Garfunkel a decade or more before, **The Ramones** exemplified so many of what were to become recognized as punk's virtues that, if they hadn't been the first guys to get it together, they'd have been vilified as bandwagon-leaping posers.

"We did our first show with The Fast at Performance Studios. For the second show, no one came back" **Dee Dee Ramone** remembers in his autobiography *Poison Heart/ Teenage Lobotomy – Surviving The Ramones*

The guys took pseudonyms for stage work, revived the leather-jacketed greaser look, learned their instruments on stage and patently gave less than two cents for audience opinion. Better yet, they acted dumber than they really were, screwed with the press, and somehow convinced the management at Sire Records to sign them.

They'd march into **CBGB's** in full greaser bad-boy gear – tight T-shirts, ripped jeans and those mean, unfashionably aggressive-looking leather jackets – and blunder on stage, putting the fear of God into half the audience.

A rough stab at tuning up would be soon abandoned before **Joey Ramone** yelled a song title (unintelligible) into the mic, Dee Dee counted in "1-2-3-4" with no reference to the eventual speed the song would kick off at and **Johnny Ramone** powered up his guitar and amp. Two or three bars into the song, everything would fall apart, and a fight might break out before, having dusted themselves down, the band would regroup to try again. It was fine entertainment, it saved rock'n'roll, and it was funny as hell (reports say that Lou Reed was once actually seen laughing during such a set, lurking deep in the shadows at the back of the club).

The Ramones on stage back in the day.

Poetry And Punk

Tom Verlaine and **Richard Hell** were the best and most garish neon boys in the New York punk poetry scene, but represented just the earliest tip of the iceberg to make the papers. **Patti Smith** and **Jim Carroll** had been working up select crowds into refined hollering on St Mark's Place with their new take on street poetics for some time – Jim constantly whipping out his heroin habit for the audience to admire, while Patti fingered her most treasured possession through the shredded pocket linings of the huge old fur coat she hid inside as she chanted / recited – before Television strolled onto the stage at CBGB's.

The kind of respectful attention their work deserved was never going to happen in the free-for-all atmosphere of a UK punk gig, and by the time poesy's seeds had sprouted on this side of the water, the school of "rant-ing poet" had opened. Typified by **John Cooper Clarke** and backed up by **Attila The Stockbroker**, **John Hegley**, **Seething Wells** and **Porky The Poet**, the Ranting Poets created a whimsical coating of folk rhyme which they'd wrap around slabs of crushing social commentary. Not so much preaching to the converted as boosting morale in the face of overwhelming opposition, the ranters made sure that there was room for humour if they were on the bill.

For the mainstream punk rocker however, poetry was always going to be an acquired taste, and one where a little would go a long way. One of the crimes most heinous in punk was for a sensitive artist to take himself too seriously, particularly risky if the audience disagreed. Class acts such as **Patrik Fitzgerald** fell victim too often to hoots of idiocy from unappreciative audiences, and with very few exceptions the poets soon turned to straightforward music or to a life outside the entertainment business.

1974 Malcolm McLaren sets his sights.

By 1974 McLaren was taking a long and careful sideways look at one of the lads working behind the counter of his shop, **Glen Matlock**.

Glen was in a band already – he played bass for the aforementioned Strand alongside **Steve Jones**, **Paul Cook** and a guy called **Wally**, who has largely been airbrushed out of the history books. Matlock had a lot of well-heeled pals from the art-school circuit, many of whom were dumb enough to spend a small fortune on Malcolm and Vivienne's designs. Slowly the wheels turned in McLaren's mind until the ideal mix of Situationist challenge, rock'n'roll and street style took shape. One day, opportunity strolled through the door of *SEX*, wearing a Pink Floyd T-Shirt, crudely defaced with the words "I HATE" scribbled above the logo. Enter **Johnny Rotten**. By the end of the year, the **Sex Pistols** had formed.

INCUBATION: 1975–1976

January 1975 Television & Blondie at CBGBs.

We can trace the roots of the punk pandemic back to the beginning of 1975, when something loud, rebellious and new crawled out of the ooze and into the clubs of New York City. From his apartment uptown in NYC, high in the Dakota building, John Lennon was overseeing the release of "#9 Dream", while back at ground level, on the Lower East Side, **Talking Heads** were rehearsing – cover versions included "96 Tears", "Love Is All Around" and "I Can't Control Myself". Taking a walk a few blocks and you could catch **Television**, supported by **Blondie And The Banzai Babes** at CBGB's ("In The Flesh" is already part of their set) or for a few dollars more you could check out **The New York Dolls** supported by **The Dictators** at The Coventry.

Elsewhere, Led Zeppelin's three-night stand at Madison Square

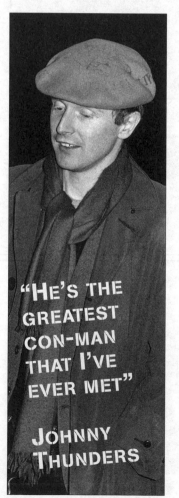

"HE'S THE GREATEST CON-MAN THAT I'VE EVER MET"

JOHNNY THUNDERS

Gardens sold out in four hours while, down the road, some 1000 fans trashed the foyer at the Boston Garden, causing $30,000 damage, apparently fed up with the wait for tickets to go on sale for Zep's February 4 concert. The mayor promptly banned the band from appearing, saving the kids from an equally interminable evening of pompous preening rock interspersed with drum solos.

February 1975 The New York Dolls split.

Storm clouds darkened the skies, the famous ravens temporarily deserted the Tower of London and an ominous rumbling (possibly related to Bob Dylan's *Rolling Thunder* tour) was heard across the UK as Margaret Thatcher deposed Edward Heath to become leader of the Conservative Party. The terrorism season began with a bomb on the Amsterdam metro and the kidnapping in West Berlin of the CDU's Peter Lorentz.

In music, **The Helium Kidz** (later XTC) recorded a bunch of demos including "Neon Shuffle". Meanwhile, Lennon's promotional gimmick – a phone interview about his *Rock & Roll* album, conducted simultaneously with twenty radio stations – completely obliterated any interest in **The New York Dolls**' revamped new red patent-leather image, funded by McLaren that set the ultimate rock'n'roll capitalists in front of a hammer'n'sickle backdrop. More intriguing even than the squeaks emitted by the boys' shiny catsuits however was Malcolm's ranting press release "What are the politics of boredom?". Weeks later the Dolls split.

March 1975 Richard Hell departs Television.

The Vietnam war entered its final phase, and North Vietnamese troops set their sights on Saigon. Londoners were queuing around the block to see The Who, Elton John and a cast of thousands in the film of *Tommy*. In New York however, you could slip into CBGB's and catch **Patti Smith**

Glen Matlock's Selection...

We raised the Pistols' original bassist from his sickbed to demand his playlist for this book. But despite not being well, he still happily provided us with a selection of classic 1970s punk on a list that also pays homage to the lost 1960s genius of Syd Barrett...

🎵 PLAYLIST

1. **BLANK GENERATION Richard Hell And The Voidoids** from **Blank Generation**

2. **LUST FOR LIFE Iggy Pop** from **Lust For Life**

3. **JILTED JOHN Jilted John** from **Jilted John**

4. **BOREDOM Buzzcocks** from **Time's Up**

5. **YOU MAKE ME CREAM IN MY JEANS JAYNE COUNTY & THE ELECTRIC CHAIRS** from **Rock'n'Roll Resurrection**

6. **ROADRUNNER Jonathan Richman & The Modern Lovers** from **Modern Lovers**

7. **GARY GILMORE'S EYES The Adverts** from **Crossing The Red Sea With The Adverts**

8. **ARNOLD LAYNE Pink Floyd** from **Relics**

9. **STAB YOUR BACK Damned** from **Damned Damned Damned**

10. **FASCIST DICTATOR Cortinas** from **The Greatest Punk Album Of All Time**

Richard Hell in his famous tin-foil shirt.

supported by **Television**, playing their last ever gigs with **Richard Hell** in the line-up. He quits the band soon after, despite the A&R buzz surrounding them, sick of having his songs cut from the set. He went on to work with Johnny Thunders and Jerry Nolan (recently released from the Dolls) in the original **Heartbreakers** line-up.

April 1975 The 101'ers and The Subterraneans play London town.

Admirable political foresight led South Vietnam's last president Nguyen Van Thieu to resign after a decade in office. In Cambodia, Australia closed its embassy just days before the last helicopter left the US embassy grounds and Pol Pot declared that the country was now the Democratic Republic of Kampuchea and that he was the prime minister. Several years of pure hell ensued for the population of the zone.

Still, if you were in New York, you could've seen **Wayne County** supported by **The Heartbreakers** playing their first gig at CBGB's, while Londoners could pop down to see **The 101'ers** (featuring **Joe Strummer**) at The Elgin. The band's *Charlie Pig Dog* weekly pub festivals cost just 10p to enter.

In West London **The Count Bishops** (muscular pub rockers) were stirring things up with a residency at The Kensington that drew several members of the forthcoming punk explosion into the same room at the same time.

Rat Scabies, **Captain Sensible** and **Brian James** were playing in the same band. Unfortunately, it was not yet **The Damned**. They were performing as **The Subterraneans**, with **Nick Kent** (a music journalist with his finger sewn onto the pulse, who'd already had a go at being a Sex Pistol) on guitar and vocals. It didn't last.

May 1975 The Stranglers get a grip.

In the month that will forever be remembered for Junko Tabei becoming the first woman to reach Mt Everest's summit, **The Stranglers'** nucleus was completed by the addition of **Dave Greenfield** and his gloomy keyboards. Elsewhere in London town, **Eddie & The Hot Rods** began their own residency at The Kensington.

June 1975 The Ramones look for a deal.

The United Kingdom voted in a referendum to stay in the European Community, while US politics was again the recipient of a slamming right hook to the jaw when just a week after Vice President Rockefeller reported having found no pattern of illegal activities in the CIA, he was back on TV to reveal the discovery of 300,000 illegally held CIA files on the activities of US citizens.

Musically, the month was a rocky mixture of diamonds and dog-dirt. Ronnie Wood replaced Mick Taylor in The Rolling Stones, and Alice Cooper fell off stage in Vancouver, breaking six ribs. In the UK Ritchie Blackmore quit Deep Purple to form Rainbow.

July 1975 The Helium Kidz move up.

In the month that Chinese archeologists uncovered 6000 clay statues of warriors dating to the 2nd century BC, **The Helium Kidz** finally changed their name to **XTC**, taking their decision after hearing Jimmy Durante shout "Dat's it! I'm in ecstasy" in his recording of "The Lost Chord" and, with Bernie Rhodes paying the bills, The **London SS** found a place to rehearse in Paddington. Across in NYC, CBGB's held two weekend-long festivals celebrating the many excellent bands currently hanging out looking for a contract. Punters willing to risk the price of a beer or two could groove to the beat of **The Ramones, Blondie, Talking Heads** and **The Heartbreakers**.

AUG 1975 Shopping at *SEX*.

Bernie Rhodes spotted **John Lydon** stomping up the Kings Road with green hair and the mythical Pink Floyd T-shirt customized with "I HATE" scribbled above the logo, and reported his sighting to pal McLaren. Meanwhile, **Alan Jones** was charged with public indecency after wearing a cowboy T-shirt from *SEX*.

In Cleveland Ohio, **Cheetah Chrome, Stiv Bators** and **Johnny Blitz** got together as **Frankenstein**, they were destined to very soon become **The Dead Boys**.

SEP 1975 Patti Smith in the studio.

In Sacramento California, Lynette "Squeaky" Fromme, one of Charles Manson's deranged followers, had her shot at assassinating US President Gerald Ford ruined by a Secret Service agent. Sara Jane Moore made another bid to kill the poor guy later in the month when he visited San Francisco.

Returning to the world of mainstream entertainment, **Squeeze** had signed to RCA, and were playing three nights every week at The Bricklayers Arms in Greenwich, and tennis star Martina Navratilova asked for political asylum, quitting Czechoslovakia for the USA. In New York, **Patti Smith** was recording *Horses* with **John Cale** at the production desk.

OCT 1975 Geldof becomes a Rat.

Ireland was in the news with the kidnap of AKZO director Tiede Herrema and, in Dublin, **Bob Geldof**'s first show with **The Boomtown Rats**.

Back in the USA meanwhile, the New Wave was beginning to tread on the coat tails of the old; **The Ramones** finally signed an album deal with Sire, and **Devo** opened for Sun Ra in Cleveland. John Lennon won permission to stay in New York despite his conviction for possession of cannabis, and Emperor Hirohito of Japan won permission to visit San Francisco despite Pearl Harbor and so forth.

The Bromley Contingent

This dismissive nickname was coined by the Sex Pistols camp to define their early audience of bored suburban kids looking for a shocking night out. Usually listed as including **Siouxsie Sioux, Billy Idol, Sid Vicious, Debbie Juvenile, Phillip Salon, Steve Severin, Marco Pirroni, Simon Barker, Sue Catwoman, Linda Ashby** and **Bertie "Berlin" Marshall**, the contingent boasted more than one hustler, trading good looks and an outfit from McLaren and Westwood for cash, drugs and a bed for the night.

In **Julie Burchill** and **Tony Parsons**' book *The Boy Looked At Johnny*, The Bromley Contingent are labelled as "a posse of unrepentant poseurs, committed to attaining fame... ".

Best seen as the interesting and slightly quaint London equivalent of the New York art monsters, their importance comes mainly from their being prepared to be seen in Malcolm's patent rubber wear. A few went on to develop a status beyond that of mere clotheshorses – as musicians, writers or artists.

NOV 1975 The Pistols take to the stage.

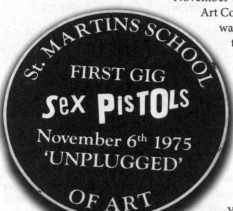

FIRST GIG
SeX PISTOLS
November 6th 1975
'UNPLUGGED'

St. MARTINS SCHOOL OF ART

Unveiled in late 2005 by Glen Matlock, this blue plaque celebrates the thirtieth anniversary of the Sex Pistols' first show.

November 6 saw the first ever **Sex Pistols** gig, at Saint Martins Art College in London. No, you weren't there. **Stuart Godard** was however, and he left **Bazooka Joe** (also on the bill that night) the next day to become **Adam Ant**. As the bandwagon snorted up its first head of speed, *Horses* appears and **Patti Smith** became the first New Wave superstar with rave reviews in the straight press (even the *New York Times* said "it will shake you and move you as little else can") and music weeklies alike (except *Melody Maker* which said "*Horses* is just bad. Period."). This was also the month in which **Charles Shaar Murray**'s groundbreaking piece on the New York scene appeared in the *NME*. "Are you alive to the sound of 75?" introduced the New York scene to a hip British readership, linking **Blondie**, **Talking heads**, **The Ramones** and **The Heartbreakers**.

Across in Ireland, **Billy Doherty** invited his old schoolmate **Feargal Sharkey** to join his new band and **The Undertones** were formed. Elsewhere on the island of Ireland, Mr Herrema, the AKZO bigwig kidnapped last month, was freed from captivity.

Back in the USA, **Pere Ubu**'s debut single "30 Seconds Over Tokyo" b/w "Heart Of Darkness" scared the crap out of Cleveland.

DEC 1975 Masters Of The Backside anyone?

Hoping, no doubt, to steer clear of bullets and bad drivers, President Ford visited China. Sara Jane Moore pleaded guilty this month to his attempted assassination, while Lynette Fromme began the life sentence she received for her own attempt. While he was out of the country, a gang of wannabe hacks launched *Punk Magazine* in NYC.

Other American tales ended more happily as **Chrissie Hynde** got a job with Malcolm McLaren (luckily not as the cross-dressing S&M transsexual front-person he had in mind for his new idea, a group called **Masters Of The Backside**) selling clothes and discouraging browsers in *SEX* on The Kings Road. As part of the rich-kid shopping experience, **The Bromley Contingent** discovered **the Sex Pistols**. Elsewhere in the city, Captain Sensible and Rat Scabies met up with **Dave Vanian** (another proposed member of Malcolm's Masters Of The Backside) and formed **The Damned** with Brian James of the London SS.

JAN 1976 ESP thwart Wayne County release.

The New Year opened with UK unemployment in excess of 1.2 million and a dozen IRA bombs exploding in London.

Things were not looking good for our team in NYC – ESP declined to publish the **Wayne County & The Backstreet Boys** album, depriving the public of "If You Don't Wanna Fuck Me, Fuck Off" and "Man Enough To be A Woman".

The London SS (not a neo-Nazi organization at all) was simultaneously allowing **Chrissie Hynde** to sit in and polish her guitar moves. In more noise news, **Malice** (later **The Cure**) were rehearsing in Crawley and **The**

Swell Maps were getting their thing together in a Solihull bedroom.

The Heartbreakers, meanehile, recorded a bunch of demos including Hell's "Love Comes In Spurts" and "Blank Generation", and Thunders' "I Wanna Be Loved".

FEB 1976 The Sex Pistols make new friends.

The Pistols opened for Eddie & The Hot Rods at London's Marquee club and wrecked the place. Equipment was trashed, Johnny Rotten hurled Jordan (*SEX* personality and shop assistant) into the audience, followed up with the mic stand and finally threw himself into the crowd. After stopping for a chat with some friends, he picked up a chair and chucked it at the rest of the band. They took this as a challenge to leap into the crowd. By the time The Hot Rods took the stage, their equipment was in pieces, the crowd was in no mood to listen and the set was ruined.

"THEY CAN'T PLAY OR NUFFINK. THEY JUST INSULT THE AUDIENCE. THEY WRECKED OUR PA. WE WAITED FOR THEM TO APOLOGISE BUT THEY HAD FUCKED OFF"

DAVE HIGGS OF THE HOT RODS

Two days later, Sex Pistols appeared at The Valentines Ball, a publicity stunt / gig organized by Malcolm and Vivien at Andrew Logan's studio in London. Jordan exposed herself while the Pistols trashed the glitterati and the cameras snapped it all for the newspapers.

The Pistols then "crashed" a Screaming Lord Sutch gig by showing up and announcing themselves as the support act. Halfway through the set somebody cut the sound from Johnny's microphone. Fisticuffs ensued. In the audience, fighting the good fight on behalf of autonomy, were Pete Shelley and Howard Devoto – they had came down from Manchester to see the Pistols and went straight back there, picking up the name Buzzcocks on the road north. They then hooked up with Malcolm and tentatively arranged a couple of gigs for the Pistols in their home town. McLaren also had a busy night; Ron Watts of London's 100 Club was in the crowd and offered him a residency at the venue.

MAR 1976 The Pistols at the 100 Club.

In the UK Harold Wilson resigned as prime minister to be replaced by James Callaghan.

Chris Spedding and Chrissie Hynde went to watch the Pistols play the 100 Club. When Glen criticized Johnny's singing, Rotten got angry, started throwing things and shruged away into the audience. Malcolm persuaded him back on stage by threatening him with the sack and no cab fare home. The performance limped along for a while but finished early. Johnny sloped off with his new best friend Chrissie.

"ROCK IS A YOUNG PEOPLE'S MUSIC AND A LOT OF THE KIDS FEEL CHEATED..."

MALCOLM McLAREN

> "I'VE ONLY HEARD IT ONCE ... I DON'T EVEN HAVE A COPY ... IF I TURN ON THE RADIO AND EVER HEAR IT, I THINK I'LL GO BERSERK"
>
> JOEY RAMONE

APR 1976 The Ramones on record.

Strikes on Liverpool docks, and among engineers in the North, pointed to growing industrial discontent in the UK. **Buzzcocks** played the Bolton Institute of Technology and, despite Pete Shelley being involved in booking the band, they were thrown off after just a couple of tunes. In more technologically focused news, Stephen Wozniak and Steven Jobs decided this was the month to form Apple Computer.

The Ramones released *The Ramones* – the best $6400 ever spent in rock'n'roll history – fourteen songs in twenty-eight minutes.

Malcolm invested £10 and booked El Paradise – a former strip club in Soho – for a Pistols gig; he planned to make it a regular Sunday session, with strippers adding to the classy atmosphere. **The Pistols** played The Nashville again (in front of numerous members of the straight and music press). To nobody's surprise, when a small scuffle broke out (allegedly provoked by **Vivienne**), the band stopped playing and dived in to help spread the love. Cameras clicked and quotes were scattered.

MAY 1976 The Heartdrops drop.

All those CBGB's gigs finally paid off for **Television**. They now had firm offers from three labels. London SS deserters **Paul Simonon**, **Keith Levene**, **Terry Chimes** and **Mick Jones** were now **The Heartdrops** and rehearsing in a Shepherds Bush squat. **The Pistols** started their Tuesday Night residency at the 100 Club, and began recording with Chris Spedding at the controls.

As **Patti Smith** brought New York style and sass to London's Roundhouse, *Metallic K.O.* – a bootlegged end-of-the-world recording of the last **Stooges** gig (Feb 74) – appeared on the streets. Despite the less-than-perfect sound, it remains a production scary and brilliant enough to be worth tracking down even three decades later.

JUN 1976 Hail The Clash.

The Pistols played Manchester Free Trade Hall. Fewer than 100 people showed up for the gig, but everyone in the crowd later formed a band. Malcolm hustled **Steve Diggle** into the gig (well, 50p is 50p) where he meets **Pete Shelley** and **Howard Devoto**. **Joe Strummer** has cut his hair and split The 101'ers, having been invited to join The Heartdrops. Paul Simonon suggested **The Clash** as a better name for the band.

In degenerate New York music biz news, **Richard Hell** left The Heartbreakers to find his inner **Voidoid**. **Billy Rath** joined in his place, and **Blondie** released "X Offender" / "In The Sun".

In the not-so-real world, Queen's "Bohemian Rhapsody" went gold.

JUL 1976 Sniffin' Glue is born.

Sniffin' Glue #1 appeared this month, under the captaincy of **Mark Perry** (see opposite). The Pistols played Hastings Pier Pavilion and turned Mari Elliot into **Poly Styrene** on the night of her 19th birthday. Later this month the Pistols recorded more demos, this time with soundman Dave Goodman at the desk, and **Adam Ant** formed the **B-Sides** with **Lester Square**, **Andy Warren** and other art-school detritus. **The Ramones**

Mark P & Sniffin' Glue

Mark Perry launched the first British punk fanzine *Sniffin' Glue* in July 1976 after seeing The Ramones, and later formed the band Alternative TV. He swiftly became disillusioned with the scene's commercialization, and closed *Sniffin' Glue* after just a dozen legendary issues, announcing that punk was already dead. To this day, he remains one of the most committed voices on the punk scene.

On leaving school in London Perry went to work in a bank. By mid-76, Mark was wishing he'd followed his school pal **Danny Baker** (see p.74) straight out of the gates of academe and into the buzzy, exciting adult world of record retail. While Mark was rubber-stamping the backs of cheques, Danny was selling vinyl to David Bowie and Marc Bolan; it must have grated a little. The regular wage was useful though, and allowed Mark to head into town every night to see a band play.

All it took was The Ramones first appearance in London to spark him into setting up *Sniffin' Glue*. The first issue boasted Blue Oyster Cult and was a mixed bag, but one that sold out almost as quickly as Mark could sneak copies through the office duplicating machine.

Adopting the pseudonym Mark P and accepting that Danny's input would make for a hipper magazine, he took a crash course in punk rock and rapidly became recognized as one of the scene's wittiest and most direct commentators. *Sniffin' Glue* was an immediate hit and one of the only media through which news of the scene and new releases was first disseminated.

As his expertise and contacts grew, he started **Step Forward Records** with **Miles Copeland** (of The Police) and put out early releases by the Fall, Sham 69, Chelsea and The Cortinas.

After a year of telling his readers to go out, get on stage and do it themselves, it was only a matter of time before he had to put his money where his mouth was and got a band together. Handing *Sniffin' Glue* over to Baker, he hid out for long enough to write a set and find a gang of similar minds before resurfacing with **Alternative TV** (see p.62).

In recent years Mark began assembling the definitive archive of his old fanzine. Published in 2000 by Sanctuary Books, *Sniffin' Glue: The Essential Punk Accessory*, is a complete reprint of the dozen originals with a hefty chunk of accompanying essays, photos and so forth. The pages drop out while you read it, in an amusing echo of the original *Glue*'s half-heartedly stapled editions, but it's still a must-have purchase.

Unsurprisingly, Mark Perry's playlist concentrates heavily on the period 1976–77, when *Sniffin' Glue* was briefly the most important music publication in Britain...

🎵 MARK PERRY'S PLAYLIST

1. 1977 The Clash
from **Super Black Market Clash**

2. **LONDON'S BURNING** The Clash
from **The Clash**

3. **GOD SAVE THE QUEEN** Sex Pistols
from **Never Mind The Bollocks**

4. **NOW I WANNA SNIFF SOME GLUE** The Ramones
from **The Ramones**

5. **RIGHT TO WORK** Chelsea
from **Chelsea: Punk Singles**

6. **INCENDIARY DEVICE** Johnny Moped
from **Basically: The Best Of Johnny Moped**

7. **ONE CHORD WONDERS** The Adverts
from **Crossing The Red Sea With The Adverts**

8. **BLANK GENERATION** Richard Hell
from **Blank Generation**

9. **NOBODY'S SCARED** Subway Sect
from **1978 Single**

10. **BOREDOM** Buzzcocks
from **Time's Up**

played a remarkable Independence Day gig supported by The Stranglers and The Flaming Groovies at the London Roundhouse. **Ian Dury** quit The Kilburns to become Blockhead-In-Chief. This month also saw the formal reunification of North and South Vietnam, while space news saw *Viking 1* land on Mars. Having recovered from Richard Hell's departure (taking most of the good songs with him) **The Heartbreakers** unveiled their new set in NYC.

AUG 1976 Chelsea set sail.

While the workforce at Grunwick's film-processing plant in London went on strike, **John Cravene** (Acme Attractions clothing) assembled

Doc Martens

Practical, proletarian, hardwearing and scary if worn correctly, **Dr. Martens** boots have been the weapon of choice for street fighters and poseurs ever since the good Doctor's orthopaedic soles made their way out of the medical wholesalers and into the high-street stores.

Fitted to steel-toecapped working boots, the AirWair soles were a hit in factories, on building sites and in locations where dangerous or corrosive chemicals were likely to be spilled. Once British skinheads realized in the early 1970s that "dangerous chemicals'" included the keg ale they used to swill down their corrosive cheap amphetamines, DMs moved from the workplace to the soccer terraces and thence onto the high streets of the UK.

There was nothing on the market so conveniently priced, comfortable to wear and reassuringly hefty; even the geekiest kid could kick to kill in his oxblood-coloured Docs, and unlike a concealed knife, they couldn't be used against the owner if a difference of opinion turned into a forthright discussion in the pub car park.

Still part of the uniform – and now available in paisley, pink and fluorescent versions – a pair of Doc Martens puts an AirWair spring in the most jaded punk rocker's step.

a band just like his rival Malcolm had; his friend **Gene October** finally had a band to play with as **Billy Idol** and **Tony James** (ex Bromley Contingent and London SS) showed up in answer to an ad in *Melody Maker*. **John Towe** (drums) joins in and **Chelsea** were up and running.

Television finally signed a deal – with Elektra – and set about recording *Marquee Moon*.

The Clash played a showcase at Rehearsal Rehearsals, their "studio" (an unheated railway warehouse at the back of London's Roundhouse) wearing the paint-splattered clothes they'd worn while redecorating, jazzed up with a few off-the-shelf slogans. Voilà, The Clash had their own look and were immediately seen as the thinking punk's alternative to the Sex Pistols.

"THE CLASH ARE THE SORT OF GARAGE BAND THAT SHOULD BE SPEEDILY RETURNED TO THE GARAGE, PREFERABLY WITH THE MOTOR STILL RUNNING"

CHARLES SHAAR MURRAY IN THE NME

Stiff Records launched, funded by a £400 loan from Dr Feelgood. "So It Goes" b/w "Heart Of The City" recorded by **Nick Lowe** for £45 is released. In the same month, **DP Costello**'s demos are played on *Honky Tonk* – the essential-listening BBC local radio show hosted by **Charlie Gillet**.

The **Sex Pistols** played their self-promoted "Midnight Special", with support from The Clash and Buzzcocks at the Screen On The Green in Islington, London. **Suzie Sue** and **Steve Severin** cornered Malcolm at the cinema and blagged the promise of a slot at the Punk Festival he was planning to put on at the 100 Club . Having seen the attention her outfit attracted from the straight press guys (she was in her full regalia – deathwhite makeup, breasts out, swastika armband and fishnet stockings), he was glad to agree. **Wire** were rehearsing in college back rooms and bedsits, developing their skills in writing some of the world's shortest tunes.

The **Ramones** were linked to a glue-sniffing death in Glasgow by the city's *Evening Times* newspaper; as a result, the band pick up some publicity north of the border.

Back on Mars, *Viking I* this month found "the strongest indications to date" of possible life on Mars.

SEP 1976 The Banshees start to howl.

While all the kids went back to school after the hottest summer in decades, Suzie Sue became **Siouxsie Sioux** and her band was rejoicing in the name of **The Banshees**. **Billy Idol** had been borrowed back from Chelsea to play guitar and teach **Steve Havoc** his bass lines, but the list of songs was looking decidedly shaky with a Bay City Rollers cover and the *Goldfinger* theme jostling with *The Lord's Prayer* for positions in the set. Days before the gig Billy announced that Chelsea objected to his playing with The Banshees – they now needed to find both a drummer and a guitarist. **Sid Vicious** and **Marco Pirroni** fitted the bill perfectly and a righteous noise was created.

The Pistols were booked to play the opening night of an upmarket new Paris disco, Bois De Boulougne (and to reveal Malcolm's new line in bondage suits). Billy Idol drove the **Bromley Contingent** across for the gig in his beaten up old van and Siouxsie got a punch from an outraged local who objects to her outfit (see-thru plastic mac with polka dots, see-thru bra, vinyl stockings, stilettos and swastika armband).

Richard Hell had assembled his Voidoids with **Marc Bell** (ex-Wayne County's band and later **Marky Ramone**), **Bob Quine** and **Ivan Julian**.

Subway Sect put the final touches to their set and debut at the 100 Club Festival while across town, **Eater** signed fourteen-year old **Dee Generate** (Roger Bullen to his proud mum) as replacement for **Social Demise** (who had trouble getting off school) to play drums.

OCT 1976 The Pistols in the studio.

Malcolm this month took £40,000 from EMI on behalf of **the Pistols**. They immediately entered the studios to work on final versions of "Anarchy In The UK".

Throbbing Gristle appeared at London's Institute of Contemporary Arts accompanied by strippers and **Chelsea** (playing as **L.S.D.** that night). Later that week **The Clash** played the venue with **Subway Sect** and **Snatch** in support. Carried away by the fun, **Shane McGowan** accidentally ripped the ring from his earlobe. The ensuing bloodbath was swiftly retold for the benefit of the press as a case of Shane's girlfriend biting his ear off.

Promoted by the record company slogan "Young Hot Loud and Stiff", **The Damned** released the first ever punk rock single – "New Rose" b/w "Help".

Patti Smith's second album – *Radio Ethiopia* – was this month in the shops, while *Wreckless Eric* hand-delivered his demo cassette to Stiff Records, went home and waited for the call. When the summons arrived he successfully held out for a two-figure deal.

NOV 1976 No fun in Lancaster

The Sex Pistols' "Anarchy In The UK" appears on EMI and was unofficially banned by daytime radio (and most night-time radio too). Everybody in **Chelsea** except Gene quit the band and immediately re-formed under the **Generation X** label.

On the streets of London, meanwhile, eighty thousand marched against public sector cuts and twenty-five thousand marched against racism. In Lancaster, the Pistols were banned from playing the university. However the band did star in a Punk Rock Special for *The London Weekend Show* – a Sunday lunchtime TV magazine show hosted by **Janet Street Porter**.

The 100 Club Festival

Monday 20th September 1976: Sex Pistols / The Clash / Subway Sect / Siouxsie & The Banshees

Tuesday 21st September 1976: The Damned / Chris Spedding & The Vibrators / Stinky Toys / Buzzcocks

Much more than just the UK scene's best line-up ever, The 100 Club Festival was the first opportunity for British punks to get together and realize that none of them were alone any more. The Bromley Contingent had thrown up a couple of acts; the Manchester mob had ventured south; the Pistols, Clash and Damned were the main attractions. Sid Vicious allegedly threw a glass during the Damned's set, which shattered, cutting one of the crowd. Sid and journalist/scenester Caroline Coon (who it was also alleged was the inspiration behind The Stranglers' "London Lady") were arrested and carted off. If everyone who claims to have attended had really been there, they could have sold out Wembley Stadium.

DEC 1976 The Pistols and Bill Grundy.

The Pistols opened the month with a drunken appearance on *Today*, the local London tea-time magazine show hosted by **Bill Grundy** (a legendary appearance which is well worth catching, and is still frequently aired; see box) while record packers at EMI refused to handle the "Anarchy" single. As the anti-punk backlash swept across the country, harmless bands like **The Vibrators** are caught up in the chaos and most of the dates for their tour of the U.K. and Europe are cancelled.

Generation X this month made their debut at Central St. Martins, London. Eleven days later, The Roxy Club opened in the city, with Siouxsie And The Banshees supporting Generation X. **Buzzcocks** start their own label (the first of the bands to do so) and released the *Spiral Scratch EP*, while **The Damned** recorded the first punk Peel session.

EPIDEMIC: 1977-1979

1977 was the year that punk went overground and spread, like a disease across the UK, and was also the year that Disco turned planet-killer. The soundtrack to the film *Saturday Night Fever* turned the **Bee Gees** into worldwide superstars in spangled jumpsuits and established them as the biggest-selling act since the Beatles. Punk was totally swamped in terms of sales, but outranked the shuffling, hustling, boogie-driven hordes in column inches, outrage and cultural impact.

JAN 1977 EMI ... say goodbye.

The backlash against punk rock diminished a little as the press moved onto their next nine-day wonder, and **The Vibrators** managed to salvage some of their cancelled tour dates. Fearsomely hungover after the New Year celebrations, the Pistols managed a little performance at Heathrow for the benefit of their entourage of press hyenas. A week later, they were off the EMI roster (three weeks into a two year deal and now £50,000 the richer after Malcolm negotiated £10,000 for breach of contract).

In the States, **Patti Smith** whirled off stage during a gig in Tampa and broke her neck (see p.295) and **The Ramones'** second album, *Leave Home*, picked up from where the first left off without missing a beat.

FEB 1977 Matlock ... say goodbye.

The modern age officially began this month as Radio Shack markets its TRS-80 – the first home computer that does not require its own dedicated power station and cooling plant.

Tony Parsons covered the world of fanzines in a piece for *NME*, while **Sid Vicious** did his first transatlantic phone interview, despite not yet officially being a Pistol. His "audition" the previous week had been a disaster. Some days later, Malcolm issued a communique to the press announcing the sacking of **Glen Matlock**. Desperate to get a credible punk act on board, Polydor threw a sizeable life-raft to **The Jam**.

MAR 1977 No more Sniffin' Glue.

The Slits – the all-female punk band comprised mainly of scene stars' girlfriends – made their debut and **Jerry Harrison** got back into the

Poor old Bill Grundy

It's rare to see such a well-established TV presenter blow himself so irreversibly off the screen, but **Bill Grundy** joined his own funeral so enthusiastically that he's become a legend of British punk.

Back in the mid 70s, Grundy was one of the hosts of a bland magazine-style show that followed the early evening news programme on the UK's ITV network. Megastars Queen were booked to appear that evening, but fate intervened and made them unavailable. Instead, fellow EMI recording artists, the **Sex Pistols**, were bundled into a couple of taxis with **Siouxsie Sioux** and a few other hangers-on and delivered, slightly drunk, to the television studios.

There was as little common ground between Grundy and the Pistols as there would have been between him and the rock royalty of Queen. However, had he been dealing with consummate professional entertainers instead of teenage guttersnipes, he might not have made quite the same mess of things.

The spot opened with a seemingly innocent introduction in which Grundy compared the band to The Stones and commented on their, and his own (apparently joking) drunkness. From then on in things spiralled downwards rapidly to a point where the whole episode became painful to watch. And just when it seemed nothing worse could happen, Grundy appeared to make a pass at the pouting Siouxsie Sioux. Legendary. Finally, the cheesy signature tune played and the credits rolled. Rotten looked at his watch, Jones started dancing to the music, and Grundy muttered an off-mic "Oh shit!" to himself.

The story made the front pages of the morning newspapers, amidst howls of outrage, including the infamous *Daily Mirror* headline "THE FILTH AND THE FURY!". The Pistols had cemented their place in television folklore.

Though immortalized in the short term by the **Television Personalities** in their tribute "Where's Bill Grundy Now?", the man himself died in 1993, aged 69.

music biz after his experience as a Modern Lover, signing up as the fourth **Talking Head**. Sniggering up their bloodstained shirtsleeves at the irony, **The Heartbreakers** signed to Track Records.

The Sex Pistols spent a few days on A&M's roster this month and pocket an alleged £75,000 for their time. **Mark Perry** announced he was giving up *Sniffin' Glue* to become an **Alternative** TV. Quitting while he was ahead (the mag had a circulation of 10,000) Mark handed over the reins of the fanzine world to such future luminaries as **Paul Morley**, whose *Out There* had been jostling for record store space with other new arrivals such as *Au Contraire* and the *Aylesbury Roxette*.

The release of *Marquee Moon* meant **Television** fans finally got to take some of the magic home with them, while the *A Bunch Of Stiffs* compilation brought **Mötorhead**, **Wreckless Eric** and **Magic Michael** together on a slab of vinyl.

APR 1977 Cash for The Clash.

In glamorous New York City, the world-famed Studio 54 Discotheque threw open its doors to a crowd of diamond-crusted elegance. Back home in London, **Sid** celebrated a successful gig at the Screen On The Green by picking up some smack and a dose of hepatitis that put him straight into hospital.

This Heat terrified the entire country into thinking the aliens had landed with their first and funky scary Peel session. Later **The Jam** and **The Adverts** were invited in to perform. **Siouxsie And The Banshees**, meanwhile, entertained a crowd at The Roxy that included the newly-named **Adam And The Ants**.

In record news, **Blondie** put out "In The Flesh", while *The Clash* appeared in the UK (in the US 100,000 imported copies were snapped up after Stateside record company dudes decided it wouldn't sell as a domestic release).

> "WE'RE AGAINST BUREAUCRACY, HYPOCRISY... AND ANYTHING ELSE THAT ENDS IN 'Y'"
>
> JOHNNY ROTTEN

Gobbing

gob *n* Informal, a globule of spittle or saliva. *vb* (intr) Brit. informal to spit. Etymology, 14c, originally meaning "a lump", from the French *gobe*, which means "a mouthful", from *gober*, the Celtic "to gulp".

Gobbing on bands as a sign of approval was the most depressing and incomprehensible aspect of punk rock ever to make it into the mainstream consciousness. Pink hair and drainpipe jeans were easy enough to defend, and the more extremely argumentative had the occasional stab at the morally indefensible wearing of Nazi paraphernalia, but nobody ever heard a rational defence of gobbing, nor ever met anyone who'd admit to doing it.

Despite the denials, somebody was sure as hell producing a ton of spittle. TV Smith's hippy-length hair glinted like a frosted Christmas tree within seconds of his approaching the mic stand; Billy Idol almost drowned in the stuff; and Joe Strummer even blamed it for the hepatitis attack that laid him low in the late 70s.

Finally, the bands decided they'd swallowed enough and began first threatening and then actually quitting the stage when the spitting started. Having seen a few persistent assholes pummelled into hamburger by people who'd paid good money to see the gig, the habit fairly quickly died out.

MAY 1977 Adam goes country.

Missing an opportunity to turn "May the 4th be with you" into a marketing slogan, *Star Wars* didn't open till the 26th of the month. In other entertainment news, **Adam And The Ants** played their first set, in a London house. Their next gig was a more guerilla affair: Adam booked into the ICA claiming to front a country band, but managed only one number, "Beat My Guest" in his leather and chains outfit, before being paid off and asked to leave quietly.

Post punk kicked off in the north of England when **Julian Cope** met **Pete Wylie** and later **Ian McCulloch** at a Clash gig in Liverpool. **The Damned** recorded another Peel session, **the Pistols** signed to Virgin and Sid got out of hospital; Nancy's been his only regular visitor.

After David Bowie released his *Low* LP, **Nick Lowe** this month retaliated with his *Bowi* EP. The joke was better than the music. In Manchester, Stiff Kittens became **Warsaw** (step two on the way to becoming Joy Division).

JUN 1977 The Silver Jubilee.

Celebrated with fireworks, bonfires on the hilltops and parties in the tenements, it was the Queen's Silver Jubilee. The cities swarmed with po-faced punk rockers kicking moodily at the cobbles trying to ignore the whole charade. In the US, *The Washington Post* announced that the US military had the neutron bomb.

Back in London, Sex Pistols **Johnny Rotten** and **Paul Cook** were beaten and robbed in separate incidents, and **The Damned** were having cancellation troubles: a planned St Albans gig (with Adverts support) was moved to Dunstable at the last moment, with Stafford, Southampton, Newcastle, Cromer, Cheltenham and Southend dates following suit. Dee Generate quit **Eater** (musical differences and diminishing publicity) just as they were heading off on tour. Luckily an older wiser head was available to step in – enter sixteen-year-old **Phil Rowland**.

As **The Jam** dropped their Union Jack motif – they kept being associated with the National Front which had co-opted the nation's banner as its own symbol – **Sham 69**'s new line up debuted with only **Jimmy Pursey** and **Albie Slider** remaining from the originals. **Rezillos** signed to Sensible Records, a label put together by Island Records man Lenny Love.

The Pistols' "God Save The Queen" stormed the charts but was denied the number one slot ... meanwhile the infamous boat trip turned into a police riot (see box opposite).

Live At The Roxy, London WC2 showcased the talent that played Covent Garden's most famous underground toilet between January and April 1977. Hidden mikes capture snatched of conversation that added as much to the atmosphere of the album as the bands themselves. It brought new vital material from bands including Buzzcocks, Eater, Slaughter & The Dogs and The Adverts, while Wire X-Ray Spex and Johnny Moped did comparatively well as a result of this vinyl debut.

Boating With The Sex Pistols

One of the all-time great promotional stunts was when **the Pistols** hired *The Queen Elizabeth* riverboat for a touristy trip up and down the river Thames; everybody on the London scene heard about it in advance and most of them turned up at the quayside hoping to get on board. In the end, the 175 invited guests made their way through the mob and, with advertising banners flapping like corporate Jolly Rogers, *The Queen Elizabeth* headed for deep water.

Having taken the money, the boat's owner decided he didn't like the cut of his clients' jib and called the police. As the vessel headed upstream it collected a flotilla of police boats, with more joining in each time *The Queen Elizabeth* passed under one of the capital's bridges. Meanwhile, the band, friends and freeloaders got stuck into the bar for a three-hour drinks session before the boat turned around and the entertainment began.

The Pistols started their set with "Anarchy In The UK", following up with "God Save The Queen" as they bobbed past the Houses of Parliament. "I Wanna Be Me", "Pretty Vacant", "No Feelings" "Problems" and finally "No Fun" did their best to entertain the crowd, crew and coppers but without totally succeeding. By "Problems" the Pistols were being tailed by six police boats and the captain was under instructions to pull over at the next available pier. The boat was boarded and "No Fun" was finally crudely shut off when someone cut the power.

Then the fun truly stopped. Some of the era's most unpleasant footage records the police assault – check it out, it's all over the documentaries, and appears in Julien Temple's film *The Filth And The Fury* (2000) – in which cameras were taken and destroyed, whilst fans, band members and innocent Virgin employees were "assisted" off the boat and into waiting police vans.

Siouxsie & The Banshees recorded for the first time in a real studio. XTC, Elvis Costello and Chelsea all did their first Peel sessions, and **The Future** agreed that **Phil Oakey** (hospital porter by trade) was the guy they needed to relieve them of the tedium of computer operation and set them on the road to stardom as **The Human League**.

"I DON'T SEE HOW ANYONE COULD DESCRIBE US AS A POLITICAL BAND. I DON'T EVEN KNOW THE NAME OF THE PRIME MINISTER"

STEVE JONES

JULY 1977 Johnny on the radio.

New York City was blacked out for 25 hours and **John Lennon** received his green card (permanent permit to stay in the US as a resident). Holding their breath in the hope of avoiding another radio and chainstore boycott, **the Pistols** sneaked out "Pretty Vacant", single number three, and the first to boast a major-label quality promotional video. Against expectations it was shown on BBC TV's *Top Of The Pops*.

Johnny Rotten's one-off radio show, *A Punk And His Music*, was aired on London's Capital Radio. 90 minutes of dub, Captain Beefheart, Tim Buckley and the like confounded expectations. **The Clash** showed up at the venue of a cancelled punk festival in Birmingham together with a bunch of fans and the local police. Moved on to Barbarella's, they borrowed a local band's kit and knocked out an impromptu set to the 500 fans in attendance. Nigel Harrison replaced Gary Valentine as bassist of **Blondie** and **The Damned** played a four-night stand at the Marquee to celebrate their first year in the business.

"ELVIS WAS
DEAD BEFORE
HE DIED AND
HIS GUT WAS SO
BIG IT CAST A
SHADOW OVER
ROCK AND ROLL
... OUR MUSIC
IS WHAT'S
IMPORTANT NOW"
JOHNNY ROTTEN

AUG 1977 Hey Hey we're The SPOTS.

August in London will be remembered for the Battle of Lewisham, the capital's street confrontation of the century, where the good guys stopped the fascists from marching. In New York the month became memorable for the arrest in Yonkers of David Berkowitz, who was accused of being the "Son Of Sam" killer. This was also the month that Elvis Presley ate his last burger.

Sid was fined £125 at Wells Street Magistrates Court for being stupid enough to carry a knife on the night he was arrested for throwing a glass. Released, he headed for the airport to join the rest of the band on their mini-tour of Scandinavia. On the Pistols' return to the UK, they found they were back on tour – but under the assumed name of **The SPOTS** (Sex Pistols On Tour Secretly).

Sham 69 signed to Step Forward Records, record with John Cale producing (Mark Perry provided the beer). **XTC** signed to Virgin (£250,000/six-album deal), **Buzzcocks** signed to United Artists. Glasgow city council banned all "punk" shows in town. **The Vibrators** relocated to Berlin. Wayne County & The Electric Chairs played the Reading Festival. They made it as far as the intro to "If You Don't Wanna Fuck Me, Fuck Off" before the weather (a sudden storm of beer cans, bottles, mud and underweight hippies) turned inclement and they left the stage.

SEP 1977 A bad month for rats.

One from the catalogue of great music business promo disasters – Mercury's Artist Development Manager **Mike Bone** left a brainstorming session with the brilliant wheeze of sending out freeze-dried, vacuum-packed dead rats with every radio promotional copy of **The Boomtown Rats**' debut single. He got it in the neck from the band, label managers and the mighty US Postal Service, which has regulations covering that sort of thing.

Ian Dury and Stiff propelled the lapel pin industry into an even higher orbit with the extremely desirable multicoloured series of "Sex &", "Drugs &", "Rock &", "Roll &". The artist-promo badge "Ian Dury &" that completed the set was never quite as popular but it got one's preferences across without all that difficult mid-gig conversation.

Alternative TV's gig at the exceedingly seedy Rat Club was taped for posterity and made available as a semi-official bootleg. Despite the atrocious quality, it stands alongside The Velvets' *Live At Max's Kansas City* and The Stooges' *Metallic K.O.* as an essential document of the time. As a final, profit-blowing initiative, Mark Perry gave away a flexi-single of "Love Lies Limp" (punk's first mention of male sexual impotence as far as we know) with every copy of his final issue of *Sniffin' Glue*.

X-Ray Spex joined the major league by signing to Virgin but lost **Lora Logic** – still young enough to see a life beyond punk, she went back to school to make her grades.

OCT 1977 The punk pack gets shuffled.

A busy month on the transfer lists with Jerry Nolan quitting **The Heartbreakers** (musical differences) and Rat Scabies dropping out of **The Damned** (musical differences, and sick of the whole damn business). Dave Berk (on free temporary transfer from Johnny Moped) jumped in to help so The Damned could finish their tour, and Rat tried out for The Heartbreakers.

The "Stiff's Greatest Stiffs Live Tour" began, and breweries all over the country introduced 24-hour production to cope with expected demand from the tour bus. **Ian Dury & The Blockheads** made their debut, while Nick Lowe, Elvis Costello & The Attractions and Wreckless Eric rounded out the bill each night. Unfortunately a monstrous musical difference of epic proportions broke out between the two founders of Stiff the very next day, resulting in Elvis Costello, Nick Lowe and Jake Riviera heading off on their own to start Radar Records.

Garth lurched away from **Buzzcocks** (musical differences) leaving them up the creek without a bassist on the eve of their UK tour.

In the US, and with a zombie-like gait, **The Cramps** staggered out of the swamp and into Ardent Studios in Memphis to record "Human Fly", "The Way I Walk", "Domino" and "Surfing Bird". Blondie signed to Chrysalis from Private Stock Records. Raw Records finally signed **The Unwanted** (remember them from the *Roxy Live* album?), **Squeeze** signed on the dotted line to A&M and **Sham 69** joined the Polydor roster.

The Pistols' album was banned by the chain stores within an hour of release on 28 October on account of its offensive title. Luckily the latest bootleg version to hit the streets – *Spunk*, which appeared just over a week earlier – came in a plain black cover. Also in the stores, *Talking Heads '77*, *L.A.M.F.* by The Heartbreakers and the *3-D* EP by XTC.

NOV 1977 Banshees on the airwaves.

Even though Wings released "Mull Of Kintyre" this month, *Never Mind The Bollocks...* was the disc spinning on right-thinking turntables all over the UK. But the Pistols' robust use of language led to most advertising and shop window displays being hurriedly torn down in panic or under duress. Zealous coppers from the anti-punk squad busted the Virgin Store in Nottingham's King Street, impounding stock and arresting the shop manager Chris Seale using an ingenious combination of the Vagrancy and Indecent Advertisement acts. In response label boss **Richard Branson** had the front window of his flagship London store filled with nothing but covers, posters and banners, all featuring the name of the band and the album. When the case came to court later in the month, the defence brought in the historical big guns to justify the use of the word, then slipped in a neat hint that this might be considered a state-sponsored attack on the band rather than their language. A few days later, Sid got drunk and tried to throw himself out of a hotel window (he showed up at rehearsals to find nobody else had arrived, and took it personally). Nancy grabbed him by the belt and pulled him bodily back into the room, where fisticuffs ensued.

The Boys recorded the first of a series of Christmas novelties as **The Yobs**. Their pedestrian remake of Chuck Berry's "Run Rudolph Run" was the official A-side but **John Peel** and everybody else who buys a copy played the flip – a punked up version of the playground fave "The Worm Song". Peel also plays the

"**I**F PEOPLE BOUGHT THE RECORDS FOR THE MUSIC, THIS THING WOULD HAVE DIED A DEATH LONG AGO"

MALCOLM TALKS MARKETING TO **T**HE **T**IMES

Records worth stealing this month include...

This Is The Modern World, The Jam's second album, Rocket To Russia, The Ramones third, Music For Pleasure, second outing by The Damned, and Pink Flag by Wire.

long-awaited Siouxsie & The Banshees session in full, the band's first opportunity to reach out to those too old or isolated to make it to one of their concerts. They increased the pressure on the major labels to get serious in negotiations.

DEC 1977 NME Readers' Poll.

As famously manipulated by **Danny Baker** and his spiky headed colleagues, the *NME Readers' Poll* for 1977 put the Sex Pistols ahead of Led Zeppelin and Genesis in the Best Group category. They also won Best Album, Best Single, Best Dressed Sleeve and Best Drummer with Johnny Rotten picking up a Most Wonderful Human Being award. The Tom Robinson Band also did well, as did The Clash, Stranglers and Boomtown Rats.

In the States, this month saw **Elvis Costello and The Attractions** make their first U.S. TV appearance, on *Saturday Night Live*, where they caused a bit of controversy by switching mid-tune from the comparatively anodyne "Less Than Zero" to the corporate-blistering "Radio Radio".

With Sid moping on his own in the back of the bus, **the Sex Pistols** were dispatched to the Netherlands for a ten-day break. On their return they laid into a tour of previously unknown suburban venues, and finish up their working year by playing a kiddies' party on Christmas Day.

1978...

JAN 1978 Jarman's Jubilee.

In unrelated Ted incidents this month, Ted Nugent "autographed" a fan's arm by carving his signature into it with a knife, and Ted Bundy killed two Florida State University students.

While **the Pistols** were doing their rock'n'roll Macbeth routine in the States (see box) and heading for a mess o'trouble, back in England, the scene was going to hell. Joke bands were appearing in every little market town, and no TV comedy was complete without a "Sid Snot" pastiche punk character. The only kids who seemed to show any genuine belief were wide-eyed weeny teenagers like those who followed Adam & The Ants and dressed for a night in the torture chamber.

Warsaw decide to adopt the more user-unfriendly Joy Division monicker ending the confusion between their appearances and gigs by Warsaw Pakt. **Ian Curtis** got righteously lubricated for the band's

Essential shopping items this month include...

White Music by XTC and the Safety Pin Stuck In My Heart EP from Patrik Fitzgerald.

Sex Pistols' Tour Of The USA

Having been held up by immigration officials just prior to the New Year while the feds checked out the band members' criminal records, **the Sex Pistols** were allowed in, and their tour of the bottom half of the US map kicked off in Georgia. It was a crap show and a rotten way to begin their intended conquest. Shaking off his record company minders (on hand to protect the deposit paid to the insurance companies as much as to defend the band against assault), **Sid** went out to buy some heroin.

The tour pushed on to Memphis, San Antonio via Austin, Baton Rouge, Dallas, Tulsa and finally San Francisco, a horribly debilitating slab of mileage zigzagging the band on endless roads across endless rural views. Sid bought himself a knife and after some experimental carpentry, started carving himself up. At the San Antonio gig he lost his temper in one of those charming hissy fits that are a part of his legend, and thumped a member of the audience with his bass ... arguably the most precise use he ever made of the thing.

The Dallas gig was booked into one of the sacred shrines of country music – Dewey Groom's Longhorn Ballroom. 500 country'n'western fans showed up to face down the 500 ill-dressed apprentice punks of Dallas and surrounding districts. Following the scent of blood, the press was on hand to capture this replay of the Alamo in living color. Alas for their ratings, peace broke out. Sid was too sick withdrawing to stand upright, much less play or abuse the audience, otherwise things went well.

At the last show, in San Francisco, the fun finally came to an end. Sid's amp was turned down so as not to embarrass him and to give the rest of the guys a chance to play without being put off by his random tones.

Four thousand fans went berserk and at the end of it all **Johnny** sat down at the front of the stage and asked "Ever get the feeling you've been cheated?" while Sid went off to buy some heroin.

A few days later, Johnny was informed that both he and Sid were now ex-Pistols. Johnny borrowed enough for a plane fare to New York, Sid made his way to Los Angeles and the other two went to Rio with Malcolm to record a single with **Ronnie Biggs**, the robber.

first gig under the new name and was thrown out of the venue before he could take the stage.

Johnny Rotten went to Jamaica at Richard Branson's expense to track down acts for Virgin's offshoot Front Line label, accompanied by filmmaker and dreadlock Rasta **Don Letts**, top punk scribe **Vivienne Goldman** and photographer **Dennis Morris**.

Peel invited **Siouxsie & The Banshees** back to record another session, while Johnny Thunders was propped against a wall in the Speakeasy and played with Peter Perrett, Patti Palladin and Sid Vicious on stage.

Jubilee by **Derek Jarman** opened in London featuring Adam Ant, Little Nell, Wayne County, Gene October, Toyah Wilcox, Jordan, Siouxsie & The Banshees, The Ants (on TV) and most of the Slits. A badly plotted or should one say, enigmatic meditation on the punk rock world of a future 1984, all the kids went to see it, nobody else really bothered.

MAR 1978 Gimmicks are us.

The Damned split up for the first time with the departure of Brian James; he was allegedly fed up with the clowning around element in the band. Stiff's profit-blowing promo scheme for *The Wonderful World Of Wreckless Eric* meant that two different versions were on sale – both at the same price. There was a regular 12" slab of plastic, or an edited 10" version that omitted "Whole Wide World" and "Telephoning Home". In a more traditional promo stunt, helium balloons were released from London, Manchester, Leeds, Liverpool and Newcastle, with free Buzzcocks album vouchers attached. Coolest promo gimmick award, however, went to **Elvis Costello**'s *This Year's Model* runout groove; there was a phone number scratched into the vinyl and the first 5000 callers got a free bonus single, "Stranger In The House" b/w "Neat Neat Neat".

APR 1978 Sid does things his way.

April gave the country's lefties, punks and level-headed music fans the chance to let off some steam and recharge morale with the first Rock Against Racism Carnival. **Sid Vicious** went to Paris and filmed the "My Way" sequence that eventually showed up in *The Great Rock And Roll Swindle* movie – it was the performance that made his legend.

John Ellis left **The Vibrators**. Ed Banger (a.k.a. Edward Garrity) left **The Nosebleeds** and is replaced by one **Steven Morrissey** (yes, that Morrissey).

MAY 1978 Factory opens in Manchester.

Easy Cure became **The Cure**; **The Skids** signed to Virgin and recorded a Peel session; Gary Chaplin left **Penetration** and was replaced by Neale Floyd, guitar slinger and long term fan of the band. Dave Allen joined **Gang Of Four**.

Just what Jimmy Pursey DIDN'T want – **Sham 69** were adopted as the official band of the resurgent and thoroughly loathsome Nazi skinheads. As anyone with an ounce of sense immediately stopped attending Sham gigs, the boneheads split into moderately evil National Front ("send 'em back to Africa!") supporters and totally evil plus stupid British Movement ("kill 'em then send 'em back to Africa!") followers.

The Nosebleeds split up, leaving Morrissey bereft. No group to play around in front of? Heaven knows he was miserable now. Across town, The Factory club opened with **Durutti Column** topping the bill.

JUN 1978 Stiff Little Fingers sign to Island.

The remaining **Sex Pistols** – Paul, Steve and Sid – were whipped into a London theatre by Malcolm, and auditioned fitfully for a new vocalist. Nobody really cared but the session was filmed and later showed up in the *Swindle* movie, and it turned Eddie Tudorpole into **Tenpole Tudor**.

Stiff Little Fingers signed to Island. Polydor finally got their corporate finger out and signed Siouxsie And The Banshees to a reasonable deal, allowing them to maintain artistic control of their music.

It had been a while since the weekly music papers reviewed the fanzine scene, and in a small twist, the *NME* looked across to the US market, giving space to *Teenage Rampage*, *La Mere* and *Gabba Gabba Gazette*. This month also saw **Television** split up.

AUG 1978 The scene goes down hill, fast.

Standards on the bandwagon dropped further still with new groups such as The Rottin Klitz, Injections, Blitz, Transmitters, Moderne Man, Raped, Dick Envy, Innocents, X Films, Giro, Cock Sparrer, Acme Sewage Co. and the like playing interchangeable, instantly forgettable ramalama "punk" rock noise that was derivative and retro-looking in a most un-punk manner.

Sid's "My Way" clip was shown on *Revolver*, the latest TV show to risk showing punk acts on a regular basis. A week later, "No One Is Innocent" was shown but in a censored format. Sid and his pals got together for a superstar jam at the Electric Ballroom – Sid sang, Nancy provided backing vocals while Rat Scabies (drums), Glen Matlock (bass)

"I'LL DIE BEFORE I'M VERY OLD... I DON'T KNOW WHY... I JUST HAVE THIS FEELING"

SID TELLS HIS OWN FUTURE TO RECORD MIRROR

Fashion And Hair

The old-school punk look, despite being very much "anything goes", was based on what could be borrowed, bought cheap or transformed with an ounce of imagination. **Bondage trousers** (with the legs loosely fastened to one another at the knee or below) were briefly in vogue and neatly encapsulate the punk ideal – only utter fools and posers would pay Chelsea prices for genuine "original" bondage strides from *SEX*; the rest of the world cobbled together their own from distressed old army trousers and dog chains. Similarly, **straitjackets** as sported by the Pistols were admired but rarely purchased.

By the beginning of 1977, articles on "dressing punk" were already hitting the women's magazines. By the end of the year, it was possible to spend hundreds of pounds on exclusive, designer jewellery based on the egregious safety-pin fad. By 1978, the mainstream had moved on, everyday punks had settled on a uniform appearance and the fashion-darlings were denying they'd *ever* worn anything from McLaren and Westwood (pictured).

By the time punk went overground, big-time, the way to instant punkness was to co-opt the Joey Ramone look of leather **biker jacket**, sloganeering T-shirt and a few **badges**. It was all too easy, particularly when wash-in/wash-out hair-dyes arrived on the scene – suddenly any Arnold could punk themselves up for the weekend and be back in harness on Monday, dressed down and dowdy for work.

At some point in the late 70s, The Clash saw De Niro in *Taxi Driver*. It coincided with the band visiting New York, the very same mean streets featured in the film, and resulted in Joe Strummer getting his hair cut Mohawk-style and creating the last of the great punk looks. It took a matter of minutes for the look to be copied, expanded to ridiculous proportions, coloured and spat out to become the icing on the postcard punk stereotype that tourists still flock to London expecting to see.

That said, the **mohawk** style (mohican in the UK) was a relatively late arrival on the scene, and never took off in a big way. Most employers looked disapprovingly enough on the music – the notion of offering a job to crazy-looking kids with no respect for the laws of morality or even gravity when it came to matters tonsorial was, at least for most straight jobs, then and now, out of the question. Much more common was a cheerfully amateurish cropped look that either spiked up of its own volition in a sweaty, beer-drenched gig environment, or could be correctly "spiked" using some additional styling medium. While certain, cakey-smelling individuals experimented with egg white or flour and water pastes, good old-fashioned CFC-destroying aerosol hairspray was usually enough to ensure that your spikes stood up sufficiently for you to pose around town, outrage public decency and freak out the normals.

A second reason for the style remaining a very visible minority taste revolved around notions of male vanity and dandyism. Anyone spending too much time on their look risked being branded a "poseur" (some, of course – notably Poly Styrene of X-Ray Spex – didn't care, and wrote songs about it). Thirdly, it required time better spent in other activities and funds better used in the purchase of records. Finally, there was the question of camouflage: bonehead adolescents with nothing better to do than isolate and torment those trying to be different exist all over the record-buying world, and a fluorescent mohican is a difficult thing to hide, even in a dark alley.

By the 1980s, in the UK at least, the high-rise mohican was to be seen mainly on those lost souls who'd washed up on London's Kings Road, wearing a uniform that was instantly recognizable as "punk", but whose sheer conformity with expectations made it anything but.

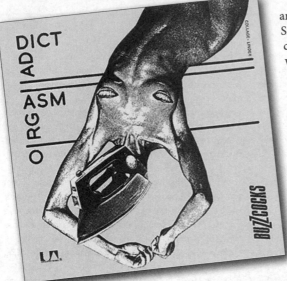

and Steve New (guitar) provided the music. Sid and Nancy were moving to NYC for the climate and their health, and this was a farewell to old pals and audience alike.

In Manchester **The Fall** released their debut, while across town **Linder** (Linda Mulvey), local hero and artist responsible for some of the best punk graphics (the "Orgasm Addict" cover was one of hers) jumped the counter and got her own band together, named **Ludus**.

SEP 1978 Slaughter And The Dogs reform.

Marky (Marc Bell) Ramone made his debut this month as big brother Tommy Ramone moved away from the kit and into the more comfortable producer's chair. Just to mess everyone up in the UK, Stiff issued a press release stating their position as "a 'new' record company, not a record museum" and deleted both Damned albums and the compilations released so far. They then rereleased their first 10 singles as a collectors' edition box set (and deleted the damn thing almost immediately). Record collectors up and down the nation felt a little dizzy and needed a sit down as a result.

In another move guaranteed to put obsessives on their mettle, Manchester's own defender of The New York Dolls' flame, **Steven Morrissey** appeared as the singer – alongside his pal Billy Duffy (ex-Nosebleeds) on guitar – for the re-formed **Slaughter And The Dogs**.

Cool low-key event of the month took place at the Project Arts Centre in Dublin where **Patti Smith** read poetry, with **The Pop Group** as the support act. Ragingly noisy event of the month went to the appearance of **Les Punks** for one night only (5 Sept) at Camden's Electric Ballroom.

Wigan council had had a ban on punk rock gigs in force for months, London's GLC would, it seems, have dearly loved to impose something similar, and across the country it was becoming more difficult to find places to play. It was not simple state-organized repression of the kids; club owners had genuine concerns for the safety of their staff, fixtures and fittings.

OCT 1978 The End Of Nancy.

Never a dull moment at the Chelsea Hotel. Stabbed by persons unknown, **Nancy** bled to death and **Sid** was arrested. Charged with second degree murder his bail was set at $50,000 – a sum beyond his means, especially since his apartment had been looted of cash in the confusion before the cops arrived – and he was shipped off to the hospital ward at Riker's Island to detox while Malcolm rushed around in ever-decreasing and ineffective circles trying to spring his best chicken.

Those with pennies to spend this month bought...

1. **CHAIRS MISSING**
   Wire
2. **PARALLEL LINES**
   Blondie
3. **LOVE BITES**
   Buzzcocks
4. **TEENAGE KICKS EP**
   The Undertones
5. **PREHISTORIC SOUNDS**
   Saints
6. **TRUE ROMANCES**
   Cortinas
7. **DISGUISE IN LOVE**
   John Cooper Clarke
8. **SEPARATES**
   999

Geoff Travis's Top Ten....

Geoff Travis opened the Rough Trade shop in London's Notting Hill in 1976. It swiftly became *the* place to pick up punk records on tiny labels which the mainstream stores didn't stock, and was particularly influential in importing hard-to-find records by American punk acts. Two years later, Travis launched Rough Trade as a record label. Among those he signed were Monochrome Set, Stiff Little Fingers, The Raincoats and the Smiths.

However, for his playlist we asked him to go back to his early days as the manager of Punk Britannia's coolest record store. "These are ten of the records from America that set the shop alight during the early days," he says.

PLAYLIST

1. 30 SECONDS FROM TOKYO Pere Ubu
from the compilation **Rough Trade Shops: 25 Years**

2. BLANK GENERATION Richard Hell
from **Blank Generation**

3. LOVE GOES TO BUILDING Talking Heads
from **The Best Of Talking Heads**

4. X OFFENDER Blondie
from **Blondie**

5. SICK OF YOU Iggy Pop
from **The Best Of Iggy Pop**

6. LITTLE JOHNNY JEWEL Television
from the expanded reissue of **Marquee Moon**

7. BANGKOK Alex Chilton
from **Bach's Bottom**

8. PISS FACTORY Patti Smith
from **Land 1975–2002**

9. JOCKO HOMO Devo
from **Are We Not Men? We Are Devo**

10. I'M STICKING WITH YOU Velvet Underground
From **VU**

Virgin finally sent Malcolm the dough and Sid hurtled off with nary a word of thanks to score. A couple of days later he slashed his arm, drank all his methadone and was on the way to join Nancy when his mum showed up. She called Malcolm, who intervened.

Saints split. Palmolive quit **The Slits** to become a full-time Raincoat. Knox dumps The Vibrators. **The Undertones** appeared on *Top Of The Pops* performing "Teenage Kicks".

DEC 1978 Dury brings the house down.

The Cure finally got to record a Peel session and, skimming the cream off their latest batch of songs, broadcast "10:15 Saturday Night", "Boys Don't Cry" and "Fire In Cairo".

The floor at Ilford Odeon gave way beneath the pogoing masses attending an **Ian Dury & The Blockheads** gig but fortunately the sheer strength of the carpet weave held up ... disaster avoided.

Sid Vicious escalated a bar room difference of opinion with Todd Smith (Patti's brother), tried to resolve matters with a broken bottle and whoops! He headed off back to Riker's for one of the worst nights of his life.

The Pretenders joined the traditional drummer swapping routine that punk bands seem to require, losing Gerry Mackleduff and gaining Martin Chambers. **The Rezillos** went one better and split into two bands. We now had The Revillos and another bunch, as yet un-named, to deal with. Safari Records give a deal to **Toyah**, possibly confusing her with Wayne County who had been on their books a while back. Spinning on the nation's turntables could be found *Public Image 1st Edition* by PiL and *A Factory Sample* EP, featuring artists including Joy Division, Durutti Column and Cabaret Voltaire.

> "PUBLIC IMAGE LTD. WOULD LIKE TO THANK ABSOLUTELY NOBODY. THANK YOU"
> PiL SLEEVE NOTES

...1979

Nº 0171
GEN. ADM. $3.50
DOORS OPEN 7.30 P.M.
SUN. EVE.
JANUARY 1
MIDWEST TICKET CO.®
SEX PISTOLS
18 OR OVER PROPER ID IS REQUESTED
SUN. JAN. 1, 1978-8:00 P.M.
$3.50
GEN. ADMISSION
THE AGORA 1730 EAST 24th STREET
WMMS NIGHT OUT
JAN. 1
TAX INCLUDED NO REFUND
1710 Nº 0171

JAN 1979 Sid Vicious on trial.

Sid Vicious's trial for the murder of girlfriend Nancy Spungen began; however, world events soon intervened to force the newspapers into covering more tragic and urgent stories as Vietnamese forces stormed in to capture Phnom Penh from the Khmer Rouge.

Gang Of Four recorded a Peel session and soon after **Joy Division** shuffled into the studio to blow a chill wind across the airwaves with their first session.

Crass's home-brewed anarchy got them and label Small Wonder into hot water with the police and the pressing plants after a foreman threatens to call the entire factory out on strike rather than allow a copy of the song "Asylum" to pass through the gates. (Honestly, you can't buy publicity that good!).

Sham 69 were forced to give up part-way through a gig by violence spilling out of control. As the BBC TV cameras rolled, a bunch of boneheads in the audience, cranked up on booze and cheap nationalism, attempted to stormtroop their way onto the stage through a swarm of security guards. Fisticuffs ensued and Jimmy, broken down in tears, led the band away.

FEB 1979 Sid Vicious is dead.

"YMCA" hit the charts worldwide, Pink Floyd debuted *The Wall* live in LA and, in the same month Sid got out of jail, bright-eyed, bushy tailed and sober after seven weeks enforced detox on Riker's island. Twenty minutes after making it back to Greenwich Village he was passed out on a bed in a friend's apartment. The next day he was dead. With the exception of a premature T-Shirt from Vivienne, it took almost a week for the exploitation of Sid's legend to begin.

MAR 1979 The New Merseybeat.

In New York, **Wendy O Williams** – ex-porn star turned chanteuse (pictured opposite) – and the other three **Plasmatics** released their debut EP on their own Vice Squad label.

Live At The Witch Trials by **The Fall** was released and **Teardrop Explodes** were leading a "New Merseybeat" according to *Sounds*, comprising, among others, Echo & The Bunnymen, Orchestral Manoeuvres In The Dark and Pink Military Stand Alone. There was apparently some stiff competition to come up with the stupidest band name.

APR 1979 Thatcher takes power.

Although nobody in the UK appreciated it at the time, Jim Callaghan's "Winter Of Discontent" would soon seem like a fondly recalled sum-

"OK McLAREN, YOU GOT YOUR CORPSE, NOW SELL IT"

TEENAGE DEPRESSION FANZINE

mer holiday. In the general election, Thatcher's gang was elected.

In an astonishing example of how rapidly the New Wave had already disappeared in the US, **Blondie**'s latest single "Sunday Girl", which went to #1 in the UK on the week of release, and across Europe in the days that followed, failed even to enter the charts back home.

The Ramones' *Rock 'n Roll High School* premiered in the same month that *Sounds* presented a photo of four lads from Birmingham sporting a very silly hairstyle indeed: first sighting of the mohican in Britain's homegrown punk crowd. It's a silly month all round though – JJ Burnel of **The Stranglers** was involved in the alleged kidnapping of a journalist with whom he used to be best mates (a joke gone wrong?), while Virgin Records was sending **Iggy Pop** on tour with **The Human League**.

MAY 1979 The Ramones vs Spector.

In the US, The Ramones began working with **Phil Spector**. The bad state of punk in the UK was becoming ever more obvious; after a couple of years on its outskirts, Gary Numan and Tubeway Army finally struck gold with their synth-heavy stomper "Are 'Friends' Electric". Another ominous sign saw the Mod Revival continuing apace. In Ireland, U2 were pulling in the crowds; and Lene Lovich was in Amsterdam with Nina

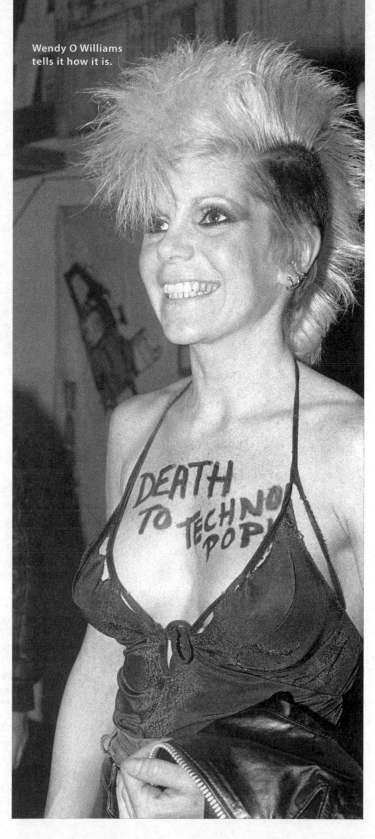

Wendy O Williams tells it how it is.

That Summer! (Arista; 1979)

A sixteen-track masterpiece compilation that stands as one of the essential recordings released during the glory days of late-70s Punk. *That Summer!* was a more expensive package than previous punk compilations, reflecting the increased importance the industry was attaching to the previously derided spikeyhead market. The set boasted a decent-quality gatefold sleeve, some reasonable photography, and a little input from the design department. The tracks it features are all widely available elsewhere, so there's no real hardship in its being unavailable on CD – just cobble it together yourself as a killer playlist – and if you do come accross a vinyl copy, it makes a great artefact to frame and stick on the wall. It's hard to beat.

THAT SUMMER

1. **SEX & DRUGS & ROCK & ROLL**
   Ian Dury

2. **SPANISH STROLL**
   Mink DeVille

3. **I DON'T WANT TO GO TO CHELSEA**
   Elvis Costello

4. **SHE'S SO MODERN**
   Boomtown Rats

5. **NEW LIFE**
   Zones

6. **ANOTHER GIRL ANOTHER PLANET**
   The Only Ones

7. **WHOLE WIDE WORLD**
   Wreckless Eric

8. **BECAUSE THE NIGHT**
   Patti Smith

9. **KICKS**
   The Boomtown Rats

10. **ROCKAWAY BEACH**
    The Ramones

11. **TEENAGE KICKS**
    The Undertones

12. **DO ANYTHING YOU WANNA DO**
    Eddie & The Hot Rods

13. **WHAT A WASTE**
    Ian Dury

14. **I LOVE THE SOUND OF BREAKING GLASS**
    Nick Lowe

15. **WATCHING THE DETECTIVES**
    Elvis Costello

16. **BLANK GENERATION**
    Richard Hell & The Voidoids

Hagen to make a film called *Cha-Cha*. Things were falling apart and, with **The Cure**'s *Three Imaginary Boys* having to fight off ska bands on one side, while facing down modern boys in sharp suits on the other, the centre couldn't hold. Even **Patti Smith** had had enough: "I really have no patience at all for so much of the crap in the punk rock scene … all this shit sticking safety pins into cheeks and all the fucking violence."

A List From Kris Needs

Under the editorship of Kris Needs, the legendary 1970s mag *ZigZag* – the biggest and the best of all the music fanzines – changed sides overnight in the tribal warfare between hippies and punks. Needs turned the title into virtually the Clash's house mag and members of the band backed him on at least one of the records he made as the Vice Creems – including the track he immodestly includes here. His acclaimed biography of Joe Strummer was published in 2005. "These were the big ones when I was steering *ZigZag*," he says of his playlist.

🎵 PLAYLIST

1. COMPLETE CONTROL The Clash
from **The Clash**

2. HUMAN BEING The New York Dolls
from **The New York Dolls**

3. TV EYE The Stooges
from **Fun House**

4. BORN TO LOSE The Heartbreakers
from **LAMF**

5. BLITZKREIG BOP The Ramones
from **The Ramones**

6. SATELLITE Sex Pistols
from **Never Mind The Bollocks**

7. NEW TOWN The Slits
from **Cut**

8. SUBURBAN RELAPSE Siouxsie & The Banshees
from **The Scream**

9. BLANK GENERATION Richard Hell & The Voidoids
from **Blank Generation**

10. DANGER LOVE Vice Creems
from **1979 single**

JUN 1979 Rotten on Juke Box Jury.

The Ramones were still recording with **Phil Spector** but had both the *Rock & Roll High School* soundtrack and *It's Alive* albums in the shops. The latter retailed at £4.99 and included 28 tracks recorded at the Rainbow, London on New Years Eve 1977. The price of 17.821428p per track featured heavily in the advertising but in more "death of punk rock" news, the album didn't even rate release in the US. Also, Rich Kids split this month.

Unknown Pleasures by **Joy Division** was album of the month on the turntable of the nation's youth, with "Nag Nag Nag", **Cabaret Voltaire's** scariest tune to date, blasting out of the better-stocked jukeboxes. In an accident surely sponsored by an anti-noise-pollution hit squad, The Lurkers' equipment van ran into a wall and destroyed everything inside.

Johnny Rotten and Joan Collins finished the month in style, appearing together on BBC's *Juke Box Jury*, reviewing the nation's latest single releases and rating them as "hits" or "misses".

As the year progressed things get quieter and quieter. It became transparent to all concerned that the first shock wave had passed. Though punk was clearly here to stay, it was also clear that punk was not going to stay the same. Roll on the 1980s.

AFTERMATH: 1980–1985

The 70s gave way to the "Me Decade" – an era of triumphant conservatism with the motto "Greed Is Good" – and punk took cover underground. By the middle of the 80s, indie bands, indie labels and indie entrepreneurs were absorbing the bulk of the UK's adolescent angst whereas US punk, which had never been particularly robust, shattered into dozens of small-scale local scenes with little sense of community.

1980

1980

Down on the mean streets of the UK's cities, politics became messier with the rise of the right-wing British Movement – a new home for former members of the National Front. Set against a background of grumbling urban discontent punk was pronounced dead and buried by the music and mainstream press.

At its heart though, the beat most definitely, went on and on; this was the year that **Minor Threat** and **Hüsker Dü** first took form, while in England, **The Sisters of Mercy** got it together. In short, the seed of 70s punk was already germinating into new fractions, new scenes. Album releases too demonstrated the fact; while the music may have come under a broadening set of banners (rather than the previous decade's all-encompassing New Wave grouping) there was still some extraordinarily robust and inventive noise being made.

With super-cop *Juliet Bravo* and robot-wise-cracker *Metal Mickey* on UK TV screens, the **Birthday Party**'s self-titled first album shows that Australia's taste for scary noise had yet to be exhausted. Moving across to the US, New York was represented by two from **Blondie** – *Eat To The Beat* and *Autoamerican* – plus the major label debut of **The Jim Carroll Band**, whose *Catholic Boy* told in plain English the shuddering, stuttering shameful life of drug addiction that Television had only hinted at. **The Feelies'** *Crazy Rhythms* – gaunt pop with well-defined cheekbones – was buried by the avalanche of publicity and fawning over **Talking Heads'** masterpiece album *Remain In Light*, but was none the worse for it. **The Cure**, meanwhile

Thr Dead Kennedys, lookin' meaner than mustard.

Essential 1980 Singles

The Pistols may have been a distant memory, but there were plenty of busy bunnies left on the scene, and morphing punk into a whole new bag of odd Plasticine shapes. Here's our pick of the singles releases in 1980.

🎵 PLAYLIST

1. **A FOREST**
   The Cure

2. **ACE OF SPADES**
   Motörhead

3. **ANT MUSIC**
   Adam and the Ants

4. **ATOMIC**
   Blondie

5. **BAGGY TROUSERS**
   Madness

6. **BANKROBBER**
   The Clash

7. **BIG MAN, BIG M.A.N.**
   Crass

8. **BRASS IN POCKET**
   Pretenders

9. **CALL ME**
   Blondie

10. **DANCING WITH MYSELF**
    Generation X

11. **EMBARRASSMENT**
    Madness

12. **ENOLA GAY**
    OMD

13. **GENO**
    Dexy's Midnight Runners

14. **GOING UNDERGROUND**
    The Jam

15. **HAPPY HOUSE**
    Siouxsie and the Banshees

16. **I CAN'T STAND UP FOR FALLING DOWN**
    Elvis Costello and the Attractions

17. **LOVE WILL TEAR US APART**
    Joy Division

18. **MIRROR IN THE BATHROOM**
    The Beat

19. **MY GIRL**
    Madness

20. **MY PERFECT COUSIN**
    The Undertones

21. **NEW AMSTERDAM**
    Elvis Costello and the Attractions

22. **POISON IVY**
    The Lambrettas

23. **RESCUE**
    Echo and the Bunnymen

24. **SPECIAL BREW**
    Bad Manners

25. **START**
    The Jam

26. **TALK OF THE TOWN**
    The Pretenders

27. **TOO MUCH TOO YOUNG**
    Specials

28. **WE ARE GLASS**
    Gary Numan

headed down the road to gloom with *Seventeen Seconds*; probably their finest moment.

Midwesterners **Devo** hit the stores with *Freedom Of Choice* while the West Coast mob offered *Group Sex* – first outing from **The Circle Jerks**, plus *Fresh Fruit For Rotting Vegetables* – **The Dead Kennedys'** first.

Taken together, **The Clash**'s *London Calling* and *Sandinista!* comprised five full-length albums – more than most bands managed in their entire career. **Elvis Costello And The Attractions**, travelling by the less-is-more route, offered up *Get Happy!!*. – although *Stations Of The Crass* (from **Crass**) defied you to do any such thing.

Other musical highlights of 1980 included **Patti Smith**'s marriage to MC5 guitarist **Fred "Sonic" Smith** in Detroit, the breakup of Led Zeppelin (who found themselves suddenly without a drummer) and Paul McCartney's marijuana hassle with the Japanese authorities – picked up with half a pound of weed in Tokyo, he was jailed for ten days before being deported.

1981

Raiders Of The Lost Ark, starring Harrison Ford, was the year's hit movie. A dark shadow, however, blotted the summer sun from the sky as corporate rock's behemoth, MTV was launched in answer to the unmanageable chaos and tiny profit margins of the alt:rock and indie scenes. Kicking off in August, MTV made an instant and radical change to mainstream pop marketing with such peculiarities as Kim Carnes' "Bette Davis Eyes"(#1 for nine weeks) and Olivia Newton-John's "Physical" (#1 for ten weeks) early video-driven successes.

Throbbing Gristle gave it up this year, to the relief of their neighbours, but the silence was short-lived as **Sonic Youth** and **Social Distortion** started jamming their way towards a new kind of rebel music.

Of the old guard, **Crass** were still ploughing away with *Penis Envy*, while **The Exploited** propped up the corpse with the release of *Punk's Not Dead*. A strong wiff of the new era came, however, with the appearance of **Kraftwerk**'s *Computer World* and **New Order**'s *Movement*.

This was also the year that saw **Adam And The Ants** at the height of their flamboyant powers, again riding the video wave created by the birth of MTV.

Essential 1981 Singles

I'm sure you've got the idea by now – what better way to sum up the-year-that-was than with a little look through our singles box. And if we had to pick just one this year, it would almost certainly be "Ceremony".

 PLAYLIST

1. **ABSOLUTE BEGINNERS**
   The Jam
2. **ALL STOOD STILL" & 1X. VIENNA**
   Ultravox
3. **KINGS OF THE WILD FRONTIER**
   Adam & The Ants
4. **CEREMONY**
   New Order
5. **DON'T YOU WANT ME**
   Human League
6. **GHOST TOWN**
   Specials
7. **GREY DAY**
   Madness
8. **IT'S GONNA HAPPEN**
   The Undertones
9. **MOTÖRHEAD (LIVE)**
   Motörhead
10. **ONCE IN A LIFETIME**
    Talking Heads
11. **ONE IN TEN**
    UB40
12. **PAPA'S GOT A BRAND NEW PIGBAG**
    Pigbag
13. **PLAN B**
    Dexy's Midnight Runners
14. **PRETTY IN PINK**
    The Psychedelic Furs
15. **RAPTURE**
    Blondie
16. **REWARD**
    The Teardrop Explodes
17. **ROCK THIS TOWN**
    The Stray Cats
18. **SGT. ROCK IS GOING TO HELP ME**
    XTC
19. **SHE'S GOT CLAWS**
    Gary Numan
20. **SWORDS OF A THOUSAND MEN**
    Tenpole Tudor
21. **FUNERAL PYRE**
    The Jam
22. **THE LUNATICS HAVE TAKEN OVER THE ASYLUM** Fun Boy Three
23. **THIS IS RADIO CLASH**
    The Clash

1982

The year that Blondie split up saw the first wave of punk retreating further after swamping Europe and both coasts of the USA. In its wake indie rock started to flex its foppish muscles, epitomized by **The Smiths**, who formed in Manchester and began their slow conquest of sensitive teenaged hearts up and down the UK. Across in NYC, **Madonna**'s life in the limelight kicked off. She later appeared in the UK as one of the first guests when youth culture show *The Tube* started to transmit on Channel 4. CDs first appeared in the shops this year, with players way too expensive for the average punter to consider.

Post-punk in one form or another made an increasing impression on the pop charts, with the newly buffed-up **Human League** topping the tree on both sides of the Atlantic with "Don't You Want Me?" and **Adam & The Ants** pop-gold "Goody Two-Shoes" helping bury even deeper any memory of his deviant past incarnation. **The Jam** did well, although neither "Town Called Malice" nor "Beat Surrender" managed to match **Dexys Midnight Runners'** "Come On Eileen", which outsold all its rivals in Britain and proceeded to a fine post-retirement career as a perpetual hit at wedding-night discos.

In the States, "I Love Rock 'N Roll" by **Joan Jett & The Blackhearts** was the best selling single of the year, and "O Superman" from **Laurie Anderson** was one of the strangest. **Michael Jackson** released *Thriller* and wiped the floor with everyone when his million-dollar promo for the title track premiered on MTV. The big movie studios took their own life and death struggle into space with *Star Trek II: The Wrath of Khan* battling *ET: The Extra-Terrestrial* for intergalactic bums on seats.

The Stranglers' "Golden Brown", "I Know What Boys Like" from **The Waitresses** and "Iron Fist" by **Motörhead** were keeping the freak flag of subversive youth flying, while paranoid rockers could rely on **Black Flag** and "TV Party" for their thrills.

1983

Punk rock was no longer a newsworthy movement, and having expired almost completely in the USA it saw a depressing swathe of big name disbandments. **Joey Ramone** was beaten up in August and underwent brain surgery – not a teenage lobotomy – as a result. In Europe, the scene continued to fragment and vanish underground while **The Cocteau Twins** and **The Smiths** championed a shy, shuffling advance of twee-pop bands such as Altered Images into the alternative spotlight. Mainstream pop continued to funnel money into the video medium. **The Police** released *Synchronicity* and made Sting another small for-

1982–83

Billy Bragg's Playlist....

The 20-year-old Billy Bragg formed his first band Riff Raff during punk's annus mirabilis of 1977. Apart from a short spell in the army in 1981, he's remained pretty much true to the cause ever since, forging a unique role as a working-class, politically motivated performer who has never forgotten his roots. He sent us his playlist via the wonders of modern technology while en route to Heathrow airport...

PLAYLIST

1. GARAGELAND The Clash
from **The Clash**

2. IN THE CITY The Jam
from **In The City**

3. 96 TEARS / GET OUT OF DENVER / GLORIA / SATISFACTION Eddie And The Hot Rods
from **Live at the Marquee EP**

4. GOD SAVE THE QUEEN Sex Pistols
from **Never Mind The Bollocks**

5. ORGASM ADDICT Buzzcocks
from **The Complete Singles Anthology**

6. NEWTOWN The Slits
from **The Cut**

7. SHEENA IS A PUNK ROCKER The Ramones
from **Rocket to Russia**

8. ALL I WANT Snatch
from **Snatch**

9. DARLING, LETS HAVE ANOTHER BABY Johnny Moped from **Basically: The Best Of Johnny Moped**

10. INTO THE VALLEY The Skids
from **Scared To Dance**

tune with "Every Breath You Take" before breaking up. Glenn Danzig disbanded **The Misfits**, going on to set up Samhain, and elsewhere, ex-Tourists, now Eurythmics **Dave Stewart** and **Annie Lennox** continued the androgynous explosion in mainstream entertainment with their "Sweet Dreams (Are Made of This)" chart and video hit. **New Order** put out their second album – *Power, Corruption & Lies* – and plunged into the real world of economics when their worldwide hit "Blue Monday" – the best-selling 12" single in history – lost money on every copy sold. The problem was a rather lovely cut-out section of the cardboard record sleeve, which made them exceptionally expensive to produce.

On TV, hits included *The A-Team* and *WWF Wrestling* – which made Mr. T and Hulk Hogan unlikely heroes to kids all over the globe.

Of the top singles out in 1983, very few had even the twinkle of that late-70s punk sound; everything was getting crisp and drum-machine-calibrated. That said, you might have spent your punk pocket money on "Everyday I Write The Book" by **Elvis Costello**, or "The Love Cats" by **The Cure**. "Tunnel Of Love" was a big hit for **Fun Boy Three** and indie pop was still bobbing along thanks to "Rip It Up" by **Orange Juice** , "This Charming Man" from **The Smiths** and **R.E.M.**'s "Radio Free Europe".

By now **Siouxsie And The Banshees** were very much their own creation and had a massive hit with their cover of The Beatles' "Dear Prudence", while Talking Heads were filling dance floors everywhere with "Burning Down The House".

1984

The world of entertainment reeled in shock when Michael Jackson's hair caught fire during the filming of a commercial. Los Angeles' reputation as a bad town for entertainers was enhanced still further when Marvin Gaye was shot and killed during an argument with his father. Later in the year Mötley Crüe's Vince Neil was involved in a serious drink-driving accident in LA, killing his passenger **Razzle** (Nicholas Dingley) of **Hanoi Rocks**.

Frankie Goes To Hollywood spent nine weeks at the top of the UK singles chart with "Two Tribes". **The Jesus & Mary Chain** released their first single, "Upside Down", injecting the UK scene with a much-needed dose of punky white noise. Meanwhile, punk-turned-national-hero **Bob Geldof** and Band Aid ended the year with their wholesome charity single "Do They Know It's Christmas".

Essential Purchases Of 1984

One man's "rock" is another man's "punk" and another man's "indie". Though the bands have largely changed and the tags most certainly have, there was still some mighty fine noise being made in the mid 80s.

🎵 ALBUM PLAYLIST

1. **THE WONDERFUL AND FRIGHTENING WORLD OF THE FALL** The Fall
2. **TWO STEPS FROM THE MOVE** Hanoi Rocks
3. **ZEN ARCADE** Hüsker Dü
4. **MEAT PUPPETS II** Meat Puppets
5. **OUT OF STEP** Minor Threat
6. **DOUBLE NICKELS ON THE DIME** The Minutemen
7. **NO REMORSE** Motörhead
8. **FROM HER TO ETERNITY** Nick Cave And The Bad Seeds
9. **LEARNING TO CRAWL** The Pretenders
10. **LET IT BE** The Replacements
11. **HYAENA** Siouxsie And The Banshees
12. **THE SMITHS** The Smiths

🎵 SINGLES PLAYLIST

1. **THE KILLING MOON** Echo And The Bunnymen
2. **HERE COMES THE RAIN AGAIN** Eurythmics
3. **TWO TRIBES** Frankie Goes To Hollywood
4. **EYES WITHOUT A FACE** Billy Idol
5. **MADAM BUTTERFLY** Malcolm McLaren
6. **MICHAEL CAINE** Madness
7. **THIN LINE BETWEEN LOVE AND HATE** Pretenders
8. **WHAT DIFFERENCE DOES IT MAKE** The Smiths
9. **SKIN DEEP** Stranglers
10. **UPSIDE DOWN** The Jesus & Mary Chain

1985

Following suit in the wave of charity recordings kicked off by Band Aid, "a galaxy of stars from the world of entertainment" was corralled into the studio to bleat out "We Are The World". The summer saw the whole episode peak with *Live Aid*; members of the Punk Rock family in attendance included The Boomtown Rats (of course), Adam Ant, Ultravox, Elvis Costello and The Pretenders.

This year also saw **The Feelies** reunite and **The Police** disband. Overall a good result. In other news, 1985 saw Mickey Mouse welcomed in China and "New Coke" appeared and then disappeared off the shelf immediately in a hail of protest. In New Zealand, Greenpeace suddenly found themselves short of a boat after French commandos sank the *Rainbow Warrior*, in Auckland harbour.

But what of punk rock? Well, as *Rolling Stone* magazine declared in August of this year...

"PUNK ... IN ALL ITS OBNOXIOUS, REBELLIOUS, SNOTTY GLORY – LIVES."

ROLLING STONE; AUG 1985

The magazine was, of course, refering to the blossoming American scene of the day, which was quietly bubbling away just off the mainstream press's radar. Some called it punk, others called it hardcore,

The Albums That Made 1985

It's funny how the big wheel turns, and while the initial punk spark of the mid 70s burned out in the States almost as quickly as it was struck, the mid 80s once again saw the tinder smouldering across the United States in preparation for the next big flame.

While all these album selections for 1985 are essential listening, it was the contributions from the likes of Hüsker Dü and Meat Puppets that set the standard for the next wave of punked-up bands.

PLAYLIST

1. LOOSE NUT
Black Flag

2. DON'T STAND ME DOWN
Dexys Midnight Runners

3. THE FIRSTBORN IS DEAD
Nick Cave And The Bad Seeds

4. FRANKENCHRIST
Dead Kennedys

5. BLACK FLAG
In My Head

6. HORROR EPICS
The Exploited

7. NEW DAY RISING
Hüsker Dü

8. UP ON THE SUN
Meat Puppets

9. 3-WAY TIE (FOR LAST)
The Minutemen

10. RUM, SODOMY, AND THE LASH
The Pogues

11. TIM
The Replacements

12. LITTLE CREATURES
Talking Heads

Black Flag's
Henry Rollins.

but whatever the moniker, when bands such as **Black Flag**, **Hüsker Dü**, **Flipper** and **The Replacements** took to the stage in their respective US hometowns, it was clear that the original punk explosion had never stopped reverberating. Here was an angry, politicized scene with a message or two to communicate and an ever-expanding fan-base. It would soon become clear to the major record labels, as it had a decade earlier, that there was something here to be milked ... and a few years down the line the realization of that cash cow came in the form of grunge.

Part One
The End
Of History

With the 80s in full swing, and the world apparently jogging its way to a greed-fuelled physical fitness, the last remaining outposts of classic 1970s punkdom either packed their kit away and vanished, or went underground, popping their heads up every few years for anniversary gigs. Punk, however, continued to haunt both the music industry and, increasingly, popular culture.

As the 1990s began to take shape it was the power-chording and snivels of grunge (see box) that led a generation of kids into a decade of three-quarter-length shorts and goatee beards, until the shotgun blast of **Kurt Cobain**'s death finally shook them out of their torpor.

Travelling alongside the grunge machine, "indie" and "alternative" rock were still pushing through and in many instances championing the DIY ethics of the original movement. In the UK bands like **Huggy Bear** and **Voodoo Queens** were shouting loud enough to be heard in both the UK music press and over the Atlantic, where the Olympia indie-punk-grrl-power scene embraced many UK bands.

In the mainstream a more traditional punk sound was being dusted down by acts like **Green Day** and **Operation Ivy**, while so-called ska punk was also on the rise at the hands of **Offspring**, **Pennywise** and their ilk.

Another large chunk of the new generation rinsed the griminess and snotty mindset of dumb uncooperativeness out of punk, dropped acid, chewed on ecstasy, and took the DIY ethos up to their home computers, where they fiddled around with some beats and came up with the rave scene. Though it is easy to dismiss the dance scene in a book about punk, one should not forget that some of the noisiest, parent-alienating music to appear during the 90s came from the likes of DIY electronic pioneers such as **Aphex Twin** – check out "Ventolin" and "Come To Daddy", they're about as punk rock as it gets.

Grunge

Here's a recipe for grunge: take a large pinch of punk rock (US or British), stew it in self-loathing and serve with a plaid shirt and baggy shorts.

Grunge killed the "hair metal" bands of the 1980s stone dead in the water, then machine-gunned their bodies for good measure. Poison disappeared, Mötley Crüe took some time out to count their millions, and even Guns N' Roses scurried off into studio limbo.

Grunge music will forever be associated with Seattle's **Sub Pop** label, which gave the whole scene a uniquely Northwestern aspect, and a home for the flotsam and jetsam of disaffected American youth who weren't satisfied with the bleak impersonality of Los Angeles. It started off as a genuine rootsy scene, with clubs and labels sprouting in Oregon and Washington State, but when **Nirvana** went supernova, the major-label marketing teams became involved and soon the world was awash with spotty long-haired kids wearing tartan outdoorsy shirts and singing songs about pain, heroin, pain, unemployment, pain and heroin.

The band **Green River** came out of Seattle and have a good claim to having invented the patent "grunge" sound. Slower, on the whole, than the basic punk rock that it was based on, grunge maintained a fondness for filthy over-driven guitars fed through wildly protesting amplification, a stereotypical loud-soft-loud-even louder routine to the verse/chorus layout and lyrics that were either precisely enunciated with bitter resentment or bellowed into an unsuspecting microphone that would sometimes give up the ghost in shock. The roots of grunge's downward shift in tempo are often traced back to the US's hardcore scene and, particularly the mid-80s output of bands such as **Flipper** and **Black Flag** (at the time of its release in 1984, the latter's *My War* set was criticized by some punk rockers for its slower, introspective groove).

A key moment came when Green River split and turned into **Mudhoney** and **Mother Love Bone**, both bands having to fight it out for audience share with arrivistes such as **Soundgarden**, **Stone Temple Pilots**, **Pearl Jam**, **Smashing Pumpkins**, **Alice In Chains** and the aforementioned Nirvana.

Nevermind was Nirvana's second album and went to the top of the charts in all right-thinking nations of the world in 1991. Nirvana were the band to aspire to and, despite the unfortunate example to American youth set by **Kurt Cobain**'s taste for heroin and messy suicide, remain champions of the movement to this day. Although grunge has been yesterday's news for years, Cobain's face stares glumly down from a million bedroom walls around the world even now.

Any of the early recordings by the bands featured in our grunge playlist – all either full-blown grunge acts or essential influences on the movement – are worth a listen. These tracks are particularly grungy, but in a good way.

🎵 PLAYLIST

1. **LOVE, HATE, LOVE** Alice In Chains
from **Facelift (Sony, 1990)**

2. **REHAB DOLL** Green River
from **Dry As A Bone / Rehab (Sub Pop, 1998)**

3. **TEENAGE WHORE** Hole
from **Pretty On The Inside (City Slang, 1993)**

4. **BAR-X-THE ROCKING M** The Melvins
from **Stag (Atlantic, 2002)**

5. **CROWN OF THORNS** Mother Love Bone
from **Apple (Lemon, 2003)**

6. **TOUCH ME I'M SICK** Mudhoney
from **The Radio Sessions (Strange Fruit, 2000)**

7. **NOTHING MAN** Pearl Jam
from **Rearview Mirror: The Best Of (Epic, 2004)**

8. **HALO OF ASHES** Screaming Trees
from **Dust (Epic, 2001)**

9. **EMOTION SICKNESS** Silverchair
from **Neon Ballroom (Columbia, 2001)**

10. **BLACK HOLE SUN** Soundgarden
from **A-sides (A&M, 1997)**

By the end of the decade, **pop punk** was the vogue, with spikey headed acts like **Sum 41, Good Charlotte** and more recently the bizarrely popular **McFly** trying hard to recapture the magic of the late 1970s in an attempt to raise some money for a few major labels who were pulling their hair out looking for the next big thing.

And while these same majors were trying hard not to panic about the growth of Internet file-sharing, the World Wide Web was becoming an important arena for the dissemination of new underground music – the DIY ethic had never been more alive.

The politics was still strong too, with examples of the militant punk rock message coming from movements such as **Rock Against Bush**, spearheaded by **NOFX**'s Fat Mike, and bands such as New York City's **Leftöver Crack** and their outspoken post-ska-punk anthems.

Which all brings us to the end of this whistlestop tour of The Punk Years. Many of the gaps in specific bands' histories should be filled in Part Two of this book, and for everything else, there's always the Internet. One thing to learn from all these recollections is that punk rock at its best is the sound of rebellion, and as such was, and is, the continuation of a tradition that can be traced right back to early rock'n'roll, the blues, and even folk music.

And punk rock seems unlikely to go away. From Seattle's continuing influence in the top left corner of the map to the cheeky, chirpy clubs and unsigned geniuses playing in venues along Brighton's seafront in the bottom right corner, punk refuses to die. Just spend a couple of hours surfing the gargantuan **MySpace.com** website community to get an idea of how much new talent is out there waiting to fill future volumes of this book.

Part Two

A Punk A–Z

A CERTAIN RATIO

Formed Sheffield, England, 1977; still spotted now and then.

Leading figures in the north of England post-punk movement, **A Certain Ratio** had credibility by the bucket-load. They took their name from the lyrics of Brian Eno's "The True Wheel"; their first album was only available on limited-edition cassette; it came out on Manchester's innovative Factory Records; and, in the best punk tradition, they were hellishly difficult to categorize.

The first hint of the group's own brand of mayhem came in 1979, when **Simon Topping** (vocals/trumpet), **Martha Tilson** (vocals), **Jez Kerr** (bass),

Martin Moscrop (guitar) and **Peter Terrell** (electronics/loops) released their first single, "All Night Party / The Thin Boys". **Donald Johnson** (drums) signed up shortly afterwards, introducing a new punk/funk sound that they made their own. When the group toured the UK with label-mates Joy Division, audiences expecting yet another evening of three-chord wonders found themselves confronted by horn sections, synthesizers and Latin-tinged funk, with Topping dressed in army surplus and yelling at the crowd like a raving lunatic as he hopped round the stage

Backed by Factory and produced by Martin Hannett, the group turned to bands such as Can and Kraftwerk and New York dance music for inspiration, creating an intelligent alternative to an

ACR, and inset left, the cover of their grooving LP *Graveyard & Ballroom*.

increasingly insular punk-rock scene. Alongside bands such as Human League and Joy Division, ACR developed their own even bleaker take on punk's "no future" credo, paradoxically producing danceable tracks of unutterable gloom. Their take on the post-punk movement produced first *The Graveyard And The Ballroom*, and then, after their first US tour, the experimental album *To Each*.

ACR flew to New York every year to recharge their batteries performing to broader-minded audiences than they found at home. However, by the end of 1982, Terrell, Tilson and Topping had left the band, and despite picking up some new tricks from the NYC urban street music scene, the rest of the group found it difficult to graft them onto the twisted industrial funk they made back in the UK. The music was disturbing, challenging and raucous, but although it perfectly encapsulated early 1980s angst, it veered a little too close to Latin jazz-funk for many punks' tastes, and the group never really broke through in a big way.

I'd Like To See You Again (1982), featuring newly signed vocalist **Carol McKenzie**, was followed in 1985 by *Force*, with the line-up strengthened still further by the addition of **Tony Quigley** on sax. Their New York gigs gave them a taste for the new, chunkier rhythms played at the Danceteria club (where they performed on several occasions, supported at least once by Madonna), and they became the only possible choice to headline the launch of Manchester's answer to the Big Apple's nightspots – the Factory-owned Hacienda club.

Leaving Factory in 1986, ACR moved to A&M; *Good Together* came out to muted applause in 1989, followed a year later by the mini-LP *Acr: Mcr*. Meanwhile, Alan McGee's Creation Records picked up ACR's back catalogue and, dusting it down with help from Graham Massey, Electronic, the Other Two and others, released a remix album, *Looking For A Certain Ratio*.

The band kept a low profile for most of the "me" decade and the fans who'd tried to keep in touch assumed they'd suddenly, silently vanished away. Instead, ACR returned in 1997 with *Change The Station*. Held together by friendship (strong enough to permit members to leave and rejoin apparently at will over a period of twenty years) and a shared interest in making new music, ACR grew from a career band into something more akin to a DJ collective as they grew from young

musicians out to change the world into a bunch of comfortably middle-aged part-timers for whom music is still more than a hobby, but perhaps less of an obsession than it used to be.

⊙ **The Graveyard And The Ballroom (Universal Sound, 2004)**

Combining live and studio recordings, the legendary first album shows ACR at the forefront of the post-punk revolution. Now reissued in pristine digital sound, it includes the A- and B-sides of the band's otherwise impossible-to-find first single, "All Night Party" and "The Thin Boys".

ADAM & THE ANTS

Formed London, 1977; not seen for years.

O nce upon a time there was a London-based band of feel-good pub rockers called Bazooka Joe, fronted by one **Stuart Goddard**. According to legend, Goddard ditched Bazooka Joe after seeing the light as shone by the Sex Pistols. He returned, backed by a bunch of the nastiest-looking rubber-boys London's nascent punk scene could spit out, with a stage act that verged on criminal assault, and managed by shop assistant turned mistress of ceremonies **Jordan**. **Adam And The Ants** were soon a very hot ticket on the UK circuit.

Early Ant-music made the most of punk's "don't be afraid of a new direction" ethic, and weren't afraid to draw on bondage, degradation and kinky S&M sex for their stage act. Shows sometimes climaxed with a shirtless Stuart, now reborn as **Adam**, on his knees being heartily flogged by Jordan, who, striding unannounced onto the stage in full dominatrix get up, would scare the living shit out of the audience. They were, though, obliged to admit that she managed to keep the beat going. After belting out "Lou" and thwacking Adam once or twice more for good measure, she would retreat to the bar and graciously accept drinks from admirers. The rest of the band – **Andy Warren** (bass), **Lester Square** (guitar) and **Paul Flanagan** (drums) – kept their heads down, their clothing black and their attitude sulky. As an image, it worked really well.

Even on the transgression-worshipping outer edges of punk, it was hard to get away with lyrics such as "Tie me up and hit me with a stick / Beat me, beat me / Use a truncheon or a household brick", and Adam trod a lonely path, singing the joys of ligotage and Italian Futurism. Unsurprisingly, although the group attracted a peculiar bunch of dedicated acolytes in white face-paint and dinky black stripes, a mass audience failed to follow. An album of sordid degradation and atrocious jokes, *Dirk Wears White Sox*, and a collection of John Peel sessions are all that remain

ICONIC SINGLE: ZERØX / WHIP IN MY VALISE (Do-It, 1980)

"Zerøx" was one of the original Ants' best songs and one that never failed them live. An everyday story of seeing the best bits of your songs stolen by musical associates, it regularly wound Adam himself into paroxysms of righteous anger on stage. Later, once he'd sold his soul to the demons of mainstream success and discovered the value of "seeking inspiration" from other people's work, it was dropped from the set. The B-side was far more interesting though…

"Whip In My Valise" takes its title from one of the most famous dirty books published by the Olympia Press: a tale of five women, four sadists and a nymphomaniac, travelling through Europe and beating breathy gasps out of every man they put under the lash. The Ants' masterwork is every bit as funny and almost as painful as the stories in the book, including such agonizing lyrics as the refrain "Who taught you to torture? (Who taught ya?)" and the unforgettable couplet "I spent a packet / On a new straitjacket".

A masterful reminder of punk's ethos of transgression and the ability to laugh at yourself, "Whip" helped to wrest polished patent leather and skin-tight rubber away from Soho's sex-establishments and wriggle it onto far more nubile bodies. For that, if for nothing else, we should all be grateful.

as evidence of the good old down-and-dirty version of the band.

When his original Ants collectively departed to become Annabella's backing band, having been tempted away by Malcolm McLaren's promises of money and success in **Bow Wow Wow**, Adam quite sensibly ditched his dreams of a pervy, punk-led sexual revolution in favour of a far more easily achieved pop superstardom. Swallowing what little pride he had, Adam went to McLaren and picked his brains for a new image.

McLaren turned to Vivienne Westwood's Pirate collection for sartorial inspiration, added a touch of highwayman chic of his own and gave us back a new improved Adam. This *"King Of The Wild Frontier"* version was washed free of any sexual menace, but still good-looking enough to moisten the underwear of the Saturday-morning TV audience. The new Ants, fronted by his old mate **Marco Pirroni**, camped along willingly enough in a set of outrageous videos that kept them at the top of the charts for three years. It was fun, it was amusing to watch, and the "Prince Charming" dance routine is still a staple at post-wedding discos. Punk, however, it was not.

When pop sales dried up, Adam went to the US, living on the royalties and playing a few cameos in TV shows to pay the rent. The Ants went on to build nests of their own, steering clear of the spotlight and growing up relatively healthy and wise. For Adam, however, the loss of fame, record sales and his hair at around the same time were all too much to bear. He returned to the UK, living a quiet, sober life before famously losing control in 2002. After a bizarre fight in a North London pub, he was committed to a London psychiatric hospital and charged with possession of a firearm. Since then, he's been sensibly keeping himself to himself, out of the tabloids and the public eye.

◉ Dirk Wears White Sox (Do-It, 1979)

The classic art-punk celebration of the late 70s, *DWWS* is full of overly clever lyrics, puns bad enough to have been cut from a *Carry On* film script and an air of rather seedy gloom and despondency. Very monochrome, very stylish.

◉ Antbox (Columbia, 2003)

Subtitled "The Definitive Story Of Adam & The Ants", this 3-CD box set promises – and delivers – the lot. All the hits are here of course (up to "Wonderful" from Adam's 1990s revival), but what makes this a must-have is the selection of previously unreleased demos dating back to his rubber-fetishist days.

🎵 PLAYLIST: ADAM AND THE ANTS

When you need to take it sleazy, to hunker down in your bondage gear and rub yourself with petroleum jelly, then you need a spoonful of vintage Ant-music – it helps the medicine go down. Most of the following come from the reissued expanded version of the first album.

1. DAY I MET GOD
from **DIRK WEARS WHITE SOX (Sony, 2004)**

2. CLEOPATRA
from **DIRK WEARS WHITE SOX (Sony, 2004)**

3. CATHOLIC DAY
from **DIRK WEARS WHITE SOX (Sony, 2004)**

4. ZEROX
from **DIRK WEARS WHITE SOX (Sony, 2004)**

5. WHIP IN MY VALISE
from **DIRK WEARS WHITE SOX (Sony, 2004)**

6. PHYSICAL
from **DIRK WEARS WHITE SOX (Sony, 2004)**

7. KICK!
from **DIRK WEARS WHITE SOX (Sony, 2004)**

8. PLASTIC SURGERY
from **ANTBOX (Columbia, 2003)**

9. DEUTSCHER GIRLS
from **ANTBOX (Columbia, 2003)**

10. PUERTO RICAN
from **ANTBOX (Columbia, 2003)**

◉ **Complete Radio One Recordings**
(Strange Fruit, 2001)

Adam's original Ants were far more disturbing than the gang of dandy pirates/highwaymen he recruited on his way to becoming a star, while the dubious sexual preferences expressed in his early lyrics set him apart from the rest of the London punk-rock gang. This collection of Peel sessions and other studio detritus casts an interesting light upon his dark obsessions, his art-school background and terrible taste in puns.

THE ADVERTS

Formed Devon/London, 1976; split up 1979.

Tim Smith had a history of songwriting and glam rock, and he had most unpromising grammar-school / West Country roots, but when he met **Gaye Atlas**, art-school romance and punk magic sparked into life. Tim became

TV **Smith**, and together with the renamed **Gaye Advert**, left Devon for London, where they found guitarist **Howard Pickup** (a.k.a. Boak) and drummer **Laurie Driver** (previously Muscat). The **Adverts** were ready to roll and played their first gig at the Roxy on January 15, 1977, as support for the newly formed Generation X.

In what seemed like a bizarre conspiracy to those who attended the same gigs as the journalists, The Adverts never got the good reviews they deserved. Though this would have been enough to stop most new acts dead in their tracks, once the band appeared on the seminal *Live At The Roxy* album, storming through "Bored Teenagers", they picked up a countrywide audience.

Their first single, "One Chord Wonders" on Stiff, was heavily promoted (posters for the tour proudly proclaimed "The Adverts can play one chord, The Damned can play three. Come and hear all four at…"), but when it failed to chart they moved to Anchor. Releasing "Gary Gilmore's Eyes" – a punk-rock masterpiece, with a *Grand Guignol* storyline about the wish of a murderer facing execution to donate his eyes to science, The Adverts were suddenly mainstream national news. Once the tabloids got hold of the song's "sick" lyrics, and spread them all over their pages, the single went straight to number eighteen in the UK charts, riding a wave of outrage and propelling Gaye to unwanted media stardom.

Gaye did her best to turn her back on publicity that relied on her looks, leaving her bass to pose in her place for the cover of their third single, "Safety In Numbers", and by the autumn of 1977, The Adverts, the band from nowhere, was back on track and on the road, touring with her all-time

hero, Iggy Pop. The new single dealt, like many of Smith's London songs, with punk's move towards conformity and uniform, and its readiness to abandon its earlier ideals. Having failed to storm the charts, missed out on streets paved with gold and proved unable to get any positive coverage in the music papers, the group found the pressure beginning to tell. Damning it with faint praise, *NME* voted "Gary Gilmore's Eyes" as the 21st best single of 1977, and the writing was on the wall.

Press response was varied when the band's debut album, *Crossing The Red Sea With The Adverts*, came out in February 1978. Although "No Time To Be 21" took the band back into the singles charts, the album peaked just inside the Top 40, and despite the undeniable quality of the music, it failed to propel them into the big league.

Live, the band were unmatched for excitement, intensity and integrity of performance. On stage, Smith soaked up his own skinny weight in spittle every night from misguided morons, Gaye created a whole new dimension of cool, Pickup thrashed around like a man electrocuted and Driver was simply magnificent. Yet punk was already waning in the USA, and although they were on tour for most of 1978, personnel problems (Driver out with hepatitis, replaced by **Rod Latler**, ex-Rings), label difficulties (leaving ABC, signing with RCA) and writer's block (leading Smith to collaborate with **Richard Strange** of less-than-punk band the Doctors of Madness) resulted in the disappearance of their hell-for-leather insistent driving music and a second album that lost them the bulk of their fans.

Looking back now that the dust has settled, *Cast Of Thousands* is not that bad an album. Good songs, clever musicianship, but too unlike their previous sound for their audience to make the leap with them. It was universally despised by the press, was lackadaisically promoted by the label and resulted in Pickup walking away from the band, to be replaced eventually by **Paul Martinez**. The ink on his contract was barely dry before a meeting was called to wind up the band. **Rick Martinez** (Paul's brother) joined as drummer for a few contractual-obligation gigs but after a final October 1979 concert in Slough, The Adverts were no more.

Although TV Smith always tried too hard, Gaye Advert's laconic basslines and "don't fuck with me" glare kept the band in touch with the real world

---

**ICONIC SINGLE:
ONE CHORD WONDERS /
QUICKSTEP (STIFF, 1977)**

Not just a fine song with an equally impressive B-side, this was one of the very first punk singles. And what a single! One guitar riff, two verses and a chorus that you can repeat all night long – this was slice-of-life punk-rock impressionism at its finest. The verses tell of every musician's pre-performance nerves, the chorus screws the fear into a small ball and throws it away without a backward glance – "The Wonders don't care. We don't give a damn".

"Quickstep" merits attention not only for its move away from the pulse-beat of punk rock (not that anyone ever attempted to match their furious pogoing to Smith's novelty rhythm), but also for its lyrics of defiance. When he wrote this, TV Smith was convinced that "Pretty soon you're going to see what punks can do". It didn't take him long to learn otherwise.

🎵 PLAYLIST: THE ADVERTS

What you need from The Adverts is the singles and a couple of album tracks. Here they are.

1. **ONE CHORD WONDERS**
from **Anthology (Devil's Jukebox, 2003)**

2. **QUICKSTEP**
from **Anthology (Devil's Jukebox, 2003)**

3. **GARY GILMORE'S EYES**
from **Anthology (Devil's Jukebox, 2003)**

4. **BORED TEENAGERS**
from **Anthology (Devil's Jukebox, 2003)**

5. **SAFETY IN NUMBERS**
from **Anthology (Devil's Jukebox, 2003)**

6. **WE WHO WAIT**
from **Anthology (Devil's Jukebox, 2003)**

7. **NO TIME TO BE 21**
from **Anthology (Devil's Jukebox, 2003)**

8. **BOMBSITE BOY**
from **Anthology (Devil's Jukebox, 2003)**

9. **NEW CHURCH**
from **Anthology (Devil's Jukebox, 2003)**

10. **CAST OF THOUSANDS**
from **Anthology (Devil's Jukebox, 2003)**

and on the right edge of cool. Smith still gigs, and still produces goose pimples of empathy when he performs "Bored Teenagers", even if his audience these days are all middle-aged.

⊙ Crossing The Red Sea With The Adverts (Castle, 1998)

As this reissued CD version of the album also includes the original versions of the band's first two singles, this is probably all the Adverts you need. Album-only tracks such as "Bombsite Boy", "New Church" and "New Day Dawning" are far from filler, though – they contain Smith's most incisive lyrics and stand as masterpieces of disaffection even now.

ALICE DONUT

Formed NYC 1987, split up, re-formed in 2004

When **Tom Antona** (scream-inducing vocals) started collaborating with **Dave Giffin** (guitar), **Richard Marshall** (guitar), **Stephen Moses** (drums, trombone!), and **Ted Houghton** (bass) as **Alice Donut**, they attempted to corner Manhattan's market for weird punk rock, sticking to their guns through six finger-blistering studio full-lengthers (plus a live album) before packing it in at the end of their 1000th gig.

Blaring out of the East Village they sprang their infectiously appealing off-centre tunes onto a waiting audience and into the studio, signing a recording contract just a few months after their first gig and, taken under the wing of Jello Biafra, releasing *Donut Comes Alive* (1988) with almost indecent haste and totally indecent lyrics.

As their fame spread – rather like an unpleasant rash – they released *Bucketfulls Of Sickness* and *Horror In An Otherwise Meaningless Life* (1989). Great title, but a sloppy, messed up recording.

It was to be but a temporary lapse of style however, as *Mule* (1990) saw them rehearsed, refreshed and sounding far more alive and involved in the music than ever before. *Revenge Fantasies Of The Impotent* (1991) combined a decently interesting title, some top-notch musicianship from a band growing in experience and confidence and all the poo-snot-weewee humour you could ask. Things were looking good and *The Untidy Suicides Of Your Degenerate Children* (1992) saw them stretching musically far beyond punk's basics into the realm of dub-influenced silly noises and found sound.

Pure Acid Park (Alternative Tentacles, 1995) was the band's final statement before Dave went off to become a professional golfer. By this point the band's sound had drifted off course and, paying too much attention to the direction Butthole Surfers – their labelmates and friendly competitors in the weirdo-punk league – were taking, Alice Donut swerved into the middle of the road.

Ted quit too, replaced by **Sissi Schulmeister** (bass, banjo!). Although Richard managed to hang on until 1995 (he went off to get a proper job, with NASA), **Michael Jung** (guitar, keyboards) took his place in the band for the last gigs in 1996.

After the split, Tomas and Sissi started a family, keeping their profile low for a while and steering clear of the music world. When Sissi, Stephen and Michael started jamming again towards the end of the decade, however, it was only a question of time until Tomas was brought back into the fold. The band re-formed officially in 2003 and released *Three Sisters* and a live DVD on Punkervision in the next year, touring the US and apparently having a wild time once again. Long live the Donut!

⊚ Donut Comes Alive (Alternative Tentacles, 1988)

One of the funniest records to come out of NYC in years, this is punk rock humour scraping the bottom of its own disgusting barrel for crude jokes that the average 8 year old would be ashamed to laugh at. Their take on Donovan's "Sunshine Superman" has yet to be beaten.

⊚ Mule (Alternative Tentacles, 1990)

Alice Donut's homage to New York City covers all those facets for which it's famous – there's murder, cockroaches, and the constant beat of a hot and sticky public transportation system binding Anton's twisted vocal mystery to the off-message punk that backs it up, Standouts include: "Bottom Of The Chain" and "Roaches In The Sink."

⊚ Revenge Fantasies of the Impotent
(Alternative Tentacles, 1991)

Another confident blast from a band doing well enough locally to ignore their purely parochial fame. Essential listens include "Telebloodprintmediadeathwhore" and an impressively even-more-deranged-than-the-original version of Black Sabbath's "War Pigs".

⊚ Dry Humping the Cash Cow
(Alternative Tentacles, 1994)

The aforementioned live album: almost as much fun as being at CBGBs for the recording is to drink a few cold, inexpensive beers from your own refrigerator (avoiding the warm, overpriced piss on sale at the venue), close your eyes and enjoy the show. When it gets to "The Son Of A Disgruntled X-Postal Worker Reflects On His Life While Getting Stoned in The Parking Lot Of A Winn Dixie While Listening To Metallica", turn the volume up to full and get some of your own back on the world.

⊚ Three Sisters (Howler, 2004)

Washboard? Trombone? Banjo? All present and as incorrect as ever. This is really one for completists and old-time fans only.

ALTERNATIVE TV

**Switched on London, 1976;
still broadcasting occasionally.**

The first publication to take any serious notice of what was happening on the punk scene in London was a scrawled and typewritten newsletter called *Sniffin' Glue*. Published illicitly on "borrowed" photocopying equipment, it carried reviews of all the punk gigs in London, was populated with random photos of sweaty, grinning kids bouncing around in front of the stage, and looked like something that any self-respecting state should try to ban.

First of the fanzines, it was the personal soapbox of **Mark Perry**, a young, committed and fearsomely eloquent writer who became, by default, one of the main voices for punk elsewhere in the media. After eighteen months of writing, editing

ATV: (L-R) Tyrone, Mark and Alex conspire to hide the drummer from the photographer

and distributing Glue, however, **Mark P** (as he was known) was finally forced, by the sheer inadequacy of other bands on the scene, to put his money where his mouth was, and actually get himself on stage instead of sniping from the sidelines.

Expectations of failure, especially on the London punk circuit where he'd made and lost a good number of friends, were high. When the new band finally appeared, assembled from the remains of an earlier and sadly unrecorded line-up that worked under the name "The New Beatles", those who came to laugh left stunned at the quality, variety, challenge and inventive tension of the music they produced.

In the midst of a teen revolution, in an age of amphetamines, rampant lust and unprotected sex, ATV came out with a floppy 7-incher. "Love Lies Limp", a reggae-beat punk-rock classic dealing with impotence, was a farewell freebie from the editor of *Sniffin' Glue*, being released in the form of a flexi-disc given away with the mag. Showing, as always, more dedication than perhaps absolutely necessary, Perry had handed over his fanzine to **Danny Baker** in order to devote himself full-time to the band, which consisted of Perry on vocals and dodgy guitar, **Alex Ferguson** (guitar), **Tyrone Thomas** (bass) and **Chris Bennett** (drums).

Like so many of the real originals in punk, Perry was phenomenally hard to categorize. He'd turned a nerdish schoolboy interest in the ragged edges of rock into a huge range of inspiration, reinterpreting Frank Zappa's "Why Don't Ya Do Me Right?" and Chuck Berry's "Memphis" into songs their owners would barely have recognized. Hitting experimental rhythms, playing with found sound and multitrack recordings, early ATV gigs owed more to Andy Warhol's Exploding Plastic Inevitable or the legendary festivals (dis)organized by the Grateful Dead back in the Sixties than to the stewpot of sweat, hormones and spilled beer of most punk performances. With Mark frequently settling backstage discussions by barging his way into Alex or Tyrone, concerts often ground to a halt while Chris untangled the flailing legs, soothed bruised egos, and – being the only one in a fit state to do so – retuned the instruments.

ATV toured the UK and ventured abroad to Europe, supporting John Cale. Impressed with the band's repertoire, he signed up as producer. The combined musical input of Cale, Perry and

the rest of the band – opinionated and argumentative to a man – ensured that the first album, *The Image Has Cracked,* covered all their bases. Part live recordings, part clinically over-produced studio pieces, it featured a couple of reassuringly ramalama punk-rock stormers alongside the tales of violence and degradation on the mean streets of Deptford: "You Bastard" had more to say than most other, longer-winded tunes of the time,

ICONIC SINGLE:
LOVE LIES LIMP (*SNIFFIN' GLUE* FLEXI)

Staying true to their stated devotion to reggae and the music of Can, the band's first release was this dub-tinged snapshot of teenage impotence and bedroom apathy. Not the stuff to take the band to the top of the charts, but ATV were always more art-punk concept than band of crowd-pleasing thrash merchants.

With slightly better diction and a more refined set of lyrics, "Love Lies Limp" could pass as one of the great world-weary songs. Too confessional for the Sinatra crowd, it would go down a storm translated into French and grunted by someone called Yves. As it is, the song broke new ground in the hitherto fiercely potent masculine world of rock'n'roll, with Perry's deadpan, ennui-drenched delivery conveying that numb, bloodless lack of feeling and absence of human connection that happens to every guy now and then.

When it was first released, the single certainly struck a chord with the speed-chomping contingent of punk rockers, famously celibate through sheer chemically induced inability. Since then, the song's empty, echo-swamped production, its gentle pace and gloriously over-detailed confessional lyrics have earned it a place in the hearts of thousands, and a painful ache in the pants for many more.

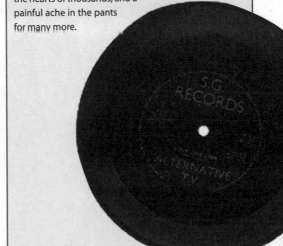

"Splitting In 2" bragged a descending guitar line to beat anything the Stooges ever produced, and "How Much Longer" hung a whole series of unanswerable questions on the state of punk from one of the scene's most twisted guitar lines. It was the longer songs, though – "Alternatives To NATO" and "Still Life" in particular – that grabbed your attention and kept hold of it. This was undeniably punk rock, and it very obviously followed no leaders.

The safe option at this point would not have involved sacking the entire band and recruiting a new bunch, ditching a good fifty percent of the crowd-friendly set or reinventing yourself as an art-punk outfit with more than a hint of jazz-hippy fusion in the mix. Perry, punk-rock to the marrow, did all the above and ended up on tour with Gong / free-festival offshoot band Here and Now. Only a few of the old crowd made the jump with him, but those who did can testify to Perry's constant refusal to be anything except punk-rock. Like some one-man Grateful Dead of the genre,

Alternative TV never really went away. For most of its illustrious history, ATV has been Mark Perry plus whoever he can talk into playing along with him. Whenever he next decides to sling it together on stage in a town near you, go check it out.

⦿ The Image Has Cracked (Anagram, 2003)

Great-value CD reissue of one of the all-time great punk-rock albums. The nine original tunes are accompanied by a whacking total of eleven bonus tracks, giving you the perfect introduction to the band.

ANGELIC UPSTARTS

Started up South Shields, England, 1977, shut down 1986, firing on all four cylinders on sporadic tours since 1992.

The Geordie answer to Sham 69, the **Angelic Upstarts** were a punk band that attracted a crowd of fighting demons, out for beer and aggravated assault rather than a few spirited yells of defiance and a night dressed up, bouncing

Li'l angels: (L-R) Mond, Mensi, Steve and Sticks

around like an idiot to that wild, wild rock'n'roll sound. Despite their admirable punk credentials and resolute stance against bonehead politics, they ended up tarred with the brush of violence that their audience brought along to their gigs and consequently their limited-vocabulary poetry never reached the audience that it deserved.

Mensi (a.k.a. Tom Mensforth, vocals) was the real punk deal: a working-class kid with chips on both his shoulders, spitting out lyrics that stank of deprivation and injustice. When he teamed up with **Mond** (guitar), **Steve Forsten** (bass) and **Decca Wade** (drums), the Upstarts were ready to have a go at any likely target dumb enough to stick its head above the parapet.

The late-1970s police force provided them with the subject they'd been looking for, and their three-chord, independently released debut, "The Murder Of Liddle Towers", brought them to the attention of Sham 69's Jimmy Pursey, a man in pursuit of the very same audience and an all-round good sport of the punk scene. Combined with Sham 69's well-known patronage of the band, the song's anti-authority stance and frankly scary intensity unfortunately began to attract less welcome attention from the scene's newest arrivals – bunches of skinheads who'd attend gigs looking for dance-floor aggro.

Jimmy shooed the boys into the studio and produced *Teenage Warning* for them. It turned out to be a fiercely committed statement, refuting all the accusations of racism and fascism that some of their followers had caused to be levelled at them, but its sheer relentlessness made it difficult listening. Trapped in a dead end of rabble-rousing statements of monochromatic simplicity, the Upstarts began a career on the road, convinced they'd make more from ticket sales and putting on a show than they'd ever pick up from royalty payments.

As a singles band, though, they were unmatched, at least for a while. "I'm An Upstart" is still one of the all-time great rebel records, and "Teenage Warning", the release that followed it, was strong enough to stand as the title track for the band's second album. *Reason Why?*, their 1983 offering, saw them reach their creative peak, delivering a set of songs that could stand, heads held high, alongside the best of the Pistols, The Clash or indeed Sham 69. They'd bolted on **Bryan Hayes** (rhythm guitar) by this point, and had seen **Tony**

Feedback replace **Ronnie Wooden** (who'd himself replaced Forsten) on bass, while Wade's drum stool was taken over, first by **Sticks** (who went on to be a Cockney Reject), then by **Paul Thompson** (ex-Roxy Music) and finally by **Max Splodge** of Splodgenessabounds.

Despite a few late splutterings of the fuse (notably "Green Fields Of France" and "Brighton Bomb") on their 1986 swansong *The Power Of The Press*, times had changed and good old-fashioned punk rock was, although undeniably still good, by now depressingly old-fashioned. Though they're still to be seen on tour now and then, their legacy is best appreciated on disc.

⊙ **Punk Singles Collection (Captain Oi!, 2004)**

Really, at seventeen tracks long, this is all the Angelic Upstarts you need. From "Liddle Towers" to "Brighton Bomb", this shows the band at their simplistic but hard-hitting and angry best.

◎ **ICONIC SINGLE:**
I'M AN UPSTART / LEAVE ME ALONE (WEA, 1979)

Although welcomed as a refreshing slap of proletarian defiance by some, for others this was disturbing evidence of declining standards. By stripping away everything except an obnoxious attitude, "I'm An Upstart" was a guaranteed crowd-pleaser, but it failed to present any challenge or demand any solutions. It's rebel music, but manufactured to meet the lowest common denominator. Nihilism like this was never going to solve problems: it could only make things worse.

There's no denying the song's power, though. The guitar tone is rough enough to blister paint, and the chords that define the tune also push the rhythm forward into a rabble-rousing unstoppable beast, topped off with an absolute cherry of a call-and-response chorus – in short, just the tune to play before the revolution kicks off.

Art-School Punk

The smart-arse end of the music spectrum blossomed under Britain's art-school system – a regime designed to soak up the unemployable creative types who would otherwise gum up the smooth running of the economy. While it gave society's square pegs an opportunity to smooth off their rough edges in order to better fit the round holes of everyday society, it's best remembered for producing more than a few genuinely valuable artists and some unforgettably fantastic rock'n'roll bands. **Adam Ant** is guilty, as are **Joe Strummer**, **Paul Simonon** and **Mick Jones** from The Clash. All four of them can be lined up as ex-art school kids alongside **Johnny Rotten** and **Sid Vicious** from the Pistols, and their evil uncle **Malcolm McLaren** had been at Croydon Art School in the sixties.

Celebrated by **The Jam** in their song of the same name, Art School is a place where you can do "anything that you wanna do", and "go anyplace that you wanna go". As the rough'n'ready greaser version of John Lennon's ghost would be happy to concur, art school was a great place to simply be a punk – it gave big kids time to play with hair-dye, grossly impractical clothing, and all kinds of weird sex in a secure environment. In addition, it provided plenty of time to sling together a band, rehearse now and then, and perhaps even learn to play a little. **"Wild"Billy Childish**, the creative beauty behind The Pop

Rivets, Thee Mighty Caesars, The Milkshakes, Thee Headcoats and currently The Buff Medways, deserves particular respect for being so stroppy that he was thrown out of art school, and **Jamie Reid**'s unmistakeable graphics for both the Sex Pistols and Buzzcocks came from an art-school background.

Art schools also attract people of genuine ability, creativity and vision, and most of them were in bands already when punk happened. Wire, for example, found themselves lumped in alongside the rest of the bands that appeared on the *Live At The Roxy* album, despite having more in common with Bebop Deluxe than Generation X, while **Talking Heads**, a band whose delicate musical tracery was way more arty than punky, had to share the bill at CBGB's with **The Ramones**.

Devo's roots go back to art school, and there was more than a touch of the bristle-hair brush to **Throbbing Gristle**. Although bands such as **ATV** and **The Fall** were the genuine article – "working-class crap that talked back", as **Mark E Smith** put it – they made the students swoon, leaving a wake of artsy fallout ranging from **Pavement** to **Sonic Youth** on one side of the ocean, and from **The Pop Group** and **Gang Of Four** to **The Band Of Holy Joy** and **The Mekons** on the other. If it weren't for the art-school input, punk would never have taken off.

ATARI TEENAGE RIOT

Formed Berlin, 1992; dissolved 1999.

"MY MUSIC TAKES PEOPLE TO PLACES WHERE THEY'VE NEVER BEEN BEFORE. SOME NEVER RETURN, AND THOSE WHO DID ARE SCARED TO GO BACK."

ALEC EMPIRE

Alec Empire is an extraordinary performer, even by punk-rock standards, and the music he creates is sometimes actually physically painful. He's the man behind noise-punk crew

Atari Teenage Riot, heroes of the silicon generation who relied even less on musicianship than had the original 1970s punks. Spiritual parent to The Prodigy, and spiritual descendant of Sham 69 (this is a keyboards-and-computer band, agreed, but one that covered "If The Kids Are United"), ATR were among the angriest punk rockers of the 1990s.

To some extent, ATR's music symbolized the revenge of German adolescents. After years of home-grown oompah music, translated Europop, super-cerebral cosmic prog rock and ghastly disco fodder from expats such as Boney M and Donna Summer, the time for the kids to get down and dirty with electronica was well overdue. When Empire hooked up his home computer and beat-up keyboards with **Hanin Elias** and **Carl Crack** in 1992, they threw together a nasty selection of greased-up sharp electronic noise, called it "Hunting For Nazis" and released it through Berlin Hardcore label Force Inc.

"Hunting…" was no one-off headline-grabbing statement: ATR showed a political commitment and streetwise appreciation of the joy of activism that had been missing from the German scene for a quarter of a century. They also understood the speechless headlong rush that anything powering out of the speakers in excess of 200 beats per minute is going to create.

Politically radical in a general anti-conservative, pro-freedom way, ATR made music to play loud and get angry to. After walking out on a deal with multinational PolyGram, their massive distorted guitar sounds and beats from the guts of Beelzebub found a listening public through Alec's own label, Digital Hardcore Recordings, which released the band's first albums.

Delete Yourself resounded with punk-rock guitar noise, tortured beyond belief and chained to the ugliest industrial drum loops the boys could find. To the delight of kids with bleeding ears, *The Future Of War* was, almost unimaginably, even harder, rougher and faster. It boasted impenetrable sheets of white noise, driller-killer drumbeats fed through awful computer distress and road-repair basslines; parents across Europe ran blindly into walls to escape the noise.

The Teenage Riot was happening worldwide by the mid-1990s as John Peel and college radio latched on to that digital hardcore groove. Never a band to measure success on a purely commercial scale, ATR achieved a huge amount by their own standards, not least their aiding and nurturing of the Berlin Techno Scene. 60 Second Wipe Out,

released in 1999, showed a degree of polish lacking from earlier outings, brought on more by advances in technology than by any search for pure undistorted waveforms. It was also the band's last statement: Carl Crack went into psychotherapy and rehab, which failed to help the concurrent mental and physical decline that finished him off before the end of the year.

Despite the lack of any obvious overlap between the music enjoyed by the loved-up kids of the new rave generation and Empire's shouted warnings of imminent apocalypse, ATR helped kick down any resistance to rave culture in the old capital city, showing bedroom kids new and disturbing things to do on their home computers with sound, vision and brutal acid beats. Though their music is always worth a listen, it has dated in a way that more conventional guitar-driven punk rock hasn't, and a five-minute burst is probably a sufficient dose for beginners. Digital Hardcore provides a more fitting memorial, continuing as it does to pour out good old-fashioned punk-rock noise from bands such as **Le Tigre** to this very day.

◉ **Delete Yourself** (Digital Hardcore, 2002)

Still available, still hardcore, still incredibly hard going, this is a twelve-track soundtrack to the dreams you'd thought you'd forgotten. ATR's blend of technology and aggression drags punk brutally into the digital age, bridging a gap of more than a decade with their masterful cover of Sham 69's "If The Kids Are United".

Electronic Punk

Punk rock or something like it shows up regularly as each new generation discovers the joys of telling the powers that be to go fuck themselves. An explosion of cheap, nasty but adequate instruments and amplification, combined with excess capacity in the rehearsal studio market made the late-Seventies punk wave possible. Just a few years later, inexpensive keyboards took the synthesizers out of the hands of the rich and progressive rockers and put them within reach of the dour student intelligentsia. The Eighties saw personal computers starting to appear on the desktops of the world, then performing on stage with the more techno-savvy bands and ultimately delivering the power of the recording studio into the grubby mitts of factory fodder and dole scum. So far, so democratic.

Our story continues with **Peter Hammill**, the least pretentious member of progmeisters Van Der Graaf Generator, who was one of the first of the old wave to break cover with his album *Nadir's Big Chance* (1975).

This enjoyed a brief burst of sales after being cited as "important" by no less an authority than **Johnny Rotten** during his one-off radio show / interview on London's Capital Radio in July 1977, but it was really the New York New Wavers who brought electronics to the party. Bands such as **Talking Heads** had few problems fitting such "poseur" instruments into the line-up, while **Suicide** used nothing else.

Rotten flirted with electronica himself as part of **Public Image Ltd.**, and later collaborated with electro-god **Afrikaa Bambataa** on his "Time Zone" single. As the price of technology collapsed, it began to fall into untrained hands and was subjected to massive disrespect, first by the hip-hop community and subsequently the ravers.

The most obvious example of a band working at the punk / electronica interface is **The Prodigy**, whose entire back catalogue is based on the bedroom laptop noodling of **Liam Howlett** (see overleaf).

⊙ **The Future Of War (Digital Hardcore, 2002)**

This is the best of the three albums in terms of the balance between ear-ripping noise and eye-gouging rage. Harder, faster, stronger and, somehow even meaner than its predecessor, TFOW has shards of white noise where before there were drums, and deep industrial machinery-core loops in place of guitars. Awe-inspiring stuff that later acts (especially The Prodigy) would find impossible to ignore.

THE AU PAIRS

Formed Birmingham, England, 1979; quit 1983.

Proudly post-punk, Birmingham's **Au Pairs** brought a focus and political discipline to their music that their Ur-punk predecessors would have been ashamed of. Difficult to listen to at times, all angular guitars, carefully honed discord and jagged rhythms, The Au Pairs suffered for their music, and were prepared to ensure their audience did too. That's not to say they were totally stony-faced and undanceable: their lyrics veered in the direction of irony, particularly once Thatcher took over ruining the country, and for a time, no agitprop fund-raising disco was complete without a rousing stomp along to "We're So Cool" or "It's Obvious".

The band picked up a certain amount of sniggering notoriety through the outspoken lesbian feminism of **Lesley Woods** and shared a musical and political soapbox with bands such as The Mekons and Gang Of Four. More often than not, however, they found themselves lumped together with all-girl groups such as The Slits or The Raincoats by a lazy music press still unable to see the stance for the gender. In fact, Lesley shared both vocal and guitar duties with **Paul Foad**, joined onstage by **Jane Munro** (bass) and **Pete Hammond** (percussion). The dramatic blending of Foad and Woods' fine, bluesy voices and differing points of view dominate the band's work.

In concert, The Au Pairs were a triumph of minimalism, using sparse lighting and forcing the impossible best from frequently atrocious PA systems to punctuate and emphasize the high points of gender-play in the stories of sexuality, passion and politics they brought to the stage. Despite being the darlings of the student unions, the gig-attending left and the mainstream music press, however, their records rarely troubled even the indie charts.

Nevertheless, the band produced two decent albums, both of which are worth a listen, if only to appreciate the extent to which they're showing their age. The thought-crime politics of *Playing With A Different Sex* (1981) or *Sense And Sensuality* (1982) strike nothing near as powerful a chord in the teenage heart today as they were originally intended to, and too many of the songs seem more like lectures to be really comfortable. The CD reissues come bundled with a whole bunch of singles, B-sides, alternate versions and entire tracks that were not previously available.

Australian & Kiwi Punk

Back in the 1970s from the comfortable perspective of the opposite side of the planet, it was easy to see Australia and New Zealand as little plots of punk rock heaven dumped down here on Earth: both nations had an enviable reputation for bluff, hearty behaviour and the kind of robust language that made punk rocking so much fun.

The music that spilled out of both nations – connected here merely as a point of geographical convenience and not to deny the many unique and distinctive features of each – seemed awash with the same rough charm that characterized their wines. Their take on punk seemed to celebrate the same mindlessly obnoxious attitude that the home-brewed plonk encouraged and many a cold London heart yearned for the endless summers of the lucky countries.

With snot-nose roots going back to the mod classic "Friday On My Mind" (recorded in 1967 by The Easybeats and later covered by both David Bowie and dial-a-punk boy band London), and movie delights including **Peter Weir**'s 1974 *Cars That Ate Paris* and the iconic outsider/rebel dude from 79's *Mad Max*, punk has an impressive antipodean pedigree musically and culturally.

But when the distant sounds of late 70s mutant rock came howling simultaneously over the horizon from LA, New York and London, Australia was only partly ready. Sydney had **Radio Birdman** (with their Stooges family connection) and **The Saints** (a home-grown Ramones who'd started hairy, stayed hairy and who pre dated the Ramones when it came to leather jackets and high speed buzzsaw rock); while under the stern thumb of **Nick Cave**, Melbourne's **The Boys Next Door** were on their way to becoming **The Birthday Party**. These few bands apart however, New Zealand and Australia contributed little that made it to the international arena, and no other bands of note.

It's a shame that it never really took off over there but, in the pre-Internet era, both countries were simply too isolated from the rest of the world. Local bands seemed content to grind out acceptable but hardly revolutionary covers of 60s classics and more recent imports. Worse still, as those few other worthwhile acts that made it onto vinyl rarely made the jump onto CD, tracking down good-quality vintage material means becoming involved in all manner of tape-swapping and copyright transgressions. One fine alternative is the two-disc set *Alternative Animals*, a music plus CD-ROM documentary recently reissued on Shock Records.

Good value, whether you want an ear-bashing or just to complete your collection.

Deciding, no doubt, that there were easier ways to make a living than preaching in poverty to the already converted, the group disbanded in 1983. Woods went on to form a band called **The Darlings** towards the end of the 1980s.

Although on occasion a bit too didactic to swallow, and despite the undeniable tendency to see everything in the stark black and white of hardcore, doctrinaire politics, The Au Pairs kicked ass and kicked it hard. The band's legacy is best seen in the film *Urgh! A Music War* (1981) –they also feature on the soundtrack – and best heard on the 1983 live album listed below.

⊙ **Live In Berlin (Essential, 1996)**

Long available only on the bootleg *Equal But Different*, this recording, made at the first Berlin Women's Festival in 1980, showcases the band at their best – confidently preaching to a crowd that's already converted. The standout track, a precision reworking of Erma Franklin's "Piece Of My Heart" will have you dancing in the aisles, singing along like a loon.

BABES IN TOYLAND

Started screaming Minneapolis, Minnesota, 1987; stopped 1998.

Punk rock from their smudged lipstick and torn tights to their speaker-straining rages, Minnesota's **Babes In Toyland** were as genuine and committed to the cause of noisy rock'n'roll as their idol Iggy Pop. Formed by guitar-torturing vocalist **Kat Bjelland**, a long-term muso who'd done time over the years in bands with Jenny Finch (L7) and Courtney Love, Babes In Toyland also featured the talents of bassist **Michelle Leon** and drummer **Lori Barbero**. Their first single earned them a support slot on Sonic Youth's European tour, and like so many stunning US bands, they found themselves more welcome abroad than at home.

The Babes' debut album, *Spanking Machine* (1990), demonstrated a similar approach to both **Hole** and L7: Kat spat out lyrics as if they were forming clots in her throat as she sang, and her guitar work had the savagery of a nicked-edge razor in a street fight. Taken in a single dose, the album leaves the listener genuinely stunned, breathless and searching for words, even today.

The band's high-voltage performance was strong enough to land them a major-label deal with Reprise, where, after **Maureen Herman** stepped in to replace Leon, their second album took shape. Capitalizing on the association with Sonic Youth, Bjelland drafted in Lee Renaldo to produce, and the result, *Fontanelle*, was just as punk as its predecessor – no big-corporate sell-out for the Babes.

Despite the appreciation shown by foreign audiences (John Peel, for example, was a champion of their work), at home the band suffered from being neither grunge nor riot grrrl enough for mainstream success. Turning their collective back on the opportunities offered by a slot on the 1993 Lollapalooza festival/tour, Babes In Toyland remained effectively silent until the release of *Nemesisters* in 1995.

A strange recording even for these past mistresses of the difficult, the new album introduced a new concept: the Babes cover version. Both "All By Myself" and "We Are Family" get the Bjelland vocal workover and come out much improved for the experience. Hardcore fans were, however, split on the wisdom of giving such uncharacteristic songs the benefit of the Toyland treatment and some saw it as evidence of a band looking for direction.

While the Babes had been in effective retirement, bands such as Hole had claimed their crown and titles, and were already taking the radio slots scheduled for Female Rock. When Herman left (to be replaced by **Dana Cochrane**) in 1996, the writing was on the nursery wall. Bjelland devoted increasing time and attention to her new project **Katastrophy Wife**, a mommy-daddy project featuring her husband **Glenn Mattson** on drums, and apart from a series of retrospective album releases, the Babes died of neglect.

This is a band that helped shatter the last few misconceptions about a woman's role in rock music. They subverted the traditional rock-chick image, turning playthings into weapons. The injustice and abuse they describe is as widespread today as it was a decade back, and their music remains as fearsomely relevant now as it was then.

⊚ **Fair Is Foul And Foul Is Fair** (Fire, 2003)

Two discs packed with fire and pain. Kat Bjelland's posse's greatest hits, and a respectful roundup of a solid career. Best and most widely available of the compilations.

BABYSHAMBLES

Formed London, 2003.

"START WITH BABYSHAMBLES AND YOUR FRIENDS WILL COME TO BLOWS"

LYRIC BY PETER DOHERTY

To eight out of ten adults over the age of 25, **Pete Doherty**'s name conjures up first his romance with model **Kate Moss**, second his tabloid drug hell and only third, if at all, his band **Babyshambles**. Picking a name for his band that's the perfect evocation of his low-rent mess of a life (combining a pun on the "s"hampagne perry that signified a classy evening out in the 60s, and the main man's disastrous personal life) is symbolic of Pete the artist – creator of thought-provoking puns and lyrics of sufficient occasional beauty to reward him with a pension from the royalties, should he live that long. The word "Babyshambles" first surfaced as a result of *The Babyshambles Sessions* – a drug-addled visit to New York and bid to get some **Libertines** (his previous band, see p.186) material hammered out, which **Carl Barât** left in a huff, fed up with his songs playing second fiddle to Pete's pipes and paraphernalia.

Scrabbling together a band of half-competent musicians from his circle of friends and via word of mouth, Pete began to play under the new name in 2003 while The Libertines were briefly back in the UK between a tour of the US and a planned stomp around Europe. When Pete began missing band appointments, meetings and whole concerts, Carl (Pete's long-term comrade in arms and fellow face of the Libertines) took charge and marched the rest of the band off to play without him.

Pete's absence on the European dates soon raised all sorts of pointed questions in the press. Pete's drug habits weren't decreasing and when Carl returned home he found his flat had been broken into and a bunch of saleable possessions missing.

Responding for once with alacrity to a reported break-in, the law showed up, looked round, asked a few questions then went straight to Pete's place where Carl's missing computer was sitting on the coffee table awaiting a buyer. Lurid tales of burglary, druggery and worse flooded the mainstream press, ever hungry for a "pop star in drug scandal" column filler, drowning out all reasonable comment on what was, after all, a halfway-qualified punk rock band, growing in confidence, with the most charismatic leader in the country. As tabloid tales of his antics increased, and he turned from asset to asshole, Pete Doherty finally officially left the Libs (which, after staggering along like a darted animal for a few weeks, collapsed sideways in a cloud of dust). When the haze cleared, Carl was said to be working on a new project to be known as **Dirty Pretty Things** (a name taken from Stephen Frears' 2002 docu-drama movie).

Pete however was diamond-hard focused by his insatiable need for cash. It meant he leapt straight back into the live concert arena, playing solo when he couldn't assemble a band and firing out sporadic broadsides from his website. Rumours of his entourage exchanging interviews and photo opportunities for cash were blended with solid reports of increasingly reckless behaviour – such as enjoying several pipes of crack cocaine in the presence of a

PLAYLIST: BABYSHAMBLES

1. **FUCK FOREVER**
   from **Down In Albion (Rough Trade, 2005)**

2. **THE 32ND OF DECEMBER**
   from **Down In Albion (Rough Trade, 2005)**

3. **PIPEDOWN**
   from **Down In Albion (Rough Trade, 2005)**

4. **KILLAMANGIRO**
   from **Down In Albion (Rough Trade, 2005)**

5. **PENTONVILLE**
   from **Down In Albion (Rough Trade, 2005)**

6. **WHAT KATY DID NEXT**
   from **Down In Albion (Rough Trade, 2005)**

7. **ALBION**
   from **Down In Albion (Rough Trade, 2005)**

8. **BACK FROM THE DEAD**
   from **Down In Albion (Rough Trade, 2005)**

9. **MONKEY CASINO**
   from **Fuck Forever 7" vinyl (Rough Trade, 2005)**

10. **BABYSHAMBLES**
    from **Fuck Forever 7" vinyl (Rough Trade, 2005)**

reporter from one of the larger-format, more reliable newspapers. Things truly went down the plug however when one of the tabloids printed a picture of Pete halfway along a line and having a whale of fun. When he was spotted in the company of Kate Moss shortly afterwards, the papers went berserk.

Somehow in the middle of all this unnecessary distraction, Pete found time to herd a band of Babyshamblers into the studio. April 2004 saw the band sneak out a self-titled limited edition single and once he'd found a line-up as stable as he was – **Patrick Walden** (guitar), **Gemma Clarke** (drums) and **Drew McConnell** (bass) – Pete was in the charts at the end of 2004 with "Killamangiro".

Pete's marching onward still, attempting to weather the publicity, and facing into the flashes like a drenched shepherd walking into the teeth of a moorland storm. Babyshambles (now minus Gemma who has returned to her previous job with **The Suffrajettes**, and with **Adam Ficek** in her place) are still trying to play live, to keep in touch with their fans and reality, and to make records, returning to the studio in 2005 with ex-Clash member and ex-Libertines' producer Mick Jones on hand to record *Down In Albion*, their full-length debut.

Selling well although accompanied by extremely mixed reviews, *Down In Albion* has so far yielded a couple of good singles ("Albion" and "Fuck Forever"). As for Pete, he's hardly the only junkie in the business, he's certainly one of the most honest, and seeing that he's the most charismatic man in UK rock at time of writing, let's hope he gets clean in time to show what he's really capable of as a musician and songwriter.

⦿ **Down In Albion (Rough Trade, 2005)**

Get your Babyshambles product while everyone in the band's still breathing. One of the most controversial albums of punk's thirtieth-anniversary year, it's also one of the strongest (apart from the opening track – the twee "La Belle & La Bête" featuring Kate Moss on vocals).

BAD BRAINS

Formed Washington, DC, 1977; changed name to Soul Brains, 1998.

P aul "HR" / "Hunting Rod" Hudson (vocals) originally got together with **Gary "Dr. Know" Miller** (guitar), **Darryl Jenifer** (bass) and **Earl Hudson** (drums) to play the bastard hybrid late-1970s musical aberration known as jazz-funk. Somewhere along the road, somebody slipped the guys a copy of Never Mind The Bollocks and that was the end for **Mind Power**, the jazz-funkers time forgot. What emerged from the wreckage was **Bad Brains**, a hundred-percent committed 1977 vintage punk-rock band that even had a taste for reggae, acquired from early exposure to the first Clash album.

The guys took a disturbingly professional and adult approach to their assault on the music biz, buying a communal house, studying and doing various jobs, before returning home for hours of character-building rehearsals, arguments, songwriting sessions and endless blues jams in E.

They kept the public away for six months while they put a shine on the songs and honed their anger, then, ready to unleash the country's only

---

🎧 **PLAYLIST: BAD BRAINS**

The most important punk band to come from the US capital, Bad Brains broke across boundaries of race, class and culture to teach the kids about the poitical importance of jumping up and down while shouting about the suckiness of the system

1. SAILIN' ON
from **Bad Brains (Roir, 2004)**

2. BANNED IN DC
from **Bad Brains (Roir, 2004)**

3. JAH CALLING
from **Bad Brains (Roir, 2004)**

4. FEARLESS VAMPIRE KILLERS
from **Bad Brains (Roir, 2004)**

5. PAY TO CUM
from **Bad Brains (Roir, 2004)**

6. HOW LOW CAN A PUNK GET
from **Rock for Light (Caroline, 1999)**

7. RIOT SQUAD
from **Rock for Light (Caroline, 1999)**

8. I AND I SURVIVE
from **Rock for Light (Caroline, 1999)**

9. I AGAINST I
from **I Against I (SST, 1993)**

10. HOUSE OF SUFFERING
from **I Against I (SST, 1993)**

Badges

O the sheer punk power of the right badge at the right time! Whether tin or cardboard, they were secret signs of allegiances best left unmentioned to employers or the overly straight-laced members of the family.

Badges became icons: **Gaye Advert** was never seen without her Iggy badge, and **Tom Robinson** wore his Rock Against Racism allegiance with pride – lines of big fluorescent-yellow discs went up and down both lapels of his schoolboy blazer. Paradoxically perhaps, punk insiders preferred smaller, subtler badges: the two-inch broad items on sale in the markets were seen as tourist fodder, retail rubbish sold to weekenders. Most desirable of all were the half-inch, limited-edition promo badges hurled by the handful into the audience by band members themselves.

Badges were there to promote bands and recordings, but they immediately became a kind of coded language; you could bet that anyone sporting more than one **Adam & The Ants** badge would be the guy to approach for a small hit of speed, while "I'm A Mess" or a **Johnny Thunders' Heartbreakers** badge indicated (sometimes) a commitment to something a little stronger. People wearing the full set of **Ian Dury** promo "Sex &", "Drugs &", "Rock &" and "Roll &" buttons were always good for a laugh, but anyone sporting a "Legalize Cannabis" badge was an undercover cop.

Perfect pieces of punk jewellery, the badges were instantly disposable chunks of glamour, at a time when home-made was just as acceptable as store-bought. They showed humour – when, for example, a syringe-decorated "Drug-Users Against The Nazis" parodied the ubiquitous Rock Against Racism arrow – outrage, political persuasion and sheer pop enthusiasm, and did it all on a budget that couldn't always stretch to buying the T-shirt and poster.

---

black hardcore punk band, they threw open the basement of their home for a free concert. It was a total roadblock of a show: word of this unique bunch of guys getting their act together behind closed doors had got round, and a crowd of the curious packed the place out.

Months of hard gigging followed, resulting in a dedicated audience, a few verbal face-offs with the police and finally a total ban from playing in their home town. As the 1970s drew to a close, the Brains rolled into NYC with a song to make them famous. "Pay To Cum" was recorded in December 1979, roaring defiance at the new decade with an uncompromising drum attack, backed up by one of the simplest power riffs in rock music and lyrics delivered with Uzi-like rapidity.

"Pay To Cum" was a slice of pure, late-1970s US punk rock. It was exciting, so fast it was barely danceable, and stuffed full of accumulated frustration and hardcore angst. What made it exceptional was the way in which it revealed absolutely nothing of the band's surprise mass conversion to Rastafarianism, after witnessing an eye- and mind-opening Bob Marley performance.

Not that Dr Know and the crew were hiding anything. If anything, they were sticking to the comparatively easy route of punk rock while they got to grips with the deceptively subtle rhythms of the new music they were planning to play. Songs such as "Sailin' On" and "Big Takeover", both of which appeared for the first time on the Brains' legendary debut release Bad Brains (ROIR, 1982; initially available only on suitably down'n'dirty cassette), showed the guys still had at least one of their flags nailed to the mast of louder, faster = better.

The Cars' Ric Ocasek recorded Bad Brains' *Rock For Light* (PVC, 1983) in his Boston studio, their last outing as a purely punk-rock outfit. Soon after its release, they announced plans to sub divide into three new bands, united under the Brains' banner but allowing them to concentrate more on righteous rasta music. Only **HR**, the outfit fronted by HR (who else?) would keep the hardcore flame burning; the others, **Zion Train** (a seven-piece, exclusively reggae band, no relation to the UK dub outfit) and **101** (comprising HR, plus Judah Selassie from Zion Train; the pair to be backed by local pick-up bands as needed) looked to Jamaica and Ethiopia for inspiration.

The plans depended on 101 making enough money to finance the other projects, and initially included a two-man pilgrimage to Africa, where HR was to acquire a second wife and, together with Judah Selassie, was to set up a 101 HQ in Nigeria to match the one that the band had put together in Brooklyn. Reality interfered, however, and *I Against I* (SST, 1986) showed that the guys had somehow lost touch with whatever makes punk rock so essential; the hardcore had slowed down and allowed its feet to get tangled in some heavy metal undergrowth. The riffs were still around, but they just didn't seem as big tree-choppingly important.

Musical differences followed in the wake of indifferent reviews, and soon Dr Know and Darryl Jenifer found themselves at the metal/rock end of a tug-of-war. At the other end were HR and Hudson, fighting for the right to reggae. Though they didn't finally leave until three years after *I Against I* (to be replaced by **Israel Joseph-I** – a.k.a. Dexter Pinto, and **Mackie Jayson**), they spent much of the time absent from the Bad Brains camp, working on their own reggae side-projects.

Sadly by the time the industry decided they were worth a gamble – Epic finally offered them a contract in 1993 – their moment had passed. They'd spent the hardcore years in distribution hell and marketing limbo, unable to go countrywide, and *Rise* sank without even a trail of bubbles. The original line-up got back together for *God Of Love* (Maverick, 1995), a last-gasp affair that again suffered mixed reviews and led to HR quitting.

Welding punk rock's immediacy and "no future" attitude to the slower-paced mysticism of Rastafarianism was never going to be easy; that Bad Brains even tried is remarkable and merit-worthy. These days there are still occasional sightings of **Soul Brains**, the name the band adopted in 1998, but their legacy deserves better than a slow fade on the oldies circuit. Always a cult, never aiming for the mainstream, the Brains are much better celebrated by digging out the reissued *Bad Brains* or *Banned In D.C.* and listening to them at their simple, unconfused best.

⊙ **Bad Brains** (ROIR, 2004)

Intense, phenomenally loud, righteous and right-on, this album delivers the dome-shattering attack promised on the cover. Includes "Pay To Cum" and "Sailin' On" from the punk end of their spectrum, and stretches all the way over to "Jah Calling" and "I Love I Jah" from their spiritual side.

⊙ **Banned In D.C.** (EMI, 2003)

Quite simply one of the best hardcore albums ever. If this best-of compilation tickles your interest, then go check out *Bad Brains* and *I Against I*.

BAD RELIGION

Formed Los Angeles, 1980.

Los Angeles' longest-enduring contribution to the wonderful world of punk rock, **Bad Religion** have, in their time, soaked up as much in the way of musical influences and bad-ass drugs as they have of Californian sun. Whether it was the musical diversity that kept them interested, or whether it was down to the drugs disguising their boredom long enough for them to realize they had a career worth continuing, is a question that can't be answered here. What matters is that for twenty years, you could be sure that by

Danny Baker

Currently earning an honest crust as a radio presenter, Danny Baker is known to most Brits as "that bloke who used to be on the telly all the time". While it is perhaps true that he smothered his own career on TV through simply saying "yes" too often when offered a job during the Eighties and Nineties, his place in the history of punk rock is assured, for he is the one who turned a fanatical interest in music into mastery of the good ship *Sniffin' Glue*. Already known for his work on the fanzine *Adrenaline*, he talked his way onto the fledgling *Glue* early on, after bludgeoning the magazine's founder Mark P into admitting that Danny was the greater expert on punk.

When Perry moved on from writing about music to actually making a joyful noise himself with ATV, Danny was there to take charge. The night that Elvis died, the snickering about the fat guy who'd snuffed it sitting on the toilet had already begun, but the fearless Baker leapt on stage at the Vortex to harangue the hypocrites and defend the memory of the young Presley. As editor, hanging out in the office next door to the Sex Pistols and downstairs from The Police, Baker took the magazine nationwide, and if the momentum hadn't dribbled away with the fickleness of the readership, could have turned it into a world-class punk-rock journal.

So, when the takings started to drop to embarrassingly low levels, Baker moved on to work at the *NME*, first as receptionist, then as staff writer. Introducing the black musical renaissance to the paper's otherwise pallid musical palette, he toured with the best of the bands of the day, even being shipped over to the US to stake out Michael Jackson for an interview.

Depending on one's memory of his Eighties TV career, Baker comes across as either excruciatingly irritating or tear-jerkingly funny. What's never been in dispute, however, is his devotion to and genuine love of music

investing your hard-earned cash in a Bad Religion album, you were going to be rewarded with some of the hardest, meanest, most intellectually stimulating music ever conceived to begin "1-2-3-4!"

Brett Gurewitz (guitar) set up Epitaph Records in 1980 to record and release the unholy racket he was making with a garage band he'd put together up in north LA. With **Greg Graffin** (vocals), **Jay Bentley** (bass) and **Jay Lishrout** (soon to be replaced by **Peter Finestone**) on drums, Bad Religion carefully assembled a set of mind-blowing power, tested the water with an EP in 1981, and borrowing $1000 from Brett's dad, hit the stores big-time in 1982 with *How Could Hell Be Any Worse?*.

From the outset, BR's work was characterized by the thought and empathy that went into the lyrics. Poignant, well-informed social commentary was never one of hardcore's major selling points, but it worked. Picking up a great local response (and a couple of new members – **Paul Dedona** on bass and **Davy Goldman** on drums), Gurewitz and Graffin gigged the new guys into shape before herding them into the studio to record *Into The Unknown*, shaking up their audience with an unusually trippy, keyboard-drenched take on the normal LA hardcore sound. It shook off a fair number too: those unable to respond to the swirling, sparkly sounds lost interest in the band, just as the band members themselves were developing a new and debilitating interest in chemical experimentation. Gurewitz took a year off to get well, while Graffin and the newly returned Peter Finestone hooked up with **Greg Hetson** (guitar, ex-Circle Jerks) and **Tim Gallegos** (bass, ex-Wasted Youth) to keep the band's name in the public eye with the self-deprecatingly titled *Back To The Known* EP, all no-nonsense high-velocity guitar+drums+shouting punk rock.

Three years of silence from the band led many to assume that it had shuffled off the scene for good. 1987's *Suffer*, a full-length set from a full-strength line-up (Gurewitz, Graffin, Lishrout, Hetson and Finestone), however, was unchallenged evidence that BR was back, badder and louder than ever. 1989's *No Control* was followed by *Against The Grain* in 1990 and *Generator* a year later, the now-traditional hardcore sound mellowing a little as the guys grew older – just enough for their trajectory to cross that of the rising alt.rock scene. Their 1993 *Recipe For Hate* originally appeared on

Epitaph, but Atlantic swooped them up and reissued the album, taking the name and the music to a worldwide audience hungry for angst.

Bad Religion was on a roll, though Gurewitz saw it more as a treadmill, jumping ship between *Stranger Than Fiction* (1994) and *The Gray Race* (1996). He stayed away for the rest of the band's major-label career, missing *No Substance* (1998) and *The New America* (2000), before finally rejoining the band after an absence of six years. Bringing them back to Epitaph – now one of the most successful independent labels in the world, thanks to Offspring and Green Day – Gurewitz set them to work and produced *The Process Of Belief* in 2002 and *The Empire Strikes First* in 2004.

Twenty years in hardcore is a kind of life sentence. Graffin, the Plato of punk, kept his sanity by working for his PhD in evolutionary biology while on the road and in the studio (his thesis – *Monism, Atheism And The Naturalist World-View: Perspectives From Evolutionary Biology* – is more rock'n'roll than its title suggests). Gurewitz turned to record production, while the rest of the guys did their time as best they could. Time served at Atlantic presumably helped pay for the remastered and reissued versions of the early albums that are the best they ever made.

⊚ How Could Hell Be Any Worse
(Epitaph, 1982)

The band's self-financed debut comes blasting out of the speakers just as mean and aggressive today as the day it was released. Beautifully rough-edged – the new remastered reissues haven't polished the sound that much – and oozing self-confidence, US hardcore never sounded better.

⊚ No Control
(Epitaph, 1989)

Best of the band's long list of studio albums with Gurewitz and the guys pulling some amazing feats out of their socks and moving away from the "four to the floor" pulsebeat in search of maybe a pinch more melody and a hint of subtlety (not too much, thankfully).

⊚ All Ages
(Epitaph, 1996)

The best way into a career collecting BR recordings is to go for this 22-track compilation, which puts all their best early material onto a single disc. "All killer, no filler" as they say, with special kudos going to "Fuck Armageddon...This Is Hell", "21st Century Digital Boy", "Do What You Want", "Atomic Garden" and "Suffer".

LESTER BANGS

Born Escondido, California, 1948; died NYC 1981.

"MUSIC IS ABOUT FEELING, PASSION, LOVE, ANGER, JOY, FEAR, HOPE, LUST, EMOTION DELIVERED IN ITS MOST POWERFUL AND DIRECT IN WHATEVER FORM."

LESTER BANGS

Patron saint of rock journalists and the music-press equivalent of Hunter S. Thompson, **Lester Bangs** gave his life, heart, lungs and soul to rock'n'roll. Born Leslie Conway Bangs, he became hooked on journalism soon after turning 21, when *Rolling Stone* began asking readers to send in reviews.

A huge influence on several generations of writers, Bangs took the essence of Thompson's "gonzo journalism" style – in which the writers and their experiences become a vital part of the story being told – and applied it to the freewheeling world of rock music, creating marvellous, essential reading for the *Village Voice, Penthouse, Creem, New Musical Express* and many other publications worldwide. Whether raving about the joys of 1960s garage bands, verbally slugging it out with **Lou Reed** , or oozing dirty thoughts after a Barry White gig, his work was invariably fantastic and enjoyable reading, full of intense personal commitment to whatever point was driving his drug-addled mind at that particular moment. Famously fired by *Rolling Stone* (for being disrespectful to musicians), it wasn't till he washed up in New York City and confronted his nemesis, Lou Reed, that he truly blossomed.

One of many writers credited with inventing the term "punk", he first scribbled it down in the title of his 1968 autobiographical novel *Drug Punk*. Whatever the merit of discussing who said it first, and what they meant by it, Bangs was one of the first "old wave" journalists to understand punk when it blew up in the mid-Seventies. He accompanied **The Clash** on their 1977 UK tour (he can

be seen lurking just offstage in concert footage), sending back a series of inspirational dispatches to the *NME* that helped capture the adrenaline and excitement for those of us who couldn't be there.

Much of his finest work – including his duel with Lou Reed, his Clash tour and a marvellous, unforgettable piece beginning "I decided it would be a good idea to get fucked up on drugs and go see Tangerine Dream with Laserium. So I drank two bottles of cough syrup and subwayed up to Avery Fisher Hall for a night I'll never forget" – is collected in *Psychotic Reactions And Carburetor Dung: The Work Of A Legendary Critic*, edited by his friend Greil Marcus. *Mainlines, Blood Feasts And Bad Taste: A Lester Bangs Reader* maintains similar standards.

Bangs died aged 33, after mistreating a cold with Darvon and Valium. *Let It Blurt: The Life And Times Of Lester Bangs, America's Greatest Rock Critic*, a biography by fellow legend Jim Derogatis, is as fine an epitaph as anyone could ask.

JELLO BIAFRA

Born Eric Boulcher, Boulder, Colorado, 1958.

Eric Boulcher's epiphany famously came to him at the Sex Pistols' last gig in San Francisco, when Johnny Rotten, sick of the whole game, finished the set sitting on stage cross-legged and despondent, for once at a loss as to what to do next. Grabbing the fallen punk-rock banner from Rotten's lifeless hands, Eric was reborn as **Jello Biafra** (the best American punk pseudonym by several hundred yards), and with the rest of the **Dead Kennedys**, spent the next few years baiting the establishment, battling obscenity charges (and ultimately his ex-bandmates) in his determination to defend his constitutional right to fight the powers that be in any manner he desired. His stint fronting The Dead Kennedys made him the de facto voice of West Coast punk rock, although his talent for self-promotion made him a name on the political scene before the band entered the studio. Challenged to put his money where his mouth was by one of the guys in the band, he gained notoriety, and serious respect amongst the armchair activist community, by standing for mayor of San Francisco in 1979 (scribbling down his policy positions while at a Pere Ubu concert).

Developing their talents for political prankster-ism, Biafra and the band spent the next few years blowing holes in accepted wisdom, challenging the status quo and making the American Right fidget uncomfortably in their underpants. The major labels were reluctant to become involved with such a broadside of loose cannons, so to take their music to the masses, Biafra set up Alternative Tentacles, the label that would release all DK recordings, as well as giving a home to some of the best West Coast rebel bands to emerge during the 1980s.

Eight years later, Biafra's cheerful exuberance had matured into something far more bitter; he'd spent the early 80s as front man for one of the most successful punk-rock acts in the world, but after falling foul of the nation's self-appointed moral defenders, he finished the decade shuttling in and out of the courtroom, handing over his earnings and gambling the future of Alternative Tenacles fighting the lawsuits that he'd attracted by getting under the skin of some powerful names.

The trouble started in 1985, when the Dead Kennedys' *Frankenchrist* album included a poster of a painting known as *Penis Landscape* by the respected artist H.R. Giger, also known for his work on the *Alien* movies. Urged to take action, the San Francisco District Attorney's office brought the city's mighty financial wherewithal to bear on the band, declaring in justification that the Dead Kennedys' case was "a cost-effective way to send a message to the music industry". Biafra's door was kicked in by the SFPD and he was dragged off to court to answer charges of "Distributing Harmful Matter to Minors".

When finally acquitted more than a year later, Biafra found himself with no money, no band, and with no friends left in the Dead Kennedys' camp. Understandably sick of the music biz and with a great deal of accumulated venom to discharge, he went into the spoken-word game, becoming a beloved and unmissable ranting attraction on the college circuit. He also fired off a set of spoken-word recordings as exciting, but in a very different way, as his work with the band. Naturally, these were issued on Alternative Tentacles, which adopted the slogan "Harmful Matter Since 1979".

Returning to the music world in the 1990s, Biafra teamed up with Al Jourgensen and Paul Barker of Ministry to make some evil, dark matter under the name of Lard. He's also collaborated more recently with NoMeansNo, D.O.A., The Melvins and the sadly missed Mojo Nixon. Never one to quit even after a serious beating (such as the one he took in 1994 when some skinheads decided he'd "sold out", broke both his legs and put him in hospital for a while), Biafra remains a big name on the anti-censorship, first-amendment scene. Standing tall, bloodied but unbowed by his continuous scrapping with the bad guys, he remains a thorn in their evil corporate sides to the present day. Long-time cham-pion of civil disobedience, and one of the USA's best-known anarchists with a small "a", he contin-ues to make sure the establishment keeps looking nervously over its shoulder and that it can never be taken entirely seriously.

◉ **I Blow Minds For A Living**
(Alternative Tentacles, 2004)

A double CD that tells the truth, the whole truth and nothing but the truth about running for mayor of San Francisco, cover-ing censorship, big oil and pacifism on the way.

BIG BLACK

Formed Chicago, 1982; disbanded 1988.

"I DO NOT CONSIDER MYSELF A 'PRODUCER' IN THE CLASSIC SENSE. I HAVE MET A FEW OF THEM, AND THEY'RE ASSHOLES."

STEVE ALBINI

The rock journalist burning with a hidden desire to make music rather than write about it has passed beyond familiarity into cliché. Fortunately, perhaps, few of them take the plunge into the limelight. When **Steve Albini** turned away from his typewriter, picked up his guitar and formed **Big Black** (initially a solo project), however, the world struck lucky. Here was a gifted hack who could actually play con-vincingly, had something to say, and an interest-ing way of expressing it.

Big Black appeared on the outer edges of hard-core, picking through the musical detritus of the fragmented post-punk scene and putting together a clanging, distorted musical monster. Joy Division was an obvious influence, but there were also distinct hints of other UK avant-gardesters PiL, Wire and The Pop Group in his sound.

The first BB release was the 1982 EP *Lungs*, a confrontational, echoing noise-fest that came almost exclusively from Steve and his pal Roland, the drum machine. In search perhaps, of better conversation, Albini recruited **Jeff Pezzati** (bass) and **Santiago Durango** (guitar) for the 1983 EP *Bulldozer*, and *Racer X* (1985). Pezzati went his own way, to be replaced by **Dave Riley** for *Atomizer* (1986).

Riley's funk-tinged input tipped the band over some kind of balancing point, and the new sound of Big Black was capable of reducing industrial-strength stereo systems to their component elements. *Atomizer* conveyed all sorts of physical and mental anguish by means of what sounds like turning the amps way past 11, fighting with the guitars like battle-axes and pressing all the buttons on the drum machine before throwing it downstairs. The ragged shreds of vocal that made it through the dense electronic undergrowth screamed tales of abuse, corruption, lies and depravity. It also brought Big Black embarrassing notoriety and unwelcome attention from the media – though it should be pointed out that there are better ways of keeping a low profile than forming a hugely loud, controversial punk-rock band.

An appropriately titled EP, *Headache*, saw them ploughing a familiar furrow in 1987, and that year's album, *Songs About Fucking*, brought the band to a planned halt while Santiago made his way through law school. Where *Atomizer* was full of boiling rage, *Songs* was a slow-cooked, simmering stew of grudges, burnt to a crisp here and there – a fitting end to a great career. Followed by a farewell tour, the best of which can be heard on the live album *Pigpile* (1992), Big Black split up. Albini went on to form **Rapeman** and **Shellac** before slipping into the comfortable producer's chair for bands such as The Pixies, Nirvana and PJ Harvey.

◉ **The Hammer Party** (Homestead, 1987)

Big Black's first two EPs, Lungs and Bulldozer, plus the Racer X mini-album, with "Cables" for good measure, all bundled together on a single CD. A brilliant, bargain-price introduction to their nasty, dark world.

◉ **The Rich Man's Eight-Track Tape** (Blast First, 1986)

Welcome reissue of the band's classic *Atomizer* and *Headache* EPs, showcasing 1980s US punk at its peak.

◉ **Songs About Fucking** (Blast First, 1987)

A must-have album on the strength of its title alone, this is just as meaty and sweaty as you'd imagine. Standout tracks include their unusual take on Kraftwerk's "The Model", "L Dopa" (with its good handful of false endings) and "The Power".

BIKINI KILL

Formed Olympia, Washington, 1990; ripped to shreds 1998.

There are those among the flag-waving purist community who would insist that **Bikini Kill** belong to the feminist hardcore genre known as riot grrrl and are nothing to do with punk rock. To which, one would respond "Bullshit!" and argue that riot grrrl was never anything more than a convenient media-applied label that split the burgeoning northwest US punk scene and reduced it to a discussion of boy against grrrl – the "divide and rule" principle in practice.

There had always been women in punk, but the riot grrrl tag came up when journalists covering the outer edges of the US discovered that in the wastelands, women were still getting up on stage to kick ass. Still, the perceived novelty value got the scene into the music press, and Bikini Kill's call for "Revolution Girl Style Now" made great copy.

Kathleen Hanna, **Tobi Vail** and **Kathi Wilcox** first teamed up at Evergreen College in Olympia at the end of the 1980s, bringing out a couple of copies of their feminist fanzine – the original *Bikini Kill* – before forming a band, having picked up **Billy Boredom**, born William Karren (guitar), on the way. Live performances had all the passion of good old-fashioned punk rock, with confrontation, challenge and audience participation unwritten extras on the set-list every single night. Kathleen had stage experience and knew how to control a crowd, but the band's ability to keep the idiot dancers to one side so that women in the audience could "go down the front" without risking physical harm was unequalled.

Recordings spread BK's incendiary word countrywide, beginning with the cassette-only release of early demo recordings *Revolution Girl Style*

Now and followed up by the *Bikini Kill* EP on local super-independent label Kill Rock Stars. Building on local momentum, riot grrrl went international in 1992 as Bikini Kill linked up with grrrls from the other side of the Atlantic, first splitting a single with British band **Huggy Bear** ("Yeah, Yeah, Yeah, Yeah" with the Bear's "Our Troubled Youth" on the other side), then touring the UK with them in 1993.

Although this tour and other, less formal collaborations drew hundreds of women into politics, music and other creative arts, riot grrrl was soon classed as yesterday's news and the press turned its attention elsewhere. Peacefully back underground

in the States, Bikini Kill worked alongside **Joan Jett** (held up as a riot grrrl icon in much the same way that Iggy Pop was saddled with his "godfather of punk" label), with Jett called in to produce their next single, "New Radio" / "Rebel Girl. Hanna repaid the favour by co-writing "Spinster" for Jett's 1994 album, *Pure And Simple*.

That same year, Bikini Kill released *Pussy Whipped*, their most accomplished, confident recording to date. Messy production, no-holds-barred lyrics and no-prisoners-taken guitar combine to create something of awe-inspiring power, beauty and danger. Punk rock to the marrow of its bones, this album should be required listening for

Bikini Kill's Kathleen Hanna.

Kill Rock Stars

Like 4AD, Bomp!, Rough Trade and precious few other companies, the Kill Rock Stars label promises a certain standard, in this case music of a particularly abrasive beauty. Founded in 1991 by Slim Moon and still proudly strident in its original home town of Olympia, in Washington State, Kill Rock Stars (KRS from here on) is the indie label yardstick *par excellence*. Putting out the music some other labels are too chicken to touch, ready to run a few risks and take the odd short cut in its desire to see good new material meet the audience it deserves, KRS has for more than 15 years been the label all others aspire to becoming.

Slim has moved the goalposts back and forth over the years; he originally saw KRS as a spoken-word operation, bringing hard-hitting "wordcore" to the frozen northwest and an audience starved for poetry. With this noble ideal in mind, he split a single with Kathleen Hanna (later of Bikini Kill, and subsequently head herself of Le Tigre) which sold as predictably badly as anyone could have told him.

Far more successful was the label's first full-length album, a compilation of local bands including Bikini Kill, Bratmobile, Unwound, and The Melvins, released under the title *Kill Rock Stars*.

The album hit the stores about the same time as all the music magazines discovered and labelled riot grrrl, and became required listening for the country's hip cognoscenti. Slim swiftly followed up his first big seller with further collections from the area called *Stars Kill Rock* and *Rock Stars Kill*, riding the waves first of riot grrrl, before alt: rock and grunge in turn took their place, and not making the spoken-word album he'd intended in the first place until 1995 when Juliana Lecking's *Big Broad* was released. (Juliana would also go on to become one of Le Tigre).

Flourishing during the 1990s as the label of choice both for sensitive young things (Elliot Smith being a notable signing) and highly strung noisemonsters (Sleater-Kinney joined the label; in 1997) alike, KRS found time to sprout a bud (the 5RC label) where a place was found for the more extreme-sounding delinquents that headed their way. Current radio darlings Deerhoof live there, alongside The No-Neck Blues Band, The Robot Ate Me and Semi-automatic. On the parent label meanwhile, things are going equally well, with recent signings Comet Gain and Rock-A-Teens helping make up for the loss to a more major label of The Decemberists, who left in 2005. The label's back catalogue yields some useful income of course, with old material from The Decemberists, Lung Leg, Bikini Kill, Sleater-Kinney, Huggy Bear, Bratmobile, Elliott Smith and Peechees, while a reissue series of classic recordings by artists such as Kleenex / Liliput and Delta5 promises to keep the label adequately funded for a while.

PLAYLIST:

1. **STATEMENT OF VINDICATION** Bikini Kill from **Reject All-american (KRS 1996)**
2. **I LIKE FUCKING** Bikini Kill from **The Singles (KRS 1996)**
3. **POLAROID BABY** Bratmobile from **Potty Mouth (KRS, 2000)**
4. **FUCK YR. FRUMPIES** Frumpies from **Frumpie One Piece (KRS, 2004)**
5. **P.U.N.K. GIRL** P.U.N.K. Girl from **The P.u.n.k. Girl Ep (K, 1995)**
6. **WHITE GIRL** Heavens to Betsy from **Calculated (KRS, 1994)**
7. **IMMATURE ADOLESCENCE** Huggy Bear from **Weaponry Listens To Love (KRS, 2000)**
8. **FUCK YOUR HEART** Huggy Bear from **Weaponry Listens To Love (KRS, 2000)**
9. **STRUMPET** Lois from **Strumpet (K, 1995)**
10. **WHO TOLD YOU SO?** Mecca Normal from **Mecca Normal (K)**

anyone contemplating adulthood. Brutal, like the best of Hole's output, wild-eyed and fierce like that of Babes In Toyland, *Pussy Whipped* can be hard going, but like all things spiritually rewarding, the effort is worthwhile.

Although 1996's Reject All American was to be their last statement, it never sounds tired or down-hearted: in fact, with all three members of the band contributing songs, and the united hardcore frontal delivery, things could not have appeared more solid. Almost a decade later, however, it stands as a lonely reminder of the movement that never really was: as the Nineties wore on, the novelty of aggressive rock'n'roll from the distaff side wore off and riot grrrl was no longer anything to make a fuss about. With the emergence of PJ Harvey, Björk, Tanya Donnelly and other gutsy women in the rock biz, the labels fell away. Bikini Kill disbanded in 1998.

⊙ Yeah Yeah Yeah Yeah **(Kill Rock Stars, 1996)**

The CD version of the first two albums. The one to play before you go to dump your cheating boyfriend – with extreme prejudice, using a .45 and a getaway vehicle.

BLACK FLAG

Unfurled Los Angeles, California, 1977; ceased waving 1986.

Nine years of hardcore ain't easy: you'd do less time behind bars for armed robbery, and maintaining a righteous fury at the sins of the world for that length of time has got to put a strain on the heart. **Black Flag** managed it, though, and kept punk alive almost single-handedly in the US until the masses cottoned on.

Black Flag was the initial idea of **Greg Ginn** (guitar) and **Chuck Dukowski** (bass), who got together in 1977 with **Brian Migdol** (drums) and **Keith Morris** (vocals). As Ginn and Dukowski had conveniently set up a label (SST) at the same time as forming the band, they had little difficulty in obtaining a release for their 1978 debut, the *Nervous Breakdown* EP. This early line-up refused to gel, and when Morris quit to form **Circle Jerks**, he was replaced by the immaculately named **Chavo Pederast**. Migdol left as well, making room for **Robo** in time for the 1980 EP *Jealous Again*.

Aware from the outset that they'd be swimming against the prevailing currents of taste in the States, Black Flag was always a hard-touring band. Black Flag believed in the power of live performance to turn lives around and make people examine their values – in short, as the hippies had it, to "blow minds". As a means of changing the world, it may work, but it's a long, slow process. Hitting the stage night after night proved too much for Pederast and he split, making way for **Dez Cadena**.

It wasn't until one **Henry Rollins** jumped on stage in 1981, however – elbowing Dez to one side and into his subsequent guitarist role while simultaneously physically making the microphone his tool, that the world really learned how hard hardcore could get. Originally from Washington, DC, Rollins made his debut during a gig in New York. Gifted with the voice of an industrial asphalt-laying machine, he turned the band in an even heavier direction – creating the context for increasingly vicious swathes of guitar and making scope for mayhem in the music.

Black Flag's constant touring led to a small but noisy countrywide audience, to a deal with Unicorn Records (a major label subsidiary) and, at last, access to some money and top-quality studios. The new line-up rushed to record their full-length debut, *Damaged*, but when Unicorn turned it down on the grounds of vulgarity, were forced to release it on their own SST label. Legal process ensued and, in the hail of suit and countersuit that followed, Black Flag effectively disappeared.

Not a band to give up, the guys simply dropped underground. Touring continued, although in a far lower key. The SST edition of *Damaged* was a hit with fans and reviewers alike, and despite being barred from using their name or logo, the band managed to release a live album *Everything Went Black*, credited individually to group members. Cadena gave up the

---

🎵 PLAYLIST: BLACK FLAG

No excuses needed for including the complete *Nervous Breakdown* EP; it's the band's most powerful material and the perfect introduction. No explanation needed for including the best three tracks from *Damaged*, and certainly no apologies for finishing it up with the first three cuts from 84's classic *Slip It In*.

1. NERVOUS BREAKDOWN
from **The First Four Years (SST, 2003)**

2. FIX ME
from **The First Four Years (SST, 2003)**

3. I'VE HAD IT
from **The First Four Years (SST, 2003)**

4. WASTED
from **The First Four Years (SST, 2003)**

5. RISE ABOVE
from **Damaged (SST, 1993)**

6. SIX PACK
from **Damaged (SST, 1993)**

7. LIFE OF PAIN
from **Damaged (SST, 1993)**

8. SLIP IT IN
from **Slip It In (SST 1993)**

9. BLACK COFFEE
from **Slip It In (SST 1993)**

10. WOUND UP
from **Slip It In (1993)**

struggle, leaving to form a group of his own – DC3 – but in the end, Unicorn went broke and our heroes got their name and ID back.

This opened the floodgates, and Black Flag embarked on a series of recordings as punishing as their live schedule had been. Slimmed down to a trio – with Ginn on bass as well as guitar, new boy **Bill Stevenson** on drums, and Rollins on glass-gargling vocals, Black Flag rush-released *My War* and *Family Man*. Drafting in **Kira Roessler** to play bass gave them time to record and release a third album in 1984, *Slip It In*. All this, added to the rough-hewn recording *Live '84* and the reissued *Everything Went Black* made it impossible to ignore Black Flag. Their thunder continued to roll as *Loose Nut*, *The Process Of Weeding Out*, and *In My Head* appeared the following year.

Stevenson left at the end of 1985, to be replaced at the drumkit by **Anthony Martinez**. This was one personnel change too many for the old war-horse to take, however, and after a swift "good-bye" live recording – *Who's Got The 10 1/2?* – released in early 1986, Greg broke up the band. SST had been taking up an increasing amount of his time, and working with bands such as **Hüsker Dü**, **The Minutemen**, **Meat Puppets** and **Sonic Youth** was proving to be more financially rewarding and emotionally satisfying than tearing up the country on a never-ending tour. Rollins went on to form **The Rollins Band**, and to carve himself niches in both the spoken-word performance and publishing fields, setting up his own imprint, appearing all over the world and still flying the flags of hardcore poetry and straight-edged punk-rock capitalism.

Black Flag's legacy of recordings shows that they had no interest in seeing their music develop. Satisfied from the outset with their world-beating compound of shouting, screaming, power-chords and velocity, they became one of the most important names in US punk/hardcore, arguably more brand than band. As ready to use humour as they were to be wild-eyed with rage, they were capable of moments of pure poetry in the middle of the loudest riffage, but never, ever, of selling out.

⊙ **Damaged (SST, 1981)**

Rollins has never sounded more intense, growling out his vocals past veins swollen to the size of ship-tethering cable, while the band clatter and twang violently through such epics of slack US culture as "Six Pack" and "TV Party".

⊙ **My War (SST, 1993)**

An interesting document with two distinct "sides", reflecting its original incarnation on vinyl. Standouts from the old-style Black Flag include the title track and "I Love You" whereas "Nothing Left Inside" is the best song Iggy never wrote.

BLACK REBEL MOTORCYCLE CLUB

Started up San Francisco 1998.

Leaving aside the question of whether you can still be punk rockers when you're discussing the point of art, have a major-label deal and thousands in the bank, the slo-mo Ramones-style moves adopted by **Black Rebel Motorcycle Club** certainly make them look the part. **Peter Hayes** (guitar) and **Robert Turner** (more guitar) first got together to make noise in San Francisco. Their early sessions were given some kind of structure by a drum machine until **Nick Jago** hooked up with them, first to form **The Elements**, then – stung by the indifference with which the name was met – changing to the **BRMC** moniker. It sounded much cooler – after all, the original BRMC was the gang that Brando tried to quit in the 1953 movie *The Wild One* – but the new name met with much the same lack of interest.

Moving south to LA the next year, BRMC grabbed a deal with Virgin and set about mixing up a slow-cooking pot of punk-tinged, psychedelic stew that owed as much to The Doors as to **The Stooges**. The band, like so many other US trailblazers, initially found themselves more appreciated in the UK than in the leviathan-like markets of their home country.

Combined with the resolute no-smiling / leather jackets / shades regime adopted when facing the media, the back-to-basics sound that the band championed made UK radio fall in love with them and their debut single, "Whatever Happened To My Rock'N'Roll (Punk Song)". This gave them a ready-made fanbase when they showed up on tour in Britain to promote the album *Black Rebel Motorcycle Club* in 2000.

Jago had grown up in Devon and was really making a return home, but Hayes came from the farmlands of Minnesota and Turner from the mountains of Santa Cruz. Confronted by incomprehensible British accents asking questions generally too dumb to be worth answering, BRMC developed a reputation for being difficult, showing up for interviews under the influence of one thing or another, and doing little to dispel the air of uncooperative menace that grew around them. The whiff of danger they gave off guaranteed a welcome on London's alternative music scene, and the guys decided to stay a while.

Although they were press darlings for most of 2002 and the year after, when they returned to the studio to concentrate on their second album *Take Them On, On Your Own*, they dropped out of sight almost completely amid rumours of dark, ill-advised habits and musical differences deep enough to require hospital treatment. They resurfaced in 2005 with *Howl*, flourishing that cool neon tan so sought after by the style-conscious underground muso.

Known across Europe for their ass-kicking live performance and devastatingly effective singles, it's time for them to go home and boot open a few doors.

⊚ **Take Them On, On Your Own (Virgin, 2003)**

Faster, tighter and more disciplined than the first album, it oozes sleaze and ill behaviour. It also brought some fine American radical thought back into rock'n'roll, giving the album an atmosphere more MC5 than Stooges in inspiration. Standout tracks include "Generation", "Six Barrel Shotgun" and (Kill The) US Government", all of which swirl and boil with anger.

BLONDIE

Formed NYC, 1974; reappear now and then.

Blondie was the name of the whole band, not just **Debbie Harry**, but it never really mattered. To her fans, both admiring girls and adoring boys, Blondie started and ended with Debbie. Who cared about her partner / muse / guitarist **Chris Stein**? Did anyone give a fig for bassist **Fred Smith** or even his replacement **Gary Valentine**? Was there no fan mail for **Jimmy Destri**, keyboard whizkid, nothing to say about drummer **Clem Burke**?

Apparently not. Although the guys were regularly lined up against a wall and shot by photographers, they appeared only as a vaguely geeky background to the gorgeous, pouting Harry. This was a real shame, because in their own pop-tinged way, Blondie the band did a lot of good for the world of rock'n'roll.

Harry came from Miami, Florida, where she learnt some chops as singer for **Wind In The Willows** (yes, they were as bad as the name suggests) and **First Crow On The Moon**, a band so obscure they landed support slots even lower on the bill than The Velvet Underground. Drifting along to early 1970s New York, she picked up work as a waitress in Max's Kansas City after a session

Deborah Harry rocks the microphone.

as a Playboy bunny girl, and parlayed that into a part-time gig as a member of **The Stilettos**, a bar-band covers act that bumped and ground its way through the raunchier end of the girl-group spectrum. Stein dropped into Max's one night and a punk-rock love story began.

Thanks to hanging out in the rock'n'roll bar in Manhattan, Stein and Harry were in tune with happenings down at CBGB's, where the Ramones, Talking Heads, Patti Smith and Television were making a new kind of sound. The band put a set together that tipped its hat towards the punk-rock sound, but had its feet planted firmly in the Sixties trash-pop world of Phil Spector and the Shangri-Las.

In 1976, Blondie hit the record-buying public with a classic pop single released on Private Stock, a label best known for its disco releases. "X Offender" sounded like a lost transistor radio classic of the Sixties: opening with one of those breathy spoken intros and bursting into life with drum rolls, Farfisa organ riffs and dirty, East Coast surf-music harmonies.

The band followed up with *Blondie*, and the multimedia blitz began. Waving a cheery goodbye with "Rip Her To Shreds", Blondie left punk behind and moved decisively into the New Wave/Power Pop camp. Chrysalis Records bought them up and reissued the first album with appropriate fanfare. Stein and Harry had their hands very firmly on the controls of the band's image, and right from the start, all picture requests went through Stein. When Harry showed up, miniskirted and waif-like, in the promo footage for "In The Flesh", she knew exactly what she was getting herself into: for the next five years, she'd be primped, painted and posed as the dress-up doll of the New Wave. Touring the US with Iggy Pop and the UK with fellow New Yorkers Television, Blondie found themselves uncomfortably strapped into the industry's money-making machine; a few ill-advised comments in Australia about drug use while on tour were the last uncensored messages anyone had from the band. From then on, the image-makers were in charge and Blondie was a product.

When bassist Smith quit the band in one of the great historic bad decisions of rock'n'roll, he was replaced by **Nigel Harrison**, who was joined by fellow new boy **Frank Infante** (guitar) as the big time hit and the dollars began to roll in. The next few years zipped by in the familiar pop vortex of tours, videos, personal appearances, recording sessions and photo-shoots. *Plastic Letters* made them a biggish name in both the UK and US, but it was *Parallel Lines* that broke them worldwide. *Eat To The Beat* had its share of good tunes, but by *Autoamerican (1981)*, Blondie was cruising, dabbling in reggae ("The Tide Is High"), and rap ("Rapture"), and ready to dissolve. The lawsuits began with Infante's protest that he was being ignored, and not invited to play on the records. Just a year later Debbie was working on her solo *Koo Koo* album, the greatest hits package was being prepared, and then – apart from the forget-

---

ICONIC SINGLE:
X OFFENDER / RIP HER TO SHREDS (PRIVATE STOCK, 1976)

Promoted through ruthlessly exploitative advertising that even Spinal Tap might have blenched at – one slogan read "Wouldn't you love to rip her to shreds?" – Blondie's first single soared above the mire in glorious tribute to The Shangri-Las, Phil Spector and the Velvet Underground.

"X Offender" is the everyday story of love between a hooker and the cop who busts her. He reads her her rights and says "Let's go", but on the way to the precinct, romance blossoms in the heart of the handcuffed perpetrator, strangely drawn to the big guy with the badge and rubber boots. As the song ends, there's no doubt in the singer's mind that she'll be offering her services to the arresting officer for free just as soon as she makes bail.

"Rip Her To Shreds" is a far more credible slice of life, with a lyric sheet that reads like a transcript from the powder room at Max's Kansas City. "Look at that hair" and "Check out those shoes!" hiss the girls as Miss Groupie Supreme catwalks through the crowd. Poor "Vera Vogue", those bitches even diss her choice of drug!

Neither track really qualifies as one hundred percent genuine punk rock, but as Blondie's first statement, this is one single you really need to hear.

PLAYLIST: BLONDIE

Like most of our featured artists, Blondie did their best work – from a punk rock standpoint – at the very beginning of their career. When given the chance to let herself go, Debbie crams all the passion of a full-tilt soul diva into the popcorny lyrics; when reined in, her voice flutters like a startled bird. Either way, the band deserve a continuing respectful listen.

1. **X OFFENDER**
from **Blondie** (Chrysalis, 2001)

2. **SHARK IN JET'S CLOTHING**
from **Blondie** (Chrysalis, 2001)

3. **RIP HER TO SHREDS**
from **Blondie** (Chrysalis, 2001)

4. **IN THE FLESH**
from **Blondie** (Chrysalis, 2001)

5. **KUNG FU GIRLS**
from **Blondie** (Chrysalis, 2001)

6. **HANGING ON THE TELEPHONE**
from **Parallel Lines** (Chrysalis, 2001)

7. **FADE AWAY AND RADIATE**
from **Parallel Lines** (Chrysalis, 2001)

8. **BANG A GONG (GET IT ON)**
from **Parallel Lines** (Chrysalis, 2001)

9. **I'M ON E**
from **Plastic Letters** (Chrysalis, 2001)

10. **(I'M ALWAYS TOUCHED BY YOUR) PRESENCE DEAR**
from **Plastic Letters** (Chrysalis, 2001)

table 1982 release *The Hunter*, which yielded a last chart single in "Island Of Lost Souls" – Blondie dropped off the radar for sixteen years.

As stardom disappeared, Stein fell seriously ill, and nobody expected to hear from the band again. Harry combined her nursing duties with a respectable solo career as a chanteuse, until, in 1998, she and a recovered Stein joined Destri and Burke for a reunion tour, a new album (*No Exit*), and a nostalgia-driven chart entry with "Maria". Riding the last ripple of the New Wave right up to the beach, *The Curse Of Blondie* was the group's 2002 salute to the new millennium, and their eighth studio album.

Apart from the iconic Harry, what really set Blondie apart form the rest of the Manhattan New Wave was the skilful way in which they integrated their danceable, pop sound with the city's underground black music. Combining hip-hop with their own (by now) otherwise fairly bland product smacked of opportunistic exploitation to some, but by bringing beats and rap to an otherwise almost exclusively white audience, "Rapture" probably did more to help hip-hop cross over than any number of didactic rants from KRS-1 or Grandmaster Flash.

⊙ **Greatest Hits** (EMI, 2002)

Blondie were never an album band: the joy they bring comes in disposable three-minute slices. Although *Plastic Letters*, *Parallel Lines*, *Eat To The Beat*, *Autoamerican* and the rest are still available (as is a pricey *Singles Box Set*), this is all the Blondie you're ever going to want to listen to more than once.

THE BOOMTOWN RATS

Formed Dublin, Ireland, 1975; done 1986.

When *NME*'s Ireland correspondent Bob Geldof jumped the counter and landed onstage singing for **The Boomtown Rats**, he suddenly found himself spokesperson for the entire Irish punk-rock contingent. Linking up with **Pete Briquette** (bass), **Gerry Cott** (guitar), **Simon Crowe** (drums), **Johnny Fingers** (pyjama-clad keyboard wizard) and **Garry Roberts** (guitar) the Rats picked up their name from Woody Guthrie, threw together a set of part-punk, part-show band numbers and headed for London.

They hit town in 1976 and, by default, became one of the big names on the scene. Like most of the other punk bands, the Rats professed to care for their audience, but they went to unusual lengths to put this into practice. During that year's long hot summer, for example, the Rats scoured London's Soho district buying up electric fans to circulate the sweat-laden air in the Marquee club, their venue for the night. As a result, Bob and the boys became true heroes to an audience that would otherwise have suffocated. A class act in all senses of the phrase.

Having the rock'n'roll chops to back up the spiky haircuts and stage-wear set them apart from most of their contemporaries too, and by the time they'd recorded and released their first single "Lookin' After No. 1" in August 1977, they were a crowd-

Celebrity Playlist: Bob Geldof

"We weren't punks. We had saxophones and ballads and harmonies," Bob Geldof says of the Boomtown Rats. "Punk was a cool metropolitan thing in London. We came straight off the boat from Ireland and were excluded from the metropolitan cabal." His playlist reflects how he felt estranged from London's punk elite of the time and found more in common with fellow outsiders such as the Feelgoods and Graham Parker...

1. **ALL THROUGH THE CITY – DR. FEELGOOD** from Stupidity
2. **DEAD END STREET – THE KINKS** from Face To Face
3. **VENUE DE MILO – TELEVISION** From Marquee Moon
4. **PERSONALITY CRISIS – NEW YORK DOLLS** from New York Dolls
5. **NEW AGE – VELVET UNDERGROUND** from Loaded
6. **DO THE STRAND – ROXY MUSIC** from For Your Pleasure
7. **PICTURES OF LILY – THE WHO** from My Generation
8. **WAR IN-A BABYLON – MAX ROMEO** from War In-a Babylon
9. **DRIVE IN SATURDAY – DAVID BOWIE** from Aladdin Sane
10. **CAN'T BE TOO STRONG – GRAHAM PARKER & THE RUMOUR** from Squeezing Out Sparks

Rat-infested hotel bedroom.

pleasing name all over the UK.

An album, *The Boomtown Rats*, was released a month later, full of the storm and chaos of that glorious year, but it proved to be pretty much the end of the Boomtown Rats as a punk band. Something happened between the debut and the release in 1978 of their second album, *A Tonic For The Troops*, which turned the band into little more than a power-pop act.

The passion remained, and the subject matter stayed contentious, but the sound had grown into a limp pastiche of Bruce Springsteen's pompous New Jersey operas. The evil story behind "I Don't Like Mondays", for example – about a California teen who had enjoyed a murder spree and later

justified it with the title line – was lost behind Bob's false histrionics and a wailing brass section. No matter, it sold by the truckload, charted on both sides of the Atlantic and took the band's third album, *The Fine Art Of Surfacing*, up the ladder of success.

The Rats' final UK Top 10 hit, "Banana Republic" – an eloquent lament at the state of an Ireland still stuck in the past – appeared in 1980, to be followed by *Mondo Bongo*, in 1981. Soon afterwards, with the Rats disappearing from the music press and record sales dwindling, Cott left the band and was not replaced. A fifth album, *V Deep*, was released in 1982 and *Ratrospective*, a six-song compilation, in 1983, but when the record company initially rejected the band's newly recorded sixth album, *In The Long Grass*, the end was unavoidably in sight. Although *Long Grass* picked up a US release on the back of Bob's high-profile involvement in charity work, its failure to chart left the Rats up the creek without a label. The group folded in 1986, and Geldof launched a solo career.

⊚ **The Boomtown Rats (Mercury, 2005)**

Still a great little punk-rock album, whining, reedy-voiced and angry. The sheer quality of the original songs (including "Lookin' After No. 1", "Mary Of The 4th Form", "Close As You'll Ever Be" and "Joey's On The Streets Again") make this a worthwhile purchase, but the addition of early demos and a live track on this remastered edition make it essential.

THE BOREDOMS

Formed Osaka, Japan, 1986

The kind of band that Quentin Tarantino stumbles across by accident, **The Boredoms** have the "zany Oriental" label stuck all over them. Though this brought them a degree of worldwide attention that they'd otherwise have missed out on, it's also distracted people from their music (which sucks, incidentally). No, really, it was bad music, pure noise-rock: fiendishly good entertainment, but listening to it hurt. The Boredoms were best appreciated as a live band, in a venue that had well-signed exit routes – there are limits to the amount of distorted guitar, found-object sounds, incomprehensible and possibly meaningless vocals, and abrasive song-structures that any mind can take without cracking.

They were formed in 1986 when **Yamatsuka** (vocals) got together with ex-**Hanatrash** bandmate

---

ICONIC SINGLE:
LOOKIN' AFTER NO. 1 (ENSIGN, 1977)

Way back when Mrs Thatcher was a fairly low-ranking opposition spokesman on education (and still known as "Maggie Thatcher - Milk Snatcher", the politician who put an end to free school milk), this anthem to what would later be called Thatcherism was The Rats' declaration of intent: a three-minute manifesto performed with tongue stuck firmly in cheek. Geldof never sounded more like the young Mick Jagger and pulled out all the stops in an almost-successful bid to convey the sincerity of his passionate delivery. While it pressed all the right buttons for a punk single of the time – a full-speed guita-driven riff-based ramalama that talks about "standing in the dole queue", it was interesting precisely because of its out-of-the-ordinary self-centredness. Catchy as chlamydia, it went to Number 11 in the mainstream pop charts, one of the best-performing New Wave singles the UK had seen. Full of clever subversive lyrics, it showed there was more to punk than simple protests of football-chant imbecility, and paved the way for the band's subsequent run of nine top-ten hits.

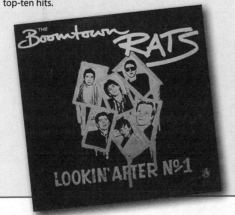

Taketani (drums) and fellow noise-merchants **Tabata Mara** (guitar) and **Hosoi** (bass) for floor-rocking sessions of aural destruction. The maniacal cacophony this line-up produced obviously lacked some finesse, because by the time the Boredoms' first full-length recording was released, the entire band bar Yamatsuka (who was flirting with the pseudonyms **Yamanta.k.a. Eye**, **Yamata.k.a. Eye**, and just plain **eYe**) had been replaced. The *Anal By Anal* EP (1986) and the 1998 full-length release *Osozeran No Stooges Kyo* (meaning "The Stooges Craze In Osozeran") were the work of Yamatsuka and new friends **Yoshikawa Toyohito** (drums), **Hira** – sometimes known as **Hilah** – (bass) and **Yamamoto Seiichi** – a.k.a. **Yama-Motor** – (guitar).

Keeping the music extreme while maintaining a rictus grin of fun at all costs, The Boredoms grabbed a new drummer, **Yoshimi Yokota** (a.k.a. **Yoshimi P-WE**), moving Yoshikawa to percussion in 1988. When he left the band the following year (replaced first by **Hasegawa Chu** and then by **ATR**), Yamatsuka was very likely the only member of the group who had the faintest idea what was going on.

A high-profile collaboration (by underground standards) with New York jazz-noise-monster **John Zorn** and his Naked City collective boosted the band's second album Soul Discharge (1990) and took them worldwide. Sonic Youth and Nirvana went on file as self-declared fans of the band, who were rejoined by Yoshikawa as co-vocalist and synthesizer player for *Pop Tatari* (1993) and *Chocolate Synthesizer* (1995). That same year, The Boredoms did Lollapalooza (the rolling-thunder alt:rock multi-venue tour that took this kind of dangerous noise to impressionable kids all across the USA). Having been championed in the UK by John Peel, they then hit the European festival circuit, memorably stunning a Friday morning audience at the Glastonbury Festival, with Yamatsuka gleefully stage-diving like it was well past midnight in a Tokyo gangster hangout.

Never easy listening, The Boredoms were unlikely to cross over into the mainstream. Briefly famous and as annoying a bunch of noiseniks as you'd ever want to play to punish inconsiderate neighbours, they showed the West what – given sufficient time – punk-rock attitudes, noise and rock'n'roll could mutate into in the land of Godzilla.

⊙ **Pop Tatari (Very Friendly, 2004)**

This prime example of their early work features standout tracks "Noise Ramones", "Okinawa Rasta Beef" and the title cut itself, but to be honest, if you like any of this stuff, you'll probably like all of it, and if you don't like it then don't waste your time trying to appreciate it. Life's too short.

THE BOYS

Formed London, 1976; split up 1981; reunited for the odd gig 1990s.

One of the first bands on the British scene, **The Boys** captured the spirit of punk rock; they stuck to it for only as long as it was fun, then ditched it for more sensible ways of making a living. Though not truly a comedy band (they had an alter-ego group, which recorded each Christmas as **The Yobs**, to cover that side of things), they had a sense of humour and were ready to use it. Unlike so many of their more po-faced contemporaries, the Boys were able to see the ridiculous side of their instant pop success and use it as the basis for songs such as "Backstage Pass".

Originally concocted by Norway's greatest ex-pat

PLAYLIST: JAPANESE PUNK

Teenage rebellion in an eastern vein.

1. FIGHTING FISTS, ANGRY SOUL
Hi Standard from **Angry Fist**

2. PUNK ROCK RADIO
Nicotine from **Session by Nicotine**

3. WHEN THE BOMBS FALL
The Blue Hearts from **Blast Off**

4. MOTHERFUCKER Bloodthirsty Butchers
from **Bloodthirsty Butchers**

5. LONESOME DIAMOND
The Pillows from **Penalty Life**

6. 21ST CENTURY RIOT
Dragon Ash from **Lily of Da Valley**

7. GET ON MY NERVES
Assfort from **Ejaculation**

8. NICE B.O.R.E. GUY & BOYOYO TOUCH
Boredoms from **Pop Tatari**

rocker, **Casino Steel** (formerly of **The Hollywood Brats** – London's very own, very lame, version of the New York Dolls), and **Matt Dangerfield** (guitarist and tenant of a conveniently bohemian flat in central London with a recording studio in the basement). Picking up a lyricist and backing singer in the shape of **Duncan "Kid" Reid** (bass/vocals), a drummer, **Jack Black**, and **"Honest" John Plain** as an extra guitarist to fill out the sound, the Boys then talked their way onto the punk circuit, stunning booking agencies into silent compliance. They played their first gig at London's Hope and Anchor pub in September 1976 with Mick Jones, Billy Idol, Tony James and Gene October in attendance. Soon they were creating enough of a buzz to blag a John Peel session, winning good-hearted reviews in the music press and a recording contract with NEMS. (A note to trainspotters: the Boys were the first UK punk band to sign an album deal.)

The lads immediately set about giving us the first of their two decent albums, *The Boys*, hurled together from the best bits of their live set and a few slower numbers with more considered lyrics. It included their first manifesto of defiance, which included the prize couplet "I don't care about rock'n'roll / I don't care about nothing at all!" Released with the unsurprising title of "I Don't Care" and a falling-down-the-stairs chorus of "Never had a hope / Never had a chance / Nobody ever taught me / To begin to understand", this was also the A-side of their first single and took them countrywide. A second single, the John Plain anthem "First Time", came out at the end of July the same year.

Both the singles and the album itself were a bit rushed and raw round the edges, and the Boys headed out to Rockfield Studios in Wales to get their heads together in the country, relax a little and take their time over *Alternative Chartbusters* (1978).

This was a far more mature album, where some great tongue-in-cheek humour and a better class of songwriting watered down the manic speed-crazed intensity.

The Boys left NEMS at the end of 1978, when, after they'd recorded an entire third album, the record company's financial difficulties meant the band were physically unable to get their hands on the tapes. Although these lost masterpieces did eventually surface (on *Odds And Sods* and *Punk Rock Rarities*), the group and the label parted company. The following year, Casino took his gang to a small town in Scandinavia to record another third album, just so that he could call it *To Hell With The Boys* ("Hell" being the name of the aforementioned small town – hilarious, huh?). Despite being almost drowned out by the groans of journalists stunned by the appalling pun, this third set was surprisingly good. The title, however, was bad enough to attract the attention of the British Home Office, and Casino Steel was deported back to Norway the following year.

Without their main man, the rest of the band assembled the distinctly bad *Boys Only* set, released to general disdain in 1981. Astute enough to read the writing on the wall, the group took this as their cue to split up and get proper jobs for the next two decades. Lured out of retirement in 1999, The Boys have appeared in the UK, throughout Europe (where they were always appreciated to a greater degree than at home) and in the Far East.

⊙ The Boys (Captain Oi!, 2003)

This latest version of the original album now stretches to 22 prime cuts, including a couple of Yobs' tunes. Though never the hardest of hardcore bands, this demonstrates The Boys' punk rock roots. Standout tracks include "I Don't Care", "Tonight" and "Soda Pressing" (geddit?).

⊙ Alternative Chartbusters (Captain Oi!, 2003)

Also including a couple of Yobs tracks, this shows The Boys moving away from straightforward punk rock and into something more poppy and better suited to their infectious sense of humour. "Do The Contract" and "Classified Susie" vie with "Brickfield Nights", "TCP" and "Backstage Pass" for standout track, but the whole album's definitely worthwhile. (NB: The two original albums can also be found in a single disc bundle, excellent value but without the extra tracks.)

BUTTHOLE SURFERS

Formed under another name in Dallas, Texas, 1977. Started surfing in 1981; apparently wiped out in 1998.

"[GIBBY'S] ACCOUNTING CAREER WASN'T BLOSSOMING AND IT DIDN'T LOOK LIKE I WAS GONNA BE A VERY GOOD STOCKBROKER, SO WE STARTED A BAND..."

PAUL LEARY

So many US punks wasted more imagination on finding a cool name for the band than they ever did on writing songs. The **Butthole Surfers**, though, were an honourable exception. As well as picking a name that effectively banned them from 99 percent of US radio shows, they set themselves up with one of the most chaotic, sick and dangerous stage acts seen in the history of rock'n'roll, and found time to write some of the most amusing titles in punk.

Gibson "Gibby" Haynes's (vocals/electronics/guitar) peculiar take on pop music had its roots in the good ol' Texas psychedelia of The Electric Prunes and The Seeds, Sixties garage punks who'd added a long streak of mean attitude to the Jack Daniels and acid cocktails they'd been ingesting. Gibby's dad was known to most of the kids across the southwestern US as Mr Peppermint – host of a TV show broadcast from Dallas – so when he hooked up with **Paul Leary** (guitar/bass/devices/keyboards) at college in San Antonio, there was already a hint of showbiz in the air. Nonetheless, like sensible young men who'd seen how tough it could be to make a living from the entertainment game, they went on to finish their studies (Gibby was doing graduate work in accounting) before appearing live as **Vodka Family Winstons** and **Ashtray Baby Heads**. The new band switched name again – to the catchy **Nine Foot Worm Makes Home Food** – before finally being forced to become **Butthole Surfers** when a radio announcer mistook the title of an early song for the group's name.

In 1981, the group signed to **Jello Biafra**'s Alternative Tentacles label, but still took another two years to record and release their debut album, *Butthole Surfers* (1983). The band had been working its way through an apparently endless series of rhythm sections before finally settling on **Paul "King Koffee" Coffey** (drums, percussion) and **Jeff "Tooter" Pinkus** (bass), with **Theresa "Nervosa" Taylor** (drums and percussion) on the reserves bench.

Gibby and the guys decided the world was ready for a return to outrageous and bizarre rock'n'roll behaviour and set out to scratch that itch with sleazy shock-rock, wild live gigs and an ever-worsening series of song titles such as "Lady Sniff", "The Revenge Of Anus Presley" and "Bar-B-Cue Pope". The Butthole Surfers reached their offensive peak in the mid-Eighties, captured on the live *PCP* EP in 1984 and followed up by the studio album *Psychic Powerless Another Man's Sac* (1985).

After recording "The Shah Sleeps In Lee Harvey Oswald's Grave" and the *Cream Corn From The Socket Of Davis* EP, there was nowhere left to explore in the realm of the offensive, and the Surfers went psychedelic. Hayes had stumbled across a vocal-mangling effects box, and his new "Gibbytronix" voice helped make *Locust Abortion Technician* (1987) the band's most unsettling album. The next year they came up with Hairway To Steven – easily their greatest title, but a recording that had no fire in its belly. *Double Live*, which followed in 1988, was a spoof bootleg as lazy as its title suggests, and despite a brace of EPs – *Widowermaker* (1989) and *The Hurdy Gurdy Man* (1990) – and a full-length album (*Ploughd*, 1991), the creative motor sputtered into silence.

The band entered its most lucrative phase on signing to Columbia in 1992. Previously as indie as they come, after a decade of ill-paid street credibility the band understandably leapt upon the big dollars when they finally appeared. They recorded *Independent Worm Saloon* (1993) with **John Paul Jones** (ex-Led Zeppelin) producing, and while they didn't disappear into the bland middle-distance of MOR adult-oriented rock, they grew increasingly MTV-friendly. By the mid-Nineties, they were just another Top Forty chart act, and of no further interest to us.

Evil, pure evil. "Lady Sniff" and "Gary Floyd" come across on this recording as two of the nastiest tracks ever committed to tape, but in a good way. Certainly among the most powerful recordings of the 1980s, this is an ideal start to your Butthole collection.

BUZZCOCKS

Formed Manchester, England, 1976; still buzzin'.

Perhaps the only band apart from The Monkees to have a TV series – the long-running pop-quiz panel game *Never Mind The Buzzcocks* – named after them, **Buzzcocks**, the seminal Manchester punk-rock band, were on the scene almost as quickly as the Sex Pistols, and like them, inspired a crossover between the worlds of art/design and music. Thanks to their chart success and sheer longevity, Buzzcocks have influenced the sound of the last three decades, from the Midwestern anxiety of Sugar to the mid-adolescent confusion of Busted. More than that, they were a band that inspired devotion among a generation that allegedly had no more heroes. People fell in love with Buzzcocks.

Manchester was as much in the economic doldrums as London when **Pete Shelley** (a.k.a. McNeish; Starway guitar) met **Howard Devoto** (previously Trafford; vocals) at the Bolton Institute of Technology in 1975. The guys recruited a drummer and soon had a pretty good though short-lived band going, covering Velvets and Stooges numbers for their own amusement. It was when Devoto and Shelley nipped down to London early in 1976 to see the Sex Pistols that they were jolted into real action.

Their first step was to book the Pistols for a one-off show in Manchester. Following the London boys' example of commitment over ability, bassist **Garth Smith** and a now-nameless drummer were roped in, and a ferocious rehearsal schedule was instituted so that Buzzcocks could play support. The Pistols duly appeared and, according to legend, pretty much everyone in the audience followed the gig by forming bands of their own. Buzzcocks' moment of triumph had to be postponed though: Smith and the drummer dumped Shelley and Devoto before the big night and they had to pull out.

Wandering gloomily through the audience, they bumped into **Steve Diggle**, local guitar hero, who

agreed to stand in on bass. **John Maher**, drums, was located through the small ads and they set about regrouping, rehashing lyrics and rehearsing the band. Buzzcocks finally got to share the stage of Lesser Free Trade Hall with Johnny Rotten in July, five months after they'd first seen him.

Having spent the rest of the summer gigging around northwest England spreading the word, Buzzcocks were an obvious choice for the ill-fated Anarchy Tour that stumbled around the country at the end of 1976. They took their experience and a few road-tested tunes into the studio soon afterwards, recording the *Spiral Scratch* EP (the first punk record on an independent punk label, their very own New Hormones).

Devoto quit the band almost immediately after it was released in January 1977, for reasons only he can fully explain. Returning briefly to college, he returned to the music scene fairly quickly as front man of **Magazine**. Shelley was by now getting used to being ditched at the altar and he quickly regrouped, moving Diggle to guitar and re-recruiting Smith on bass; wobbly voice and sawn-off Woolworth's guitar notwithstanding, Shelley himself moved to the front of stage as lead singer.

Buzzcocks signed to United Artists in September 1977 and rush-released "Orgasm Addict" to an immediate radio ban but priceless publicity. Smith found himself replaced by more-permanent bassist **Steve Garvey** and "What Do I Get?" took them into the charts early in 1978.

Like the Pistols, Buzzcocks could offer a unique sound and crisp image that set them apart from the ramalama drones that followed in their wake. Both the audio and visual aspects of the band were emphasised for the March 1978 release of *Another Music In A Different Kitchen*: the band were immaculately dressed and looking prettily into camera, the sleeve design was mirrored in the matching carrier bag that was the reward of early purchasers and a firing-all-guns-at-once publicity campaign thrust them into the nation's hearts.

The pressure stayed on for the rest of the year, as the band and the label rode the wave. *Love Bites* hit the shops just six months after their first album and suffered slightly from being bashed out too hurriedly. A lot of the band's trademark wit and wordplay had disappeared, to be replaced by a distinctly non-punk wistfulness. From "Ever Fallen In Love (With Someone You Shouldn't Have Fallen In Love With)?" through "Nostalgia" and "Sixteen

Again", Buzzcocks were looking back, and not even in anger. The album was still loaded with top punk-tinged pop music, though: "Just Lust" soars cheekily above the more miserable "Love Is Lies", and both "Love You More" and "Noise Annoys" were chart singles – the album was hardly a last will and testament.

Its successor, *A Different Kind Of Tension*, was a creaky and ill-assembled affair, however. Yielding only one single – "I Don't Know What To Do With My Life", its UK release was dampened down by the band being on tour in the US. In the States, its release was overshadowed by *Singles Going Steady*, an ill-timed compilation, but one well worth having nonetheless.

Buzzcocks' popularity at home was booming, but booze, drugs and general wear and tear were putting the band at risk. When United Artists were taken over by EMI in 1980, the band had released just three singles in more than twelve months. Record company economics, politics and the culture of revenge meant that a planned fourth album was ultimately shelved permanently, as Shelley decided to break up the band rather than bow his knee any further to major-label high-ups.

Setting out in 1981 on solo careers, Shelley struck lucky with "Homosapien", while Diggle formed **Flag Of Convenience** with Maher. Thereafter, nothing much happened until 1989, when a revival of interest spurred them to re-form for a US tour. Older, balder, but obviously not a great deal wiser, the band stayed together. Shelley, Diggle and Maher recruited bassist **Tony Barber** (all-round punk-rock firebrand and motivator, he's also played with **Alternative TV**) to record *Trade Test Transmissions* in 1993, *All Set* in 1996 and *Modern* in 1999. This second-generation Buzzcocks looks set to keep going until forced by legislation to pack it in for good.

◉ **Singles Going Steady (EMI, 2001)**
◉ **The Complete Singles Anthology (EMI, 2004)**

Depending just how up to date you want your Buzzcocks, either of these compilations should be snapped up. Though easily capable of maintaining song quality across a full-length recording, Buzzcocks were always best as a singles band, and these are singles collections. Go and buy one.

◉ **Time's Up (Grey Area, 2000)**

Gorgeously gritty pre-fame recordings by a band of inept musicians blindly groping their way towards a new music of strange, twisted, guitar-led beauty. One for completists and the desperately curious.

◉ **Another Music In A Different Kitchen / Love Bites (EMI, 2003)**

From Shelley's cheeky two-note guitar solo (lifted straight from "Times Up", recorded more than a year earlier and dumped at the end of the album's intro) to the sudden cut-off of "Moving Away From The Pulsebeat", there's not a duff tune or wrong note played.

 ICONIC SINGLE:
SPIRAL SCRATCH EP
(NEW HORMONES, 1977)

A four-track dispatch from the northwest outpost of punk rock, *Spiral Scratch* was announced to the world through a half-pompous, half Dada-manifesto-style press release and a few blotchy 1/16th page adverts in the music weeklies. Kicking off 1977 in style, this January release on the band's own New Hormones label was all that most ever heard of Howard Devoto's time with them. By the time Buzzcocks made it out of Manchester, Devoto had quit in disgust at seeing the changes in a scene he'd help to build. "What was once unhealthily fresh is now a clean old hat", he said, stomping off in a huff to found Magazine.

Devoto's disaffection notwithstanding, the rest of the world was only just getting into punk, and was reluctant to follow him to a joyless life under the floorboards. The few in the know jumped through all kinds of black-market hoops to buy the record or scrounge copies on cassette. Now it's out on CD, there are no scratches and no jumps and it sounds absolutely marvellous.

Really, there's a big hole in your collection if *Spiral Scratch* is missing. Four tracks of unassailable punk genius that manage to convey urban defiance tinged with a delicious ripple of self-doubt. Devoto's delivery makes deciphering the words part of the pilgrimage (refer to *It Only Looks As If It Hurts*, the collected lyrics, if you must), but the titles ("Breakdown", "Time's Up", "Boredom" and "Friends Of Mine") give useful pointers to the seeker. With their staccato guitar bursts, weedy-sounding solos and quavering vocals leaning for support on the band's meaty rhythm section, these tunes defined Manchester punk.

🎵 PLAYLIST: BUZZCOCKS

If I seem a little jittery I can't restrain myself from weighting the Buzzcocks' list heavily towards the early stuff. *Spiral Scratch* remains at the head of many punk rock playlists for some good reasons – it's never been bettered and is still the most honest piece of work to make it past Manchester's city limits.

1. **BREAKDOWN**
from **Spiral Scratch (New Hormones, 1977)**

2. **TIME'S UP**
from **Spiral Scratch (New Hormones, 1977)**

3. **BOREDOM**
from **Spiral Scratch (New Hormones, 1977)**

4. **FRIENDS OF MINE**
from **Spiral Scratch (New Hormones, 1977)**

5. **WHAT DO I GET**
from **Singles Going Steady (EMI, 2001)**

6. **AUTONOMY**
from **Singles Going Steady (EMI, 2001)**

7. **ORGASM ADDICT**
from **Time's Up (Grey Area, 2004)**

8. **OH SHIT**
from **Time's Up (Grey Area, 2004)**

9. **YOU TEAR ME UP**
from **Time's Up (Grey Area, 2004)**

10. **LOVE BATTERY**
from **Time's Up (Grey Area, 2004)**

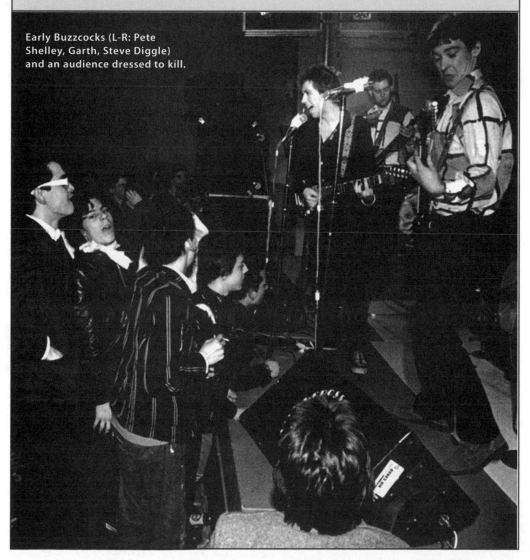

Early Buzzcocks (L-R: Pete Shelley, Garth, Steve Diggle) and an audience dressed to kill.

CABARET VOLTAIRE

Formed Sheffield, England, 1973; split 1994.

One of the most highly regarded of the British "without whom" bands, **Cabaret Voltaire** helped shape the early stages of punk in the UK, insisting on there being room for a witty and artistic no future.

They never fitted in easily with the lumpen punk-rockers, having roots and memories that went back to the experimentalist, free-form mad-hats of the late Sixties. Taking their name from one of the world's least-comfortable stage events, the original Dadaist literary Cabaret Voltaire in World War I Zurich, they also nodded collectively in the direction of previous arty/musical luminaries, from Hugo Ball to Andy Warhol. Although they were present at punk's birth, the members of Cab Volt soon tired of the conformist, uniform-wearing brat it grew into, and like so many of the great brains and personalities that made punk so much fun, they moved on.

In the meantime though, they did liven up the scene. Formed well before the punk explosion, the band had been performing and recording for years and had a far better idea of how to blow an audience's mind than did the bulk of their peers. Frequently sharing the bill with totally unmatched thrashers who had difficulty finding three of the four chords they claimed to understand, **Richard H Kirk** (guitar/vision), **Stephen Mallinder** (bass) and **Chris Watson** (tapes) gave the crowds of entertainment-hungry punk-rock kids an introduction to the sharp industrial end of performance art. Already partly disoriented by cheap lager, potent sticky black hash and Doctor Martens laced up a bit too tightly, a late-1970s Cab Volt audience was assaulted by great blasts of noise, and

unless rendered unconscious by the shock, would never forget it. Huge waves of sound were formed by loop upon loop of tape, with the output force-fed to amplifiers distorted beyond legal limits. People were stunned, confused and rendered a trifle deaf.

They signed to Rough Trade in 1978, pretty much as soon as the UK's most indie label set up shop, and given the freedom to do so, started hitting the public with something more enduring than a hazy Friday night memory of a dingy club on the outskirts of town. Continuing the original definition of punk as being able to include almost anything provided it was done in the right spirit, the first CV releases contained as much primitive electronica as they did heads-down punk-rock guitarness. The band happily quoted Can, Stockhausen and James Brown as influences at a time when it was social death to be able to see further than The Velvet Underground, and beat a path that Throbbing Gristle, The Pop Group and 23 Skidoo were able to tread in their wake.

Titles such as "Baader Meinhof" and "Do The Mussolini (Headkick)", and the full-length recordings of the period – *Mix Up* (1979), *Voice Of America* (1980) and *Red Mecca* (1981) – emphasized the confrontational side of the music, which Cabaret Voltaire reluctantly handed over to Rough Trade after handcrafting it at their own Western Works Studio in Sheffield.

Watson quit the band for a proper job in 1981, leaving Kirk and Mallinder to face the Eighties pop industry alone. As the decade progressed, they picked up a new deal with another UK independent, Some Bizarre, and took both "Sensoria" and "James Brown" to the indie singles charts as their music turned away from the storms of punk to embrace a danceable solution to teenage revolution. In 1986, they flitted over to Chicago to hang out and record *Groovy, Laidback & Nasty* with Marshall Jefferson, one of the big cheeses in house music.

By this point, though, nobody would link them to the punk-rock noisemakers of the previous decade, and although three full-length albums of electronic music appeared in the 1990s on Instinct records, the Cabaret can be assumed to have closed.

⊚ **The Original Sound Of Sheffield: The Best Of Cabaret Voltaire 1979–1982 (Grey Area, 2002)**

Covering the band's earliest and most creative phase, this "best of" package ignores anything they've done in nearly a quarter of a century. However, it gives the listener a rock-solid base from which to start by including such stern beauties as "The Set Up" and "Do The Mussolini (Headkick)", both of which date back to their time with Rough Trade.

⊚ **Live At The YMCA 27.10.79 (1979, reissued Grey Area 1999)**

Great electro-rock gig recorded, of all places, at the YMCA in London's Tottenham Court Road. A visceral record of Cab Volt at their best, this is as raw and street-level as a dachshund's scrotum, joining ATV's *Live At The Rat Club*, Joy Division's 28th Feb 1980 Preston set and Suicide's *23 Minutes Over Brussels* in capturing one of the period's essential live sets.

JAMES CHANCE

Born Milwaukee, Wisconsin, 1953 as James Sigfried, a.k.a. James White.

Though no punk rocker himself, if it hadn't been for the spikyheads, **James Chance** would have never made it past the front door of even the lowliest New York nite-spot without having his squawking sax rammed up where the sun never dares show its face.

Punk mutated over time, one section twisting off to become New Wave and then power pop, another breathing new life into the free-festival avant-garde rock ideal, and a third growing into something monstrously akin to jazz. This last became known in New York and to the music press as No Wave, a short-lived movement that welcomed James Sigfried (also known as James White and James Chance) and his free-jazz musical leanings with open arms when he breezed into town.

James Chance And The Contortions dressed sharp – suits, ties, dapper to the max – but played dangerous, painfully sloppy, skronking, funk-laced

noise music that you only really listened to if you thought it would increase your coolness quotient. James (vocals/sax) blew up an ugly storm, aided by **Adele Bertei** (organ), **Pat Place** (guitar), **Jody Harris** (guitar), and **Don Christiansen** (drums).

Anyone who has listened to Chance torment a saxophone will find it easy to believe that he often ended up in fights with the audience, but more surprising to hear perhaps that he frequently started them himself. Punching out the paying customers, however, was but one facet to the band's confrontational stance. Hectic, violent and sometimes scary club appearances led to a recording session with Brian Eno, and four tracks on his seminal *No New York* compilation (1978, now available again as a CD reissue).

Buy The Contortions, the band's only full-length outing, came out in 1979. Deciding that No Wave was over, James then reinvented himself as **James White**, and the band, minus Bertei, as **The Blacks**, to release *Off White*, a weird disco-influenced take on his old noise-and-screaming routine.

The Blacks disappeared soon after, with James making sporadic appearances and even more occasional live recordings ever since. Just as he seems to be making a commitment to regular live performances, Tiger Style's *Irresistible Impulse* has collected all the official material he recorded as Chance or White in 2003, bundling it with a bunch of rarities as a three-disc set. The same label brought out *Sax Education* in 2004 – a double CD consisting of a hits collection coupled with a previously unreleased live performance recorded in 1981 for Radio Holland.

⊙ **Buy The Contortions / Off White (Munster, 2005)**

If you must buy any of this odious pretentious noise, then this package gives the best value. A horrible noise from beginning to end and a waste of the planet's dwindling resources

CHELSEA

Formed London, 1977; split up but completely reformed 1977, underground during the 1980s, back as mean as ever since the 1990s.

Chelsea was one of the early punk bands thrown together in a frenzy of bandwagon-jumping in late 1976. Like many of their contemporaries, they had one good song, a snotty attitude and little experience. Still, at least their front man, **Gene October**, knew how to strike a pose and dominate an audience. If the rumours that he had previously performed as a young stud in a number of gay porno films are correct, being covered in saliva might have made a pleasant change. He also had a booming, grown-up and powerful singing voice, not unlike that of Joy Division's Ian Curtis.

The rest of the original line-up was guitarist **Billy Idol**, **Tony James** (bass) and **John Towes** (drums), both of the latter coming from London SS. After a few gigs, these three deserted October to form **Generation X**, with Idol later becoming an MTV staple. October then roped in **Carey Fortune** (drums), **Martin Stacy** (guitar) and **Bob Jessie** (bass), with the last two soon replaced by **James Steveson** and **Henry Daze**. Not surprisingly, the band went through almost as many line-up changes as The Fall, later including **James Stevenson**, who eventually followed tradition by jumping ship for Generation X. With some two dozen members going through the band in the

space of a few years, you'd be hard pressed to find any punk rocker back then in London who wasn't at some point a member of Chelsea.

Chelsea's first single, "Right To Work", had a shambling stop-start guitar riff, which gave a nicely raw backdrop to October's growling and shouting. The lyrics were a bit political for the average punk's taste, but it was all fine rabble-rousing stuff, good to dance to and with a chorus to bellow at the ceiling in the nasty, sweaty clubs. Nothing that followed ever really matched it.

They spent most of 1977-78 touring the UK and overseas, which delayed their first LP, *Chelsea*, until 1979. By this time, most of their class-of-'76 contemporaries were already working on their second albums or trying to make it in the States. October's concerns about unemployment, alienation and urban squalor were worked over by the band, but by 1979, punk audiences were looking for something a little more profound than Chelsea's yob rock. And the band was losing credibility due to October's posturing before the music press and the band's increasingly obvious lack of talent.

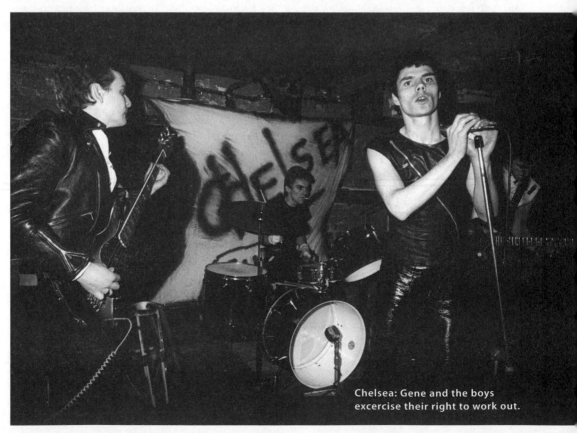

Chelsea: Gene and the boys excercise their right to work out.

Plagued by personnel changes, Chelsea should really have retired after the second LP, 1980's *Alternative Hits*, which was little more than a collection of re-recordings of their early singles. As usual, the original versions were better and the three-minute manifestos rapidly lost impact when heard sequentially. Chelsea continued recording throughout the Eighties, but none of their stuff from this period can be recommended. They were a great live band in the late Seventies, but by the late Eighties, they were a joke.

Chelsea re-formed briefly for the flurry of punk revival gigs of 1996-97. The long period of inactivity appeared to have recharged their batteries as October and the boys menaced their way across stages around the UK and back into the hearts of the old school. Great gigs, great opening comments – no "Hello London, it's great to be back", just a simple, yet elegant "Fuck off!" – great memories of good times long dead.

⊚ **The Punk Singles Collection** (Captain Oi!, 2003)

This superbly edited compilation clocks in at 23 tracks, most of which you really want to hear. From the magnificent "Right To Work" to the saddening "The Last Drink", this is an all-killer collection.

CIRCLE JERKS
Formed Los Angeles, 1979; jerked off in 2003.

Add the Ramones to Jan & Dean, shake well and distil the resulting gloop into a four-piece with bad attitude, powerful amplification and just a touch of the high-school jock. *Et voilà*, your **Circle Jerks** are ready to serve.

When **Keith Morris** (vocals) quit **Black Flag**, he took a cutting of that band's sense of humour along with him. Teaming up with ex-**Red Kross** man **Greg Hetson** (guitar), **Roger Rogerson** (bass) and **Lucky Lehrer** (drums) allowed his precious hardcore shoot to flourish and develop into the immensely noisy, downright funny and deeply, deeply offensive band he'd created, named after an otherwise unmentionable prep-school practice.

Taking their place alongside other hardcore heroes on the circuit such as **Fear**, **The Germs** and **X** (as well as Black Flag), Keith and the gang picked up a large and enthusiastic audience, and were soon regarded as one of the top names on the West Coast scene.

Group Sex, their first album, came out in 1980 and was a fourteen-track taster of their own little corner of skateboard hell. With tracks clocking in at no longer than 1'35" this was punk knocked clean of all excess and taken to a new level of minimalism. It helped land them a slot in the Los Angeles punk documentary film *The Decline Of Western Civilization* (1981), and a small piece of the immortality action too.

By 1982 and their second album *Wild In The Streets*, the humorous side of the Circle Jerks was becoming more obvious. Tongue-in-cheek cover versions of desperately inappropriate pop standards such as "Put A Little Love In Your Heart" were delivered at several hundred miles per hour, with everything turned up to mosh-pit levels and such glowing enthusiasm that the joke took quite a while to get old.

Golden Shower Of Hits (1983), saw the joke worn wafer-thin through being rubbed in the face of the audience. Despite the slam-dance versions of "Along Comes Mary," "Afternoon Delight," "Having My Baby", and "Love Will Keep Us Together", this third album stalled and spiralled into a distant puff of dust like Wile E. Coyote running off a cliff in pursuit of the Roadrunner.

The band went quiet for a couple of years, during which Hetson joined **Bad Religion** for something to do and to pay the rent (he continued playing in both bands until the mid-1990s). It lurched back into life in 1985 with two new members – **Keith Clark** (drums) and **Zander Schloss** (bass) – reborn as just another hard-rockin' band on the West Coast scene. *Wonderful* (1985) and *VI* (1987) saw them struggling for direction, and despite a stopgap live album (*Gig*, 1992), they were written off and listed missing.

Just as the ink was drying on their obituary however, Mercury Records stepped in to offer them a major-label deal and oversee the release of their first new studio album in eight years. *Oddities, Abnormalities And Curiosities* was by no means a return to their punk roots, but it had its moments, including a bizarre cover of the Soft Boys' "I Wanna Destroy You", with vocals shared between Clark and soft-core popstrel Debbie Gibson, a dedicated fan.

It all went haywire for the Jerks again afterwards though, with Clark in particular paying for his years on the road in a series of debilitating illnesses, culminating in a 1999 diagnosis of diabetes. It took another four years for him to return to live performance, and although he's been seen since then with jazz-punk outfit **Midget Handjob**, with Henry Rollins and even back with the Jerks, there's no punk rock left to detain us any longer.

⊙ Group Sex (various reissues available)

The album now clocks in at well over its original sixteen minutes, and in some versions, contains as many as 28 tracks. Try this, and if you like it, there's plenty more where it came from.

John Cooper Clarke and his great punk rock hairstyle / earring combination.

JOHN COOPER CLARKE

Born Manchester, England, 1949; still with us.

"YOUR TYRES ARE KNACKERED / YOUR KNACKERS ARE TIRED."

"PSYCLE SLUTS", JOHN COOPER CLARKE

If evidence of the open-mindedness of punk is ever required, then its tolerance of atrociously bad rock bands jumping onto its bandwagon, amused acceptance of the most pretentious of performance artists, enthusiastic welcoming of incomprehensible Rastafarian millennial chants and cheerful heckling of the poetry of **John Cooper Clarke** should be sufficient.

When punk kicked off, Clarke had to quickly kick his folk-rock roots under the carpet, where they joined many another musician's embarrassing past, creating an alter ego that was equal parts Sixties hipster and Seventies biting social commentator. The perfect warm-up for an evening of four-to-the-floor punk-rock madness, he'd shamble on stage with a carrier bag of scrawled poems, picking them at random and reading them out despite the crowd, laughing at the more amusing abuse and cheerfully ignoring the rest.

In 1977 he took his bag of words to **Martin Hannett** and recorded "Psycle Sluts" an echo-drenched recording in two parts, and, having started setting his poetry to music, he never looked back. Opening for groups such as the Sex Pistols, Buzzcocks and Elvis Costello helped push his 1978 debut album, *Disguise In Love*, and follow-up single, "Gimmix".

There was never likely to be a mass market for poetry, and despite the appreciation shown by the press for both his live album *Walking Back To Happiness* (1979) and second studio effort, *Snap, Crackle And Bop* (1980), he parted company with his label after the disappointing sales of *Zip Style Method* (1982).

Writing off most of the Eighties and the bulk of his teeth as he struggled with heroin addiction – a situation not helped by the romantic relationship he was simultaneously pursuing with Nico (as described in James Young's book *Nico: Songs They Never Play On The Radio*) – Clarke paid the bills through gritty live appearances, but mislaid the bulk of his audience. It took him until the next decade to clean up and revive his act, get back to writing and to reinvent himself as an elder statesman of the glory days of punk.

⊚ **Word Of Mouth, The Very Best Of… (Sony Special Marketing, 2002)**

Although the musical accompaniment does its best to provide an atmosphere, it never comes close to the beery, cheerful heckling and abuse of Clarke's best performances. Still, it contains his most instantly recognizable pieces, from "I Married A Monster From Outer Space", "Psycle Sluts" and "Beasley Street" to "Heart Disease Called Love".

THE CLASH

Formed London, 1976; disbanded 1986.

Often seen as punk's second-ranking band, The Clash, like Avis, tried harder. While the Pistols spurted loose gobs of anarchy, The Clash were tightly focused on "real" political issues. Whereas the Pistols were seen as Malcolm McLaren's puppets, The Clash kept their equally domineering manager better concealed and were seen as more independent. The Pistols wore clothes from Sex, The Clash had theirs run up for them by friends who were handy with a sewing machine. Whatever the realities of the situation, there was an artistic tension between the bands that produced punk rock of the highest quality from both.

The London flat of **Matt Dangerfield** (The Boys) boasted a rudimentary recording set-up and attracted jobless musicians like a dropped ice cream draws the flies. This loose collective – later nicknamed the **London SS** (the "SS", it should be emphasized, stood for Social Security) – was where **Mick Jones** (guitar hero), **Nicky "Topper" Headon** (drums), **Keith**

🎵 PLAYLIST: THE CLASH

Trimming out all the fat from The Clash's back catalogue still leaves a playlist several days too long to be included here. However, ten tracks do somehow wriggle their way to the top of the pile as follows.

1. **WHITE RIOT**
from **The Clash (Columbia, 1999)**

2. **DENY**
from **The Clash (Columbia, 1999)**

3. **I'M SO BORED WITH THE U.S.A.**
from **The Clash (Columbia, 1999)**

4. **POLICE & THIEVES**
from **The Clash (Columbia, 1999)**

5. **COMPLETE CONTROL**
from **The Essential Clash (Sony, 2005)**

6. **CLASH CITY ROCKERS**
from **The Essential Clash (Sony, 2005)**

7. **CAPITAL RADIO ONE**
from **The Essential Clash (Sony, 2005)**

8. **(WHITE MAN) IN HAMMERSMITH PALAIS**
from **The Essential Clash (Sony, 2005)**

9. **THE GUNS OF BRIXTON**
from **London Calling (Columbia, 1999)**

10. **LOST IN THE SUPERMARKET**
from **London Calling (Columbia, 1999)**

Levene (guitar, later of **Public Image Ltd**) and **Paul Simonon** (later to emerge as bass player for The Clash) first met up.

Jones and Simonon recruited **Joe Strummer** (guitar/vocals) from pub-rockers **The 101ers**. Before long, they had a charismatic manager, **Bernie Rhodes** – a man who re-registered his car to CLA 5H and who figured that it would be good for the lads' image if they arrived at a gig in a military-style armoured vehicle – and were locked away on starvation wages to rehearse in a draughty studio in the middle of a London winter. Bernie was well aware of McLaren's plans for the Pistols and wanted a slice of the action for his own team.

When the scene's most radical band signed meekly to CBS, swearing "to corrupt them from within" as they were dragged off to sell their souls, their stance began to be offset by doubts. Even some true believers felt that Strummer (real name John Mellors) came from too privileged a background to be genuinely angry, while Jones's South London childhood was considered suspiciously overdramatic.

By the time they first came to major attention touring with the Sex Pistols on the infamous Anarchy In The UK Tour, Topper and Levene had quit. Lovable **Terry Chimes** stepped in at the last minute to drum on the first album (and was given the wonderful pseudonym "Tory Crimes" on the sleeve). *The Clash*, the best album of 1977, was recorded in just three weekends. The music was angry punk rock, played fast and furiously. A treble-heavy mix and production ensured that the lyrics were generally comprehensible and that their messages got through.

The Clash certainly appeared to care about their fans – they produced some remarkably inexpensive LPs and you could almost always afford a ticket when they toured – but their ambition was to crack America, which explained their acceptance of dubiously qualified Blue Öyster Cult producer **Sandy Perlman** to look after their second LP, *Give 'Em Enough Rope* (1978). It came under withering critical fire from the British music press, with "sell-out" being among the milder accusations levelled against what is, in retrospect, a fine album.

Opening with a triple-whammy in the shape of "Safe European Home", "English Civil War" and "Tommy Gun", the band moved on to "Julie's Been Working For The Drug Squad", the tongue-in-

cheek tale of a formidable British acid cartel, and "Drug Stabbing Time", one of the great tributes to the joys of life on the road. Granted, Jones's "Stay Free" was skin-crawlingly twee, and the remaining tracks could be classed as filler, but it scarcely merited the venom it received. Besides, it paved

ICONIC SINGLE: COMPLETE CONTROL (CBS, 1977)

One of the most powerful songs of its era, and nothing less than a rallying cry for the heroes of punk's brave new world, "Complete Control" is also an archetypal punk-rock song that makes its point succinctly, telling its story with little embellishment and not much of a solo in about three minutes from start to end.

When The Clash finally jumped onto the CBS money train, they muttered about "changing the system from within" and hinted that the end of corporate rock was now within their grasp. Nobody believed it of course, but the political gesture was appreciated. Their embarrassingly low position in the pecking order was revealed, however, when the band were shipped over to play some badly received gigs in the Netherlands; while they were out of the country, CBS took it upon themselves to release a second single, "Remote Control", which, although acceptable as an album track, didn't cut it as a single.

When the lads found out how they had been misled by the suits at CBS HQ – distracted from the small print by a big handful of cash, like mugs from the back end of nowhere – their self-belief was dented, but strengthened. This single, opening with a martial guitar riff that echoes the anger in the Pistols' near-contemporary "Holidays In The Sun", drips with anger. Backed up by the most solid rhythm section in British punk, Joe never sang a bitterer vocal and Mick's guitar sounds ready to leap from its case and bite the throat of the nearest executive.

A goose-pimpling song even now, more than 25 years later, it still works its magic as the perfect "getting ready for a gig" tune.

the way for their planned world domination.

Having conquered an enormous home audience through good PR, great records and a barnstorming headline set at London's 1978 Rock Against Racism festival in Hackney, The Clash turned their attention to America, visiting the States twice in 1979. That year also saw them managing to fit in the writing, rehearsal and recording of *London Calling*, a double LP sold at the price of a regular single album, recorded with veteran producer **Guy Stevens**. Critics and fans alike loved it, while the heavy-metallist accusations that had accompanied *Give 'Em Enough Rope* died away: the band's love of reggae showed in "Guns Of Brixton", they got historical with "Spanish Bombs", there was an R&B classic in "Brand New Cadillac", and even Mick Jones's weedy voice survived well on "Lost In The Supermarket". It also produced their biggest hit singles to date – the title track in Britain, and "Train In Vain (Stand By Me)" in the States.

They went one better and brought even bigger lumps to the throats of CBS executives by releasing a triple album just in time for the Christmas market. *Sandinista!*, sold at the price of a double LP, was the band's "experimental" album, an attempt to kick over their past traces, to shake off the fans who couldn't see beyond the three-chord drone of four years earlier, and get them played on college radio. It worked too, although the use of brass bands, disgustingly syrup-voiced children, and even some C&W fiddle playing was considered cruel and unusual punishment in some quarters. It was mauled by critics, and even old-time fans felt it was too long and sprawling, but it certainly had some marvellous moments – "The Magnificent Seven", the wonderful "Hitsville UK", the pacifist "The Call-Up" and the wobbly oldie "Junco Partner".

Bernie sent his boys to the Far East and Australia in 1981, a year which was otherwise quiet for the band. On returning to the UK in March 1982, they linked up with Guy Stevens again to record *Combat Rock* (1982), which turned out to be the final album from the original line-up.

Dismissed by the more purist critics and old-school fans, it succeeded in its commercial intent, particularly in America, where both "Should I Stay Or Should I Go?" and "Rock The Casbah" reached the Top 10. When Strummer disappeared on the eve of the band's Know Your Rights UK tour, dates were postponed for three weeks before it was revealed as a publicity stunt.

Strummer returned to the ranks, but then Headon was fired, to be replaced once more by Terry Chimes. When Chimes himself was sacked and replaced by **Pete Howard** in early 1983, things began to fall apart. Matters came to a final head when Mick Jones was given the boot a few months later, resurfacing in 1985 with **Big Audio Dynamite**.

A last-gasp Clash, formed of Strummer and Simonon plus jobbing guitarists **Vince White** and **Nick Sheppard** (ex-Cortinas), squeezed out the superfluous *Cut The Crap* album in 1985, a recording of little interest bar "Dirty Punk" and "This Is England". Effectively The Clash were no more.

Strummer embarked on a solo career, and grew up to be one of the grand old men of punk rock. His recording career continued with a new band, The Mescaleros, until his sudden, unexpected death in 2004. Mick went through a fling with technology during his time with BAD and finally emerged as a producer, notably with **The Libertines**. Simonon is now a respected artist based in London and occasionally pops up on talking-head history of punk programmes.

The Clash's back catalogue has continued to sell, but they resisted the temptation to re-form and tour the stadiums, even after an unexpected number-one UK hit in 1991 with the reissued "Should I Stay Or Should I Go?", which had been featured in a Levis commercial. Throughout their career, The Clash were obliged to pull off something exceptional time after time. And that's just what they did, more or less redefining punk's agenda by channelling teenage angst into the worlds of mainstream and revolutionary politics.

◉ The Clash (CBS, 1977)

It's undeniably raw, but it's also pure, coming from a time when "I'm So Bored With The USA" had yet to become a cliché. *The Clash* is an indispensable document of early UK punk, full of inescapable guitar hooks and ready-to-wear slogans.

◉ Give 'Em Enough Rope (CBS, 1978)

Opening with the awe-inspiring power-guitar riff of "Safe European Home", this shows a more considered approach, and an appreciation that louder does not necessarily mean better.

◉ London Calling (CBS, 1979)

A mature and well-constructed album from the cover (a clever Elvis parody) to the running order, this is The Clash at their peak. The 25th anniversary reissue comes with an extra disc of interesting demos.

◉ **From Here To Eternity** (CBS, 2001)

At last, the live recording that proves just how strong, tight, and thoroughly lovely they were back in the Seventies.

THE CORTINAS

Started Bristol, England, 1976; scrapped 1978.

One of the first of the "second wave" of British punk bands, and the first to sign to Step Forward Records (run by Mark P. of Alternative TV), **The Cortinas** motored into the public consciousness straight down the M4 from Bristol, a city not otherwise celebrated much in the annals of punk rock.

They started off as school friends in a common-room band, jamming through hyped-up R&B standards to keep out of the lunchtime rain, but soon graduated to burning up the local club scene with their own speedy take on Sixties garage-band classics. Clubbing together with Mr Swan Senior as acting manager, **Daniel Swan** (drums), **Dexter Dalwood** (bass), **Mike Fewings** (guitar), **Nick Sheppard** (guitar), and **Jeremy Valentine** (vocals) headed for London in search of a recording contract and directions to the Roxy.

Hitting town at exactly the right time for a punk band that knew its chops and had a set ready, the Cortinas were an immediate hit. Their music was cut back to the bone, played loud, fast and snotty: just what the kids were waiting for. Major-label A&R men circled above them, but in the end, credibility won out, and "Fascist Dictator" eventually appeared on Step Forward. The rest of 1977 went by as a set of snapshots: the obligatory John Peel session, unforgettable gigs supporting Blondie, Television and The Stranglers, all culminating in their greatest statement, "Defiant Pose".

So far, they had not put a foot wrong, and when their new and more professional management took them aside and re-signed the band to CBS, all they were able to see was the bigger-league gigs they were being invited to play, the extra marketing budget, and a golden future for all concerned. However, stripping the story to its essentials, signing to CBS ruined the band. *True Romances* was, as its title suggested, a step away from punk; although Valentine was still cheerfully bellowing at the microphone like an angry rhino, this was a pop record. The album's two best tracks, "Heartache"

and "Ask Mr Waverley", were released as a single (it sank without even a trail of bubbles) and at the end of 1978, the Cortinas split up.

Although most of the band members went on to join other musical projects, and were seen here and there throughout the 1980s, their big moment was definitely when they said "yes!" to the cover design for "Defiant Pose".

◉ **ICONIC SINGLE:**
DEFIANT POSE (STEP FORWARD, 1977)

If ever a record sold on the strength of its picture sleeve, it was this. Though the song itself is a fine upstanding piece of in-yer-face snottiness, boasting the full complement of trebly guitars, beat-'em-to-death drumming and vocals that are ripped through with rage, it's the sleeve that made this single such a desirable object.

"Defiant Pose" (b/w "Independence") appeared at the end of 1977. Although the record cover was designed by Hipgnosis, who'd created memorable record sleeves for punk's greatest enemies (Pink Floyd, Genesis and ELP), it is undeniably one of the lasting images of punk – a middle-aged, middle-class couple look distressed and disapproving as their teenage son vomits his last three meals onto the kitchen floor. As a work of art, its value lies in the precise attention to grating detail: wallpaper clashes violently with tablecloth, the mother's dress, apparently woven from the purest polymers, lies flaccid across her shoulders like a collar of raw meat, father's watch glints with a mocking masculinity at his spineless pose, featureless outfit and ineffective moustache. If this boy's been living on speed and cigarettes for the last few days like a good punk should, the decor alone would be enough to induce projectile puking.

The back cover features a portrait of the band by Jill Furmanovsky. Behind the forced punk sneers and studied lack of interest of the fresh-faced punks themselves lies an enormous farmhouse-style kitchen, filled with the comforts of late Seventies living. Still, they never did claim to be council-estate kids escaping a life on the dole.

PLAYLIST: ELVIS COSTELLO

As he so frequently used to insist, he's not angry … he's bubbling lava, livid and raging hot.

1. OLIVER'S ARMY
from **Armed Forces** (Demon; 2002)

2. WATCHING THE DETECTIVES
from **My Aim Is True** (Demon; 2001)

3. PUMP IT UP
from **This Year's Model** (Demon; 2002)

4. I CAN'T STAND UP FOR FALLING DOWN
from **Get Happy** (Demon; 2003)

5. EVERY DAY I WRITE THE BOOK
from **Punch The Clock** (Demon; 2003)

6. GREEN SHIRT
from **Armed Forces** (Demon; 2002)

7. TRAMP THE DIRT DOWN
from **Spike** (Rhino; 2001)

8. SHIPBUILDING
from **Punch The Clock** (Demon; 2003)

9. HIGH FIDELITY
from **Get Happy** (Demon; 2003)

10. (THE ANGELS WANNA WEAR MY) RED
SHOES from **My Aim Is True** (Demon; 2001)

ELVIS COSTELLO

Born Declan McManus, London, 1954.

"THE ONLY TWO THINGS THAT MATTER TO ME … WRITING ALL THESE SONGS, ARE REVENGE AND GUILT. THOSE ARE THE ONLY EMOTIONS I KNOW ABOUT."

ELVIS COSTELLO

The angriest young man in punk rock was **Elvis Costello**, no contenders. Spitting almost as much frothy cotton wool at the punters as they were sending in his direction, his early gigs put a whole new slant on punk's famous battering down of the audience-performer barrier. He materialized, apparently fully formed and carrying a songbook crammed full of bitter lyrics, sweet tunes and sour outlook when *My Aim Is True* came out on Stiff Records – the sure-fire hit label of the time – in 1977.

Only in myth and movies do musicians leap on stage out of nowhere; the rest have to pay their dues, just like DP Costello – computer-programmer for Elizabeth Arden by day, folk singer by night – did in the UK clubs during the early 1970s. Turning his attention to the more popular and equally passion-soaked genre of country rock in the middle of the decade, Costello performed with a covers band called Flip City, at the same time recording a series of solo demos of his own material. When they reached the ears that mattered at Stiff Records, DP was renamed Elvis, and there was a new king on the block.

In one of those occasional strange, yet meaningless coincidences that litter the history of rock'n'roll, the backing band booked for the first

 ICONIC SINGLE:
LESS THAN ZERO (STIFF, 1977)

The sheer volume of venom poured into the lyrics of "Less Than Zero" make it impossible not to lump this in with the anger and cynicism of the punk movement. Though they touch on the assassination of a Kennedy, mention the aged British fascist Oswald Mosley and are set against a backdrop of casual afternoon sex, the immediate impression it gives is one of nausea and depression, a worn-out feeling at the end of a stale day. Still, it's got a catchy beat and you can certainly dance to it.

My Aim Is True (then known as "*Clover*") sessions, went on to become Huey Lewis And The News, even though Huey himself was elsewhere at the time.

Anyway, back to the plot. With Nick "Basher" Lowe in charge of production and working at his usual high velocity, the first single was ready to go by April. Elvis recorded the album in just 24 hours, spread out over the sick days and holiday he'd built up in his day job. By July, Elvis was a professional musician, backed by **The Attractions** – **Steve Nieve** (keyboards), **Bruce Thomas** (bass) and **Pete Thomas** (no relation) on drums. As the summer grew hotter, and with the album doing much better than the first two singles (reaching number fourteen in the UK charts), it was time to take the music to the masses and go on tour.

Stiffs Live, the autumn 1977 package tour featuring Elvis and The Attractions plus Nick Lowe, Ian Dury and Wreckless Eric, was the label's high-water mark. When it was over, Elvis quit alongside his mentor Jake Riviera and Nick Lowe to form Radar Records. As a parting gift, his last Stiff single, "Watching The Detectives", charted at number fifteen.

Elvis was obviously far too talented a songwriter to stay within punk's fairly limiting borders for long, but he kept his reputation as the most caustic kid in town for the next two years and two albums. Kicking off 1978 with *This Year's Model*, Elvis and The Attractions rode the wave of punk-rock resentment they'd observed welling up while on tour, knocking out a back-to-basics set of hard-hitting tunes. *Armed Forces*, following in 1979, and was even tougher, spattering anti-personnel lyrics with glee and abandon.

1979 was also the year Elvis outgrew the confines of punk: moving first into production (starting with the first Specials album) and then into a widening circle of musical exploration – including Sixties soul, country ballads, collaborations with lounge-king Burt Bacharach and sensitive orchestral numbers. Across the decades, he's maintained the hit-and-miss, "integrity above certainty" attitude of his early years, and still undeniably slings a mean lyric when inspired and in the mood. However, although Elvis lives, he ain't no punk rocker no more.

⊙ My Aim Is True (Demon, 2001)

Bulked out to a massive 26 tracks, the reissued album shows Elvis when he was younger, angrier and a lot more intense than the extremely gifted songwriter he became. Blisteringly irate, from "Welcome To The Working Week" to "Poison Mood", with standout tracks including "Miracle Man", "Alison", "Angels Wanna Wear My Red Shoes", "Less Than Zero" and "Watching The Detectives".

Cowpunk

If what they say is true, even cowgirls get the blues. So it follows that cowboys go punk now and then. Cowpunk is easily imagined as the Ramones jamming with Johnny Cash; its "maximum sturm und twang" sounds sweet to the ears of the young, pissed-off and rural in the same way that hip-hop strikes a chord in the urban soul. Faster, harder-hitting and capable of far better jokes than the dreary interminables of the alt.country genre that followed it, Cowpunk flourished during the 1980s, but although bands sporadically spring up to keep the sound alive, it has since largely withered away for lack of attention.

▣ PLAYLIST:

1. **BREAKFAST** Mary Prankster
from **Blue Skies Over Dundalk** (Fowl Records, 1998)

2. **PISS AND VINEGAR** The Legendary Shack Shakers
from **Believe** (Yep Roc, 2004)

3. **SKINHEAD BLUES** U.S. Roughnecks
from **$20 and Two Black Eyes** (Epitaph, 2004)

4. **LONESOME JOHNNY BLUES** Cracker
from **Kerosene Hat** (Cracker, 1994)

5. **COWBOY LOVE** The Reverend Horton Heat
from **It's Martini Time** (Universal, 2002)

6. **16 DAYS** Whiskeytown
from **Strangers Almanac** (Universal, 1998)

7. **FOLSOM PRISON BLUES** Pronghorn from **Now That's What I Call Dogshite vol.1** (Hogbitch, 2001)

8. **HELP THERE'S A FIRE** Jason & the Scorchers
from **Midnight Roads & Stages Seen** (Mammoth, 1999)

9. **DIM LIGHTS, THICK SMOKE, AND LOUD, LOUD MUSIC** Beat Farmers
from **Tales of the New West** (Rhino, 2004)

WAYNE / JAYNE COUNTY

Born Dallas, Georgia, circa 1947; Wayne became Jayne in 1980.

When asked for a short biography, Jayne said: "Go to my website!!! Just take some of the info off the back jacket of the book or something!!! Or write something about me from memory! You know how I am the most sexiest, talented, and most beautiful woman you know, and that I single-handedly started both the glam and punk scenes!!!" She's a monster talent, she's never sold out and she still rocks like a motherfucker. Before Jayne, however, there was Wayne.

Wayne County was the weirdest, fiercest vision ever to appear on a rock'n'roll stage. As early as 1972, this dragged-up Lenny Bruce was astonishing New York's blasé rock scene with his filthy lyrics and demented stage antics. Andy Warhol and **David Bowie** courted him, and for the emergent punk generation he was an inspiration. When it came to outrage and attitude, nobody could beat Wayne County. Starting out in New York as the DJ at Max's Kansas City, he was a punk rocker before the term had been invented, wearing trash-bag dresses, heading up a band called The Electric Chairs, singing "If you don't want to fuck me baby, fuck off" and wielding a mic-stand with intent and haphazardly dangerous lack of precision in New York's clubs before Television had plucked up the courage to poke a nose round the door at CBGB's.

As so often happens, New York had to wait to be fed the next big thing before it would bite of its own accord, and so, packing up his frills, foundation and foul language, Wayne went to London. Signing up to Safari Records just as punk was about to explode, his debut album – *The Electric Chairs* – appeared in 1978.

His "Eddie And Sheena" single told a heartbreaking tale of a punk girl in love with a Teddy boy, going some way to stopping the rival gangs knocking lumps off one another at the weekends. He continued recording, releasing *Storm The Gates*

Wayne (drinking) and The Chairs relax backstage.

Of Heaven in 1978 and *Things Your Mother Never Told You* in 1979. Wayne was never really going to be mainstream radio material though, and as punk rock died down, he managed to save enough money for something he'd always wanted. He moved for a while to Berlin and emerged, transformed, as Jayne County.

◉ Rock 'N' Roll Resurrection (1981)

Jayne's first album was a live recording powerful enough to keep her on the road for another couple of decades. An autobiography, *Man Enough To Be A Woman*, appeared in 1996, and in 1999, she recorded a new version of "Fuck Off", snappily named "Fuck Off 2000".

◉ Rock 'n' Roll Cleopatra (RPM, 2004)

Most easily available of the compilations, this is an excellent twenty-track scamper through Wayne's closet. Includes the brilliant "Wonder Woman", the title track, "I Had Too Much To Dream Last Night", "Mean Muthafuckin' Man", "Fuck Off", "Eddie And Sheena Pts 1 & 2", "Toilet Love" and of course "Man Enough To Be A Woman".

THE CRAMPS

Created New York City, 1976; currently undead.

"WE DON'T FEEL LIKE OUR MUSIC IS FOR EVERYBODY. IT'S FOR THOSE WHO CAN IDENTIFY WITH BEING A HOODLUM, A MISFIT. NO ONE ELSE SHOULD BE EXPECTED TO LIKE IT."

MS POISON IVY

Born in the shadow of a howling dog one moon-drenched night down in the swamps, **The Cramps** want to eat your children raw to the sound of the devil's own rockabilly beat.

More prosaically, for the last three decades they've taken it upon themselves to bring psychobilly – their own term and one that fittingly describes their unique sci-fi B-movie take on the ramalama rhythms of punk – to the world. Where regular-flavour punk embraced the "slice of life" style of cinéma vérité and documentary photographers, The Cramps' music looked to flying saucers, late-night TV and eerie-mutant-zombie-teenage goo-goo muck for its inspiration. In short, much like The Addams Family, it was really rather ookie.

Paying their dues on the seedy stages of Max's Kansas City and down the road at CBGB's, **Lux Interior** (stilettos/vocals) and his partner in crime, the evil dominatrix **Poison Ivy** (disdain/guitar), started to create "bad music for bad people" back in 1976. As the only two permanent members of the band, they set the controls for Coolsville, building a real cult following on the way.

IRS Records collected their early singles as the Gravest Hits mini album, followed shortly afterwards by their first full-length recording, *Songs The Lord Taught Us*. When **Bryan Gregory**, the band's original noise-guitarist, quit, he was replaced periodically over the next three decades by Julien Greinsnatch, ex-Gun Club Kid **Congo Powers** and a series of others – lonely, unmourned characters for the most part, who disappeared forever on moonless nights.

Kid Congo kept his blood in his veins long enough to record *Psychedelic Jungle*, and, after a nasty scrap over royalties, a live set recorded at the Peppermint Lounge, New York, released as *Smell Of Female* (Enigma Records). By the end of the eighties, the line-up had more or less stabilized into Lux, Ivy, **Slim Chance** (bass) and **Harry Drumdini** (drums), delivering *A Date With Elvis*, *Stay Sick*, *Look Mom No Head*, *Rockinnreelinina uklandnewzealnd* (a live concert recording), and *Flamejob*. Style, humour and kicks mean a lot to the Cramps – they cut their first album at Sam Philips' Sun Studios, they can use the term "squares" without irony and they don't bring no cat down.

Though a Cramps gig is an unforgettable and mind-expanding experience, the band are much more than simply kitsch, and a lot more dangerous than they look. They've earned the right to use their menacing, outsider attitude and still take no shit in their wild-eyed celebration of sex and getting righteously fucked up. Creating tunes for you to howl at the moon with, The Cramps are the real deal and won't ever let you down.

◉ Off The Bone / Songs The Lord Taught Us (EMI, 2003)

An excellent-value 35-track 2-CD collection, combining the group's first album with a compilation that itself included the earlier *Gravest Hits* EP. Features more echo than you'd

Snarl for the camera, darlin'. The Cramps' Ms Ivy and Lux hog the lens, with Miriam and Bryan in the rear.

📱 PLAYLIST: CRAMPS

With *Off the Bone* and *Songs the Lord Taught Us* available as a two-for-one from EMI, we're spoiled for choice. The following ten will see you marching widdershins round a black cat bone just to get your mojo working again.

1. **HUMAN FLY** from **Off the Bone & Songs the Lord Taught Us (EMI, 2003)**

2. **WAY I WALK** from **Off the Bone & Songs the Lord Taught Us (EMI, 2003)**

3. **DOMINO** from **Off the Bone & Songs the Lord Taught Us (EMI, 2003)**

4. **SURFIN' BIRD** from **Off the Bone & Songs the Lord Taught Us (EMI, 2003)**

5. **FEVER** from **Off the Bone & Songs The Lord Taught Us (EMI, 2003)**

6. **DRUG TRAIN** from **Off the Bone & Songs the Lord Taught Us (EMI, 2003)**

7. **GOO GOO MUCK** from **Off the Bone & Songs the Lord Taught Us (EMI, 2003)**

8. **SHE SAID** from **Off the Bone & Songs the Lord Taught Us (EMI, 2003)**

9. **GOOD TASTE** from **Off the Bone & Songs the Lord Taught Us (EMI, 2003)**

10. **STRYCHNINE** from **Off the Bone & Songs the Lord Taught Us (EMI, 2003)**

get shouting "Fuck you!" in the British Library, and guitars so twangy they might be strung with pantyhose. Unmissable. Stop reading this now: go out and buy it.

◉ **How To Make A Monster (Vengeance, 2004)**

Another magic 2-CD set (the second one hundred percent live) of old songs dusted off, some demos, and other difficult-to-locate items.

CRASS

Convened Epping, England 1977; dissolved 1984, reconvened 2002.

■■he band most likely to lead a march on Parliament with a view to burning the place down to the ground, **Crass** gave new meaning to the word "commitment" as applied to musicians flirting with politics. Whereas their contemporaries – The Jam or The Clash, for example – were dab hands with a slogan and weren't averse to rabble-rousing lyrics, Crass deliberately turned their backs on fame, devoted what little fortune they acquired to agitprop purposes and were more likely to include a diagram on how to make a Molotov cocktail with their recordings than any well-meaning but ultimately futile set of chord diagrams.

Deciding in advance (presumably at a communal meeting) that they would disband in Orwell's 1984, they were able to concentrate on filling their fixed term with as much direct action, tinged with hardcore punk rock, as humanly possible. Crass

were tarred very early on with the "poor little rich kids" tag, particularly when one of the family homes was given over to the establishment of an anarchist commune. They nevertheless strove to live up to the ideals they championed, and to encourage others to join them.

Not that they made their message easy listening by any means: in addition to wearing their politics very much for show, they made the most gloriously raucous and challenging punk rock of their era. Crass gigs were a sea of black leather and whitewashed slogans and, given the traditional anarchist stance of opposition to whatever "The Man" is offering, were often more like rallies than traditional gigs.

Through a blistering series of recordings (on their own, fiercely indie Crass Records label, of course) they laid out cogent, reasonably well-thought-out alternatives to the Western late-capitalist way of life, and then spread hellishly loud cries of rage against the evils of war, organized religion, sexism and state oppression over the top. British punks found the new hot-chilli Crass-flavour veggie-punk-burger very appealing – hardly a surprise when the bland competition came from the likes of the corporate-friendly Clash, miserably elitist Pistols, dinosaur-rock-ish Stranglers and the overly styled Jam. Much to their own amusement, Crass became a success.

But first, back to the commune: deep in leafy Epping Forest, in unfashionable east London, **Steve Ignorant** (vocals) and **Penny Rimbaud** (drums)

🎵 **PLAYLIST: CRASS**

Not to be taken too seriously unless you're tooled up with military hardware and have a bunch of loyal cadres trained in ninja skills watching your back. If you're ready, clad in black don't look back, it's time to chant down Babylon with anarcho-syndicalist truths.

1. YES SIR I WILL
from **Yes Sir I Will (Crass, 1995)**

2. REALITY ASYLUM
from **Feeding of the 5,000 (Crass, 1999)**

3. DO THEY OWE US A LIVING
from **Feeding of the 5,000 (Crass, 1999)**

4. PUNK IS DEAD
from **Feeding of the 5,000 (Crass, 1999)**

5. BANNED FROM THE ROXY
from **Feeding of the 5,000 (Crass, 1999)**

6. YOU PAY
from **Feeding of the 5,000 (Crass, 1999)**

7. SO WHAT
from **Feeding of the 5,000 (Crass, 1999)**

8. YOU'VE GOT BIG HANDS
from **Stations of the Cross (Crass, 1995)**

9. WALLS
from **Stations of the Cross (Crass, 1995)**

10. BIG MAN
from **Stations of the Cross (Crass, 1995)**

were inspired by cider and the Sex Pistols to get a band together. Nailing the "do-it-yourself" ethos to the mast (though the sheer number of flags they sailed under eventually made it impossible to see the mast, find a direction or agree a course), they set to writing songs that their untrained mates could strum along with.

Drowning stage fright with snakebite and learning the game as they went along, they took their first five-song set on the road. Famously banned from the Roxy in London (an event soon turned into a halfway-decent song) and wild enough to provoke a riot in a Carmelite convent, they found a circuit of pub gigs and fund-raisers and began raising the money to fund their drinks and recording bill.

Everything about their debut release, *Feeding Of The 5000* – from the stark graphics of the cover design through the drum beat, guitar patterns and delirious vocals – shouted intensity and sincerity. The title referred to the minimum number of copies they could have pressed up and the disc itself was a 12" 45rpm EP / mini-album that deliberately fitted into none of the contemporary musical pigeonholes. The cover – the first of their famous series of fold-out sleeves combining lyrics, agit-prop info and a poster for the bedroom wall – was too clever to be straightforward punk, while the music was too damn noisy for them to be listed alongside the art-school bands. Crass and their product were hard to pin down.

Feeding came out on the independent Small Wonder label, with "Reality Asylum" originally intended as the opening track. This had to be pulled, however, after someone in the pressing plant got wind of the lyrics. The entire piece was replaced by a silent track, listed on the cover as "The Sound Of Free Speech". Eventually rerecorded and issued as a single, "Reality Asylum" is anything but a typical punk-rock tune. It rises from a lone female voice chanting the lyric as if it were an incantation or spell, to an almost unbearable mess of distorted guitar. As a way of annoying Christians, or indeed of scaring the pants off anyone with a hint of belief in the afterlife, it was hard to beat. The track begins: "I am no feeble Christ, not me. He hangs in glib delight upon his cross, upon his cross, Above my body, lowly me...".

The B-side of the single, "Shaved Women", continued the band's exploration of shocking evil noise

**ICONIC SINGLE:
NAGASAKI NIGHTMARE / BIG A LITTLE A (CRASS, 1980)**

The definitive single by the UK's most uncompromising punk rock act; confronting the horror and sheer human outrage of nuclear attack, this double A-side was catchy, repetitive anti-war propaganda of the finest kind.

Eve never sounded more defiantly afraid, even as she's scorched, irradiated and blown to smithereens by "Nagasaki Nightmare" and its combined blast waves of tormented guitar, feedback and heinous sound effects. The lyrics constantly return to the image of a city in which families burned alive, and children played innocently unaware of death creeping towards them from above. Studied in isolation, the words give only the smallest hint of the song's crescendo power, whereas the lyric sheet to the flip – "Big A Little A" – leads you to expect polemic of considerable complexity and length.

However, the tune kicks off in cheery mood, with a chorus of kiddy voices chanting the opening couplet. It's not until Steve gets hold of the lyrics and hurtles recklessly headlong with them as fast as he can – a trick which only gets better when he runs out of words and has to resort to sputtering "They're out to get you get you get you get you get you get you get you!" – he had never produced anything as raw. The guitar'n'bass combine in a shock and awe assault with Penny's confrontational drum'n'saucepan salvoes creating an irresistible call to arms (which would then be snottily refused, of course). Managing to splatter poison over God and those who serve the churches, the Queen, police, armed forces, Prime Minister and Britain's policy towards Ireland in one catchy pop song is a feat yet to be beaten – although Britney's supposed to be working on something.

The original vinyl is long since unavailable of course but both tracks can be heard as part of the band's incongruous greatest hits compilation: *You'll Ruin It for Everyone* (latest reissue on Pomona, 2001).

as a way of luring in the punters. Hammering out a message bemoaning the pathetic state of female independence, it resurfaced on the *Stations Of The Crass* album.

For anyone of the punk persuasion claiming a degree of commitment to the good fight, all this was hard to resist. It also introduced **Eve Libertine** (vocals), **Gem Stone** (backing vocals), **N. A. Palmer** (rhythm guitar), **Phil Free** (lead guitar) and **Pete Wright** (bass). Rimbaud contributed radio, tape and drums, while the rest of the commune – Ignorant and **Joy De Vivre** – were credited as "Members Of Crass Not On This Recording".

Huge line-ups like this were rare in live music, due to the costs of paying a swarm of musicians, but Crass were never in it for the money. Their uncompromising attitude to "straight" society meant that they'd never be much more than a safety valve for disaffected youth – to the band and their fans, the most important things were the freedom and joy of live fast punk rock.

The band and fans alike adopted the all-black look, restating the anti-art, anti-fashion ideals of punk's earliest days, although the graphic work of newly-recruited communette **G. Sus** (a.k.a. **Gee Vaucher**) looked suspiciously schooled and studied.

Although most of the band's output was hardcore speed guitar, they also experimented with cut-up tapes, film/video/audio collage and even the odd disco beat. But nothing could conceal their evil anarchist message, and seen as an annoyance by the powers that be, they grew to live in constant fear of having the front door kicked in by the Flying Squad.

Stations Of The Crass (1979), with its huge fold-out cover illustrated by photos of Crass graffiti on various bits of London Underground real estate, was the first album on Crass Records. The contents were as quick to assimilate as the spray-can sloganeering celebrated on the sleeve: easily digested statements covering the usual wild anarchic spread of topics. Subsequent albums were more focused, though: *Penis Envy* (1981) concentrated on the anarcho-feminist viewpoint, while *Christ: The Album* (1982) targeted the Church, but it wasn't until the Falklands / Malvinas war had ended and the band put out "How Does It Feel To Be The Mother Of A Thousand Dead?" that Crass's name was mentioned in parliament. A

short and unsuccessful attempt at prosecuting the band left Mrs Thatcher and her goons exposed as liars and fools.

The final track on *Penis Envy* was "Our Wedding", a satire on slushy pop-song love stories that "Creative Recording And Sound Services" (spot the acronym) offered to Loving magazine, who duly passed it on to their readers as a freebie flexidisc. What those readers thought of the "listen to the wedding bells, say goodbye to other girls" refrain must be left to the imagination, as must the dialogue from the meeting in which the executives who'd accepted the disc and recommended it as "a must for that happy day" tried to explain how they'd not seen through the hoax.

By now, Crass were banned from BBC radio, were ignored by the music press and never invited to play the established venues. Despite this, thanks to a never-ending series of squat parties and benefit gigs – the band helped to boost the youth membership of the then-moribund CND, turning it into a powerful anti-military protest group once again – Crass had a larger and more dedicated following than ever. The album *Yes Sir, I Will* (1983) was the band's most traditionally "anarchist" album, a passionate yell of defiance at established authority and the obedience that keeps the system in place.

True to their word, Crass disbanded in 1984, after a final gig in support of the striking miners. Rimbaud and Vaucher retired back to Dial House – the long-term anarchist hotbed plonked incongruously in Epping – and eventually bought the place. Ignorant went off to sing with third-wavers **Conflict** before forming a band of his own, **Schwartzeneggar**, in 1992. Joining The **Stratford Mercenaries** in 1997, he contributed to their albums *No Sighing Strains of Violins* (Southern, 1999) and *Sense of Solitude* (Southern, 2000). Libertine went off to explore performance art, Wright built himself a houseboat and Rimbaud worked on his writing.

All went still and quiet until 2002 when **The Crass Collective** surfaced as the *éminences grises* behind "Your Country Needs You", a concert of "voices in opposition to war" held at London's South Bank Centre. Scaling down their ambition from world revolution somewhat, a year later saw them renamed as **Crass Agenda** and actively defending a North London jazz club.

Since June 2005 they've been calling themselves **Last Amendment**.

Whether history condemns Crass for slumming it or not, it should also give the band due credit for trying so hard and believing so deeply in the power of punk rock. We never did get to overthrow the system with Crass manning the barricades, but it wasn't because of lack of effort on their part. Their record label, meanwhile, gave a voice to a whole swathe of bands that would otherwise – for a variety of political reasons and on the grounds of taste – never have had a hearing.

◉ Feeding Of The 5000 (Crass, 1999)

Reissued with "Reality Asylum" reinstated as the opening track, this is the original and best of the band's recordings. Standouts include "Do They Owe Us A Living", "Punk Is Dead" (remember, this was in 1978!), "General Bacardi" and the magnificently snide "Banned From The Roxy"

◉ Stations Of The Crass (Crass, 1999)

Stretching out over more than thirty tracks, this suffers perhaps from trying to cover too many issues. Well before the end, listeners are likely to be suffering from combat fatigue, or else so imbued with revolutionary fervour that they'll already be out on the streets.

D

THE DAMNED

Formed, London, 1976; disbanded 1988; re-formed 1997; still extant.

oved and loathed in roughly equal parts by the cognoscenti, **The Damned** still star today in the longest-running soap opera in punk-rock history. Cursed by some for their confidently camp take on punk, others are just as staunch in their defence of the lads as true believers in the "get it right or get it wrong, having a laugh is what we're about" school of rock'n'roll.

As with so many of the early British punk bands, if you scratch the Damned hard enough, you eventually dig down to the **London SS**, a loose collective of musicians and layabouts that hung around town forever on the brink of getting things together and performing, but never quite having the get-up-and-go to leave the studio. **Rat Scabies** (wild-man drums, also called Chris Miller), **Brian James** (incendiary guitar, real name Brian Robertson) and **Captain Sensible** (bass/guitar/drums/vocals/anything, answers to Ray Burns) were all veterans, and when they lassoed **Dave Vanian** (vocals/vampire outfit, real name Dave Letts) from the crowd of strangely dressed young things looning about in London's weirder clubs, the original and classic line-up was in place.

Initially, the musical impetus came from James, whose death-trip-rocker chic went perfectly with his taste in tunes: stripped-down, riff-heavy power-chord attacks on the nervous system, the bastard hybrid offspring of MC5 and the Stooges. Constant touring knocked the rough edges off their performance and they were soon competent enough for Vanian's amphetamine-vampire shtick to share the stage with the Captain's fancy-dress

antics and Scabies' drunken drumming. James hurled himself from one pose into another, apparently oblivious to the playground action happening all around.

Politically though, they had a lot to learn. The band was thrown off the Pistols' Anarchy In The UK tour for, allegedly, being prepared to play gigs even if the Sex Pistols had been banned. Whatever the truth, and however strong the band's declaration of total lack of interest in anything except playing a few concerts, selling some records and getting too close to available female fans, for some time they found themselves answering awkward questions from the press.

As far as the music was concerned, though, things could not have been much sweeter. Played fast, loud and for the most part through the cheapest PAs in the world, The Damned's sets were lapped up by the young punk crowd, and the band soon found themselves signed up with Stiff Records by Jake Riviera. Produced by Nick Lowe, "New Rose" (the first-ever punk-rock single) was rushed into the shops, and before long, they became the first of the new boys to release and chart with an album, *Damned Damned Damned*, also bashed out by Lowe in 1977.

As the original punk album, there were standards to be set. Most of the tunes hurtled out of the speakers at speeds far beyond the capabilities of most tyro bands (leading to jealous accusations of fiddling with the tape speed), and told simple stories of everyday happenings on the punk-rock scene – meaningless sex, cheap drugs, going out to gigs and falling in love. Tributes were paid (for example, the Stooges' "1970" was renamed "I Feel Alright" and closed the album) and statues were kicked over (after The Beatles' "Help" had received a going-over from The Damned, it needed six

🎵 PLAYLIST: THE DAMNED

Long-since written off as little more than a punk rock cabaret act, The Damned have resurrected their reputation simply by keeping on keeping on going. All the following are available on *PLAY IT AT YOUR SISTER* – the Stiff years box set released in 2005. Alternatively, try and track down the original slabs of vinyl, as listed below.

1. SEE HER TONITE
from **Damned Damned Damned (Stiff; 1977)**

2. NEAT NEAT NEAT
from **Damned Damned Damned (Stiff; 1977)**

3. SO MESSED UP
from **Damned Damned Damned (Stiff; 1977)**

4. BORN TO KILL
from **Damned Damned Damned (Stiff; 1977)**

5. 1 OF THE 2
from **Damned Damned Damned (Stiff; 1977)**

6. SO MESSED UP
from **Damned Damned Damned (Stiff; 1977)**

7. PROBLEM CHILD
from **Music For Pleasure (Stiff; 1977)**

8. STRETCHER CASE
from **Music For Pleasure (Stiff; 1977)**

9. MELODY LEE
from **Machine Gun Etiquette (Chiswick; 1979)**

10. SMASH IT UP
from **Machine Gun Etiquette (Chiswick; 1979)**

months in hospital to recover). It set a bar for the Pistols and Clash to aim at while The Damned stole ahead of the pack yet again, heading across the Atlantic to New York, where they appeared at CBGB's, created a few scandals with some of the girls on the scene, and generally had fun without ever trying to crack the entire country.

On their return, **Lu Edmunds** joined as second guitarslinger, just in time to see things go temporarily but disastrously wrong. *Music For Pleasure* was shredded by the press, and soon afterwards Scabies left the band. His replacement **Jon Moss** (ex-London, soon to be Culture Clubber) barely had time to adjust his hi-hat before an excess of pique early in 1978 had everyone walking off in different directions, vowing never to work together again.

The next few years saw a blizzard of new personnel joining and leaving, with legal battles over the rights to the name "Damned" causing appearances under the name **The Doomed** to be advertised for a few months. Although James was never to be lured back into the band, a core crew of Vanian and Sensible, sometimes assisted by Scabies, kept the band afloat. With Sensible stepping sideways to play guitar, **Lemmy** (from Motorhead) took over on bass, to be replaced by **Algy Ward** (ex-Saints), then **Paul Gray** (once a Hotrod) in 1980. Despite the chaos, these were great times for The Damned. 1979's "Love Song" and "Smash It Up", taken from *Machine Gun Etiquette*, went Top 20 in the UK. A third single, "I Just Can't Be Happy Today", failed to chart, but grew to be recognized as one of punk's great statements.

The Black Album followed in 1980, a rambling four sides of vinyl that, as usual, divided the critics into those who saw it as a crime against music and others who simply disliked it. Compared to The Clash's tight, disciplined double-album *London Calling*, released the previous year, this was a noodling, experimental affair. There'd been no place for seventeen-minute long epics like "Curtain Call" back when they'd filled the Roxy club; Vanian's "Dr Jekyll And Mr Hyde" was surely little more than a music hall routine; and who'd let the Captain near the microphone?

It went down well with the kids, though. The Damned's original audience had grown out of their punk-cabaret routine, but a new generation of spikyheads was buying their records, attending the gigs, and keeping the lads in lager. Far from seeing him banned forever from singing, the Captain even went solo for a while, taking "Happy Talk" from South Pacific into the charts before finally quitting the band in the wake of *Strawberries* (1982). Baling his sinking ship with both hands, Vanian switched **Roman Jugg** from keyboards to guitar, drafted **Bryn Merrick** in to play bass and managed to wring *Phantasmagoria* (and mega-selling single "Eloise") from them.

Although *Anything* appeared a year later, *Phantasmagoria* was really the last gasp from a long-dead horse. Their records were selling, but not to punk rockers. There was a definite risk of the band becoming punk's answer to Fleetwood Mac and moving from respectable penury into the mainstream.

Numerous Damneds appeared in the Nineties, but they were so far from punk that they and their works can safely be ignored. It took a new century, a conveniently timed punk revival and the attentions of US label Nitro to bring the rotten old corpse back to life. *Grave Disorder* (2001) saw the Damned find a fitting role on the nostalgia circuit. **Pinch** (drums) was never going to find as high-profile a gig anywhere else, **Patricia Morrison** (once a Sister Of Mercy) was, thanks to being married to Vanian, likely to stay on board playing bass, **Monty Oxy Moron** (keyboards) appeared to be unemployable in the outside world, and to great joy, the Captain was welcomed back.

Causing a small furore in the press at the end of 2004 when the lads were invited to switch on the Christmas illuminations in Cambridge, The Damned – an everyday story of punk folk – still draw a huge audience and are almost as much of an institution as The Archers.

 Smash It Up: The Anthology 1976-1987 (Essential, 2002)

Thirty-five tracks, including "Curtain Call". You don't need anything else until you're word-perfect on the lyrics to this.

 Machine Gun Etiquette (Big Beat, 2004)

Machine Gun Etiquette is now available in a somewhat fleshed out 25th anniversary special edition. It's been reissued, enhanced and is now twenty-tracks long – still as much a masterpiece as it ever was.

Alley of the Damned:
(L-R: Rat, Brian,
Captain, Dave).

ICONIC SINGLE: NEW ROSE / HELP (STIFF, 1977)

Not just a great record, this was the first punk record and has become an icon in all the history books (including this one). Inseparably woven into the story of Stiff Records and the whole independent label explosion, by the time most interested parties had heard the tune, it was already impossible to obtain, having been deleted as part of the label's strict back-catalogue policy. Luckily, French label Skydog picked up the licence and made it available again to a breathless punk-hungry British public.

An instant pop hit from the moment Scabies' mad war-drumming and Brian James's dirty, fuzzy guitar riff lurched out of the stereo, "New Rose" sums up everything you need to know about punk rock. According to the lyrics, there is a love song in there somewhere; don't bother looking for it, just jump up and down. A lot.

THE DANDY WARHOLS

Formed Portland, Oregon, 1994; still dandy.

The Nineties poster band for stoner chic and slacker rebellion, the **Dandy Warhols** notched up wild success in the decadent charts of Old Europe, whereas in the wild northwest of their native country, they could only just about get arrested.

Not so much a punk band as a band of punks, the Dandys are one of those bands that would never have found their way out of the bars of Portland if The New York Dolls and Heartbreakers had not painted the signposts for them in the Seventies. Their music is a thieves' cavern of pilfered styles, riffs and attitude, and on stage, they use handfuls of style to cover up enormous gaps in talent. **Courtney Taylor** (guitar/vocals) is the consummate rock frontman, and just to ice the cake, someone – probably **Zia McCabe** (keyboards/bass/percussion) – gets nekkid.

Far more punk than some of their more obvious contemporaries, The Dandy Warhols turned their reputation for shambolic bad behaviour and parlayed it into a deal with a local label. Their first single, "Little Drummer Boy" (1994), created a buzz, and *Dandys Rule Ok* (1995) turned that buzz into a growl loud enough to draw the major labels away from their LA home. When the momentum had built high enough to take "TV Theme Song" onto MTV, the Dandys cashed in, took a massive advance from Capitol Records and turned it into cocaine and tequila. **Peter Holmstrom** (guitar/vocals) had signed on for the ride, as had **Eric Hedford** (drums/keyboards/vocals). Well, wouldn't you?

Though far from being the only band in history to do something so dumb, and indeed, not the only band to have their first album for a major label rejected and returned (Capitol apparently wanted something with "songs" on it, the philistines!), the Dandys were probably the first band to take two such heavy beatings and come back with a wide, country grin, ready to take some more.

Armed with a good set of tunes, Taylor took the band back to the studio and spent the last of the advance money recording *The Dandy Warhols Come Down* for 1997. This time, the record they delivered met whatever standards the label was demanding and the roller coaster started up again.

You've got to love a band who can make a pop song called "Not If You Were The Last Junkie On Earth". Things had moved on since Lou Reed's epics of the heroin lifestyle, and with so many promising artists having turned blue in the recent past, smack was way past its days of glamour. Evidently triggered by the stupid tragedy of a kid who, unable to cope with being parted from a lover even for a week, used the time to develop a habit, "Not If You... " probably did more to stop addiction than a fifty-foot-high pile of well-meaning leaflets. The accompanying video was a beautifully shot parody of any Sixties game show – here, though, the dancers wore syringe costumes, the Busby Berkeley routines were performed by nurses with thrashing OD patients rocking around on gurneys, and the prizes included a car crashed into a tree, a home emptied of all possessions and finally, your own grave. The deadpan delivery of such obviously heartfelt lyrics added regret and even some sympathetic understanding, and turned the song into a punk-rock classic. *Come Down* also gave up the singles "Every Day Should Be A Holiday" and "Boys Better".

Things were looking good for the Dandys when the relationship between Hedford and Taylor finally exploded into open "musical differences". Hedford left, to reinvent himself as **DJ Aquaman**, and was replaced by one of Taylor's cronies, **Brent de Boer**. The Dandy Warhols lived up to their reputation as a band of stoner slackers with no interest in pursuing a career for the next three years, performing locally to their home town, keeping their name in the papers with an occasional interview (Taylor gives quotes like a two-tongued professional sex worker gives head) and very obviously not working at the follow-up.

When it did finally surface in 2000, however, there was genuine gold hidden amongst the other shiny facets it held. *Thirteen Tales From Urban Bohemia*'s secret was the irresistibly catchy "Bohemian Like You". It found a space on daytime radio, but also sneaked into the ear of a nameless advertising executive. Much like **Chumbawamba's** "Tubthumping" a couple of years earlier, the track developed a life of its own and began to turn up in the strangest of corporate places – it backed a scene from an episode of *Buffy The Vampire Slayer*, then the US *Monday Night Football* programme began using it, and finally Vodafone UK bought it to accompany a multimedia advertising campaign. The band used the funds this generated to splurge on a sizeable chunk of Portland real estate, fitted out as recording / film studios (and the coolest place for a party).

Borrowing its title from Kurt Vonnegut's perceptive tale of modern interplanetary manners, *Welcome To The Monkey House* (2003) saw Nick Rhodes of Duran Duran – a band inexplicably respected in the US – roped in to produce. A predictably smooth sound oozed out of the speakers as a result, with "The Last High" coming in almost comatose (but still a killer tune). "We Used To Be Friends" was the album's other top groove, and was a lot more lively.

To judge by the Dandys' most recent release, *Odditorium Or The Warlords Of Mars* (2005), urban bohemia remains alive and screamingly well in the wild north northwest. "Smoke It" may have failed to chart in the UK, where the band's appeal first bloomed, but taking its starting cue from what sounds like a bodged rehearsal tape concocted by The Fall was an extremely promising signal, and the band can't be written off yet.

⊙ Dandys Rule OK (Capital, 1998)

Pun-tastic titles including "Coffee And Tea Wrecks" and "Lou Weed" go some way to hiding the genuine intelligence and louche posing that characterise the Dandys' output, but not enough to disguise it completely. Artful as smoothing an eyebrow as you pass by a mirror

⊙ Come Down (Capital, 1998)

Unflappable as Bogart and including such classics as "Not If You Were The Last Junkie On Earth", "Cool As Kim Deal" and "Hard On For Jesus", this is perfection pulled somehow from the wreckage of a week-long binge.

DANZIG

Born aeons ago in the pits of hell… or 1955, New Jersey, depending on who you believe.

"RELAX AND ENJOY THE MUSIC."

GLENN DANZIG

Mild-mannered Glenn Anzalone appeared on this earth on June 23, 1955. At some point in the following two decades he adopted his true identity and turned into **Glenn Danzig** – the greatest prankster on the US punk scene. Glenn gets his kicks by acting like the king of the demons, and his best joke is convincing kids to take him seriously. Still, whether he's a punk rocker these days or not, there's always room in a book like this for the man who claims he wants to "collect the heads of little girls and put them on my wall" and whose solo project, *Black Aria*, was an overcooked porridge of classical operatics apparently intended to invoke the fall of Satan from heaven.

But to go back to the beginning, once upon a time, there was **The Misfits**, a punk-rock band so extreme and spooky they could have scared the colour back into Dave Vanian's cheeks. Formed by Glenn and his pal **Jerry Only**, they spent six years making one hell of a racket in the name of rock'n'roll. When The Misfits misfired for the last time in 1983, Glenn took his white pan-stick make-up with him to form first **Samhain** (seminal early goth crew) and then, in 1987, **Danzig**.

There have been two Danzigs. The first – comprising Glenn, ex-Samhain member **John Christ** (guitar), ex-Rosemary's Babies **Eerie Von** (bass), and **Chuck Biscuits** (drums), formerly of D.O.A., Black Flag, and Circle Jerks – gave Glenn the freedom to indulge himself and wallow in gore. The second, formed in 1994, features Glenn plus ex-Prong member **Tommy Victor** (guitar), **Castillo** (drums) and **Josh Lazie** (bass), and it's this line-up that's been responsible for everything since *Blackacidevil*, released on Halloween in 1996.

Having convinced both bands to play under his surname, Glenn had their balls so firmly gripped that he could lead them musically in any direction he chose. Whereas The Misfits used to sing about the good old days of the horror film, Glenn's new bands went a lot further back in search of evil inspiration, getting biblical with tales of Cain and Abel, picking up hints from Edgar Allen Poe and conjuring up angels grievous in the extreme.

Samhain had played with some disturbing occult ideas, but it was Glenn's return to his heavy metal / punk / hardcore roots with the Danzig line-up that took his music to the masses for the first time. Danzig was an MTV-friendly band, knocking out miniature masterpieces of video nasty aimed squarely and point-blank at the receptive heads of the *Beavis And Butthead* generation. If the kids were dumb enough to believe in his "Evil Heavy

Metal Overlord" routine or take his theatrical flirting with the dark side seriously, he could hardly be held responsible.

Despite all the shock-horror "We're so evil!" posturing, there's no denying Glenn is punk rock to the core of his bartered soul: his CV is a list of fights won and lost, labels and management departed and dismissed. Glenn could have been a big success if he'd knuckled under; instead, he remains nothing more than a cult. These days, he's even managing to put two decades of bad blood behind him and to collaborate with Doyle, his spar from the Misfits era. He's dabbled in movies, owns a "dark" comic book publishing company called Verotik, has tried orchestral work and still makes it out on the road often enough to give recurring nightmares to impressionable punklings all over the USA.

Glenn's sinister sensibilities were often overwhelmed by the hellish thunder cooked up by the other members of the group, but when they got the balance right, Danzig were a damn fine band.

⊚ Danzig III: How The Gods Kill (American, 1992)

Powerful, blood-dripping stuff from The Evil One Of New Jersey, and the band's best-selling album, this comes with scary artwork from H.R. Giger (see Dead Kennedys entry) and some of Glenn's best tunes. Anyone past the age of trick or treat who takes this stuff seriously, however, is advised to seek professional help or listen to a New York Dolls album.

⊚ Blackacidevil (E-Magine, 1996)

Selling his soul to the grim lords of electro / industrial dance, Glenn sacked the rest of the band and cobbled together an album of techno-tinged goth rock, with lyrics that will either shiver your spine or tickle your funny bone. Competent cage-rattling stuff throughout, however, with standouts including "Satan's Child", "Bleedangel" and "Ashes".

⓪ Circle Of Snakes (Regain, 2004)

With Glenn writing all the material and producing, it's not surprising to hear the old fraud occasionally becoming self-indulgent. Although this album has its share of duff decisions, items such as the title track, "1000 Devils Reign", "When We Were Dead" and "Black Angel, White Angel" are worthy of your attention.

THE DEAD BOYS

Loud and snotty in Cleveland, Ohio, 1976; laid to rest in 1980.

The Atlantic Ocean has long been known for its two-way musical trade: R&B was picked up by The Rolling Stones and The Beatles, who resold them to the US, indirectly creating a hundred American rock groups who batted the music right back to Blighty. With punk too, the reverberations went on and on: Television's look and The Ramones' music led to The Clash, the Pistols, The Damned and Generation X in England. They in turn spawned Midwest monsters like the Dead Boys.

Scientists in the future will debate the wisdom of mixing Iggy's excesses with the teenage enthusiasm and physical robustness of The Dead Boys, all amped-up with imported singles and over-written attitude reports from London's front-line clubs. Some would see it as meddling with forces best left beyond the understanding of mankind; most

A Stiv in Cheetah's clothing.

would agree, at least, that **The Dead Boys** were by far the youngest, loudest and snottiest punk rockers the Seventies ever saw.

When The Dead Boys showed up at CBGB's in 1977 to support the Damned on their first US visit, the New York punks must have felt like an isolated party of settlers, wagons huddled in a ring, with whooping, painted spikyheads roaring in on all sides. The Midwestern invaders cared not a jot for the finer art-punk stylings of Tom Verlaine or the Talking Heads crew, were absolutely not going to join in any watered-down "New Wave" and were ready to go for gold by grossing out.

Their gory details are spread out elsewhere in print (*Please Kill Me* by Legs McNeil is a good starting point), but to start back at the beginning, we move to Cleveland, Ohio and fabled pre-punk master group **Rocket From The Tombs**. If everyone who now claims acquaintance with the band had actually gone to see them play, RFTT would have given Led Zeppelin a run for their money. What actually happened when **Cheetah Chrome** (Gene O'Connor, guitar) and **Johnny Blitz** (a.k.a. John Madansky, drums) hooked up with **Peter Laughner** (vocals/visionary) and **Crocus Behemoth** (later **David Thomas**, here providing weird vocals, acid strangeness and impressive stage presence) was a short-lived band of sporadic brilliance, blown apart by lifestyle and philosophical disagreements as much as by the usual musical differences.

RFTT built up a local following in Cleveland and around, but split into two camps before their lasting magic could spread to either coast. Laughner and Thomas went off into the long grass to make wailing animal music as **Pere Ubu**, and terrify the children of a generation of hipster parents. Meanwhile, Chrome and Blitz put together a short-lived heavy-metal monster called Frankenstein – a band brought to hideous twitching life by **Stiv Bators** (Steve Bator, vocals/obscene behaviour/Nazi memorabilia). Hearing word of the new scene in New York via the East Coast pony express, however, the trio hired **Jimmy Zero** (William Wilden) as second guitar and **Jeff Magnum** (a.k.a. Jeff Halmagy) on bass and blagged a regular spot at CBGB's, having no doubt made up and learnt their set on the way to the big city. (Bators had previously met Joey Ramone and motormouthed him into an introduction to **Hilly Crystal**, the owner of the club; signing

Hilly as manager probably helped them get their foot in the door too.)

The Dead Boys were an unforgettable live act. Musically they knew their stuff, and at the beginning of their career at least, they played a tight, powerful, loud and defiantly snotty set (despite Bators or Chrome sometimes receiving oral pleasure on stage courtesy of an enthusiastic fan or two – a practice which must mess up one's vocal delivery). Rushed into the studio by Sire Records, *Young Loud And Snotty* (1977) did good business on release and things looked good for the boys. "Sonic Reducer" was picked up in the UK for the then-essential compilation album *That Summer* (issued on the now-defunct Vertigo label) creating a welcoming buzz for the Boys on the far side of the Atlantic.

Unfortunately, the temptations offered by the big city caused the dream to curdle; drinking led to bitching led to worse and their second album, *We Have Come For Your Children* (1978), suffered for it. Wrecked in part by the wrong choice of producer (**Felix Pappalardi**, ex-bass player for arch-hippies Mountain), responsibility for the album's faults must be shared by the label, the management and by the band themselves. "Ain't It Fun" excepted, the second album reeks of cheap drugs, physical excess and a lack of interest. It sold badly even in the band's hometowns of Cleveland and New York.

As punk fizzled out in the US, Blitz nearly joined it, narrowly escaping permanent wipeout in a mugging. While The Dead Boys stood idly by, forced off the road, North American punk turned into something so unpleasantly macho that even Bators and Chrome lost interest. In 1979, soon after Blitz was back on his feet, the band decided to split up and wave goodbye to the music business.

The band re-formed sporadically throughout the 1980s, with various line-ups either defending the faith or going through the motions, depending on one's point of view. Bators showed up in the UK, first as a member of **The Wanderers** (a bunch of ex-Sham 69 lads who released *Only Lovers Left Alive* in 1981 before falling apart) and then as one of the **Lords Of The New Church**, alongside Brian James (ex-Damned), a position he kept until 1988.

Most of the Boys went back to Ohio, although Cheetah Chrome, still in the music game, went to Nashville, and Bators died in Paris, the city he moved to after the New Church was dissolved, in a 1990 road accident. Never one to quit, at the time of his death he was said to be involved in putting together a punk/junkie supergroup with Dee Dee Ramone and Johnny Thunders. Dealers across Europe must have shed a tear at the thought of so much lost income.

⊚ Young, Loud And Snotty (Sire, 2000)

Essential document, seminal, piece of history etc, etc. These days, the song that stands out on this record is an old Rocket From The Tombs number ("Sonic Reducer"), dusted down and speeded up for a punk audience. A lot of the rest boils down to Midwestern rock, flavoured with overlong MC5-style solos and Iggy Pop-like vocal interjections.

⊚ Night Of The Living Dead Boys (Bomp!, 1994)

Contractually obliged to deliver one last album after splitting up, the lads threw together this live recording at CBGB's in a fit of pique, with Bators deliberately making his vocals largely inaudible (though his encouraging yell of "Suck it!" comes through loud and clear). Despite themselves, the band performed an incendiary farewell set, and when Bators re-dubbed his vocals in the studio for this reissue, he rescued it.

DEAD KENNEDYS

Born San Francisco, 1978; died after a hail of lawsuits 1985.

A s the echoes of Johnny Rotten's farewell sneer "D'you ever get the feeling you've been cheated?" died slowly away in the 1978 night after the Pistol's final concert, **Jello Biafra** stomped through the Winterland car park, deep in thought. Like so many others who had sniffed the Pistols' festering breath, he'd been infected with the "do-it-yourself" ethos and was itching all over with his desire to get a band together.

By June, San Francisco had its latest punk-rock band, **The Dead Kennedys**. With Biafra on vocals, **East Bay Ray** (guitar), **Klaus Fluoride** (bass), and **Ted** (a.k.a. **Bruce Slesinger**) on drums, they spent a year learning their instruments, putting together a set and playing local venues with increasing success. Once Biafra had formed a label – Alternative Tentacles – they had all they needed to release their first single.

"California Über Alles" sold well enough to become a local hit, and to attract the attention of John Peel across the Atlantic. It sounded like nothing the British punk scene had heard before and

was as refreshing and welcome as the bugle sound of the cavalry coming to the rescue.

While waiting for something better to do in 1979, Biafra ran for mayor of San Francisco. He came a very creditable fourth on a well-thought-out absurdist platform designed to appeal to the free-thinking / snotty / awkward squad sectors of the electorate (his policies included requiring businessmen to wear clown suits to work).

Fresh Fruit For Rotting Vegetables followed in 1980, by which time, the Kennedys were well enough established to tour across the States and throughout Europe. Ted split, to be replaced by **D.H. Peligro**, who kept the drum-stool warm while recording the *In God We Trust Inc.* EP and the breakthrough album *Plastic Surgery Disasters* in 1982.

North America in the Eighties was as plump and full of targets for punk-rock destruction as Thatcher's Britain was, and the Dead Kennedys were often spoilt for choice. Reagan, organized religion and US foreign policy came in for regular doses of withering hardcore. After a while, having such a coherent and eloquent spokesman and such a large following made the band a target for the moral guardians. When *Frankenchrist* (1985) included the *Penis Lanscape* poster by respected artist **H.R. Giger**, it became the trigger for a newly formed organization calling itself Parents Music Resource Center (PMRC) to take legal action, and in 1986 the Dead Kennedys were tried for "distribution of harmful matter to minors".

Bedtime For Democracy sneaked out in 1986 but the lawsuits dragged on until 1987, and despite all the charges eventually being dropped, the hiatus killed the band stone-dead. Biafra stayed politically active, putting together a new career on the spoken-word circuit. A large chunk of the 1990s was lost in legal disputes between Biafra, East Bay Ray and the others, and although this seems to have come to an end, there's still enough bad blood between them to preclude any reunion.

⊚ Fresh Fruit For Rotting Vegetables
(Cherry Red, 2001)

Their first and best album, *Fresh Fruit* remains US hardcore punk rock's most impressive statement. From the opener, "Kill The Poor", to the closing ear-ringing bars of "Viva Las Vegas", this is pure, treble-heavy, politically correct fun. Now expanded to a two-disc set with extra singles.

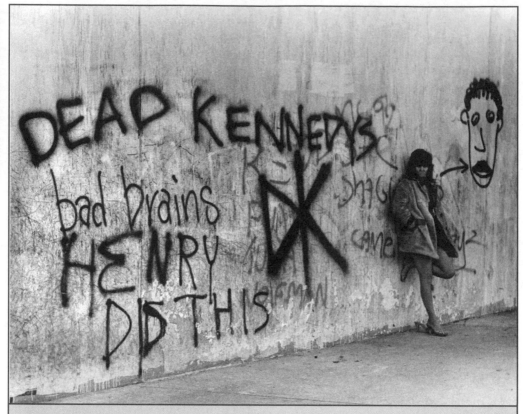

🎵 PLAYLIST: DEAD KENNEDYS

Jello Biafra's scream and East Bay Ray's clanging guitar together summed up the frustration infecting the US West Coast as the 70s gave way to the 80s. Sad to say most of their concerns are as relevant today as they were back when they were still fresh fruit.

1. **KILL THE POOR** from **Fresh Fruit for Rotting Vegetables (Cherry Red, 2002)**

2. **LET'S LYNCH THE LANDLORD** from **Fresh Fruit for Rotting Vegetables (Cherry Red, 2002)**

3. **HOLIDAY IN CAMBODIA** from **Fresh Fruit for Rotting Vegetables (Cherry Red, 2002)**

4. **CHEMICAL WARFARE** from **Fresh Fruit for Rotting Vegetables (Cherry Red, 2002)**

5. **VIVA LAS VEGAS** from **Fresh Fruit for Rotting Vegetables (Cherry Red, 2002)**

6. **TAKE THIS JOB AND SHOVE IT** from **Bedtime for Democracy (Decay, 2001)**

7. **CHICKENSHIT CONFORMIST** from **Bedtime for Democracy (Decay, 2001)**

8. **BUZZBOMB** from **Plastic Surgery Disasters / In God We Trust Inc. (Decay, 2001)**

9. **NAZI PUNKS FUCK OFF** from **Plastic Surgery Disasters / In God We Trust Inc. (Decay, 2001)**

10. **TOO DRUNK TO FUCK** from **Give Me Convenience Or Give Me Death (Decay, 2001)**

⊚ Plastic Surgery Disasters / In God We Trust. Inc. (Decay, 2001)

Fantastic value 2-CD package of guitar-driven, hyperactive, indignant, teeth-gnashing rock'n'roll. "Buzzbomb" and "Winnebago Warrior" stand out for their well-crafted sharphoned attack, but for sheer outrage it's hard to surpass "Government Flu" or "Nazi Punks Fuck Off".

⊚ Give Me Convenience Or Give Me Death (Decay, 2001)

If you want to maximize your bangs per buck then this, the inevitable greatest hits compilation, is the best place to begin. It includes the band's most important singles, essential album cuts and all the anarcho-satirical-insurrectionary rhetoric you could wish for.

DESCENDENTS

Descended to Los Angeles, 1979; split and reunited a couple of times, but ultimately re-ascended in 1996.

One of the most influential US punk bands of the late Seventies, if only because of the lack of worthwhile competition, **Descendents** fought to defend punk rock's humour and melody in the face of the overwhelming and sour-faced hardcore axe-grinding firepower that was to dominate the Eighties scene.

"Ride The Wild", the band's 1979 kick-off single, was a false start. Recorded by the trio of **Frank Navetta** (guitar/vocals), **Tony Lombardo** (bass/vocals) and **Bill Stevenson** (drums), it blended The Beach Boys with Buzzcocks in a uniquely sunny take on punk, but did little to make the guys a name. When they blipped onto the world's radar again in 1981, they were equipped with a new secret weapon, known at first only as Milo.

Milo Auckerman (vocals/whacky behaviour) was the depraved, delinquent uncle of the LA punks. Follower of few creeds, setter of trends, and all-round bad example to the kids who adored him, Milo injected the Descendents with vitamins F, U and N and put a lot more pop into their punch. He helped herd the band round the relentless touring circuit, contributed lyrics and vocals to the 1981 *Fat* EP, and stuck with them for two years before living up to the title of their debut album *Milo Goes To College* and taking himself off, like a fast-food-crazed behemoth, to do a degree. With Milo away, Stevenson took a gig with **Black Flag** and so Navetta and Lombardo took an enforced break from the business.

With the band having been up in the air for so long, it was hardly surprising that a few pieces fell off when it next descended, crash-landing in the punk-rock no-man's-land of 1985. Stevenson found that Navetta was not ready to come back to the band, and replaced him with guitar-for-hire **Ray Cooper**. This line-up assembled and released the frankly more pop than punk album *I Don't Want To Grow Up* before ditching Lombardo in favour of **Doug Carrion** (ex-Anti). This lot moved even closer to the big pop sound and included a Beach Boys cover version, "Wendy", on their first full-length release, *Enjoy!*.

At this point, Stevenson discovered **ALL**, a kind of total-focus philosophy running on willpower, and bringing it to the band, he oversaw the 1987 release, also called *All*. So far, so LA-LA-land, but punk dies when exposed to deep thoughts, and the album was described as "patchy" even by the most devoted followers. Public reaction led to the band splitting up again and to Stevenson forming a new band of his own called, predictably, **ALL**.

A couple of live albums sneaked out – *Liveage!* in 1987, and *Hallraker* in 1989 – but essentially the band was dead until 1996, when Stevenson and Milo put together another band, signing up **Steven Egerton** (guitar) and – from the remnants of ALL – **Karl Alvarez** (bass) to record *Everything Sucks* and take it on tour.

⊙ Two Things At Once (SST, 1991)

A bargain: two full albums for the price of one (even if one does deliver fifteen tracks in just over twenty minutes). This essential twin-set bundles *Milo Goes to College* together with the *Bonus Fat* album, providing a refreshing total-immersion experience. Start your Descendents addiction here, then when you're good and hooked, go buy the rest and spend a day weeping because you never saw them live.

DEVO

Left the primeval slime, Ohio, 1972; crawled back into it 1990; re-emerged briefly 2000.

There's little room for philosophy in rock'n'roll, and even less in that tight little thicket we call punk, unless you take it to ludicrous extremes. Latching onto the ideas contained in an extremely dodgy paperback (*The Beginning Was The End* by Oscar Kiss Maerth) and writing a whole series of tunes based on them qualifies **Devo** as ludicrous extremists of the highest order, and as welcome members of this book's roster. Maerth's book argues that what is conventionally seen as evolutionary progress is in fact a retrogressive de-evolution brought about by our ancestral habit of eating the brains of our fellow primates. Whatever, it made a great hook from which to hang creations such as "Smart Patrol" and "Jocko Homo".

Devo began as just another college rock'n'roll band in the early Seventies when **Gerald Casale** and **Mark Mothersbaugh** first hooked up at Kent State University. **Bob Lewis**, who was to become Devo's manager (and who ended up suing the band over intellectual property rights some years later) joined to make up a trio and the jam sessions began. Early

🎧 PLAYLIST: DEVO

Akron's finest export (apart from tyres, Chrissie Hynde, The Black Keys and Alcoholics Anonymous – founded in the city in 1935), Devo started weird but sadly as the de-evolution kicked in they shrivelled up to nothing more than an above-average covers band, having run out of ideas sometime early in the 80s. At the outset though, they were the strangest thing that even Eno had found himself dealing with.

1. JOCKO HOMO
from **Hot Potatoes (the best of Devo) (Virgin, 1993)**

2. MONGOLOID
from **Hot Potatoes (the best of Devo) (Virgin, 1993)**

3. SATISFACTION
from **Hot Potatoes (the best of Devo) (Virgin, 1993)**

4. WHIP IT
from **Hot Potatoes (the best of Devo) (Virgin, 1993)**

5. COME BACK JONEE
from **Hot Potatoes (the best of Devo) (Virgin, 1993)**

6. SECRET AGENT MAN
from **Hot Potatoes (the best of Devo) (Virgin, 1993)**

7. DAY MY BABY GAVE ME A SURPRISE
from **Hot Potatoes (the best of) (Virgin, 1993)**

8. **S.I.B.** from **Q;Are We Not Men? A:We Are Devo (Virgin, 1993)**

9. **GUT FEELING** from **Q;Are We Not Men? A:We Are Devo (Virgin, 1993)**

10. **SPACE JUNK** from **Q;Are We Not Men? A:We Are Devo (Virgin, 1993)**

Devo tunes drew parallels between the brain-eating apes they'd read about and the "straight" US society they observed from the dorm window. It took the US National Guard and their infamous slaughter of protesting Kent State students, however, to put some iron into their dippy-hippy souls and to turn the trio from a frat-boy joke into a vaguely menac-

ICONIC SINGLE:
JOCKO HOMO (STIFF, 1977)

A marvellous descending synthesizer riff – once heard never forgotten – crashes like Frankenstein's monster falling drunk down the stairs straight into the hardcore de-evolutionary lyric. Managing to be funny and serious at the same time, the song's perverse, catchy rhythm invites you to twitch along regardless and ignore comparisons with a spider monkey cranked up on dubious-looking pills. Lose yourself to the de-evolutionary jig!

ing and decidedly subversive rock'n'roll band.

Mark recruited his brothers **Bob** (guitar) and **Jim Mothersbaugh** (home-made weird electronic drumkit). Gerald recruited his brother, **Bob Casale**, also on guitar. Perhaps frightened off by too many Bobs, Jim left, so **Alan Myers** came in to play drums and hit strange electronic percussion devices. Gerald and Mark meanwhile got together a bunch of new tunes that pointed up the evil conformity and rigorous intolerance of mainstream US apple-pie living.

The new tunes mimicked society's lock-step march to the rhythms of repression, stealing the technical precision of synth-based music from the progressive rockers and using its robotic beats as the basis of a whole new style of onstage behaviour, something like dancing but without any of its joy. Their Middle-American weirdness was a lot more palatable than the full-strength product being offered at the same time by San Francisco's Residents, a band to whom they were often compared. In another of those strange yet meaningless rock'n'roll coincidences, both groups recorded versions of the Rolling Stones' "Satisfaction".

Their own Booji Boy records label issued a couple of singles here and there, tricked out with noises gleaned by wiring up electric toasters to amplifiers, overdriving home-made synths and performing unnatural acts on kids' toys. Mark created a whole Booji Boy persona, complete with scary baby face and his own little jigging dance. Devo gigged, recorded and messed around with sound in this manner for the next four years until striking gold in 1976, when Iggy Pop took David Bowie to the Ann Arbor film festival.

The stars fell in love with *A Short Film About De-Evolution*, little more than an extended promo video for the band. With Bowie and Iggy behind them and Brian Eno on board as producer, Devo soon metamorphosed from local-hero pond-life into short-lived but beautiful creatures of the punk-rock underground, with a Virgin Records deal and bags of credibility.

Q: Are We Not Men? A: We Are Devo! appeared on bright blue vinyl, emphasizing the band's pose as mutant outsiders rejected by the straight world, and was an immediate hit with the UK punks. The band toured Europe, selling out big venues in London and other capital cities while the brief flurry of interest lasted, before going home to concentrate on *Duty Now For The Future* (1979) and *Freedom Of Choice* (1980). These continued the exploration of de-evolution in their lyrics but were successful purely because of their kick-ass electronic poppiness.

"Whip It" made a cult of the band and the video – which explored transgressive S&M sex in a way that Madonna hadn't even dreamed of – won them heavy rotation on the new MTV network. It also kicked off a short burst of controversy when *Rolling Stone* magazine, getting hold of the wrong end of the stick, accused them of promoting fascism, conformity and sterile subservience.

Though they went on through the Eighties – releasing a series of albums depressingly predictable in their own slow return to the swamplands of traditional rock – and even cobbled something together for Lollapalooza in 1996 and 1997, Devo are best remembered for their role as the missing link between Kraftwerk and Kylie.

These days, Mark runs Mutato Muzika, a one-stop shop for theme tunes, jingles, videos and production, with Gerald, Jim and all the Bobs. They went into the studio as **The Wipeouters** in 2001 to record a one-off surf music single, "P Twaaang" before happily marching back, in lockstep and wearing flowerpot hats, to Mutato.

⦿ **Q: Are We Not Men? A: We Are Devo! / Devo Live (Virgin 1993)**

Magnificently good-value reissue clocking in at 21 tracks of disciplined madness. Sing along with "Space Junk", retch as "Gut Feeling" sticks in your mind like phlegm in the throat, and get that old-time religion feeling on with "Slap Your Mammy".

THE DICTATORS

Born New York Fuckin' City, 1974; died New York Fuckin' City, 1978.

New York's answer to MC5, but without the endless politics and drug busts, **The Dictators** were proto-punk rock'n'roll monsters who, had they not been confined by local statute to the island of Manhattan, might well have taken over the world. As it was, their contribution to punk history boils down to little more than a spat with Wayne County and a couple of good singles.

1974 was a prime year for NYC music, spawning The Ramones, celebrating the art-poetics of Television and permitting **Andy/Adny Shernoff**, (keyboards/bass) and **Richard Meltzer** (sidelines cheerleader) to get together with **Scott "Top Ten" Kempner** (guitar), **Ross "The Boss" Funichello** (more guitar), **Mark Mendoza** (bass), **Stu Boy King** (drums) and ex-wrestler, ex-roadie **"Handsome" Dick Manitoba** (vocals/crowd-baiting). The band was cheerfully blue-collar in its aspirations and their gigs happily celebrated pizza, beer and TV, while across town the intelligentsia swooned over Patti Smith, Jim Carrol and Television.

The group's musical influences included mod-flavoured Sixties rock from the UK, and US garage bands of the same decade. Adding their unique blend of nasty spice and bad-taste flavourings, The Dictators created fantastic, snotty, high-energy rock'n'roll to their own recipe, earning valiant support at their live gigs but proving sadly incapable of converting it into record sales or company support. Much like the British pub-rockers who cut a path for the punks to follow a year later, The Dictators made it easier for the bands that followed in their footsteps to make it from the garage to Max's Kansas City, CBGB's and beyond.

A little good fortune might have helped, though: they first lost Mendoza, who went off to earn millions as a Twisted Sister, then had to recruit **Richie Teeter** when Stu Boy went AWOL. Their singles picked up little or no airplay, record companies didn't want to take risks on a local joke band, and they'd pissed off the majority of critics. When punk rock was finally ready for takeoff and The Ramones, Blondie, Patti and Television were queuing for their boarding passes, The Dictators were all in the photo-booth, gurning like fools for pictures that only they would understand.

The band put out three full-length albums in their initial four-year stint together, and although mainly of curiosity value to today's punk-rock explorers, they contain enough maximum R&B energy to illuminate a city block. These days Handsome Dick has a bar on Manhattan called Manitobas, Kempner is a solo act and Funichola, formerly with **Manowar**, is now a session player and part-time member of punk/metal/ wrecking crew **Manitoba's Wild Kingdom**, along with Shernoff (freelance producer by day, rocker by night) and of course Handsome Dick himself. Rumour has it that they're still playing a more powerful version of "Search & Destroy" than The Stooges ever managed, and long may it remain so.

⊙ Manifest Destiny (Wounded Bird, 2004)

A roaring, unleashed beast of an album – pure rock music spelled out in big, metallic capitals. Go listen to "Sleepin' With The TV On", "Hey Boys", "Science Gone Too Far!" and their marvellous chrome-plated, whitewall tyred, pimped-up version of "Search & Destroy".

⊙ Go Girl Crazy (Sony 2001)

With the big cover picture showing off Handsome Dick in his prime, pumping-iron outfit, getting ready to flex his sweaty muscles for you, it's amazing this never topped the album charts. As it is, the album's contents are even sweeter than the sleeve suggests, with magic from NYC in every note of "Teengenerate", "Weekend" and "(I Live For) Cars And Girls".

⊙ New York, New York (ROIR, 1998)

Gives you fifteen tracks of live energy (and a handy sample from all three studio albums) with the guys at their motherfuckin' peak. Get a beer, pull up a smoke, throw back your head and yell!

⊙ Blood Brothers (Wounded Bird, 2005)

If recent concert appearances are anything to judge by, then The Dictators will still be playing somewhere within 25 miles of the Statue Of Liberty when the Day of Judgement comes. This pristine new recording shows that nothing much short of naval gunfire or Armageddon is going to slow them down.

DIM STARS

Started twinkling in New York City, 1992; only come out intermittently.

Sonic Youth's Thurston Moore and Steve Shelley got together with **Don Fleming** from **Gumball** for this side-project. What turned **Dim Stars** into more than just another one-off New York jam session was the presence of **Richard Hell**.

Hell had retired from the music biz years before, but crawled out from under his slab to record three EPs and a full-length self-titled album with the band, which performed music very much in the old **Voidoids** tradition – lots of distorted angular guitar riffs, stop-start rhythms and the vocal yelpings of a loon.

D.O.A.

Dead on arrival in Vancouver, Canada, 1978; sporadically resuscitated from the 1980s to present.

Punk took root in the most unexpected of places once it escaped the posers who haunted the minuscule underground clubs of night-time New York, Los Angeles or London, and became mainstream news. Vancouver, for example, doesn't spring to mind as a big rock'n'roll town, yet thanks entirely to the tireless **Joey "Shithead" Keithley** and his long-running outfit **D.O.A.**, punk has flourished in the northern wastes. Keithley got the punk-rock bug lodged in his pants way back in 1978. It nested and has stayed there, lodged warm and comfy, ever since.

D.O.A. has had its share of personnel swaps over the years, with Keithley being the band's only permanent feature. However, long-term collaborators such as **Chuck Biscuits** on drums (ex-Black Flag / Danzig / Social Distortion) and **Dave Gregg** (guitar) have helped to give cohesiveness to the band's sound and its otherwise sporadic career.

Taking the DIY ethic and its "learn while you earn" philosophy to heart, D.O.A. issued their first EP, *Disco Sucks*, as soon as they'd written down the chords, learned the lyrics and booked some studio time. They followed it up with a brace of albums that many long-time fans consider D.O.A.'s classic recordings, *Something Better Change* (1980) and the following year's *Hardcore '81*. (A popular compilation of both releases plus early tracks, *Bloodied But Unbowed*, appeared in 1984.) Since the beginning, Keithley has been unafraid to voice his political opinions – a renowned D.O.A. slogan among their faithful is "Talk-Action 0" – and this landed him in jail at one point.

D.O.A. would go on to sporadically issue albums throughout the Eighties and Nineties (including such highlights as 1982's *War On 45*, 1985's *The Dawning Of A New Error*, 1993's *Loggerheads* etc.). The group also found time to collaborate with another outspoken punk leader, former Dead Kennedys front man Jello Biafra, on 1990's *Last Scream Of The Missing Neighbors*.

Like Biafra before him, Keithley took the plunge and attempted to enter politics, running as a candidate in Canadian provincial and civic elections for the Green Party in 1996. Keithley also runs his own indie record company, Sudden Death Records, and issued an autobiography in late 2003, titled *I, Shithead: A Life In Punk*. D.O.A. continues strong to this day, as evidenced by such releases as *Win The Battles* (2002). As a result of Keithley's hard work, D.O.A. is often name-checked as an important influence by other hardcore/punk bands, including such notables as Green Day, The Offspring, Rancid, and Propagandhi.

⊙ **Bloodied But Unbowed / War on 45**
(Restless Records; 1993)

Although a swift search online will find you the entire D.O.A. catalogue in various formats both practical and collectable, this compilation packs a double-strength hit of Vancouver's punk rock espresso into a single cup by bundling Alternative Tentacles' 1983 *Bloodied But Unbowed* compilation (which itself comprised *Something Better Change* from 1980 and the following year's *Hardcore '81*) plus the original set that made up 1982's *War On 45* mini album. This set can't be beaten in terms of value for money or as an intro to the band.

THE DONNAS
2gethR 4evR since 1993, Palo Alto, California.

All of **The Donnas** were born in 1979 – the year after punk was first declared dead. Fourteen years later the kids had formed a junior high school band called Ragedy Anne, and after just a month of playing together, had entered a hometown Battle Of The Bands. Following a dodgy name-change (appearing for a while as bitch-queens of heavy metal **The ElectroCutes**), they parlayed this early success and a growing local reputation into a headline-stealing major-label contract as soon as they left high school.

First though, they had to become The Donnas. **Darin Raffaelli** (ex-Supercharger) had seen The Electrocutes playing live and thought they would be a suitable vehicle for the all-girl-Ramones material he'd been sitting on. He turned Brett Anderson into **Donna A** (vocals); Allison Robertson into **Donna R** (guitar); Maya Ford into **Donna F** (bass); and Torry Castellano to **Donna C** (drums). With a musical agenda straight outta 1977 (guitars set to "buzzsaw", everything turned up louder than everything else, "dumb" posing and an interest in intoxication), The Donnas gave nods of appreciation in the direction of both The Ramones and The Stooges, waving bye-bye to The Runaways as they cruised past, leaving their memory stained and bedraggled in the dust.

They played on as The Electrocutes for a while, even releasing the full-length album *Steal Yer Lunch Money* in 1996, before finally becoming The Donnas the following year and releasing their eponymous Rafaelli-penned debut. *The Donnas* was a big hit, selling sufficiently well for the band to take a year off high school studies to go on a Japanese tour. Darin's Svengali-esque influence led to invidious comparisons with Kim Fowley and The Runaways. As a result, and in the wake of strong denials from both sides, the original partnership dissolved and Darin moved to a more decorous, arm's-length relationship with the band. He still had a finger in The Donnas' pie, though, and co-wrote some of their follow-up, *American Teenage Rock'N'Roll Machine* (1998).

Copping their juvenile delinquent / baddest girls in school routine from a bunch of old Shangri-Las singles and *St. Trinian's* movies, the

The lovely Donnas.

Donnas combined the essence of early Blondie with a fierce "Tina Turner goes punk" routine, creating a rude four-letter alternative to the boy bands' own cock-rock posings. Their white-trash jailbait routine couldn't last forever, though, and as the band grew older and more confident, their music moved closer to mainstream rock.

While all-girl bands with the "show me what you got, boy" attitude have become a perennial feature of the music scene, the early Donnas had something special.

◉ **The Donnas** (Lookout, 1998)

The original eight-legged all-girl punk-rock backlash starts here, with tracks such as "Hey, I'm Gonna Be Your Girl", "Get Rid Of That Girl", "Do You Wanna Go Out With Me" and "I Don't Want To Go To School".

THE DRONES

Started droning Manchester, England, 1976; buzzed off 1981.

One of the many things Manchester has to answer for is **The Drones**, a band of pub-rock chancers who leapt onto the passing bandwagon of punk in a blatant grab for the next big thing. They were, however, far from being the only band to do so, and while they had nothing much to say, they had an exciting way of saying it. Sometimes dumb slogans are just what you want to hear.

MJ Drone (vocals/guitar), **Gus "Gangrene" Callender** (guitar/vocals), **Pete Perfect** (drums), and **Steve "Whisper" Cundall** (bass) were originally known as **Rockslide**. When punk kicked off, they speeded up a bunch of old tunes, wrote a few new ones and were able to hit the circuit with just enough confidence and ability to keep them ahead of the pack for a while. Up against local competition from **Slaughter & The Dogs**, **Buzzcocks**, **The Fall** and Warsaw (later to become **Joy Division**), The Drones forged the most conventional punk identity in town, and their gigs were like a jolt of speed delivered by a mad nurse screaming in your ear.

As well as putting on a fine stage show, the lads soon went into the studio and released "Temptations Of A White Collar Worker" on their own OHMS records. This raised the stakes: The Drones were a local band, they knew how to play, they could handle an audience and now they had a record out. All over town, other bands bought the single in a spirit of solidarity, dismissed it in a spirit of envious contempt, and got their acts together in a spirit of panic.

"Temptations…" sold more than ten thousand copies, landing them a John Peel session and a deal with Valer Records. As punk went nationwide, The Drones picked up an audience of their own through playing support to bigger-name bands such as The Stranglers, selling twenty thousand copies of their first Valer single "Bone Idol" / "Just Wanna Be Myself" and through their appearance on the *Live At The Electric Circus* album, released in 1978 to commemorate Manchester's most punk-friendly venue. "Persecution Complex" was a great song, they paid their dues with tribute versions of the Stooges' "Search And Destroy" and old Who numbers, and they even got themselves arrested after turning their PA up to full volume and deafening the street outside.

So where did it all go wrong, and why don't we celebrate The Drones in the same way that we remember the Pistols or The Ramones? The simple answer lies in the album *Further Temptations*, which saw them stripped of their punk-rock credentials and reduced to the rockist ranks. The sleeve was wrong, the songs were substandard, the production was weak, and suddenly The Drones were perceived as stinking like three-day-old fish. Even the marketing and gossip came across like something from *Spinal Tap*: the sleeve featured a model wearing blue body paint and a dog collar, the press launch pack included similar dog collars for the hacks, and in the aftermath of the party, a salty story that we needn't go into here went round about the relationship between the band and their cover model. This was just tacky, and whatever else it was about, punk rock had nothing to do with sexual oppression.

Matters didn't improve when Valer went bankrupt. Floundering without a record company behind them, The Drones reverted to pre-punk rock, hiring a keyboard player and – for the love of Johnny Rotten – dancing girls to perform onstage with the band. Signing Paul Morley, the man later better known as the *NME*'s most hardcore theoretical journalist, as manager probably didn't help either. Morley's management skills were unable to lift the band from the bottom rungs of the punk circuit, and despite staggering on into the early 1980s, The Drones never regained their buzz.

It was no surprise, though, to see them re-form in 1997 for a short series of twentieth-anniversary gigs. The line-up was identical to the one that first ground out a bottom-heavy rumble back in 1977, with the ironic exception of original bassist

Cundall, who was apparently reluctant to give up work and family commitments to act like a mental teenager again.

⊙ **Further Temptations** (Anagram, 2001).

Now more than twenty tracks long, this album has aged pretty badly. Given that it wasn't great in the first place, this is one for the specialist collector only.

THE DROPKICK MURPHYS

Formed Boston, Massachusetts, 1995; still scoring goals.

Irish-American punk crew **The Dropkick Murphys** were originally based around a hard core of **Mike McColgan** (vocals), **Rick Barton** (guitar) and **Ken Casey** (bass), knocking out fierce punk rock with a Celtic twang with whichever drummer they could persuade to sit in with them. When **Matt Kelly** showed up in 1997 and proved able to keep a righteous beat going and keep smiling through the raging music around him, the band gelled and set about becoming the loudest, proudest bunch of plastic paddies on the East Coast.

Setting out their stall with a crop of fine EPs – *Fire And Brimstone, Tattoos And Scally Caps* and *Boys On The Docks* – the Dropkick Murphys finally signed to Hellcat Records for their 1998 full-length debut *Do Or Die*. After three years of limited success, McColgan decided to get a real job, and was replaced by **Al Barr** for *The Gang's All Here* (1999) and *Mob Mentality* (2000), a split release with fellow local punkateers **Business**. Barr's arrival opened the gates to a whole new sound for the Murphys as the four-man basic setup grew into a less wieldy but fuller-sounding seven-strong band: Barton left and was replaced by **Mark Orrell**, with **James Lynch** (guitar), **Spicy McHaggis** (bagpipes), and **Ryan Foltz** (mandolin) signing up as well.

Sing Loud, Sing Proud gained loads of greeniepoints by hosting **Shane MacGowan** and was issued in early 2001. It also featured a guest appearance from **Colin McFaull** (Cock Sparrer), and was the band's first solo production, with Casey taking over after previous releases had been put through the studio by Rancid's Lars Frederiksen.

In 2002 the band were still banging loud and hard on their Irish roots, releasing Live On St. Patrick's

Day From Boston, Ma. Playing loud and hard in front of a home crowd made this the Dropkick boys' most convincing recorded statement. The guys invested body and soul, blood, sweat and tears in the set and sent the crowd home roaring with Fenian rebellion in their hearts.

Still wowing the crowds, if preaching to the converted at the same time, The Dropkick Murphys are one of the East Coast's most enjoyable and powerful bands. Blackout (2003) sent them off straight down the same old furrow, bellowing the chorus to "Kiss Me I'm Shitfaced" as they went.

Whether their Celtic-punk-brothers-in-arms shtick would stand up next to genuinely angry, genuinely Irish people such as Stiff Little Fingers is another matter, but for a great night out cursing the injustices of the world, they'll not be beaten.

⊚ Sing Loud, Sing Proud (Epitaph, 2001)

The album that saw the Boston boys break out of their home town and onto the national stage. This is wide-eyed and legless Plastic Paddy Punk writ very large indeed, but concentrating on jigs and reels rather than misty-eyed sentimentality.

⊚ Live On St. Patrick's Day From Boston, MA (Hellcat, 2002)

Playing a greatest hits set to a home audience, this is passionate, fun-loving, whiskey-fuelled entertainment from The Dropkick Murphys at their uproarious best.

⊚ The Warrior's Code (Hellcat, 2005)

The Murphys' latest recording makes no concessions to the new audience they've gained from having their music featured at various sports events. Featuring a brace of boxers on the cover, this is a fine demonstration of two-fisted guitar aggression that will batter you into submission over fourteen rounds.

THE DURUTTI COLUMN

Joined up Manchester, England, 1978; still marching.

One of the few Manchester bands to escape being crushed when punk fell to pieces, **The Durutti Column** were never really card-carrying members, more one of those bands that would never have existed had it not been for the do-it-yourself ethic of punk. **Vincent "Vini" Reilly** (guitar/vocals/ anything) is the man behind the Column, a band that traces its roots to local legends **Ed Banger And The Nosebleeds**.

The Nosebleeds were one of many cabaret-band crossovers that punk spawned early on in the UK, and at one point gave a home to Morrissey. Reilly blew into the band like the mysterious stranger hitting town in a spaghetti western, oozing a slick and expert guitar-slinging style that the other young punks could merely dream of matching.

Tony Wilson (Manchester's Mr Big in the music biz) was managing the Nosebleeds, but in January 1978 he extracted Reilly and his diamond-rare skills to team him up with **Phil Rainford** (vocals), **Dave Rowbotham** (guitar), **Tony Bowers** (bass) and **Chris Joyce** (drums). Taking the group's name from a series of 1960s French Situationist comic-strip posters entitled *The Return Of The Durutti Column* – originally a Spanish Civil War unit led by revolutionary anarchist Buenaventura Durruti [sic] – Reilly

---

🎧 PLAYLIST: THE MANCHESTER MOB

The UK's second city of punk dished out enough bands to fill this book. When you're in the mood for some northwestern soul then there's nothing that'll beat a bit of Mancunian misery.

1. CITY HOBGOBLINS The Fall from **Palace of Swords Reversed (CD reissue Cog Sinister; 1998)**

2. I CAN'T CONTROL MYSELF Buzzcocks from **Time's Up (Grey Area; 2000)**

3. SONG FROM UNDER THE FLOORBOARDS from **Correct Use Of Soap (reissued Virgin; 1994)**

4. CRANKED UP REALLY HIGH Slaughter & The Dogs from **Do It Dog Style (Captain Oi; 2000)**

5. PSYCLE SLUTS – PARTS 1 & 2 John Cooper Clarke from **Disguise In Love (reissued Sony; 2005)**

6. AT A LATER DATE Joy Division from **Short Circuit (reissued Caroline; 1990)**

7. PERSECUTION COMPLEX The Drones from **Short Circuit (reissued Caroline; 1990)**

8. NAG NAG NAG Cabaret Voltaire from **Nag Nag Nag (reissued Mute; 2002)**

9. KILL Alberto Y Lost Trios Paranoias from **Snuff Rock (Mau Mau; 1991)**

10. DO THE DU A Certain Ratio from **The Graveyard and the Ballroom (Universal Sound; 2004)**

The Factory:
Where Northwestern Punk Was Assembled

Tony Wilson was ready, towards the end of the 70s, to mutate into the city's punk-rock mogul. His time at the regional TV company had brought him into contact with some of the New Wave's most interesting and inspirational characters and, not without an eye on making some dough from the scene, he launched himself as Manchester's Mister Music.

His original money-spinning idea was nothing much more than a once-a-week disco, with a band on towards the end of the evening; hardly ground-breaking stuff. His second was to give catalogue numbers to everything his new organization – Factory – produced

The venue was known as The Russell Club for six nights a week – it's now The Lighthouse – a down-at-heel address in a part of town that even now is still struggling to find an identity to be proud of. As The Factory however, for one night a week, Royce Road attracted a crowd. Everyone in Manchester played there. Wilson's weekly events started here in 1978, when Joy Division opened the club, and he soon expanded his empire into larger, more salubrious premises, with a nightclub and record label (also called Factory) to look after. Visiting acts from London and overseas soon came to know it as the most important underground club in the north of the country.

The new club, a joint project with New Order called The Hacienda on Whitworth Street, opened in 1982 and for fifteen years was arguably the country's best night out. When it closed in June 1997 (under a withering fire of "drug hell" headlines and gangster tales) it stayed empty until the end of 1998 when the demolition crew moved in. The fabric of the old venue was auctioned off (bricks came in at £5 each) for charity and a new development, of trendy, expensive-looking flats – also known as The Hacienda – was built in its place.

and the lads were let loose to make their own kind of music, far from the four-to-the-floor pulsebeat of punk rock.

This first line-up recorded just two tracks before Wilson's handpicked team went off to become **The Mothmen**. Reilly kept the name and fell under the spell of demon producer **Martin Hannett**, spending endless days and long dark nights closeted in Factory Records' studio (with Wilson now running the label, studio time came free), essentially jamming along to Hannett's tireless drum machine. A more human input, from **Phil "Toby" Tolman** (who provided a less indefatigable source of percussion) and **Peter Crooks** (bass), was bolted onto Reilly's guitar work, and after some drastic editing, *The Return Of The Durutti Column* appeared, with its suitably enigmatic title amusingly aided in mischief by the record's sandpaper-coated sleeve (another idea swiped from the Situationists).

Though Reilly remains an important name to drop, his inward-looking fascination with (some admittedly mesmerizing) guitar noodling led him quietly off-stage before fame was able to crush his sweet hands. Without the punk spotlight to bleach the fragile elegance of his work, he's now playing better than ever, but has left anything we'd recognize as snot-nosed rock'n'roll far behind.

⊙ **The Best Of The Durutti Column (Warner, 2004)**

The best place to begin any exploration of the development of Reilly's work over the last 25 years or so. Reilly left punk rock behind years ago, but when he does "aggressive" you can see his roots showing. Working with some inspired choices of guest vocalist, he has never lost the attitude or single-minded determination to make his own music in his own way that typified the movement in its earliest days.

IAN DURY AND THE BLOCKHEADS

Ian Dury born London, 1942; died 2000.

Punk rock gave a home and a welcome to a whole bunch of freaks, weirdos and outsiders who were bent away from the normal in mind or body. **Ian Dury**, part-crippled by polio yet still looking distinctly "useful", creator of heart-wrenchingly beautiful imagery and the foulest of curses, professional Cockney and celebrator of the golden age of music-hall variety theatre, qualified on all counts and was in from the beginning.

One of the UK's many art-school musicians, Ian had started out on the pub-rock circuit with **Kilburn And The Highroads** – a well-respected but ultimately inessential band – before forming **The Blockheads** and signing to Stiff soon after it opened for business.

Ian was no spotty teenaged oik – his art-school background had included not just a qualification, but a subsequent teaching post at the respected Canterbury Art College – and he recruited an appropriately mature set of musicians to back him up as he returned to the music scene on the crest of a scummy punk-rock wave. The Blockheads he found were a roguish bunch of extraordinarily skilled musos, easily capable of keeping pace with Ian's eerie Cockney geezer routines, following him from neo-music-hall tunes down into the foul language and worse smells of the punk-rock gutter. Sticking with **Chaz Jankel** (piano/guitar) and **Davey Payne** (sax) from the Highroads, Ian put together a swift debut, *New Boots And Panties* (1978), using session musicians before settling on **John Turnbull** (guitar), **Mickey Gallagher** (piano), **Norman Watt Roy** (bass) and **Charley Charles** (drums) and taking the show on tour. New Boots grew to be the party soundtrack of the year, with "Plaistow Patricia", "Blackmail Man" and "Blockheads" – all outstandingly powerful punk-rock songs – jostling for space with less aggressive crowd-pleasers such as "Wake Up And Make Love With Me" and "I'm Partial To Your Abracadabra".

New Boots sold over a million copies in the UK, and the singles that followed including "Hit Me With Your Rhythm Stick," "Sex & Drugs & Rock & Roll" and "Reasons To Be Cheerful (Part 3)" all went into the Top 10. Seen at home as a slightly seedy cross between a comedian and **Keith Moon** playing Uncle Ernie in the film of *Tommy*, Dury's dry wit, clever lyrics and bursts of rage meant that he was impossible to export. Although he never really left the music world, he concentrated for most of the Eighties on an acting career (his movie credits include the pawnbroker in Total Recall, and appearances in Peter Greenaway's *The Cook, The Thief, His Wife And Her Lover* and Roman Polanski's *Pirate*), while the royalties from his sublime singles continued to add up.

By the mid-1990s, however, Dury's health was failing, and he was diagnosed with colon cancer. When the disease spread to his liver, Ian went public with his intention to fight his illness as long as he could, partly as an encouragement to others, partly to make preparations, while he was still able, for the family he would leave behind. A hectic and hastily planned tour followed, with the old Blockheads reunited and Ian summoning up his outrageous rhymes and frightening anger for audiences across the country that wished him eternal life and strength. Sadly, this was not to be, and Dury died on March 27, 2000.

New Boots And Panties
(Edsel, 2004)

Even for balding ex-punks who treasure the original vinyl version, the strength of the extras makes this reissue a must-have. Expanded with three bonus tracks and a full disc of demos, this is a crystal-clear, digitally remastered party in CD form. Download this little lot onto your MP3 player and put some razzle in your pocket!

ICONIC SINGLE:
SEX & DRUGS & ROCK & ROLL
(STIFF, 1977)

Not included on the original release of *New Boots And Panties*, this is the tune that made him a star and a hero to a crowd that was supposedly anti-both. Easily the finest title for a single in the history of music, "Sex & Drugs & Rock & Roll" also inspired a very collectable set of badges and an interminable series of punning headlines in the music press. It's not a conventional punk-rock song by any means – there are no power-chords, it has a jolly little melody, it even boasts a dreamy sax solo and a proper middle eight – but it was so elegantly subversive, and so precise in its encapsulation of punk's ideals that it was an immediate underground hit before it entered the mainstream.

Danceable, singable and very catchy, it was the soundtrack to a great many lives as the Seventies turned into the Eighties. It remains a radio favourite, and if you don't know it already, you should.

EATER

Happy when formed in London, 1975; blown out by 1979.

"WE ... TOLD ALL THE GIRLS IN OUR SCHOOL THAT WE HAD THIS BAND. GIRLFRIENDS WERE SUDDENLY EASIER TO FIND."

ANDY BLADE

In a lot of ways, **Eater** was the ultimate punk band, with the best of all punk-rock histories. Scrambling onstage at the very start of the movement, Eater played support to a lot of the groups that would go on to be big-name successes, without ever coming within reach of the big time themselves. They went on to grab some notoriety mainly because they were all in their mid-teens (the drummer was just 14 when he joined), did a few tours and had a touch of the rock'n'roll lifestyle. They recorded everything they had to say on a couple of singles and a quickly released album, then split up and more or less disappeared. That's the way it ought to be done.

Andy Blade (guitar/vocals) formed Eater in 1975 with his school pal **Brian Chevette** (guitar), naming the group after a line from Marc Bolan, "Tyrannosaurus Rex, the eater of cars". They drafted in **Ian Woodcock** (bass) and our 14-year old hero **Dee Generate** (drums). Dee was introduced to the band by The Damned's **Rat Scabies**, and went on to use his friendship with Scabies to hang out and be photographed with London's punk-rock elite.

Taking punk's ethic of learning your instruments in front of an audience to heart, Eater tormented crowds around town, being seen as little more than a joke until they muscled their way onto the seminal *The Roxy, London WC2* compilation. Catapulted into a kind of stardom simply because there were so few punk records around, Eater and their aptly titled track "Fifteen" – with lyrics adapted from Alice Cooper's "Eighteen", played over the standard buzzsaw and jackhammer backing – was played all over the country at punk and New Wave gigs.

Signing to The Label, the band released "Outside View", an idiot-savant slice of high-rise living, and the undeniably classic "Thinking Of The U.S.A.", before peaking with *The Album*. A mish-mash of re-recorded singles, better-than-expected new material and high-speed cover versions (including attempts at "Sweet Jane" and "Waiting For The Man" so awful that one can imagine Lou Reed declining the royalties if he heard them), it didn't sell particularly well.

After Eater released the live EP *Get Your Yo-Yos Out* – an obvious but brilliant pun on the Stones' *Get Yer Ya-Yas Out* – Dee was sacked and went back to school, his homework eighteen months late. He's quite possibly still in detention and cleaning blackboard dusters. His replacement **Phil Rowland** had just about learned the songs when, in the face of declining press coverage and slow concert ticket sales, the band finally folded in 1979. While Blade had a solo career on the outskirts of punk for the next fifteen years and Rowland moved on to join **Slaughter And The Dogs**, the rest of the band simply vanished away.

◉ All Of Eater (Creativeman, 1995)

Fearsome collection of all the studio tracks and demo recordings the band ever made. Not for listening to at one sitting, this is, however, a valuable and wildly funny historical document from a time when even this kind of noise seemed a positive step forward.

EDDIE AND THE HOT RODS

Revved up Canvey Island, England, 1975; blew a gasket 1981; periodically back on the road ever since.

" ...LIVE, THEY WERE ONE OF THE MOST EXCITING BANDS IN LONDON."

MARK P

As John the Baptist was to Jesus, so **Eddie And The Hot Rods** were to British punk. Any venue that had experienced fans of the Essex invaders would have had few problems managing the punk-rock audiences that followed. With slightly better timing, the band could have sprung a mod revival on the London scene and stolen a march on **The Jam**. As it is, they arrived just as pub-rock was facing last orders, falling into the gap between bar-room brawlers like **The 101ers** and **Kilburn And The Highroads** and the bridge-burning revolutionaries of the next generation. Although the Rods were by no means failures – a top-ten hit, and four assaults on the Top 40 meant a lot of money back in the Seventies, when chart records sold by the hundred thousand – their legacy is one of what-might-have-been and what-should-have-happened.

Formed as part of the peculiar burst of musical creativity which struck Essex in the mid-Seventies, the Hot Rods Mark 1 were assembled in Southend-on-Sea early in 1975 by **Dave Higgs** (guitar), **Barry Masters** (vocals), **Pete Wall** (guitar), **Rob Steel** (bass – swiftly replaced by **Paul Gray**), **Steve Nicol** (drums) and **Lew Lewis** (harmonica), though Lewis was thrown out of the group before they made much of an impression. And **Eddie** was, according to legend, a dummy that suffered a fearsome beating every night as part of the band's stage performance (although **Ed Hollis**, the band's original manager, who also introduced them to the music of MC5, **The Stooges** and the rest of the Detroit underground, might have a different point of view).

Spurred into action by the success of fellow Canvey Islanders **Dr Feelgood**, the Hot Rods put together a similar high-octane R&B set, but being on average about fifteen years younger, they played it with the kind of amped-up gusto not heard since the heady days of **Geno Washington And His Ram Jam Band** in the 1960s. The Rods hit the road on the pub-rock circuit, where, like Washington, they picked up a pill-popping audience of bug-eyed teenagers ready, willing and able to party all night.

The Hot Rods' brand of maximum R&B hadn't been seen in London since the glory days of the 1960s, when **The Who**, **The Yardbirds** and **The Pretty Things** were fighting for headlines, duelling with one another using virtuoso skills, ear-blasting volume, pyrotechnics and onstage outrageous behaviour as weaponry. At a time when audiences were more used to sitting on the floor at gigs and nodding their heads in appreciation at particularly sensitive harpsichord frills, jumping around on stage, whipping up the crowd and celebrating the adolescent abandon that comes when you mix teenaged hormonal overload with amphetamines and beer was terribly unfashionable. However, when their debut EP *Live At The Marquee* started to pick up airplay on local radio and John Peel's show, even the more conservative music weeklies had to pay some attention.

While the dinosaurs of mid-Seventies rock journalism were making up their minds what to say about them, Eddie And The Hot Rods went on doing what they enjoyed most – entertaining the crowds, knocking out the records, and tearing around the country on a high-pressure, sweat-filled tour. "Teenage Depression", their first chart single, was a typically high-octane cut that piled on the pressure from the start. It sold well just on radio play, and when the record appeared in a then-rare picture sleeve (showing some kid about to blow his brains out), it was adopted wholesale by London's handful of young punks as the nearest thing in the shops to a proper rallying cry. Ex-Kursaal Flyer **Graeme Douglas** (guitar) joined in time to mellow the group's raucousness a little and to help get the first Hot Rods album, also called *Teenage Depression*, out on the streets by June 1976.

The follow-up to "Teenage Depression" was "I Might Be Lying", which inexplicably looked back to medium-paced R&B. When it failed to storm the charts, the band must have sensed there was a bit of a teen-rebellion bandwagon around the corner, because their first single of 1977, "Do Anything You Wanna Do", seemed custom-designed to jump on it.

While it pressed all the right buttons lyrically, however, "Do Anything …" owed far too much musically to Bruce Springsteen to be seen as anything more than a tribute to the New Jersey troubadour. Likewise, the negative, tried-and-

ICONIC SINGLE:
TEENAGE DEPRESSION (ISLAND, 1976)

"I'M SPENDING ALL MY MONEY AND IT'S GOING UP MY NOSE" LYRIC

Kicking off with a guitar riff that sticks like glue and itches you into dancing, and one of the best-ever punk-rock opening lines, "Teenage Depression" was a sign of something new and interesting going on in music. It had a great picture cover of some kid about to blow his brains out and there was a rare purity to the music: no synthesizers, no false histrionics, just a guy from southeast England telling us a bit of the story of his life. It had a resonance that no amount of flute-wanking songs from the wood was ever going to match and it sold a bundle of copies.

It's not much more than a snottier-than-average rock'n'roll tune really: what set it apart from the output of The Kursaal Flyers, the Feelgoods and their mates is the snapshot of reality it encloses, the lack of pretension in its lyrics and the raw unadulterated energy of the delivery. The Hot Rods were very careful never to try to position themselves as a punk band, but they attracted an audience of spikyheads on the strength of this single.

By the time it made it to the stores, though, the graffiti had been sprayed on the wall for the Hot Rods and their pub-rock pals, and it was only a matter of time before their retro sets were replaced by punk's no-future routine.

failed story of "Quit This Town" was too much of a bring-down for an audience aiming to storm the barricades just as soon as the drugs kicked in, and their home audience began to look to punk rock for their aural stimulation.

In another mistimed stab at success, Eddie And The Hot Rods spent most of 1977 trying to crack America. Despite recording with ex–MC5 vocalist Rob Tyner and touring with The Ramones, Talking Heads and Tom Petty, they returned home poorer but wiser to find the punk-rock revolution they'd helped create in full swing without them.

Although they headlined the Reading Festival in 1978, they'd missed their chance, and were seen as irretrievably "old wave". Subsequent releases failed to sell in the numbers demanded by a major label, and in 1981 the band split.

After a couple of false starts in 1984, and again in 1995, Eddie And The Hot Rods fired up their motor again in 2000. Fronted by Barry with just as much energy as he'd shown in the Seventies, the new Hot Rods toured on the nostalgia circuit for a couple of years until they'd picked up sufficient interest to release a completely new album, *Better Late Than Never*, in 2004.

⊙ Do Anything You Wanna Do (Spectrum, 2000)

Cheap and cheerful, this budget-priced compilation – latest in a never-ending chain of CDs forever rehashing the same old hits – should satisfy all your Hot Rods needs. Includes "Do Anything You Wanna Do", "Teenage Depression", "96 Tears", "I Might Be Lying" and "Quit This Town".

⊙ Get Your Rocks Off Live (Jungle, 2002)

For the full Hot Rods experience, however, you need to hear them live and, frankly, they never sounded better than they did the night this set was recorded. Knocking several kinds of stuffing out of their peers, and packed with standout rock'n'roll tunes, this is the best of the in-concert collections available.

THE EIGHTIES MATCHBOX B-LINE DISASTER

Occurred Brighton, England, 1999; ongoing.

Proof, if any were needed, that the punk-rock spirit lives, **The Eighties Matchbox B-Line Disaster** make just the sort of modern psychedelic noise and have just the kind of attitude to spur a new generation of kids into thumbing their noses at authority and turning their backs on the State.

Formed by **Guy McKnight** (vocals), **Andy Huxley** (guitar), **Marc Norris** (guitar), **Sym Gharial** (bass), and **Tom Diamantopoulo** (drums) on the night a new millennium began, TEMBLD didn't actually take up their instruments in anger until a year later. They kicked off with a double B-sided single ("Morning Has Broken" / "Alex") that out-Ramoned The Ramones, and a swift circuit of the country's seedier venues – billed as the "We Love The Tour" tour – that attempted to derange audiences with stroboscopic lighting (an unconscious tribute to The Velvet Underground) and amps turned up loud enough to make your ears bleed. Elements of The Birthday Party's sound fought with hints of The Cramps' style to create something beautiful and unique.

All this was essential preparation for *Horse Of The Dog*, their well-received and extraordinarily noisy good-fun debut album, released on their independent No Death label in 2002. A ten-track juggernaut, heavy on the echo, distortion and twang, *Horse Of The Dog* served up an appetizing, 25-minute stew of Elvis Ghastly punk, Southern-fried psychobilly and powerful electric noise that went down as well on national radio and at festivals as it had in the sweaty back rooms of Brighton's club scene. Thanks in part to the notoriety that inevitably comes when a single ("Celebrate Your Mother") rejoices in the pleasures of inter-generational, incestuous intercourse, TEMBLD ruled the music press, live scene and awards ceremonies, hitting the charts three times in a row with "Psychosis Safari", "Chicken" and "Mister Mental".

The Royal Society followed in 2004, ploughing very much the same furrow and going gold in the process, with celebrity endorsement from Foo Fighters front man Dave Grohl. Provided the temptations and excesses of life on the road (the band did more than 200 gigs in one recent twelve-month stretch) don't make them old before their time, we can expect many more important lessons to emerge from this disaster.

⊚ **Horse Of The Dog** (MCA, 2002)

The kind of disc that turns simple fans into proselytizers of the worst order, *Horse Of The Dog* takes just 25 minutes to play and recruits converts to the cause of loud'n'dirty punk rock every time it's played. Stinking of the garage, filthy like a gutter, this album is the epitome of primal, back-to-the-ooze blues.

Ten tracks to love, with standouts including "Celebrate Your Mother", "Psychosis Safari", "Morning Has Broken", "Team Meat" and "Presidential Wave".

ELECTRO HIPPIES

Shocked into life Liverpool, 1985; slipped into patchouli past tense 1989.

You've got to tip your hat to any bunch of musicians prepared to use the "H" word in their name *and* release a forty-track album called *The Only Good Punk Is A Dead Punk*, so here we honour the Electro Hippies, probably the only Ultrafast Hardcore Death Metal act in the book.

As the Hardcore Death Metal Underground is such a closed shop, personnel details and dates are impossible to fix precisely. However, at some point, the band has included an **Andy** who provided vocals and guitar, both a **Dom** and a **Jeff Walker** on bass, and a brace of drummers – **Simon** and **Gaz Farrimond**.

In a headline-grabbing moment, they recorded a split single with Napalm Death. Each side lasted just one second, making it officially the worst-value music purchase in the world. Listening to their greatest moment, a 3'50" version of Hawkwind's "Silver Machine", the immediate impression is that of listening to a younger brother and his school friends mess up a good song just for the sake of making a hell of a noise.

⊚ **Peel Sessions** (Strange Fruit, 1987)

Championing Electro Hippies was one of the late great John Peel's least comprehensible decisions, but he was always overly fond of Liverpool (the band's hometown) and perhaps that goes some way to explaining it, This collection of nine bass-driven assaults' comes with vocals vomited from the bowels of hell.

THE EXPLOITED

First spiked their hair in anger East Kilbride, Scotland 1979; steeped in super lager, they are likely to go on forever.

When the misguided electorate of the UK exercised its democratic right to undergo nearly two decades of Thatcherism, it also let loose the country's hardest-hitting punk-rock acts. While England's anarchist horde was led by

🎵 PLAYLIST: GRINDCORE

Don't blame us if your ears begin to bleed and your eyeballs start to melt.

1. FOREVER FALLEN **Bolt Thrower** from **For Victory (Earache, 1999)**

2. SWARMING VULGAR MASS OF INFECTED VIRULENCY **Carcass** from Choice Cuts **(Earache, 1999)**

3. FEEL LIKE MAKING LOVE (YES, A BAD COMPANY COVER!) **Today Is The Day** from Live Till You Die **(Relapse, 2005)**

4. I LIKE DRUGS AND CHILD ABUSE **Anal Cunt** from It Just Gets Worse **(Caroline, 1999)**

5. DENIAL OF EXISTENCE **Brutal Truth** from Extreme Conditions Demand Extreme Responses **(Earache, 1999)**

6. TAKE THE STRAIN **Extreme Noise Terror** from **From One Extreme to Another (Anagram, 2003)**

7. CHRISTBAIT RISING **Godflesh** from **Streetcleaner (Earache, 1993)**

8. FROM ENSLAVEMENT TO OBLITERATION/ SUFFER THE CHILDREN **Napalm Death** from Peel Sessions **(Strange Fruit, 1991)**

9. DEAD SHALL RISE **Terrorizer** from **World Downfall (Earache, 1999)**

10. FILL THIS PLACE WITH BLOOD **Vengeance Rising** from **Human Sacrifice (Star Song, 1993).**

Crass from rural-ish Epping, just outside London, Scotland's wildest response came with a banshee wail from **The Exploited**, who first assembled in East Kilbride – a proud, tough and fiercely industrial town near Glasgow, where teething babies chew iron bars and the coppers go around in twos for safety (and that's when they're inside the police station) – but moved to Edinburgh in short order, attracted by the larger number of venues prepared to let them play.

The Exploited came together when a bitterly disillusioned ex-soldier called Walter David Buchan, known for the rest of this entry as **Wattie**, (gruff, occasionally screaming vocals) linked forces with **"Big John" Duncan** (guitar), whose more than 280 lbs of honed musical talent was only matched by his complete lack of respect for authority. Teaming up with **Dru Stix** (drums, real name Glen Campbell – no relation) and **Gary McCormick** (bass), The Exploited threw together a few rabble-rousing chants and a book of chords, stirred them well and produced three singles, all on their own Exploited label.

"Army Life" b/w "Fuck A Mod" summed up most of the band's philosophy. "Barmy Army" and "Dogs Of War" followed at irregular intervals while the band roared, growled and scrapped their way to the top of the local punk heap. Signing to local indie label Secret and capitalizing on the incredible strength of local response, the band recorded the *Punk's Not Dead* set – the opening salvo in the Edinburgh Revolt – in three days flat.

Punk's Not Dead was the rallying cry the leftover rump end of punk had been waiting for. Blasts of polemic were spattered around in all directions as Wattie's sawn-off shotgun vocals took out chunks of the establishment. Starting with the Royal Family and slowly working their way through the slime of corruption, police, "justice" system, state arrogance and the like, they saved their most powerful weaponry for then Prime Minister Margaret Thatcher in their touching song "Maggie".

Wattie's time as a squaddie – not such a strange career-move considering the lack of options available in East Kilbride at the time – lent a unique bitterness to his pacifism (another of the band's enduring themes). While he was always apparently quite prepared to get involved in a punch-up, and was known for brawling with the riot police during a tour of Germany, The Exploited's comments on the futility of war and the hidden agendas that cause it had a resonance born of their singer's time in uniform.

The album's barely contained aggression complemented the band's booming reputation as the most exciting rock act (never mind just punk rock) in the country. On the strength of album sales (it went to #20 in the national charts) and the promising performance of "Dead Cities", the first single taken from it, in one of those remarkably pleasing twists on conventional reality, they were booked and appeared on the BBC's flagship teeny-pop music programme, *Top Of The Pops*. Their incendiary performance was the perfect backing track to the long summer of 1981, when the cities of the UK were intermittently aflame and riots

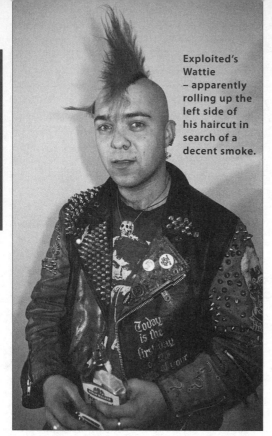

Exploited's Wattie – apparently rolling up the left side of his haircut in search of a decent smoke.

Despite Duncan's departure being just the first in a never-ending series of line-up changes – particularly around the drum kit as Dru was replaced by **Danny Heatley**, **Steve Roberts** and then **"Wullie"** (Wattie's brother William) – they went on to produce *Troops Of Tomorrow* (1982), *Let's Start A War (Said Maggie One Day)* in 1983, *Horror Epics* (1985) and *Death Before Dishonor* (1987). By this point, Wattie was the only member of the band who actually remembered when they started and where their roots lay. He kept an immoveable hand on the tiller, refusing any musical compromise and sneering at the idea of changing course lyrically through to the end of the decade and beyond, reappearing in 1990 with *The Massacre*, and again in 1996 with *Beat The Bastards*.

Since then, The Exploited have reunited for sporadic tours, and remain one of the country's most powerful live attractions, spitting out a uniquely appealing blend of venom and humour whenever they hit the stage. In 2001, Cherry Red released *Rock & Roll Outlaws / Sexual Favours*, an outstanding documentary plus live footage DVD that tails the band round Europe through two years of hangovers, hi-energy performances, parties and previously unseen footage from Wattie's own collection. Highlights include their *Top Of The Pops* appearance, and in-concert versions of "Army Life", "Maggie", "Punk's Not Dead", "Let's Start A War" and "Dead Cities".

were the order of the day. The band toured with **Discharge**, **Chron Gen** and **Anti Pasti**, doing their best to stir things up.

Like the rest of punk, The Exploited had a pretty rough time of it as the Eighties struggled forward. When Duncan left at the end of 1982 – first to become a **Blood Uncle**, then spending a short while hanging out trading licks with a bunch of Seattle kids calling themselves **Nirvana** – the band lost a lot of momentum.

◉ **Punk's Not Dead (reissued Snapper Classics, 2004)**

The Exploited's first album, initially released on Secret Records in 1981, was notorious for its muddy mix and rushed production. More than twenty years later, Snapper have remastered it, and the result is a high-pitched, race-tuned, roaring beast of a record that'll be the pride of your collection.

🔊 PLAYLIST: THE EXPLOITED

A dream playlist if you're angry and need to rid your head of all rational thought.

1. ARMY LIFE from
Singles Collection (Snapper Classics, 2005)

2. (FUCK A) MOD SONG from
Singles Collection (Snapper Classics, 2005)

3. EXPLOITED BARMY ARMY from
Singles Collection (Snapper Classics, 2005)

4. I BELIEVE IN ANARCHY from
Singles Collection (Snapper Classics, 2005)

5. DOGS OF WAR from
Singles Collection (Snapper Classics, 2005)

6. DEAD CITIES from
Singles Collection (Snapper Classics, 2005)

7. Y.O.P. from
Singles Collection (Snapper Classics, 2005)

8. TROOPS OF TOMORROW from
Singles Collection (Snapper Classics, 2005)

9. SEX AND VIOLENCE from
Singles Collection (Snapper Classics, 2005)

10. PUNK'S NOT DEAD from
Singles Collection (Snapper Classics, 2005)

THE FALL

Descended to Manchester, England in 1977; still here, never going to leave.

"IF YOU CAN'T DELIVER IT LIKE A GARAGE BAND, FUCK IT."

MARK E SMITH, 1989

The mightiest of all the punk acts in terms of longevity, commitment, productivity and sheer gritty quality of work delivered, **The Fall** are still, to quote John Peel, "the yardstick by which all other bands must be measured". **Mark E Smith** (vocals, inspiration, random acts of musical mayhem), the band's fearsomely talented leader, is also its only constant feature – after almost three decades with scarcely a week off, the accumulation of musical differences, band members growing up, and sheer bloody-mindedness in the camp means that virtually an entire generation of Manchester musicians has passed through The Fall. Their output makes uneasy listening from beginning to end, but like it or not, it has left its mark everywhere in the modern indie / punk / alt:rock world, and for that reason if no other, it merits a close look.

The Fall's official website lists some 25 studio albums, the recently demoted, and now unofficial website for the band totals up more than ninety full-length recordings, and as the group's thirtieth anniversary looms, there are already more than two minutely detailed biographies in the shops. What follows, then, can be nothing more than a broad-brush sketch of their career.

Smith has been the driving force of The Fall since the outset in 1977, when the band was noth-ing more than a part-time outlet for our hero to look forward to after a day's work at Manchester Docks. Coming to punk from a background of heavy metal, prog and the "krautrock" experimentalists (Can, Faust and Neu! being particularly obvious influences), he and his pals in the band created a unique version of New-Wave noise, combining back-to-basics rock'n'roll –"Container Drivers" from 1980's *Grotesque*, the band's third album, being recognised as the first genuine "Mancabilly" tune – with Smith's hallucinatory, strangely prophetic and generally unsettling lyrics.

From the cover of the first single "It's The New Thing" (see p.139), it was clear that something unusual was going on. The Fall was obviously a "punk" band, but they were literate enough to take their

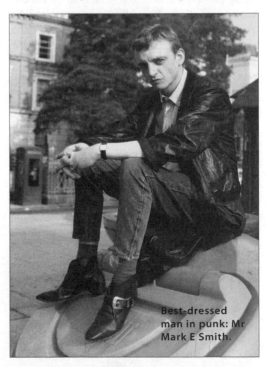

Best-dressed man in punk: Mr Mark E Smith.

🔲 PLAYLIST: THE FALL

It's simply impossible to summarise a thirty-year career in ten tracks, but this will serve as a useful introduction to new converts, might yet persuade the unbeliever and is anyway the ideal backing track to any commute.

1. PSYKICK DANCEHALL
from **Dragnet (Castle, 2004)**

2. NO XMAS FOR JOHN QUAYS
from **Totale's Turns: It's Now Or Never (Castle, 2004)**

3. CONTAINER DRIVERS
from **Grotesque: After The Gramme (Castle, 2004)**

4. NEW PURITAN from **The Complete Peel Sessions Box Set (Castle, 2005)**

5. WHO MAKES THE NAZIS?
from **Hex Enduction Hour (Castle, 2005)**

6. TEMPO HOUSE
from **Perverted By Language (Castle, 2005)**

7. CREEP from **The Wonderful And Frightening World Of The Fall (Castle, 2005)**

8. SPECTRE VS RECTOR from **Live In London: The Legendary Chaos Tapes (Castle, 2004)**

9. CAB IT UP from **458489 B-Sides** (Beggars Banquet, 1990)

10. STRYCHNINE from **The Twenty Seven Points** (Cog Sinister, 1995)

---

name from one of Albert Camus's lesser-known novels. Musically too, this was no simple standard 4/4 piece: twinkly toy-sounding pianos rubbed up against a biscuit-tin drum kit in an opening refrain, before everything – drums, keyboards, wild spiralling guitars and Smith's wonderful drawling vocals – hurtled into the melody, jostling for position in a glorious, confusing, delightful mess. Listeners reached the end breathless.

BBC London DJ Danny Baker deserves credit for being the first to champion the band in the nation's capital, but it was The Fall's total capture of John Peel that turned them from a local phenomenon into a nationwide cult, which in turn went international and even saw them troubling the lower reaches of the "real" charts, all without selling out.

Peel greeted the first Fall recordings like they were long-lost children, and played *Live At The Witch Trials* and *Dragnet* (both 1979), followed by *Grotesque* and their first live album, *Totale's Turns* (both 1980), until the vinyl wore through to transparency. His tactic of playing The Fall until the audience grew to share his uncritical love of their material paid off. As the Eighties progressed, Smith and The Fall – generally comprising **Craig Scanlon** (guitar), **Stephen Hanley** (bass), with **Karl Burns** (drums) sometimes assisted, sometimes replaced by **Simon Wolstencroft** (drums) – grew in confidence and ability, touring like crazy, recording whenever the muse settled on Smith's shoulder and hiring/firing extra hands as the situation required.

This was the band's golden age, with a series of progressively more twisted and inspired albums leading to ever more widespread touring, and

for Smith, an ever-broadened songwriting mind. Touring Iceland – for all kinds of occult reasons, popular with **Killing Joke**, Echo & The Bunnymen and The Fall at that time – Smith stopped off long enough to get a few tracks down for the epic *Hex Enduction Hour* (1982), while "Marquis Cha Cha" from *Room To Live* (1982) saw him commenting on British foreign policy at the time of the Falklands Crisis.

A tour of the USA, on the other hand, introduced Smith to his future wife, **Brix** – nicknamed for her love of The Clash's "Guns Of Brixton" – who was then a bassist in a group called Banda Dratzing. Smith was taken by one of her songs, and before she knew it, Brix was married and a member of The Fall. Although her influence was controversial, the band entered its mellowest and financially most secure period, scoring chart success in the UK with cover versions of The Kinks' "Victoria" and R Dean Taylor's "There's A Ghost In My House".

It was *Perverted By Language* (1982), closely followed by *The Wonderful And Frightening World Of The Fall* (1984) that, in the end, proved to be the cream of this prime series of recordings, although the darker corners of *This Nation's Saving Grace* (1985), *Bend Sinister* (1986) and *The Frenz Experiment* (1988) did nothing but add to the band's reputation as serious reporters of doom.

While Mark and Brixie posed for photo shoots costumed as Napoleon and Josephine, airbrushed and made-up, before driving home in matching his'n'hers BMWs, The Fall launched sideways into a collaboration with radical ballet artist and choreographer **Michael Clark**. Based (and why not?) on the accession to the British monarchy of William of Orange in the 1688, *I Am Kurious, Oranj* (1988) was not quite the soundtrack album to Clark's ballet, but something similar. The "Prole Art Threat" Smith had howled about back on *Slates* (1981) had, it seemed, become reality.

Their continuing preparedness to take musical risks was demonstrated again when keyboard player **Simon Rogers** joined the fun (first as a session musician, then as full-time band member before moving on to production duties). He made an instant and growing impression on The Fall's sound – smoothing off a lot of its rougher edges and bringing greater emphasis to melody, yet without ditching the primal soupy drum'n'bass bottom end that defined it. Nobody, thank the gods below, tried to make Smith take singing lessons.

It couldn't last. It didn't last, and when Brixie quit the Smith household – later surfacing on the arm of classical violinist *enfant terrible* Nigel Kennedy – she was out of the band and Smith began producing some of his bitterest and most melancholy work. After the divorce, Brix went on to form Adult:Net before returning to The Fall and her previous role as the little grain of sand in Smith's oyster. Meantime, **Martin Bramah** (who had been in the original line-up more than a decade before) took her place, joining the tour and recording sessions for *Extricate* (1990): he'd gone again by the release of *Shift-Work* (1990).

Sporadically brilliant and essential ever since, The Fall remained in the public ear mainly thanks to John Peel's continued support. *Code: Selfish* (1992) and *The Infotainment Scan* (1993) were packed with gems, *Middle Class Revolt* (1994) less densely so, but *Cerebral Caustic* (1995) saw a stomping return to form, with Smith's visions rendered even more acid by Brix's return. Since then, the albums have come with the ominous regularity of a dripping tap – *The Twenty-Seven Points* (1995), *The Light User Syndrome* (1996), *Levitate* (1997), *The Marshall Suite* (1999), The Unutterable (2000), *Are You Are Missing Winner* (2001), *The Real New Fall LP* Formerly "Country On The Click" (2003) and most recently, *Fall Heads Roll* (2005). Meanwhile, Smith has branched out into solo, spoken-word recordings with *The Post-Nearly Man* (1998) and *Pander! Panda! Panzer!* (2002), keeping his day job with The Fall going at the same time.

Circling his fiftieth birthday ever more closely, Mark E Smith long ago gave up speaking for anyone but himself – he never was a teen idol, he never preached, but he told some great stories and still does. His band not only drew up the template for punk rock, they built the prototypes, tested them, set up production facilities and are even now working on refinements for next year's model. The last working remnant of Manchester's proud industrial heritage, The Fall merit all kinds of praise from the outbreak of noiseniks that followed, such as Public Image Ltd., Pavement, Sonic Youth and Sugarcubes.

 ## Grotesque – After The Gramme
(Castle, 2004 Reissue)

The deluxe, expanded edition of the best of the band's earlier albums, *Grotesque* demonstrates all The Fall's major strengths. Smith yelps at local bureaucracy in "Pay Your Rates", lays into expatriate workers in "English Scheme", delivers two of his best horror epics with "New Face In Hell" and "Impression Of J Temperance", and goes completely, magically barmy on "C 'n' C's Mithering" and "Container Drivers". Add the languid croon

ICONIC SINGLE:
IT'S THE NEW THING (FORWARD, 1977)

Quirky keyboards and a drumkit apparently constructed from bedsprings and biscuit tins provide the opening, softening you up for a mad, guitar-driven sprint of an intro and then the first appearance of that voice: hard to describe, impossible to forget and far too tempting to imitate, Mark E. Smith's awesome singing is something you either "get" immediately or never at all.

Dedicated fans will swear to the difficulty, even after prolonged and repeated exposure, of converting unbelievers to the Fall's music, but many jolly hours have been spent in the attempt. Originally on *Live At The Witch Trials*, "…New Thing" is available on various Fall albums, so saddle up and give it a blast.

of "Gramme Friday" and "NWRA", and you've got a real treat of a recording. The bonus tracks, previously released as singles, are all worth having too.

☉ Hex Induction Hour (Castle, 2005 Reissue)

This has been boosted up to a 2-CD set with otherwise unavailable alternate takes – including all the versions of "And This Day" anyone's likely to want, and "Jazzed Up Punk Shit" – which sounds just like you imagine it does. The standout tracks, however, remain "The Classical" and "Hip Priest".

☉ Perverted By Language (Castle, 2005 Reissue)

Another expanded 2-CD set. More than superficially chirpy, particularly on "I Feel Voxish" and "Eat Y'self Fitter", it features some of Smith's best lyrics, with "Tempo House", "Garden" and "Hexen Definitive/Strife Knot" still foxing the best efforts to completely comprehend them.

☉ The Wonderful And Frightening World Of The Fall (Beggars Banquet, 1998 Reissue)

Just the one disc at the time of writing, but with so many highlights, it has never seemed anything less than a complete statement. Smith goes mystic on "Elves", turns psychedelic when reminiscing about "Pat Trip Dispenser" and gets down'n'messy with "Lay Of The Land", "Two By Four" and "God Box".

☉ Cerebral Caustic (Castle, 2005 Reissue)

The best post-divorce but back in the band album ever made, with Smith and Brix coming to terms with their new relationship. Standout track is, of course, the fiercely galloping "Don't Call Me Darling".

FEAR

Came over us in Los Angeles in 1977; split, re-formed and stayed together.

Hardcore is a lousy vehicle for comedy – either the best jokes go in the chorus, and lose all trace of humour as they're bellowed to the roof night after night, or the wit stays in the verse, and nobody can understand what's being said. That has never stopped **Fear** from trying, although a lot of their "humour" leaves a bitter taste. One of the world's most enduring of punk bands, Fear has been our companion for as long as we can remember, helping to shape the Los Angeles sound of expensive instruments driven through ruthlessly overwrought amplification.

Formed in Los Angeles by front man **Lee Ving** (vocals/mayhem/abuse), Fear's original line-up of **Philo Cramer** (lead guitar), **Derf Scratch** (bass), and **Johnny Backbeat** (drums) kicked around garages and rehearsal studios, toying with **Burt Good** (guitar), replacing Backbeat with **Spit Stix** and generally having fun while putting together a set.

Criminal Records put out "I Love Livin' In The City" in 1978, but Fear kept away from any full-

---

Fast Product

Whizzing around Edinburgh, Scotland from 1977

"WE'RE INTERESTED IN ANYONE WHO'S GOT SOMETHING TO SAY AND ALL WAYS OF SAYING IT."

FAST PRODUCT COMMUNIQUÉ, 1977

Bob Last wrote the quote above in December 1977 as part of his first paranoiac rant from his bunker in Keir Street Edinburgh. Tipping a stylistic hat to the then fashionable taste for manky old amphetamines imbibed in huge quantities, the communication goes on to challenge posers, disco dross and 12" limited edition disco-punk collectors' items before finally getting to the point – Bob's new label had a couple of releases planned for the New Year.

The few who read beyond Bob's opening tooth-grinders found that he'd signed a band from Leeds and another from Sheffield. The happy, happy few that

actually went out in the January cold to find this new Fast Product were rewarded with The Mekons' EP "Never Been In A Riot" / "32 Weeks" and "Heart + Soul" and 2.3's "Where To Now?" / "All Time Low". Fast Product released a mere dozen catalogue items but threw a shadow far bigger than you'd expect.

Late one night, Bob came up with the idea of "ear comics" – short-run, ephemeral (and ironically, incredibly collectable) 12" single samplers that gave Joy Division, DAF and others sadly less well known their first vinyl outing. The label also dealt in "Subversive Commodities", packaging recordings in thought-provoking images, wrapping records in challenging manifestos and providing a blueprint that any aspiring independent record label could follow.

Quality releases continued to dribble out of Scotland as Sheffield yielded The Human League, Leeds gave up The Gang Of Four and local band Scars (whose single "Horrorshow" was sampled this year for Lemon Jelly's "The Shouty Song"). When the fun was over, Last closed Fast (finishing with the UK debut by The Dead Kennedys) and became the man behind Pop:Aural, another label, with an entirely different philosophy and history all its own.

length album commitments until 1982, when they were invited to sign on the line by Slash Records. In-between times, they had grown into the West Coast's tightest live act, with all the punk-rock moves perfectly orchestrated and a grossly unpleasant shtick that aimed to offend majorities just as much as minorities. Fear gigs were loud, fierce, confrontational and very moist as the crowd sweated, drooled, flailed arms and spilled their drinks, while Ving slobbered and snarled his venom past the mic into the front rows.

Actor, comedian and bad-behaviour expert **John Belushi** fell head over heels in love with Fear in a cocaine-driven epiphany, having observed their wild performance in the LA punk documentary *The Decline of Western Civilization* (1981). He made a point of hooking up with members of the band and finally persuaded *Saturday Night Live* into letting them appear on the 1981 Halloween show. True to form, Fear showed up with an entourage of skinheads who slam-danced with such enthusiasm that some thousands of dollars of damage to expensive broadcasting equipment ensued.

Countrywide exposure, boosted by the frisson that comes whenever anyone swears on TV in the US, finally convinced Slash to put up the money for an album's worth of Fear, and *The Record* appeared to excellent critical reviews in 1982. Sales were good enough for "musical differences" to appear and cause cracks to form. Scratch was the first to jump and a merry-go-round of bassists followed. He was replaced first by **Eric "Kitabu" Feldman** (who played on "Fuck Christmas", Fear's doomed stab at once-a-year royalty cheques), then **Flea**, on a break from the Red Hot Chili Peppers, and finally the Dickies' old four-string wizard, **Lorenzo Buhne** The band's confusion over who'd be playing the low notes was not helped when Spit Stix showed up in Europe and took a short-term gig with Nina Hagen. As 1982 and 1983 drifted past, Fear stayed quiet – Cramer put together a side-project called **M'Butu Ngawa**, and Ving went back to Hollywood to talk his way into a few character parts in the movies.

By 1985, the band was back in the studio, working on the admirably titled *More Beer* album. It appeared to a far less enthusiastic response than *The Record* had received, possibly because they had neglected to keep audience interest alive, possibly because their aggressively macho posture was finally perceived as being the antithesis of what punk stood for, but most likely because it wasn't a very good record. Whatever the reason, sales weren't great, and Fear gave it all up in 1987.

Nothing in the music biz is forever, and Fear was back on the road in 1991. Ving, Stix and Cramer were joined for this outing by yet another bass player, **Will "Sluggo" McGregor**, who lasted long enough to appear on the *Live... For The Record* album that resulted. When Fear split up again two years later, Ving formed a completely new group, **Lee Ving's Army** with **Sean Cruse** (guitar), **Scott Thunes** (bass) and **Andrew Jaimez** (drums).

Perhaps hoping that nobody would notice, in 1995 Ving quietly turned his Army into yet another Fear, took them into the studio and squeezed *Have Another Beer With Fear* from them. Musical differences intervened again, and soon yet another bass player was required. **Mondo Lopez** came in as Thunes departed, holding open the door for Cruse to leave and have his seat warmed by **Richard Presley** Long past their overindulging period, this line-up of middle-aged men flogged Fear's long-dead horse into a last semblance of life in 2000, when they surfaced with *American Beer*.

⊙ **The Record** (Rhino, 2000)

If your idea of fun includes mind-scrambling volume and lyrical attacks on your own side, then this might be just what you need. Easily their best record, and if you can take their hate-mongering as "ironic", worth a listen.

FEEDERZ

Started feeding in Phoenix, Arizona, 1977; fed up by 1987; but still snacking.

"THE SIMPLEST SURREALIST ACT CONSISTS OF GOING DOWN INTO THE STREET, REVOLVER IN HAND, AND SHOOTING AT RANDOM INTO THE CROWD..."

ANDRÉ BRETON

Frank Discussion – owner of US hardcore's best-ever stage-name – gave a new definition to the phrase "confrontational performer"

Feederz at feeding time.

punk rock, laced with a stew of influences ranging from Zappa to Beethoven, to San Francisco.

He left the original gang back in Arizona, picking first on **DH Peligro** (who took over drums, though he later played bass for the Dead Kennedys) and **Mark Roderick/ Rodriguez** (bass) as his new Feederz, ushering them into the studio to produce *Ever Feel Like Killing Your Boss?* (Flaming Banker, 1984) – an album

when, backed by **Art Nouveau** (a.k.a. John Vivier, drums, deceased) and **Clear Bob** (a.k.a. Dan Clark, bass) at the first **Feederz** show, he whipped out an assault rifle and sprayed the audience with gunfire. Granted he was using blanks, there were no reported injuries and those who were there are still doubtless retelling the tale – but, unforgettable thrill and blood-fizzing buzz apart, it must have been the most frightening experience in punk-rock history.

It was a promising start to a career combining great music with serious politics, refracted through the unique anarcho-Situationist lenses through which Frank views the world. Coming from the same prankster background as his friend **Jello Biafra**, Frank's Feederz recordings and live appearances share the **Dead Kennedys'** "once heard, never forgotten" approach to claiming and maintaining an audience's attention. Having ditched the weaponry, Frank has been known to perform shows with his head shaved to the scalp and decorated with cockroaches glued – wriggling legs and antennae upwards – to his pate.

1980 saw The Feederz' first, best and most notorious song challenge the freedom of speech statutes until it creaked at the seams. "Jesus Entering From The Rear" is arguably the single most blasphemous song ever written (although Crass's "Reality Asylum" might just pip it at the post), and it's certainly one of the funniest. Arizona probably has laws forbidding that kind of thing, and with the added fallout from one of his better pranks (he arranged for thousands of students to receive official-looking documents announcing a fraudulent essay contest), Frank took his

more notorious for its Situationist-style sandpaper cover, designed to rub up neighbouring products the wrong way, than for its tunes or the admirable sentiments they conveyed. (A sample from the sleevenotes: "Recording Music is Ruining the Music Industry – Keep Up the Good Work.")

Frank fell into a routine of disappearing periodically before resurfacing with an all-new Feederz line-up, while continuing to spearhead their campaign to abolish society through performance-punk and challenges to authority. Having twisted the tail of Christianity with their first single, and discovered the fun to be had with covers on their first album, The Feederz, now consisting of Frank plus **Jayed Scotti** (timbale player – another member of both the DKs and Feederz crew), took on the entire American people, together with anyone who considered themselves to be of good taste, with the release of their second album, *Teachers In Space* (1984), the cover of which showed a photo of the *Challenger* space shuttle disaster on the cover. Unsurprisingly, the album sold in the high dozens.

Frank kept the band actively irritating the powers that be until 1987, when, sick of the whole affair, he retired from the punk biz.

Frank was last definitely spotted in Seattle, where having qualified as a *babalawo* – a Santerían high priest – he was magically bringing about the end of society according to plan. After a series of gigs in the summer of 2004, he is currently rumoured to be in Mexico with the Zapatista Army of National Liberation.

◉ Ever Feel Like Killing Your Boss?
(Broken Rekids, 2002)

The CD reissue of the classic Feederz debut boasted the same sandpaper-cover gimmick as the original vinyl album. The music, if the obvious cliché can be forgiven, is equally abrasive. "Have You Never Been Mellow" is the only Olivia Newton-John song the band ever covered, for which she should be grateful, while "Jesus Entering From the Rear" is as remarkable as ever.

◉ Vandalism: Beautiful As A Rock In A Cop's Face (Broken Rekids, 2002)

Frank Discussion's new material is just as offensive as the old stuff, a refreshingly honest splash of cold water in a sea of warm piss. As for a review, how about this God's-eye view from the Feederz site (www.feederz.com): "When the idea occurred to me to create the world, I foresaw that one day someone would make a recording as revolting as *Vandalism: Beautiful as a Rock in a Cop's Face*. Therefore, I thought it better not to create the world."

THE FEELIES

Formed New Jersey, 1976; lost touch in 1992.

You have to love a punk band that's literate and pretentious enough to lift its name from mind-expansion enthusiast Aldous Huxley. Jim Morrisson's California stoners became The Doors after at least glimpsing the title to Hux's *The Doors Of Perception*, but they were university dudes. The Feelies were the next logical evolutionary step for the movies as seen by Huxley in his novel *Brave New World* – set in a futuristic dystopia where a tranquillized society is doped into docility by a gently benevolent dictatorship. Just a little bit intellectual, just a little bit subversive, very punk rock indeed.

The **Feelies** first assembled in 1976 when high school pals **Bill Million** and **Glenn Mercer** (both guitar/vocals) decided to quit screwing around and really put a band together. Original bass and drums came from **John J.** and **Dave Weckerman** respectively, but they were replaced early in 1977 by **Keith Clayton** (bass) and **Vinny Denunzio** (drums). Mercer and Million were at the controls, however, and steered the band towards the traditional New York drone of the Velvets and their children, particularly the slightly paranoid take on it given by Jonathan Richman in his less whimsical moments.

Nerdy, brainy punk rock was just what the East Coast excelled at, and The Feelies found a warm welcome in the big city. *Village Voice* gave them a headline to die for when it called them "The Best Underground Band in New York" in 1977 and they developed a reputation as the kind of punk-rock group that Woody Allen would adore. By 1979, **Anton Fier** had taken over from Denunzio on drums, and word about the band had found its way across the Atlantic to West London, where Rough Trade signed them up for the "Fa Cé La" single.

Having developed a taste for British indie labels, the guys settled on Stiff Records as the vehicle for their 1980 debut *Crazy Rhythms*. Self-produced, the album twitched and stuttered like some misunderstood piano genius overcome by stage fright at a glitzy reception – the nervous fingers of the individual band members can almost be heard drumming on the mixing desk. Its lack of confident coolness simply added to the album's charm and the band's continuing influence can be traced back to this, their most brilliant and exciting recording.

Unwilling or unable to come up with a suitable single to cash in on the album's reception, the Feelies split soon after. Mercer and Million peeled off to work on a movie soundtrack and a couple of on/off bands back in New Jersey. Fier went first to **Lounge Lizards** and then to brain-rockers the **Golden Palominos**, while Weckerman had showed up in **Yung Wu**. Mercer and Million didn't perform under the Feelies' name until 1983, when they called in Weckerman, **Brenda Sauter** (bass) and **Stanley Demeski** (percussion) to play a few gigs timed to fit around the holidays. They went down well enough, and had developed such a reputation in the meantime to agree to try a second album, this time with Peter Buck of R.E.M. producing. *The Good Earth* appeared in 1986, a fine, competent, professional recording, but about as punk-rock as *The Eagles Greatest Hits*. It went down well with the critics, though, and landed the band a deal with A&M, who released *Only Life* in 1988 and *Time For A Witness* in 1991.

The Feelies played their final show in 1991 at Maxwell's in Hoboken, New Jersey. Million split for Florida soon after, without leaving an address with anybody in the band. Mercer and Weckerman stayed together, showing up first in **Wake Ooloo** and later in **Sunburst**, but by this time their punk days were well and truly over.

⊙ Crazy Rhythms (Stiff, 1980)

Listen to it, fall totally in love with them and weep bitter tears, for you never got to see them play live. It's not punk rock, it's jangly pop-coloured New Wave material that's too soft and sweet to associate with most of the other recordings recommended in this book. Standout tracks include "Fa Cé La", the title track and the two cover versions – The Beatles' "Everybody's Got Something To Hide Except Me And My Monkey" and The Stones' "Paint It Black".

PATRIK FITZGERALD

Born London, 1958.

Like John Cooper Clarke, **Patrik Fitzgerald** was an example of just how accommodating the early punk-rock scene could be. Looking like a middle-class student tosser searching for street cred, he showed up on stage with an inability to pronounce his R's, toting a scrappy old acoustic guitar, and wearing sandals and bright red trousers – four good reasons why he might have been lynched and left hanging from the nearest lamppost. On the whole, though, Patrik's distinctive punk-folky delivery of songs from the dodgiest streets in town won him an audience that was prepared to listen – even if they frequently yelled "Wanker!" at him between numbers.

Fitzgerald actually came from honest Irish working-class stock, was born in the East End that inspired him and was ready to use his guitar as a club if necessary to make his point. By a happy coincidence, he was also a regular customer at Small Wonder, a record shop in Walthamstow that happened to run a record label of the same name. In early 1977 the two got together and put out the EP *Safety Pin Stuck In My Heart* with a beaten-up pic of Patrik on the cover. Looking and sounding like a prototype of the character created a few years later by **Rik Mayall** for British TV's anarchic situation comedy *The Young Ones*, Fitzgerald certainly had a unique style.

The *Backstreet Boys* EP (1978) offered much the same lyrical agenda, and in 1979, he signed to Polydor, who released the *Grabby Stories* album. By this time, however, punk was getting a bit too boisterous for anyone's good, and increasingly frustrated with the boneheads who were making it hard for him to complete a live set, Fitzgerald turned to overseas tours to make a living. He certainly wasn't going to survive on the royalties

ICONIC SINGLE:
SAFETY PIN STUCK IN MY HEART
(SMALL WONDER, 1977)

"Safety Pin" made Fitzgerald an instant hit with any lonesome punk rocker aching for a boyfriend/girlfriend. The lyrics veer through the iconography of early punk – bleeding, amateur piercings; dog-chains worn as jewellery; recycled items of school uniform serving again as part of the costume for a night out; home-altered flares stitched lovingly into drainpipe / bondage stylistic disasters drenched in fluorescent zips bought cheap from Woolworths. Fitzgerald evokes each in turn as emblematic of the ways in which he doesn't love the person he's singing about. All he loves, it transpires, is the extreme punk-rock "beat beat beat beat beating" he receives. There were traces of Wreckless Eric in Fitzgerald's vocal style, but his guitar chops were resolutely station-busker standard and really only there at all to give him something to hide behind.

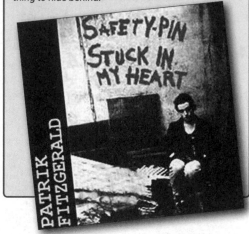

from his albums. *Gifts And Telegrams* (1982) sold appallingly, *Drifting Towards Violence* (1983) performed even worse, and when his pop-tinged stab at the charts *Tunisia Twist* (1986) failed even to get a review in most of the papers, Fitzgerald quit the business.

⊙ The Very Best Of Patrik Fitzgerald
(Anagram, 1994)

These 31 tracks are all you're ever likely to need from the original and best punk poet. Along with "Safety Pin...", you'll find the rest of the tracks from his 1977 EPs, the best of his first albums and sleeve notes by the man himself.

FUGAZI

Screamed into Washington, DC in 1987;
roared off into the sunset in 2001;
currently off the road.

Hardcore has a reputation as being mainly the preserve of brain-damaged jocks with greater mental capacity between their thighs than their ears. However, **Fugazi** – an acronym first used by American troops serving in Vietnam, signifying "Fucked Up, Got Ambushed, Zipped In" – go a long way toward dispelling that unfair judgement. As experienced musicians, **Brendan Canty** (drums), **Joe Lally** (bass) and **Ian MacKaye** (guitar/vocals) were ready to rock from day one, but after just a couple of performances, they brought in **Guy Picciotto** (guitar/vocals – like Canty, ex-**Rites of Spring**), making the band a four-piece outfit.

MacKaye had previously served in **Minor Threat** but was now outnumbered by ex-Rites members, and the band's first release, the *Fugazi* EP, owed much to the sounds that Canty and Picciotto had been accustomed to making. Lyrically though, it took hardcore into another dimension: politically correct and sensitive lyrics, eerie, stop-start jumping rhythms and enough indie righteousness to halt a Ku Klux Klan rally in its tracks.

A second EP followed in much the same vein, and was later collected with the now equally impossible-to-find first EP on the *13 Songs* compilation. Fugazi's first genuine full-length release, however, was *Repeater* (1990). An awesomely powerful expression of defiance and snot-nosed liberal rebellion, it confirmed the band's place in punk's avant-garde.

By 1991 and the release of *Steady Diet Of Nothing*, Fugazi was a tour-hardened act of undeniable power. The new material was just as hard-hitting and equally lyrically incisive, but was now being played with greater skill and more attention to delivery. Fugazi had moved on from the broadsword-style slash and thrust to a more considered, cold-blooded and sniper-like precision.

By 1993, though, they were back on the viking trail, and *In On The Killtaker* echoed with the sound of pig-stickers, battered shields and valour on the field of battle. The songs were just as angry as the music sounded, with amplifiers on "stun", guitars turned up to "pain", and drums at the "really fucking pissed off".

As the 90s wore on, Fugazi's message of "peace and love, yeah, but stick it to the Man" was rendered increasingly inaudible by the dumb-ass antics in the moshpit, and both tours and recordings became less frequent. *Red Medicine* appeared in 1995, *End Hits* didn't follow until 1998, and apart from a documentary soundtrack packed with tasty out-takes and demos from the band's best years, nothing was seen or heard of Fugazi until *The Argument* album and *Furniture* EP appeared in 2001. Since then the band has been on semi-permanent vacation. Everyone's older, some are wiser and one has even branched out into punk-rock fatherhood.

Although they were the champions of a kinder, more considerate hardcore, and less interested than most in screwing the last dollar from the fans, Fugazi were above all a kick-ass outfit, ready to walk it like they talked it and brave enough to give it up and move on when the time was right. All of them need something beyond Fugazi to pay the rent and, although Joe Lally is currently running a website that sells a zillion live recordings of the band in their prime, Fugazi-heads are advised not to hold their breath for new material any time soon.

⊙ 13 Songs & Repeater (Dischord, 1990)

Their earliest and purest recordings, digitally remastered. Although every track has its moments of delight, "Merchandise" stands out for the bitterness of its lyrics, shredding the modern Western way of life, while "Blueprint" and the title track growl and snarl like untamed hungry dogs. Turn it up!

GANG OF FOUR

Called to order Leeds, England, 1977; motion to disband carried 1984; reconvened 2005.

"GANG OF FOUR IS THE FIRST ROCK BAND I COULD TRULY RELATE TO. THESE LIMIES ROCKED MY WORLD."

FLEA (RED HOT CHILI PEPPERS)

Old punks never die: they just fall out with each other, get rich, move overseas and then get back together a few years later to make more money playing comeback concerts. But that's enough about the Sex Pistols: we're discussing the most radical of punk rockers here – Leeds' **Gang Of Four**, a band whose members fell out with each other, found satisfaction in other careers and then got back together for a stunning reunion just for the fun of it.

The lectures for fine art students at Leeds University left plenty of time for old schoolfriends **Jon King** (vocals) and **Andy Gill** (guitar) to sit around drinking gin and writing songs together. Together with **Dave Allen** (bass) and the scene's scariest-looking drummer, **Hugo Burnham**, resplendent in boiler suit and skinhead crop, they coalesced into the Gang Of Four, a band that made some of the country's most outlandish post-punk noise.

And it was, undeniably, the sound they made that first drew attention – the dour, quirky, revolution-ary stance they adopted in their interviews, lyrics and stage act came second. From the solid sheets of feedback that launched "Love Like Anthrax", the standout track on their debut *Damaged Goods* EP, Gang Of Four were impossible to ignore.

Although the music they produced could never be pigeonholed, it was impossible to imagine it existing without the precedent of punk. Defiantly funky in a virtually whites-only zone, the Gang's tunes were punctuated by echoing, warehouse-sized spaces that gave the words time to sink in and allowed drunken adolescents in unwieldy Doc Martens the chance to get into the groove. While Gill's guitar fell back in the mix, humming politely in the background as it awaited its cue to unleash hellish waves of feedback, the drum and bass team created a dark, angular hybrid of edgy punk noise and apocalyptic dub.

"Anthrax" made sufficient impact for the Gang to accept a relatively lucrative major-label deal and feed their new ideas through the latest studio kit. The resulting album, *Entertainment!* (1979), seethed blood-red from its cover and bubbled with resent-ment like a vindictive home-brewed chilli sauce. Gof4's occasionally preachy politics were made a lot easier to digest by their "danceable solution to teen-age revolution" approach (to quote Roxy Music). They rarely overdid the radical banner-waving, real-izing that their audience was already ninety-percent on their side anyway; instead, they illuminated dif-ferent points of view, showed that liberation came in as many forms as repression and played some kick-ass tunes on the way to the barricades.

When "At Home He's A Tourist", an innocuous groover from *Entertainment!*, was released as a single, it headed strongly up the charts. The Gang were invited to appear on the BBC's *Top Of The Pops*, but on condition that a reference to condoms in the song was changed. As Gill told Jason Gross of the *Perfect Sound Forever* webzine (www.furious.com/perfect/gangoffour.html):

> *…their producer said "Look, I'm sorry but you can't use the word 'rubbers'. That's not permissible. You're going to have to go and re-record your backing track."*
>
> *We said "Fuck it, OK." and changed the line so it was "Packets you hide."*
>
> *We thought it was fine. But they told us "No, we want you to use the word 'rubbish' so that it's less obvious that there's been a change, a censorship."*
>
> *I think at that point, we told them to shove it.*

On the grounds that it was hardly an incitement to dope, guns and fucking in the streets, Gof4's principled stand in defence of freedom of expression summoned up memories of dilemmas faced over similarly inoffensive sentiments a decade before by Mick Jagger and Jim Morrison. The band picked up more publicity, sales and street credibility through refusing to knuckle under to the BBC's dictates than they'd ever have received by simply doing their stuff politely like all the other mime artists.

Paying their dues and building up a sizeable record-buying fan base at the same time, the Gang toured UK universities and played the benefits circuit, appearing at countless Rock Against Racism fundraisers. Prompted to have a crack at America, they descended into tour-bus hell, straining long-term friendship to the limit. Two years passed before the guys had assembled an album's worth of material for the follow-up; the heavy touring and pressures of success were delaying their great leap forward.

Despite its shiny cover and optimistic title, *Solid Gold* (1981) was anything but. A couple of standout tracks – "Cheeseburger", an overcooked, greasy slab of life on the road, and "Paralysed", an empty-sounding paranoid return to top form – couldn't disguise the fact that they'd spread themselves too thinly and lost their grip on the punk-funk scene. **Talking Heads**, **Pere Ubu** and **R.E.M.** had cut off their retreat, while back home, **The Pop Group** swiped their audience with their own cunningly danceable mix of radical politics and polyrhythms.

Musical differences surfaced, and in the screaming wake of "To Hell With Poverty" – the Gang Of Four's hung-over hymn to feedback and the good life – Allen quit to form **Shriekback**, another post-punk set of noiseniks exploring the distorted electronics route to heaven, with **Barry Andrews** (ex-XTC). New bassist **Sara Lee** joined in time for *Songs Of The Free* (1982), an album that directly addressed the Anglo–Argentinian war over the Falklands / Malvinas islands.

When Burnham quit at the end of the year, he was replaced, ignominiously, by a drum machine. Although this allowed musos around the world to dig up the joke about how drum machines were better than their human counterparts (because with a machine, you only have to punch the instructions in once – ha!), it was an undignified and short-term remedy for a band such as the Gang Of Four. The three-piece did record an album with the rhythm box, however, and *Hard* (1983) tried to move them into the mainstream. It

🎵 PLAYLIST: GANG OF FOUR

1. **ANTHRAX**
from **Return The Gift** (V2, 2005)

2. **AT HOME HE'S A TOURIST**
from **Return The Gift** (V2, 2005)

3. **DAMAGED GOODS**
from **Return The Gift** (V2, 2005)

4. **ETHER**
from **Return The Gift** (V2, 2005)

5. **HE'D SEND THE ARMY**
from **Return The Gift** (V2, 2005)

6. **I LOVE A MAN IN A UNIFORM**
from **Return The Gift** (V2, 2005)

7. **NATURAL'S NOT IN**
from **Return The Gift** (V2, 2005)

8. **NOT GREAT MEN**
from **Return The Gift** (V2, 2005)

9. **TO HELL WITH POVERTY**
from **Return The Gift** (V2, 2005)

10. **WE LIVE AS WE DREAM, ALONE**
from **Return The Gift** (V2, 2005)

Garage Punk

Garage bands and garage punk mean exactly what you'd expect: a bunch of kids getting it together in the garage to drink, smoke and make an unholy racket. They've been cropping up on both sides of the Atlantic with cheerful regularity for the last forty years or so, and have been responsible for pretty much all the important developments in rock'n'roll since then.

It's a broad church though – a garage band formed in wealthy suburban California is going to sound completely different from a bunch of council-estate kids slamming around next to the old man's toolbox and fold-up workbench on a cold rainy night in Sheffield: for a start, the kids in America are likely to have more room to mess around in than the British kids. Those big, "Pleasant Valley Sunday" bungalow ranch-style places have room to rehearse an orchestra, whereas back in Sheffield, any attempt to strike a rock-hero pose will cover the drummer in loose screws and pour lubricating oil into the bass amp.

Garage rock was initially just a convenient term under which to file the zillions of American one-song groups that crept to the surface with three chords and a fuzz-pedal in the wake of the "British Invasion". While a lot of it comprised innocent cover versions of mainstream pop laments and teen dance-crazes, there was a darker version being brewed up in the less well-furnished garages on the poorer side of town by no-good delinquents with bad attitudes and tattoos, who played guitar but looked more ready to rumble with a bike chain. These guys were garage punks, playing punk rock before it became known as such.

William Burroughs said "I always thought a punk was someone who took it in the ass", and for years, punk was prison slang for any sexually submissive guy. It later grew into a term for a street hustler or juvenile delinquent (hello there, Tom Verlaine and Richard Hell). Although the expression "punk rock" was initially coined by Dave Marsh in Creem magazine (applying it to the magnificent Tex-Mex snot-nose rhythms of **? And The Mysterians**), it was **Lenny Kaye**, rock journalist, guitar man and garage-rock obsessive who brought the term "punk-rock" into mainstream use when he assembled his legendary *Nuggets* collection. Kaye's notion of punk referred back to Frank Zappa's "Flower Punk" character, which itself was a development of the "rotten, worthless, or snotty" dictionary definition, and included such masters of the divinely dumb as **The Flaming Groovies** (whose "Shake Some Action" is still three minutes of shameless pleasure). Lenny went on to play guitar for **Patti Smith**, neatly linking the Sixties originators with the Seventies generation.

Back in the UK, a few glorious months saw more locally grown talent charging up the charts – Them praising "Gloria", The Troggs salivating over their "Wild Thing" and The Animals begging "Don't Let Me Be Misunderstood", for example. When the kids had finally been chased out of the garages by their irate parents, they ended up hiding from the rain in the boozer. Damp, sweaty pub rock was the Seventies' British response to the cool breeze blowing through the garages across the Atlantic. Connected by a shared and almost universal inability to turn exciting live performance into record sales, garage punks on both sides of the ocean did their best to earn thirty minutes of local fame, a couple of free beers and the chance to grapple with star-struck girls who thought they were in love.

Garage rock reappeared in the 1980s under a different label and then went back underground, before popping up as grunge in the 1990s and again, hailed as a return to blues-influenced basics, in the current decade. Bands such as **The White Stripes**, **The Hives**, **Black Rebel Motorcycle Club**, **Billy Childish**, **The Datsuns**, **The Kills**, **The Libertines** and **The Von Bondies** all got their kicks on petrol fumes before hitting the big-time stages.

PLAYLIST

Most of the original and best of the Sixties US garage bands are collected on Lenny Kaye's aforementioned *Nuggets*. The original double vinyl has been expanded into a 4-CD set with a big booklet full of facts and pictures of stupid bands looking goofy. Here are some of the best tracks.

1. YOU'RE GONNA MISS ME
13th Floor Elevators

2. LET'S TALK ABOUT GIRLS
The Chocolate Watch Band

3. PSYCHOTIC REACTION
The Count 5

4. I HAD TOO MUCH TO DREAM (LAST NIGHT)
Electric Prunes

5. HEY JOE
The Leaves

6. TALK TALK
The Music Machine

7. FARMER JOHN
The Premiers

8. OH YEAH
Shadows Of Knight

9. DIRTY WATER
The Standells

10. INCENSE AND PEPPERMINTS
Strawberry Alarm Clock

did not succeed, and the band broke up, leaving a live album, *At The Palace* (1984), in their wake.

For the next six years, the Gang lay low. In 1990, however, an album of essential Peel sessions, recorded in the band's glory days, and *A Brief History Of The Twentieth Century* (a serviceable compilation of cuts from their entire career) stirred up enough interest for Gill to strap on his axe and call King. Recruiting some new Gang members, they recorded *Mall*, but the album sold badly and the project failed.

The 1995 reissue of *Entertainment!* gave Gill and King sufficient excuse to get together again under the Gof4 name and record *Shrinkwrapped*, but again, the reunion proved premature and it died on the shelves.

In 1996 Andy hooked up with doomed INXS vocalist **Michael Hutchence**, co-writing and producing his solo album and finishing it off after the singer's death. Sara went on to be much in demand as a session player, performing low-register miracles for, among others, the B-52s. The band's name was kept alive by another retrospective, *100 Flowers Bloom* (1998), a 2-CD collection of hits and bits. Then, in 2004, came the shock announcement of a reunion and mini-tour featuring all four members of the original line-up. Their warm-up recording, "To Hell With Poverty 2005", demonstrated their still awesome familiarity with a killer guitar line and a dance beat.

Cited by **Franz Ferdinand**, **Futureheads** (with whom Gill has been working on production) and others as seminal, influential and so forth, Gang Of Four have seen their minimalist, stripped-down sound come back into vogue. While their return put a little iron into the soul of their now middle-aged fan-base, however, any hopes of a permanent reunion were immediately dismissed. Even before the tour started, the band members – who all have new careers – made it clear that this was to be the last time. As Burnham put it: "We have a strong creative legacy, and the last thing we wanted to do is go out and fuck that up by doing a half-hearted job."

⦿ Entertainment! (EMI/Warner, 1995)

Never bettered in a career now stretching into its third decade, Entertainment! still shows all the spit, fizz and buzz of high-powered electrics, sexual politics and dour thought-crime. Perverse, reedy melodica blasts sneak in between the shards of feedback, providing an aural parallel to the subversive Situationist-style imagery of cowboy meets Indian on the cover. Boasts rerecordings of "Anthrax" and "Damaged Goods", the latter with a guitar riff whose edgy angularity and attack reflects the band's growing confidence.

GENERATION X

**Lost boys in London, 1976;
lost the plot by 1981.**

D espite a shameful reputation as the band that launched **Billy Idol** and his series of soft-porn S&M videos in the 1980s, now that all the mudslinging has long since finished, it's fair to say that **Generation X** were a pretty good punk band with some cracking little tunes. Recognized from the start as a triumph of style over substance, the band took its cool name from a seminal pop-sociology study of disaffected youth in Sixties Britain by Jane Deverson and Charles Hamblett (the Douglas Coupland novel came much later). A unique marketing campaign swung into action, making Idol an international star and the band among the most successful of the original

▣ PLAYLIST: GENERATION X

1. ANDY WARHOL
from Kiss Me Deadly (EMI, 2005)

2. DANCING WITH MYSELF
from Kiss Me Deadly (EMI, 2005)

3. FRIDAY'S ANGELS
from Valley Of The Dolls (EMI Gold, 2002)

4. KING ROCKER
from Valley Of The Dolls (EMI Gold, 2002)

5. KISS ME DEADLY
from Kiss Me Deadly (EMI, 2005)

6. READY STEADY GO
from Perfect Hits (Chrysalis, 2003)

7. STARS LOOK DOWN
from Kiss Me Deadly (EMI, 2005)

8. VALLEY OF THE DOLLS
from Valley Of The Dolls (EMI Gold, 2002)

9. WILD YOUTH
from Kiss Me Deadly (EMI, 2005)

10. YOUR GENERATION
from Kiss Me Deadly (EMI, 2005)

ICONIC SINGLE:
YOUR GENERATION / DAY BY DAY
(CHRYSALIS, 1977)

"'YOUR GENERATION' IS ABOUT FORGETTING THE PREVIOUS GENERATION."
BILLY IDOL.

Every new youth trend has to spend some time dancing on the graves of its ancestors. Pete Townsend wrote "My Generation" to exorcise the morality of those who'd grown up in World War II. The attack in Generation X's first and best single, "Your Generation" is as deliciously unfocused as The Who's was, and provided you're of a certain age with hormones working overtime, just as perfectly relevant to your everyday existence.

It's a storm of heartbeat-accelerating drums, a flash of sheet-lightning guitars with Idol screaming his heart and soul out like he's been snatched up andcarried away by the teeth of a gale. It is, in short, a rush.

"Day By Day" is one of Gen X's few genuine slice-of-life, jot-down-some-words-and-get-it-on-tape punk-rock tunes – a full-strength stripped-down hog of a tune that condemns petty suburban jealousies and menial production-line jobs, a pretty but meaningless juxtaposition which doesn't detract in the least from the song's enduring appeal.

Idol's stab at The Who's old theme is as guitar-driven wild and willful as Townsend's was, but he'll still be able to sing it when he's a pensioner without the lyrics painting him foolish from top to toe. Bellowing "Day By Day", he never sounded meaner or more intense. Both tracks are on the *Perfect Hits* compilation, which is, of course, in your collection already.

London punk rockers, in chart terms at least.

Generation X burst onto the mainstream scene after an incubation in the punk-rock underground that had lasted just a few short weeks. Far too good-looking to seem anything but a music-biz put-up job, Billy and the boys were mistakenly perceived as just another professionally assembled boy band, chosen for their chiselled cheekbones and moody sneers, and no doubt miming all the way to the bank.

It wasn't exactly that cynical an operation however. **William Broad** had a genuine claim to have been on the scene from the very beginning, having transformed himself into Billy Idol as part of the **Bromley Contingent**, the gang of suburban kids that hung around the Sex Pistols (and who were so succinctly destroyed in the lyrics of "Satellite"). The rest of the band initially comprised **Tony James** and **John Towe** (the drum and bass respectively of ultra-credible fellow punks **Chelsea**) plus **Bob Andrews** (guitar). They had a set together and were on stage at London's Roxy club just in time for the end of 1976: very hip, very street.

It didn't take the very small London scene to realize that Billy was an archetypal poseur whose tougher-than-thou lyrics were based more on stories swiped from the sensational Sunday papers than on any hard time spent living on his wits. Where Billy came from, the "mean streets" were broad avenues only slightly less leafy than the main drive of a country house hotel, and his ragged tales of wild fights involving a hundred punks were seen to have come straight out of his fevered imagination – or his rear end, depending on opinion.

This lack of credibility made them pariahs among the elite, and so the band went pop. They cleaned up their act, learned to play a little more competently, discarded anything that might distress the parents whose money would ultimately pay for their singles, and started to cash in. "Your Generation" gave them their first taste of the good life, charting in mid-1977. A swift change of drummers saw ex-**Subway Sect** man **Mark Laff** join the team, taking them into a period of teeny-punk pop stardom that ran from their debut album *Generation X* (1978), through a brace of chart-troubling singles "Ready Steady Go" and "King Rocker", and then on into *Valley Of The Dolls* (1979).

A year later, they'd lost a few syllables (now recording as Gen X), some hair and their slim boyish beauty. After a powerfully rocking, yet chirpily obvious ode to self-abuse ("Dancing With Myself"), Laff split, to be replaced by **Terry Chimes** (already ex-**Clash** and a drummer for hire). Andrews jumped ship at the same time, making room for **James Stevenson**, another Chelsea alumnus, but when Kiss Me Deadly (1981) disappeared from the stores almost before it had been released, Gen X admitted defeat.

Idol had bigger fish to fry on the US scene and a date in his diary with a new television channel to be called MTV; Chimes returned to The Clash and James went on to be part of Sigue Sigue Sputnik.

⊙ **Perfect Hits 1975-1981 (Chrysalis, 1999)**

All the top pop punkery you'll ever need. Even after all this time, it's still a great record to play if you plan to party. Fidteen classic cuts, including "Your Generation" and "Dancing With Myself".

GERMS

Briefly infectious in Los Angeles, 1980.

"I CAME INTO THIS WORLD LIKE A PUZZLED PANTHER, WAITING TO BE CAGED"

"MANIMAL", LYRICS BY DARBY CRASH

It was inevitable that Los Angeles, the world capital of excess and self destruction, would spew up a band like the **Germs** sooner or later. In **Darby Crash** (front man extraordinaire), the city of angels finally brought to life a creature so obviously doomed that it's a wonder the band ever made it out of the emergency ward, much less into the rehearsal rooms and recording studio. Darby, previously answering to Bobby Pyn, and before that to Paul Beahm, had a hotline to full-strength chest-baring madness on stage that pulled ever more extreme performances from the rest of band, ultimately making them the hottest act on Sunset Strip. Though **Belinda Carlisle** (later to be a Go-Go) started off as the band's drummer, the line-up that made all the best music consisted of Crash, **Pat Smear** (guitar), **Lorna Doom** (bass)

and **Don Bolles** (drums). Smear did most of the on-stage posturing, while Darby did his stage-diving, self-mutilation routine, an act combining the worst of Iggy Pop's stunts with all the dreadful folderol of performance art. Despite the unnervingly simple rock'n'roll songs they attempted, the band would sometimes drift off-message and gigs would descend into an unpleasant mess of bodily fluids and spilt beer.

If it weren't for Joan Jett – a long-time fan – there'd be no Germs studio material to back up their legend. Although they have a cameo in *The Decline Of Western Civilisation* (1981), Penny Spheeris's perceptive documentary on the LA scene, hardly any live recordings survive (a shame, but having read the above, would you have wanted to risk your own precious tape recorder trying to bootleg a drug-fuelled riot?). Fortunately, Jett corralled them simultaneously into one place long enough to record *GI*. The album showed lots of good-quality badly behaved LA promise and more snarl than the competition could summon up, with Smear desperately attempting to ape Crash's every yelp, while Doom and Bolles did pretty much their own thing in the background.

As is so often the case with bands based in LA, the drugs then got in the way of the music, and buzzing with a head full of gear and a pocket full of dollars, Crash headed for England. Apparently mislaying his memory on the way back, he set up as a solo performer in 1980 before informing the rest of the Germs that the party was over. By the time they realized what was going on, he'd hit his veins one time too many (on the tenth anniversary of John Lennon's assassination – another of those rock'n'roll coincidences that mean so little), and ended up dead.

Smear, of course, went on to the big time when he showed up first in Nirvana and subsequently as a Foo Fighter.

⊙ **MIA Complete Discography (Rhino, 2000)**

Each of the thirty tracks here is a classic of early raw hardcore punk. The collection kicks off with both sides of the Germs' first single ("Forming" and "Sex Boy") and delivers all the raw sound of tomorrow that you could ask for.

⊙ **Media Blitz (Cleopatra, 1993)**

Stick this little CD in your machine and you'll discover some strangely compelling and untamed live performances by Darby Crash – LA's answer to Sid Vicious – and the band.

VIC GODARD / SUBWAY SECT

Congregated Mortlake, England, 1976-81;
underground since then,
but still seen sporadically.

Despite appearing on the same 100 Club punk festival bill as the Pistols, The Clash and those poor Suburban Studs (see p.27), **Vic Godard** was never a punk rocker. He had all the credentials of poverty, boredom and dissatisfaction with the world, but unlike most of the speed-freak maniacs with whom he found himself associated, Vic had class and soulboy style. More lounge lizard than bombed-out anarchist, he shared a decadent, deadpan delivery with Peter Perrett of The Only Ones and sang stories of a life detached from the world and debauched beyond care, on nodding acquaintance with the New Wave nutters, but keeping them, as much as possible, at arm's length.

Still, it was at a punk gig that he was "discovered': Godard was one of the Pistols' earliest followers, part of a loose-knit collective of up-all-nighters drawn initially to Bowie and Kraftwerk and then, through audience osmosis, into the first days of punk. **Malcolm McLaren** had seen him on the edge of the crowd on numerous occasions and invited him to form a band and appear on the bill at his punk festival. He passed their management onto the overwhelmed **Bernie Rhodes**, who had his hands full already trying to establish The Clash, and sent Godard off to find a band and whip them into shape.

The **Subway Sect** that resulted comprised Godard (vocals), **Rob Symmons** (guitar), **Paul Myers** (bass) and **Paul Packham** (drums), who performed a laconic set in glorious monochrome grey – no histrionics, no stage set, no bad attitude. Surrounded by a fluorescent whirlpool of art students, poseurs and the like, they were doomed to have limited appeal and a devoted if sparse audience.

Fitted uncomfortably onto the bill for The Clash's 1977 White Riot tour, however, the Sect took their shtick onto the road. Nobody in the band could play at the outset, but this little concession to the prevailing ethos aside, none of them was particularly interested in punk's standard issue sped-up rock'n'roll noise. Instead, and again like The Only Ones, they let the lyrics do the talking and kept the amplified instruments in the background, from where they contributed a thoughtful, more mature music than their contemporaries could even dream of. Their unique style was based as much on Motown bands as the MC5 or Stooges, and looked back to a far wider range of influences than most of the bandwagon crew would dare confess to.

The band's earliest compositions showed them to be of the New Wave, however, with "Out Of Touch" in particular pointing towards the kind of sparse, echoing, twangy, twitchy music that XTC and The Cure would develop independently and shortly after.

There was no urgent hurry to get the guys into the studio – in fact, by the time they recorded "Nobody's Scared"/"Don't Splitit" there'd been personnel changes – new guitar player **Rob Miller** and new drummer **Bob Ward** were on board already, and before setting off to record the full-length debut, Bernie Rhodes dismissed all the old guard, going out to find **John Britain** (guitar), **Colin Scott** (bass) and **Steve Atkinson** (keyboards) to fill out the sound for "Ambition" / "Different Story". Despite "Ambition" topping the indie charts and selling twenty thousand copies, the album was finally completed with the aid of session musicians and put on hold until a suitable label could be found. It eventually sneaked out as *What's The Matter Boy* in 1980.

With little to do but wait for success to come knocking, the band began to rot. Unwilling to join in the unseemly scramble for the spotlight, the newly renamed **Vic Godard And The Subway Sect** grew a fashionable but counter productive reputation for not caring about their career. It meant their audience had to make do with the occasional single release and the odd tour of the country's less salubrious venues whenever Godard could be bothered to scratch together a band. He pressed on until 1981 before giving up the idea of a full-time job as a musician, returning to work for the Post Office. The detritus of the band went on to flourish briefly as **JoBoxers**

Since then, Godard's output has become ever more interesting, presenting his devotees with a series of challenges, starting with Cole Porter-esque sets of lounge pop a good decade before it became fashionable, then recording a disappointing jazz album, *T.R.O.U.B.L.E* (released in 1986, two years after it was made). He stayed off the scene completely for a few years before hooking up with **Edwyn Collins**, who produced *End Of The Surrey People* for him in 1993. His most inspired period recently was spent with **The Long Decline** – a joint project with **Mark Perry** of ATV, which released an album of the same name in 1996.

⊙ Vic Godard And Subway Sect: Singles Anthology (Motion, 2005)

All you want from the man with the bag of letters.

⊙ What's The Matter Boy? (Decca, 2000)

Despite the obvious overlaps with the essential singles collection above, and the fact it was polished up professionally, this does at least capture Vic and his mates in the early days.

GREEN DAY

Dawned Berkeley, California, 1989; their sun has yet to set.

F uture generations will continue to argue whether an act can sell ten million albums and still make any claim to being a punk-rock turn. In the absence of any decision, **Green Day** choose to ignore the entire issue and get on with making good-time pop-tinted punk for kids to get off to.

Billie Joe Armstrong (guitar, vocals) got his first axe, a blue Stratocaster that he still uses, at the age of 11. It gave him some much needed cool when local scallywag and older kid **Mike Dirnt** (born Pritchard) rented a room at the Armstrongs' place, and the two guys were soon thrashing out collaborative tunes about growing up in the suburbs and the usual adolescent anxieties. Picking Green Day as a band name (after spending a day puffing on green weed and giggling like fools) and recruiting **Al Sobrante** (drums, previously known as John Kiffmeyer), they started hassling local venues for the chance to play.

Meanwhile, up in the Mendocino Mountains, 12-year-old Frank Edwin Wright III decided that he'd rather answer to the stage name **Tre Cool**. Teaming up with his pal Lawrence Livermore, he formed The Lookouts. Livermore put up some dough, formed Lookout Records and began releasing his new band's material to back up the gigs they landed.

It wasn't long before Green Day met The Lookouts at 924 Gilman Street, hub of the Bay Area scene in industrial back street Berkeley, and Armstrong hassled to be auditioned for a deal with Lookout. Legend has it that Livermore took pity on them for being dumb enough to arrange to play an audition for him in a house with no electricity and that, after loaning them a generator, he signed them on the spot. Whatever the truth, Green Day released both their debut EP, *1000 Hours*, and first album *39/Smooth* on Lookout.

Sobrante left the band shortly after the album appeared, Tre Cool stepped in and the perfect pop-punk line-up was complete. Green Day's sound was born at that moment in 1990, and fifteen years further on, it hasn't changed one bit. Sales weren't fantastic, but they grew steadily, with the band playing every tiny club on the West Coast and taking two years to build up a fan-base before recording their second album, *Kerplunk*.

Realizing that their next step would need the facilities offered by a major label, Green Day left Lookout and signed with Reprise in 1993. Having spent all of five days recording their second album, the guys took an extravagant five weeks to get *Dookie* exactly right. Delivering a 14-song set in just 39 minutes, it was a West Coast sun'n' fun-packed response to the first Ramones album. It sold a million in just a few weeks (current sales exceed ten million) and made the band a worldwide name through heavy rotation on MTV for "Welcome to Paradise" and "Longview".

As the Nineties rolled on, Green Day seemed unstoppable. Alternating small scale club gigs with arena appearances and festival sets – the band vs. crowd mud-fight at Woodstock in 1994 is one for the history books – and with Billie Joe dropping his trousers on stage with disturbing regularity, the best-loved brats in the universe looked set to carry on the bad behaviour indefinitely.

Although it ultimately sold in the millions, *Insomniac* was not as instantly appealing as *Dookie*, possibly because the guys were exhausted after years on the road and were in the process of starting families. *Nimrod* didn't appear till 1997, but sold by the bucketload to an audience that had been waiting for another chance to show their devotion with dollars.

When *Warning* appeared in 2000 however, it aroused fears that the guys were growing up. They had never experimented with the deeper end of philosophical musings and their usual style of music didn't lend itself to simply providing a background for introspection. Self-analysis apparently led to some degree of self-loathing, and although they tweaked their familiar sound to provide a more fitting accompaniment to this heavier set of subjects, they headed dangerously close to folk-rock at times, scaring the bejaysus out of their spikyheaded fans.

A 2001 compilation – *International Superhits* – concentrated on the early stuff, cleansing the palate and short-term memory of the band's later studio noodlings. With their most recent offering, *American Idiot* (2004), yielding up a bouncy single in the title track, a return to navel-gazing lyrical ineptitude with "Boulevard Of Broken Dreams", and a jaunty if bitter-sounding "Holiday", it remains to be seen whether Green Day will ever go back to mining the seam of punk-rock gold they uncovered at the start of their career.

Dookie (Reprise, 1994)

The album that made them international stars. Full of tongue-in-cheek hilarity, high-speed thrashing and adolescent angst.

International Superhits (Reprise, 2001)

Excellent and good-value compilation. An essential if your car doesn't have a multi-changer CD player or you can't afford all the original albums.

American Idiot (Reprise, 2004)

The latest from the boys at time of writing, this demonstrates the enduring appeal of a buzzsaw guitar, a chorus you can sing along to and a hip-looking sneer. Not the most punk-rock album in history, but worthwhile.

PLAYLIST: GREEN DAY

1. **BASKET CASE** from **International Superhits (Reprise, 2004)**
2. **LONGVIEW** from **International Superhits (Reprise, 2004)**
3. **MINORITY** from **International Superhits (Reprise, 2004)**
4. **GOOD RIDDANCE (TIME OF YOUR LIFE)** from **International Superhits (Reprise, 2004)**
5. **BRAIN STEW** from **International Superhits (Reprise, 2004)**
6. **REDUNDANT** from **International Superhits (Reprise, 2004)**
7. **HOMECOMING** from **American Idiot (Reprise, 2004)**
8. **BOULEVARD OF BROKEN DREAMS** from **American Idiot (Reprise, 2004)**
9. **WAKE ME UP WHEN SEPTEMBER ENDS** from **American Idiot (Reprise, 2004)**
10. **HOLIDAY** from **American Idiot (Reprise, 2004)**

HALF MAN HALF BISCUIT

Half-formed in Birkenhead, England around 1980-82; half-serious ever since.

Hanging out, wasting time and having fun way over there on the distant edge of punk, you can spot **Half Man Half Biscuit**. A band of cult status and savage whimsy, much beloved of St John Peel, and holding cheerily on to the punk-rock tenets of making the most out of basic instrumental skills and having a laugh while you do so. These days their appearances are fewer and further between than their fans would like, but with almost a quarter-century of goodwill to draw on, they raise the roof above any stage they choose to shamble onto.

It was Peelie, in fact, who inspired Birkenhead's **Nigel Blackwell** (guitar/vocals) to form a group as an alternative to his otherwise tearaway lifestyle. After a couple of false starts, he stole **Neil Crossley**, the rhythm guitar player from ace local punk rock band Venom, and got him to play bass. The pair obviously weren't going to get very far as a duo, so Nigel's brother **Simon Blackwell** (guitar) and **Paul Wright** (drums) – both from another local band, Attempted Moustache – got in on the act. With **David Lloyd** (keyboards) as a last-minute addition, Nigel herded them all into Vulcan Studios (where he worked as a caretaker) to rehearse for free and record £40 worth of amateurish messing about that pointed out the absurdities of everyday life and poked fun at the cultish micro-celebrities of British TV.

Slightly expanded and pressed onto vinyl, these sessions became *Back In The D.H.S.S.* (1985). Thanks almost exclusively to the consistent support of John Peel, it went on to become the big-

gest-selling indie album of 1986. The title of their follow-up – *The Trumpton Riots* EP (1986) – was enough to make it a must-hear for anyone who'd ever wasted time and brain cells on the anodyne animated kids' TV programme set in the fictional town of the same name.

Clever puns and unforgettable titles have been a feature of the band's output since the days of "All I Want For Christmas Is A Dukla Prague Away Kit" and "Architecture And Morality, Ted And Alice". Parochial selections such as "Dickie Davies' Eyes", however, meant they would never be much of an attraction on the international tour circuit, and the lads went off to find better things to do with their time in 1987. *Back Again In The D.H.S.S* (1987) kept the interest alive for a few years until, in 1990, they changed their collective minds and re-formed, albeit as a part-time project – two gigs a month and an album every couple of years.

The first of these, *Mcintyre, Treadmore And Davitt* (1990) was, to be fair, a more polished product than previous HMHB albums. It might have been too smooth for Lloyd and Wright, who had slipped off before *This Leaden Pall* appeared in 1993. **Carl Alty** took over drums, and when Simon Blackwell left in 1994, Crossley moved onto guitar, making room for **Ian Jackson** (bass). During all this personnel chaos, the band somehow kept its sense of humour and eye on the funny side of life, even managing to record and release *Some Call It Godcore* in 1995.

By the time the *Eno Collaboration* EP appeared in 1996 – Eno, naturally, was notable by his absence – Alty had been replaced by **Carl Henry**. Jackson had moved on too, so Crossley returned to the back row, where he continued to be a useful bass player. **Ken Hancock** came off the substitutes' bench, exchanged a high five with Neil and

Comedy Punk

Not only was there a great deal of self-referential, self-deprecating humour in the early days of punk rock – with The Ramones, The Dead Boys, Adam & The Ants, X-Ray Spex and the Sex Pistols being the highest-profile acts involved – the sheer exuberance of the movement's stereotypical snarling rock'n'roll made it an obvious target for parody.

Some of this – particularly the keenly observed spoofing of Alberto Y Lost Trios Paranoias – managed to poke fun while maintaining a degree of dignity, and a few tracks even sounded like they meant it, maaaaan. Most, however, descended to one-joke acts like Australia's Johnny Vomit & The Leather Scabs. The UK – with its long tradition of comic song and music-hall parody – yielded up some of the more enduring jokes, with **Jilted John**'s single of the same name going to the top of the charts.

Jilted John was the alter ego of comic **Graham Fellows**, and his whine of misery, backed up by a badly tuned acoustic guitar apparently recorded in his bedroom, was picked up by school jesters and office fools in companies the length of the country. Thanks to Tony Parsons and the "Gordon Is A Moron" chorus, the tune became Single Of The Week in NME, and Fellows' droopy face and equally droopy hair appeared on the cover of both *Oh Boy* and *My Guy* magazines. Gordon and Julie, the girl who jilted

John, recorded "Gordon's Not A Moron" in reply, but the joke had worn off and it didn't sell.

UK punk's best joke came through Crass – see p.108 for the full story of their "Wedding Bells" single – a band not overly famous for its sense of humour (though they had their moments). **John Cooper Clarke**'s entire career was based around making gangs of punk rockers laugh hard enough to spray cider out of their noses while Splodgenessabounds (comprising **Max Splodge** and as many friends as could be crammed on stage) had a chart hit with "Two Pints Of Lager And A Packet Of Crisps", although some of their best jokes had to be seen live to be believed.

Honourable mention must also go to Britain's Peter And The Test Tube Babies, Toy Dolls, Tenpole Tudor, Half Man Half Biscuit, Ian Dury And The Blockheads, Captain Sensible, Ivor Biggun And The Red Nosed Burglars, and Attila The Stockbroker, while the USA contributed Devo, The Dickies, Wayne/Jayne County, The Meatmen, GG Allin (hilarious provided you were nowhere near the guy), GWAR, The Tubes, NOFX, The Dead Milkmen, occasional Dead Boys numbers and a bunch of frat-rock acts hastily re-clad in spiky haircuts and leather jackets, none of which need trouble us here.

Germany's **Die Totenhosen** may well be hilarious, but only a German punk would know for sure.

🎵 PLAYLIST: COMEDY PUNK

1. JILTED JOHN Jilted John
from **True Love Stories (Castle, 2005)**

2. KILL Alberto Y Lost Trios Paranoias from **Snuff Rock: The Best Of The Albertos (Mau Mau, 1997)**

3. MICHAEL BOOTH'S TALKING BUM
Splodgeness... from **Splod... (Captain Oi!, 2001)**

4. STUDENT WANKERS Peter & The Test Tube Babies
from **Loud Blaring Punk Rock (Dr Strange, 1997)**

5. EVIDENTLY CHICKEN TOWN John Cooper Clarke
from **Snap Crackle and Bop (Sony, 2005)**

6. SPACE JUNK Devo from **Q: Are We Not Men? a: We Are Devo!/Devo Live (Virgin, 2003)**

7. IF YOU DON'T WANNA FUCK ME, FUCK OFF
Wayne County & The Electric Chairs
from **Cleopatra (RPM, 2004)**

8. BEAT ON THE BRAT The Ramones
from **The Ramones (Rhino, 2001)**

9. ALL THIS AND MORE The Dead Boys
from **Young Loud & Snotty (Bomp! 1998)**

10. REASONS TO BE CHEERFUL (PART 3)
Ian Dury & The Blockheads
from **The Best of Ian Dury & the Blockheads (Rhino, 2002)**

took over as lead guitar in time for *Voyage To The Bottom Of The Road* (1997), *Four Lads Who Shook The Wirral* (1998), the brilliantly titled *Trouble Over Bridgewater* (2000), *Cammell Laird Social Club* (2002) and, most recently, the epic *Saucy Haulage Ballads* EP (2003), yet another sandwich of cheese on wry.

⊙ Back In The D.H.S.S. / The Trumpton Riots EP (Probe Plus, 1994)

Back to the roots of this seminal, funny and enduring band. If you like this, you'll love the rest; if you don't, then you won't.

⊙ ACD (Probe Plus, 1994)

Expanded still further with a bunch of live tracks, this is the CD issue of the *Back Again In The D.H.S.S.* album.

⊙ **Trouble Over Bridgewater (Probe Plus, 2000)**

With a tracklisting of such syllable-clattering beauty that one suspects the involvement of Mark E Smith, this is HMHB at their punky, puckish best.

HANOI ROCKS

Rocked the world from London to Tokyo via Helsinki, 1980-85.

"BORN TO BE SUPERSTARS, THERE IS NO DOUBT THAT HANOI ROCKS WILL ONE DAY BE AS FAMOUS AS COCA-COLA AND BIG MACS."

SOUNDS, 1982

If you only invest in one Finnish glam/punk band as a result of looking through these pages, then let it be the divinely decadent **Hanoi Rocks**. Self-consciously trashy but in a good way, Hanoi Rocks kept one eye on the mirror while copping all their moves from The New York Dolls, lifting riffs from the Stooges and greasepaint outrage from Alice Cooper.

Andy McCoy (guitar/vocals) and **Nasty Suicide** (guitar/vocals) had been together in a band called **Briard** during their days at school together, releasing a few punk singles – of which "I Really Hate Ya" and "Fuck The Army" stand out – in the years 1976–79. **Michael Monroe** (vocals/keyboards/saxophone/ harmonica) was a well-known face on the Helsinki music scene; according to McCoy, "his hair almost covered his whole arse and even in winter he wore T-shirts." Prising him away from the half-dozen or so other Helsinki bands that had claims on his time, Suicide put together the first Hanoi Rocks line-up in 1980, with Monroe, **Stefan Piesnack**, **Peki Sirola** and **Nedi**. McCoy joined up soon after, bringing **Sam Yaffa** (bass) along with him, and in a flurry of personnel changes, shifting musical directions and career emphasis, Hanoi Rocks (version 2.0, comprising McCoy, Monroe, Suicide and Yaffa), moved their base to the bright lights and big city of Stockholm, where they encountered **Gyp Casino** (drums) and several months of abject poverty.

Things began to improve for the band when a couple of the guys managed to find jobs and/or girlfriends. With regular food coming in, and an apartment that was, if not luxurious, then at least warmer

The ozone-depleting hairstyles of Finland's fantastic Hanoi Rocks.

than sleeping in shop doorways, the band gradually thawed out enough to start wearing lurex and makeup again, rehearsed to keep warm, and finally landed a few gigs around town. A tour of Finland (where they became near instant superstars on the strength of their clothes sense) led to their first single "I Want You" b/w "Kill City Kills". Together, these financed their debut album *Bangkok Shocks Saigon Shakes Hanoi Rocks*, recorded in Stockholm and released in March 1981.

The next logical step was to conquer the UK. A tour was arranged, mismatching what appeared to be a bedraggled gang of drugged-up Scandinavian peacocks with ultra-dour Wishbone Ash – a British rock band with a fan-base not celebrated for its broadmindedness when it came to different styles of music. To those music journalists dispatched as punishment to cover Wishbone Ash on the road, however, Hanoi Rocks were a blessing from the demons below and the guys picked up a lot of favourable press.

Oriental Beat (1982) was recorded in London and was their first truly international success. Audience reaction during the band's first headline UK tour was so extreme that although **Nicholas "Razzle" Dingley**'s wide-eyed declaration (after a gig at London's Marquee club) that he was ready to break Casino's arms if it meant he would be able to replace him in the band was perhaps a little excessive in its enthusiasm, it gave the group a chance to swap drummers. Casino went on to form **Road Rats**, and played many times on the same bill as Hanoi Rocks back in Finland.

At this glum stage of the early 1980s there was no place for such a bunch of preening poseurs in the regimented world of post-punk, and Hanoi Rocks was claimed by the Metal crowd, feted in *Kerrang!*, living in London's unglamorous Tooting and still occasionally going without food. A spandex-clad glam punk rocker has to look elegantly wasted, sure, but preferably without drooling and bending double with hunger every time he passes a burger joint.

Thankfully, a Far Eastern deal with Phonogram took the guys to a world of Technicolor larger-than-lifeness, where audiences expected their stars to look like wasted space aliens and potentially lethal cocktails of local drugs were readily available. Seven-hour sets in front of concert audiences of unprecedented hugeness in India led on to crowd reaction of unmitigated craziness in Tokyo,

but little in the way of album sales. European interest was drying up too, in the wake of the shoddy *Self-Destruction Blues* LP, their 1983 collection of B-sides and alternate versions.

Heading home with their tails held somewhat low, Hanoi Rocks recorded *Back To Mystery City* (1984), an album that, despite the glittering touches added by Mott The Hoople's **Dale Griffin** and **Overend Watts**, made it to the shops only in the Scandinavian heartland.

In a move typical of the Rocks' belief that "more has to mean better", another ex-Mott, Ian Hunter, was roped in for the follow-up, *Two Steps From The Move* (1984). Realizing perhaps that if any more British rockers were allowed in to assist they might well launch a takeover bid, and in another stab at the success they were convinced they deserved, Hanoi Rocks cashed in on their latest album's moderate worldwide appeal, and headed for the USA, Los Angeles and that good ol' rock'n'roll hedonism.

Sometime during the fourth day of Mötley Crüe's party to celebrate the release of their third album, Dingley accepted a lift from Crüe's Vince Neil. Two hundred yards down the road, he was killed when Neil ploughed his 1972 Ford Pantera into an oncoming car. Neil was later convicted of manslaughter. Hanoi Rocks' next release was *All Those Wasted Years* (1985), a very acceptable live set recorded at London's Marquee club that served as well as any spoken tribute to Dingley's life and work.

The publicity surrounding Dingley's death did nothing but good for the band's sales and popularity. Their version of the old Creedence Clearwater Revival song "Up Around The Bend" took their wasted, sleazy rock to an MTV audience, but without the madcap loon drumming behind them, the rest of the band lost heart. This was meant to be a rock'n'roll party; nobody was supposed to die. Terry Chimes (ex-Clash) took over the kit for the band's next performances – televised across Europe from Helsinki – and, liking the vibe, stayed with them.

Yaffa, on the other hand, had decided to leave by this point. His replacement, René Berg, made an inauspicious start. According, again, to McCoy's autobiography, "René couldn't get his guitar case open and asked me to help him. I managed to open it and lots of pills were flowing out: red, yellow, black and blue pills, pills in all colours and in all shapes. I thought, oh shit, we've got another junkie in the band." Whatever the true nature of Berg's chemical recreations, his life with the band was nasty, brutish and short. Taking an instant dislike to his domineering ways, the rest of the Rocks dressed him in black, stuck him on a short lead to keep him in the shadows by his amplifier and did their best to pretend he wasn't even there, failing even to announce him to the crowd.

After the *Rock'n'roll Divorce* album, taped at Hanoi Rocks' last live performance and described in between songs by Monroe as "boring, fucking boring", the band finally dissolved. In the aftermath, Chimes, McCoy and Suicide formed the short-lived **Cherry Bombz**, Yaffa joined **Jetboy**, and Michael recorded a solo album *Not Fakin' It* (1989)). There was almost a reunion in 1994 when Monroe, Suicide and Yaffa appeared as **Demolition 23**. Joined by guitarist **Costello Hautamäki**, **Lacu** and **Timpa**, McCoy and Monroe took the name Hanoi Rocks on tour again in 2002 and recorded *Twelve Shots On The Rocks*, but neither tour nor album created much interest.

⊙ **Up And Around The Bend – The Definitive Collection (Sanctuary, 2004)**

Making the 4-CD box set released in 2001 rather redundant musically – although a box set is of course a joy in its own right – this gives you a cool forty tracks of rock'n'roll sleaze at its purest and most addictive.

HAPPY FLOWERS

Planted Charlottesville, Virginia 1983; hardy perennial.

When **Charlie Kramer** (guitar) met **John Beers** (vocals), it was only natural that they'd go on to form a band together. After all, their alter egos – **Mr. Anus** and **Mr. Horribly-Charred Infant** – had been together as part of The Landlords (champions of Virginia's hardcore scene) for a month already, and it was a meeting of similarly disturbed minds.

Happy Flowers gave these two degenerates the chance to give vent to the kind of soul-searing, wailing music that seethed away inside them. They spent six months rehearsing their brutal shards of sound wrought from the living flesh of tormented instruments, played as a background to vocals that were evidently extracted from tortured children using hot, sharp implements before coming out

with the *Songs For Children* and the equally terrifying *Now We Are Six* EPs.

Happy Flowers honed their material on stage, jumping in whenever one of the acts booked to play Muldowney's, Charlottesville's premier lesbian bar, failed to show up – even though Mr. Anus would often have to be dragged through the crowd to the stage, screaming "I don't want to play! We're the worst band in the world!", John Peel's musical radar picked up their signal, and after a tour of Europe taking in half a dozen countries (and setting back transatlantic relations by a decade), they were invited to record a session for his show, later released on Homestead Records, the label still responsible for disseminating their dangerous music.

More psychotherapeutic exercise than a band, Happy Flowers went on to frighten the daylights out of all who heard them with *My Skin Covers My Body* (1987), *I Crush Bozo* (1988), and *Oof* (1989), caring little for the conventions of songwriting and even less about how their audiences would be able to sleep after hearing them. Hometown gigs – and there were many – were occasionally boosted by the appearance of Mr. Surrogate Roadie (a.k.a. **James McNew**, bass player of **Yo La Tengo**) on drums.

Despite doing everything except be quiet to discourage them, Happy Flowers acquired an audience of fiercely devoted followers, not sufficiently numerous to boost *Lasterday I Was Been Bad* (1990), their fourth and final album, into the charts, but certainly strong enough to suggest that hospitals for the criminally insane might be releasing their inmates before they were quite ready for the world outside the walls.

Four years after Happy Flowers split up in 1987, Mr. Surrogate Roadie joined them onstage again for their "fourth anniversary of breaking up" tour, supporting his other band, Yo La Tengo. This success was repeated a mere ten years later when Happy Flowers' most extensive tour of the United States (four days) kicked off to stunning audience reaction; people knew the material well enough to call out requests, and some poor fools actually knew the lyrics.

⊙ **Making The Bunny Pay 1987**

Collecting the first two scary EPs onto one very scary disc. Includes "Mom And Dad Like The Baby More Than Me", "I Wet The Bed Again", "Mom, I Gave The Cat Some Acid" and "All The Toys Hate Me".

HEARTBREAKERS

Heart started beating New York, 1975; finally broke in 1990.

"2 DOWNERS BEFORE THE OVERDUBS"

ENGINEER'S NOTE, MAY 16, 1977

Bad-ass dudes from every parent's worst nightmares, **The Heartbreakers** were a bunch of rebellious, rock'n'roll delinquents with switchblades, black leather jackets and more heroin habits than strictly necessary for a four-piece band. Like so many rebels without much of a cause, they lived fast and died young.

Although it was his soon-to-be bandmate **Richard Hell** (bass/vocals, ex-**Television**) who would give him the label, **Johnny Thunders** (gui-

Hardcore Transatlantica

To some extent, **hardcore** can be defined as the concentrated rage, speed and rebellious attitude that remains when the wit, charm, experimentation and strange beauty of punk has been boiled off. In a field known already for its lack of subtlety, hardcore dominated a good few acres with longhorn, lowbrow down'n'muddy bad-ass rock.

Hardcore first began to show up as a separate phenomenon in the confusion that followed the **Sex Pistols** break-up. Its genesis came partly from the sudden lack of direction showed by most of the herd animals on the scene, coupled with the new generation's need to outperform the originals they hoped to replace. Punk rock, like most other kinds of music, is dominated by alphamale primates. Hardcore punks had a need to pound their chests louder, harder and faster than their rivals; and although arguments could usually be reduced to the minimum – "We're more hardcore than you are!" "No, you ain't!" "Yes, we are!" – definite differences grew up between the UK and US hardcore contingents.

UK hardcore had its roots in the squatting, anarcho-fearsome wing of alienated city-dwelling youth; kids who were ready to hurl a Molotov cocktail at the next passing cop car or drink it if it failed to show up. British hardcore punks boasted a "nothing left to lose" swagger, bragged of street fights, arrests and overdoses, with typical acts **Crass**, **The Exploited**, GBH and Discharge happy to tear any US hardcore act limb from limb simply for daring to be American at the height of Reaganomics and the Cold War.

Whether they were showing off their subversive sympathies or simply didn't understand the words, many US hardcore fans paid top dollar for over-priced imported vinyl, the lyrical content of which would have caused a flurry of state surveillance to descend on the purchaser's unfortunate family had the feds lent a tutored ear to it. Whatever the reason, the imports seemed to trigger an explosion of politically committed North American hardcore acts. Although the term soon became so overused as

to be almost as broad-brush as "punk" itself, hardcore US included fire'n'brimstone bands such as **Dead Kennedys**, **Circle Jerks**, **Germs**, **Feederz**, **Black Flag**, **Bad Brains**, **D.O.A.** and **Minor Threat**. Though the first signs in the USA came from a suburban hardcore scene, lampooned before it even existed by The Tubes in their "White Punks On Dope", and which whined through luxurious equipment about the angst of growing up well-heeled and misunderstood – the new bands recruited city kids on the whole, guys and girls from blue-collar households who had never seen the inside of a two-car garage and who had paid for their equipment out of their own pockets.

The movement spread on both sides of the Atlantic as the Seventies gave way to the "me decade", moving underground as selfish greed became the mainstream fashion. By the time it reached Vancouver, Canada – where DOA's "Hardcore '81" track was written – it had developed into a tight-knit sub-underground movement in its own right. The teenaged punks of the 1980s were as keen to burn the bridges connecting them to the past as the 1976 vintage had been, and their passion for the new ultra-disciplined, ultra-fast sound of hardcore, delivering cop-killer bullets of righteous outrage separated them from the creaking leather jackets and increasingly leathery skins of the old-school bands. These were the kids who built the mosh pits, who dared to stage dive and slam dance, and who had a totally inexplicable taste for the skateboard. Hardcore bands typically toured themselves into psychosis and threw themselves about with tendon-snapping abandon on stage, issuing sporadic singles on labels so ferociously indie that even the FBI didn't have their address.

However, in the pursuit of ever-higher velocity and increasingly grotesque on-stage histrionics, a lot of bands crossed over into heavy metal, and in a move to make tons of dollars, the big labels began to circle overhead. Co-opting the most accessible aspects of the hardcore sound and bolting on as much emotion as the produc-

tar, born Genzale) was established in his role as "the Dean Martin of heroin" after his hell- and hair-raising stint in **The New York Dolls**. Together with his brother-in-infected-arms **Jerry Nolan** (drums, also ex-NY Dolls) and **Walter "Waldo" Lure** (guitar), the new band kinda clotted together in NYC when Thunders and Nolan – still raw and smarting after their escape from Dolls' manager **Malcolm McLaren**'s clutches – bumped into Hell (still smarting and raw after his songs were cut

one by one from the Television set) to form the most pissed-off trio of musicians ever to hang out at Max's Kansas City. Deciding to go down the "supergroup" route, they hired the talented but inexperienced Lure, rehearsed over a few dozen beers and so forth, put together a set, and against everyone's expectations, absolutely blasted the cobwebs out of even the most jaded New York City clubgoers.

Maybe having Nancy Spungen (cue clap of

ers could extract from bands generally numbed up with heroin, grunge was born, swept the globe and virtually erased hardcore overnight. In the fallout, pop-punk crossover acts such as Green Day have vacuumed up a lot of hardcore's traditional demographic and today's hardcore crew are surviving on pockets of local interest rather than continent-wide adulation.

American Hardcore: A Tribal History by Steven Blush (the most complete book on the early days of the US side of

things) describes the movement as "punk rock adapted for suburban teens", a description we'll go along with. Together with *The Decline Of Western Civilization* (1981) – the best movie on the early LA flavour of hardcore – it covers all the major moments of any importance Stateside. The UK scene is less well written up, possibly because the audience quite often eats anyone who produces a notebook. Just go and buy the greatest hits of all the UK bands above.

🎵 PLAYLIST: HARDCORE UK

1. FOUR MINUTE WARNING Chaos UK
from **Total Chaos (Anagram, 1998)**

2. FUCK RELIGION FUCK POLITICS FUCK THE LOT OF YOU Chaotic Dischord from **Riot City** Years:1982-1984 (Anagram, 2003)

3. FUCK YOUR NATIONALITY Disorder
from **Under The Scalpel Blade (Anagram, 1996)**

4. ULTIMATE SACRIFICE English Dogs from **To The Ends Of The Earth (Step 1, 1999)**

5. DEAD CITIES Exploited
from **Singles Collection (Snapper Classics, 2005)**

6. SICK BOY GBH
from **Dead on Arrival: the Anthology (Castle, 2005)**

7. THUGS IN UNIFORM Oi Polloi
from **Total Anarchoi (Step 1, 1999)**

8. NO RETURN One Way System
from **Singles Collection (Anagram, 2003)**

9. FUCK THE TORIES Riot Squad from **The Complete Punk Collection (Anagram, 2005)**

10. THATCHER'S FORTRESS Varukers
from **Massacred Millions (Fall Out, 2001)**

🎵 PLAYLIST: HARDCORE USA

1. LIGHTS OUT Angry Samoans
from **Inside My Brain (Triple X, 1997)**

2. PAY TO CUM Bad Brains
from **Banned In DC (EMI, 2003)**

3. WORLD UP MY ASS The Circle Jerks
from **Group Sex (Porterhouse, 2004)**

4. WORLD WAR 3 D.O.A. from **Something Better Change (Sudden Death, 2003)**

5. DICKS HATE THE POLICE Dicks
from **Dicks 1980-1986 (Alternative Tentacles, 1997)**

6. FUN AND GAMES Government Issue
from **The Complete History (Dr Strange, 2000)**

7. THE BIGGEST LIE Hüsker Dü
from **Zen Arcade (SST, 1995)**

8. ONE DOWN THREE TO GO The Meatmen from **We're the Meatmen ... And You Still Suck!!! Live (Caroline, 1994)**

9. THAT'S HOW I ESCAPED MY CERTAIN FATE Mission of Burma from **VS (Rykodisc, 1997)**

10. I SAW YOUR MOMMY Suicidal Tendencies
from **Suicidal Tendencies (Frontier, 2002)**

Billy, Waldo and Johnny tune up.

thunder from the gates of doom) review the first gig was a risky proposition, but she loved it, writing up the band's July 1976 debut at CBGB's for *New York Rocker* magazine in a gushing full-page piece (in a subplot that finishes right here, she "fell in love" with Nolan, following him to London with the band and meeting Sid Vicious as a result). Thunders meanwhile hired Leee Black Childers (NY producer/mover/shaker) as the group's manager and man with a reasonably full wallet.

Hell had already suffered enough fallout from guitar-hero egomania, so when Thunders started putting on airs and swanning round like the group's leader, Hell quit sharpish and went off with a handful of good songs to become clan chief of the Voidoids. **Billy Rath** took his place on bass, leaving all the vocal and front-man duties to Thunders, just the way he wanted it. As soon as Rath had learned his chops, Childers decanted them onto a plane to London (on one-way tickets and with no work permits) to join the infamous and ill-fated Anarchy In The U.K. tour, which should have seen the Sex Pistols, Clash, Damned, Buzzcocks and Heartbreakers kicking the Bay City Rollers off the charts for good.

While the tour collapsed under the weight of tabloid press disapproval, the boys hit the streets of London, scored and retreated to the comparative comfort of their hotel rooms. In the aftermath, the band played a set of gigs around the capital– partly to sell themselves to the record labels, partly to buy themselves some supplies – succeeding on both counts when Track Records produced the kind of contract they approved of: money upfront and access to a studio.

L.A.M.F. hit the shops in the autumn of 1977, and despite containing some of the punk scene's most powerful recordings – this was a band of some considerable experience, with enough talent and Big Apple swagger to force most of their peers to cower when they passed – the mix was terrible. Nolan, sick of this and other antics springing unbidden from Thunders' ego, quit and flew back home. **Terry Chimes** (ex-Clash and one of the most capable drummers for hire on the scene) stepped in so that the band could honour the gigs they had been contracted to play, but in one of punk rock's epic "final straw" moments, Track Records went broke and Childers resigned as manager.

Lure and Rath took what little money there was and followed Nolan back to New York. Thunders remained in London for a while, played a few gigs and, in his own good time, sauntered back home himself, just ahead of the deportation order. By the late summer of 1978, The Heartbreakers (with **Ty Styx** – drums) were playing again, doing one-night stands for as much cash as they could get.

Thunders went more or less solo for a few years, crumbling into deeper addiction, recording and playing live, but never with anything resembling a solid line-up behind him (fixed definitely, solid, no). The real Heartbreakers reunion didn't happen until 1984. Even then, Lure quit and returned to his job on Wall Street (*sic*) soon after meeting what was left of the Johnny Thunders he'd once known. Despite both the 1979 and 1984 London reunion gigs being recorded and released as blisteringly hot live albums, fans were delighted when Thunders and Tony James (ex-Generation X and not terribly famous for his skilled production work) laid hands on the old *L.A.M.F.* tapes. The revised mix went a long way towards reviving Thunders' reputation and introduced the Heartbreakers to a new gen- eration of kids, but the old band never got back together and all they could do was listen to the records and sigh at what they'd missed.

After a reunion show at the end of 1990 came to little, Thunders of course went on to die in New Orleans in 1991 and Nolan in early 1992, with their hard-drug lifestyle the major factor in their early and sordid demise. Remember, kids: just say no. You know it makes sense.

⊙ **Live At Max's Kansas City (Max's Kansas City, 1979).**

Back on his home turf, Johnny and the gang swagger and snarl their way through a monstrously powerful set, stopping only to hurl abuse at the paying customers.

⊙ **D.T.K. L.A.M.F. (Jungle, 1984).**

Must-have twin-pack, featuring the remastered studio album bolted on to a 1977 live set from London's Speakeasy club. Both recordings sensibly let Johnny's scrawny junkie whine and his rock-god guitar-playing run the show. The initials, by the way, stand for "Down To Kill, Like A Mother-Fucker", evidently an old New York gang challenge.

RICHARD HELL (AND THE VOIDOIDS)

Hell on Earth since 1949, in Lexington, Kentucky.

"PLEASE KILL ME"
RICHARD HELL T-SHIRT

One day they might put up a statue, or at least a commemorative plaque to Richard Meyers. Adopting the stage-name **Richard Hell**, he became the young man who to some extent is to blame for inventing punk rock.

Had he been dealt some more (or perhaps fewer) whacks to his head as a young man, Hell might have stayed on the rails. He grew, however, from a troubled child into a troublesome teenager, and by the time he was old enough to have dif- ficulties with the law, he was just plain trouble. More or less incarcerated in a private school, he bonded with fellow wannabe rebel Tom Miller and an escape plan was hatched. Going over the wall with all the careful preparation that a pair of 16-year-olds could muster, they were of course

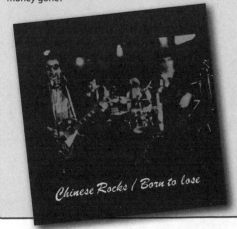

ICONIC SINGLE:
CHINESE ROCKS (TRACK RECORDS, 1977)

With all the people concerned now past caring, it seems irrelevant to continue fretting about poor Dee Dee being robbed of his writing royalties and credit: this is the defin- itive version of the first punk-rock song from America to cause any major ripples on the British scene. Richard Hell perhaps deserved a co-author credit, but Thunders, Nolan, Lure and Rath (whose names appeared on the original sleeve's back cover) certainly don't – whatever, it sold 20,000 copies. Lyrically sharp and precise, musically just perfect for the subject matter, and not a second too long, "Chinese Rocks" is simply the best song about hero- in ever written: a hot and sticky New York summer night, the plaster's falling off the wall, your girlfriend's crying in the shower, you can scarcely breathe and where's all the money gone?

Chinese Rocks / Born to lose

apprehended (although not until some weeks later, by which time they'd made it an impressive way across country to Alabama) and sent home. A couple of months later, Richard turned his bookstore paycheck into a bus ticket and, with his mother's permission if not her blessing, headed to New York City, arriving just in time for Christmas and the cold weather.

For the next few years, Hell and Meyer – who, now known as **Tom Verlaine**, and grown old enough to do what he liked, had also made his way to the Rotten Apple – lived the kind of sordid hustling existence captured in the movie *Midnight Cowboy*. At first, as a pair of well-spoken, privately educated young men with a scholarly interest in books and poetry, they managed to hold down jobs as bookstore clerks to keep the wolf a decent distance from the door. Bookshop jobs are famously underpaid, though, and even with the generous discount and shoplifting opportunities they offer, it was hard for the two young poets to make a living, particularly as New York City was awash with heroin at the time, and both boys had succumbed.

Feeling "too itchy for life" (Hell's bio) as 1972 shifted unnoticed into 1973, the guys decided to become rock'n'roll musicians. Verlaine was already pretty handy as a guitar-slinger and picked out a snazzy-looking DanElectro bass as the ideal prop for Hell. **Billy Ficca** was recruited up from Delaware and for the recording of six glorious tracks only, **The Neon Boys** flickered into life.

Hell's contributions included "Love Comes (In Spurts)", short haircuts all round and some astonishingly inept bass riffs.

Enter **Terry Ork** – NY scenester and acquaintance of the rich and famous. Already the guys' employer (he was manager of Cinemabilia, where the boys were earning an honest crust), in 1974 he not only offered them his loft as a rehearsal space, but also supplied the Neon Boys' missing ingredient, a second guitarist, in the shape of **Richard Lloyd**. **Television** was born, a far better name and a vastly superior band. In a sweet arty move prefiguring the entire video-installation racket that came in the early Eighties, the stage at their first gig had a backdrop of TV sets, each tuned to a different station apart from one showing the display from a roving camera sent out into the crowd.

Television's career is detailed on p.319, but cutting to the chase, after a successful regular gig at CBGB's and another at Max's Kansas City (with **Patti Smith**), Television found Hell surplus to requirements and he left the band. Pausing only to impress Malcolm McLaren with his spiked-up hair and torn T-shirt look – one he maintained he shared with Rimbaud – and turning down the chance to go to England and front a proposed band to be known, say, as the Sex Pistols, Hell linked track-marked arms with **Johnny Thunders** and **Jerry Nolan** to form **The Heartbreakers**.

Another false start for Hell but vital fuel for the small spluttering flame of punk, The

The usual suspects: L-R Robert, Richard, Ivan Julian (2nd guitar) and Marky Bell.

Heartbreakers injected a healthy shot of professionalism and stagecraft into the scene, and Hell stayed with them for most of 1975, helping steal "Chinese Rocks" off poor Dee Dee Ramone before the drugs got too much in the way of his creativity. In a final attempt to find "an outlet for passions and ideas too radical for any other art form", he finally jumped ship.

Hell (bass/vocals) had invented the term "void-oid" and written a short novel of the same name back in the days when he still sat at the same deli table as Verlaine (they used to call one another by constantly changing pet names of the pattern "this-oid and that-oid" in the way close pals do). Recruiting **Robert Quine** – a long-term friend of Hell who died in 2004, and this book's only lawyer/guitarist – plus **Marc Bell** (drums, an ex-Electric Chair, later reborn as Marky Ramone) and **Ivan Julian** (more guitar), **Richard Hell And The Voidoids** set about polishing their three-song set – "Blank Generation" "You Gotta Lose" and "(I Could Live With You) (In) Another World" – for the EP that Terry Ork had agreed to finance.

Richard presumably persuaded good old Terry to shell out for the band's stage outfits too. Ever the showman, Hell wrestled the band into the spectacle of identical $50 suits for the first Voidoids gig at CBGB's in November 1975. When the *Blank Generation* EP appeared on Ork records early in 1976, punk's original anthem at last began to spread the good word from HQ in NYC.

As a New York band with a punk-rock following, the Voidoids were naturally snapped up by Sire. The label funded the 1977 debut album (same name as the EP, and featuring all but one of the tracks from the original session) before sending the gang on tour. The final all-night recording sessions were tense but hilarious, as detailed by Lester Bangs in *Psychotic Reactions and Carburetor Dung*. Washing up soon after in the UK, supporting **The Clash** and rendered a little on-edge by the whole European experience, Hell was reported as diving for cover when a joker in the audience set off an explosive firework and being taken to task for his lack of commitment to the "Please Kill Me" T-shirt he was wearing. Whatever his thoughts at that moment, by the end of the year he had had enough of the music business.

Returning to the USA, sick of being spat on for a living and still shaking off the drugs prob-

lems, Hell put the Voidoids on part-time while he decided, in the words of Quine, whether "to be a rock star…or just go die". A band called the Voidoids recorded sporadically (losing Quine to a part-time gig with **Lou Reed's** band around the time of *Destiny Street*'s release, the act was now just Richard "and friends" most of the time), and played live now and again, before it softly and silently vanished away in 1982, with *R.I.P.* (1984) – the usual collection of outtakes, alternate ver-

---

ICONIC SINGLE:
BLANK GENERATION EP (SIRE, 1977)

"I WAS SAYING LET ME OUT OF HERE BEFORE I WAS EVEN BORN."

OPENING LINE OF "(I BELONG TO THE) BLANK GENERATION"

The reputation of the track "Blank Generation" has grown with time, to the point where it is now seen as the punk movement's first real anthem. Even though Hell has insisted in the intervening years that "blank" indicated a space you could fill with your own obsession, he nevertheless gave an extra label to a swathe of kids who saw no future, no point and no reason to do what they were told. Musically, the recording starts off fighting, and keeps punching all the way from the title-cut's jolting guitar, which rips you into distressing shapes before another guitar kicks in with a sneer, sending a bubble that explodes right at the centre of the rock'n'roll lobe in your brain.

Long unavailable on vinyl, but just a few buttons away from becoming a playlist, the EP comprised "Blank Generation" itself, "Another World" and "You Gotta Lose". Put them together and walk that stray-cat strut in time to the best slow-paced punk-rock tune to make it to vinyl that year.

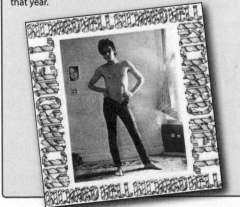

sions and studio-floor detritus – a poor epitaph.

When the Voidoids disappeared into the void, Hell returned to poetry, prose and his old love of publishing short-run works. He'd set up *Genesis: Grasp* and *Dot Books* back in his early New York days, having bought a secondhand tabletop printer on a whim, and before he turned rock'n'roller was a published and vaguely respected poet. It still wasn't going to pay the bills, though, even when the dealer's account was no longer a consideration, and the cheque he received for his role as Madonna's boyfriend in *Desperately Seeking Susan* (1985) must have been extremely useful. Spoken word gigs, combining poetry and war stories from his time as one of the hardest-living characters to have survived the punk era, slowly built him a new audience and a reputation as an arresting performer.

He showed up again on the outskirts of music in the Nineties as a member of part-time Sonic Youth offshoot project **Dim Stars**, contributing to their eponymous album. Realizing that just a taste wasn't going to be enough, he made the calls, reassembled the original Voidoids gang and recorded "Oh" (2000), their first and only Internet release, subsequently issued on the compilation *Beyond Cyberpunk* (Music Blitz).

⊙ **Blank Generation (Warner, 2000)**

Originally on Sire and released in 1977, this is Hell's only essential album. Mostly masterpieces, the album's standouts – "Down At The Rock And Roll Club", "Blank Generation" and "Love Comes (In Spurts)" – give a fascinating picture of New York City fun. Equally interesting, and worthy of repeated listens, are tracks where Hell either reveals his personal torment or projects himself poetically into the tortured New York personae behind the lyrics.

HOLE

Opened up 1989, Los Angeles; filled in, 2002.

More often cited for her reputation as the worst rock'n'roll girlfriend in the world than for the music she has produced, **Courtney Love** (born Michelle Harrison in 1964 to a pair of flaky hippies) overcame childhood trauma of epic proportions, substance misuse, physical abuse, family break-up and the suicide of husband Kurt Cobain in order to become a successful songwriter and performer. And although **Hole** was always more than just Courtney's band,

it was driven by her need to exorcize a bunch of personal demons.

Love had a taste for the limelight: she'd appeared in the films *Sid & Nancy* (1986) and *Straight To Hell* (1987), and had paid her dues scrapping it out with Kat Bjelland in **Babes In Toyland**. Hole was formed in 1989 by Love (vocals/guitar) and **Eric Erlandsen** (guitar/vocals). They swiftly found a rock-solid rhythm section in **Jill Emery** (bass) and **Caroline Rue** (drums).

Booking **Kim Gordon** (Sonic Youth's bass player) to produce Hole's debut was a masterstroke. Gordon extracted every last ounce of passion from the band and put Love through the emotional mangle. *Pretty On The Inside* appeared in 1991. An album so full of anger and emotion in search of release that it was likely at times to leap right out of the CD player to bite you on the ass, it set new standards of growling and howling for the already noisy Riot Grrrl movement. Hot, sweaty and at times downright scrappy-sounding guitar-based punk rock, it was the best thing to come out of LA in years. It won the band an instant audience in the UK, and led indirectly to Love meeting and marrying Kurt Cobain, and starting a family with him.

The band was essentially dismissed while she wed and bred, and it was another few years before she called Erlandsen and set about hiring and drilling a new Hole. **Kristen M. Pfaff** (bass) and **Patty Schemel** (drums) got the job, Love and Erlandsen wrote the songs and Hole's follow-up recording *Live Through This*, appeared in 1994. Coming so soon in the aftermath of Cobain's death in April, the album was lost in the media maelstrom swirling around Love and seeping into her private life. Worse still, the songs it contained – although they were less confrontational than those included on the debut, and showed a promising degree of refinement, even maturity – were virtually ignored even by the music papers.

As the wife of a prominent rock'n'roll suicide, Love was a prime target for vilification. In the eyes of lazy journalists and sensation-seeking editors, her music came second to linking her to Yoko Ono-Lennon, Linda McCartney, Nancy Spungen, and Jeanine (David St Hubbin's girlfriend in *This Is Spinal Tap*) as one of those women who'd interfered in groups and screwed things up for the boys. Yet tracks such as the album's standout cut,

"Doll Parts", showed a willingness to turn down the volume on the rage and let the self-analysis and doubt seep through.

When Pfaff died after a heroin overdose, her place was taken by multi-talented **Melissa Auf Der Maur**, who joined for the extensive tour that followed the album and which helped push "Doll Parts" into the US Top 60. Love flirted with acting – appearing in *The People Vs Larry Flint* (1996) among other productions – prescription drugs, motherhood and childcare for a while, growing up and calming down a little.

In 1998, four years after Cobain's death, Hole released *Celebrity Skin*. Immediately dismissed by many early fans as Love's pension-plan recording, it lacked the bite seen in previous releases, veering at times unpleasantly close to pop. Still, with **Billy Corgan** (of Smashing Pumpkins) on board as musical consultant, it was expected to do well. Schemel quit the band, necessitating the recruitment of yet another drummer from the apparently endless supply of musicians just hanging around waiting for a gig in LA. **Samantha Maloney** (ex-Shift) took the gig, did the tour and sat back openmouthed with the rest of the band as the album went platinum.

Auf Der Maur, shaken to her bones by the noxious atmosphere of booze, hard drugs and rampant egos, quit Hole for a spot with Smashing Pumpkins. Amidst a legal storm of contractual wrangling and copyright-ownership suits with the remainder of Nirvana, Love formed a new band (**Bastard**) without winding up Hole first. Best described as "on hold" at time of writing, the group has probably expired through neglect. Courtney's undeniable talent as a musician is twisted into sharp focus by the blurry swirling chaos she attracts around her, and although she still has much to say, it's unlikely she'll return to the old band as a means of expressing herself.

⊙ **Live Through This** (Geffen, 1995)

Hole at its wide-open best, neither too raw to eat nor too sophisticated to satisfy the appetite. Music made by girls, for girls – but don't let that stop you if you're of the alternative gender – there's meat and two veg for everyone in tracks such as "Violet", "Miss World", "Jennifer's Body" and "I Think That I Would Die".

⊙ **Celebrity Skin** (Geffen, 1998)

Hole's most professional-sounding set, led by Love at her most regal, was named after a low-rent mag that printed paparazzi pix of C-list stars showing some unexpected flesh. There's a

similar conflict between the album's sweetish, pop-like, lighter-weight items (mainly the five tunes co-authored by the ubiquitous Billy Corgan) and Love's lyrical subject matter – addressing drug abuse, spousal abuse and the continuing emotional fallout from her husband's suicide. Still a fine album with sprigs of subtlety growing up in the cracks between the power chords.

HUGGY BEAR

Rolled up in Brighton, England, 1991; quit the game in 1994.

Britain's welcoming party for the US riot grrrls was hosted by **Huggy Bear**. Celebrating their own take on revolution, girl-style, Huggy Bear's collective mind was broad enough to let boys into the group, and sharp enough to keep the media at arm's length. **Chris** (vocals), **Niki** (bass/vocals), **Jo** (guitar), **Jon** (guitar) and **Karen** (drums) ditched their surnames and released a cassette-only collection of demos on Wiija. Following up with a series of hard-hitting small-venue gigs and a TV appearance on *The Word* that ended in a riot, Huggy Bear had the A&R men in a muck sweat.

The UK music press and major labels salivated at the idea of a girlie version of punk rock springing up simultaneously on both sides of the Atlantic, and did their best to ignore the fact it had come into being without any hype, not even a single three-Martini lunch. Apart from teasing Nude Records with an agreement to sign (but only if they dropped Suede, their biggest act, first), Huggy Bear decided to stay indie and remain with Wiija.

The band's first "proper" release was the beautifully titled *Rubbing The Impossible To Burst* EP in 1992. Scorching politico-lyrical rants spread thickly over power-station guitar output were in fashion that season and the record did well enough for riot grrrl to go officially transatlantic. When **Bikini Kill** arrived for a joint tour and split single with Huggy Bear, the whole shebang was treated by the local music papers like some kind of Cold War summit conference. A second, now impossible-to-find EP *Kiss Curl For The Kid's Lib Guerillas* appeared soon after. Thankfully, *Taking The Rough With The Smooch* appeared in 1993, collecting all the band's previous releases into a single handy CD package.

The band was silent for a year before breaking cover towards the end of 1994 with the *Long-Distance Lovers* and *Main Squeeze* EP releases. Outstanding in their own right, they helped set the stage for the group's one and only full-length project, *Weaponry Listens To Love*, the album that closed the year and the group's history.

Karen was next spotted with **The Phantom Pregnancies**, Niki and Jo went on to join **Blood Sausage**, Chris resurfaced as a part-time member of **Skinned Teen** and Jon briefly strummed for Brighton's best-kept secret, **I'm Being Good** – an impressive, hard-working outfit whose *Poisonous Life* (Infinite Chug, 2000), *Sub Plot* (Infinite, 2002) and *Family Snaps* (Jonson Family, 2005) all deserve a listen.

◉ Taking the Rough With The Smooch (Kill Rock Stars, 1993)

As mentioned above, this will bring you up to speed on the Huggies' first two years' output. With as much effort going into the titles as into the musicianship, it sounds patchily brilliant, with standouts including "Dissthentic Penetration", "Shaved Pussy Poetry", "Pansy Twist", "Herjazz" and "Carn't Kiss".

◉ Weaponry Listens To Love (Wiija, 2000)

Leaving behind their original cute-core image, this is the sound of a confident professional team. Although tracks like "Immature Adolescence", "Fuck Your Heart", "Erotic Bleeding", "Sixteen And Suicide", "Obesity And Speed" and "Why Am I A Lawbreaker" showed enormous skill and growing maturity, their promise was sadly never realized.

Most of Huggy Bear:
L-R Chris, Jo and Niki.

🎵 PLAYLIST: RIOT GRRRL

Partly a genuinely independent transatlantic network of (generally) young women with a shared interest – expressed either as musician, audience-member or fanzine journalist – in loud, punk noise; and partly a label created by mainstream hacks in search of the next big theme, lazily applied to bands with little in common apart from a right-on, feminist attitude, some token female component and hardcore lyrical determination not to knuckle under, **riot grrrl** (or grrl) was as exciting as it sounds and looks in print: a whirl of breathless high-speed guitar thrashing, trashing the rancid worlds of adolescent love, sex, male supremacy, middle-of-the-road politics, and boredom. It's punk rock for girls, mainly by girls. Here are ten classic tracks.

1. OH YEAH! Babes in Toyland
from **The best Of (WSM, 2004)**

2. I LIKE FUCKING Bikini Kill
from **The Singles (Kill Rock Stars, 2001)**

3. POLAROID BABY Bratmobile
from **Pottymouth (Kill Rock Stars, 2000)**

4. FUCK YR. FRUMPIES Frumpies
from **Frumpie One Piece (Kill Rock Stars, 2002)**

5. CALCULATED Heavens to Betsy
from **Calculated (Kill Rock Stars, 1994)**

6. CARN'T KISS Huggy Bear from **Taking The Rough With The Smooch (Kill Rock Stars, 2000)**

7. WARGASM L7
from **Bricks Are Heavy (London, 1999)**

8. GLAD I'M NOT YEW Lunachicks
from **Babysitters on Acid (Go Kart, 2001)**

9. 24,900 MILES PER HOUR 7 Year Bitch
from **Gato Negro (Imports, 1996)**

10. DIG ME OUT Sleater-Kinney
from **Dig Me Out (Matador, 1997)**

HÜSKER DÜ

First recalled Minneapolis, 1979; just a memory since 1988.

Named after a Norwegian board game – it means "Do you remember?" – popular in the frozen states of the Mid-West, **Hüsker Dü** did their best to erase all memory of the music that had gone before in a blizzard of year-zero thrash-punk rock that sounded far too loud and abrasive to have been created by a mere trio. Although all the tunes came from **Bob Mould** (guitar/vocals) and **Grant Hart** (drums), their unique sound would have been impossible to achieve without the input of **Greg Norton** (bass). The guys met at the record store where Mould had a job, and finding they had much in common, formed a band that leant back hard on the trebly, urgent sound of Buzzcocks' early recordings and kept the faith with an unmatched series of three-minute masterpieces.

The guys hurtled out of Minnesota in 1981 on the back of "Statues", an extraordinarily powerful single that breathed some warmth back into the rapidly chilling body of hardcore. Land Speed Record screamed out of the snowbound horizon in 1982, followed by the single "In A Free Land", *Everything Falls Apart* and the *Metal Circus* EP (both 1983), a combined assault that made their name across the USA and as far as the UK. It is certain that without the influence of Hüsker Dü, the entire US hardcore scene would have died on its knees. Bands as diverse as the Pixies and Nirvana could never have achieved their great success if Hüsker Dü hadn't been there first.

The 100 Club
100 Oxford Street, London

A friendly basement venue with one of the best addresses in town, **The 100 Club** has hosted a fair amount of punk in its time, although it started as a jazz den and has given a platform to heavy rock acts and the cream of world musicians. A cavernous booming room, wider than it is deep, it is not fantastically well suited to hugely amplified electric rock – though quelling the dodgy acoustics with tightly packed crowds and whacking them with lashings of volume seems to help matters. It first became popular in the 1950s as a cool, relaxed place for sweet music that went on long after the rest of London closed down for the night, satisfying an after-work trade of catering workers, waiters, actors and musicians. During the 1960s, it was often busier at lunchtime – when the capital's keen teens used to pop downstairs for an hour's discotheque session before returning to the office or shop floor – than in the evenings, but of course to people like us, it's best known as the venue for Malcolm McLaren's famous 1976 Punk Festival (see p.27).

Hüsker Dü's crisp, neat approach showed a return to the form and discipline that had characterized hardcore punk in its earliest days. Songs started with a roar, sped through a quick riff of verse and chorus and screeched to a parachute-assisted halt at the end of the measured mile. College radio and a relentless touring schedule helped break the band in the US, and Hüsker Dü's crowd-pulling power exploded. Still, it nearly all went totally wrong when they rediscovered the double concept-album for *Zen Arcade*, their 1984 outing. The loosely thrown together story of a kid who hates his life, leaves home, then hates his new life even more, it ended with "Recurring Dreams" a monstrous fourteen-minute epic that would have had them drummed ceremoniously out of the guild of punk rockers had it not been such a fantastic song.

New Day Rising (1985) ditched the idea of song cycles in favour of a return to more familiar buzz-saw beauties. Backstage, however, things weren't as friendly as they seemed. The creative partnership was beginning to fall apart. Gritting their teeth, however, the band released the marking-time, less-than-perfect *Flip Your Wig* in 1985, their masterpiece *Candy Apple Grey* in 1986, with *Warehouse: Songs And Stories* – another double album, but worth the effort – appearing the following year. In 1988 the familiar "musical differences" finally became irreconcilable and Hüsker Dü split up. Mould went on to do pretty much exactly the same as he'd done before, first working solo and then, from 1991, with his new band **Sugar**. Hart went solo too before creating **Nova Mob**, while Norton, sick of the whole business, retired and became a chef.

⊙ Zen Arcade (SST, 1997)

Punk rock à la Hüsker Dü, with sidetracks into folk-rock, R&B and some extraordinary anger.

⊙ Warehouse: Songs And Stories (Warner, 1992)

From the sickly coloured stage set on the cover to the stark black and white imagery of the classic closing track, "You Can Live At Home Now", this is as unpleasant and yet as welcome as recovering from a hangover. Retaining their rawness, the band skilfully gives way here and there to the label's pleading for a more radio-friendly sound, without otherwise compromising at all.

⊙ Candy Apple Grey (Warner, 1992)

Mould's afterburner-assisted vocals deliver shards of intense focused rage. The guitar and drums are blinding too.

Punks Of The Us Midwest

The wind streaming south from the Arctic and down across Canada passes little to warm it up to friendlier temperatures, and whipping across the Great Lakes before it enters the US just makes it more unpleasant to deal with. Small wonder, then, that some of the best, raw and teeth-grindingly angry noise to surface in the last few decades has come from this part of the world. Midwest punk has some interesting ancestors of course: through the Sixties and Seventies, **The MC5** thought the White Panther Revolution was going to happen in Detroit and **The Stooges** did what they could to bring about the city's physical destruction by sheer volume while **Pere Ubu** tried to weird the place out of existence. When punk rockers erupted like teen zits on the face of the great nation, there was no doubt that the Midwest would provide a bountiful crop.

🎵 PLAYLIST: MIDWEST PUNK

1. **THE BIGGEST LIE Husker Du** from **Zen Arcade (SST, 1995)**

2. **SONIC REDUCER The Dead Boys** from **Young Loud And Snotty (Sire, 1999)**

3. **WALKS IN COLD Naked Raygun** from **the Jettison EP (Quarterstick, 1999)**

4. **RACER X Big Black** from **Hammer Party (Touch & Go, 1986)**

5. **BODY BAG The Effigies** from **Remains Nonviewable (Touch & Go, 1995)**

6. **DIET PILL L7** from **Bricks Are Heavy**

7. **THE UNION FOREVER The White Stripes** from **White Blood Cells (XL, 2001)**

8. **C'MON, C'MON The Von Bondies** from **Pawn Shoppe Heart (Reprise, 2004)**

9. **SHOUT BAMA LAMA The Detroit Cobras** from **Life Love and Leaving (SFTRI, 2001)**

10. **SEETHER Veruca Salt** from **American Thighs (Hi Rise, 1999)**

IKARA COLT

Foaled in the East End of London, 2001; galloping on.

Skinny, snotty, wearing old school uniform and making a manically intense speed-driven noise on stage, **Ikara Colt** are without doubt the most exciting prospect of this decade's garage-punk revival. As punk rock mutates into its next generation, the band shows that the music remains essentially the same: it's got to be fast, loud, young, mean and rebellious.

Admittedly the degree of threat presented to the establishment by **Jon Ball** (bass), **Claire Ingram** (guitar), **Paul Resende** (vocals) and **Dominic Young** (drums) – a bunch of guitar-wielding art students covered in paint and named after a fictional racehorse – has yet to be established, but like Crass and the heroes of the late Seventies, Ikara Colt refuse to accept that "guitars and microphones are just fucking toys!" and if there's a way to bring down Babylon with high-powered amplification, then this is the mob with the best chance of doing it.

One of many acts to make a breakthrough thanks to BBC Radio – with Steve Lamacq and John Peel ahead of the pack as usual – Ikara Colt made a deal with Fantastic Plastic Records and began their attack. "Sink Venice" started a ripple of interest in 2001. When "Rudd" appeared early the following year, the ripple had become more of a torrent and the band swung into a series of higher-profile gigs, including well-received appearances at Glastonbury and the harder-to-please Reading Festival.

Chat And Business (2002), Ikara Colt's debut album, won them even more widespread support, which was boosted by the band's stunning appearances in support of Six By Seven and Idlewild, and a headlining tour with Matchbox B-Line Disaster and fellow modern punkeurs The Parkinsons. Ball quit in 2003, leaving time for his replacement Tracy Bellaires to learn the old songs and record a bunch of new ones with the band for *Modern Apprentice* (2004).

⊙ **Chat And Business**
(Fantastic Plastic/Epitaph, 2002)

From standout opening track "One Note" through the searing pace of "Pop Group", "City Of Glass" and "Sink Venice", this is a modern classic.

⊙ **Modern Apprentice (Fantastic Plastic, 2004)**

"Wanna Be That Way" could have been written on a greasy 1970s cigarette packet and recorded in an afternoon by a bunch of drunken mates fooling around. There is simply no higher praise.

171

THE JAM

Kicked off Woking, England, 1975; kicked out, 1982.

Forget all the mod versus punk versus soul boy rubbish that still clings to the name and legend of **The Jam** and listen to the music. **Paul Weller** (vocals/guitar), **Bruce Foxton** (bass/

The mighty Weller.

vocals) and **Rick Buckler** (drums) were a punk band before the label was invented, just like The Small Faces, The Kinks and The Who – from whom they took so much – had been before them.

Unlike most of their contemporaries in the first wave of British punk, The Jam admitted to a history that went back before Year Zero was declared, happy to keep old numbers such as Martha And The Vandellas' "Heatwave" and even their own version of the novelty hit "Batman" – the theme from the Sixties TV series – in their repertoire, at least until Weller's songwriting had given them the luxury of an entirely self-penned set. The guys (including, at the very beginning, fellow guitar player **Steve Brookes**) started out in school, jamming through rainy lunch breaks with thrashed-out, high-speed covers of The Who's greatest hits, and versions of vintage Sixties Motown numbers.

Stylishly turned out, managed by Mr Weller Senior and, in truth, a well-brought-up bunch of lads, The Jam were seen initially by punk's own snobbish elite as a bunch of outsiders divorced from the rest of the movement – bandwagon-jumpers from way out of town, and too posh to have any understanding of the mythical "streets". True enough, Weller had never had to peddle his rear end on the Piccadilly meat rack, Foxton was more interested in getting his next pint than in chasing the dragon and Buckler never appeared on the front page of a Sunday tabloid shamefacedly leaving a brothel, but there was sharp, polished steel beneath the mohair suits and an irony in Weller's adoption of the British flag that was more subtle, but along the same lines, as the theory that led some to believe the swastika was now an acceptable accessory.

Leaving credibility issues aside, The Jam were the most exciting band, visually at least, on the

PLAYLIST: THE JAM

These are all available on the special edition of *Snap!* (Universal, reissued 2006), but if you're chasing down the albums, details are as below.

1. IN THE CITY
from **In The City (Polydor, 1997)**

2. AWAY FROM THE NUMBERS
from **In The City (Polydor, 1997)**

3. MODERN WORLD
from **This Is The Modern World (Polydor, 1997)**

4. BILLY HUNT
from **All Mod Cons (Polydor, 1997)**

5. "A" BOMB IN WARDOUR STREET
from **All Mod Cons (Polydor, 1997)**

6. DOWN IN THE TUBE STATION AT MIDNIGHT
from **All Mod Cons (Polydor, 1997)**

7. SMITHERS-JONES
from **Setting Sons (Polydor, 1997)**

8. ETON RIFLES
from **Setting Sons (Polydor, 1997)**

9. GOING UNDERGROUND
from **Snap! (Universal, 2006)**

10. FUNERAL PYRE
from **Snap! (Universal, 2006)**

scene. Serious, committed and professional enough to start taking on regular gigs while Paul was finishing school, The Jam, ferried about by Paul's dad, already had stage experience when punk exploded and were well aware of the seedy temptations of the fleshpots of London. Years of practice meant that the band had a natural telepathy that none of their peers could match, and it made their stage act the tightest around. Well dressed, with none of the dribbling sneers of their rivals to turn the sensitive stomach, The Jam made smart-sounding, tightly focused punk pop tunes that were witty, intelligent and, best of all, intelligible.

Weller and Foxton had boy-band good looks to spare – even Buckler buffed up pretty well for the photo shoots and had his admirers – and having whipped up a bit of a frenzy on the live circuit in London and around the country, the band were soon signed to Polydor and wiping the floor with the other punk-rock bands.

Weller's chunky opening riff to "In The City" still packs the rush that it demonstrated when it first hurtled out of tinny transistors and booming jukeboxes across the country in 1977. The track bounced straight out of nowhere into the lower reaches of the UK Top 40, and with a little money behind them, The Jam followed up just a month later with the *In The City* album, recorded in just eleven days. Swaggering like a pilled-up mod on Brighton promenade in the certainty that it looked and sounded fan-fuckin'-tastic, *In The City* sold well and, in the absence of much other product in the shops worth listening to, became a punk essential.

No matter how strong the writing team, it is tough to produce two killer albums in a year, and when *The Modern World* hit the stores towards the end of 1977, it picked up a lot of unnecessarily barbed reviews for being less hard-hitting than its predecessor. It gave the band a Top 20 single with "This Is The Modern World", however, and helped to disguise the bitter taste left after the band tried – and failed – to find a niche in the USA.

Life back home was no bed of roses, however, and after a difference of opinion with a group of rugby players, the band's tour had to be postponed while Weller's hands healed enough for him to play guitar again. The Jam's most powerful single, "Down In The Tube Station At Midnight", a tense, dramatic slice of urban violence, appeared at the same time, oozing spite at the racist assholes and mindless thugs who made life in London hazardous for anyone looking a bit alternative at the time.

As Weller's confidence in his writing grew, he turned away from broad punk themes of alienation and injustice to concentrate more on the minutiae and miseries of British life. Like Ray Davies, he became almost defiantly English, and while this resulted in The Jam becoming superstars at home, it made them harder to export. Weller's devotion to the British pop magicians of the Sixties culminated in a searing cover of the Kinks' "David Watts" on The Jam's third full-length release *All Mod Cons*, released in 1979.

The cynicism and world-weariness reflected in the multi-layered pun of the title didn't stop the album pounding into the charts. Meanwhile, The

🔲 CELEBRITY PLAYLIST: PAUL WELLER

"He's not particularly a fan of the music," a spokeswoman told us when we asked for Paul Weller's punk playlist. An alternative list of the records that influenced him to form The Jam reinforces the point – it seems the Modfather was always a bit of a pop traditionalist and an old-fashioned soul boy, who never quite went the full course with punk's 'year zero' philosophy...

1. TIN SOLDIER Small Faces
from **Small Faces**

2. WATERLOO SUNSET The Kinks
from **Something Else By The Kinks**

3. FIRE BRIGADE THE MOVE
from **Flowers In The Rain**

4. TWIST AND SHOUT The Beatles
from **Twist and Shout EP**

5. MY GENERATION The Who
from **The Who Sings My Generation**

6. SO SAD ABOUT US The Who
from **A Quick One**

7. MUSTANG SALLY Wilson Pickett
from **Wicked Pickett**

8. PRETTY LITTLE BABY Marvin Gaye
from **The Master**

9. BACK IN MY ARMS AGAIN The Supremes
from **More Hits By The Supremes**

10. CHEQUE BOOK Dr Feelgood
from **Down By The Jetty**

💿 ICONIC SINGLE:
DAVID WATTS / "A BOMB IN WARDOUR STREET (POLYDOR, 1978)

This double A-side 7" boasts a storming cover of the Kinks' "David Watts" – the start of Weller's overt fascination with the mod mythos. The flip bashed around a repetitive one-two riff on guitar and drums, while the lyrics of this song describe yet another increasingly familiar scene of nightclub violence. The setting is long-dead and much-lamented punk venue The Vortex, where a fight breaks out as our hero (his head's been kicked in and blood's starting to pour) tries to defend the honour of his date (fifteen geezers have her pinned to the door). As the song builds to its climax, the lyrics move outside, showing how idiotic testosterone-driven violence builds like the blast from the bomb in the title leading to genocide, war and goodness knows what else.

Jam's continuing string of singles chart successes spawned an irritating new fan-base of mini-mods who turned the front of stage area from mosh pit to kindergarten. Despite the financial success and the teenybopper adulation, Weller stayed true to punk rock's initial ideals of keeping the music basic and singing about what you knew. "Eton Rifles", a song that sprayed Britain's class system, militarism and culture of privilege with a burst of withering fire, made the Top 10 as the "me decade" dawned, while the album it came from, *Setting Sons*, went into the Top 5.

The Jam had never really conformed to official, Ministry Of Punk standards, however, and spent the next few years enjoying the pop-star lifestyle. "Start", musically best described as a tribute to the Beatles' "Taxman", entered the charts at number one and *Sound Affects* went to number two in the album listings. Resolutely refusing to cheer up, the boys punched out "Funeral Pyre" and "Absolute Beginners" in 1981, before a nervous collapse forced Weller to rest for a few months on doctor's orders.

Evidently he spent his enforced break soaking up classic US soul music and playing endless R&B, as *The Gift* (1982) showed just how far the gang had progressed in a few short years. Horns blared, soulful guitar licks stroked up and down the spine of the listener and everybody had a good time. Released as a double A-sided single, "Town Called Malice" c/w "Precious" took The Jam once again straight to the top of the charts, resulting in the band being invited to perform two songs in a single edition of BBC TV's *Top Of The Pops* show. With The Gift performing a similar balancing act at the top of the album charts, there was little left for the band to achieve. Weller had outgrown the sound of The Jam, and quitting ahead of the game, the band announced their break-up in October 1982.

Weller went on to form **The Style Council** with **Mick Talbot** (previously with the best-named mod band ever to come from Merton Park – the Merton Parkas), which continued his string of hits but was nowhere near a punk band. He's since gone solo and retains his pessimistic outlook. Buckler played for a while with **Time UK** before returning to his furniture business, while Foxton, after the solo album *Touch Sensitive*, made the leap back into punk rock, playing bass with **Stiff Little Fingers** on their first and subsequent revival tours.

⊚ **The Very Best Of** (Polydor, 1997)

The title says it all. If you don't know the work of Britain's lost punk superheroes, then this is the one to start with.

⊚ **All Mod Cons** (Polydor, 1997)

The lads playing as a band with the world at their feet. Not quite a concept album, more pointed than your average "no future" ranting, it looks wistfully back to a golden age of mod that never existed. Delicious.

⊚ **In The City** (Polydor, 1997)

The original and best.

THE JESUS AND MARY CHAIN

Started arguing as a band, East Kilbride, Scotland, 1983; agreed to differ, 1999.

James Reid (guitar/vocals) and his brother **William** (ditto) made the most glorious feedback drenched fuck-you guitar-based noise of the 1980s, brimming with fraternal tension, envy and that slow-burning loathing that only a family environment can really create. When early demo tapes of ferocious stormy rock'n'roll failed to win them the major-label adulation they clearly thought they deserved, they changed the name from the admittedly good **The Poppy Seeds** to the far more memorable **The Jesus And Mary Chain**, called in **Douglas Hart** (bass) and **Murray Dalgliesh** (drums) and headed for London.

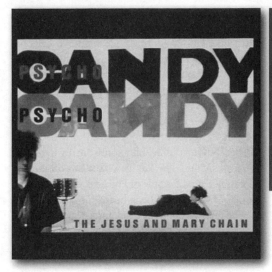

In a very punk rock move, they started crashing other bands' gigs, showing up early and announcing themselves as the support act before piling on stage and letting rip with overwhelming sheets of sharp-edged, wailing, fuzzed-up feedback. One famous guerrilla appearance of this kind had them thrown off by the venue manager less than four minutes into their set. Desperately cool in the same manner as their heroes, The Velvet Underground, they had a similarly limited impact in terms of record sales, but were in some respects just as influential on a scene turning to stone.

Even their headline appearances tended to last only fifteen to twenty minutes before equipment malfunction, behavioural breakdown or substance abuse on the part of the band or audience brought proceedings to a sudden stop. Stick-thin, clad in black and with a propensity for sunglasses after dark and indoors, they were just what the London scene needed; the old town was overdue a shock from the outside, and a bunch of don't-care-'bout-you Scottish guys with awful attitude problems and a distinct lack of respect for the way things were generally done were on the scene to provide it.

Creation Records' Alan McGee, long-time champion of the awkward squad in music, gave them a deal, releasing their first single, "Upside Down", in 1984. Its barbed-wire distortion and electrifying feedback of doom knocked the wax from the ears of the critics and blew dust from a million tormented speakers. A month later, they'd moved to rival label Blanco Y Negro and swapped Murray for a loan of **Bobby Gillespie** (Primal

Scream's singer), releasing "Never Understand", "You Trip Me Up" and the breakthrough single "Just Like Honey" in the space of a few weeks.

There was a huge buzz about the band by now, centred on London but radiating across the whole of the country. *Psychocandy*, which appeared in November 1984 (still less than two months since their debut), kicked off with a roar of distorted amplification and slaughtered the critics and record-buying public. Like some deadly hybrid of surf music and The Stooges, mixed to demotion effect by a mad disciple of Phil Spector, nothing so cool and sneery had been heard for years.

The guys went on the road, forced to spend even more time in one another's company between gigs and finding the pressure hard to deal with. Bobby went back to the Scream and **John Moore** (guitar/drums, depending) signed on in his place. Gigs were still at this point frequently descending into genuine chaos as the crowds rose to the band's bait of full-on noise and total indifference to audience reaction.

"April Skies", the taster single from the Mary Chain's second album did not hit the stores until 1987, and *Darklands*, which followed shortly afterwards, showed the Reid brothers experimenting with lower levels of distortion, a virtual absence of feedback and with audibly comprehensible lyrics. Having dispensed with the band for the purposes of recording, the Reids had to weather the wave of disappointing reviews and lack of sales on their own. In an attempt to win back the feedback fans, *Barbed Wire Kisses*, a 1988 collection of B-sides plumped up with some new material, followed with embarrassing speed while the Reid brothers returned, chastened, to the studio.

Automatic (1989) attempted to reach a compromise. With the distortion reined in, the vocals brought forward in the mix and a more "accessible" approach to the songwriting, the band struck lucky. "Head On" sold well and picked up a lot of useful airtime across the Atlantic, breaking the band on the college radio circuit.

By the release of *Honey's Dead* in 1992, the Reids had bought themselves a studio, which, in a rather obvious and less than tasteful manner, they'd named The Drug Store. They'd also recruited **Ben Lurie** (guitar) to join them as the third permanent member of the crew. The rock'n'roll lifestyle was by this point interfering with their career – punk rock was harder to produce in the fug of fame that enveloped them in London – and *Stoned And Dethroned* (1994) was too gentle an album to add much to their hell-raising reputation.

It is a truth almost universally acknowledged that adding boyfriends or girlfriends to the already ego-filled sphere surrounding a successful rock act leads to disaster – and when Jim found he was expected to share his vocal duties with bro' William's main squeeze – the admittedly stunningly gifted **Hope Sandoval** of Mazzy Star – it must have hurt a little. Whatever other effect it had, Hope's voice contributed to the album's generally softer sound as the mellower J&MC looked once again to "breaking America". Touring at home and overseas helped occupy the Reid brothers – although switching allegiance back to the Creation label and rowing over Sandoval's continuing contribution to the act also kept them busy – until "Cracking Up" served as a taster for *Munki* (Creation, 1998).

There's been no new J&MC product since then, although the brothers have been far from idle in the meantime. Jim signed up for a short ride with his pals from **Death In Vegas** (whose later collaboration with **Iggy Pop**, "Aisha", is an absolute must-have piece of guitar madness) before assembling **Freeheat** with **Ben Lurie** (guitar, ex-Mary Chain), **Nick Sanderson** (drums, ex-Earl Brutus) and **Romi Mori** (bass, ex-The Gun Club) bashing out some fine back-to-essentials rock. Their debut album *Back On The Water* (Planting Seeds Records, 2006) combines live and studio recordings in a seventeen-track introduction to the band.

While Jim charmed the press, romanced Sandoval and generally did the suave rocker thing for a few years, William kept the banner of evil music fluttering. He started by releasing the artwork for his debut album in advance of the record itself. Featuring our hero stark bollock naked and sporting a hard-on (of sufficient rigidity, frankly, to merit the photo – who wouldn't be proud of such a beast?). Creation Records legal department burned every copy of the picture it could find and refused outright to let it onto the streets. Will flounced off and self-released *Finbegin* – albeit with a sleeve toned-down to comply with the obscene publications act – on Hot Tam in 1999. Following up a year later with *Saturday The Fourteenth*, William's ear-wrenching feedback and experimental effing around won him few converts but lost him even fewer.

With only the Peel Sessions (Strange Fruit. 2000) and compilation *21 Singles* (Blanco Y Negro, 2002) showing up in the stores in the eight years since *Munki*, perhaps that's the end of the J&MC. Brotherly love is a powerful emotion though…

◉ Psychocandy **(Blanco y Negro. 1984)**

White noise hadn't sounded this good since the time of The Velvets – no home should be without it.

◉ Peel Sessions **(Strange Fruit. 2000)**

Blasting, fiery, paint-blistering versions of some the band's most exciting music, delivered without overdubs or pretensions. "In A Hole" and "You Trip Me Up" kick off a further set of 21 great cuts. Standouts include "Just Like Honey", "Some Candy Talking", "Psycho Candy" and "My Girl".

◉ 21 Singles **(Blanco Y Negro, 2002)**

An essential purchase, this compilation is, without doubt, the finest slice of angsty emotional punk rock to come out of Scotland in the last two decades. From "Upside Down" to the cheeky cynicism of "I Love Rock'n'Roll", there's not one duff track in the whole collection.

JOAN JETT AND THE BLACKHEARTS

Born Philadelphia, Pennsylvania, 1960.

"I HOPE ONE DAY PEOPLE DON'T LOOK AT WOMEN LIKE THEY'RE OUT OF THEIR MINDS WHEN THEY WANT TO PICK UP AN INSTRUMENT AND PLAY."

JOAN JETT

J oan Jett first came to public attention in the mid-Seventies as one of **The Runaways**, the glam-punk girl band "discovered" by US impresario and general music biz entrepreneur/fixer **Kim Fowley**. Thirty years later, she is revered as the godmother of Riot Grrrl, a national treasure, gay icon and one of the rockingest rock chicks in history.

Having acquired her first guitar aged just thirteen, she was playing "Cherry Bomb" with the Runaways less than two years later. Feted in Europe but written off as just a novelty act at home, the band split up in early 1979 after four studio albums and a recording made live in Japan.

By this point, though, Jett had been fronting a band for two years, had recorded with the **Sex Pistols**, produced **The Germs'** first album and was ready for more. Adopting the ever-popular leather catsuit look, she neatly kept the heavy metal boy fans on her side while exploring the more interesting punk-rock aspects of her muse. Still, she was saddled with her former band's bubblegum reputation, and her self-financed 1980 solo debut *Joan Jett* (released in the US as *Bad Reputation*) was turned down by more than twenty US labels before it found a European release. The single "Bad Reputation", taken from the album, sold well enough for her to set up her own label, Blackheart Records, with her producer and long-time friend **Kenny Laguna**. Jett recruited a new band in 1981 – a bunch of guys to take on tour and to boss around in the studio – and in one form or another **Joan Jett And The Blackhearts** has existed ever since.

Punk rock might be Jett's preference, but it was the dinosaurish classic rock of "I Love Rock And Roll" (1981), previously recorded by British one-hit wonders The Arrows, that made the industry take her seriously. Propelled by MTV, it sold in truckloads (some 14 million copies worldwide) and gave her a million-selling album of the same name. Another top-ten cover version, the steamy "Crimson And Clover", was a far juicier confection than the Tommy James And The Shondells' original, and heavy MTV rotation made her a teenage fantasy figure around the world.

Glorious Results Of A Misspent Youth (1984) boasted a return to her roots and one of the mid-Seventies' best punk moments with a rerecorded "Cherry Bomb". It helped rally round the riot grrrls, who had adopted the Runaways as heroines from an earlier era, and who elevated Jett to virtual sainthood when *Good Music* appeared in 1986.

The music might well have been good, but it wasn't punk. The entire punk scene was going through a patch of diminished popularity and Jett had taken the opportunity to mellow out a little, even taking on a few movie roles. She kept her hand in at the studios, however, releasing *Up*

Your Alley in 1988 and taking two singles from it – "I Hate Myself For Loving You" and "Little Liar" – into the Top 10.

Putting The Blackhearts project to one side, Joan worked solo for most of the Nineties, beginning with *The Hit List*, an inspired covers album, in 1990 and following up with *Notorious* the year after. Stepping off the recording-touring-recording treadmill, she helped nurture the new wave of riot grrrl bands and found time to join Seattle punk act **The Gits** after the murder of their lead singer.

⊚ **Fit To Be Tied: Great Hits By Joan Jett (Blackheart Records,1997)**

A fine fifteen-track introduction to the punk from Philly, blasting off with "Bad Reputation" and "Light Of Day", she pays her dues with ""I Love Rock & Roll", gets mean'n'sleazy through "Crimson And Clover", and boots ass with "Roadrunner" and "Cherry Bomb"

Jordan

Pamela Rooke (born 1958) invented **Jordan** when she was 14 years old and growing up near Brighton on England's south coast. On a trip up to London a few years later, elegantly clad in gold stilettos and a see-through skirt, she strolled into the Sex boutique on the Kings Road, Chelsea and was hired on the spot. Malcolm McLaren and Vivienne Westwood had stumbled onto the perfect assistant for their anti-shop: an audacious and comparatively bullshit-free girl who would happily wear their creations and taunt visitors into making extravagant purchases.

Jordan wore her Mondrian-inspired make-up and Sex threads on her daily commutes from the seaside and was regularly upgraded to first class for her own protection. Becoming a member of the **Sex Pistols**' inner circle, she had her top ripped off by an enthusiastic Johnny Rotten at one early gig and practised her most regal sneer on the Pistols'"God Save The Queen" promotional boat trip. She later teamed up with fellow bondage-fashion fan **Adam Ant** as co-vocalist and manager of the early Ants, and the two of them subsequently appeared in **Derek Jarman**'s 1978 film *Jubilee*, in which Jordan, playing the post-apocalyptic historian Amyl Nitrate, performed an unforgettable Nina Hagen-esque, bump-and-grind operatic version of "Rule Britannia".

A few years of fun and games proved sufficient, however, and in 1984, claiming there was no challenge left in punk, Jordan quit the London scene. She moved back home to train as a veterinary nurse, run an animal sanctuary and breed Burmese cats.

JOY DIVISION

Recruited Manchester, England, 1977; replaced by a New Order in 1980.

"WILSON, YOU CUNT! YOU BASTARD! YOU PUT THE BUZZCOCKS AND SEX PISTOLS AND ALL THOSE OTHERS ON THE TELLY, WHAT ABOUT US?"

IAN CURTIS INTRODUCING HIMSELF TO TONY WILSON IN 1978

When Buzzcocks' Howard Devoto and Pete Shelley arranged a **Sex Pistols** gig at Manchester's Lesser Free Trade Hall, **Peter Hook** (low-slung bass/percussion/vocals) and **Bernard Albrecht** (guitar/keyboards/vocals, born Bernard Dicken, later settled on Bernard Sumner and generally known as Barney) were in the audience. Like many others at the gig, they wandered out into the night determined to form groups of their own and to take over the world by means of punk rock and sheer effort of will.

Naturally, the first thing they needed was a good punk name, and when Pete Shelley mentioned seeing a litter of abandoned and extremely dead felines in his neighbourhood, they decided to call themselves **The Stiff Kittens**. An ad placed in a record store brought them **Ian Curtis** (vocals/lyrics/guitar, also at the Pistols gig), **Steve Brotherdale** (drums) and a much better name. Now working as **Warsaw** (after David Bowie's track "Warszawa"), the band made its debut at Manchester's Electric Circus in May 1977, sharing the bill with Buzzcocks and Penetration, and recorded a set of demos before Brotherdale quit. His replacement, **Steven Morris**, signed on and stayed while Warsaw (irked at the press coverage given to – and possible confusion with – a mob called Warsaw Pakt) changed names once again to become **Joy Division**.

Taken from Karol Cetinsky's World War II novel *The House of Dolls*, in which "joy division" was a

great feeling of belonging would dissolve into isolation, depression and ultimately suicide.

Still, it was all fun and games at the start. Gigging all over the north of England with occasional forays to the bright lights of London, the band picked up **Rob Gretton** as manager and a loyal following of kids riddled with post-industrial angst, Cold War horror and an acne-driven inability to get laid.

Another set of demos, made in preparation for a first album, was abandoned after a misguided engineer, John Anderson, added some synthesizer lines of his own creation to the pure, if basic guitar/drums sound the band was perfecting. The first Joy Division release – the EP *An Ideal For Living* – did not appear until the summer of 1978, but it created enough of a stir for the band to record a John Peel session for the beginning of 1979. Manchester scenemeister **Tony Wilson** soon became involved, signing Joy Division to his Factory label and teaming them up with legendary producer **Martin Hannett** to record *Unknown Pleasures*.

The ideal soundtrack to the UK's gloomiest decade in living memory, *Unknown Pleasures* hit the G-spot of every thoughtful, serious music journalist in the country. Peering down on the competition from a substantial height, the album had the word "masterpiece" stamped all over it, from the fashionably monochrome cover (by artist of the moment Peter Saville) and weighty titles to Ian's vocal melodramatics and startling studio effects. It didn't sell remarkably well at first, but it drew the crowds, as did the increasingly grotesque stories of Curtis's epilepsy. Never the calmest of on-stage characters, Curtis used to jerk around in

slang term for the forced prostitution units set up in some Nazi concentration camps, it wasn't the most inspiring of names. It nevertheless proved adequately mournful for a band that would go on to take punk rock into a whole new ballpark, where rage gave way to tortured introspection and anger to melancholy, and in which the movement's

---

🎵 PLAYLIST: JOY DIVISION

1. SHADOWPLAY
from **Unknown Pleasures (London, 2000)**

2. DISORDER
from **Unknown Pleasures (London, 2000)**

3. INTERZONE
from **Unknown Pleasures (London, 2000)**

4. ICE AGE
from **Still (London, 2000)**

5. GLASS
from **Still (London, 2000)**

6. THEY WALKED IN LINE
from **Still (London, 2000)**

7. SISTER RAY
from **Still (London, 2000)**

8. TRANSMISSION
from **Still (London, 2000)**

9. LOVE WILL TEAR US APART
from **Substance 1977-1980 (London, 1999)**

10. ATMOSPHERE
from **Substance 1977-1980 (London, 1999)**

the spotlight as if controlled by malevolent puppet masters fighting one another for control. Doused in stroboscopic stage lighting, he was provoked into a genuine fit on more than one occasion, each of which would leave him drained, weakened and more depressed than before.

Touring halted briefly while the band began recording its second album, releasing "Love Will Tear Us Apart" in April 1980 and resting up briefly before heading out to the USA. Curtis's personal life was in enough of a mess for suicide to be considered, and whether in a gesture gone wrong, or a serious bid that turned into horror, he took his own life by hanging in May, aged just 23.

Joy Division ceased to exist at that moment. The band had always agreed that there would be no personnel changes, and attempting to replace Ian would be almost as grotesque as his death had been. Albrecht (now surnamed Sumner) took over vocals in **New Order**, the group he formed with Hook and Morris.

New Order, of course, went on to have its own place in the history books, but in the wake of Curtis's death, the Joy Division juggernaut acquired a momentum of its own. *Closer* went into the album Top 10, dragging *Unknown Pleasures* into the chart in its train, while a reissued "Love Will Tear Us Apart" went Top 20 in late 1980 (charting again in 1983), and *Still*, a respectable collection of rarities, went Top 5. The juggernaut continued throughout the 80s and into the present: "Atmosphere", a track so gloomy it verges on self-parody, entered the Top 40 in 1987, and *Substance* (1988) – more of a cash-in compilation than *Still* had been – went Top 10. More recently, there has been the 1995 compilation *Permanent: Joy Division*, the tribute album *A Means To An End*, and a Curtis biography, *Touching From a Distance*, written by his widow, Deborah.

Twenty-five years after Ian's death, New Order began to include the occasional Joy Division number in their live appearances. Impressed by the reception they received, the band has recently played a series of sets comprising nothing but old JD material. Nobody will ever match the booming presence of Ian, and Bernard wisely avoids trying to, but the music is as vital and as relevant today as it was back then, and it still sounds like it was written yesterday.

◉ Unknown Pleasures (London, 2000)

Unknown Pleasures set new standards for punk rock. Permitting themselves the use of synthesizer and overdubs and virtually disowning the raging punk anger they had started with, the band give themselves over to Martin Hannett's production magic. Curtis's lyrics echo and reverberate in your mind long after the music has turned to silence

◉ Closer (Factory, 1980)

Promising so much, the release of this recording was initially overshadowed in the storm surrounding Curtis's death. Later listenings show the band to be developing into a unique, vital focus of attention for a disaffected generation. Dark and rich like a connoisseur chocolate bar, it's also far too much to consume in one sitting.

◉ Preston Warehouse: 28th February 1980 (Factory, 2003)

Ghouls will note that this is the last live recording Joy Division ever released. It's also, without doubt, one of the most powerful in-concert performances in the rock archives. Raw with wrong notes, scarred by equipment wars, together with *Les Bains Douches 18 December 1979* (Factory, 2003) it gives a picture of just how heart-stopping a bit of punk'n'rock'n'roll can be.

◉ Still (London, 2000)

Standout tracks on this, the best of the early JD collections (apart from the 4-CD box set *Heart And Soul*) are those taken from the last-ever gig the band played, recorded during May 1980 at a concert at Birmingham University. These include the only live version ever taped of "Ceremony" and a stunning, overwhelming take on The Velvet Underground's "Sister Ray" that challenges the original in terms of instrumental attack and vocal aggression.

◉ ICONIC SINGLE: LOVE WILL TEAR US APART (FACTORY, 1980)

Written as a response to "Love Will Keep Us Together", the relentlessly upbeat song by The Captain And Tenille, this is the true sound of despair distilled into a few short minutes of harrowing beauty. The track was recorded just two months before Ian Curtis killed himself, while he was under intense romantic pressure and suffering from epilepsy and the side-effects of the medication he was taking for it. The title is engraved on his tombstone.

KILLING JOKE

Formed Notting Hill, London, 1978;
still sporadically active.

"I HOPE YOU REALIZE THAT YOUR EFFORTS TODAY ARE ALL QUITE FUTILE."

JAZ GETS THE AUDIENCE ON HIS SIDE AT A LONDON RALLY FOR CND

Dark, rich and intense, **Killing Joke**'s music comes in heavyweight slabs, and even more than other brands of punk rock, is best experienced at brain-scrambling volume, under the influence of alcohol and other stimulants, in a crowded venue with stroboscopic lighting. Still kicking down doors after more than a quarter of a century, Killing Joke have dug deep into the bitter, twisted soul of rock'n'roll, returning each time with gems of evil sparkle and grim brilliance.

Notting Hill in the late 1970s was nothing like the later fabrication assembled by Hollywood. Largely untouched by the gentrifying hand, recession, inflation and unemployment had hit the area hard, and anyone as foppish as Hugh Grant daring to saunter its boulevards of broken dreams would have risked a kicking. So when **Jaz Coleman** (vocals/keyboards), **Geordie** (guitar), **Youth** (bass) and **"Big Paul" Ferguson** (drums) first began brewing up their musical storm there in 1978, it reflected the anger, fear and tension they brought home with them from outside.

Coleman and Ferguson had briefly been part of **The Matt Stagger Band**, Martin Glover (aka Youth) had done time with punk traditionalists **The Rage**, and they found Geordie (born Kevin Walker) under a rock on the way into town. Ferguson had once described Coleman's voice as "the sound of the Earth vomiting", and with all the essential earth-moving amplified equipment in place, the band began to make extreme music to give it the backing it deserved. Like the aftermath of an industrial accident in a dangerous goods factory, Geordie exploded his sharpened fragments of guitar noise, Youth set off barely muffled explosions of subsonic bass and Ferguson's ear-bursting drum sounds hurtled around picking off the wounded.

A girlfriend and true believer fronted the money for Killing Joke's recorded debut late in 1978. The *Almost Red* EP soon led to a stunning John Peel session that made them famous throughout the UK overnight. English audiences soon got used to the band's extreme graphics, which employed images culled from the Nazi era crosscut with religious figures and scenes of degradation. Sectarian Glasgow, however, banned them from playing after a particularly inflammatory poster for the gig threatened to set the audience at one another's throats even before the guys crossed the border into Scotland. The ensuing controversy, together with the release of "Wardance" in 1980, took the band into the international league.

The band's reputation for doom and gloom fitted perfectly with the prevailing mood of pre-apocalyptic depression and fear, and Killing Joke hit just the right sort of nerve with their follow-up singles "Psyche" and "Follow the Leader". They were an instant hit on the live circuit, spending a couple of years getting the mood right and the audience prepared for their first album, *Killing*

Joke (1981). Black and heavy as an opium-laced chocolate fudge cake, it fed the cravings of the fans, and with hit tracks "Requiem" and "Wardance", it drew in new believers ready for their second recording. Delivering more of much the same sort of barely articulate ill-focused rage, *What's THIS For...!* (1981) captured the delicate sounds of nature throwing up with the same precision as the debut, and it took the band out on tour again, to explore the world and frighten those they found in it.

It was while rampaging across Europe that Killing Joke hooked up with **Konrad "Conny" Plank**, the legendary producer / madman who had famously recorded Can, Neu! and Moebius. Plank provided the inspiration for their third album, *Revelations*, encouraging Ferguson's love of the occult, and drawing out for the first time the fascination with Masonic imagery which later inspired a number of songs (killing-joke.com has reams of information on the secretive group, some of it possibly true). Apparently in fear of a predicted apocalypse, Ferguson and Geordie fled briefly to Iceland soon after the album appeared. As they waited a few months for the world to end, they checked out the local music scene, hooking up with local punks Theyr (later to gain fame as The Sugarcubes). Youth joined the guys briefly during their frozen sojourn, but found little to interest him, and after a few months of the world stubbornly refusing to end, quit.

Killing Joke remained in Iceland to record and release a swift live EP, *Ha*, followed by *Fire Dances* (1983). The music was as primal as ever, and appealed to glands buried deep and reached only by the back routes of the central nervous system.

New bassist **Paul Raven** made his presence felt by the space he left for the rest of the instruments to leap through, and there was more emphasis on ear-searing treble and massively percussive attacks of tribal beat.

Night Time (1985) was Killing Joke's most successful recording, and gave them chart success with "Love Like Blood" and "Kings And Queens". *Brighter Than A Thousand Suns* continued the band's blind groping towards a warmer, more mature sound; with age and experience, it seemed, they had developed a taste for less aggressive stimulants. Persisting with their potent brew of dub and punk, they still sounded as if they drank fresh human blood by moonlight, but you could now imagine them driving to the sabbath in a warm and well-equipped 4x4. Without Youth and with increased mellowness, however, the band lost its grip on its audience. Ultimately, it all became a little too comfortable and the band splintered before Ferguson released *Outside The Gate* (1988). Essentially a prog rock solo album, it was a less than fitting epitaph to the band that had rendered so many people so joyously and temporarily deaf.

Killing Joke spluttered through the early Nineties, reassembling at the beginning of the decade with new drummer **Martin Atkins** (ex **Public Image Ltd**) for *Extremities, Dirt & Various Repressed Emotions*, which included the splendid "Age Of Greed" and "Inside The Termite Mound". After a one-off performance entitled *Exorcism*, recorded inside the Great Pyramid (pretty ookie, huh?), a trio of Ferguson, Geordie and the prodigal Youth reformed for *Pandemonium* (1994) and *Democracy* (1996), recorded with **Geoff Dugmore** on drums. They were, however, wasting their time chasing a new generation of kids already besotted with grunge. They left their mark elsewhere in history, influencing the industrial sounds of **Ministry** and **Nine Inch Nails** as much as the gloomy goths that were their most obvious legacy. Youth used his time away from the band well, forming **Brilliant** with Ferguson while the others were scaring the Icelanders. As the Nineties wore on, he reinvented himself as a super-producer, remix genius and bassist for **The Orb** and a bunch of other ambient electronicists. Coleman developed a career as composer in residence for the New Zealand Symphony Orchestra (the country where he now lives most of the time).

Nirvana were younger, prettier and easier to assimilate than the scary-looking uncles the Joke had grown into. Having helped steal their fans, **Dave Grohl** joined the band briefly (on drums of course) for *Killing Joke* (2003). Although this was their second eponymous recording, it came with a bright yellow cover, so you wouldn't mistake it for the grey masterpiece of the early Eighties.

Together with *Unperverted Pantomime* (2003), a compilation of rarities and B-sides, it trod the same old paths of fear, hatred and cynicism – all good stuff, but without the punk-rock roar. One for the completists only.

⊙ Killing Joke (EMI, 2005)

Remastered in the wake of the band's re-formation and successful tour supporting Mötley Crüe – the band's 1981 debut is a roaring, booming, drum-and-bass-heavy warning of imminent apocalypse. Featuring "The Wait" (later covered by Metallica) and "Wardance" (virtually their signature tune), this album refuses to compromise in terms of lyrical attack or sonic assault.

⊙ What's THIS For...! (EMI, 2005)

If this were prog rock rather than dark punk, it could be called a progression in the way it explores and develops individual themes from the debut. As it isn't, we merely recommend turning the volume up loud enough to make your eyeballs jiggle in their sockets. Includes a live version of "The Fall Of Because" – the song that inspired one group to name themselves after it, later turning into Godflesh.

⊙ Love Like Blood (Brilliant Classics, 2002)

Still the best of the available compilations, this gives you the best of the early singles, with a creamy topping of selected delicious album tracks.

L7

Formed Los Angeles, 1985; last seen 1999.

"HATTY TOLD MATTY / 'LET'S DON'T TAKE NO CHANCE. / LET'S NOT BE L7 /COME AND LEARN TO DANCE.'"

"WOOLY BULLY", SAM THE SHAM AND THE PHARAOHS

Donita Sparks (vocals/guitar) and **Suzi Gardner** (guitar/vocals) started off hanging out and drinking together before the idea of a band ever cropped up, way before the invention of riot grrrl. Gardner had previously played in local band **The Debbies** and helped weed out the dweebs before they picked out **Jennifer Finch** (bass) and **Roy Koutsky** (drums). Jennifer had worked with **Sugar Baby Doll** / **Sugar Babylon** – a band with two names that had also hosted **Courtney Love**, later of Hole and **Kat Bjelland**, later of Babes in Toyland.

Putting together a punchy set of punk-rock tunes, the band picked a cool name, taken from a 1950s expression meaning "square", as in uncool. (You make a letter "L" with the thumb and forefinger of your left hand, make a number 7 with the thumb and forefinger of your right hand, bring them together and you make a square – dig?). Then they hit the club scene in their adopted home town.

Initial comparisons with Suzi Quatro, The Runaways and even Heart were soon seen to be lazy journalism as L7 won the soul of right-thinking punk-rockers up and down the West Coast. Signing in 1987 with Brett Gurewitz's ultra-credible indie label Epitaph and supporting his band, Bad Religion, on a US tour, L7 tightened up all the loose bolts on their set and burned into the studio to record their first album, *L7*. Released in the autumn of 1988 and full of high-speed, angry noise, it was a righteous punk album and a suitable tribute to the good work of Koutsky, a drummer just a bit too male to suit the rest of the group. His place at the traps was taken by **Demetra "Dee" Plakas** (ex-Problem Dogs), and she fitted in just fine.

The arrival of Plakas signalled a change to the then super-successful SubPop label and the release of *Smell The Magic* (1990). This new album was just as intense as the first had been, but the raw edges had been knocked off and the band seemed a little less angry with the world, if perhaps a little more cynical and better informed. It sold by the bucketload, winning them a place on Nirvana's European tour and in the hearts of UK audiences. However, *Smell* showed a move away from punk and a slide sidewards towards the Seattle-friendly sounds of grunge. Hardly surprising and not necessarily a bad thing, but unfortunately the echoes of *Spinal Tap* in the title extended some way into the music and stopped little short of pomposity.

In 1991, the band deflected accusations of self-importance by founding Rock For Choice, an organization defending women's rights to have an abortion. Then, deciding to risk the inevitable accusations of "selling out", they jumped ship to Slash/Reprise, grabbing the chance to make a major-label masterpiece. *Bricks Are Heavy* (1992) roped in **Butch Vig** (star producer of the era and the man who'd delivered Nirvana's *Nevermind*) and yielded a fantastic single, "Pretend We're Dead". A hit with both critics and fans around the world, the album briefly propelled L7 into the stratosphere.

It was no coincidence that one song from the album featured in Oliver Stone's *Natural Born Killers* (1994). "Shitlist" – the record selected from a jukebox in a diner as Mallory's theme by her partner in crime Mickey – was head and shoulders above most angry girl music, providing the perfect accompaniment to a put-upon young lady kicking the living crap out of a bunch of red-necked old perverts.

The band followed up the album with a notorious appearance at the Reading Festival. After the traditionally torrential rain had rendered the festival site treacherous and the audience uglier than normal, one mud-throwing member of the crowd finally provoked Donita into dropping her pants and hurling a used tampon back out at them.

As if that wasn't enough, L7 then swaggered on to UK TV screens like the Sex Pistols reborn. Booked to perform on Channel 4's post-pub young adult showcase *The Tube*, the band kicked ass and Sparks stripped off, entering punk-rock legend in just three and a half minutes. Carrying off such an obviously planned stunt with panache and humour was punk rock to the core, and the kids who saw the show spread the word.

The band continued to tour the world and even showed up in a knowing cameo as **The Camel Lips** in John Waters' movie *Serial Mom* (1994) before returning to the studio to record their next set, *Hungry For Stink* (1994). It hit the streets with easily the best album title of the year and a killer opening track, "Andres".

Jennifer quit to finish college in 1996, leaving the remaining partners to record *The Beauty Process: Triple Platinum* as a trio. They were joined by **Gail Greenwood** (ex-Belly) for the tour to promote it, but when L7 parted company with the label, she returned to her East Coast base. Although she never worked on any studio recordings, Gail's contribution can be heard on *L7 Live: Omaha To Osaka* (1998).

Though riot grrrl had been and gone by this point, and punk was once again in the doldrums, L7 headed for the straight-no-chaser rock'n'roll

audience. First, they founded their own Wax Tadpole label (a name taken from a track on their debut, itself inspired by the translated ideogram allegedly once used to promote Coca Cola in China). Then, recruiting **Janis Tanaka** (ex-Stone Fox, Auntie Christ and Fireball Ministry), the newly independent L7 released *Slap-Happy* in 1999. It failed to set the charts alight, however, and since then, apart from *The Best Of L7: The Slash Years* (2000) and occasional appearances on the rock circuit, the band has essentially shut the store.

◉ **Bricks Are Heavy (London, 1999)**

Originally released back in 1992, this is still the best of the band's albums: eleven urgent, fast, punk-rockin' tunes that are angry, wild and oozing poison. As it includes "Wargasm", "Pretend We're Dead", "Diet Pill" and "Shitlist", you are instructed to buy it and play it until you are word-perfect.

◉ **The Best Of L7: The Slash Years (London, 2000)**

Twelve more tracks, with some overlap from the album above, that nevertheless deserve a place in your collection. As it says on the insert, "play loud for maximum effect".

LAUGHING CLOWNS / ED KUEPPER

Formed Sydney, Australia, 1979; stopped laughing in 1985 (Ed's still out there somewhere).

H anging out in Sydney, far from his birthplace in Germany, **Ed Kuepper** was just into his twenties and waiting for something good to happen when punk first broke out. Hooking up with **Chris Bailey** and taking **The Saints** – the city's first punk band – to success across in the UK before most kids in Sydney had even heard the word, he was there at the very beginning and instinctively knew what it was about.

The Saints fell apart in London during 1978 and Ed cashed in his royalties for a ticket back home. Bringing some international credibility to an Australian scene dismissed or simply ignored by the bulk of the US and European media, he formed **Laughing Clowns** with **Jeffrey Wegener** (drums), **Robert Farrell** (sax), **Ben Wallace-Crabbe** (piano) and Ben's brother **Dan** (bass).

Deliberately difficult to classify, the new band made something best described as jazz-punk, music that was decidedly arty-crafty, with difficult rhythms, awkward time signatures and downright weird song structures, releasing a number of EPs before going full-length with *Mr. Uddich Schmuddich Goes To Town* (1981). The album's dour vocals, courtesy of Kuepper, were its most arresting feature. Low-pitched and mean-tempered, he growled through his nose, backing up his more extreme statements with overpowering waves of discordant threshing-machine guitar.

Kuepper and Wegener tinkered with the line-up, adding a trumpeter here, an extra sax player there. Then, having showered the competition with a bunch of fine singles and a magnificently titled compilation *Reign Of Terror/Throne Of Blood*, they relocated the whole band to London for a while – a move that led to the compilations *Laughing Clowns* and *Laughter Around The Table* on UK label Red Flame. Kuepper and Wegener finally settled on **Louise Elliot** (trumpet/sax), **Chris Abrahams** (piano) and either **Peter Walsh** or **Paul Smith** (bass) to make up the quintet, but their killer live act, bitter lyrics and devoted gig audience were not enough to take Laughing Clowns into the big league. *Law Of Nature* (1984) was a critical hit but a dud in the stores, and the follow-up *Ghosts Of An Ideal Wife* (1985) performed even worse. In the face of rejection, the band split up.

Kuepper went solo, and in a burst of berserk productivity over the next decade, released more than a dozen albums, mainly studio recordings. He's slowed down a little in recent years, and has managed to steer clear of his punk past most of the time, although at one point he toured with soundalike band **The Aints**.

In the last twenty years, Kuepper has never once let a dud onto the market, although each release has varied wildly in style from the one before. Since the mid-Nineties, he's stayed mainly in Australia, mainly on tour and mainly not selling a great deal of records. This is despite having a devoted, if unusual following composed of balding punk rockers in faded gig T-shirts and jazz fans with an even worse dress sense.

⦿ **Golden Days When Giants Walked The Earth (Hot, 1995)**

Best and most easily available of the compilations.

THE LIBERTINES / DIRTY PRETTY THINGS

Libertines formed London 1996; relaunched as Dirty Pretty Things 2005.

"I LIKE THE SMELL OF MY GRANDMA'S SOAP – I USED TO SIT IN THE BATH AND EAT IT."

CARL BARÂT, INTERVIEWED BY BBC SOUTHAMPTON, 2002.

Prime movers of Britain's recent punk resurgence, **Pete Doherty** (vocals/guitar/ class 'A' press and police problems) and **Carl Barât** (guitar/vocals/some degree of restraint) waded through almost unbelievable squalor to eventually surface as **The Libertines**, press darlings of 2001/02. Granted it was a squalor of their own making, but, hailed as the latest and greatest hope of British punk by a music media desperate to find a band to pitch on top of its latest self-created bandwagon, **The Libertines** were blown out of the water before they had a chance to blossom. Another case of too much attention, much too soon – and the drugs didn't help.

Barât was born in 1978 and split his childhood years shuttling between his father (who worked in an arms factory) and his mother, who had embraced pacifism and left the old family home for a commune in rural Somerset. He met Doherty through Pete's sister Amy, a fellow student on his drama course, who shared a squat with her brother in London's fashionable Bethnal Green. The guys discovered they had much in common musically and had a shared taste in drugs. Each owned a mixed bag of half-finished songs and, nailing his scrotum to the mast of certain fame, Barât quit his job to move into another, even more dilapidated squat with Doherty, ostensibly to work on finishing the set.

Together with Barat's sudden lack of salary and the household's continuing need for powders and potions, the move to Camden Town brought the songwriting to a regular halt as, according to their own legend, they went out hooking to buy off the monkey. Sordid, squalid and shocking, but that's what a heroin / crack habit does to you.

Anyway, they were far from being the first bunch of punk rockers with a drug problem to deal with, and the experience of living in a house with no locks – in fact in a house without a door to fit one to – and no money added genuine grit to their first set of material. The beautifully deadpan music was littered with drug references, degradation and the algebra of need, and songs such as "Skag And Bone Man" came straight out of the pure punk-rock lives they were living. Working together, Barât and Doherty joined the English songwriterly tradition of The Kinks, The Who, The Small Faces and Blur.

In the meantime, survival was the most important thing on their minds. Once the guys had bought themselves a beer, the occasional ill-rewarded pub sets they landed weren't even paying enough to cover their nonexistent rent. Having given room to almost every wannabe rock'n'roll star in London, Barât and Doherty finally agreed on backup from **John Hassall** (bass) and **Gary Powell** (drums) and had discovered writing the material and living the life proved to be the easy part of being a successful punk-rock act – the hard part was convincing someone to listen to the material. The Libertines' shambolic gigs – part music-hall knees-up, part football-terrace brawl – were drawing larger and more enthusiastic crowds and the band was soon on the front pages of all the music mags, and began to feature in the mainstream press.

Inspired by the repeated experience of being turned down (or worse, ignored) by some record company fool in designer jeans and a self-mocking T-shirt, the lads' bitter "Death On The Stairs" was among the set that finally led the band to a deal with Rough Trade and studio time with **Bernard Butler** (ex-Suede) behind the producer's desk. The resulting double A-sided single, "What A Waster"/ "I Get Along", hit the UK charts and earned them the kudos of having **Mick Jones** (ex-Clash) produce the band's debut album *Up The Bracket*, released in October 2002. Jones' influence turned them from a bunch of losers into a tight, focused and dedicated group, prepared to work for endless hours on a guitar solo to get it exactly right. With Jones behind them providing encouragement and a standard to live up to, The Libertines were ready to create music they could still be proud of twenty years down the line.

The Libertines spent much of 2003 on tour (spending spring in the US as part of the Coachella circuit and the summer hitting the road in Europe), with Doherty making ever more sporadic appearances as he finally achieved an income to match his appetites. Ultimately, having chosen drugs in favour of the band he'd always apparently wanted more than anything else in the world, he was sacked. In an ugly coda to this part of the story, he was subsequently busted for breaking into Barat's flat and stealing the portable valuables – presumably cashing it in for powdered fun – while The Libertines were adding Japanese visa stamps to their passports.

Left behind in England and out on pre-trial bail, Doherty dithered between solo appearances and fronting a new band with no fixed membership, trading under The Libertines' name while Barât and his lot were out of the country. As unchal-

Dirty, pretty thing: Carl Barât.

lenged master of the early-post-millenial gimmick of guerilla gigging, Pete had little trouble attracting crowds or spreading the word of the new outfit's new name. Punning on the brand name of a once highly advertised drink, **Babyshambles** (see p.71) began trading on Doherty's notoriety.

While the Libertines bandwagon rolled on, with Barât and the rest releasing "Don't Look Back Into The Sun", Doherty pleaded guilty and was sentenced to six months behind bars. Appeals and time served meant that he was back on the streets and back in The Libertines in time for the Rough Trade 25th Anniversary bash held in London in October 2003.

Doherty's self-confessed addiction to heroin and crack made him a liability to both his bands. The pressures of fame combined with the easy availability of money to render him a bloated travesty of all that punk rock was about. He turned increasingly to the Internet to issue incoherent statements and to announce secret gigs – some of which he actually managed to attend. Barât and the others were under the same kinds of strain, but were fortunate enough to keep a lid on most of their obsessions for long enough to work on a follow-up album, hidden away from their friends, fans and suppliers in northern France.

Back home early in 2004, Barât and Doherty found themselves back in the singles charts with "For Lovers" – a beautiful pension-plan of a song recorded by their pal Wolfman. Babyshambles released their first, self-titled single, and if he'd only kept his nose out of the bag, Doherty could have had a magnificent year. Instead, he spent it flirting with journalists, exchanging ever-more lurid "My Drug Hell" stories for his next hit, and on a pointless set of abortive stints in rehab clinics at home, in France and finally in Thailand.

Both the band and their fans grew increasingly fed up with not knowing whether Doherty would turn up to gigs, or whether he would be in any fit state to perform if he did. June was a write-off as his Love Music/Hate Racism appearance was cancelled, followed by potentially huge and much anticipated sets at Glastonbury, the Isle Of Wight and Meltdown festivals. When Doherty was busted yet again (for a switchblade knife discovered by police during a "routine" traffic stop), the band threw up their hands and continued without him, **Anthony Rossomando** taking his place temporarily "until Pete got his addictions under control".

As "Can't Stand Me Now," hit the charts in August, Doherty was back in court, pleading guilty and escaping jail with a fine and the promise to keep trying the rehab. *The Libertines* was released shortly after and the band, without Doherty – who had Babyshambles to occupy him – went on the road.

The Libertines stop/start history jolted and spluttered on until February 2005, when, with Doherty ricocheting around in rehab/tabloid/supermodel hell, Barât put The Libertines on hold, signed a solo deal and promptly reappeared with a new band.

Dirty Pretty Things was originally the name of a club night Barât hosted, and had itself been the title of a movie. Reluctant to throw it out while there was still some life in it, he recycled the name, sticking it onto the new band (although even that remains in doubt at time of writing, with another British band claiming to have dibs on that moniker already). In the autumn of 2005, Barât took the band – former Libertines **Gary Powell** (drums) and **Anthony Rossomando** (guitar), plus **Didz Hammond** (bass/ vocals, ex-The Cooper Temple Clause) first to Italy for a few "unannounced" dates, then to Paris for a "secret" headline show (word must have got out somehow, the place was rammed). By November the band were in the studio, recording their self-titled debut with Dave Sardy producing. Picking up where The Libertines left off, the album, unreleased at the time of writing, is predictably predicted to be a classic by label boss Alan McGee.

◉ **Up The Bracket (Rough Trade, 2002).**

Intelligent, spunky punk-rock noise that descends directly from the same family tree as The Clash and The Jam.

◉ **The Libertines (Rough Trade, 2004)**

The album's standout track "Can't Stand Me Now" is one of the all-time greatest buddy songs, and, along with "Whatever Became Of The Likely Lads", provides an elegant summary of Barat's relationship with his troublesome sidekick.

LIGHTNING BOLT

Formed Providence, Rhode Island, 1995; still striking.

One-time art-school punks, **Lightning Bolt** have been exploring the drone'n'bass end of the spectrum for the past ten years. Now well rid of the education system, they still get together to summon up their mega-heavy drum-laced noise and make extreme music for extreme people.

Much beloved of cerebral muso types, the Bolt's three-part art/hardcore attack initially comprised **Brian Chippendale** (drums, gymnastics), **Brian Gibson** (bass), and **Hisham Bharoocha** (vocals). When Bharoocha left (perhaps uncomfortable at being outnumbered by Brians), Chippendale took over, clamping the mic in his jaws, feeding his voice through a mess of effects pedals and keeping up a righteous noise on the drums at the same time. Intelligible or not, the duo were the most exciting punk-rock act on the East Coast in years, and they found themselves at the centre of a small vortex of Rhode Island bands as the Nineties wore on, influencing and gigging with everyone from Six Finger Satellite, Men's Recovery Project and Arab on Radar, to Ruins, Landed, Locust and Melt Banana.

Ride The Skies appeared in 2001 on the tail of a series of now completely unobtainable singles and pretty much explored every nook and niche available to a two-man noise factory. The great improvisation and undeniable telepathy it demonstrated, however, very quickly grew monotonous. *Wonderful Rainbow* continues their experimental punk-rock death-metal jazz-fusion and is just as frenzied, improvisational, violent and spontaneous as its predecessor. Whether this stuff is ever played on the home stereo is debatable, but live, particularly on the nights when they aim to be the loudest band ever and really crank up the PA, they kick ass for miles around.

⊚ **Wonderful Rainbow (Load, 2003)**

Pulling out all the stops and including everything but the kitchen sink (which was already being used by Fatboy Slim), Lightning Bolt's music really does all sound the same. Though in concert they regularly tear the roofs off tha sucka, whenever they go into the studio the recorded output sucks, big time. This is the least unpleasant of their albums.

LONDON

Formed where you'd expect, 1976; split up 1977.

"...WE WERE PROBABLY ONE OF THE FIRST PUNK BANDS TO USE IRONY. THE GUITAR INTRO TO 'SUMMER OF LOVE', FOR EXAMPLE, IS MEANT TO BE A PISS-TAKE."

COLIN WIGHT

London formed, recorded, did everything the marketing men said and then died on their feet, virtually unknown to the mainstream of punk fans, all in less than two years.

When Robert Stigwood, owner of the RSO record label, decided he needed a punk band on his roster, he turned to his young friend **Miles**

London calling.

Tredinnick to arrange things. Miles became **Riff Regan** (vocals) adopting the surname of the heroic police inspector from TV cop drama *The Sweeney*, and recruited **Jon Moss** (drums) **Dave Wight** (guitar) and **Steve Voice** (bass, confusingly). The new band threw together a set of covers and self-penned disposable pop-punk tunes, bought themselves some suitably outrageous stage threads and hit the circuit.

Simon Napier-Bell, infamous London pop scenester and manager at large, jumped at the chance to manage such a gorgeous and marketable team of lads and signed them up on the strength of a secondhand review of their first live gig. With Stigwood and Napier-Bell on their side, London swiftly found themselves headlining far larger venues than they deserved and attracting the kind of press that only money could buy.

In fairness, they were not entirely relying on smoke and mirrors for their success. The set was good, the guys were growing more confident and developing some competence on their chosen instruments, and having signed a presumably more lucrative than normal deal with MCA Records, their debut, "Everyone's A Winner" sold well, receiving encouraging airplay from John Peel.

It didn't chart though, and neither did the follow-up, a massive multi-cut beast that sported "Summer Of Love", "Siouxsie Sue", "No Time" and their gorgeously amphetamined cover of the Easybeats' 60s mod classic "Friday On My Mind". "Animal Games" released in November 1977 was their last stab at the Top 40.

Animal Games the album, finally released in 1978, stands as the legacy of one of the UK scene's greatest "might have been" bands. London disintegrated after Moss was drafted in to replace Rat Scabies in **The Damned**, only for his new group to collapse into drunken arguments and split up almost before he'd warmed up his drum stool. Although Moss later surfaced in Culture Club and went on to fame and fortune of a different kind, it was as a member of London that he learned the ins and outs of the music business.

⊙ **Animal Games (MCA, 1978)**

One for punk completists only, as not even their most loyal fans of the group played this album twice. The couple of singles that qualify as listenable are worth tracking down on other compilations rather than here.

LONDON SS

Never really formed in London, mid-1975; never gigged, kind of split up early in 1976. Didn't record anything worth hearing either.

"... BERNIE (RHODES) BROUGHT MALCOLM MCLAREN DOWN TO SEE US REHEARSE AND MALCOLM WAS LIKE 'THIS IS GOING TO CHANGE THE WORLD? NOT REALLY!'"

MICK JONES

London SS was a seminal and loosely knit gathering of musicians that would have been called a collective if anyone had dared to use such a hippy-tainted word. It centred on **Mick Jones** (later Clash, Big Audio Dynamite), **Tony James** (later Chelsea, Generation X and Sigue Sigue Sputnik) and **Bernie Rhodes** (clothes salesman, scenester and later manager of The Clash). The lads used to spend hours in a greasy spoon café in Praed Street called the Paddington Kitchen, supping tea and playing the jukebox – soon stocked mainly with records of their own choosing – between stints of directionless rehearsals under the café (a few horrible-quality bootlegs exist, but they're not worth buying).

Potential recruits were located by postcard advertisements pinned up around the record machine and then quizzed in the café on their knowledge of bands such as The New York Dolls, Stooges and MC5, before being led downstairs to rattle and roar their way through the band's ramshackle repertoire of Sixties pop and beat-group classics.

If legend is to be believed, most of London's loose-end musicians sooner or later turned up to rehearse and kick out a few jams. **Paul Simonon**, for example, met Mick Jones through a drummer friend who'd gone down to Praed Street in search of his destiny. The audition was loose enough for Simonon to be invited to have a bash at singing, and apparently Bernie was sufficiently impressed for him to draft

Simonon, with Jones, into the much more successful band that appeared a few months later.

Keith Levene (later Public Image) was introduced to the set-up through his schoolmate **Viv Albertine** (later Slits). **Terry Chimes** tried his hand as drummer (it didn't work out, although he eventually played on the first Clash album), as did **Nick "Topper" Headon**. Topper took the gig when it was offered, but left after a week, only to return to The Clash some time later. **Chrissie Hynde** (then a journalist, later a Pretender) hung out with the kids, **Brian James** and **Rat Scabies** joined the club for a while before becoming Subterraneans and finally getting a gig with The Damned, and **Glen Matlock** was in on the scene before he became a Sex Pistol. It was Matlock, in fact, who encouraged Jones and Simonon to go and see the 101ers (featuring **Joe Strummer**) at Hammersmith's Red Cow music pub. A few weeks later, with Bernie's help, the future members of The Clash were finally all in the same room at the same time.

It was around this time that the collective began to disintegrate, yielding The Clash, The Damned and all the other bands mentioned above. As the breeding-ground for London's punk scene, the SS – which stood for Social Security, not for anything nastily Nazi – has a permanent place in the rock'n'roll Valhalla, and still owe the price of several teas to the Paddington Kitchen.

LYDIA LUNCH

Born Lydia Koch, Rochester, New York, 1959.

"THERE'RE ENOUGH HAPPY ASSHOLES OUT THERE, WHY SHOULD I BE ANOTHER ONE"

LYDIA LUNCH

Lydia Lunch was the black-clad vampire magnet around which the New York No Wave swirled. Never exactly a fully paid-up card-carrying member of the punk community, she hung out on its artier, more poetic edge, scaring the hicks and hissing menacingly. Once seen never forgotten, once heard always remembered, she has

been terrifying recording engineers and audiences alike since the mid-1970s, and was responsible for bands including **Teenage Jesus And The Jerks** (see p.319), Beirut Slump, The Devil Dogs, 13:13 and Eight Eyed Spy.

Teenage Jesus started out in 1976 with the 16-year-old Lydia screaming, wailing and bashing crap out of her guitar. Two years later, **Brian Eno** recorded the band for his No New York compilation alongside fellow noisepests The Contortions, Mars and DNA.

By the 1980s Lydia was essentially a solo artiste, performing her own material backed by a bunch of hired guns. Occasionally dispensing altogether with the musicians, she's earned a great deal of respect for her spoken-word performances and recordings. Some of this material verges on punk rock, but it's all a bit too self-centred and self-consciously artistic to genuinely claim the label.

It has led her, however, to a series of collaborations with some of the world's more interesting musicians, including **Nick Cave**, members of The Weirdos, Einstürzende Neubaten, Marc Almond and Thurston Moore. She founded her own label, Widowspeak, in 1984, before working with Clint "Foetus" Thirlwell on *Honeymoon In Red* (1987) and the dangerous, sexually charged *Stinkfist* in 1989. She also formed the all-girl noise band **Harry Crews** with Kim Gordon and has shared the stage with **Henry Rollins**.

In 2002, *Hysterie*, a video of her musical projects with other artists, was shown at the Athens film festival. Far from easy listening, her work is very much an acquired taste.

⊙ **Teenage Jesus & The Jerks** (Atavistic, 2001)

The band once played a three-song concert that was over in three minutes. This unfortunately goes on a while longer but, once the pain recedes, it gives way to a relatively pleasant throbbing. Serious explorers of the New York No Wave phenomenon, however, will find plenty of delights contained herein, with highlights including "Red Alert", "Burning Rubber", "Baby Doll" and "My Eyes".

THE LURKERS

Formed London, 1976; split 1979. Re-formed in 1987, still lurking somewhere.

Cheerfully continuing West London's tradition of producing good-time, style-conscious singalong rock'n'rollers (see The Who, The Faces etc), **The Lurkers** swaggered into the centre of town in 1976 with the brash false confidence of newly-recruited sailors out on their first shore leave. Taking more than a cue from **The Ramones** and tuned into the zeitgeist with sufficient accuracy to jump onto the punk bandwagon before its paint dried, they romped and strolled like **The New York Dolls** crossed with **Slade**, but faster… much faster. **Howard Wall** (vocals) dominated the venue whenever the lights hit him, throwing himself into impossible shapes and sometimes almost ripping his trademark tight white trousers, but never losing his mod-based dignity. With **Pete Stride** (guitar) by his side, ripping impossibly rapid chordwork from his machine at the front of the stage, solid, quick-fingered backup from **Arturo Bassick** (bass, of course) and riotous support from **Manic Esso** (drums), Wall and the band led the audience through a greased-lightning set covering love, hate, confusion, relationship breakdown, personal politics and dog-ugly girls (well, nobody's perfectly politically correct) in about twenty minutes, including encore.

The band built up a loyal following on the London and provincial circuit, signing to Beggars Banquet for their majestic first single "Shadow" (see below). Bewitching and converting almost everyone who heard it, "Shadow" picked up some limited local radio play that helped spread the word. As their popularity increased, a series of killer singles – "Freak Show", "Ain't Got A Clue", "I Don't Need To Tell Her", "Just Thirteen", "Out In The Dark" and "New Guitar in Town" built them an audience of over-emotional heartbroken teenagers, looking for something that would stop their hot angry tears. Listening to "Love Story" or "Ooh! Ooh! I Love You" (B-sides to "Shadow" and "Ain't Got A Clue" respectively) would stiffen their bottom lips long enough for black or purple to be applied before they returned to the search for romance down at the rock'n'roll club.

Bassick and Esso quit the band after "Shadow" but before *Fulham Fallout* hit the shops in 1978, leaving The Lurkers as a two-man vehicle. John Peel was an early convert but the band's increasing popularity saw them attracting an ever younger, less discriminating audience, and led to appearances alongside one-hit novelty acts on BBC TV's *Top Of The Pops*. The strain of hiring and firing almost every warm, breathing rhythm section in the land, touring up and down the country with occasional forays into the rest of Europe, and working their way through a phenomenal number of young female admirers eventually took a toll on Stride and Wall too, though

they continued to cause mayhem until they and their audience, but more importantly, the record company, had developed different interests.

The Lurkers gave it up for a couple of years after *God's Lonely Men* (1980) sank without trace, reforming too soon – in 1982 – to have really been missed. Since then, various line-ups, mainly shepherded together by the returned Arturo Bassick, have shuffled into the studios or, less frequently, out on the road. Bassick has never given up the ghost of punk rock, but most of his old band mates retired into proper employment, where there's not quite as much oral sex but at least they take home a regular wage. Despite the thrill that comes from spinning "Shadow" loud enough to scare the neighbours, or catching them live, The Lurkers really lost most of their relevance at the beginning of the 80s.

Their legacy includes a set of live albums best ignored and various repackaged greatest hits sets. Both the studio recordings are worth grabbing if you see them, but a decent compilation will serve most needs.

The Beggars Banquet Punk Singles
(Anagram, 1999)

Best of the current bunch – and it includes the B-sides. Standouts aplenty including "Shadow", "Love Story", "Freak Show, "Be My Prisoner", "Ain't Got A Clue" and the otherwise difficult to find "Fulham Fallout Firty Free".

ICONIC SINGLE:
SHADOW (BEGGARRS BANQUET, 1977)

Starts out with the cutest hook in punk rock – a one-finger, single-string illustration of the chord sequence, followed immediately by an overwhelming roar of distorted guitar chords, with drums and bass guitar thrashing away in a bid to make themselves heard. The lyrics tell the old story – girl finds new boy, old boyfriend gets jealous, borrows a gun and lays plans to kill his replacement – all the details you need for a classic "slice of life" punk-rock piece, not a word out of place, three choruses and a solo, clocking in below the three minute mark. Perfect.

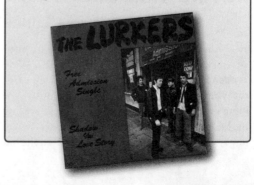

M

SHANE MACGOWAN

Born Kent, England (no, NOT Ireland), 1957; incredibly, still with us.

"You've got to have someone to deal with all those people who are into Gary Numan and the Gang Of Four."

Shane O'Hooligan, 1978

The greatest living Plastic Paddy, **Shane MacGowan** ruined his mother's festive season by appearing, squawking, clench-fisted and with no control over his bowels, on Christmas Day 1957. Now, as he approaches the end of his fifth decade after a lifetime of abuse, degradation and rock'n'roll, depressingly little has changed.

A fiercely intelligent and creative child, MacGowan turned bad as he hit his teens, expelled from school after being caught with drugs, and spending time as a working hustler on London's Piccadilly meat-rack before attending his first Sex Pistols concert in 1976 and finding salvation.

Renamed as Shane O'Hooligan, he appeared in almost all the early footage shot of punk London in 1976–77, bouncing brainlessly and joyously drunk with a Banshee hanging off him. The story of him losing an earlobe at a gig when someone else in the crowd bit it off is apocryphal – in fact, he suffered no more than a cut on the head from a broken bottle, which clearly didn't deter him from putting a band together himself and getting in on the fun.

Deciding the world needed a band called **The Nipple Erectors** until persuaded that perhaps **The Nips** would stand more chance of appearing on *Top Of The Pops*, MacGowan hustled a recording session from someone on the scene and produced "King Of The Bop". This, to be honest, could have been recorded in the mid-1950s, and apart from a certain breezy, drunken delivery and a sneer so wide it should have received an Arts Council grant, added little to the state of play.

With music delivered with joyful sloppiness by **Shanne Bradley** (bass), **Blondie Douglas** (guitar) and **Ringo Watts** (drums), the single appeared in early 1978, and managed to attract the attention and sponsorship of no less than The Jam's Paul Weller, who stepped in and kept them together, more or less, until 1980. Neither "All The Time In The World"

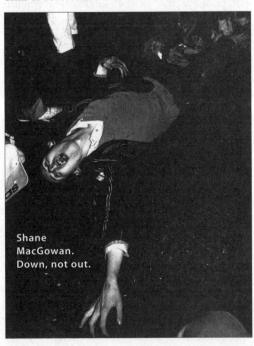

Shane MacGowan. Down, not out.

193

🎧 CELEBRITY PLAYLIST: MOBY

Once labelled the "Iggy Pop of techno", there are few musical genres Moby has not embraced in his career. No surprise, then, that when asked for his punk playlist, he came up with perhaps the most eclectic list in this book and insisted on annotating it for us, too...

1. **BANNED IN DC Bad Brain** from **Banned In DC**
"One of the best hardcore punk songs ever recorded. I remember listening to this over and over when I was in high school and missing a class as a result of my obsession with this song."

2. **MY RULES Void** from **Faith/Void**
"Another DC hardcore band. Incredibly sloppy and chaotic, but somehow embodying that perfect punk ethos of sounding as if it's about to implode."

3. **WHITE MAN IN HAMMERSMITH PALAIS** **The Clash** from **The Clash**
"Arguably the best Clash song every written, and that's saying something, as the Clash wrote and recorded about 100 flawless songs. But this is epic, and it's almost like five songs in one. Kind of like the 'Bohemian Rhapsody' of punk rock."

4. **WHY Discharge** from **Why**
"I remember first hearing this and thinking that it sounded like the end of the world. I recently went back and listened to it again, and yes, it still sounds like the end of the world."

5. **SO WHAT? Anti-Nowhere League** from **We Are The League**
"OK, a bit of comedy. Well, I assume it's comedy. Every time I hear this song it makes me laugh. I hope that was the intention..."

6. **SEX BOMB Flipper** from **Sex Bomb**
"Another big slice of chaos. With the only lyric being 'she's a sex bomb my baby, yeah', in the early 80s this was the punk rock version of 'Louie, Louie' with every hardcore band doing their own version of it live."

7. **TRASH New York Dolls** from **New York Dolls**
"Is this punk rock? In my mind it is. It's degenerate and fun, as most good punk rock should be. And without the Dolls you never would've had the Sex Pistols.

8. **COMMUNICATION BREAKDOWN** **Led Zeppelin** from **Led Zeppelin**
"I'm sorry, but this is punk rock. Go back and listen to it – punk rock before there was punk rock. Even the title sounds like something that The Ramones or Dead Boys would've come up with."

9. **LOS ANGELES X** from **Los Angeles**
"X's first three albums have held up amazingly well and they still stand as probably the best lyricists in the history of punk rock. This is, in my mind, their signature song."

10. **FUCK CHRISTMAS, FUCK YOU Pork Guys** from **a limited edition single**
"OK, I'm just throwing this into the list for the hell of it. I played drums in the pork guys, and we were funny and noisy and absurd. The only lyric to this song is 'fuck Christmas, fuck you'. Good luck trying to find it, as we only made 100 copies."

---

nor "Gabrielle", the follow-up singles, did very much in terms of sales or legend-building, and The Nips went their separate ways. MacGowan washed up as a part-time guitar man for his pal Spider Stacy's band, **The Millwall Chainsaws** (named after an imaginary bunch of football hooligans from British soccer's most notorious club), working in a record store to pay the rent and food bills.

When the Chainsaws split up too, MacGowan and Stacy formed **Pogue Mahone**. Gaelic for "Kiss My Arse", the name showed the lads' resistance to conformity and initially carefree attitude to radio play and TV appearances. Someone with an eye on the finances suggested that once again, something less provocative should be chosen, and the band became **The Pogues**. MacGowan and Stacy surrounded themselves with a bunch of hardened musicians with a general thirst and a talent for welding the energy of punk onto the heartfelt passion of traditional folk music. **James Fearnley** (accordion), **Jem Finer** (guitar), **Cait O'Riordan** (bass) and **Andrew Rankin** (drums) signed on for the voyage into territories unknown and hit the tour circuit.

Frenetic, wild and free, even by the considerably high energy levels of the average early 1980s performance, The Pogues kicked some serious ass live in concert, and they soon built up a following of such dedication that a coup might have easily been possible. Luckily for the powers that be, MacGowan and the gang were having far too much fun to dish out revolutionary justice, taking on chart acts and serious musos alike and simply outplaying, outclassing and outperforming them.

His greatest hit was "Fairytale Of New York" – a pension-plan Christmas tune that is as reliable an indicator of the forthcoming festivities each year as the appearance of overpriced toys in the TV commercial breaks. A sparky, boozed-up and vicious argument in the drunk tank turns into the most warming, cinnamon-spiced love story as MacGowan and **Kirsty McColl** trade insults and memories and the music swells like a sentimental lump in the throat: "You're a bum, you're a punk, you're an old slut on junk" and "You scumbag, you maggot, you cheap lousy faggot" – phrases to cheer the heart and warm the soul every time.

All that energy comes at a price, however, and MacGowan spent quite a few years devoting himself to booze and drugs – even investing a chunk of his royalties in a pub so that there was always somewhere he could sit around and drink without risking being thrown out onto the streets. As so often happens, the chemicals began to interfere with the performance, and as the Eighties rolled into the Nineties, there was always a good chance that the ticket-buying public would feel cheated as MacGowan showed up drunk, incapable or not at all. With half the audience cheering his excess and the other half trying to enjoy the music, there were constant disappointments, and after screwing up a tour supporting Bob Dylan, MacGowan found himself sacked by his own band at the end of 1991.

With not even a band to distract him, MacGowan turned his attention even more fully to the bottle and was roundly expected to drink himself to death. He surfaced occasionally – managing to record a stunningly powerful version of "What A Wonderful World" alongside **Nick Cave** – but kept out of sight for a few years until the dust had settled and he was able to start again.

Nearer sober than he'd been for over a decade, MacGowan formed The Popes in 1994 and began to tear the roof off again wherever he played. The new band – comprising **Berni France** (bass), **Tom McAnimal** (banjo), **Paul McGuinness** (guitar), **Kieran 'Mo' O'Hagan** (guitar), **Colm O'Maonlai** (whistle) and **Danny Pope** (drums)– released *The Snake* in 1995, forming ties with members of The Dubliners and inviting ex-Pogues Finer and Stacy to join them whenever the fancy took them. Just as fun-loving as any other of MacGowan's projects, the new band even persuaded **Johnny Depp** to provide guest vocals on their debut, "That Woman's Got Me Drinking".

Having taken "Haunted," a duet with **Sinéad O'Connor** into the charts, MacGowan worked with ex-Clannad member **Máire Brennan** on the follow-up, "Lonesome Highway", which appeared in 1997, and stumbled through an on/off relationship with The Popes that continued into the new millenium.

Although he takes his own legend a little too seriously and sometimes appears to be the punk-rock Dean Martin, when it comes to uplifting songs of wild rebellion, world-weary ballads and epic tales of alcoholic mayhem, MacGowan's yer man.

⦿ **Rum, Sodomy & The Lash** (WSM, 2004)

Produced by Elvis Costello, and as enjoyable as fourteen swift pints of stout. Now available in a deluxe, remastered version, expanded with six bonus tracks (including the four that made up the *Poguetry In Motion* EP), this becomes an even more important piece of plastic. There's also a bargain box set on sale, with *Rum Sodomy And The Lash*, *If I Should Fall From Grace With God* and *Peace And Love* in one neat package but they seem to be the old, non-remastered versions.

⦿ **If I Should Fall From Grace With God** (WSM, 2004)

Also available in a deluxe, remastered version, expanded with six bonus tracks, this is perhaps a more restrained Pogues album. Most of the band sound as if they're keeping at least one foot on the ground, most of the time. The delicate melodies that sometimes make it through to the front of the mix are worth the entry price on their own, but seeing that you get "Fairytale Of New York", "The Broad Majestic Shannon", "Lullaby Of London" and "Turkish Song Of The Damned" thrown in as well, you can't say this isn't a bargain.

MAGAZINE

First published Manchester, England, 1977; folded 1981.

"I SHOW PEOPLE WHAT THEY WANT TO SEE ... THEY MAY NOT BE AWARE OF WHAT THEY WANT TO SEE – BUT I WILL SHOW THEM EVENTUALLY..."

HOWARD DEVOTO, 1977

Howard Devoto (vocals) started **Magazine** in what could quite easily have been construed as a fit of righteous pique after walking out of Buzzcocks. It must have been something serious if it caused him to quit the band he'd formed with his old art-school pal Pete Shelley, especially when it was on the very brink of success. Whatever the truth, Devoto escaped the constricting uniform of mainstream punk rock when he left the group and was free to explore the music world in his own way and at his own pace, unearthing strange and unsettling lyrics from under the floorboards of his mind.

First, though, he needed a band. **John McGeoch** (guitar/sax), **Barry Adamson** (bass), **Bob Dickinson** (keyboards, replaced by **Dave**

Formula) and **Martin Jackson** (drums) were swiftly recruited, a set was thrashed out, and Howard borrowed Buzzcocks' PA for his new band's unannounced first appearance at Manchester's legendary Electric Circus.

To give the now outfit the best possible start, Howard signed up **John Leckie** to produce, figuring correctly that someone who'd worked with artists of the stature of Chris Spedding, Mott The Hoople, Be-Bop Deluxe, Pink Floyd and XTC would not only know what all the studio buttons and knobs actually did, but also he'd be ready to pull the optimum performances from the less-than-experienced Magazine crew. Leckie turned the band's first single "Shot By Both Sides" from a recycled tune (compare its ascending guitar line to that of Buzzcocks' "Lipstick") into a blared declaration of bravado.

Devoto and the boys hurried back to record *Real Life* on the back of their first single's success, shooing it into the shops as quickly as they could. Despite the rush, the album's rough edges were almost smoothed

---

ICONIC SINGLE:
SHOT BY BOTH SIDES (VIRGIN, 1978)

Although given the unmistakable stamp of Magazine by the band's instantly recognizable sound, "Shot By Both Sides" was a Devoto/Shelley composition, and the tune ended up backing Buzzcocks' own "Lipstick" not too many months after this gritty slab of alienation hit the shops. Notable for its focus on Howard's recurring themes of paradox and contradiction, the protagonist is alone in the heart of a crowd, surrounded yet unable to lose himself.

Deep philosophizing aside, this is a magnificent track, darkly evil and jerkily boisterous at the same time. It kicks off with a threatening guitar line before storming into a blizzard of words, first muttered then shouted, and a whirlwind of full-powered punk-rock noise.

---

out of sight without losing any of the band's passion and explosive technique. Filled with edgy Mancunian energy, it set a new standard for thought-provoking, high-speed, sarcastic and witty punk music. Live, they were mesmerizing, with Devoto stalking the stage and terrifying the crowd, a vicious light show and fearsomely powerful amplification that scattered cold, jagged fragments of sharp guitar.

After a strange interlude during which McGeoch first joined the Banshees and then became a large part of Visage with Adamson and Formula, Magazine returned to the studio, and with a vengeance. For a while, Magazine and Buzzcocks seemed to be in competition, sharpening one another like knives and producing ever more successful singles with increasingly fine musicianship. After Jackson left and was replaced by **John Doyle**, Magazine shot back into the studio to work on *Secondhand Daylight*.

Devoto's songwriting had matured quickly and his deceptively simple lyrics outlined far deeper questions about emotions and relationships than most would have expected from a Manchester punk outfit. This more considered version of punk for thoughtful grown-ups was immensely successful. It helped sell *The Correct Use Of Soap* to an audience that would have shuddered to think of buying a punk-rock record. They were lured in by Devoto's menacingly deadpan version of Sly And The Family Stone's "Thank You (Falettinme Be Mice Elf Agin)" and "Sweetheart Contract", which took Magazine into the lower reaches of the charts again, but marked the end of McGeoch's time with the band; he rejoined Siouxsie and the Banshees, making room first for **Robin Simon** (ex-Neo and Vox) and subsequently **Bob Mandelson** (ex-Amazorblades).

Magic, Murder And The Weather hit the shops and simultaneously served as the band's epitaph. In the aftermath, McGeoch went on to do a stint with Public Image Limited, before dying unexpectedly young in 2003. Adamson fled to The Bad Seeds and has subsequently had an extremely successful solo career. Devoto dissolved the band and went solo for a while before forming **Luxuria**, a decidedly non-punk duo with the flamboyant but otherwise unknowable **Noko**, in the mid-Eighties. A complete collection of Devoto's lyrics – *It Only Looks As If It Hurts* – was published in 1990, and is well worth the very small asking price.

PLAYLIST: MAGAZINE

All the following are included on the *Rays & Hail* compilation (Virgin, 1993) or on the original albums as listed below.

1. A SONG FROM UNDER THE FLOORBOARDS from **The Correct Use of Soap (Virgin; 1994)**

2. BACK TO NATURE from **Real Life/Secondhand Daylight (reissue EMI; 2003)**

3. BECAUSE YOU'RE FRIGHTENED from **The Correct Use of Soap (Virgin; 1994)**

4. DEFINITIVE GAZE from **Real Life/Secondhand Daylight (reissue EMI; 2003)**

5. I WANT TO BURN AGAIN from **The Correct Use of Soap (Virgin; 1994)**

6. MOTORCADE from **Real Life/Secondhand Daylight (reissue EMI; 2003)**

7. PERMAFROST from **Real Life/Secondhand Daylight (reissue EMI; 2003)**

8. RHYTHM OF CRUELTY from **Real Life/Secondhand Daylight (reissue EMI; 2003)**

9. SHOT BY BOTH SIDES from **Real Life/Secondhand Daylight (reissue EMI; 2003)**

10. THE LIGHT POURS OUT OF ME from **Real Life/Secondhand Daylight (reissue EMI; 2003)**

The Marquee Club
90 Wardour Street, London

Though initially based on Oxford Street, and now relocated to some godless suburban backwater in the north of town, The Marquee's golden years were spent at this dark, sweaty, under-ventilated, overpriced address in the middle of Soho. Everybody played the Marquee, and from early 1977 it hosted an apparently endless stream of punk gigs. Queueing for entry opposite the Peters Edition music publishing company, endless wannabe pop stars were inspired to pick Peter Sedition as a stage name.

Well placed at the southern Soho end of Wardour Street and cherished for its bargain price entry, it often shared audience members with The Vortex, another fine, inexpensive venue at the northern, Oxford Street end.

◉ Real Life (Virgin, 1988)

The standout track "Shot By Both Sides" still generates the mad, twitchy amphetamine rush of a Saturday night on the town full of risk and excitement. "The Light Pours Out Of Me" is a pure anthem and the rest of the tracks, particularly "Parade", "Definitive Gaze" and "The Great Beautician In The Sky" all hint at the band's skill, showing that Magazine was much more than just a smartypants version of Buzzcocks.

◉ Secondhand Daylight (Virgin, 1988)

Considered by many to be the best of the Magazine albums, this demonstrates the stark majesty of Devoto at his most impressive. Includes "Permafrost", one of the most blood-chilling songs to come out of the post-punk era.

◉ The Correct Use Of Soap (Virgin, 1988)

First issued in 1980, this shows Magazine loosening up a little, daring to smile, shrugging their shoulders and, aligning themselves for once with prevailing musical trends, experimenting with a little funk. The two obvious standout tracks "Thank You (Falettinme Be Mice Elf Agin)" and "Song From Under The Floorboards" (perhaps the only UK pop chart entry with a title inspired by Dostoevsky) are crowded by the set's other excellent tunes.

◉ Rays & Hail 1978-1981: the Best of Magazine (Virgin, 1993)

Covering all the most important singles from the band's most successful period, but with enough odds and ends to make it a genuine introduction to this most enigmatic of late/post punk bands, Rays & Hail has to some extent been made redundant by later, more luxuriant box sets and retrospectives, but its sheer concise precision means it remains the best-value starter pack on the market. Naturally it includes "Shot By Both Sides", "The Light Pours Out Of Me", "Permafrost" and "Song From Under The Floorboards" but these are only the bait to draw you onto Howard's barbed hooks such as those hidden in "Motorcade" "Rhythm of Cruelty" and "Back to Nature".

Max's Kansas City
213 Park Ave. South NYC.

"THINK IT'S SWELL PLAYING MAX'S KANSAS / YOU'RE LOOKING BORED AND YOU'RE ACTING FLASH / WITH NOTHING IN YOUR GUT / YOU BETTER KEEP YOUR MONTH SHUT."
"NEW YORK", SEX PISTOLS

Now a delicatessen, this used to be the kind of place where Truman Capote and Andy Warhol could watch Lou Reed and Iggy Pop snorting the dandruff from David Bowie's head while the New York Dolls took turns taking care of Debbie Harry in the back room, listening to the latest hot sounds being spun by DJ Wayne County... or so the legend goes. And now it's a deli. Shame.

The place was a labyrinth of increasingly exclusive rooms and tales of the regulars who turned it from just another dodgy-looking music club into a haunt for the beautiful people are told at their best in *Please Kill Me*, Legs McNeil's oral history of punk.

THE MEKONS

Descended to Leeds, England, 1977; beamed up 1981. Re-formed 1984, moved to the USA early 1990s, still occasionally visiting our galaxy.

Part II.

"I NEVER LISTEN TO MUSIC AND NEITHER DO THE MEKONS. THEY MAKE IT INSTEAD. EVERYBODY HAS TO DO SOMETHING."

LESTER BANGS

The Mekons have been with us for almost forty years, as long as any other punk band, and understandably, have undergone a few changes along the line. Initially a shambolic assembly of pals from Leeds University, the Mk I line-up comprised **Jon Langford** (drums) and **Tom Greenhalgh** (guitar) – the only two who have been Mekons since the beginning – plus **Andy Corrigan** and **Mark White** (vocals), **Kev Lycett** (guitar) and **Ros Allen** (bass). The band started out just hanging around and jamming improvised semi-political or just downright funny lyrics over awfully executed punk-rock rhythms. These early songs were as painful to hear as a scared kid's first driving lesson, but they were having more fun making music than they were following their studies, and decided to take their dumb show on the road, with no expectation of the cult fame and small fortune that it would bring them.

Refreshing though this attitude was in a scene riddled with bandwagon-jumping wannabes, they found themselves a record deal with minuscule label Fast Product, joined a tour organized by the label's owner and issued a single that vanished. Refusing to drown, it made its way to the safety

The Mekons en masse.

of the label's first and only compilation – a full-length album that included debut releases by Human League, Scars, 2-3 and **Gang Of Four** as well as the Mekons' unbelievably sloppy "Never Been In A Riot" / "32 Weeks". Hilariously inept and anarchic in the most fun way imaginable, and a tongue-in-cheek riposte to the ultra-hip Clash and their "White Riot" track, it became a favourite with John Peel and persuaded them to push on with a follow-up album.

The Quality Of Mercy Is Not Strnen (1979), with its cover photo of a monkey almost producing Shakespeare, was one of the last flowerings of proper early punk rock in the UK. Packed with humour, impotent rage, ribaldry and half-baked politics and played with a joyful aplomb that more than compensated for

198

PLAYLIST: MEKONS

1. WHERE WERE YOU
from **Mutant Pop: Various Artists (Fast Product, 1980)**

2. I'LL HAVE TO DANCE THEN (ON MY OWN)
from **Mutant Pop (Fast Product, 1980)**

3. NEVER BEEN IN A RIOT
from **Mutant Pop (Fast Product, 1980)**

4. 32 WEEKS
from **Mutant Pop (Fast Product, 1980)**

5. LIKE SPOONS NO MORE from **The Quality Of Mercy Is Not Strnen (Caroline, 1992)**

6. JOIN US IN THE COUNTRYSIDE from **The Quality Of Mercy Is Not Strnen (Caroline, 1992)**

7. WHAT ARE WE GOING TO DO TONIGHT from **The Quality Of Mercy Is Not Strnen (Caroline, 1992)**

8. WATCH THE FILM from **The Quality Of Mercy Is Not Strnen (Caroline, 1992)**

9. LONELY AND WET from **The Quality Of Mercy Is Not Strnen (Caroline, 1992)**

10. DAN DARE from **The Quality Of Mercy Is Not Strnen (Caroline, 1992)**

any lack of technical ability, it became an instant cult classic – an album that listeners either adored immediately or loathed forever.

Staying on the road, presumably to avoid gangs of outraged musicians armed with pitchforks and carrying flaming torches, The Mekons ran into a withering hail of second-generation bands and their fans, seemingly more interested in fighting among themselves than chanting down Babylon, setting termites at the foundations of the establishment or even having a laugh. It helped sharpen up the musicianship, and The Mekons, as much as their peers in the Gang Of Four, were responsible for the bleak and frightened white-boy funk sound that would dominate the 1980s underground and inspire bands such as the **Red Hot Chili Peppers** a decade later.

Certainly their second album, *The Mekons*, showed them less relaxed, even more obviously politicized, apparently on edge and looking over their shoulders while playing – never an easy task. They'd also embraced the new electronic revolution and had rounded out their sound mainly with tinny cheap synth effects, with the occasional swirling keyboard line to make it all seem worthwhile. It didn't go down tremendously well with the increasingly hidebound punk-rock crowds, however, and their follow-up, *The Mekons Story* (a compilation of rarities and alternate versions) was wilfully audience-baiting, full of slurred drunken rants, evil percussive noise and raw chord progressions.

By 1981 the lack of focus and jokey minimalism were beginning to wear thin, and The Mekons went underground and concentrated on side projects, most notably Langford and two pals who gigged and recorded briefly as **The Three Johns**.

When the band resurfaced in 1985 with *Fear And Whiskey*, it was, surprisingly, as a rather fine country'n'western band. An awful fate for a group that had started so well, the new Mekons' interest in lonesome cowboys and twanging romantic balladry lost them their audience like a snake shedding its skin. They picked up a new crowd, but they're not our kinda folk and they don't take too kindly to the likes of us.

⊙ Punk Rock (Quarterstick, 2004)

If it weren't for its dubious availability, *The Quality Of Mercy Is Not Strnen* would be the first choice here, but *Punk Rock* features the most desirable tracks from the same era (including "32 Weeks", "This Sporting Life", "Never Been In A Riot", "Lonely And Wet" and "Dan Dare"), making it a very acceptable alternative intro to the band at their nutty, art-school, weird and wired best.

THE MEMBERS

Opened for membership in leafy Surrey, England, 1977; went limp in 1983.

The Members were a stereotype: a bunch of bored suburban teenagers, the type that made up British punk's foot soldiers. While the central London elite bitched about who was shagging who, and whether the Roxy was more "authentic" than the Vortex club as the place to be seen, bands such as The Members hopped cheerfully onto the bandwagon heading towards the front line, played their sets in foul-smelling trenches of unbelievable unpleasantness and lived or died on audience reaction. Although they followed the embarrassingly common route of unsuccessful Eighties revival and eventual rebirth as zombies on the oldies circuit, The Members managed two standout singles before being shot down, and as a result, their name liveth for evermore.

Nicky Tesco (vocals), **Jean-Marie "JC" Carroll** (guitar), **Gary Baker** (guitar), **Adrian Lillywhite** (drums), and **Christopher Payne** (bass) first appeared ranting against the fascist National Front on *Streets*, a compilation album released by the Beggars Banquet label, with "Fear On The Streets" a piece of ear-popping ramalama guitar-driven anger.

The guys blagged a deal with Stiff Records and released "Solitary Confinement", a far from standard punk-rock tune in early 1978. Running through a fairly standard "kid moves to the big city, discovers streets are paved with shit, gets very lonely" story, it started slow, veered towards white-boy reggae (à la Police) and generally refused to conform. The single's relative success, boosted by airplay from John Peel, led to a more substantial deal with Virgin, who bought and cajoled "Sound Of The Suburbs" into the Top 20, helped by an enormous advertising campaign, and eventually into classic status (the promo copies are very collectable).

Tesco was a natural front man, well able to cope with the song's multiple direction and rhythm changes, and he inspired adoration among a fanbase much younger than that accumulating around older bands like the Pistols or The Clash. Baker quit, however, and was replaced by **Nigel Bennett** before they recorded *At The Chelsea Nightclub*, their first LP, released in 1979 and skilfully produced by Lillywhite's brother Steve, who went on to work for U2 but was then just a tyro with only a couple of credits to his name.

The Members' taste for jumping rhythms in mid-song allowed them to experiment with various aspects of dubology, but they were unable to convince the record company that it was a direction they should continue to follow. The Members' second single, "Offshore Banking Business", was initially refused a UK release, though it went on to sell well around the world, by punk standards at least, and was even banned in Dubai (some street-credibility, eh?). Its importance lay in its prescience: The Specials and Madness were already drawing crowds, the Two-Tone label was about to begin its chart assault and the whole home-grown reggae scene was poised to take flight, with UB40, Aswad and the like already forging their own, Caribbean-rooted sounds.

Bands with their fingers on the pulse such as The Members, The Ruts and The Police knew that punk audiences were also into reggae. When Rasta Don Letts started spinning the tunes at the Roxy, there simply were not enough punk records available, and he brought in some of his own tolerably weird collection of dub to fill the gaps between acts on stage. Thus dub and punk came together, and not surprisingly, some of the aspects of rebel music struck a chord in the oppressed souls of the UK's bored teenagers. Their record label was less sure and insisted on the safer option of releasing the disco-tinted "Romance" / "The Ballad Of John And Martin" against the band's wishes, and soon after, Payne dropped out of the band in the middle of a tour, pleading nervous exhaustion. Carroll's brother stood in for a while, as did **Paul Gray** (ex-**Eddie & The Hotrods**) and when their next album *1980 The Choice Is Yours* failed to perform in the stores, the band were dropped.

A brief rebirth in the early 80s with the US-

> ### ICONIC SINGLE:
> ### THE SOUND OF THE SUBURBS
> (VIRGIN, 1979)
>
> Still a hit on daytime radio in the UK, The Members' greatest hit celebrates life on the outskirts of town rather than taking punk's usual stance of challenge and criticism. Searing a trail through the pre-packed boredom and plasticized conformity of life with a two-car garage, it found an audience with surly office fodder up and down the country, hitting the charts and giving the lads their first big exposure in the music weeklies. Adopted in 2001 by a sportswear manufacturer for one of their pointless branding advertisements, it enjoyed a brief revival and hopefully provided a handy lump sum for the band's retirement.

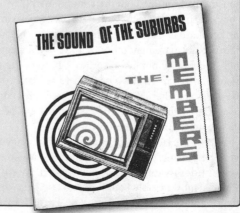

friendly *Uprhythm / Downbeat* album (released for some reason as *Going West* in the UK) came to nothing, being a stab at grabbing the disco crowd that fell flat, and the Members went off to find proper jobs in 1983.

⊙ Sound Of The Suburbs (Virgin, 1995)

Although *At The Chelsea Nightclub* (Caroline, 1991) and *1980 The Choice is Yours* (Caroline, 1991) both have their moments of brilliance, most of the tunes they carry are sounding tired and dated. Much better to opt for this excellent-value compilation which, as it has the band's greatest hit (plus "Offshore Banking Business" and their original Stiff Records single "Solitary Confinement") on it, will probably be all The Members you really want to hear.

MINOR THREAT

**Emerged Washington, DC, 1980;
no longer a threat, as of 1983.**

S traight Edge is the hardest branch of the big old punk-rock tree to understand. A movement seemingly dedicated to self-expression, the embrace of freedom, sexual autonomy and a reluctance to deal with the mainstream world would appear to have little place for its po-faced celebration of sober self-denial. In fact, preaching of any kind – ascetic or Dionysian – is about as anti-punk as you can get. However, in a small corner of Washington, DC, one of the most corrupt cities on Earth, **Ian MacKaye** (vocals) and his pals formulated a musical philosophy that championed abstinence and confronted the realities of the drugs trade with the awesome roar of righteous punk rock played with all instruments set to "hardcore".

Ignoring his obvious problem with other people having fun, MacKaye showed an admirable determination to succeed in rock'n'roll. He formed his first band, The Teen Idles, while still at school and founded his own Dischord record label on graduation. When the group split up, MacKaye and drummer **Jeff Nelson** hooked up with **Brian Baker** (bass, ex-Government Issue) and **Lyle Preslar** (guitar), and **Minor Threat**, the country's angriest four-piece, was ready to go. Kicking off with a couple of seminal, essential and vital hardcore punk-rock statements, "Minor Threat" and "Straight Edge", the band stormed up and down the East Coast of the USA inciting audiences to radical good behaviour and whipping up a fanbase of committed stoics.

Although Baker quit in 1982 (going on to play with both The Meatmen and Dag Nasty), his replacement **Steve Hanses** was hired and trained in time for Minor Threat to record their only full-length album, *Out Of Step*, released in 1983. The abum's relative success, plus the attention it drew to the band, its philosophy and MacKaye himself sat uncomfortably on his puritan shoulders and he dissolved the group later in the year.

MacKaye and Nelson stayed in the business, however, continuing to run the label they'd started and playing together in Egg Hunt for a while, releasing a single before moving apart musically. Nelson played in a number of locally successful bands before opting to concentrate on the label. MacKaye, of course, went on to wider success, moving through a number of groups before finding his permanent home in **Fugazi**.

Minor Threat's melodic, yet fast, passionate and almost desperate-sounding pleas for responsibil-

🎵 PLAYLIST: STRAIGHT EDGE

For those who like their rock'n'roll without the sex'n'drugs.

1. DRINK DRUNK PUNK Anti-Flag
from **Die For The Government (New Red, 2005)**

2. START TODAY Gorilla Biscuits
from **Start Today (Revelation, 1997)**

3. WHAT'S WRONG WITH ME In My Eyes
from **Nothing to Hide (Revelation, 2000)**

4. SCREAMING AT A WALL Minor Threat
from **Complete Dischography (Dischord, 1999)**

5. SO FUCKING BLIND Project X from **Straight Edge Revenge (Plastic Head Music, 1997)**

6. NO THANKS Screaming For Change
from **Uniform Choice (Wishing Well, 1999).**

7. NO GUTS NO GLORY Slapshot
from **Step On It (Taang, 1995)**

8. HARDCORE PRIDE Ten Yard Fight
from **Hardcore Pride EP (Plastic Head Music, 1997)**

9. TEXTBOOK CASE With Honor
from **Heart Means Everything (Stillborn, 2004)**

10. YOUTH CREW Youth Of Today
from **Can't Close My Eyes (Revelation, 2004)**

ity and sobriety continued to echo around the US hardcore scene for the rest of the Eighties. A peculiarly American phenomenon, Straight Edge spectacularly failed to take root in the rest of the punk-rock world.

⊙ **Complete Dischography (Dischord, 1990)**

Like it says. Everything the band ever recorded: 26 tracks of hard-core straight-edged preaching. Remember, kids, just say no.

THE MISFITS

Failed to adjust to society, Lodi, New Jersey, 1977; finally assimilated 1983.

The band you'd expect to see on the kids' jukebox upstairs at the Addams Family household, **The Misfits**, like The Damned across the Atlantic, delved into the blacker, camp-er, gothic/horror-movie end of punk rock, found themselves a ludicrously devoted following and set about scaring the bejaysus out of the record industry and fans alike.

Glenn Danzig (vocals), **Jerry Only** (a.k.a. Caiafa, bass) and **Manny** (drums) – just Manny, OK? – first got together in 1977 to record "Cough Cool" / "She", releasing the record on their own

label. From the start, they stood out from the iden-tikit punk bands springing up all over the East Coast through their attention to detail – such as melody and intriguing lyrics – even if technically they were as average as the others. The guys felt they had created a surefire monster mix of great heartbeat-enhancing power-guitar tunes and dis-tinctly odd subject matter, all set off by Danzig's unmistakeable voice – the bolts on the neck of the monster.

Having ditched Manny in favour of **"Mr. Jim" Catania**, the band hired **Frank "Franché Coma" LiCata** (guitar) and, hiding ineptitude with veloc-ity and intensity of attack while disguising a bunch of wrong notes behind Danzig's bull-throated howls, The Misfits built up a set packed with late-night B-movie references. Throwing out nods to the classic monsters of vintage horror flicks, they cranked up the speed and hurtled from studio to gig and back in a six-year frenzy of crowd-baiting, worship-attracting mayhem.

Musical progression was never really part of the plan, and kicking off with the *Bullet* EP (1978), the guys glued all the amp settings at max and set about recording the kind of evil-tinted fun-time tracks that no respectable record company would touch. They signed **Bobby Steele** (guitar) from the

Misfits: Glenn (L) and Doyle (R). Not actually that scary.

PLAYLIST: MISFITS

If you don't want to sell your soul in exchange for the full set of original albums, these are all available on *The Misfits Collection Vol.1* (Caroline, 1999).

1. **ASTRO ZOMBIES**
from **WALK AMONG US (Rhino; 2000)**

2. **DIE, DIE MY DARLING**
from **EARTH A.D/WOLF'S BLOOD (Plan 9; 2000)**

3. **GHOUL'S NIGHT OUT**
from **EVILIVE EP (Caroline; 2000)**

4. **HOLLYWOOD BABYLON**
from **Static Age (Caroline; 1999)**

5. **I TURNED INTO A MARTIAN**
from **WALK AMONG US (Rhino; 2000)**

6. **MOMMY CAN I GO OUT AND KILL TONIGHT**
from **EARTH A.D/WOLF'S BLOOD (Plan 9; 2000)**

7. **NIGHT OF THE LIVING DEAD**
from **WALK AMONG US (Rhino; 2000)**

8. **TEENAGERS FROM MARS**
from **Static Age (Caroline; 1999)**

9. **WHERE EAGLES DARE**
from **Legacy of Brutality (Plan 9; 1999)**

10. **WOLF'S BLOOD**
from **EARTH A.D/WOLF'S BLOOD (Plan 9; 2000)**

Whorelords to add extra beef to the front, landed a regular spot at CBGB's, and picking up another new drummer (**Joey Image**) like some punk-rock Spinal Tap, set about the studio again, releasing a brace of EPs – *Horror Business* and *Night Of The Living Dead* – before heading across to the UK to join The Damned's 1979 tour. This really did not work out as planned: the tour was cancelled and Danzig was arrested after getting into a fight in a pub. Sick of the chaos and short of funds, Image split and **Arthur Googy** took his place. If Image had waited a short while, he could have had company on the flight home, because after one "musical difference" too many, Steele was sacked, to be replaced by Only's kid brother Paul (who worked under the name **Doyle von Frankenstein**).

When the new bunch of Misfits lurched back to the US it was back to the old routine of trying to make enough money from gigs to record the next single, sales of which would pay for promoting the next tour and, with luck, feeding the band now and then. A flurry of live dates and a couple of singles yielded enough cash to record *Walk Among Us*, the first full-length Misfits album, after four hard years trying to break into the money pipeline that had swirled around Blondie, The Ramones and the other CBGB's bands.

After the group had virtually sold their bodies on the streets and their souls to the gods below to record the album, it was just another typically shitty trick of the universe that, once it was ready, the big labels started sniffing around. It was a pity not to have the debut out on their own label, but signing with the corporate beast meant their record would be easily available across the whole country. All they had to do was convince a few DJs and a few million kids in the badlands far from the cities that their campy-vampy punk rock was cool and they would live like kings.

The universe wasn't finished messing with The Misfits yet, though, and "musical differences" caused Googy and the band to part company. The timing messed royally with the schedule for the planned follow-up album, and while the *Evillive* EP (featuring **Henry Rollins**) was a fantastic stopgap, released to keep the audience happy while they found a new guy to hit the skins, the momentum had been lost. **Robo** took the job while *Earth A.D. / Wolfsblood* was being put together, but was replaced almost immediately by the so-brilliantly-named-that-he-had-to-be-mentioned **Brian Damage**.

The album finally made it to the stores in the autumn of 1983, but sales were lukewarm and Damage had barely adjusted his stool to the most comfortable height before Danzig, sick of the whole affair, told everyone to go home. "Die Die My Darling" made a last grab for the fans' collective throat, like the not-quite-dead monster of a thousand horror movies. Then The Misfits were no more.

Danzig went on to form **Samhain** with Eerie Von – another of the great punk-rock stage names – and pursue a career in the bogeyman business (see the earlier entry under his own name). Once The Misfits were dead and buried, however, the tomb robbers began unearthing rarities and alternate versions, live recordings and long-vanished B-sides from who knows what unwholesome sources. As Danzig's solo career blossomed during the Eighties, fans began to hunt out his earlier work, a process repeated later when first Metallica covered "Last Caress" and "Green Hell", and then Guns'n'Roses did a version of "Attitude". When the old-school fans from the New York days added their support, it all added up to an audience numerous and well heeled enough to justify a lush mid-Nineties box set with four discs of material.

Less welcome was the reunion that took place about the same time. Jerry Only and his bro' Doyle hired a singer (most definitely *not* Danzig) and a new drummer to take the old songs out to a new audience, and in what many saw as sacrilege, to record under the old Misfits' name. The new guys released *American Psycho* and *Famous Monsters* towards the end of the 1990s.

◉ Walk Among Us (Rhino, 2000)

Spooky. Psychotic. Evil. Maladjusted and marvellous. Includes "Mommy, Can I Go Out And Kill Tonight?"

◉ Earth A.D./Wolfsblood (Plan 9, 1990)

Ooky. Less immediately intriguing than *Walk Among Us*, the second album is more conventionally "punk rock".

◉ Legacy Of Brutality (Plan 9, 1985)

All the early stuff that the labels wouldn't release, assembled here on the guys' own label. Standout cuts include "Angelfuck" and "She".

MOTÖRHEAD

Formed London UK 1975

A t first glance, the idea of an avowedly heavy metal band with all the technoflash skills so despised by the new generation appealing to a punk crowd seems absurd. Stir in the fact that the band was formed by the son of a religious minister, who'd previously been a part of the über-hippy commune/band Hawkwind and it looks even weirder. Then you see the word "Lemmy", and it all falls into place.

Ian "Lemmy" Kilminster (later Kilmister) had left Hawkwind when his taste for amphetamines clashed with the prevailing swords'n'sorcery vibe of acid and marijuana. Grabbing up his biker jacket, his bass and his dignity, Lemmy got together with two like-minded souls, named

his band after his best Hawkwind song and launched Motörhead. His partners in crimes against the hearing were both ex-Pink Fairies and ex-Hawkwind: **Larry Wallis** and, initially, **Lucas Fox**. Fox soon left, making space for **Phil "Philthy Animal" Taylor**, who better fitted the band's appetite for mayhem and whiz.

Early recordings show the band exploring the room they'd built with their unique sound. Far louder than Spinal Tap's mythical "eleven", Motörhead booted new life into standards such as "Louie Louie" before getting down to their eponymous single. A vital and exciting track that will get you a speeding ticket every time it comes on the car radio, Motörhead celebrates *la vita amphetamina*, where four- or five-day marathons of no sleep and nothing to eat except spearmint gum are just routine. "Speed Metal" was just one of the pointless labels slapped onto the band by the music press, but whatever its relevance in the greater scheme of popular musical history, it does quite neatly sum up the appeal of early Motörhead, at a time where there wasn't much else worth hearing.

It struck several chords in the speed-scorched brains of hardcore punk rockers in the UK and made the band's name. Though later claimed, with much justification, by the Heavy Metal kids, Lemmy was more at home at punk-rock gigs where wide-eyed youths unable to blink or control their tongues would virtually form a queue to shake his hand and buy him a drink.

JOHNNY MOPED

Kickstarted in Croydon, England 1976; sputtered and ran out of juice 1978

Johnny Moped, the leader of the group of the same name, remains one of UK punk's most enigmatic characters, difficult to find, yet seminal in the development of at least two of our other featured artists, **The Damned** and **The Pretenders**. ("Moped", by the way, is short for "motor-pedal" and is the generic name for distinctly uncool low-powered motorcycles. It's pronounced accordingly, and is definitely not the same as "moped" as in "Morrissey moped gloomily around Manchester for months after the New York Dolls split up" – but we digress.)

Genetic Breakdown formed and were playing before the new music had been given the label "punk rock". The band comprised Johnny Moped (born Paul Halford, front man antics/rough'n'ready vocals), **Dave Berk** (drums), **Fred Berk** (keyboards), **Xerxes** (more vocals), **Ray Burns** (guitar) and **Phil Burns** (bass) – was little more than an excuse to take over the Burns family house, drink a few dozen beers and make an unholy racket. Whereas most bands rehearse in order to improve their performance, growing slowly more competent and professional-sounding, Genetic Breakdown were followers of jazz/rock improvisers Soft Machine and made a virtue of never playing the same song the same way twice. Moped and Xerxes, meanwhile, soon developed the kind of lyrical agility that rap superstars would be jealous of thirty years or so later.

Having once had to resort to paying a couple of local kids to hang around and pretend in order to play in front of an audience, it was apparent that Genetic Mutation were going nowhere. Burns started hanging out with kids from London, cut his hair, invested 20p in a pair of fluorescent-rimmed toy sunglasses and became **Captain Sensible**. The rest of the crew called themselves after Moped and played their first few gigs supporting Burns' new band, The Damned.

After a few sets playing for both the Mopeds and The Damned, Captain Ray made it clear that the old band needed a new guitar-slinger. The Berk brothers put the word around and **Chrissie Hynde** showed up (going by the rather silly punk name of Sissy Bar at the time) for an audition. She had been a member of The Unusuals with the Berks way back before Genetic Mutation had started but was rejected in favour of the more skilled and better-named **Slimy Toad**, and retreated back to her second-best choice, The Pretenders. The Mopeds put together a set of mad, high-speed, bounce-off-the-ceiling rockin' tunes, padded it out with a couple of tongue-in-cheek ballads and set about ruining the evenings of quiet drinkers in search of a peaceful pint, playing all the boozers in the Croydon area foolish enough to give them access to a stage.

After the local pubs grew wise, the Mopeds had to move up to London and found themselves contributing "Hard Lovin' Man" to the *Live At The Roxy, London WC2* compilation, together with one of Johnny's rants on bludgeons and maces. Signed in short order to Chiswick, they recorded a pair of fine punk-rock cuts, "Incendiary Device" b/w "No-One", the first of which was a little too near the knuckle for radio play. It left "No-One" to pick up the credit, and as a piece of suburban alienation set to an ear-melting manic guitar assault, it worked well.

Although largely written off by the *NME* as nothing more than a comedy punk routine, like a zillion others bashed together by cynical old club acts, Johnny Moped was a big hit with the crowds. The debut album *Cycledelic* appeared in 1978 and performed with merit in the lower reaches of the charts. The second cut lifted from the album, "Darling, Let's Have Another Baby", was picked as single of the week by all the music papers and things looked promising.

Strangely ill-chosen bookings led to unpredictable audience reactions: a good night meant being drenched in spit; a bad one meant beer. Johnny's reluctance to stand and be gobbed at understandably grew, and as the fun started to wear off, the band was increasingly off the road, packing it in by the end of 1978. When fellow Croydon resident (and ex-member of The Drug Addix) Kirsty McColl covered "Darling, Let's Have Another Baby" in the early 1990s, the arrival of Johnny's first worthwhile royalty cheque put the old band to bed for good. *The Search For Xerxes* came out in the wake of Kirsty's single, rehashing a lot of material from 1978, but there were no gigs played to support it and the guys, mainly grown up and gainfully employed, kept their heads down.

◉ **Basically: Studio Recordings & Live At The Roundhouse 19th Feb '78 (Chiswick, 1995)**

Twenty-nine slices of punk rock at its funny, outrageous, experimental, deranged, rock'n'rolling best, and a more than acceptable replacement for the currently unavailable *Cycledelic*. Standouts? Try "No One", "VD Boiler", "Little Queenie", "Darling, Let's Have Another Baby", "Hell Razor" and "Incendiary Device".

MUDHONEY

Dripping, from the comb to the dirt, in Seattle, USA since 1988.

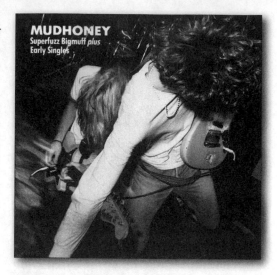

The **Mudhoney** story begins in the early Eighties, when distortion-loving noise merchants **Mark Arm** (vocals/guitar) and **Steve Turner** (guitar) began thrashing out a fuzzy version of the Sixties garage sound in Seattle, first in **Mr. Epp and the Calculations** (a high-school homework avoidance project that after a couple of EPs, played its final show in 1984), then as **Green River**. For the new band, Arm decided to concentrate on his singing rather than his guitar-playing, and **Stone Gossard** (guitar) completed the line-up alongside **Jeff Ahmet** (bass) and **Alex Vincent** (drums). Together they took the feel-no-pain, emotional detachment of punk and bolted it on to the bombastics of heavy metal. This ghastly hybrid sounded new and exciting, yet with strong hints of safe and familiar musical turf – no mean trick – and became known as grunge before taking over the world.

Green River's contribution to grunge amounted first to a pair of EPs – *Come On Down* (released just after Turner quit and was replaced by new guitar-man **Bruce Fairweather** in 1985) and *Dry As a Bone* (1987). The latter was released on a new local independent label, **Sub Pop Records**. The group managed to squeeze out one album, *Rehab Doll* (1988), then split up in a mess of egos.

The split freed Arm up to spend more with **The Thrown Ups**, a "just for laughs" side-project he'd started with Turner and **Ed Fotheringham** (vocals), but soon he and Turner were hammering out harder-edged, more seriously intentioned material – without Fotheringham, but with **Matt Lukin** (bass, ex-**Melvins**) and **Dan Peters** (drums) on hand. Naming themselves after the **Russ Meyer** film (which none of them had actually seen), Mudhoney set about making dreadfully distorted guitar statements that added Sixties garage sneer to Seventies punk sneer, sprayed it over a heavy-metal base and finished it with a few hard lacquer coats of glam-rock arrogance.

Shunning, however, any hint of glam's taste for lurex, and spurning hair-metal's penchant for eye-liner and hairspray, the new foursome looked and sounded like angry mountain men. At first, Sub Pop must have thought a militia insurrection was under way, but having finally recognized Arm and Turner under the plaid shirts and work boots, they signed the new band and got them into the studio, releasing their debut single in 1988.

"Sweet Young Thing (Ain't Sweet No More)" – the everyday story of a teen girl overdosing on Mum's pills – came backed with "Touch Me I'm Sick", without question the best title to come from the wild Northwest in a generation. For once, the effort expended on finding a great title was matched by the quality of the song – lyrics were washed almost out of sight by the guitar rush, while the rhythm section, taking its name extremely seriously, belted seven colours of tartan out of both bass and drums. There were just three verses, three choruses and a middle eight – in short, a very enjoyable punk-rock experience and an essential listen.

When the *Superfuzz Bigmuff* EP (the names of a pair of fine and useful guitar effects pedals, but also good for snickertastic sub-jock humour) followed a few months later, Sub Pop leapt at the chance to beat the pack to the stores with that new Seattle sound, flooding college rock and alt: rock indie radio stations with a shit-or-bust profit-gambling promo blitz. Soon Mudhoney and the rest of the roster were taking grunge countrywide. Thanks in part to John Peel and his BBC pals, it brought them to Europe, where they toured supporting **Sonic Youth**.

By 1989, the band were back in Washington State, heroes returned from conquering the old world and proud parents of a bouncing full-length eponymous first album. They took the opportunity to rest up and enjoy the adulation for a while - an understandable choice, but one that did not help Sub Pop at all. Juggling as many bands as they could sign while trying to corner the market in acts that wore lumberjack outfits sent the label into a financial tailspin for a while. When the situation improved, the band came back to work and handed over *Every Good Boy Deserves Fudge* (1991).

While they'd been waiting to get back to the studio, however, **Nirvana** had been swiping the Mudhoney audience (aided notably by Soundgarden, Pearl Jam, Mother Love Bone and the rest of the newly bearded grunge hairies). Pausing only to bitch at Sub Pop before signing to a major label and having a lot of ground to make up, the group swapped *Piece Of Cake* (1991) for the poisoned chalice offered by Warner.

Moving to Warners made their music increasingly self-indulgent, and while *My Brother The Cow* (1995) and *Tomorrow Hit Today* (1998) have their moments, they didn't sell well enough for the band to stay on the new label. After the band were dropped by the label, Lukin retired, and most who cared at all assumed that Mudhoney's filthy sweetness had dried up to a dirty, sticky paste.

In 2001 though, Mudhoney were gigging again, playing smaller venues with help from **Steve Dukich** (temporary bass, ex-Steel Wool). Finding **Guy Maddison** (full-time bass) put the guys back on the road, and into the studio again. *Since We've Become Translucent* (2002) and audience reaction at live gigs gave them the energy to record *Under A Billion Suns*, a ranting new album, full of political rage, in 2006.

As midwives to the birth of grunge, their importance to the continuing history of punk is obvious.

Better still, they brought some of the humour and irony of punk to a bluff and hearty heavy-metal culture and made it bearable to listen to again. Their new position as elder statesmen of grunge won them a gig co-curating the **All Tomorrow's Parties** festival in Britain in May 2006.

⦿ Superfuzz Bigmuff & Early Singles (Sub Pop, 1991)

All recorded before 1992, the original EP was a six-track slice of slacker rock heaven. This adds the earlier singles, blending garage passion with the ironic wit of punk and blowing it all out under high pressure through a great big Marshall stack. It's a feast of fuzz-drowned jet-airliner roars that Hawkwind would have loved (that's meant as praise by the way). Rock music doesn't get much better than this.

Mudhoney's Mark Arm – doin' it for the kids at 2006's ATP festival.

NAPALM DEATH

Exploded in Ipswich, England, 1982; yet to be fully extinguished.

"OUR ROOTS ARE PUNK, BUT I WOULDN'T REALLY CONSIDER OURSELVES A PUNK BAND. WE'RE JUST EXTREMELY FAST AND POWERFUL THRASH WITH FILTH METALLIC BITS."

JUSTIN BROADRICK, 1987

Not punk as we generally understand it, **Napalm Death**'s output is more akin to an all-out assault on all the senses, best filed under extraordinarily heavy metal, and then forgotten about.

Originally known as **Civil Defence** when they first lined up to make noise back in 1982, the band made a below-the-radar appearance on a Crass Records compilation, *Bullshit Detector #3*. Becoming noted for personnel changes of such complexity that even The Fall could look on with envy, they next inflicted their self-created grindcore revolution on the record-buying public in 1987, when *Scum*, on their own Earache label, hit the streets. While **Mick Harris** kept his arse firmly planted on the drum stool for the whole session, the first half of the album was the result of **Justin Broadrick** (guitar) messing around in the studio with **Nick Bullen** (vocals/bass), while

musical differences meant the second side – we're going back to the days of vinyl here kids – was down to **Lee Dorrian** (vocals), **Bill Steer** (guitar) and **Jim Whitely** (bass).

The sheer awful strangeness of Scum led John Peel to invite them into the studio to record a

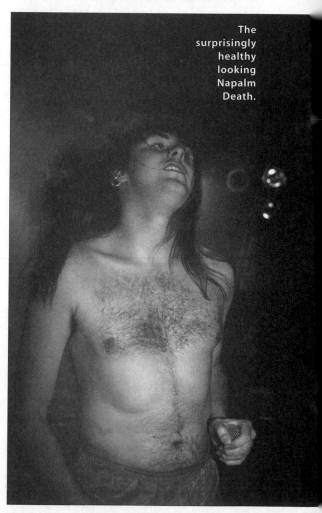

The surprisingly healthy looking Napalm Death.

Nazi Punk

"HOW MUCH LONGER WILL PEOPLE WEAR / NAZI ARMBANDS AND DYE THEIR HAIR?"
ATV, "HOW MUCH LONGER"

A few ill-conceived T-shirts, some dodgy choices of armband and a couple of badly thought-out lyrics apart, Nazi punk was always a contradiction in terms. In the UK, Siouxsie and Adam Ant were known for their fetish-like attraction to certain icons of the Third Reich, but their devotion was more to Dirk Bogarde's stylishly costumed roles in *The Damned* (1969) and *The Night Porter* (1974) than to the ultra-conformist racism of Hitler's National Socialists. Still, there's no avoiding the facts – "Love In A Void" *did* once contain the line "too many Jews for my liking", and Adam And The Ants' early works "Deutscher Girls" and "Puerto Rican" both expressed reactionary sentiments best ignored.

Sid Vicious's notorious swastika T-shirt came straight off the racks at Sex, Malcolm McLaren and Vivienne Westwood's frock shop on the King's Road, and can be seen at least in part as a facet of McLaren's promotional campaign for the Pistols. Certainly, by the time the mainstream press found out that some of the country's pop kids had been flaunting the crooked cross in the faces of an older generation that had died in the war for their benefit, the scene had moved on. There was enough violence on the streets of London already; nobody needed to up the ante with Nazi symbols.

Much the same flirtation/rejection took place in the US, where, after a few dumb schmucks were hailed with ridicule and worse for wearing it, the swastika as a fashion accessory simply became uncool. The hammer/sickle iconography of state capitalist "communism" just didn't attract the same kind of shock and awe from the straights, and the punks of America had to find some other way of freaking out the street.

Those pop kids who found comfort in the jailhouse-tattooed arms of right-wing politics soon drifted off to get military-style cropped haircuts and wear the uniform of the skinhead revival. Whichever side of the Atlantic they found themselves polluting, those who tried to combine the free-form autonomy of punk with the "I was only following orders" mindset of the Nazis were treated to a resounding chorus from the Dead Kennedys' greatest contribution to the debate: "Nazi Punks Fuck Off".

---

session of enduringly strange awfulness, which won them a worldwide audience of sorts. The music produced under such difficult conditions naturally sucked. Fortunately, most of the band's "songs" lasted only a number of seconds, but even so, a little Napalm Death goes a long way. *From Enslavement To Obliteration*, originally released in 1988, will give you more than fifty tracks to choose from.

Since Harris's departure in 1992, there have been no original members in the line-up, which, as the band is still releasing recordings as of 2004, is pretty punk rock. The music, though, with unintelligible vocals hurled out of the speakers, all the instruments distorted beyond legal limits and the drummer apparently plugging himself into the AC current in search of rhythm and inspiration, is just a pain in the auditory canal.

⊙ **Leaders Not Followers: Part II**
(Century Media, 2004)

Pretty much any Napalm Death album is a good place to start, and this recent covers album comes well recommended by those who can stand to listen to it. If you like it, go buy more, you weirdo!

THE NEW BOMB TURKS

Formed State University, Columbus, Ohio, 1992; still bombing now and then.

"I THINK ANY SHOW THAT WE COME OUT ALIVE FROM WITHOUT ANY BROKEN BONES OR BROKEN EQUIPMENT IS A GOOD SHOW."
MATT REBER

As fine and offensive a gang of punk purveyors as you could wish to meet, **The New Bomb Turks** gladly turned their backs on the benefits of a university education to follow the long and lonely path of hardcore. Championing the speed-crazed, balls-out hurtling flavour of traditional hardcore through the Nineties and into the present, **Eric Davidson** (vocals), **Jim "Motherfucker" Weber** (guitar), **Matt Reber** (bass) and **Sam Brown** (drums) cheerily turned their college-honed wit and venom onto the broad swathe of targets offered by late-era Western capitalism, happy to point their fingers, giggle and walk away, knowing that punk rock wasn't going to bring down Babylon any time soon.

Starting out as part of the treble-heavy, high-velocity school of American punk, the NBTs wove their own musical influences into what would have otherwise been pretty average material, bringing chunks of swampy rockabilly, sleaze and degradation into the mix, and stirring in a heap of words to make people laugh or even think for themselves. Full-length recordings have been sporadic and of varied quality – New Bomb Turks were always primarily a live band and the old-fashioned 7" vinyl single was their preferred medium.

Taking their name from a minor character played by a minor actor in an almost unknown movie – *The Hollywood Knights* (1980) – was a typically knowing NBT joke. They relished a kind of frat-boy humour that tipped just a little too far towards old-school jock-strap rock to be genuine, certified, dyed-in-the-wool punk rock, but *!!Destroy-oh-boy!!*, their 1993 debut album, injected a serum of pure monkey glands into the flaccid member of punk in the USA of the 1990s. They backed it up with a set of blistering live appearances and devotional cover versions (ranging from Hawkwind to The Modern Lovers) that helped to tie up a few loose ends, gain the guys an informed, enthusiastic fan-base and provide the material for the magnificently titled *Drunk On Cock* EP.

Information Highway Revisited tipped a wink at the Dylan fans and showed the band had more than thrash-warp chainsaw-guitar riffing to back up their skilled lyricism. *Pissing Out The Poison: Singles And Other Swill* summed up the band's indie period, leaving everything neat and tidy for their move to Epitaph Records and a stab at the bigger time. *Scared Straight*, *At Rope's End* and *Nightmare Scenario* failed to sell that well, however, and in 1999 The New Bomb Turks took a break.

Since then, apart from the odd tour – the group appeared as recently as March 2005 – and an album, *The Night Before The Day The Earth Stood Still* (2002), not much has been heard from the

NBT. Musical progression was never part of the deal, and apart from a few cuts from *Information Highway Revisited*, has never been explored by them, so grab the first album you see and give it a whirl. If you like it (and we're sure you will), buy more. It's as simple as that.

⊚ !!Destroy Oh Boy!! (Crypt, 2002)

Sixteen tracks of heavenly hardcore, wit and drollery from the Midwest. The New Bomb Turks' lighthearted take on punk rock was a much-needed foil to the hard-assed Straight Edge crowd on the East Coast and the newly-politicized tattoo-clad jocks ruling the West. Singalong jollities include "Born Toulouse-Lautrec", "Tattooed Apathetic Boys", "We Give A Rat's Ass", "Mr Suit", "I'm Weak" and "Cryin' Into The Beer Of A Drunk Man".

⊚ Pissing Out The Poison (Crypt, 2002)

With no reason to mess with a winning formula, the Turks' most recent recording shows they've yet to change their tune. Years of practice and access to better equipment means that like it or not, they've actually improved the sound, but this still sounds like it was written rehearsed and recorded in a drunken 48-hour binge. Magnificent.

NEWTOWN NEUROTICS

Formed Harlow New Town, England, 1979. Succumbed to neurosis 1988.

"WE WANT ... TO STOP THE ROT WITHIN BRITAIN AND THE WESTERN WORLD ... AND WE'RE GOING TO DO THAT WITH OUR NEXT SINGLE..."

STEVE DREWETT

A genuine example of the mythical bedroom epiphany when the kid realizes that the new single he's just bought is one he can pick up his guitar and play along to, **Steve Drewett** (guitar/ vocals) had his eureka moment when he heard The Ramones' "Blitzkrieg Bop". Rounding up a rhythm section in the shape of **Colin Dredd** (bass) and **Simon Lomond** (drums) – sadly for fans of groovy stage names, the first drummer **"Tiggy" Barber** left the band – and labelling the group **Newtown Neurotics**, Drewett built a little bit of anarchy in the Essex suburbs just outside London, based on steaming live performances and a righteous outrage at the newly elected Thatcher regime.

Their late 1979 debut "Hypocrite" was a splendid bit of ranting, now and then bursting out with anger, but maintaining a healthy degree of serious disgruntlement throughout. "When The Oil Runs Out", which followed the next year, saw the band moving away from their earlier ill-focused "teenage rebel" stance and towards the delivery of more direct political messages.

This went down very well with sections of the music press, with Chris Dean (of The Redskins and *NME*) offering them a deal with his C.N.T. label and hosting a few less-than-challenging interviews before "Kick Out The Tories" / "Mindless Violence" appeared in 1982 and hammered their banner irremovably to the mast. (It wasn't all "power to the people", though – their next release was "Licensing Hours", a plea for a relaxation in the law covering pub opening times)

Their first album, *Beggars Can Be Choosers* (Razor, 1983), saw them delivering a huge and nutritious dose of derivative but otherwise thoroughly wholesome punk rock. Hints of Steve's first love, The Ramones, battle it out with a dose of The Clash (their three-piece heroes) and a taste of The Stooges in a rounded, professional and undeniably big fun debut.

Like many of their punk/New Wave contemporaries, the Newtown Neurotics grew increasingly politicized by the stinking 1980s atmosphere, and it showed up in their music, which, although remaining spirited and uplifting, was increasingly dominated by slogans. It's impossible to criticize the commitment of a band that supported the anti-apartheid struggle, the battle to save the GLC (London's local authority and a thorn in the side of the Thatcher government) and Red Wedge (a short-lived umbrella group of left-leaning wandering minstrels that included Billy Bragg, The Style Council, The Redskins and ranting poet Attila The Stockbroker), but it became increasingly easy to ignore the endless messages in their music.

Dropping "Newtown" from their name in 1985, the newly labelled Neurotics handed *Repercussions* to Jungle Records, following up with *Kickstarting A Backfiring Nation*, the UK's best live album of 1986 and one that can still inspire a stirring in the long-dormant agit-prop glands of ageing Reds.

However, it signalled a development in the band's musical palette, introducing horns to the mix and politely showing the old punk-rock sound the way out of the studio.

Taking the idea of preaching to the converted to its logical extreme, The Neurotics hopped over the border into East Germany in 1987 and 1988, going down a storm by delivering sentiments that the authorities would have approved of in the international vernacular of very loud rock'n'roll. Taking music to the kids is all very worthy, but this wasn't punk rock – this was the very opposite, doing what you were told.

The music press in the UK had not escaped untainted from the growing political polarization evident in the readership it served, and had come down unanimously on the correct side of the fence. It made the inky weeklies of the period pretty heavy going, as readers were now expected to have a working knowledge of Marxist theory in addition to the usual "what brand of guitar does he use" trivia, but it meant that the Neurotics and their comrades were generally welcomed as visiting high-ranking apparatchiks and given an appropriately easy ride. *Is Your Washroom Breeding Bolsheviks?* (1988) was their best title and final album, and was greeted like an army with banners by the *NME*, although the record-buying public on the whole gave it one careful listen before filing it thoughtfully away.

The Neurotics gave it all up soon after – Dredd fell victim to pleurisy and was unable to continue on the road, and after a swift set of farewell gigs with a stand-in bassist, the band split up. Drewett went on to form **The Indestructible Beat**, last heard of in 1993.

NEWTOWN NEUROTICS

⊚ Beggars Can Be Choosers **(Razor, 1983)**

Their finest hour, or thereabouts. Includes their version of The Members' classic "Solitary Confinement", which, reworked as "Living With Unemployment", became one of the band's best numbers, always delivered with passion. "No Respect" stands out lyrically, as "Newtown People" does musically.

NEUROTICS

⊚ Repercussions **(Jungle, 1986)**

Heavier messages (Falklands war = bad, striking miners = good) delivered at a more considered pace by a more mature set of musicians, this is a more grown-up album all round. Their initial sparse sound is bulked out by some massive horn work.

Is Your Washroom Breeding Bolsheviks?
(Jungle, 1988)

This is an example of what can happen to a nice young punk band if it hangs around with no-good skinheads: the punk-rock spirit has been washed away by the influence of The Redskins' Motown-lite sound.

NEUROTICS AND FRIENDS

Kickstarting A Backfiring Nation (Jungle, 1987)

Performed live in front of an audience (although recorded in the studio), this is a useful live summary of their earlier albums, with a fine version of The Flaming Groovies' "Shake Some Action" re-jigged into "Take Strike Action". Be warned – there's poetry between the tracks (including the only known recorded appearance of one Porky The Poet, now working under his own name – Phil Jupitus).

45 Revolutions A Minute: Singles 1979-1984
(Jungle, 1990)

Described by the label as "the virtually complete singles collection", this is an excellent career summary, less overtly worthy than the albums themselves.

THE NEW YORK DOLLS

Formed exactly where you'd expect in 1971. Split in 1975, spluttered on until 1977. Don't mention the revival of 2004.

"WITH THE DOLLS, IT WAS JUST LIKE THE STREET PUT ON STAGE, YOU KNOW?"

RICHARD HELL

One of the great cult godparents of our beloved punk rock, **The New York Dolls** more or less invented punk by adding bad attitude to glam rock, wowing the kids and winning a teenage heart-throb following, before exuberantly losing the lot to musical differences exacerbated by drug problems.

In the early Seventies, a devotion to the slap-and-glitter world of glam was enough to give right-thinking folks the jitters. Stirring in the snotty attitude distilled from a bunch of New York street kids with the guts and balls of the hardest of drag queens made them filthy, gorgeous, delicious, decadent and just a little bit dangerous all at the same time. They singlehandedly revived the street corner rock'n'roll tradition in the rotten Apple and paved a road for The Ramones, Blondie, Television, Talking Heads to tread a year or so later.

In the US, they attracted the kind of following that was the right age for Donny Osmond, but which found him a little insipid. In the UK, they found a more mature kind of fan: the kind of weird druggy/pervy misfit that builds a cult following. Still, you can't beat a mixed-up fan-base like that, and the Dolls' blend of Rolling Stones-style dirty guitar and leering vocals with a fey cross-dressing non-threatening boy-band coquettishness touched their followers in all the right places.

They had a magical mix of personalities from the start: **Johnny Thunders** (guitar) played his instrument like it was a sneer, **Sylvain Sylvain** (more guitar) had all the style and moves, **David Johansen** (vocals) was a natural-born-killer front man and, in **Billy Murcia** (drums) and **Arthur Kane** (bass), the Dolls had a rhythm section solidly bolted to the floor by booze and downers. They fumbled together a set of raw NoooYawk girl-group hits, bad-boy ballads, classic R&B cover versions and drug-fuelled rants of their own, fine-tuning their instrumental skills in front of a rapidly growing horde of paying customers crowding into the shabby surroundings of the Mercer Street Arts Centre and then the marginally less skanky Max's Kansas City.

The sheer strength of their appeal to a bunch of decadent Manhattan socialites, drunks and outlaws simultaneously captivated and repelled the record companies. This kept them out of the greater public eye in the US until their triumphant 1972 appearance at Wembley in London turned into an instant disaster, when Murcia died at a post-gig party in stupid, life-wasting and avoidable circumstances. Hustled back home before the press or police could get too close, the Dolls kicked off their few months of fame in the worst possible way.

Jerry Nolan came to the rescue. Well respected on the scene in New York and a total fireball of a drummer, he hustled his way into Murcia's chair, counted off a "1-2-3-4" and sprang the band back into life. **Todd Rundgren** was roped in to produce, Mercury Records put up the money and The New York Dolls burst out in a shocking pink cover to brighten the summer of 1973. Still a great album to play and enjoy more than three decades later, the

Syl (L) and Johnny (R):
Too much too soon.

🎵 PLAYLIST: NEW YORK DOLLS

1. **TRASH**
from **New York Dolls (Polydor, 1998)**

2. **PILLS**
from **New York Dolls (Polydor, 1998)**

3. **FRANKENSTEIN**
from **New York Dolls (Polydor, 1998)**

4. **JET BOY**
from **New York Dolls (Polydor, 1998)**

5. **PERSONALITY CRISIS**
from **New York Dolls (Polydor, 1998)**

6. **LOOKING FOR A KISS**
from **New York Dolls (Polydor, 1998)**

7. **BAD GIRL**
from **New York Dolls (Polydor, 1998)**

8. **SUBWAY TRAIN**
from **New York Dolls (Polydor, 1998)**

9. **WHO ARE THE MYSTERY GIRLS**
from **Too Much Too Soon (Mercury, 1994)**

10. **HUMAN BEING**
from **Too Much Too Soon (Mercury, 1994)**

debut was a critical hit, but it performed abysmally in the stores. Too Much Too Soon, which followed a year later, bombed just as spectacularly, despite the magic of legendary girl-group production wizard **George "Shadow" Morton**. Mercury released the band from their contract, and in a moment of madness on an otherwise routine sales-trip, Malcolm McLaren decided to become their new manager.

By this point, the Dolls had been flogging their collective booty around the world for the best part of two years, and they'd matured from snotty but essentially good kids into a set of petty, jealous, adult drunks addicted to all kinds of problem behaviours.

In 1972 they'd been cheerfully on tour, getting merrily high and stealing the teenage girls waiting at the stage doors for Alice Cooper to appear; by the time McLaren dressed them up in red patent leather and propped them up in front of a hammer and sickle flag, they were stealing money for drugs and ignoring the fans almost totally.

The sweaty, nervous atmosphere that at least half the band exuded all the time didn't help at all in landing a new deal, and having paid for a course of detox here, a new hairdo there, new boots and guitar strings all round, McLaren took the guys on tour down to the hot, sticky, backwoods badlands of Florida. Nolan and Thunders could not cope with the mosquitoes and headed back to the welcoming concrete of Manhattan where they could buy drugs, pausing momentarily to quit the band before catching the bus north. They went on to form **The Heartbreakers**, but that's another story. In their absence, the rest of the guys ditched McLaren and sent him home to mess with the lives of the **Sex Pistols**, hiring stand-ins and sidemen for another two years before Johansen went solo as **Buster Poindexter**, the cabaret song-and-dance man he'd always wanted to be.

Their legend lived on, boosted to godhood by the punk rockers of the late Seventies and the celebrity devotion and respect showed by stars including Morrissey (who had run the UK Dolls fan club before the idea of singing for a living ever occurred to him). He took the chance to invite the surviving three Dolls to headline his 2004 Meltdown Festival in London. Not a dry eye in the house, of course, and the DVD is a fine present for balding chaps of a certain age, but it ain't punk rock, it's nostalgia – even if Kane did tragically finally succumb to a lifetime of abuse just days later, dammit.

⊙ **New York Dolls (Polydor, 1998)**

A genuine classic and never once out of print since its release. This is a record that might well convince you to start a band of your own. Get down in the garage and have a stab at "Personality Crisis", "Pills", "Looking for a Kiss", "Trash" or

"Frankenstein". Just try and keep the other rock'n'roll behaviour associated with this bunch of degenerates at arm's length.

⊙ **Too Much Too Soon (Mercury, 1994)**

Relying on a few raunchy old-school R&B covers and giving Johansen his chance to show off as an old-school vaudeville wannabe, the Dolls' second album bombed even worse than the first on original release. Nevertheless, in retrospect it has grown to be seen as another essential document of an earlier, more innocent time. Cool cruising proto-punk comes in the form of "Babylon", "Who Are The Mystery Girls", "Human Being" and Johnny T's workout "Chatterbox". Johansen gets all showbiz through "Stranded In The Jungle" and "Don't Start Me Talkin'" while the whole ensemble tries hard to sound sweet and innocent on "(There's Gonna Be A) Showdown". That they fail dismally in this last effort in no way diminishes what is a great, fun, rock'n'roll record.

999

Formed London, 1977; still occasionally seen reunited for a tour.

One of the best, first-wave British punk bands, and one that gets extra points for being there at the kick-off, **999** started gigging all the way back in January 1977. Granted, they were known as The Dials at the time (later going through a phase as 48 Hours, and then becoming The Fanatics, before hitting on 999 as the band name), but things were very fluid back then. Main man **Nick Cash** (guitar/vocals) was, for example, still known to the fans as Gene Carsons

Nick Cash of 999, smartly dressed for the occasion.

PLAYLIST: 999

All of the following can also be found on *The Punk Singles 1977–1980* (Captain Oi!, 2001).

1. I'M ALIVE
from **999 (Captain Oi!; 2000)**

2. QUITE DISAPPOINTING
from **999 (Captain Oi!; 2000)**

3. NASTY! NASTY!
from **999 (Captain Oi!; 2000)**

4. NO PITY
from **999 (Captain Oi!; 2000)**

5. EMERGENCY
from **999 (Captain Oi!; 2000)**

6. ME AND MY DESIRE
from **999 (Captain Oi!; 2000)**

7. FEELIN' ALRIGHT WITH THE CREW
from **Separates (Captain Oi!; 2000)**

8. TITANIC (MY OVER) REACTION
from **999 (Captain Oi!; 2000)**

9. HOMICIDE
from **Separates (Captain Oi!; 2000)**

10. SUBTERFUGE
from **Separates (Captain Oi!; 2000)**

(although fans of Kilburn And The Highroads had known him best as Keith Lucas) and **Pablo LaBrittain** (drums/percussion) was answering to Paul Buck.

Some of the best-known faces on the scene, including John Moss (London, Culture Club), Chrissie Hynde (The Pretenders) and Tony James (Chelsea, Gen X, Sigue Sigue Sputnik) auditioned for the band before **Guy Days** (guitar/vocals) and **Jon Watson** (bass) signed up, and 999 were soon strutting their stuff on London's sparse collection of punk-friendly venues.

The band's tremendous early live gigs were backed up by getting their stuff onto the market before most of the competition had even thought about studio time. They hit off with "I'm Alive", a splendid declaration of intent to misbehave and kick against the pricks of everyday life. Despite the song's almost embarrassing Charge of the Light Brigade attack – everything turned up to eleven, virtually no bass, histrionic vocals and gibbering delivery, 999 became, by default, a big name on punk club turntables.

Firing out singles on all sides (having your own label – LaBritain records, with only one 't' – helped), 999 looked set to hit the top. They got a major-label deal, signing to United Artists before Buzzcocks got a look-in, and put out a finely-honed self-titled first album of pop-art delight. 999 shoved their way into the singles charts five times before a car accident put Pablo LaBrittain out of action. He left the band to recover and took all their good luck with him.

Stand-in drummer **Ed Case** was recruited, in fine punk-rock style, from the audience, and accompanied the rest of the lads on their first jaunt

to America. By this time – March 1979 – however, punk in the USA had stalled, and 999 returned home with their tails between their legs. Even when LaBrittain came back (he rejoined alongside Case, bringing the band up to a five-piece), 999 failed to regain momentum. When United Artists went bankrupt in the early Eighties, their

ICONIC SINGLE: NASTY! NASTY! (UA, 1977)

Having ditched their initial, ferociously independent stance and LaBritain label, 999's first single for their new company, United Artists, was 1977's "Nasty Nasty", a finely honed rant on the mindless violence that was, even then, already scouring the punk community.

It's an uncompromising aural assault that bursts into madly pogoing life from the very beginning, and says, in well under three minutes, everything there is to say on the subject. Far from easy listening even by the standards of the time, there's an innocence about the trebly sound and everything-turned-up-to-11 school of production that preserves its sense of urgency and delivers it raw and twitching even today.

home audience had dispersed, and although the band were briefly on Polydor, they slumped idly from one small label to another, experimenting bravely but pointlessly with more contemporary sounds, until, in 1985, Watson called time and pulled down the shutters.

They reconvened for business and gigs a couple of years later, but it was with a new bassist – **Danny Palmer** – and without much success. Although they still show up on the bill of punk revival shows now and then, their glory comes from their singles and essential-purchase first album.

⊚ 999 (Captain Oi!, 2004)

The first UA album saw the lads dressed up to the 999s in bright pop-art colours, and the clean-cut look no doubt helped them on their way to chart success. However, the meat and veg of the recording, which blended instantly appealing tunes with tracks that were darker, deeper and obviously based on personal experience, showed that there was more to the group than slick management, a few good haircuts and some decent set decoration.

⊚ The Punk Singles (Captain Oi!, 2003)

Does exactly what it says on the wrapper, with 21 choice cuts lifted from the band's best A- and B-sides. Excellent-value compilation and probably all the 999 you'll ever really want.

NIRVANA

First appeared as Nirvana in 1987; stopped dead in 1994.

"NOBODY DESERVES TO HAVE THEIR PERSONAL LIFE PRIED INTO LIKE I DID, AND NO ONE DESERVES TO HEAR ME WHINE ABOUT IT SO MUCH."

KURT COBAIN

A band that crawled from the mass of oppressed, ignored and bored youth of North America and made some of the angriest music ever to come out of the country. Single-handedly, they grabbed the nation's kids by the collective scruff of their necks and made them listen to punk rock until they understood it,

creating a new market for groovy late-70s revival sounds and thrusting alt.rock into the mainstream at the same time.

The story kicks off in the wild, wild Northwest. In 1985 Aberdeen, Washington State was just as rough and ready as Aberdeen, Scotland had been when its founders first washed up at the top left-hand corner of the map. When sensitive, troubled kid from a broken home **Kurt Cobain** (vocals/guitar) met relatively stable but unhappy-in-the-middle-of-a-cultural-desert **Chris (born Krist) Novoselic** (bass), they bonded over their misery and decided to become **The Stiff Woodies**, with Cobain drumming, Novoselic on bass and friends roped in to sing or play guitar depending on ability. Their choice of name was hardly Wildean in its wit, but was an adequate tribute to the guys' shared musical influences (mainly **The Melvins** from Olympia, a town just up the road in US terms). The Woodies became **Skid Row**, Kurt finally moved to guitar/vocal/front man, Skid Row became **Nirvana** and a series of drummers were employed, with **Aaron Burkhart** replaced by **Chad Channing** replaced by **Dan Peters** (Mudhoney) replaced by **Dave Grohl** (ex-Scream), who didn't come aboard until the band's first album was on the streets.

Before Grohl arrived on the scene, however, Nirvana had built a cult following playing live. They turned this good reputation into a set of demos and then into a deal with Sub Pop. "Love Buzz", a cover of Dutch pop band Shocking Blue's least memorable hit, was accompanied by a ghostwritten back-story that represented our tender heroes as little more than hosed-down lumberjacks. However, *Bleach* – its title a knowing tribute to an essential item for the cleaner–living junkie – found them the underdog audience of relative losers they'd been searching for: a fanbase of college students fed up with pointless excess but still well heeled enough to fork out for albums, music journalists looking for the next "real" scene to report on, and depressive loners across the States and into Europe. Nirvana were a particular hit in the UK, where a taste for the band's grunge (q.v.) music already existed and a John Peel session was all it took to get the word out to the kids.

Back home, meanwhile, producer **Butch Vig** tightened the nuts and bolts on their ramshackle

sound for their next single, "Sliver". He remained at the controls for the sleeker, six-song demo that landed them Grohl as their new full-time drummer, alongside a delicious quarter-million dollar contract with a major label. Vig was part of the winning team and stayed on to record *Nevermind*. Released at the end of 1991, it sold zillions worldwide, helped by "Smells Like Teen Spirit", with its superbly simple guitar riff and enormously popular video.

Within the band though, success wasn't proving to be all that much fun. Cobain had started misbehaving in front of the TV cameras, appearing in drag, in a mess and even refusing to mime properly on the BBC's *Top Of The Pops*. It went down immensely well with the fans, who loved to watch a bit of pointless rebellion and snapping at the hands that dished out the grub, but despite

the guys' obvious comradeship and mutual support, there was very obviously something going wrong.

What the band did not need right at this moment was for Cobain to go off and marry **Courtney Love** of **Hole**. There had been no rock'n'roll couple so obviously doomed since Sid Vicious had stepped out with Nancy Spungen, and despite Love's pregnancy, rumours of heroin abuse by both expectant parents wouldn't go away. Although *Insecticide*, a stop-gap compilation of B-sides and rarities appeared in 1992, the press invasion and battle for custody of Frances Bean, their newborn child, kept Cobain and the band out of the studio – if comfortably still in the limelight – until 1993.

Steve Albini was appointed as producer and set about wringing *In Utero* from a band tired, strung out and devoting too much time to activities unmusical to perform at their best. Albini was later replaced behind the desk by Scott Litt, who was called in to put a shine onto the album prior to its release in September 1993.

Cobain continued to flirt with drugs and suicide attempts until the following April, when he finally put a shotgun to his head and fired, gaining the same dumb immortality assigned to Sid Vicious, Jimi Hendrix and Johnny Thunders. On his way out, Cobain made plaid shirts and heroin fashionable, both heinous crimes for which his memory should be smeared with mud. Those blue eyes, that tortured soul and his lovely, lovely angst, however, means that he'll stare down from thousands of bedroom walls for years to come.

MTV Unplugged In New York, the band's 1994 posthumous release, topped the charts worldwide as a kind of tribute to another misunderstood kid

🔘 PLAYLIST: NIRVANA

1. SCHOOL
from **Bleach (Sub Pop, 2002)**

2. ABOUT A GIRL
from **Bleach (Sub Pop, 2002)**

3. FLOYD THE BARBER
from **Bleach (Sub Pop, 2002)**

4. SMELLS LIKE TEEN SPIRIT
from **Nevermind (Geffen, 1991)**

5. IN BLOOM
from **Nevermind (Geffen, 1991)**

6. COME AS YOU ARE
from **Nevermind (Geffen, 1991)**

7. LITHIUM
from **Nevermind (Geffen, 1991)**

8. BREED
from **Nevermind (Geffen, 1991)**

9. RAPE ME
from **In Utero (Geffen, 1993)**

10. DUMB
from **In Utero (Geffen, 1993)**

from the wrong side of the tracks who got too much too soon and didn't know how to deal with it. Legal problems kept a proposed box set out of the stores for more than a decade, yet the band's reputation refused to fade and a swathe of LOUD-soft-LOUD grunge kings stomped the planet like so many rich yet still miserable dinosaurs. Bands such as The Vaselines, The Melvins, The Raincoats and even The Meat Puppets saw their own stock and sales rise in the wake of Cobain's blessing, a very good thing, as is Nirvana's legacy of hard-rocking sly humour, punk individualism, self-loathing in small doses and a refusal to knuckle under.

⊙ **Bleach (Sub Pop, 2002)**

Raw, mean and scabby as a junkyard dog, Bleach is the consummate slacker album and defines the difference between punk's attitude of "change what you can, burn down the rest" and the grunge route of growing your hair too long to see what's happening, taking heroin so you can't feel the outside world and playing guitar so loud you can't hear it either. It's a brilliant piece of work, though, with "About A Girl", "School" and "Love Buzz" (a cover of the Shocking Blue track) framing Cobain's last glowing embers of innocence and naivety.

⊙ **Nevermind (Geffen, 1991)**

Although the subtitle to this album might be "Fame is misery and fortune doesn't bring any happiness", Nevermind remains the band's most exciting and powerful set. From the opening riff of "Smells Like Teen Spirit" to the shock of the hidden track that crashes into the room long after "Something In The Way" has faded out, it drips with studied cool and elegant juxtapositions. Electronic distortion and percussion-led rioting swap place with gently acoustic, slow-paced meditations, creating a synergy of emotional effects.

⊙ **In Utero (Geffen, 1993)**

While Cobain devoted a great deal of time to enjoying his self-medication, he maintained enough focus to whip himself and the guys back into the studio, tossing off this raw-edged, snarling set of unbelievable, heartfelt anger through a haze of painkillers. Personal issues and an increasingly sour view of the world outside mean the whole set oozes bile (particularly "Serve The Servants" and "Milk It", two well-observed sketches of the demands of fame), with scant relief coming from the Nick Drake-like ballad "All Apologies".

⊙ **Unplugged In New York (Geffen, 1994)**

Singalonga Nirvana in the "round the campfire" setting of an MTV Unplugged gig. The acoustic version of "Where Did You Sleep Last Night" is worth the price by itself; other highlights include "Polly", "Pennyroyal Tea" and "On A Plane".

⊙ **With The Lights Out (Geffen, 2004)**

Just the thing for the ageing punk in your life, a 3-CD + DVD box set of grunge, most of it previously unavailable. The ideal map of how not to cope with fame and fortune, despite having nothing to do with the ethics of punk rock.

NOFX

Formed in Berkeley, California, 1983; still with us.

"WE HAD TO SIPHON GAS AND SELL ACID ON TOUR TO GET BY, BUT IT WAS SO FUN…"

FAT MIKE BURKETT

A sterling example of the healthy West Coast reaction to the tight-assed nay-sayers of the easterly Straight-Edge movement, NOFX started out as a powerhouse trio – **Fat Mike Burkett** (vocals/bass), **Eric Melvin** (guitar) and **Erik Sandin** (drums, also answers to Erik Ghint and Erik Shun) - in the liberal hothouse of Berkeley, moving across the bay to San Francisco when they started getting gigs there. Sandin took his punning pseudonyms (Arrogant and Erection – geddit?) with him when he quit in 1985, making room for **Scott Sellers** (drums), who lasted long enough to record the No F-X and So What If We're On Mystic? EPs (both on Mystic Records) before packing his traps. His replacement, after a two-week temporary called **Scott Aldahl** sat in, turned out to be Erik Sandin, again.

Sick of percussionists-excuse-me, the guys played out with **Dave Allen** (vocals) until he died in a car accident. NOFX then decided to try **Dave Casillas** (additional guitar) instead, and soon came up with The P.M.R.C. Can Suck On This EP, which was released on Fat Mike's own Fat Wreck Chords label in 1987. Things had changed again by the time NOFX's first full-length album, S&M Airlines appeared, however: first they had moved to Epitaph (keeping Fat Wreck Chords going as an indie label sideline), and second, they had lost Allen and replaced him with **Steve Kidwiller** (guitar). Although Kidwiller hung around for a while – contributing to both Ribbed (1990) and Liberal Animation (recorded in 1988 but not materializing in the stores until three years later), the guys found themselves training up **El Hefe** (guitar/trumpet, known to his folks as Aaron Abeyta) to take his place.

Having at last hit upon a stable line-up, NOFX shifted up a gear and set about dominating as much of the Nineties punk revival as they could. 1992's *White Trash, Two Heebs And A Bean* had moments of irresistible pop-punk brilliance, and *Punk In Drublic* (1994) finally saw the band hitting gold for sales of a gazillion copies.

The guys could afford to coast through to the end of the decade, slipping out *Heavy Petting Zoo* in 1996, *So Long & Thanks For All The Shoes* in 1997 and *Pump Up The Valuum* (2000) - all on Epitaph - to round off the millennium, shifting significant units through their Fat Wreck Chords releases, *The Longest Line* EP (1992) and *I Heard They Suck Live* (1995), at around the same time.

A diet that's all gravy will make you fat and lazy in the end, and this decade has seen the band reclining a little too heavily on their laurel-wreathed feather beds. The 2002 compilation (plus one new track) called *45 Or 46 Songs That Weren't Good Enough To Go On Our Other Records* was good value but evidence of idleness, while the split album they shared with Rancid (BYO *Split Series, Vol. 3* - each band recording half a dozen of the other's tracks) was cute, but had little to offer the fans in search of new NOFX tracks.

Better came with *The War On Errorism*, appearing in the same year but apparently recorded by a younger, more vital and far more conscious gang. Full of well-chosen observations on the US political scene and the country's foreign policy, it was just one more step on the long march to **Punk Voter**, an umbrella group of punk bands that tried to get kids to vote Dubya out of office. Despite seeing Warmonger the Younger re-elected in 2004, the group remains active in trying to convince young people that it's worth their while registering to vote – even though, as we all know, if voting could bring about political change, it would have been made illegal. Returning to the musical world full-time in 2006, NOFX next released the EP *Never Trust A Hippy* with the full-length *Wolf In Wolves' Clothing* following a month later.

⊙ S&M Airlines (Epitaph, 1989)

An admirable example of a band following the "earn while you learn" route to professional full-time musicianship. The occasionally sloppy playing (no bad thing in itself but it sometimes interferes with the drama of the music) is more than compensated for by the lyrics – Mike's groan-wrenchingly awful puns hide some novel and sensible ideas that America should take seriously. Includes "You Drink, You Drive, You Spill Nothing But A Nightmare (Sorta)".

⊙ The Longest Line EP (Fat Wreck Chords) 1992

Introducing El Hefe and the solid line-up still entertaining our troops today. Some tracks – particularly "Kill All The White Man" aren't anywhere near as funny as they're probably intended to be, but given the band's continuing stance against racism and in favour of real reggae, the guys get away with it – just.

⊙ I Heard They Suck Live (Fat Wreck Chords) 1995

Brilliant title, outstanding performance and a crowd-pleasing set packed with hits. Dating from more than ten years ago, it remains, nevertheless, a pretty good guide to what you can expect from a NOFX gig.

NOMEANSNO

Formed Victoria, British Columbia, Canada, 1980.

"Hey you! Let's brew!.../Tastes like an import / Crack another cold quart."

NoMeansNo, "Blitzkrieg Hops"

Hanging out in the less populous, jazzier corner of punk rock's musical playground, **NoMeansNo** is the creation of **John Wright** (vocals/drums/ keyboards) and his brother **Rob Wright** (vocals/guitar/bass), a combination that means live performance is out of the question. OK, they call on **Andy Kerr** (guitar) to provide an extra set of arms and cut down on the studio time, but essentially NMN is the Wright Brothers' toy.

They've been issuing enigmatic, upsetting music since 1980, mostly on vinyl – "SS" / "Here Come The Wormies" was their debut single – but thankfully, mostly collected on compilation CDs too. Great titles such as "Betrayal, Fear, Anger, Hatred" and "Small Parts Isolated And Destroyed" convey only a general and very rough idea of where their weirdness has its roots and the musical directions they pursue. Imagine a battle of the bands scenario with Wire up against Motorhead, with Devo refereeing and all three groups onstage simultaneously. It's an acquired habit, but tasty, very tasty.

◉ Wrong (Wrong/Alternative Tentacles, 1989)

The debut recording shows that the band's terrifying mix of jazz, squawking rock and desperate sub-human blues growling was part of the plan from the start. Highlights include "It's Catching Up", "The Tower" and "Oh No Bruno!". The 2004 reissue has been expanded to fifteen tracks of madness.

◉ Why Do They Call Me Mr. Happy? (Alternative Tentacles, 1993)

The mid-1990s were far from kind to the band, judging from the content of this extraordinarily angry piece of work at least.

Still, you have to have a track called "Cats Sex and Nazis" in your collection and this gives you "Land Of The Living", "Madness And Death" and "Kill Everyone Now" too.

◉ People's Choice (Wrong, 2004)

This splendid compilation is probably the easiest introduction to such a difficult bunch of artists with such an extensive back catalogue. Includes "Now", "Sex Mad", "Give Me That Knife", "Body Bag", "Angel and Devil", "Rags 'n Bones" and a live version of "The Day Everything Became Nothing" that raises goose pimples.

THE OFFSPRING

Conceived in the heavenly sounding Garden Grove, Orange County, South California, 1984; born 1987, still springing.

I n a lot of musical fields, the lack of progress or development points to a similar lack of ideas. With **The Offspring** however, you can be certain that they fossilized through choice. The guys know what they like, know how to do it, and long ago had all the controls on their equipment welded down tight to avoid any unwelcome, unnecessary change to their sound. With uncountable fans apparently equally enthralled by their permanent adolescence, why should they mess with a winning formula?

Credit is owed to The Offspring for their colours-nailed-to-the-mast devotion to punk when all around them were getting into plaid shirts and heroin – although given that founder-members **Brian "Dexter" Holland** and **Greg K.** (born Kreisel) met in the mid-1980s through the high-school cross-country running team, a teenage taste for opiates and heavy clothing was never a realistic proposition. Together with another couple of jocks, they became **Manic Subsidal**; a good name, but a false start. While Holland polished his barely amateur guitar skills sufficiently to permit him to consider writing the songs for the band, **Kevin "Noodles" Wasserman** (patently mad guitar) and **Ron Welty** (drums) sneaked into the line-up,

bringing a healthy taste for beer with them and dismissing the rest of the Subsidals to leave the current Offspring line-up.

Rolling into and out of the studio less than an hour later (to judge by the sound quality) in 1987, The Offspring recorded "Born To Kill". It took a full two years for them to parlay the single's popularity and their local live success into a deal with local label Nemesis, releasing *The Offspring* in

The Offspring...
springing off the
stage.

221

🎵 PLAYLIST: OFFSPRING

1. SELF ESTEEM
from **Greatest Hits (Sony, 2005)**

2. COME OUT AND PLAY (KEEP 'EM SEPARATED)
from **Greatest Hits (Sony, 2005)**

3. GOTTA GET AWAY
from **Greatest Hits (Sony, 2005)**

4. ALL I WANT
from **Greatest Hits (Sony, 2005)**

5. GONE AWAY
from **Greatest Hits (Sony, 2005)**

6. PRETTY FLY (FOR A WHITE GUY)
from **Greatest Hits (Sony, 2005)**

7. WHY DON'T YOU GET A JOB?
from **Greatest Hits (Sony, 2005)**

8. THE KIDS AREN'T ALRIGHT
from **Greatest Hits (Sony, 2005)**

9. JENNIFER LOST THE WAR
from **The Offspring 1st album (Nitrro, 2001)**

10. CAN'T REPEAT
from **Greatest Hits (Sony, 2005)**

1989. Using it as a springboard to Epitaph Records and wider distribution, they went nationwide on the alt:rock scene with *Ignition* (1992).

Skate-punks supreme, convinced from the out-set that they had a surf-born boss sound to drive the kids Waikiki-wild, the band spent a decade in the undertow before climbing on top of the board with "Come Out And Play" from their third album

OI!

"OI! IS WORKING CLASS, AND IF YOU'RE NOT WORKING CLASS YOU'LL GET A KICK IN THE BOLLOCKS."

STINKY TURNER OF COCKNEY REJECTS, 1980

Once the British press declared punk dead at the end of the Sex Pistols' spree across the USA, they were left with a bunch of noisy, stroppy bands but no convenient pigeon-hole in which to file them – hence the invention of **Oi!** as a term to describe the late Seventies wave of aggressive, back to basics, anti-everything, punk-rock groups.

With most of the new arrivals still just getting their sets, stage names and chord charts sorted out, Oi! never had time to put down any roots, and most bands lumped together under its banner in the early Eighties changed swiftly into blatantly political skinhead groups or leaned towards a depressing punk-rock underground of formulaic bands regurgitating the stale buzzsaw guitar sound of the previous decade.

"I LIKE PUNK AND I LIKE SHAM / I GOT NICKED FIGHTING DOWN WEST HAM."

COCKNEY REJECTS, "POLICE CAR"

It started out well, though, despite the dumb tag – a hack journalist's brainwave of what a real working-class

movement might call itself, apparently derived from *hoi polloi* but just as likely to be a reference to the closing choruses of Ian Dury's "Blockheads". Oi! came with the clear-cut idea of bringing middle-class punk theory to the working-class football crowds (back in the days when soccer was still a working-class pastime) and to the skinhead mob forming a large section of the new bands' audiences. If the kids were united (by filling their cultural desert with ideas cribbed from ill-digested Situationist graffiti, decayed socialism or anarchist sloganeers), then they'd never be divided.

Unifying the skinheads and punks was a plan doomed from the outset, though. Whereas the bulk of late Seventies skinheads were little better than fascist thugs – tough little doggies, but obedient, conditioned and too ready to follow a master's orders – punk rockers reacted instinctively against authority, questioned all orders and refused to cooperate, all as a matter of course. The two groups shared a taste for music of a raucous, aggressive, provocative bent, but it was nowhere near enough common ground on which to build a genuine movement.

"ALL YOU KIDS, BLACK AND WHITE/TOGETHER WE ARE DYNAMITE"

– ANGELIC UPSTARTS, "KIDS ON THE STREET", 1981.

Garry Bushell (a journalist on his way from socialism to knee-jerk right-wing petty-mindedness) was the first

Smash (1994). The track's enormous success came in part from the heavy rotation it received on MTV, partly from the coincidental return to popularity of stripped-down punk with a grunge-stuffed audience. It remains their best-selling studio set and is one of their two best albums.

Whatever the reasons, Smash boomed across the nation and into Europe – where, thanks to MTV, the band saw its profile soar– selling nine million copies and making a move to a major label inevitable.

Columbia were the lucky winners, swapping a monstrous advance for the chance to sell Ixnay On The Hombre (1997) and Americana (1998). The lead single from the latter, "Pretty Fly For A White Guy" was the track that finally wore away any remaining British resistance. The Offspring played more or less live on the BBC's Top Of The Pops TV showcase, winning hearts and minds through their geeky looks and novelty keyboard/percussion setup. Americana sold in truckloads, and blending their unique punkish pop with some nifty studio tricks and some well-thought-out musical hooks, remains the other of their two best albums.

Since then, The Offspring have been a worldwide brand, ubiquitous as McDonald's. Conspiracy Of One (2000) and Splinter (2003) kept the old flag flying, selling in satisfying quantities even without disturbing the singles charts. Welty finally left the band in 2003, his place instantly taken by **Adam "Atom" Willard** (ex-Rocket From The Crypt).

⊙ **Greatest Hits (Sony, 2005)**

Sixteen tracks of Orange County punk rock sung by one of the world's most over-qualified musicians – Holland is chasing a PhD in molecular biology – and performed with a delicious stab at dumb insolence.

---

to link "street punk" acts such as **Angelic Upstarts, Cockney Rejects** and **Cock Sparrer** under the Oi! umbrella he'd invented. Soon he found it broad enough to include bands such as **Demob, Vice Squad, The Business, The Last Resort** (named for a punk/skinhead boutique in London's Spitalfields Market), **The 4-Skins** (not as witty as their name suggested) and **Infa-Riot**, all delivering almost incomprehensible rants, punctuated by bad guitar solos and clearly enunciated profanities. All good stuff, but hardly revolutionary.

Skrewdriver is generally seen as the band that won the movement its bad name – despite the broad anti-establishment pose of the bands, with Angelic Upstarts being particularly noisy about their left-wing politics, Oi! gigs were pulling in an increasing percentage of neo-Nazi skinheads. Skrewdriver's well-publicized transformation from a run-of-the-mill punk act into champions of white supremacy was followed by an impromptu audience vs. locals street fight in London's Southall District after a 1981 Oi! event held in a nearby pub. When closing time came, the more belligerent members of the audience turned violent. Local shopkeepers and members of the Asian community took the brunt of the skinhead aggro, while the pub (The Hamborough Tavern) had a little trouble with a firebomb attack.

Although certain members of the Oi! tribe were quick to denounce the riot and racism, the appearance of the Strength Thru Oi compilation around the same time destroyed their good work. The title was an obvious pun on the old Nazi "Strength Through Joy" slogan and organization, and the cover featured a photo of a bonehead-about-town who had gained fame of sorts when he was sentenced to four years in prison for racist violence. Oi! went worldwide to some extent, with outbreaks of right-wing punkery particularly noticeable in the US as the Eighties began, but it withered away as more mainstream hardcore acts of a more acceptable political stance grew in number during the middle of the decade.

🎧 PLAYLIST: OI!

1. I'M AN UPSTART Angelic Upstarts from **Angel Dust: The Collected Highs (Anagram, 1999)**

2. POLICE CAR Cockney Rejects from **The Very Best Of... (Anagram, 1999)**

3. RUNNIN' RIOT Cock Sparrer from **The Best Of (Recall, 2004)**

4. STAND STRONG STAND PROUD Vice Squad from **The Very Best Of... (Anagram, 2005)**

5. WORKING CLASS KIDS Last Resort from **Violence In Our Minds (Harry May, 2002)**

6. A.C.A.B. (ALL COPPERS ARE BASTARDS) 4-Skins from **The Best Of (Recall, 2001)**

7. DRUG SQUAD Infa-Riot from **The Best of (Captain Oi!, 2005)**

8. OFFICIAL HOOLIGAN Anti Social from **Battle Scarred Skinheads (Captain Oi!, 2002)**

9. POLICE BRUTALITY Criminal Class from **Blood On The Streets (Captain Oi!, 2000)**

10. GLC Menace from **GLC – R.I.P. (Captain Oi!, 2003)**

THE ONLY ONES

Came together London, 1976; lonely ones 1981.

"I WAS NEVER THE SORT OF PERSON WHO ACTUALLY GOT THINGS TOGETHER. I ENJOYED WRITING SONGS BUT NEVER THOUGHT ABOUT MAKING A CAREER..."

PETER PERRETT

Skilled musicians who found themselves swept up onto the punk bandwagon as it passed by, **The Only Ones** owed much more to The New York Dolls than to The Ramones. If it hadn't been for the gutter charm and charisma of **Peter Perrett** (guitar/vocals, well-crafted songwriting, puppy-dog eyes), the band could have evolved into something like Squeeze or Dire Straits, their near-neighbours and contemporaries on the mid-Seventies southeast London bar scene.

The Only Ones were saved from that ignoble fate by Perrett's "little boy lost on a chemical fog of his own creation" appeal (a style popularized by Syd Barrett of Pink Floyd and championed today by Pete Doherty of The Libertines). Concealing the sordid past of **Mike Kellie** (drums), an ex-member of Spooky Tooth who'd worked alongside Peter Frampton, the band kept **Alan Mair**'s balding pate out of the publicity shots long enough to develop a reputation for the hardest, most sordid rock'n'roll in history – bleaker and more tortured than Joy Division and delivered with tormented angst by a long thin guy in a moth-eaten fur coat reaching down past his knees. **John Perry** (guitar) balanced his relative inexperience with onstage exuberance, the attack he brought to the show and the devotion he delivered in the studio.

Perrett, though, had the words "rock star" written all over him. He was good-looking and waif-like, dangerously angry about something and struggling hard to say it. A classic, too-much-too-young rock'n'roll junkie icon like Johnny Thunders or Keith Richards, he came alive in front of an audience, but seemed lost when the lights went out and the people went home. Towards the end of 1977, The Only Ones' set of doomed romance and chemical obsession yielded "Lovers Of Today", their debut single on their own Vengeance label, which came out just in time to attract the attention of major label A&R scouts sniffing round the backside of London waiting for the next big thing to pop out. CBS won the fight and *The Only Ones* appeared in 1978. It gave the band their only enduring hit, "Another Girl Another Planet", a thinly disguised love-poem to the joys of illicit pharmaceuticals, and was in all respects an advertisement for what's best euphemistically described as an alternative lifestyle of late nights, empty bottles and rambling conversations about not very much.

Even *Serpents Shine*, the self-produced follow-up didn't appear until 1979, with the guys spending the interim capitalizing on the limited fame that came from the first album's short time in the Top 50, facing one another across the bus on an endless tour that led them up and down the country and across into continental Europe. The internal tensions that come as part of the touring schedule were evident in the album's raw, even unfinished feel, and leached into the edgy, tension-filled songs it contained.

ICONIC SINGLE:
ANOTHER GIRL ANOTHER PLANET
(CBS, 1978)

Doctors should experiment with the opening of this song as an alternative therapy for mainline drug-users. It starts off distant, wistful and almost silent before punching wide every blood vessel in the body all at once as the guitar-led rush kicks in. The opening line of "I always flirt with death / I look ill but I don't care about it" destroys any fiction that this is a song about conventional boy-girl fleshy love – this is about the total devotion and algebra of need that only addiction can bring. Beautiful and deadly.

Pain-killing chemicals do not tend to help in this kind of situation, and despite pulling in a professional, **Colin Thurston**, to produce, and inviting **Pauline Murray** of Penetration to provide guest vocals, the best feature of *Baby's Got A Gun* was its title. It vanished pretty much without trace on release in 1980 and the band was dropped by CBS, splitting up as a result.

A spinechilling rumour that Perrett was working as a cab driver circulated for most of the 1980s and early 90s until, to everyone's surprise, he resurfaced in 1995 as **The One**, with a new band and a new set of songs. It wasn't the right time for him to come up for air, however, and *Wake Up Sticky* tanked, despite being welcomed by *Q* magazine as "the record he should have made sixteen years ago". "Another Girl…" gets regular airplay to this day, and the compilations, rarities collection and so forth are still there on the record-store shelves waiting to be bought and enjoyed, but there's been nothing new to listen to since then.

◉ Only Ones (Sony, 1994)

Putting a good ninety percent of their eggs into the basket of their debut recording, The Only Ones came up with a masterpiece. Standout tracks are harder to pick as, from the opener "Whole Of The Law" to the final cut "Immortal Story", there's not a single duff moment. Naturally, rockers such as "Another Girl Another Planet" and "Language Problem" (which verges on the Voidoid in terms of musical dementia) stick in the mind but haunting tracks like "Breaking Down" or the eerie pairing of "Beast" and "Creature Of Doom" return and echo in the mind long after the disc has been returned to its cover.

world. **Jesse Michaels** (vocals) hooked up with **Tim "Lint" Armstrong** (guitar), **Matt "McCall" Freeman** (bass) and **Dave Mello** (drums) and cooked up a ska-tinged high-energy set. Like their contemporaries on the US scene – particularly The Mighty Mighty Bosstones – Operation Ivy's take on ska was harder, faster and less political than the Jamaican originals or UK revivalists that had inspired them. It hit the right chord with the local kids, though, and scored them a deal with Lookout, the Bay Area punk label of choice. Extensive touring gave them an appropriately large, if still underground following, which, together with the critical approval given to their first recorded output, led to EMI offering them a deal.

With immaculate timing the band then split up, allegedly under the pressure of deciding whether to go for corporate gold or stay pure, broke and indie. By the time their debut album *Energy* was released at the end of 1989, the band had gone off in different directions. Tim and Matt went on to much bigger things in Rancid, keeping the ska-punk flag flying throughout the Nineties.

◉ Energy (Lookout, 1998)

The best of the late-Eighties ska-punk albums to come out of California, Operation Ivy's only full-length recording delivers the goods by the truckload with this full-to-the-brim 27-track beast. Well-paced and put together, with slower tracks such as "Bankshot" and "Junkie's Running Dry" offering breathing spaces between knees-up ravers such as "Take Warning", "Unity", "Bad Town", "Gonna Find You" and "Jaded".

OPERATION IVY

Operation launched Berkeley, California, 1987; ivy poisoned in 1989.

"WELL, AS TO WHAT I THINK OUR BAND WOULD BE REPRESENTED BY, I'D HAVE TO SAY A LAWNMOWER."

JESSE MICHAELS

Short-lived and more of a ska band than a pure punk-rock troop, **Operation Ivy** is nevertheless sure of its place in history simply because it went on to give **Rancid** to the

THE OTHERS

Born on a whim, as the result of a dare, London 2002

"IF I RUIN IT ALL NOW I ONLY HAVE MYSELF TO BLAME, I AM IN CONTROL OF MY OWN DESTINY."

DOMINIC MASTERS

Perhaps the first real punk band of the 21st century, **The Others** have the world patent on guerrilla gigging – a five-minute wonder that kicked off in 2004 – and a devoted teenaged following that make Tarantino's Crazy 88 look like girl guides. Fronted by **Dominic Masters** (guitar/atrocious vocals), a guy so in touch with his fans that he knows most of the 853 Kamikaze Division – the kids who go to every gig – by name, The Others are working below the music-industry radar, cheeking the adults and having just as much fun as they can before everyone has to grow up and get serious. Playing on the London Underground, on the back of a lorry, in a funeral parlour, behind a tree in Regent's Park and so forth – with all appearances publicized by text messages and hurried Internet chats – has got to be the best fun a band can have in public. Masters is taking all the interviews and most of the flak, but has let it be known that **Johnny** plays bass and **Martin** drums (he also organizes the post-gig parties)

Reminiscent of The Clash's early tours, dozens of names go onto the guest list, hardly anyone has to pay for a ticket, and a winning smile and the right attitude will get the stranded somewhere warm and safe to sleep overnight. Crowd involvement means that most live events are ramshackle, stop-start affairs where amps are pushed over, strings break and there are simply too many people bouncing around onstage for the band to reach their instruments properly.

Masters' crew attracts the same kind of dedicated unwashed passion that the Pistols did, and pleases the crowd like Sham 69 at their height. However, they're best compared to today's other hot punks in town, The Libertines: they're a similar age, they're equally "risky" and "dangerous" to a fascinated tabloid press and they're equally happy to talk about aspects of their desperately fucked-up backgrounds.

The gutsy, street-fighting debut single "This is For The Poor" starts off with a riff lifted directly from Swell Maps' vintage classic "Read About Seymour", before kicking into a cool, modern, direct dedication to just the kind of people they want to attract. Winners of the newly created "John Peel Award For Musical Innovation" at the *NME* awards, The Others will either take over the world or die trying.

⊙ **The Others (Poptones, 2005)**

Includes "William", the sentimental "Almanac", "Psychovision" (rockabilly), "How I Nearly Lost You" (a cheery-sounding drug-induced weepie), "Johan" (a love song to Masters' partner), "Community 853" (if the kids were united...) "Darren Daniel Dave" (just say no, kids!), "Stan Bowles" (love of QPR and Pete Doherty) and "Southern Glow", a classic urban ass-kicking tune.

JOHN OTWAY

Born Aylesbury, England 1952; still going strong.

Although **John Otway** would never do anything as crass as allying himself to a movement like punk or New Wave, he's been entertaining a rowdy, boisterous audience of fun-loving fans since his earliest outings with **Wild Willy Barrett** in the pre-punk misty dawn of the mid-Seventies. Grizzled old rocker **Pete Townshend** was an early convert and contributed extra guitar to the Otway & Barrett duo's self-titled debut album.

There was no way to beat the old-wave vibes out of Wild Willy Barrett – he was steeped in patchouli oil, reeked of afghan coats, was beardier than most of Tolkien's wizards and a technical superflash guitarist whose mastery of his home-made instruments and their accompanying array of effects pedals ought to have sat badly with the "anything goes" attitude of the punk rockers, but nothing diminished the crowds drawn to their gigs through word-of-mouth rumours of the outrageous Otway's stage behaviour.

Like some folk-rock Iggy Pop, Otway was known to climb to the top of the PA stack during live performances, on one memorable occasion launching himself from the top of a speaker to hang, by one hand and both ankles, from one of the girders supporting the venue roof. In his other hand he held the microphone, and although Willy Barrett had to take an unexpected solo while John did his exercises, neither of them missed a beat. Otway came in with the lyrics right on cue. Screaming at the audience, the half-human/half-bat beast sounded angry as if woken red-faced and sweaty from an unusually enjoyable dream.

Understandably this kind of high-risk performance made Otway a bit of a star and won the duo a deal with Polydor. When "Cor Baby That's Really Free" went Top 30 in the UK in the middle of 1977, he blew the takings on a chocolate-brown Rolls Royce, split up with Barrett and began almost three decades of increasingly cultish behaviour.

Reuniting sporadically with Barrett – who contributed to "DK 50-80", a just-in-the-Top 50 single from 1980, and "Headbutts" from 1982 – Otway's income has come mainly from live appearances,

John Otway
and the zombie
remains of Wild
Willy Barrett.

who must mingle a little awkwardly with the large number of police officers he can usually count on drawing to his live shows, along with a perennially renewable student audience. Beating himself on the head with a microphone as part of "Headbutts" every night for the last 25 years or so has perhaps taken some of the sharpness off his wit, but at least the manufacturers have provided an endless series of heavyweight professional kit for him to damage himself with.

Adding increasingly weird cover versions to his set list ("House Of The Rising Sun" and "Green Green Grass Of Home" being particularly worthwhile tracking down) has kept his act fresh, and as long as Otway himself remains interested, a splendid time is guaranteed for all. Having booked and filled the Royal Albert Hall in 1998 for a spurious anniversary gig, he promoted himself back into the charts in 2002 with "Bunsen Burner", a unique take on "Disco Inferno" that went to Number 9. Otway spent the resulting money buying back the chocolate-brown Roller he'd treated himself to in 1977, just to prove he'd learned nothing from all those years in rock'n'roll. At the time of writing he's promoting the John Otway Big Band World Tour and shows no sign of slowing down.

⊙ **John Otway & 'Wild' Willy Barrett/ Deep And Meaningless (Rotator, 2004)**

The first two Otway/Barrett albums on a 2-for-1 CD. Strictly speaking this is folk-rock, and without a holographic projection of Otway's antics to liven up the proceedings, this much O&B can begin to drag. Still, it's a bargain and includes such highlights as "Racing Cars (Jet Spotter Of The Track)", "Louisa On A Horse", "Really Free", "Beware Of The Flowers", "Oh My Body Is Making Me" and two versions of "Riders In The Sky". It's punk of sorts... different sorts.

THE OUTCASTS

Cast out Belfast, Northern Ireland, 1977; played out 1978.

B est known as "that band from Belfast… no, not Stiff Little Fingers – the other lot", **The Outcasts** were formed in mid-1977 when

and with titles such as "Beware Of The Flowers (Cause I'm Sure They're Going To Get You Yeh)", "Oh My Body Is Making Me" and "Louisa On A Horse" played alongside his astonishing, unforgettable take on Bad Company's "You Ain't Seen Nothing Yet", he's managed to stay in the business without troubling the charts or big labels.

His output is virtually hallmarked "eccentric English rocker; file under 'quirky'", and he draws predictably peculiar groups of strangely affiliated fans – the "Beware Of The Flowers Motorcycle Club" (www.bewareoftheflowers.co.uk) for example,

brothers **Greg Cowan** (bass/vocals), **Colin Cowan** (drums) and **Martin Cowan** (guitar) made too much noise for the family home to contain them any longer. Stuffing their instruments into carrier bags and supermarket trolleys, the lads – accompanied by **Colin "Getty" Getgood** (guitar) shuffled off to make their debut appearance in a pub, with a confidence-boosting second gig at the city's "punk" venue, the Pound Club, soon after.

However cool and exciting it might have seemed to the guys themselves and their limited fan-base, The Outcasts' studied punk-rock swagger and generally snottier-than-thou attitude didn't go down tremendously well with the establishment, nor with those conducting the just under civil war-level hostilities prevailing on the streets. Nobody was going to take them seriously as insurrectionists for dressing a bit funny on streets where the AK-47 was a common fashion accessory. Still, they managed to win the tag "The Band You Love To Hate" from the local press, and turned notoriety into a deal with IT Records, resulting in "You're A Disease" b/w "Frustration" and "I Don't Want To Be No Adult" (reissued 1996 on French label Combat Rock). Moving across to Good Vibrations for their one and only album gave them access to a wider audience, but it was an opportunity lost. By the time the LP was released, punk had visited Northern Ireland, seen it was far too serious and heavy for snot-nosed yobs, and moved on.

◉ Self Conscious Over You (Captain Oi!, 2004)

The album's strong tracks (including the title cut) are stompy and anthemic but too plodding for an audience cranked up on adrenaline and swift enough to dodge bullets. These days, they sound just fine. Look out for "Just Another Teenage Rebel", "Love You For Never", "Gangland Warfare" and "Cops Are Coming".

THE PARKINSONS

Kicked off in Coimbra, Portugal, 1994; still kicking against the pricks.

"WHY DO WE PLAY THE TOILET VENUES? THIS IS THE JUNGLE AND WE ARE THE TIGERS! THIS IS OUR HOME..."

VICTOR TORPEDO

Y ou wait thirty years for punk to hit Portugal and then from out of nowhere, **The Parkinsons** show up – with the most extreme show you've ever seen. Life's like that sometimes.

Victor Torpedo (guitar/vocals) and **Pedro Xau** (drums or bass) linked up with fiery frontman **Alfonso Pinto** (a.k.a. **Al Zheimer**) to form **The Tedio Boys**, releasing three albums under that name in the mid-1990s. Word-of-mouth publicity – there aren't that many bands who arrive unannounced to play on the top of city office blocks – landed them the job of playing Joey Ramone's birthday bash in 1997, which is where we pick up the trail.

Building on a reputation as Portugal's most chaotic group, the newly renamed Parkinsons became the support band of choice for visiting acts that included The Fall and Jon Spencer, until the demands of becoming famous and making a fortune led them to move their base to London. There they stumbled over **Chris Low** (ex-Apostles) a handy drummer who took over hitting things so that Xau could move to bass full time.

Getting naked once will get your name in the papers; taking it to the level of normal everyday onstage behaviour, as the Parkinsons did, will get you an article or two describing you as "the next big thing", a fan-base among the scribbling classes and an instant audience who understand that onstage nudity, the occasional fight, and a sizzling live set is as near as we're going to get to that elusive original punk-rock spirit.

So far, so seen it all before. The Parkinsons, however, stood out from the rest of the 1990s shock-merchants by actually having a set of songs worth hearing: their fire and urgency was a rare thing indeed. Famously, if anonymously described by one journalist as "making At The Drive-In seem like The Corrs", the Parkies played the 100 Club in London and wrung an admission from Mark Perry of ATV and *Sniffin' Glue* that Torpedo was "the finest guitarist he had seen since The Clash's Mick Jones".

Support and headline appearances across Europe did nothing to quiet the rising roar of approval, but most who know the band picked up on them in 2002, when *A Long Way To Nowhere* appeared. Album of the year to most right-thinking folks, it drew the crowds to every stage they appeared on during the 2003 festival season.

By then, however, it seemed that a little too much fame and fortune had landed in the band's collective lap, and during the quiet period at the end of the year, Pinto and Low decided to leave. **Jet** and **Eric Baconstrip** replaced them, stepping neatly into the breach and picking up the beat without a hitch.

⊙ **Streets Of London EP (Fierce Panda, 2002)**

This three-track EP captured the band at their most exciting – on the brink of making it big and with the world on its knees in front of them. "Bedsit City", "Somerstown" and "Pill" are individually worth whatever price you pay for the whole three-pack of punkness.

⊙ A Long Way To Nowhere (Fierce Panda, 2002)

The instant-classic first album – kicking off with the growling masterpiece that is "Primitive" and roaring through a short but fearsomely intense set (nine tracks in 27 minutes). Listening to this album is as exhilarating as sticking your dumb head out of a train window at 90mph.

⊙ Reason To Resist (Curfew Records, 2004)

Moving to Curfew gave the Parkinsons time to plan their next moves. Nobody in the band wants to see it go mainstream and they've seen how "too much, too soon" can wreck a career. Just as ear-piercingly honest, raw and intense as the first album, it's informed much more by the experience of living in good old London Town.

PAVEMENT

Hit the streets Stockton, California, 1989; cracked 1999.

"CRICKET IS SO SOOTHING – AND KIND OF KINKY."

STEVEN MALKMUS

Beautifully experimental, happy to jam feedback together with pure noise, cryptic of lyric and twisted of logic, **Pavement** started out as a studio-only setup. Childhood buddies **Steven Malkmus** and **Scott Kannberg** got together towards the end of the 1980s (recording initially under the pseudonyms of "S.M." and "Spiral Stairs") and headed downtown to Louder Than You Think Studios – owned by **Gary Young**, a local ex-hippy, full-time acid-casualty and part-time drummer – who took their $800, sat in as drummer and became part of the band. The EP that resulted, *Slay Tracks (1933-1969)*, was a glorious, stop-start shamble through the back streets of the Pavement mind and the beginning of the "Lo-Fi" strand of US music that was to dominate the underground there for the next decade.

Following up with *Perfect Sound Forever* (1991), the band's clever, sly and deliriously quirky music began to make its way out into the world. Laconic of delivery, strikingly difficult and unusual, Pavement started out as punk as you can get – when the band recorded a first full-length album, *Slanted And Enchanted* (1992), their brazen "tribute" to the patented disorganization of The Fall's sound reportedly turned Mark E. Smith a peculiar incandescent red.

Faced with an overwhelmingly positive reaction to their first recorded outings (John Peel had his copy of *Slay Tracks* and made sure the band became known in the UK), Pavement moved out of the studio and onto the live circuit, leaving a trail of newly formed, thought-provoking bands in their wake.

Young took to life on the road with enthusiasm and gusto, adding novel sparks to otherwise predictably indie gigs by greeting the audience individually at the door to the venue, or by showing off his skill at performing handstands in front of the crowd, or by handing round salad bowls, or by falling down drunk onstage. He quit the band in 1993, taking much of the punk-rock spirit with him, and was replaced by **Steve West**.

Crooked Rain, Crooked Rain, released the following year, certainly showcases a more polished sound, and the album yielded the inordinately catchy track "Cut Your Hair", which swerved perilously close to becoming a mainstream hit.

Slanted And Enchanted introduced **Mark Ibold** (bass ex-Dustdevils) and **Bob Nastanovich** (percussion) – one of West's old pals – to the line-up.

Though Pavement moved on to become just about the biggest band on US college radio, and sold a shedload of records, they managed to avoid mainstream success, carrying off the extraordinarily difficult task of staying underground despite being known to anyone with an interest in the scene.

Having the band's two driving minds live on opposite sides of the continent undoubtedly helped keep things good and unsteady, and their habit of dashing from lo-fi to highly polished production helped keep them out of the charts. *Wowee Zowee* (1995) was just as bone-idle and rambling as anything from the *Slay Tracks* EP, just as obscure in its references and just as intriguing to unpick, whereas *Brighten The Corners* (1997) saw a return to comprehensible lyrics with relatively singalong tunes – leading some to utterly unflattering comparisons to the blander meanderings of R.E.M.

Terror Twilight (1998) was the band's final statement and virtually a solo album; West's songs had left no room for any contribution from Kannberg or the rest of the band, and after the usual flurry of misinformation and denial, Pavement split up, with West making the announcement on stage at London's Brixton Academy in November 1999.

Westing (By Musket And Sextant)
(Drag City, 1993)

Splendid and essential collection of the band's earliest EPs.

Slanted & Enchanted Luxe & Reduxe
(Big Cat, 2003)

Boasting a ludicrous number of bonus tracks and issued along-side a double DVD, *Slow Century*, this is easily the best lost weekend you'll have in a long while.

Crooked Rain, Crooked Rain (Domino, 2004)

Another fantastic reissue with more bonus features than the original had tunes. Another weekend lost in lo-fi reverie.

PEECHEES / BRATMOBILE / COLD COLD HEARTS

Bratmobile hit the road in 1991, becoming PeeChees and Cold Cold Hearts 1994–99. Reverted to Bratmobile 1999–2003.

Alongside Bikini Kill, **Bratmobile** were a vital plank of the scaffold supporting riot grrrl in the American Northwest at the start of the Nineties. However, they blew a lot of their vital energy answering dumb questions from lame journalists about a movement that really didn't exist, when they should have been blowing speakers and minds with their amped-up high-powered punk rock.

Alison Wolfe (vocals) met **Molly Neuman** (drums) at university. They collaborated on seminal fanzine *Girl Germs* before forming Bratmobile with **Erin Smith** (guitar). The band debuted at the grandly named International Pop Underground Convention organized by Calvin Johnson (ex-Beat Happening) and held in Olympia, Washington – the capital city of riot grrrl and grunge – in 1991. Having performed whatever the grrrl-approved phrase for tearing the roof of the sucka might be, they knocked out some cool singles and finally squeezed out an intense full-length album – *Pottymouth* – in 1993, having patched it together from sessions recorded here and there over the previous two years.

Sadly, the band members couldn't have lived further apart while remaining in the continental United States if they'd planned it, and the logis-

tics finally proved insuperable. The wheels fell off Bratmobile almost as soon as 1994's *The Real Janelle* EP and their *Peel Sessions* EP (both well worth tracking down by all fans of distaff-led punking) hit the stores, and the old jalopy was towed back to the garage.

Neuman found herself in San Francisco in 1994, where she joined **Christopher Appelgren** (vocals, Neuman's future husband and co-owner of Lookout! Records – see the **Green Day** article on p.153 for more family ties), **Carlos Canedo** (guitar) and **Rop Vasquez** (bass) and formed **PeeChees**. A full-strength, double-shot, unfiltered punk rock band like PeeChees stood out from the crowd in mid-Nineties San Francisco, and the new gang found little trouble turning a fierce live reputation into a deal with Neuman's old pals up in Washington at Kill Rock Stars. Their back-to-the-roots, frill-free four-to-the-floor punk rock was a refreshing sea breeze to a West Coast scene turning stagnant, with both the debut, *Do The Math* (1996) and follow-up, *Games People Play* (1997), performing respectably in the shops.

As Neuman's arms and drumming grew ever stronger (she was a part-time member of The Frumpies too), Wolfe and Smith formed **Cold Cold Hearts** with **Lora McFarlane** (drums). McFarlane was soon replaced by the experienced rhythm section of **Katherine Brown** (drums) and **Nattles** (bass), who had worked together in **The Cutthroats**. Scoring a Kill Rock Stars deal with the same kind of ease that Neuman had found, the group released their debut *Cold Cold Hearts* in 1997.

PeeChees and Cold Cold Hearts both had their moments of exquisite delight, but nothing really came close to the joys of Bratmobile, which with communications eased by the Internet and access to reasonable interstate travel, reunited in 1999 and toured the US in support of **Sleater-Kinney** (another bunch of groovy dames from the top-left of the US map). They took advantage of their time together to write and record *Ladies, Women, and Girls*, which appeared in 2000, following up on a wave of new fans with *Girls Get Busy* (2002).

BRATMOBILE

Pottymouth (Kill Rock Stars, 2000)

Featuring a unique (and definitely worthwhile) cover version of The Runaways' "Cherry Bomb" and sixteen other slabs of punk-rock attitude played with delirious aplomb, this is one of the fin-

John Peel

"...IT'S POSSIBLE THAT JOHN CAN FORM SOME KIND OF NIGHTMARISH CAREER OUT OF HIS ENTHUSIASM FOR UNLISTENABLE RECORDS."

SCHOOL REPORT, 1950s

Britain's most influential radio presenter, champion of our kind of music and the epitome of English eccentricity in its refusal-to-conform guise, **John Peel** was the greatest English DJ and the man without whom none of us would be interested in this kind of thing.

Born **John Robert Parker Ravenscroft** just before the outbreak of World War II to a rather posh family from just outside Liverpool, he was expensively educated at Shrewsbury – a private establishment for boys – where he showed an admirable lack of diligence, dedication or talent for learning. Released into the similarly stifling embrace of the armed forces, he stumbled through his national service, emerging in 1959 with a hearty contempt for petty rules, a deep-seated loathing of hierarchies and a determination not to follow his father's respectable but dull career in the cotton business.

He followed him as far as the US, however, where he tried the textile industry and insurance sales before talking up his assumed Liverpool accent (totally dissimilar to that which school had inculcated) into a close personal friendship with The Beatles and became John Ravencroft, DJ and Midwest hipster's guide to the swinging British invasion of the mid-Sixties.

Returning more or less to the UK, he spent a summer on board ship, anchored just outside British territorial waters, broadcasting one of the first underground music shows from a pirate radio station, where he spent his spare time with fellow genuine musical devotee **Kenny Everett** "feeding acid to the seagulls" and finding the name **John Peel**. The BBC spiked the pirate stations' guns in 1967 by starting Radio 1 – its first dedicated pop music channel – and hiring the cream of their talent, John Peel included.

"RIGHT PLACE, RIGHT TIME, WRONG SPEED"

BADGE SLOGAN CELEBRATING PEEL'S PERENNIAL INABILITY TO MASTER THE TOOLS OF HIS TRADE.

His radio shows became increasingly influential, directing tastes, introducing new genres and occasionally showcasing astounding errors of judgement, from his national network debut until his death almost forty years later. In addition to his regular "festive fifty" Christmas show of listeners' favourites, he introduced his essentially white audience to reggae, championed punk rock, played death metal until he kind-of understood it, experimented with grindcore, loved the more inventive hip-hop acts, worshipped Liverpool Football Club, forced Vivian Stanshall and Ivor Cutler's spoken-word pieces onto the air, jigged about to various styles of African pop and of course became **The Fall**'s earthly prophet.

His parallel career (nominally journalistic commentary on music but frequently dwelling more on the uniforms of the **Dagenham Girl Pipers**) led him to a role in talk radio that he carried out alongside his role as musical arbiter of taste for at least three generations. Always at the alternative end of rock music, he fell in love with "Anarchy in the UK" and played it to death on his late-night show. He was the first Radio 1 presenter to play "God Save the Queen", first to host a session by **The Damned**, first to play untold tracks mentioned in these pages and the only nationally broadcast DJ to stick up for happy hardcore (a late rave genre his kids enjoyed). After John announced a craving for a curry on air one evening in 1983, aspiring unknown **Billy Bragg** wrapped a mushroom biryani around a copy of his demo, delivered it by hand to the BBC studios and went on to international success.

"TEENAGE DREAMS, SO HARD TO BEAT"

LYRIC CARVED ON PEEL'S GRAVESTONE, FROM HIS ALL-TIME FAVOURITE, THE UNDERTONES' "TEENAGE KICKS".

Genially developing a niche in the public consciousness, Peelie matured from everyone's best source of friendly expertise about the latest cool sounds into a kind of weird but beloved uncle who knew far too much and who was far too enthusiastic about those adorable slices of musical plastic. As he grew older, his juggling of several radio shows, live appearances (he carried an emergency copy of Status Quo's "Down Down" as his "never fails" dancefloor-filler), writing and musical research – itself a Sisyphean task with more than 24 hours of demos and new releases arriving every day – became more difficult, and he confessed that moving his Radio 1 show from a 10pm start to an 11pm kick-off was killing him. This was despite broadcasting as often as he could from his home, known to his fans as Peel Acres, a thatched cottage in Stowmarket, Suffolk, surrounded by enough land to hold parties, play his records as loud as he wished and store his unbelievably huge collection of records.

Working for the BBC provided him with the audience and income he desired, but security came with strings attached – he claimed not to enjoy his obligatory stints in front of the camera as co-presenter of *Top Of The Pops*, but everybody else found them unmissable TV. Nobody who saw it will forget his slow-motion, deadpan attempt at the twist after introducing yet another musical banality, nor his comment after George Michael and Aretha Franklin's appearance on the show performing "I Knew You Were Waiting For Me". He said: "Aretha Franklin – that woman could make any old rubbish sound good. And I think she just has."

Peel's way of warming up a cold, wet UK Summer festival audience was to have them chant abuse at him for a rousing five minutes or so, adding to their discomfort and encouraging them to scream more loudly by playing a cheesy pop hit at the same time (and at the wrong speed). He once said: "I've always imagined I'd die by driving into the back of a truck while trying to read the name on a cassette, and people would say, 'He would have wanted to go that way'. Well, I want them to know that I wouldn't." Although he would perhaps have preferred to expire at the turntables, mid-apology for playing an untitled German white label at possibly the incorrect speed, he pegged out totally unexpectedly from a heart attack while on a working holiday in Peru, weighed down, one hopes, by a satchel of rare grooves purchased in a Cuzco store built of adobe, with a mangy dog scratching itself sitting outside.

His wife Sheila (affectionately known as "The Pig" because of her laugh) finished his autobiography *Margrave Of The Marshes* (Bantam Press, 2005), with the rest of the family. It became a bestseller in the UK and is a recommended read for anyone who's read this article all the way to the end.

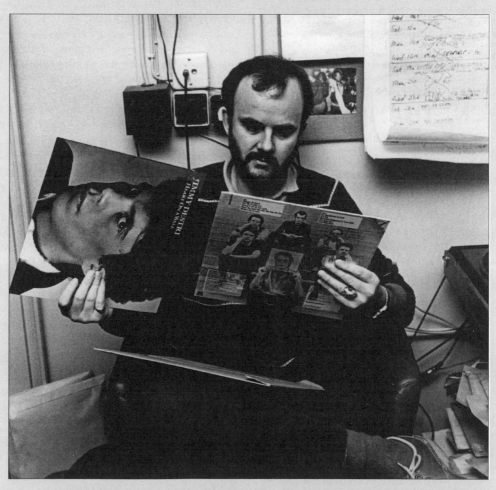

est collections of riot grrrl rage. "Polaroid Baby", "Cool Schmool", "Bitch Theme", "Juswanna (FUK U)" and "P.R.D.C.T." (Punk Rock Dream Come True) are among the album's other highlights.

◉ Ladies, Women And Girls (Lookout, 2000)

Slightly sweeter production values maybe? A little more attention to the boring technical details here and there perhaps? It's difficult to be certain, but if nothing else, this is a purely perfect set of righteous anger set to some of the best guitar rock created in years. "Eating Toothpaste"? "Gimme Brains"? It's like The Ramones opted for gender reassignment instead of psychotherapy.

PEECHEES

◉ Do the Math (Kill Rock Stars, 2000)

Sheer heart-attack-inducing fun, likely to cause hysterical laughter, red faces and palpitations – try "Pepper", "Do The Math", and "Beer City" for starters.

COLD COLD HEARTS

◉ Cold Cold Hearts (Kill Rock Stars, 2000)

Clocking in at just over twenty minutes for the whole eleven-track package, this album emphasizes loud, delicious, raw punk quality over quantity. Loud, pop-tinged buzz guitar, frantic bass and drumming from the deepest unconscious, all blended in a life-affirming mix. Top tracks are "Five Signs: Scorpio" and "State Trooper In The Left Lane Nattles".

PENETRATION

Entered Ferryhill, Co. Durham, England, 1976; pulled out, 1979.

"I NEVER WEAR A SKIRT. SKIRTS ARE RESTRICTING ONSTAGE ANYWAY AND WHY SHOULD I WANT TO SHOW MY LEGS OFF?"

PAULINE MURRAY, 1978

Punk rock didn't take long to crawl up the spine of England to the post-industrial wastelands of the North. It took root in Manchester, Sheffield, Liverpool, and the Northeast as well as spreading across the border into Scotland. **Penetration**, County Durham's most famous punk-rock export, was as tough a band as could be expected from an equally no-nonsense town battered by some of the country's fiercest weather.

Like many others in this tome, the band was formed after the Pistols' 1976 gig in Manchester. The band made its live debut at the Rock Garden in Middlesborough in October that year and was stunning from the start. **Pauline Noname** (a.k.a. **Murray**) fronted the band – cool as Patti Smith, as confident as Debby Harry and as exciting as Iggy Pop (from whose song the band had taken its name), she dominated the stage, anchored to the spot by her unrelenting fist gripped tight round the mic stand. Backed up by co-founder **Robert Blamire** (bass), **Gary Smallman** (guitar) and **Gary Chaplin** (drums), she battered a set of originals (padded out with the odd cover version – notably Patti's "Freemoney" and Buzzcocks' "Nostalgia") into amateurish shape, and headed down to London, playing the Roxy early in 1977, supporting Generation X and the Adverts.

Despite all the essentials being in place, Penetration never realized their potential. London was already awash with exciting bands, and Penetration, despite being one of the most vital acts on the live circuit, simply got lost in the rush. Their debut single "Don't Dictate" / "Money Talks" (1977) picked up excellent reviews, and Moving Targets, which followed soon after, sold reasonably well, but the sparks they kicked up failed to set the scene afire and Chaplin quit. It took both **Neale Floyd** (guitar) and **Fred Purser** (guitar/keyboards) to replace him on stage, but replacing his songwriting skills was beyond them. "Firing Squad" (1978) and the soaring loveliness of "Life's A Gamble" did the usual Penetration trick of turning rave reviews into lousy sales figures. After a disappointing reaction to their admittedly disappointing second album, Coming Up For Air, the band announced that they were splitting up onstage at Newcastle City Hall – a gig recorded and released posthumously (the album came out first as Race Against Time and then, confusingly, as Penetration on the 1993 reissue). Pauline went on to be an Invisible Girl before going solo, but never recaptured the verve and thrill of her period as British punk's greatest female singer.

◉ Moving Targets (Virgin, 1990)

Staying true to punk's original ethos of creativity above blind following of trends, Penetration's debut LP demonstrates flair, originality and talent – as well as knocking out some great no-messing Northern rock. The CD now features five tracks not included on the luminous vinyl original, including "Don't Dictate" and the 1978 single "Fire Squad".

PERE UBU

Seized power in Cleveland, Ohio, 1975; lost it in 1979… or maybe 1982…

"ROCK MUSIC IS A NON-LINEAR, NON-NARRATIVE, NON-VERBAL ART FORM. WHY DO YOU APPROACH IT AS IF IT WERE LOGICAL AND EMPIRICAL?"

DAVID THOMAS

Once upon a time in mid-1970s Ohio a band called **Rocket From The Tombs** made its way briefly to the top of the post-industrial slagheap at the centre of Cleveland, played a handful of gigs to a raggedy-assed crowd of freaks and imploded in a drizzle of urban decay. While some of the radioactive mess ended up as **The Dead Boys**, taking "Sonic Reducer" and "Ain't It Fun" from the old set-list, a couple of splotches of detritus from the old band – **David Thomas** (a.k.a. **Crocus Behemoth**) and **Peter Laughner** – stayed in touch and to re-form as **Pere Ubu**.

Taking their name from the lead character in Alfred Jarry's *Ubu Roi* (written in 1896 as a teenage stab at a pompous schoolmaster), Pere Ubu cheerfully adopted the play's surrealism and anarchy and made them part of the act. David's idiot-savant warble bounced horribly off the demented guitar noise provided by Laughner and **Tom Herman**, with **Tim Wright** (bass), **Allen Ravenstine** (keyboards), and **Scott Krauss** (drums) doing their best to be heard over the others.

The new band set out its stall with a pair of bracingly different and downright robust singles; "30 Seconds Over Tokyo" and "Final Solution", scary new music for a public still struggling to wash the last Eagles album out of its ears, but the laughter of genius to those searching for something new to believe in. The band's fusion of arty-sounding weirdness with the muscularity of raw'n'nasty garage rock landed them a degree of local notoriety and a residency at fashionable Max's Kansas City in New York.

Laughner's pursuit of the weird, the excessive and the ill-advised had caused problems as far back as his days in RFTT. When he found money in his pocket and New York outside his front door, temptation too often got the better of him and, despite making unearthly efforts to quit, his continual relapsing into binges of alcohol and other drugs eventually led to his being sacked. Watching his band go on to wider success without him can't have helped his self-esteem, and within a year he was dead, aged just 24.

Wright split shortly after Laughner's departure, going on to smaller, noisier things with **DNA**, and was replaced by **Tony Maimone**. "Street Waves" together with the band's noisy welcome from the New York papers and international music press led to a major-label contract and *The Modern Dance* (1978). Even today, this immensely influential recording stands out on the cold and lonely outskirts of rock'n'roll: the vocals are a blend of hysteria, melancholia, depression and ecstasy, the instruments fade in and disappear without warning in a decidedly hallucinatory manner, and taken as a whole, this is still a damn fine recording to play somebody else's kids just before bedtime. It sold slowly but steadily, spreading the avant-garage word and the band's strangely infectious humour around the world.

Dub Housing was even better. A dark album where forgotten corners hid weird muffled vocals, it managed to be louder, faster, softer and slower than its predecessor, turning innocent burbling into menacing nursery rhymes and leaving gut-churning images to scare you at night.

Kicking off with the threat/promise of Thomas singing "It's meeeee again", *New Picnic Time* (1979) moved the band firmly into the post-punk / lo-fi era. Self-indulgence was taking the place of a genuine desire to experiment and, despite all the art-rock fripperies, it demonstrated that it was time for a change.

The band did in fact split up briefly, with Herman deciding to give up his place in the band to **Mayo Thompson** (ex-Red Krayola) rather than return to record The Art Of Walking (1980). Standout tracks "Go" and "Misery Goats" aside, it was a disappointing album. Herman's absence meant the band had to rely on the new boy for the whole guitar aspect of the recording, and it was no great success. The disappointment showed through in the lacklustre live shows given to promote the album, where all the fun seemed to have been squeezed out of Thomas before the tour began, and in the wake of the whole dismal affair, the band split up again, this time for five years.

The Pere Ubu that emerged after the break-up comprised Thomas and Krauss plus **Jim Jones** (guitar) and **Chris Cutler** (drums). The new line-up recorded the almost-pop *The Tenement Year*

in 1988, following up with the even more lavish *Cloudland* (1989).

Like a slowly sinking sailor desperately patching up his holed craft to keep afloat, Thomas kept replacing the band's departing members, recording a set of Ubu-by-numbers albums, *Worlds In Collision* (1991), *Story Of My Life* (1993) and *Ray Gun Suitcase* (1995) before *Datapanik In The Year Zero* (1996) – a gorgeous five-disc retrospective – put him back on the crest of his own peculiar wave again. The interest and extra dollars provided by the box set led to Thomas and Herman working together again for the first time in years to record *Pennsylvania* (1998) and *St. Arkansas* (2002).

Apparently, like the poor and The Fall, Pere Ubu will always be with us, bless their shambling, warbling hearts, and we should be grateful that they're still out there in the cold, pushing envelopes and scaring the kids.

⊚ Terminal Tower (Cooking Vinyl, 2000)

All the early singles that you'll never be able to afford collected together on a handy CD.

⊚ The Modern Dance (Cooking Vinyl, 2000)

Including an old RFTT number ("Life Stinks"), Pere Ubu's debut is darker, more disturbing and a lot more interesting to listen to thirty years down the line than the bulk of its contemporaries.

⊚ Dub Housing (Cooking Vinyl, 2000)

Spectacular, fearsome, ominous, depraved and delightful. Includes the outstanding "Codex" and "Caligari's Mirror".

Pere Ubu – creators of absurdist masterpieces.

PLAYLIST: US PUNK INTELLIGENTSIA

1. **NON ALIGNMENT PACT PERE UBU**
from **The Modern Dance (Cooking Vinyl, 2001)**

2. **NOTHING IS TRUE JIM CARROL**
from **Catholic Boy (Atco, 1999)**

3. **LAND: HORSES / A THOUSAND DANCES / LA MER(DE) PATTI SMITH** from **Horses (BMG, 2005)**

4. **FRICTION TELEVISION**
from **Marquee Moon (Rhino, 2003)**

5. **BETRAYAL TAKES TWO RICHARD HELL**
from **Blank Generation (Warner, 2000)**

6. **SHINING SILVER LIGHT WEIRDOS**
from **We Got the Neutron Bomb (Frontier, 2005)**

7. **BREAK IT ALL FEEDERZ** from **Vandalism: Beautiful As a Rock in a Cop's Face (Broken Rekids, 2005)**

8. **IN THE MOUTH A DESERT PAVEMENT**
from **Slanted and Enchanted (Big Cat, 2003)**

9. **BABY DOLL LYDIA LUNCH**
from **Teenage Jesus & the Jerks (Atavistic, 2001)**

10. **UH-OH, LOVE COMES TO TOWN TALKING HEADS** from **Talking Heads: 77 (WEA, 2006)**

◉ **390 Degrees Of Simulated Stereo (Rough Trade, 1989)**

Recorded live in Cleveland, London and Brussels, this is an essential peek into the band's early days. Includes mesmerizing and visceral versions of classics such as "30 Seconds Over Tokyo", "The Modern Dance", "My Dark Ages" and "Heart Of Darkness".

◉ **One Man Drives While The Other Man Screams (Hearpen, 2004)**

Another splendid early live collection covering the late 70s to early 80s *Dub Housing* era, this includes "Heaven", "Navvy", "Ubu Dance Party" and "Codex".

PETER & THE TEST TUBE BABIES

Conceived Brighton, England, 1978; still in nappies.

"...IF ANYBODY TELLS YOU TO DO SOMETHING, YOU ALWAYS WANT DO THE OPPOSITE. THEN PUNK ROCK CAME ALONG AND SAID 'YES! WE'RE GONNA FUCKING DO IT'."

PETER BYWATERS

Joyful no-hopers who hopped on the bandwagon back in the 1970s and will still cadge a ride on it every time there's a punk revival, **Peter And The Test Tube Babies** epitomize the

slightly drunk, game-for-a-laugh tendency of the movement we know and love.

Initially conceived as a live band by ex-manager **Peter Bywaters** (vocals), **Derek "Del" Greening** (guitar), **Chris "Trapper" Marchant** (bass) – previously in The Cornflakes, the band Peter had managed – and **Nicholas "Ogs" Loizides** (drums), **P&TTTB** made their debut with "Elvis Is Dead" on the *Vaultage* compilation (still available in the shops, kids!), but then hid their masterful blend of humour and insult behind the doors of places where they could get a drink for the next four years. They picked up a devoted, if frequently confused and argumentative fan-base, with songs that included the joyfully offensive "(We Hate All You) Student Wankers", undeniably their greatest moment.

"Banned From The Pubs" in 1982 saw them committing to vinyl again, and having developed a taste for laying down tracks in the studio, they released two albums virtually at once: *Pissed And Proud* was followed by *The Mating Sounds Of South American Frogs*.

Reluctant to appear overly committed to the work ethic, however, it took them another four years to put *Soberphobia* together. They've re-formed and released the occasional disc ever since, but have never even remotely approached the wit and wisdom of their first recordings.

◉ **Pissed And Proud (Anagram, 1995)**

Rough as a badger's behind, played through overdriven amps, underpowered for the task they're set, screaming roaring vocals delivering sheer hooligan style, heart-attack inducing puns, insults and bad taste jokes, all beautifully shrouded in high-energy punk rock. Saying it with a permanent swagger and sneering grin, Peter & The TTBs never bettered this.

⊚ The Mating Sounds Of South American Frogs (Captain Oi!, 2002)

There are several different CDs of this album doing the rounds right now. This more recent version offers the best value for money, and clocks in with a weighty nineteen tracks that include early singles releases that can be difficult to find elsewhere…

⊚ The Punk Singles Collection (Anagram, 2004)

…although this compilation, 20 tracks of lovely lovely noise, might help. It's got it all: among others "Banned From The Pubs", "Moped Lads", "Zombie Creeping Flesh", "Smash And Grab", "Trapper Ain't Got A Bird", "Rotting In The Fart Sack" and, as if that wasn't enough great titles to be getting along with, "Vicar's Wank Too".

THE POGUES

Kissing cousins in London since 1982.

"WE SHOULDN'T BE ALLOWED TO GET AWAY WITH BEING DRUNK ON STAGE."

SPIDER STACY, 1991

The same whiskey-scented demon that drove **Shane MacGowan** to form **The Nipple Erectors**, a punk/rockabilly band, in the 1970s led him to combine Irish folk music with punk rock in the 1980s.

After his earlier mob shrank down to The Nips before disappearing completely, MacGowan found himself still desperately inspired to create, but without a band to lean on. Legend has it that he literally stumbled across **Spider Stacy** when the latter was playing his tin whistle busking for change in the Underground back in 1982. Rather than suggesting Spider put his whistle away where the sun don't shine, MacGowan called on **Jim Fearnley** (guitar, ex-Nips) and **Pogue Mahone** – Gaelic for "kiss my arse" – the world's only acoustic punk-rock folk trio was born.

Early pub gigs and impromptu street performances gave way to a more conventional recording/touring routine as the trio expanded into a fully tooled-up six-piece band, adding **Jem Finer** (banjo/guitar), **Andrew David Ranken** (drums) and **Cait O'Riordan** (bass). The larger line-up and growing popularity of the band led to a shortening

of the name and it was as **The Pogues** that they released *Red Roses For Me* (1984).

The band never fitted the conventional image of a traditional folk group, but they had a broader agenda than the average punk outfit – they were always happy to cover political themes, Christmas music (albeit of the most profoundly gutter-dwelling kind) and wild careering tributes to trades and lifestyles long since gone by ("Greenland Whale Fisheries", would be a good example) – and consequently a far wider appeal than either. Crowd sizes and audience drunkenness began to grow alarmingly as Pogues gigs descended from concerts into bacchanals.

Philip Chevron (an old pal of MacGowan's from his days in the Nips and more recently a Radiator From Space) joined up in 1985, in time to record The Pogues' most accomplished recording Rum, Sodomy And The Lash. Produced by Elvis Costello, who went on to marry O'Riordan, and named after Churchill's apocryphal dismissal of "the great traditions of the Navy", it made the band's name even more solid on the live circuit and led to a year away from the studio.

The Poguetry In Motion EP of 1986 had them back on form, but O'Riordan left and was replaced by **Darryl Hunt**, and **Terry Woods** (banjo) joined, adding more rusticity to The Pogues' already rural sound. They were next seen in *Straight To Hell*, Alex Cox's 1987 film, and changed label, moving to Island, before really finding their feet again with *If I Should Fall From Grace With God* later that year. The album was a hit on both sides of the Atlantic, and yielded an enduring pension-plan of a song in "Fairytale Of New York", the romantic Yuletide duet MacGowan shared with **Kirsty MacColl**.

MacGowan looked a mess in the video, a situation only partly explained by make-up and the character he was playing – and as the money rolled in, his intake of booze and other noxious chemicals increased. By 1988 he was missing gigs – famously not showing up when the band supported Bob Dylan – and by the release of *Hell's Ditch* (1990), he was effectively out of the band, with Stacy and Finer singing in his place.

MacGowan's wilderness years must have been made even less bearable by Joe Strummer standing in for him. Strummer's voice had the requisite

PLAYLIST: POGUES

1. TRANSMETROPOLITAN
from **Red Roses For Me (WSM, 2004)**

2. BOYS FROM THE COUNTY HELL
from **Red Roses For Me (WSM, 2004)**

3. DARK STREETS OF LONDON
from **Red Roses For Me (WSM, 2004)**

4. STREAMS OF WHISKEY
from **Red Roses For Me (WSM, 2004)**

5. GREENLAND WHALE FISHERIES
from **Red Roses For Me (WSM, 2004)**

6. TURKISH SONG OF THE DAMNED
from **The Ultimate Collection (WSM, 2005)**

7. THE OLD MAIN DRAG
from **The Ultimate Collection (WSM, 2005)**

8. DIRTY OLD TOWN
from **The Ultimate Collection (WSM, 2005)**

9. THE SICKBED OF CUCHULAIN
from **The Ultimate Collection (WSM, 2005)**

10. THE IRISH ROVER
from **The Ultimate Collection (WSM, 2005)**

rawness, but he'd not lived the life that MacGowan had seen and he was never more than a temp, and Stacy finally took over full time.

MacGowan formed **The Popes** and kicked around the live circuit when able to drag himself out of his pub and onto the bus, while in the meantime The Pogues disbanded after two consecutive albums stiffed.

For the reunion and tour of 2001 however, everybody was friends again. The band – now much older, wiser and looking for a decent pay-cheque at the end of the day – fiddled and strummed away liked demons behind him. It was all very nostalgic, but not very punk.

In their day, The Pogues were a fearsome punk-rock act, spitting sparks, funny, political, offensive and dangerous. MacGowan's face, however, turned from one of the most recognizable on London's punk scene into that of a poster boy for Alcoholics Anonymous. Rock'n'roll can do that to you if you let it.

⊚ Rum Sodomy & The Lash (WSM, 2004)

So street cred you can taste the grit as you sing along. Includes "The Old Main Drag" and "A Pair Of Brown Eyes".

⊚ Poguetry In Motion (WEA, 1996)

Three tunes to get drunk by: sing merrily with the "London Girl", feel the wistfulness of "A Rainy Night In Soho", then neck a dozen beers to "The Body Of An American".

⊚ If I Should Fall From Grace With God (WSM, 2004)

Includes the awful folkiness of "The Broad Majestic Shannon," but makes up for it with "Turkish Song Of The Damned" and "Fairytale Of New York".

THE POISON GIRLS

Grew venomous in Brighton, England, 1977; retired 1985.

"I WANTED A GOOD TIME. I WANTED TO GET OUT OF THE HOUSE AND ENJOY MYSELF..."

VI SUBVERSA

Purveyors of hot songs plump with unashamedly sleazy sexual desire and fleshy delight, **The Poison Girls** were the combination of a wise woman old enough to be the kind of parent most punks in the UK would have given a limb to have grown up with, and a backing band – **Richard Famous** (guitar) and pals as required – sensitive enough to give her room to work her magic. For boys, listening to **Vi Subversa** (vocals/guitar/poetry/songwriting) was the punk equivalent of being seduced by that yummy mummy Mrs Robinson in *The Graduate* (1967). She was a great and empowering symbol for girls too, causing everyone to question their roles both sexually and politically. Never stars, never courting adulation, the band became one of punk rock's most effective conduits of anarchy and subversion.

The Poison Girls' interest in black leather extended beyond the conventional biker jacket and Doc Martens, and despite hooking up with labels of diehard street credibility (Small Wonder, Crass Records and UK Xntrix), they created thought-provoking music, far from the ramalama thrash of conventional punk, choosing a pace more suited to the message. Lyrically too, they steered clear of the anarchist community's passion for sloganeering and cheap point-scoring, choosing instead to use subtlety and ironic wit. Poison Girls kept going until the end of the 1980s, gradually losing any trace of punk music, but staying ever committed to a world made better through naughty hugs.

Anarchists in the UK, and their anarcho-punk fellows were beginning to feel a renewed strength under the Thatcherite regime, just as the powers-that-be were on the attack arresting troublemakers for meeting with persons unknown, in places unknown and at times unknown to plot who knows what.

Putting their political beliefs on the line, Crass and The Poison Girls split a single in 1980, with the cash raised going towards the "Persons Unknown" defence fund – Crass took the A-side with their "Bloody Revolutions" while Subversa contributed the powerfully worded track "Persons Unknown" on the reverse side. The London Anarchist Centre was opened on the rest of the proceeds (it endured a year before closing in a mess of ideology and spilt lager).

A one-off Poison Girls reunion gig in London in 1995 sold out on the strength of a few small ads and massive word-of-mouth publicity, proving that they were more than just an interesting footnote to the history of punk: Poison Girls still have a devoted following, and although Subversa is now growing old disgracefully somewhere in Spain, the ideas she helped to plant still sprout like violent-coloured weeds in the most inconvenient patches of the music business's well-tended lawn.

◉ Hex (Crass, 1979)

Immaculate credentials (production: Crass's Penny Rimbaud, guest vocals: Crass's Eve Libertine), and an excellent introduction to Subversa's theories of SexPol and AgitProp.

◉ Bridge (Crass, 1980)

An angrier set of songs and the ideal intro to the PG manifestos. Music that'll prepare you for an argument or a night on the barricades.

◉ Statement (Cooking Vinyl, 2004)

Limited edition 4-CD box with the complete recordings – five LPs, eight EPs and singles, plus seven previously unreleased songs. Plus an outline of the history of the band, and a lyric sheet.

THE POLICE

Joined the force in London, 1977; dismissed 1984.

"I COME FROM A FAMILY OF LOSERS ... I'VE REJECTED MY FAMILY AS SOMETHING I DON'T WANT TO BE LIKE."

STING

Forget Malcolm McLaren's rock'n'roll swindle – **The Police** were guilty of serious deception from the very beginning. Admittedly, any band formed in 1977 by a bunch of thin, angsty-looking guys with bleached hair and leather jackets was going to end up filed under "punk", but The Police were a manufactured boy band with pop stardom on their minds, just like *NSYNC, The Clash, the Sex Pistols or Westlife, and their punkiness was strictly superficial.

Stewart Copeland (son of Miles II, ex-CIA spook and brother of Miles III, the hidden face of Step Forward and I.R.S. records) was an ex-college boy from California who'd done time in Curved Air, one of the oldest wave of pop rockers. He met up with **Gordon "Sting" Sumner** (jazz-rock fiend and ex-teacher) at a club in London and the guys set about plotting fame and fortune. Picking **Henry Padovani** as the third member of the gang, they began a series of pub dates around town before releasing "Fall Out" on their own label in 1977.

The look was in place, the music ticked all the correct boxes and the single sold more than 50,000. Then in 1978, booked to play a "punk" band in a chewing-gum commercial the lads took the cheque from Wrigleys, bleached their hair and watched their last trace of credibility trickle down the drain.

Replacing Padovani with **Andy Summers**, the oldest man in punk rock, meant that all subsequent publicity photos would have to be in soft focus. Andy was a fantastically good guitar player – he'd worked with Eric Burdon, Neil Sedaka, Zoot Money and Kevin Ayers, for example – and was ready to dress the part. However, being more than ten years older than his bandmates – born in 1942, he was older than Pete Townshend, Mick Jagger, Rod Stewart and other rock dinosaurs the punks were in the process of replacing – he was never going to pass as a lean, mean, teenaged punk-rocking machine.

Still, the music they made was appealing enough – their twitchy white-boy stab at reggae worked really well with their fairly conventional "boy meets girl" pop lyrics and they soon signed to A&M. "Roxanne" stiffed on its first release in early 1978 and *Outlandos D'amour*, which followed later that year, had to crawl up the charts. However, their second single, "So Lonely", did the trick. A flurry of TV appearances beamed the trio into households across the country, radio play grew overnight, and before long, the rereleased "Roxanne" was in the Top 20. *Outlandos* was caught up in the rush and was swept into the Top 10 albums.

The Police wagon was rolling, but like so many police wagons, it had a bunch of arrogant drunks in the back – hurling insults, badly aimed punches and threats at one another like a Friday night party on its way to the lock-up. Copeland was one of the hardest-hitting drummers in the business, was no songwriting fool and was the manager's brother; Sting had an excellent voice, a gift for writing lyrics, and most importantly, control of the microphone on stage. Mix in an unimaginably large raft of money and, well, arguments are bound to break out.

Sting kept his distance from the band for the second half of 1978, acting in *Quadrophenia* (1979) – the Who's Mod movie and one that was set to spark the next big thing in youth cults on its release – and *Radio On* (a 1980 road movie set on the endless highways of the British Midlands). While they kept the happy faces on for video shoots, photo sessions and most interviews while recording and promoting *Regatta De Blanc* (1979) and *Zenyatta Mondatta* (1980), rumours in the biz and press about the backstage bickering and studio shouting-matches refused to go away.

By the release of *Ghost In The Machine* (1981), any pretence at playing punks had long been ditched. Sting was digging up album titles from the writings of the philosophers, Copeland was practising the Vulcan death glare, and Summers was practising his jazz chords. *Synchronicity* (1983) ensured that the hits kept coming until a sudden massive explosion of petulance in mid-1984 led to the three stomping off in different directions at the height of their suc-

cess, never to re-form except for a few charity gigs in 1986, and a one-off in 1992 when Sting married Trudie Styler.

⊙ **Greatest Hits (A&M 1992)**

Punk for people who don't really like punk, blended with reggae for people who don't really like reggae, played by three guys who grew to detest one another. Nonetheless, tracks such as "Roxanne", "Can't Stand Losing You" and "So Lonely" have a resonance that cannot be denied.

IGGY POP

Popped out as James Newell Osterberg, Muskegan, Michigan 1947

"I'VE PROBABLY BEEN SPIT ON MORE THAN ANY PERSON ALIVE OUTSIDE OF, I WOULD SAY, A MEMBER OF THE PRISON SYSTEM"

IGGY REMINISCES IN I NEED MORE (2.13.61, 1982)

Some folks have this notion about how their god looks after fools and little children, while others will charitably extend the protection to include drunks. **Iggy Pop** has been drunk, foolish, childish and much worse in his time, and whatever's looking after him has been working thirty hours a day, ten days a week since the mid-Sixties. Be it angel or demon, the poor thing could probably use the break that his charge, by marginally slowing down the pace as he approaches the age of 60, is at last allowing.

Young Jimmy Osterberg grew up in genteel yet comparatively restrained circumstances in Ann Arbor. He took his first steps on stage as part of a high-school band, playing for various combos in and around Detroit (picking up the nickname Iggy while drumming for The Iguanas) before dumping everything and everyone he knew to go to Chicago at the age of just 17. He planned to learn and worship at the feet of legendary drummer **Sam Lay**, who had worked with everyone from blues harmonica genius Little Walter through Paul Butterfield to Bob Dylan.

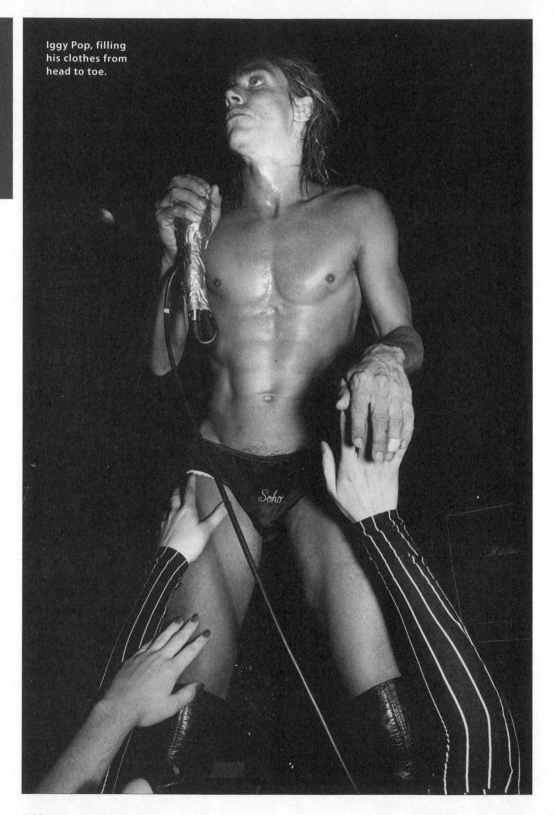

Iggy Pop, filling
his clothes from
head to toe.

A few months later, he was back in the Motor City, reborn as a singer and guitarist. Reuniting with **Ron Asheton** from The Prime Movers (one of Iggy's going-nowhere Rolling Stonesy early outfits), he reinvented himself as Iggy Pop and headed up a new band, The Psychedelic Stooges, who debuted on Halloween 1967, bringing the Summer of Love to a final and definite conclusion.

Having a front man with more guts than talent can be a double-sided blade for any band to juggle, and having mislaid the "Psychedelic" part of their name, **The Stooges** descended in a few years from beer-drinking, dope-smoking loons into whiskey-driven subhuman junkies, more interested in the next skin pop than in their next pop hit. Iggy's on stage antics grew increasingly extreme as, feeling no pain, he rolled in broken glass and knocked out his own teeth with the microphone in his struggle to genuinely connect with the crowd. Having ridden out of the Midwest on the tail of the **MC5**, as the Seventies began to turn rancid, The Stooges suddenly found themselves with no label, no management and no record to sell. Though it's told in more detail elsewhere (see p.12), by the end of January 1974, The Stooges story was over and Iggy was a mess.

Precise details of his life in the period that followed are hard to nail down and would in any case have less of an impact than the handful of astounding anecdotes that have survived. At weekends, Iggy was let out of the hospital he called home to tape the vocals for *Kill City*, a joint project with **James Williamson**, but it wasn't until David Bowie's intervention that our boy managed to break out of the nosedive he'd gone into.

The boys had met before – first in New York, and again in London when Bowie helped out in the mix and production of the *Raw Power* sessions with The Stooges in 1972. It didn't take a genius to connect Iggy with Bowie's **Ziggy Stardust** or uncover the Beckenham boy's admiration of the genuine US-manufactured rock'n'roll template, and when the opportunity to step in once again presented itself, Bowie invited Iggy to join the *Station To Station* tour before overseeing the 1977 production of both *The Idiot* and *Lust For Life*.

With the former boasting all the soul and emotion of a dying insect and the latter fairly oozing good health, redemption and clean living, they might easily have come from two completely different artists. That the same man knocked out both these championship recordings in the space of twelve months is remarkable, and yet another demonstration of how completely heroin screws its lovers. Between the two releases, Iggy turned away from the numbed-up android stomp of "Dum Dum Boys" and the barbiturate disco-stumble of "Sister Midnight", and rediscovered something beautiful and precious to take its place. *Lust For Life* twinkled with the delights of a chemical smile – from the cover picture of a healthily tanned Iggy, beaming from ear to ear like some punk-rock Alfred E. Neuman, through the presence of **Mark Volman** and **Howard Kaylan** (backing vocals, a.k.a. Flo and Eddie), to the master puppetry of Bowie himself, the album yelped and skittered with traces of cocaine.

After the rigours of heroin withdrawal and beating a goofball habit that had seen him drooling in a Hollywood gutter, however, nobody was going to deny Iggy a little enjoyment and relaxation while he returned to physical health. Besides, nothing

🎵 PLAYLIST: IGGY POP

1. NIGHTCLUBBING
from **The Idiot (Virgin, 1990)**

2. FUNTIME
from **The Idiot (Virgin, 1990)**

3. SISTER MIDNIGHT
from **The Idiot (Virgin, 1990)**

4. SUCCESS
from **Lust For Life (Virgin, 1999)**

5. LUST FOR LIFE
from **Lust For Life (Virgin, 1999)**

6. THE PASSENGER
from **Lust For Life (Virgin, 1999)**

7. SOME WEIRD SIN
from **Lust For Life (Virgin, 1999)**

8. I'M BORED
from **New Values (Arista, 2000)**

9. REAL WILD CHILD (WILD ONE)
from **Blah-Blah-Blah (A&M, 2004)**

10. T.V. EYE
from **T.V. Eye Live (Virgin, 1994)**

else on earth was going to make him play endless games of ping-pong with Bowie in the studio's relaxation area.

Iggy's miraculous redemption chimed well with the two stunning sets of work that comprised his year's output, and saw him transformed from sad ex-glamster on the skids into "The Godfather Of Punk ". *TV Eye* – the live album that followed – was recorded halfway through Iggy's mutation from slug to butterfly and is, together with *Live At The Paris Hippodrome 1977*, packed full with the roaring bull swagger of a person totally convinced of his imminent recovery and snorting after the shiny new future just down the road.

Signing to Arista and cutting Bowie's apron-strings perhaps a little too soon, Iggy returned to the fray with *New Values* in 1979. Despite the return of abrasive guitarist James Williamson, it was an over-smooth production that satisfied his fans without winning him many new converts.

His status as punk's grand unbeaten master of chemical athletics, however, kept his reputation afloat throughout the early 1980s, despite the star-studded tragedies of *Soldier* (1980) and *Party* (1981). Many a thoughtful tooth was sucked when *Zombie Birdhouse* appeared in 1982; Iggy linked up with old pal **Chris Stein** (taking leave of absence from Blondie in order to model his label-owner's hat, bass-player's sash and producer's credentials simultaneously) and was given carte blanche. In some kind of mid-life crisis, Iggy was apparently possessed by the spirit of Jim Morrison (The Doors' deceased shaman, a long-time inspiration to Mr. Pop), delivering an album's worth of pompous poetics and deep thoughts.

Urgent intervention was indicated, and Iggy rushed to Dr Bowie's private clinic in Switzerland to record *Blah-Blah-Blah* for A&M in 1986. It saw an end to Iggy's pursuit of eternal youth, with a grim determination to be the meanest hombre on the block taking its place. A solid mid-paced album, its cover showed Iggy looking rugged in a vaguely Clint Eastwood style and indicated a reassuring return to form. Perhaps predictably, *Instinct*, (1988), his next outing, sucked.

Brick By Brick (1990) saw him on yet another label – Virgin being his latest – and firing magnificently on all cylinders. *American Caesar* appeared in 1993, and was an even stronger set, wilder and far more exciting than a middle-aged man was

supposed to be. *Naughty Little Doggie* (1995) saw him kicking sparks off the cobbles as he strutted in front of a hard-rocking band and jammed with some of the best grizzled old punks still capable of thrashing out the chords, whereas *Avenue B* (1999) showcased Iggy the crooner, winding up the millennium in style and sounding like the bastard spawn of Frank Sinatra and Lou Reed.

Iggy put his solo career on hold temporarily after *Beat 'Em Up* (2001) to re-form The Stooges and drag their lardy behinds round the world in a tour / pension-fund extravaganza. Keeping the old team together for *Skull Ring* in 2003, he's been on the road and apparently thriving on it ever since, making the most of the royalty cheques accruing from the excellent compilations *Penetration* (2005) and *Million in Prizes: The Iggy Pop Anthology* (2005).

Outside the music business, Iggy's developed a useful sideline in cameo roles for off-centre Hollywood productions, appearing in *Cry-Baby* (1990), *Dead Man* (1995), *Crow II: City Of Angels* (1996) and *Coffee And Cigarettes* (2003).

⊚ The Idiot (Virgin, 1990)

Stunning set of songs, with Iggy doing a fine impression of a man on the outside after taking one too many pills for his own good. Highlights are "Sister Midnight", "Nightclubbing", "Fun Time", "China Girl" and "Dum Dum Boys".

⊚ Lust For Life (Virgin, 1999)

Quite simply the best album he's recorded in the last thirty years. Highlights are hard to pick, so here's the full, fantastic list: "Lust For Life", "Sixteen", "Some Weird Sin", "Passenger", "Tonight", "Success", "Turn Blue", "Neighbourhood Threat" and Fall In Love With Me".

⊚ TV Eye Live (Virgin, 1994)

Searing performance of a set blending Stooges numbers with early versions of some of Iggy's best solo cuts. A mere eight tracks long, but they're all marvellous and one or two feature David Bowie as part of the backing band. Full tracklisting is: "TV Eye", "Fun Time", "Sixteen", "I Got A Right", "Lust For Life", "Dirt", "Nightclubbing" and "I Wanna Be Your Dog".

⊚ Million In Prizes: The Iggy Pop Anthology (Virgin, 2005)

An incomplete introduction to the man who did it all before you'd even thought of it, but still the best of the compilations on the market. Two discs' worth of Stooges / Pop genius coming in at a bumper 38 tracks in total. Splendid party music and not too many duff numbers.

THE POP GROUP

Grouped together in Bristol, 1977;
went pop! in 1981.

"CULTURE IS WORK AND DUTY IN THE WEST, AND ANYTHING NATURAL IS A CRIME."

GARETH SAGER 1979

Bristol's scariest and most legendary musical export blended punk with funk, and Iggy Pop with Nietzsche to weave dark sounds like nothing heard before. Formed, like zillions of other bands in this book, as part of the comedown after seeing the Sex Pistols play, they soaked up and reformatted dub, jazz and proto-punk influences for four years, split up in a dignified manner and went on to new and exciting projects.

The Pop Group was formed by and attracted an audience of teenaged brainiacs and weirdos. Beating out the West Country's most fascinating rhythms, bellowing chunks from philosophy books and generally featuring at least one member clad in a frighteningly old dressing-gown, they actively hunted out the waifs and strays not soaked up by the highly absorbent sponges of disco, Rod Stewart or his dinosaur-rock cronies. As **Mark Stewart** (vocals) put it: "Basically, we're a bunch of 18-year-old kids, like any others...There must be thousands of kids like us who are beatniks at heart. At school I used to look at everyone and wonder if they thought the way I did. Why was everyone else so weird?"

Stewart first hooked up with **Gareth Sager** (guitar) and **Bruce Smith** (drums), adding **Simon Underwood** (bass) and **Jon Waddington** (extra guitar) a little further down the line. They hacked out the usual set of covers (a little Jonathan Richman here, a little T Rex there), but added a new and unusual dimension, with a huge swathe of influences reflecting their own musical backgrounds and Bristol's city/port crucible of communities.

Although they played their first gig at Tiffany's (home of the disco beat in the city), no group comprising such a broad range of refuseniks was ever going to fit comfortably into the conventional routine of building support, releasing a record and touring to support it in the shops, and The Pop Group's real career began as a series of events more like underground "happenings" or performance art than the normal concert format. Their awe-inspiring debut "(She Is) Beyond Good And Evil", for example, was unveiled in a disused church in 1979, played on a continuous loop to a select and invited audience, before going on general release and ultimately selling some very respectable thousands of copies. Politically spot-on, it captured the widespread rage and disbelief caused by Mrs Thatcher's recent election victory, but was a mere taste of the hell that was to follow. "We Are All Prostitutes" (1979) was a terrifying scream of a band sent mad by the folly and dangers of the world around them. Backed with an Amnesty International report into British military involvement in the torture of Irish Republicans, it picked up airplay from John Peel and sold well into an audience of the already converted, but is still the kind of song you'd play as a lullaby only to other people's children.

Under the circumstances – with the Cold War hotting up, the arms trade running amok, and the usual roundup of atrocities coming in on the news every day – there was not surprisingly quite a taste in the market for the music of paranoia, and The Pop Group's bad-trip acid funk, tinged as it was with free-form jazz riffing, screaming, incidental noise and chaos, hit a resounding chord at the thinking end of the post-punk universe.

Radar Records agreed to fund the recording of Y, the debut album, on the strength of little more than a handshake. Released to genuine approval from the critics in 1979, it showed just how much a little extra time in the studio could add to an album. Although superstar producer John Cale started the project, he soon made room for Dennis "Blackbeard" Bovell – big name on the UK reggae scene and then also fronting one of the country's best-known reggae acts, Matumbi – and it's his influence that is most noticeable in the final product as the album's various messages loom out of the murk of The Pop Group's trademark dubbed-up funky punk rock. It wasn't quite what the guys at the label (and their paymasters at Warner Music) had been expecting, however, and plaudits or not, the band found themselves momentarily between labels.

For How Much Longer Do We Tolerate Mass Murder? (1980) required a move to Rough Trade Records. With the nature of its contents signalled by both the title and the cover (a cute photo of two kids kissing, set over pasted-together newspaper clippings of doom and nuclear disaster), it again sold – like most mixtures of pop and polemic – mainly to an audience already convinced of the justness of its cause, but was even less easy listening than its predecessor had been. Shards of brittle guitar fell in splinters around leaden sheets of untreated noise in an atmosphere of toxic hate. Arguments within the band had already surfaced in interviews published in the music press and there were signs that the guys were beginning to move in different musical directions as the personnel moved out of its teens and into its twenties.

After a career defined by the number of benefit gigs they'd played and anti-establishment causes they'd championed, it's fitting that the Pop Group rode off into the sunset on the back of a truck after one last appearance at a CND rally in Trafalgar Square, never to appear again.

⦿ Y (WEA International, 2005)

Produced by Dennis Bovell, the Pop Group's debut showed off the band's affection for the quirky disorientation of dub reggae, summoning canyons of bass unavailable to their peers. An ugly, unholy noise to some, the laughter of genius to those with ears to listen.

⦿ For How Much Longer...Do We Tolerate Mass Murder? (Victor Japan, 2006)

Whereas most of the bands in this book would be happy to count The Stooges among their influences, those who'd cite "krautrockers" Can and Neu!, neoclassical maestros of the calibre of John Cage or apocalyptic ranters The Last Poets are considerably thinner on the ground. Blending all their influences on one album makes for a delicious messy argumentative and strong brew of music.

PORK DUKES

Formed Witham, Essex, England, 1977; crackling around the reunion circuit since 1980.

"...I AM A REAL BELIEVER IN DIY MUSIC – MAKING MUSIC IS MORE PREFERABLE THAN JUST 'CONSUMING' IT, DON'T YOU THINK?"

HORENDUS STYLES

Enigmatic rotters, and purveyors of some of the most puerile cheap filth in punk rock – no easy boast – the **Pork Dukes** have been around forever. A mostly tongue-in-cheek band formed as stress relief by a bunch of prog rockers (bored, presumably with playing the dulcimer in 13/17 time), the band comprises otherwise respectable folk-rockers and progressive musicians, did a song called "Throbbing Gristle" and inspired **Neil Megson** to become **Genesis P. Orridge**. These few solid facts and a discography apart, the data on the Dukes is scanty, self-contradicting and plagued with deliberate disinformation.

Attempts to keep the membership's real identities secret – in the hope of their maintaining some shred of prog credibility – were only partly successful. Details dribbled out through careless interview talk and some kind of family tree could be pieced together. **Colin** and **Stewart Goldring** (of Gnidrolog) were the backbone and became **Horendus** and **Vilos Styles**. **Nigel Pegram** (of Gnidrolog and Steeleye Span) became **Germun LePig**, and the trio formed a part-time covers band (featuring **Del** on vocals). Del became too much of a liability – apparently having developed a taste for fighting with the audience – so the band left him and set out to become **The Street Kings**.

Legend has it that "Bend And Flush" b/w "Throbbing Gristle", credited to The Pork Dukes, was added as a joke by an unnamed worker to the Caroline International Records catalogue for 1977. Two thousand copies were ordered pre-release, sales that the simple lack of a band or record could not be permitted to impede. The guy behind Caroline called a drummer on the circuit, our man Germun Le Pig, and the rest is punk-rock historical magic. **Rick Kemp** (of Steeleye) was complicit in some way at some point. At one time they had a drummer called **Bonk**, and lost a drummer – **Rocky Rhythm** – to the Revillos. It might even have been the same guy.

Musically, they were a more than competent punk-rock band, going through the motions, throwing all the right poses and, admittedly, entertaining their audiences immensely. Lyrically though, their output is full of lame schoolboy jokes and the kind of filth that gets pre-teens hot and bothered.

With the joke starting to generate income, an album was soon required and *Making Bacon* (1977) hit the shops shortly after. Existing ever since as an on/off act when the money's right and the guys can get the time off work, The Pork Dukes are not to everyone's liking, but can – given sufficient beer and sympathy – provide a rowdy and enjoyable night out.

⊚ **All The Filth (Vinyl Japan, 2000)**

A Sunday joint of a set – 22 tracks of punk rock's answer to the lewd rugby song. Includes the aforementioned "Bend & Flush" and "Throbbing Gristle" alongside such titles as "You're Just A Bunch Of Wankers", "Telephone Masturbator", "Making Bacon", "I Like Your Big Tits – Let's See If It Fits", "Tight Pussy", "Cocksucker Blues" and "Stuck Up You".

⊚ **Kum Kleen (Damgood, 2003)**

Worthwhile compilation of rare or unreleased tracks from 1976–1980. The four live tracks from the *Filthy Nasty* EP, which have not been available for years, are worth the price of entry alone. There are also six cuts that have never before been released: though unlikely to change your life, they offer an alternate view of this band at work.

pragVEC

Came together February 1978; fell apart 1979.

"I WAS IN A BAND BEFORE THIS AND SOME OF THE PEOPLE WHO CAME TO WATCH US I JUST DID NOT WANT TO ENTERTAIN. I WANTED TO SCARE THEM."

SUE GOGAN, 1978

Both London-based post-punks **Susan Gogan** (voice) and **John Studholme** (guitar) had been in **The Derelicts** (expired May 1976) before they met **Nick Cash** (drums – not the same one as in 999 – although this Cash did try out for them and soon found that the guitar man for 999 had nicked his name) a year later and formed **pragVEC**. A final member, **David Boyd** (bass), soon joined and pragVEC played their first gig at London's Acklam Hall in April 1978.

Based, almost stereotypically in a London tower block, they played loud but briefly through 1978 and 1979, recorded a bit and disappeared before it all got too boring. Marvellous!

Their music came from out on the art/punk borders – Fall and PiL territory – and a lot of the band's studied anonymity and obscurity grew from a shared fascination with the concept of band as brand. Sue says now that "the idea of pragVEC was that it was a name that would look well on the side of an articulated truck, a corporate ID – and we would have a second office, next door to NASA. Reflecting our devotion to P.K. Dick!" (Philip K. Dick, the science-fiction novelist).

Gig highlights included "Your Your Lay Lay", their Burroughs/Dylan tribute, where cut-up copies of the original lyrics were shuffled to give gems such as "Why stay, lady? Why stay? Him dirty eat you." Toying with the journalists, another punk stand-by, centred mainly around the endlessly repeated "Where did you get your name from?". Depending which definitive answer you read, pragVEC was taken from the writings of Camus, derived from the local brew of North Kensington, was the name of an Eastern European computer system, Polish for toilet cleaner or newspeak for foolishness.

Recorded output was limited, sporadic and terse. Their debut, *Existential*, an EP on their own Spec Records, sold four thousand copies despite being cursed as "interesting" by most reviewers. John Peel was a fan – obviously – and the recording created waves of sufficient height to surf them into touring with fellow cheerful weirdies Wire and Magazine.

Punk kudos accumulated effortlessly. In addition to producing a single for The Atoms (a band formed by one-time anarcho-comic Keith Allen), they recorded three Peel sessions, and toured with Monochrome Set and Manicured Noise.

"Expert"/"Follower", was released in mid-1979, selling five thousand copies, but failing to propel the band into the next league. A Europe-only deal to release their back catalogue on a single 12" single led to a short November residency in Paris that culminated in Cash leaving the band. The deal backfired when the record appeared on the UK market, and then, as the New Year came round, Boyd decided to leave too, leaving Gogan and Studholme to hook up with **Suresh Singh** (drums/percussion) and **Jim "Foetus" Thirlwell** (keyboards). Although Thirlwell later commented "I played with them for about ten months and it was really disgusting. After that I decided I was never working with anyone again," the new team hung together long enough to add **John Glyn** (sax) and become the Spec Records house band. At the beginning of 1981, they played London's ICA (venue of choice for the avant-garde) as **Spec Records**, appearing with Cabaret Voltaire.

Things grew a little tangled at this point. pragVEC had effectively ceased to exist, but the membership nucleus of Gogan and Studholme had developed a kind of open musical relationship, coming together and moving apart in an apparently endless series of conglomerations under different names. Spec Records plus Glyn, for example were known as **Vince Quince And His Rialto Ballroom Detectives**, Studholme and **Keith James** worked as **Couch Potatoes**, **Major Eddie** comprised Studholme, Keith James and **Gary Hill**, while alongside **Deirdre Creed** (bass), **Daniel** (drums) and **Andy** (sax), Studholme and Gogan appeared as **The Shells**, playing the Notting Hill Carnival in 1982. Their only full-length recording, *Spec Records Present No Cowboys* (1980), was credited to most of these pseudonyms and semi-bands, all based round the pragVEC nucleus.

The new arrivals of the 1980s washed away all trace of the band, with little being heard until, in the wake of being described by Jim Thirlwell as "The Dolly Parton of Postmodernism", Gogan turned to country music, and appeared in 1990 at an alt.country gig in Dublin's Garden Of Delight.

pragVEC's name has become a legend (**Half Man Half Biscuit** even recorded "pragVEC At The Melkweg" – a venue they never played, incidentally) and copies of their earlier works have been changing hands for silly amounts of money. However, all that is set to change at press time, with Cash (still a working musician, currently with **The Unmen**) and Mute Records planning a reissue of the back catalogue that will, one hopes, make some sense of their chaotic legacy.

THE PREFECTS/ THE NIGHTINGALES

Head boys 1976; expelled 1980.

"HELP ME PLEASE HELP ME I'M SO WEEDY I'VE GOT VD PLEASE HELP ME I'M SO WEEDY I'VE GOT VD"

COMPLETE LYRICS TO THE PREFECTS' "VD"

John Peel said **The Prefects** were better than The Pistols or The Clash. Despite having him on their side, however, the Midlands' finest contribution to early punk rock was a band so obscure that they actually split up a full year before they released their first record.

After auditioning and rejecting Nikki Sudden (later of Swell Maps) and Chris Collins (later comedian Frank Skinner), brothers **Paul Apperley** (vocals/drums) and **Alan "Roots" Apperley** (guitar) combined their garage band duo with **Robert Lloyd** (vocals/guitar/harmonica) and his pal **PJ Royster** (bass) at the beginning of 1977. The new outfit dived headlong aboard the punk rock bandwagon, naively swallowing the New Wave's egalitarian myths and cheerfully prepared to enter the arena with no money, no contracts, no record deal and no management to fight their corner.

Part II.

Naturally, they were shafted by music-biz sharks at every turn.

Lloyd brought some useful contacts to the band – along with new bass-player **Graham Blunt**, who replaced the swiftly dismissed PJ – and The Prefects' shambling, improvisational punk rock was soon signed up as bottom of the bill to a line-up including The Jam, Buzzcocks, Subway Sect and The Clash. After just four gigs played at small hometown venues (with a set list featuring the intensely unpopular "Birmingham's A Shit Hole"), The Prefects suddenly found themselves in the big time – opening the "White Riot" tour at London's Rainbow Theatre in May 1977 – receiving a (small) can of warm beer each in payment.

The band toured for the rest of the year (setting fire to **The Jam**'s Union Jack backdrop at one gig, stealing beer from Bo Diddley's rider at another), making little money but gaining an impressive reputation. They played the closing weekend of Manchester's **Electric Circus**, but refused to allow their performance to appear on the *Short Circuit* compilation that resulted from the festival. Audiences had to wait until late summer 1978 – when they recorded "Things in General", "Escort Girls", and "Agony Column" in the first of their Peel sessions – to hear the band other than live through a cheap, distorted PA system. The session's masterpiece cut however, and the one that made the band's reputation was "The Bristol Road Leads to Dachau". Ditching the post-pubescent humour that characterized tracks such as the 10-second epic "VD" and their remarkable stab at "Bohemian Rhapsody", Lloyd led the band through a brittle 10-minute account of the pub bombings that had traumatized Birmingham, and which was reminiscent of **Alternative TV**'s meandering "Alternatives To NATO" or **Throbbing Gristle**'s more comprehensible nightmarish epics.

The original line-up had already undergone some minor changes and rejigging, and personnel swaps were to become a feature of the band's career. For the second Peel set, recorded the following May, there were a few more Prefects to be herded into the BBC's Maida Vale studio. **Eamon Duffy** was the latest bass player, drums came from **David Twist** and/or **Andy Burchell**, with **Dave Whitton** (sax) rounding out the sound of "Going Through The Motions", "Faults", "Total Luck" and "Barbarellas" (Lloyd had learned between the first and second session that bands were paid by the BBC according to the number of musicians that showed up, and had bulked out the line-up for a few dollars more). Pausing only to tidy up the personnel roster by replacing all the other drummers with one **Joe Crow** and slimming down to a more manageable 4- or 5-piece semi-permanent set-up, they continued to plough their lonely furrow on the far side of the punk-rock farm for the rest of the year, gigging around the country and sometimes even getting paid.

"Faults", clocking in at around 90 seconds and slamming into rather than merely touching all the regular punk-rock bases was the session's most immediately accessible track. "Going Through The Motions", however, summed up the band's punk-rock attitude better than any inky manifesto from the Art-Punk theoretician brigade could do. Consisting purely of the title repeated at mind-numbing length over a drum and bass riff, the band put it together with the intention of irritating their audience into leaving the venue. The band's cheery ineptitude finally caught up with them as punk's decade petered out into the second dark age of the Eighties. The robustly amateur approach they had chosen meant that they never had a record company chasing them for product, or any royalty cheques to keep the band together when the gigs began to dry up. Soon after the second radio session, The Prefects handed in their badges.

It took more than tragic break-ups to keep Lloyd out of the music game, however, and he formed **The Nightingales** with the Apperley brothers, Crow and Duffy, signing to Rough Trade in the immediate aftermath. The new outfit was nothing like a punk band, and though it went on to produce some excellent post-punk wordy but witty pop – fine if you like that sort of thing – the Nightingales needn't trouble us further.

In a move that must have grated with Lloyd and the rest of the new band, Rough Trade put out The Prefects' only single in June 1980 – "Going through the Motions" b/w "Things in General", licensed from the Peel sessions recordings. When Strange Fruit finally cottoned on to the treasure they held, they put out the complete set of Prefects' session recordings on a single album, only to delete it almost immediately.

The sessions have been sporadically available since, with the most recent version appearing in 2004, but despite the joyful reception the band received when they reunited for a set of dates in 2001, too many years had passed for a new surge of momentum to build up. There's a semi-official, partly licensed sort of bootleg available now and then called *Prefects Live In Birmingham, October 1978*. Originally recorded onto cassette, the sound is so-so, but the music is superb – one to look out for.

⊚ **The Prefects Are Amateur Wankers (Acute, 2004)**

...or so said Clash/Subway Sect manager Bernie Rhodes. The band's entire sessions are at last available again on this delicious CD, topped up with a couple of live cuts salvaged from the Electric Circus weekender. Each track is an essential slice of punk history.

THE PRETENDERS

Pretending on and off since formation in London; 1978

"DON'T THINK THAT... TRYING TO LOOK FUCKABLE WILL HELP. REMEMBER YOU'RE IN A ROCK'N'ROLL BAND – IT'S NOT "FUCK ME", IT'S "FUCK YOU!"

CHRISSIE HYNDE

Never a punk band, but the very epitome of what was meant by "New Wave", **The Pretenders** started out like a slightly more rock'n'roll version of Blondie, but ended up with as many casualties as the New York Dolls. And they seemed so nice, too!

Chrissie Hynde (guitar) came from Akron in Ohio, the same town as Devo (sharing a band back in the day with Mark Mothersbaugh, head spudboy). Like them, she got the hell out as soon as she could. Heading for London in her mid-20s, she started out working for Malcolm McLaren at Sex on the Kings Road. Jumping soon afterwards from the frying pan right into the blast furnace, she then fell in with Nick Kent – dark lord of the London music press – who helped her get her foot in the door of the *NME*.

Hynde was soon just another laidback mid-1970s groover, hanging out with the rest of the journalists at London's Speakeasy, waiting for the celebrities to show up. Showing a lot more get up and go than the rest of the scribblers, she absorbed some of the new "do it yourself" spirit and found herself on stage, first alongside **Chris Spedding** (hot session-guitarist *du jour* and the guy who allegedly created the Sex Pistols' sound), but soon fronting her own punk-rock outfit, **The Berk Brothers**.

It didn't take her long to realize that only a genuine berk would stay in such a dead-end band, however, and leaving the Berks to become **Johnny Moped**, by 1978 Hynde was fronting **The Pretenders**. After much shuffling through the detritus of the London music scene, she settled on **James Honeyman-Scott** (guitar), **Pete Farndon** (bass) and **Martin Chambers** (drums).

They charted in 1978 with their debut, "Stop Your Sobbing", a cover of a Kinks' oldie, and moving to self-penned compositions, kept up the pressure throughout 1979 with "Kid" and "Brass In Pocket". *The Pretenders* was released in 1980 (including a fine cover of The Only Ones' "Lovers Of Today") and went to the top both in the UK and across in the US. The Pretenders' brand of power pop with a tough and gritty female edge struck home big-time on both sides of the Atlantic with a series of smooth grooves. Hynde's part-autobiographical, easily accessible soft-rock balladry blended seamlessly with Honeyman-Scott's excellent if complicated guitar work, and riding along on the crest of the New Wave, they were soon giving the Debbie Harry/Joan Jett crowd cause for concern.

Hynde met Ray Davies, author of "Stop Your Sobbing" when the band toured the US in 1980, and carried away on a tide of romance, she took her eyes off the road for a moment too long. *Pretenders II* (1981) seemed to tread water, looking again at the old "boy meets girl" routines of mainstream pop. Predictably, however, it sold in truckloads and kept the charts busy with "Message of Love", "I Go to Sleep" and "Talk Of The Town".

Farndon found himself sacked and without a band in the middle of 1982 and two days later, Honeyman-Scott died of an overdose. Knocked understandably sideways into the long grass by these events, Hynde dropped out of sight. In early 1983, just as Hynde was getting herself back into condition to return to the cut and thrust of the pop

PLAYLIST: PRETENDERS

1. **BRASS IN POCKET**
   from **Greatest Hits (WEA, 2000)**

2. **DON'T GET ME WRONG**
   from **Greatest Hits (WEA, 2000)**

3. **KID**
   from **Greatest Hits (WEA, 2000)**

4. **BREAKFAST IN BED - UB40 & CHRISSIE HYNDE**
   from **Greatest Hits (WEA, 2000)**

5. **MESSAGE OF LOVE**
   from **Greatest Hits (WEA, 2000)**

6. **TALK OF THE TOWN**
   from **Greatest Hits (WEA, 2000)**

7. **WATCHING THE CLOTHES (DENMARK STREET DEMO)** from **Pirate Radio Box Set (Rhino 2006)**

8. **PRECIOUS (REGENT PARK DEMO)**
   from **Pirate Radio Box Set (Rhino 2006)**

9. **TATTOOED LOVE BOYS**
   from **Pirate Radio Box Set (Rhino 2006)**

10. **WHAT YOU GONNA DO ABOUT IT**
    from **Pirate Radio Box Set (Rhino 2006)**

biz, Farndon too succumbed to a fatal overdose.

Most of that year was a write-off. Hynde recruited **Robbie McIntosh** (guitar, ex-Manfred Mann's Earth Band) and **Malcolm Foster** (bass), and having beaten them into shape, had to be content with topping the charts at Christmas with the frankly saccharine "2000 Miles".

Learning To Crawl kicked off the New Year in style, and the new line-up was able to put most of the catastrophic past few months to one side. It wasn't a great singles album, giving up just the Christmas hit and "Back On The Chain Gang", but it sold zillions and made Hynde's wedding in May that year (to Jim Kerr of Simple Minds – she misplaced Ray Davies somewhere in the last couple of paragraphs) just that little bit happier still. The new Pretenders were a more conventional old-school rock band than the first line-up had been, and musically, their history from here onwards has little to do with the glorious punk revolution.

The band appeared at Live Aid in 1985 and Hynde guested on **UB40**'s ghastly cover of "I Got You Babe", but it wasn't until 1986 that the next Pretenders album appeared. Get Close was effectively a Hynde/McIntosh project, lacking direction, guts or anything special to say. "Don't Get Me Wrong" charted, as did Hynde's 1988 follow-up with UB40, a far more convincing cover of Dusty Springfield's (originally Baby Washington's) "Breakfast In Bed".

Hynde split up with husband Kerr in 1990 and released *Packed!* with another bunch of Pretenders that same year. It stiffed. She came back again in 1994 with *Last Of The Independents* and a chart single, "I'll Stand by You." A pointless and unsatisfying live album, *Isle Of View*, was the band's

only release in 1995, and The Pretenders stayed undercover again until *Viva El Amor* (1999) and *Loose Screw* (2003).

Chrissie Hynde, the great Pretender.

Although their respectable legacy finished at the start of the 1980s, the Pretenders' influential blend of sharp-edged New Wave ideals with unmatched pop sensibilities made Hynde a star on the bedroom walls of boys and girls alike.

⊙ The Pretenders (WEA, reissued 1990)

The band's earliest, rawest material, perfectly depicting the New Wave sound that pinned them to the scene's map. A classic that should be in every collection.

PUBLIC IMAGE LTD

Created London, 1978; effectively destroyed in 1983, but read on…

Take another look at the footage of the Pistols' final gig, right near the end, where Johnny Rotten perches on the edge of the stage asking the crowd if they've ever felt cheated. Freeze-frame right after the question and look. He's already left the band – you can see it in his eyes. The story of exactly why Rotten quit comes later in the alphabet, but for the moment, it suffices to say that he had little to gain by staying with them and a bile-duct stuffed to bursting with reasons to go his own way.

Having watched punk rock turn into a dark circus where the laughs were punctuated by acts of violence or drug-induced deaths, Johnny Rotten reverted to his real name of **John Lydon** and remodelled himself from punk-rock scarecrow into an avant-garde artiste. The first line-up for the band was pulled together from old pals and new acquaintances and was robust enough to stop him vanishing completely up his own inflated opinion of himself. **Keith Levene** (guitar), **Jah Wobble** (bass) and **Jim Walker** (drums) were more than a match for his excruciating vocals and ran him a close second on the debut **Public Image Ltd** release, "Public Image". Levene had been on the scene since the beginning (allegedly he was the unruly subject of The Clash's song "Deny") and Lydon had known Wobble (**John Wordle** in real life) before the Sex Pistols started; neither was going to take any rock-star preening too seriously.

This almost democratic approach meant that the first album (called Public Image – Lydon was apparently a firm believer in branding – but also known as First Edition) pulled in all directions but turned out strong. There were straight-ahead punk-rock

tracks to keep the old school interested, plus enough spleen-venting to knock a hole in the ozone layer. He was still a very angry young man indeed.

Metal Box / Second Edition initially made the news more for its packaging than its content. Released as three 12" 45s in an embossed circular tin, it came with the bass mixed high enough to demolish expensive dental work and screw up most high-end stereo systems. Grossly impractical to actually play and listen to in this format, it was soon reissued as a more conventional double album (though the tin and original mix reappeared in miniature when the album was reissued as a CD). Putting the packaging to one side though, we're left with a phenomenally powerful recording that gives Lydon and Wobble room to indulge their dub fascination, has space for a pastiche of *Swan Lake* and ends with what might once have been called a large dollop of self-indulgent prog-rock rubbish.

Nevertheless, if the band had quit at this point, there'd be statues of them in our parks and streets named in their honour. The truth however is less palatable. Wobble left the band, and when Walker did the same, **Martin Atkins** signed on as the new drummer. To keep the name alive while the new guys learned the set, the band rush-released *Paris Au Printemps*, a satisfactory but uninspiring live recording.

Deciding rashly to press on without a bass player, PiL released the sonically and mentally unbalanced album *The Flowers Of Romance*. More extreme than *Metal Box*, it is held together by sheer force of will, relentless drumming and the ravings of Johnny Lydon, screeching like a zombie who's caught its yarbles in a coffin lid.

Levene jumped ship in 1983, just before "This Is Not A Love Song" gave the band its first worldwide dance-floor hit. Lydon cobbled together a new line-up and headed for Japan to cash in. *Live In Tokyo* resulted and disappeared, thankfully without trace, soon after. Work had begun on *This Is What You Want…This Is What You Get* before Levene left, and his guitar parts were erased before it was released. Levene's album Commercial Zone followed soon after – his own version of the sessions and a much more interesting album all round.

By the time *Album* (also issued as *Cassette* and *Compact Disc*) was released, PiL was a pretty interesting but otherwise standard rock band. Lydon ditched the noise, rage and aggression that brought him fame and turned into a TV-friendly, cuddly

Uncle Punky, happily bellowing "anger is an energy" almost like he still meant it, maaaan.

Happy? saw Lydon working alongside **Lu Edmonds** (underrated star guitar of The Damned's second coming), **John McGeogh** (ex-Magazine, Banshees) and **Bruce Smith** (ex-Rip, Rig And Panic) in a musicianly extravaganza of dance-floor-filling skill. All good fun, but it wasn't punk rock any longer.

Although Lydon has continued to release albums under the PiL banner, the band has, since 1983, been little more than a series of session musicians roped in to make the sounds that Mr Lydon wants them to. Johnny went back to being Rotten by name but, when he appeared on a celebrity torment TV show set in Australia in 2004, he had apparently given up his rotten behaviour. Chosen to face ordeal by ostrich, he jumped at the chance to take on a few "overgrown budgies" and charming the British audience, became the bookies' favourite to win.

It took a few days more for his old "anger is an energy" spirit to surface, but when it appeared, it took him over completely. Bored by the company and the lack of anything interesting to do he turned petulant, petty and ultimately spiteful. Despite calling the TV audience "fucking cunts" when they missed an opportunity to vote him off the show, when he walked off the set a few days later, throwing any chance of picking up his appearance fee overboard, he walked into the hearts of millions. He's seen by the tabloids as a spiky-headed Peter Pan Of Pop and though that means he gets sympathetic treatment these days, he's too canny and has too long a memory of what else the papers are capable of to be bothered with them very much.

⊚ Public Image: First Issue (Virgin, 1988)

As fine a piece of spleen-venting as anything committed to plastic, the first PiL album has its share of screaming rants from the newly renamed John Lydon, but is more than just his rite-of-passage recording. With Keith Levene, Jim Walker and Jah Wobble standing shoulder to shoulder alongside our hero, PiL knock out a particularly confident debut, which offers Lydon's two-part views on religion, "Annalisa", "Low Life" and "Attack", as well as the stirring "PiL Theme".

⊚ The Greatest Hits...So Far (Virgin, 1990)

Not too much overlap with the band's debut and collecting their most important pre-1990 tracks together, this is a splendid primer on what Johnny did next. Includes "Death Disco", "Careering", "This Is Not A Love Song", "Rise" and "Seattle".

Following the showbiz tradition of opening with a grand theme tune, PiL aimed to make a big entrance, striding up to the Music Industry saloon, booting open the door, striding up to the bar, ordering a shot of whiskey and glaring round at the other bad hombres.

It opens with perhaps the most recognizable bassline of the last twenty-odd years, a siren / percussive riff from Jah Wobble that sounds like an alarm call, and, as any DJ will tell you, acting like one too – drop this anywhere in the Western world and you'll see a herd of middle-aged ex-hellraisers twitch like a bunch of meerkats. Drop it at the right time of the evening and the herd will stampede onto the dance floor to have a bash at reliving their more supple youthful moves. Very entertaining.

A few brief vocal introductions follow before Lydon lets rip with a hugely mocking slack-jawed bellow of laughter, Levene wades in with a mesh of jangly distortion pulled from his guitar and we're away for three minutes of rage in heaven. Lydon's lyrics clearly intend to close the previous chapter of his life in the music game, revealing a young man only a few months older but left decades wiser by his experiences. As for the rest of the band – apparently given instructions to pillage, destroy and leave no two stones standing on one another – they lay into an otherwise fairly standard bit of rock music with aplomb, violence and glee, turning it from a rough diamond into a hard, shiny perfect jewel.

"The Cowboy Song" – which appeared on the B-side of the original – is so blatant a piece of filler that it actually works as a piece of entertainment. Worth a listen if you need a smile.

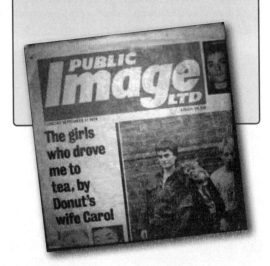

Punk International

With the exception of Belgium's pride – **Plastic Bertrand** and his pop punk assault "Ça Plane Pour Moi", which entered the UK charts in 1977 – French-language punk rock never really took off. Even though France had provided the Situationist International and the excellent examples of anarchy in action seen during the Paris revolution in 1968, when the continental European New Wave did genuinely break on the shores of Britain it came via **Little Bob Story**, **Stinky Toys** and **Métal Urbain**, none of whom managed to break out of the Francophone ghetto.

Bob Story and the band (a hard-working R&B crew straight outta Le Havre), were co-opted as part of the movement by journalists desperate for stories that backed up their theory of punk as the new world order. Their act was no more punk than the sweaty, high-intensity boogie offered by **Eddie & The Hot Rods**, **Dr Feelgood** and the rest of the Essex R&B revival that immediately predated punk. Still, they were happy for the attention and were pleased to line up alongside their Parisian comrades-in-arms, Stinky Toys.

Stinky Toys were a great proposition but one that failed to live up to the hype. After choosing such an excellent band name, the band screwed up by letting **Elli Medeiros** (vocals) near the microphone. Perhaps selected more for being easy on the eye than for the quality of her singing (which wasn't even bad enough to be interesting, she just sounded dull), they scored reasonably highly as a "live in concert" proposition but the band's debut bombed like an irritated US president and they were never heard of again.

Métal Urbain weren't much better, although they at least made an effort to pick the right kind of stage names – the band boasted input from a changing cast that included **Eric Débris** (keyboards, electro-percussion),

Claude "Clode" Panik (vocals), **Rikky Darling**, **Hermann Schwartz** and **Nancy "Pat" Lüger** (guitar), with **Zip Zinc** and **Charlie H** (keyboards). Their taste for electronica didn't sit well with the prevailing mood, though, and despite a clutch of albums and an industrial splinter group – **The Metal Boys**, who were, if anything, even worse than their name suggests, they never made a lasting impression.

With German punk of the 1970s more or less the exclusive domain of **Die Toten Hosen** as far as international coverage was concerned, Dutch and Scando-punk even less noticeable and the remainder of the continent failing to register at all, non-Anglophone punk from Europe has had the same kind of limited success on the international stage as any other kind of "foreign-language" rock and is best tracked down in the world music section of your friendly local record store.

Japan's unique and highly experimental scene (see The Boredoms, p.87) is thriving but confined almost entirely to a Japanese-speaking fan-base, living almost exclusively in the cities; in a similar way, most of the world's urban centres will have a punk network of some sort playing gigs well below the mainstream's radar.

Coincidentally, the faux-gypsy, cod-Ukrianian schtick of **Gogol Bordello** is, at the time of writing, the hottest ticket on the UK live circuit, and the band's "immigrant punk" pose has made them a bigger success in this country than at home in the USA. Like **Les Négresses Vertes**, **Mano Negra** and **Rashid Taha** (champion of Algerian-French punk attitude and the guy who covered **The Clash**'s "Rock The Casbah"), however, they're seen as little more than a novelty act by the majority audience, and their appeal is unlikely to endure much beyond their next album.

Part II.

RADIATORS FROM SPACE

Descended on Dublin in 1976; left our galaxy in 1981. Seen sporadically since.

"THE ULTIMATE IN BAD TASTE"

THE SUNDAY PEOPLE, 1977

When **Philip Chevron** (guitar/songwriting/spokesman) put together the **Radiators From Space** (after ditching such other band names as Rockette, Hell Razors and Rough Trade), he had the cream of the Dublin scene to choose from. Fortunately he left them alone, and chose **James Crash** (drums), **Peter Holidai** (guitar/vocals), **Mark Megaray** (bass/vocals) and his old ally **Steve Rapid** (vocals) instead. Chevron and Rapid had previously worked together in glam-rock act **Greta Garbage And The Trashcans**, and were keen to try this new ultra loud, noisy, smelly punk rock that they'd read about.

On the strength of a blistering single, "Television Screen" (which still drips all the energy of Eddie And The Hot Rods and shows a pretty similar take on the world), this gang of well-intentioned but unskilled musicians – minus Rapid, who remained at home – hoofed it across the Irish Sea to London with the admirable intention of showing the city kids that there was more to punk rock than towerblocks, anarchy and dole queues. There was the added attraction of being near their record company – Chiswick – right at the centre of things.

TV Tube Heart (1977) was a speed-fuelled rock'n'roll rampage, and it hit the stores before anything by bigger-named seminal bands – including The Clash, Siouxsie And The Banshees, The Jam and The Stranglers – had left the mixing desk. Dangerously overloaded with volume, passion and intensity, it offered a challenge to the innumerable orthodoxies confronted by growing up in an Ireland hidebound by political and religious convention.

Musically ramshackle though, it managed to appear simultaneously unfinished and over-produced, and failed to win the band the size of audience they probably deserved. Those who followed the Radiators live on tour, however, saw them grow increasingly confident and develop into capable and imaginative musicians. Following the advice of the label, the newly-initiate wizards of melody dropped the "From Space" from their name and signed up with **Tony Visconti** – skilled producer with years of experience – to oversee *Ghostown*. Visconti smoothed all the rough edges off the Radiators, bringing in his trademark string section, sax-player Ruan O'Lochlainn and guest vocals from Mary Hopkin (ex-Eurovision pop chanteuse), and he normally ends up with the blame for the album's content and lack of performance sales-wise.

Chevron saw the album as a "midnight walk through Dublin with the ghosts of the city's past", and it certainly picked up some remarkable reviews – "possibly the most significant Irish rock album ever" according to *Hot Press*, and "a literate, nouveau pop masterpiece…astonishing, immaculate" in *Sounds* – but with buyers hard to convince, the record stalled after a few weeks. In fact, and now that nobody cares any longer, it's safe to call *Ghostown* a fine, if uninspired powerpop album. It contains a bunch of good, toe-tapping tunes and an ironic 1950s flashback section that just about curdles fresh milk into cheese. Interesting but hardly essential, it ushered the Radiators into obscurity.

With the new decade, the audiences in London turned to new styles of music, none of it unfortunately that being peddled by the Radiators. Facing wholesale rejection of their new melodic/ironic direction, they retreated first back to Ireland, then across for a European tour before, firing off one last single "Song Of The Faithful Departed", splitting up in 1981. Chevron showed up again first alongside Elvis Costello and subsequently as a Pogue, and the Radiators reformed in 1987 for an AIDS benefit, and again in 2003 for a Joe Strummer memorial gig. Deciding they liked the taste, they stayed together as a band, touring throughout 2004 and to promote their reissued albums in 2005.

⊙ **TV Tube Heart (Big Beat, 2005)**

The original and best album by the boys. More reminiscent of Eddie & The Hot Rods' lightning-pace high-energy R&B than yer actual punk rock, this is a magnificent party record, loud, stomping and glorious.

RADIO BIRDMAN

Started circling over Sydney, Australia in 1974; shot down in 1978.

"...I THINK IT IS NECESSARY FOR ME TO HAVE VARIED EXOTIC AND 'HARD CORE' EXPERIENCES ... IF ONLY TO AVOID HAVING BORING MEMORIES WHEN I'M OLD."

DENIZ TEK, 2001

Never quite punk enough for the purists, yet just a tad too hardcore for the mainstream to take, **Radio Birdman** fell uncomfortably between a pair of stools, hit their head on the way down and never completely recovered their balance. The music they created was equally unsettled and disturbing, challenging the hard-rock, denim-clad establishment, causing it a set of unpleasant itches it was never able to scratch. Screwed over by the music biz, they became a cult band and remain an impressive name to drop even now, though they would probably have preferred international superstardom, hot and cold running groupies and a guitar-case full of cocaine.

Deniz Tek (songwriting/guitar/vocals) formed the band with reformed surfer **Rob Younger** (vocals/attitude/hair) when he washed up in Sydney. With another foreigner, Canadian **Chris Masuak** (guitar) and local boys **Warwick Gilbert** (bass), **Pip Hoyle**

(keyboards/vocals) and **Ron Keeley** (drums) completing the line-up, Birdman was go!

Originally from Michigan, in fact from Iggy Pop's home town of Ann Arbor, Tek brought a healthy dose of Midwestern American dumb into an already adequately anti-intellectual Sydney scene. With Younger, he created a hybrid beast formed partly from Tek's Detroit background of MC5 and Stooges gigs (even the band name appeared to be a misquote from Iggy's apocalyptic rant "1970" – a song that features the lyric "radio burnin' up above", but which sounds like "radio birdman up above") and partly from the heads-down no-nonsense industrial-strength heavy rock of the local scene.

Although Brisbane's Saints were signed to EMI on the strength of a self-released single, and went on to become the first band that came to mind when the subject of Oz punk reared up, Birdman were there first, with their *Burn My Eye* EP, a short, sharp kick in the nuts brimming with guitar roar and whisky-sodden piano. You can't argue with titles like "Smith And Wesson Blues" or "Burn My Eye".

Scrounging free time from Trafalgar Studios where they'd recorded the EP, the band put together a proto-punk full-length set and released it locally as *Radios Appear*, a title taken from "Dominance And Submission" by Tek's heroes Blue Öyster Cult.

Sire signed them up for international stardom, rereleased *Radios Appear* with a new cover and a few new tracks in 1978, and then ignored them. The band recorded *Living Eyes* as an immediate follow-up (moving halfway around the world to darkest Wales to do so), but such was the interest in the other big-name acts on the label (which was home to The Ramones and Blondie, for example) that it stayed on the shelf until 1981. Though still teeth-grindingly tough and masculine, the music was now out of fashion, and soon after it was finally released, the band split up and went off in different directions.

Masuak went on to **The Screaming Tribesmen**, Gilbert became one of **The Lime Spiders**, Tek stayed in the industry for a while, raging briefly against the machine in **New Race** with Younger, ex-Stooges guitarist Ron Asheton, and ex-MC5 drummer Dennis Thompson. When that band folded, he went off to become a surgeon for the US Navy (what a bedside manner!) before returning to live performances in the 1990s. Younger stayed in music too, first as part of the ultra-heavy **New Christs** and later working as a producer.

A 1996 reunion tour featuring all the original members received such excellent reviews that the guys have repeated it three or four times since, riding a wave of nostalgia admittedly, but winning over new, younger fans, attracted by their intensity, passion and skill.

⊙ Radios Appear (Sire, 1978)

Their debut kicks off with a blistering surge through the Stooges' "TV Eye" and never looks back. The standout track "Do The Pop" shows the band's tongue-in-cheek awareness of tinny punk rock, but its lasting appeal lies in heavyweight rockers like "Descent Into The Maelstrom" and "New Race", the surf-driven "Aloha, Steve & Danno" (the best song about wasting time in front of crap TV ever) and "You're Gonna Miss Me", an old 13th Floor Elevators rocker.

⊙ Living Eyes (WEA Australia, 1981)

Recorded in Wales, presumably under a leaden sky, the follow-up was already slower and more mature. It's still angry enough, with revised versions of three tracks from their debut EP, and there are giggles a-plenty in "More Fun", but this is still to be filed under "dark, sweaty rock".

⊙ The Essential Radio Birdman: 1974–1978 (Sub Pop, 2001)

All the above, and more – at a bargain price, too.

THE RAINCOATS

First worn in London 1977, hung up 1984. Re-formed 1994-96, sporadic appearances since.

"...PLAYING WAS AN EMOTIONAL THING. WE WOULD STRUGGLE, WE WOULD CRY, WE DIDN'T REALLY KNOW WHAT WE WERE DOING HALF THE TIME."

GINA BIRCH

Feminist icons, much championed by Kurt Cobain and Courtney Love, but more importantly a kick-ass punk-rock band, The Raincoats made some of the roughest music and sang with some of the best voices on the scene. Never much more than a cult back at the time when money was the least important thing on anyone's mind, they've grown in importance in the intervening period.

Ana Da Silva (vocals, guitar) and Gina Birch (vocals, bass) leapt at the chance to recruit Palmolive – a.k.a. Paloma Romero – (drums) on her way out of The Slits, and when Vicky Aspinall showed up for audition carrying her violin (the gals had advertised for someone who played an unusual instrument), the trio became a quartet. Add in manager/guru Shirley O'Loughlin, and the five-headed beast became a living, breathing band with a wild fiddle shriek and a deep guitar growl.

Live, the line-up generally comprised most of the four musicians above, but there was always room on stage for contributions from other players, and early gigs tended to involve even more dodging around between songs than the long-suffering punk audience was used to. This apparent amateurism disguised the genuine democracy that the band had adopted and it would be a mistake to see Raincoats gigs as anything less than experimental "performances".

Debut single "Fairytale In A Supermarket" appeared on Rough Trade, as did The Raincoats (1979), to much critical approval. Musically profound, disturbing, challenging and still essential, vital listening, it sold respectably enough without troubling the charts, and contained a blistering version of the Kinks' "Lola" that involved so much gender-bending that listeners got motion sickness. As an all-female, fiercely independent and experimental band, The Raincoats pushed all the right political buttons too, picking up an audience of earnest young student types who mixed uneasily with the spiky-haired mosh-pit contingent.

Palmolive left the band almost as soon as work started on the second album and Odyshape (1981) was written without the regular input of a drummer. Input from Robert Wyatt, however, more than made up for her absence, and Ingrid Weiss, who finally took over, soon picked up where Palmolive had left off.

More touring followed, giving the personnel the chance to work through their emotional turmoil in front of a paying audience, and occasional single releases (such as "Running Away", a cover of the Sly And The Family Stone track, in 1982 or "Animal Rhapsody" in 1983) kept interest alive around the world. The Kitchen Tapes (1983) – a live recording originally available only on cassette – helped crystallize the myth of The Raincoats, but their final official full-length release, Moving (1984), revealed just how quickly the group had fallen apart. A genuine (for once) case of musical differences had finally become fatal and The Raincoats ceased to be.

Almost a decade later, however, Kurt Cobain of Nirvana, a long-time fan of emotional distress, tracked down Da Silva to an antiques shop in Notting Hill and persuaded her and Birch to re-form the band. **Anne Wood** took over violin duties, and in the absence of Palmolive – variously reported as getting her head together in India or as having joined the mad evangelists of Texas – **Steve Shelley** (borrowed from Sonic Youth) hit the drums.

The new Raincoats opened for Nirvana on their 1994 tour, going on to record the *Extended Play* EP and *Looking In The Shadows* (1995), with **Heather Dunn** now beating out the rhythm. They followed up with a tour under their own name, picking up a rapturous welcome completely out of proportion to their original impact.

⊚ The Kitchen Tapes (ROIR, 1998)

Recorded live in concert, with all the extra excitement and reductions in sound quality that usually implies, this remains, nevertheless, The Raincoats' most essential recording. Highlights include "No One's Little Girl", "Only Loved At Night" and "Rainstorm". while "Dance Of Hopping Mad", "Animal Rhapsody" and "Puberty Song" boom with a power they never achieved in the studio.

⊚ Odyshape (Rough Trade, 1994)

An essential possession for anyone with an interest in the history of punk rock or of women in music, for fans of Nirvana and teen-age rebels past and present, this is a stunning debut. Rock music at its best, this blends anger with sarcasm, humour and righteous wit, with highlights including "Only Loved at Night", "Odyshape" itself, "And Then It's OK", "Red Shoes" and "Go Away".

THE RAMONES

Became a family in Forest Hills, Queens, New York, 1974; dissolved da brudderhood in 1996.

"IF YOU'RE SOMEONE LIKE ME, LIKE AN OUTLAW, YOU'LL NEVER FIT IN. I DUG MY OWN GRAVE, I'M EXCOMMUNICATED FROM HAVING A NORMAL LIFE..."

DEE DEE

To misquote John Lennon's famous statement about Elvis, before **The Ramones**, there was nothing. Granted, Patti Smith signed her record deal before the boys inked theirs, and sure, Television played CBGB's before the Queens posse made it downtown, but Smith, Verlaine and the gang were literally the avant-garde, marking a path for the main force to follow. They were poets and artists – creatures too rarefied and intellectual to appeal to the hoi polloi. The Ramones were the first band to look and act like punks, who played as dumb as Joe Schmoe on the street corner and who played music of such perfect simplicity that it erased all trace of anything that had come before. When The Ramones hit town, the calendar went back to year zero.

When the band stumbled onto the stage at the Performance Studio in NYC on March 30, 1974, they were already sporting the leather-jacketed, bad-attitude greaser look that became a trademark. Back then they had little clue how to play, some small idea of how to start a song, but not much practice in how to finish one, and absolutely no idea that they were starting a whole new rock'n'roll movement.

They also appeared as a three-piece, with some of the personnel in the wrong place – **Johnny Ramone** (guitar), born John Cummings, was OK, but **Dee Dee Ramone** (bass/vocals), a.k.a. Douglas Colvin, was out of his depth with so much responsibility, and **Joey Ramone** (drums), known to his parents as Jeffrey Hyman, was obviously far too tall to sit behind a drumkit. Two months later **Tommy Ramone** (drums) joined the family business (born Tommy Erdelyi, he had until then been "managing" the band) and Joey switched to vocals.

The Ramones were possibly the only band in the history of rock'n'roll able to make the claim that their drummer was the least dysfunctional member of the band. **Dee Dee** was a maladjusted, drug-addicted German-born army brat, already one of the better-known young delinquents in the middle-class Forest Hills section of Queens, New York, when he met **Johnny**, who was messed up in an entirely different way. A veteran of military school and hallucinogens, Johnny quit alcohol, drugs and other excesses after hearing a voice from above one day asking what he was doing with his life. **Joey** had a whole bunch of medical conditions to deal with, including obsessive-compulsive disorder (he had to be led across airport concourses to avoid him stopping to count the blobs of discarded chewing gum on the floor) and the inability to eat anything except pizza.

Ramones were the shock troops of a revolution that was still in the planning, and like all good battalions, they had a uniform. Their look was based on the greasy street-corner hoodlums of 1950s parental nightmares – leather biker jackets, ripped jeans, T-shirts and baseball boots, and they leaned on the shabby detritus of American suburban culture for inspiration. Part Stooges, part Shangri-Las, they made the best and fastest punk-rock pop in the world.

Things were stirring in old New York, and a lot of new bands with little time for the silks, glitter and charades of the established acts were knocking out back-to-basics, rootsy, uncomplicated music looking for inspiration in the home-grown tunes of the 60s and more recent trends seen in the UK pop charts.

In the wake of Television's success in bringing a thirsty young audience downtown, The Ramones scored a residency at CBGB's. They spent the next few months honing their stagecraft sufficiently for them to be able to manage a twenty-minute set without stopping to settle temporary differences with their fists onstage, and building up a head of steam among the city's musical movers and shakers. Signed to Sire (once label boss Seymour Stein was convinced that he wasn't about to hire a bunch of neo-Nazis) and with more professional management in place, The Ramones were able to take their show across to London in 1976 and thrill the European crowds. Alongside Blondie and a few others, they won an international audience that would sustain them when the slumming aristocracy of the Manhattan rock scene took their fickle asses back to the disco, leaving punk to bleed to death on the streets where it had been created.

Joey and friend.

Chasing down the details of history is not the most punk-rock activity in the world – we're all about "no future!" and "no more heroes!" – but when The Ramones made it onto the stage at CBGB's, they had been a band for almost six months and it was remarkable how little their professionalism and ability had come on in such a space of time. Even so, it was obvious that The

The Ramones was as much of a manifesto and banner for the new breed as the first Pistols or Clash albums, the first of three full-length recordings that by themselves were enough to secure the brudders a table in rock's Valhalla. *Leave Home* and *Rocket To Russia* kept the accelerator pedal stamped firmly down but by 1978 and

Road To Ruin, the wheels were already coming loose. Although the album allowed the guys room to play around with their bubblegum and girl-group influences, Tommy quit to become a producer full time, making room for **Marky Ramone** (previously Marc Bell of The Voidoids) and for reasons best described as purely mercenary, the band became involved with the movie *Rock & Roll High School* (1979). In retrospect, it's a very funny parody of the Newton-John/Travolta "high-school rebel" genre, but it was misunderstood at the time and Dee Dee, bless his heart, denied any memory of the shoot.

The connections formed between the Ramones camp and Hollywood led them to recording with Phil Spector, the legendary producer whose "wall of sound" had been such an obvious influence on the boys' New York heartbreak ballads. Although End Of The Century sold well and yielded "Baby, I Love You" – the Ronettes cover Joey had been born to sing – it was a stressful and difficult project (it's not often that the producer pulls a gun on the band members, at least not these days) that had Dee Dee returning to his favourite paths to oblivion and Johnny gnashing at his leather straps. Dee Dee had a drastic opinion of his relationship with Spector: "The worst shit I ever wrote was in that album."

Richie Ramone (né Reinhardt) took over as drummer when Marky moved on but when Dee

Dee left (to detox again, vowing to clean up for good this time) and **C.J. Ramone** (Christopher John Ward) came in, there were finally too many cracks for the ageing edifice to stay upright. Dee Dee came out of his stupor and reinvented himself for a short while as Dee Dee King, new rapper on the block.

For reasons of taste, decency, and respect to the legend, it's best to skip over most of the rest of the band's recorded output, even though by doing so, we ignore more than fifteen years of work. Although "Bonzo Goes To Bitburg" (an angry response to Ronald Reagan's 1985 visit to a cemetery stuffed with SS corpses in Germany) finally buried the accusations of neo-Nazi leanings, over time the punk spirit had died in the band, and their audience had grown up. Live in concert, The Ramones were an always impressive, always unmissable gig, thrashing their way through countless sets of strings and who knows how many custom-ripped pairs of jeans. On record, despite moments of brilliance (such as the theme song for the 1989 movie of Steven King's *Pet Sematary*), they lost the ability to cut it after their session with Spector, sounding in their later recordings like a covers band of dubious ability.

In the early 90s, Marky dried out, and, readmitted to the band, stood alongside Johnny while he did the same. Dee Dee was still denying anything was wrong and Joey's obsessive-compulsive disorder was under control. They gritted their teeth and edged back into the maelstrom with an in-concert collection called *Loco Live*. It did OK and again showed the band as unbeatable onstage, but the follow-up *Mondo Bizarro* stiffed at the stores.

Through spending countless miles on the same tour bus, they grew to detest one another. When Johnny stole Joey's girlfriend (OK, they did go on to get married, but it was still a shitty thing to do to a guy in your own band), they effectively ceased talking, despite working together for a further fourteen years. Behaviour like this means putting the monthly payslip in front of doing what's right – and that just ain't punk rock. But The Ramones had mutated into creatures of their own comic-strip mythology long before then. Acid Eaters, an album of cover versions was an interesting, if pretty sad document of a band so far past its use-by date that health inspectors were queueing up to close them down. After 2,263 shows, fourteen studio records, five live records and one classic film, they played their final gig on August 6, 1996 at Hollywood's Palace club, and recorded it for a live album released the following year.

Joey Ramone died (lymphatic cancer) in April 2001. Dee Dee died (drugs overdose) in June 2002. Johnny hung on until September 2004, when cancer got him too. With Marky the only long-serving member still breathing, it was appropriate that he supplied most of the home-movie footage that made up the non-concert sections of *Raw* (2004) – a fantastic and gorgeous retrospective on-the-road DVD, padded out with some atrocious miming and far-from-hilarious TV appearances.

The Ramones (Sire, 2001)

Starting out with a full-speed dash through the "Blitzkrieg Bop", "Beat On The Brat" and "Judy Is A Punk", this is still one of the all-time great Saturday night and dressing-to-kill albums. Fourteen singalong anthems, extended to more than twenty tracks on the remastered CD reissue.

Leave Home (Rhino, 2001)

Includes "Pinhead", "Swallow my Pride", "Suzy Is A Headbanger" and "Gimme Gimme Shock Treatment". To misquote "Judy Is A Punk", this is a case of second album, same as the first.

Rocket To Russia (Rhino, 2001)

"Cretin Hop", "Rockaway Beach" and the anthemic "Sheena Is A Punk Rocker" (which took them to the UK Top 30).

It's Alive (Sire, 1996)

The Ramones gave the biggest, loudest and best fun punk concerts, as much celebrations of the New Wave as they were traditional rock'n'roll gigs – the crackle and hum of high-powered amplification stretches out towards the whine of guitar feedback. Moments before it reaches ear-slicing volume, a figure lurches forward stage left and howls "WUNTOOFREEFOUR". As the drums kick in with guitar drone of the finest kind, the crowd turns into a boiling cauldron of bubbly pogoing homogeneous enjoyment. The singer peers out from behind the mic stand and begins his deadpan review of the wilder side of punk-rocking, headbanging, fun-loving cretins, pinheads and cartoon Nazis. This is the best of the live albums.

Hey Ho Let's Go – Anthology (WSM, 2001)

Crammed with 57 tracks on just two discs, it couldn't be anything but a Ramones collection, and if you're unwilling or unable to shell out for the good studio albums above, this is an excellent start.

ICONIC SINGLE:
BLITZKRIEG BOP (SIRE, 1975)

Kicking off with the monumental "Hey ho! Let's go!" chant, this was the first punk recording that many people ever heard. Few were totally unchanged by the experience. Released in the US at the end of 1975 and appearing a few months later in the UK, it tells you everything you need to know about punk rock in one simple hit. Three chords and a bunch of lyrics whose meaning is never made entirely clear, this track is as exciting as a ride on the old Atom Smasher rollercoaster down at Rockaway Beach. Rattling through the chord changes, pausing for breath and to yell "Hey! Ho!" with the guys before another heart-pounding blast at the end of the road. Absolutely the most fun you can have with your clothes on.

Rancid and rotten to the core.

RANCID

Formed from the poisoned leavings of Operation Ivy, California, 1990; presumably gone off by now.

It would be too cynical, too hard-bitten and mean to write off **Rancid** as simply the best Clash tribute act on the circuit, but quite understandable. From the onstage pose to the sound of the guitars, Rancid's routine has all been done before, but never with such raging success. Their refreshing fizz of guitar and drums sells by the case around the world in a way that their spikyheaded ancestors would find incomprehensible.

Matt "McCall" Freeman (bass) and Tim "Lint" Armstrong (vocals/ guitar) had grown up together in the spit'n'sawdust town of Albany in the San Francisco Bay Area, and had worked together previously in **Operation Ivy**, a band that shared with The Clash an interest in reggae rhythms and noisy white-boy angst. Signing like-minded new boy **Brett Reed** (drums), the trio headed for the studio and knocked out an EP, *I'm Not The Only One*, in 1992 and *Rancid*, their full-length debut, the following year.

Carving out a substantial audience for their fre-

netic live shows, and adding more beef to their sound with the addition of ex-UK Subs **Lars Frederiksen** (guitar), put Rancid into just the right state of mind to go into the studio. The new four-piece debuted with the *Radio Radio Radio* EP, then proceeded to blow the doors off with their high-powered follow-up *Let's Go*.

Brimming with confidence and covered in macho tattoos, the guys widened their musical remit, bringing in chunks of reggae and even full-on ska riffs to add contrast and depth to their faithful punk thrashes. Granted, so did The Clash, but Freeman and Armstrong had their previous Operation Ivy experience to show as justification when challenged by the authenticity police. They found room for more sentimental lyrics and slower-paced tunes drawing on some genuine hard times in their own backgrounds, with Frederiksen adding his own slice of true European grit: "I saw my mom hold down weekend jobs after working all week … just so we could have shoes".

The guys' variously Dickensian pasts were to continue providing inspiration, as was the legacy of The Clash. *…And Out Come The Wolves*, their 1995 release, was littered with guitar lines very obviously borrowed from their mentors, with otherwise inexplicable references to British culture (since when has any American thought of dialling 999 in an emergency?) and the usual reggae touches. Lyrically, though, it was their finest set – honest, unpretentious, oozing sincerity and delivered via a great set of tunes. After a fierce inter-label bidding war (which inspired the album's title), the lads had decided to stay indie and stick with Epitaph, their first home. The record went platinum, prompting the usual breast-beating about how it was impossible to be punk with all that money floating around.

Choosing to ignore the discussion, Rancid invited all their friends from the US hardcore scene to contribute to *Life Won't Wait*, a star-studded ska party album. More Madness than Clash for once, it sold a predictable bundle, but signalled a goodbye to the rudeboy sound.

The next album came out harder than hardcore in 2000 and was the second to be called *Rancid*. Cramming in a monster 22 tracks, it saw the band return to their rock'n'roll roots, knocking several shades of stuffing out of those who'd written them off as overfed and past their best.

With solo projects and family life making increasing demands, it took a couple of years get all the guys back into the studio at the same time. When their sixth studio album, *Indestructible*, appeared on WEA in 2003, however, fans worldwide heaved a collective sigh of relief. The band might have aged a few years, but the music stayed true, clean and pure. The Clash / reggae influence is still worn as a badge of honour in "Red Hot Moon", they show off their punk-rocking chops on the booming "Out Of Control" and tweak everybody's political nipples with "Ivory Coast" and "Spirit Of '87". A further album is in the pipeline at the time of writing.

⊚ **Rancid (Epitaph, 1993)**

Life-affirming bouncy punk rock by heroes for heroes. From the speed-driven rush of "Whirlwind" to the bouncing glee of "Ricochet Rabbit" via the burning, overdone sincerity of "Unwritten Rules", this has to be among the greatest debut albums of the 1990s.

⊚ **Let's Go (Epitaph, 1994)**

Wise men, dullards and bores say "if it ain't broke, don't fix it", and so it went for Rancid's second album. Arguably as much fun as the second Ramones album, it skips from thrash to ska and back again, with Matt adopting the worst faux-cockney accent since Damon Albarn. The joyful "Nihilism" fights it out with "The Ballad Of Jimmy & Johnny" for most cheerfully dumb tune on the album.

⊚ **...And Out Come The Wolves (Epitaph, 1996)**

More of the same really. Standout tracks include "Lock, Step & Gone", "Olympia WA." and "Time Bomb".

RAZORLIGHT
Formed London 2002, still sharp and brilliant.

"FIRSTLY, I'M A GENIUS."
JOHNNY BORRELL

Great new bands need a frontman or main spokesperson with more front than Eastbourne, more rabbit than *Watership Down* and more balls than a country house in summertime. Razorlight have all that and more in **Johnny Borrell** (vocals/guitar), the ubiquitous face of 21st century Britpunk.

Borrell used to rely on the skills and input of **Björn Ågnen** (guitar/vocals), **Carl Dalemo** (bass) and **Christian Smith-Pancorvo** (drums) to turn his dreams of stardom into pop reality, but since 2003, he has also had the marketing department

---

PLAYLIST: RAZORLIGHT

1. **ACTION**
   from **Rocknroll Lies 7"** (Mercury, 2003)

2. **GOLDEN TOUCH**
   from **Up All Night** (Vertigo, 2005)

3. **IN THE CITY**
   from **Up All Night** (Vertigo, 2005)

4. **LEAVE ME ALONE**
   from **Up All Night** (Vertigo, 2005)

5. **RIP IT UP**
   from **Up All Night** (Vertigo, 2005)

6. **ROCK'N'ROLL LIES**
   from **Rocknroll Lies 7"** (Mercury, 2003)

7. **STUMBLE & FALL**
   from **Up All Night** (Vertigo, 2005)

8. **UP ALL NIGHT**
   from **Up All Night** (Vertigo, 2005)

9. **VICE**
   from **Up All Night** (Vertigo, 2005)

10. **YEAH YEAH YEAH**
    from **Rocknroll Lies 7"** (Mercury, 2003)

and hype machine of a major label to help spread the word and dismiss any but the most brown-nosing of comparisons to Tom Verlaine, Television and the New York art-punk crowd.

Despite the band being feted as darlings of the 2004 SouthBySouthwest festival in Texas, Smith-Pancorvo jumped ship ("musical differences"), making room for **Andy Burrows** (drums) on the *Up All Night* recording sessions. This, their full-length debut, hit the shops at the end of summer that same year, and despite the smoke and mirrors of well-trained troops of crack publicists, has continued to produce hit singles. It's far too soon to say whether the boys will progress far outside the range of Borrell's egotism, but while it lasts, the sound of Razorlight is a crisp, well-turned-out New Wave joy.

⊚ **Up All Night** (Vertigo, 2005)

Splendidly arrogant first statement from the best, most swaggering outfit to surface from London's recent crop of neo-punk bands. "Up All Night", "Rip It Up" and "Stumble & Fall" stand out as the album's most instantly appealing party tunes, but there's plenty here for the more cerebral music fan – especially anyone in love with the sound of vintage Television, because parts of this set sound just like Verlaine and Lloyd reincarnated in Shepherds Bush, West London.

THE REDSKINS

First went red in York, England, 1982; peeled off 1986.

"...IN TWO OR THREE YEARS' TIME ... AN UPSURGE IN WORKERS' MILITANCY WILL BRING A CRISIS... THE CONFRONTATION'S INEVITABLE BUT THE OUTCOME ISN'T."

CHRIS DEAN, 1982.

Certainly not a punk-rock outfit, these guys doled out hefty slabs of political polemic set to a sound more big-band swing than buzzsaw guitar. They can certainly be lumped in

for honourable mention under New Wave Acts That Tried To Make A Difference, and because they were one of the very few skinhead acts to take a stand against the boneheads.

Chris Dean (vocals/guitar) and **Nick King** (drums) had already worked together in Dean's first shorthaired and right-on act, a band called No Swastikas formed in York in 1981. King was brave enough to stay on board when Dean brought in his comrade **Martin Hewes** (bass) from the notoriously unfunky Socialist Workers Party, changed the name of the band to The Redskins and headed for London to mix it up verbally and physically with the forces of evil. Their mission to wrest the frankly cool skinhead image from the far Right was probably doomed before it started, and their gigs ultimately became dangerous places to hang out, but their role as consciousness-raisers in the artistic community's response to the Thatcher regime and the associated rise of fascism makes them part of the history of Us against Them.

Hewes' paranoid range of stage names, which included Martin Militant, Martin Leon and Martin Bottomley, probably served to keep the Man off his back, and Dean was already better known to the world at large as the *NME* journalist X Moore. Small wonder, then, that their debut single "Lev Bronstein" celebrated another man with a pseudonym, better known as Leon Trotsky. Released in July 1982, it was produced by another lefty, John Langford of The Mekons & Three Johns. It sold almost exclusively to the already committed, but together with the band's surging reputation as a passionate live act, and the overwhelmingly positive reaction to their first Peel session, it convinced the boys to keep on keeping on, and to expand the line-up by bolting on a trio of brass players – **Ray Carless** (tenor sax), **Trevor Edwards** (trombone) and **Kevin Robinson** (trumpet).

The band's next single "Lean On Me!" was released in 1983 and was the first to demonstrate their peculiar affection for the exclamation mark. It won them a transfer from Leeds-based indie label CNT to Decca, who put out "Keep On Keepin' On!" in October 1984 against the background of the miners' strike. Journalist Garry Bushell, now best known for championing Oi! music and for his loony-right rantings in the tabloids, was moved to call this Trotskyist incitement to revolutionary action the best single of 1983.

The Redskins, together with acts including The Style Council, Test Dept. and Billy Bragg, played a large part in fundraising for the strike, performing endless benefits up and down the country. This level of commitment and evident lack of cynicism sat badly with the mainstream media and music press alike, and before long, the backlash set in. Before long, attending their gigs became a test of courage, especially after a mob of neo-Nazi skins swinging bike chains invaded the stage at a festival in July 1984, after causing trouble in the crowd for most of the afternoon.

The Redskins devoted so much time to the miners that their next single "Bring It Down! (This Insane Thing)" wasn't recorded until the strike ended in March the next year. King left the band, and was replaced temporarily by **Steve White** of The Style Council (he played on "Bring It Down!"), before ex-Woodentops member **Paul Hookham** was voted in full-time. The video for "Bring It Down!" featured super-Stalinist comic Alexei Sayle and took the song into the Top 40.

"Kick Over The Statues!" was released anonymously after an act of ultra-punk nefariousness in which the masters were sneaked out of Decca's hands and into those of Abstract Records (who released it to coincide with a Redskins tour, and gave all the royalties to the comrades in South Africa). It was their best song, and the high point of their career. "The Power Is Yours" was a downbeat affair, appearing naked, without even an exclamation mark to hide behind, and served as a poor introduction to *Neither Washington Nor Moscow* (1986).

"It Can Be Done!", a remix of the album version, turned out to be their very final statement, and The Redskins eventually decided to give up the struggle at the end of 1986, after four long years on the barricades.

⊙ **Neither Washington Nor Moscow (Decca, 1986)**

Funky, punky and still the dance album of choice at old-school lefty parties when the Bulgarian red wine's been circulating for an hour or two, NWNM sounded dated on release with its soapbox preaching taken straight from the *Socialist Worker* editorial page. Since the end of the Cold War, it's sounded positively prehistoric. If you still find this sort of thing relevant then you'll particularly enjoy "Kick Over The Statues", "Go Get Organized" and "Keep On Keepin' On".

THE REPLACEMENTS

Stepped into the breach Minneapolis, Minnesota, 1979; kept going till 1990.

These magnificently sloppy champions of Midwestern punk rock initially came together thanks to a mother's love, her exasperation with her kids, and her desire to save them from a career in delinquency … so she chose rock'n'roll. Good decision, Mom!

Bob Stinson (guitar) was 20, and already playing when not sitting round getting wasted and was probably glad for the company when his 12-year-old half-brother **Tommy Stinson** (bass) showed up for rehearsal dragging a stack of equipment funded from the family purse. Tommy learned his chops pretty quickly, and soon, together with Bob and **Chris Mars** (drums), he was part of **The Impediments**, who happily ruined any chance of a quiet evening stroll for anyone living in the neighbourhood by knocking out a chaotic racket in the classic garage-band mould.

Paul Westerberg (vocals/guitar/songwriting), lonely, misunderstood genius and high-school dropout, heard the new band from down the street. When he battered his way through the noise to let them know their vocals were awful, they agreed and challenged him to do better. Westerberg was a mean rock'n'roller himself, but with deep streaks of sincerity, self-examination and sensitivity, qualities that had all been lacking until he showed up.

Pretty soon the guys were being paid to drink beer and play punk rock in clubs around the twin cities, challenges they rose to and overcame with aplomb and gusto. Legendary for gigs of heroic drunkenness and unforgettable brilliance, but not simultaneously, they were so often banned from returning to local venues that they finally had to ditch their first moniker and become **The Replacements**.

Sorry Ma, Forgot To Take Out The Trash, their 1981 debut, is still a marvellously appealing slab of sloppily magnificent punk music, crammed with teenage angst, love gone wrong and celebrations of the joy of life in one of the coldest parts of the whole USA. It clocked in at under thirty minutes, but left listeners so dazed that not a single complaint of lack of value for money was to be heard.

The album led to some cool gigs – Hüsker

🔲 PLAYLIST: REPLACEMENTS

Another thirty-track playlist? Yeah, well, The Replacements were masters of brevity too.

1. TAKIN' A RIDE from **Sorry Ma, Forgot To Take Out The Trash (Restless, 2002)**

2. CARELESS from **Sorry Ma, Forgot To Take Out The Trash (Restless, 2002)**

3. CUSTOMER from **Sorry Ma, Forgot To Take Out The Trash (Restless, 2002)**

4. HANGIN' DOWNTOWN from **Sorry Ma, Forgot To Take Out The Trash (Restless, 2002)**

5. KICK YOUR DOOR DOWN from **Sorry Ma, Forgot To Take Out The Trash (Restless, 2002)**

6. I BOUGHT A HEADACHE from **Sorry Ma, Forgot To Take Out The Trash (Restless, 2002)**

7. RATTLESNAKE from **Sorry Ma, Forgot To Take Out The Trash (Restless, 2002)**

8. I HATE MUSIC from **Sorry Ma, Forgot To Take Out The Trash (Restless, 2002)**

9. JOHNNY'S GONNA DIE from **Sorry Ma, Forgot To Take Out The Trash (Restless, 2002)**

10. SHIFTLESS WHEN IDLE from **Sorry Ma, Forgot To Take Out The Trash (Restless, 2002)**

11. MORE CIGARETTES from **Sorry Ma, Forgot To Take Out The Trash (Restless, 2002)**

12. DON'T ASK WHY from **Sorry Ma, Forgot To Take Out The Trash (Restless, 2002)**

13. SOMETHIN' TO DÜ from **Sorry Ma, Forgot To Take Out The Trash (Restless, 2002)**

14. I'M IN TROUBLE from **Sorry Ma, Forgot To Take Out The Trash (Restless, 2002)**

15. LOVE YOU TILL FRIDAY from **Sorry Ma, Forgot To Take Out The Trash (Restless, 2002)**

16. SHUTUP from **Sorry Ma, Forgot To Take Out The Trash (Restless, 2002)**

Dü headlining, for example, with **The 'Mats** (short for **The Placemats**, short'n'funny for **The Replacements**) second on the bill. Bigger crowds and venues led to more money rolling in, which led to the second album, *Hootenanny*, and also to the beginning of serious substance abuse within the band. *Hootenanny* helped take their reputation for boozy magnificence countrywide. It was even less of a punk album than the first had been though, as the lads began to play around with different instruments, styles and influences.

The mid 80s were the high point of The Replacements' career, but although *Let It Be* (1984) is now considered to be their best album, filled with small pop gems from Westerberg and his rapidly blossoming songwriting skill, recording it was a series of increasingly dangerous experiments in insobriety.

With Hüsker Dü leading the way, the group went to a major label to step up onto the next level. Recording *Tim* in 1985 was just too much for Bob and his inability to turn down a drink, and he left the band soon after. He was replaced by **Slim Dunlap** around the time the band returned to the studio to make *Pleased To Meet Me*, released in 1987.

The band's subsequent work turned out to be pretty shitty. Neither 1989's *Don't Tell A Soul*, nor the 1990 release *All Shook Down* (essentially Westerberg's first solo album – despite the rest of the guys showing up as session artists) approached their previous punk excellence. By this point, Mars was losing patience with Westerberg's increased confidence and his assumption of the group's driving seat, and after one argument too many, he packed his kit and left. One last, low-profile tour followed, and sensing the pointlessness of continuing as a band in name only, The Replacements played their last show on US Independence Day 1991.

Bob overdosed fatally in 1995, and Tommy did much the same a decade later, whereas Westerberg went solo, releasing *14 Songs* in 1993, *Eventually* in 1996, *Suicaine Gratifaction* in 1999, Stereo in 2002 and *Folker* in 2004.

◉ Sorry Ma, Forgot To Take Out The Trash (Twin\Tone, 1981)

The blistering debut. Includes "More Cigarettes" (another great unrequited love song), "Takin' A Ride", "Customer", "Hanging Downtown", "Kick Your Door Down" and "I Bought A Headache" (best-ever summary of a night out and the hangover to follow). Blistering bellows of just-post-adolescent ranting about life's stupidities and the unfairness of it all.

◉ Let It Be (Twin\Tone, 1984)

Cleaned up like it was gonna meet your parents, the remastered version of *Let It Be* still sounds like the entire personnel was drunk from several days before the sessions began until some time after the mixing was finished. Play and enjoy.

THE REZILLOS

Edinburgh's finest 1976–1985;
revived in the 1990s

"WE'RE DEFINITELY NOT A PUNK BAND! HAVING FUN IS WHAT WE ARE ALL ABOUT...."
HI-FI HARRIS, NME, 1977

The world never had a chance to appreciate The Knutsford Dominators because they changed their name to **The Rezillos** before their first gig. Formed at the Edinburgh College of Art, the band was firmly rooted in the fun and games tradition of the earliest punk rock (despite the quote above), always ready to poke fun – especially at themselves, camp as Christmas at the day-glo factory.

One of the best good-times party bands of the late 1970s New Wave, they kicked off when **Fay Fife**, a.k.a. Sheilagh Hynde (vocals) and **Eugene Reynolds** (real name Alan Forbes) got together in an explosion of shiny metallic fabric, pop art and fluorescence to knock out fun-time classic cover versions from the 1960s. **Luke Warm**, a.k.a. Jo Callis (guitar), **Mark "Hi-Fi" Harris** (guitar), **Dr. D.K. Smythe** (bass), **Gale Warning** (backing vocals) and **Alan "Angel" Patterson** (drums) were swiftly recruited, and as the first wave of punk washed over the granite city, the band picked up impetus to work on their own material – soon knocking 'em dead with self-penned jumping joints including "Flying Saucer Attack", "(My Baby Does) Good Sculptures" and "Top Of The Pops". As fame beckoned and final examinations threatened, personnel changes were inevitable. **William Mysterious** (born William Donaldson) took over bass and added saxophone (though not simultaneously), Harris left in 1979, replaced by **Kid Krupa**, and Angel made room for **Rocky Rhythm**.

The success of their singles and unforgettable look of day-glo chaotics made the band's name much bigger than it deserved, and in the aftermath of *Can't Stand The Rezillos* the group split into two factions. Fife and Reynolds carried on pretty much regardless as **The Revillos**, picking up a new band and turning into a full-time party act named **Rev Up**.

Callis and the others ditched their fun stage names and became dour three-piece The Shakes before Callis jumped ship to join The Human League. The old band regrouped after a fashion in 2002 and toured the US, bringing joy and laughter to the colonies one last time.

⦿ **Can't Stand The Rezillos (Warner, 1996)**

Now includes the complete first album (including magic cover versions of The Dave Clark 5's "Glad All Over" and Gerry & The Pacemakers' "I Like It"), plus an overdose of thirteen live tracks from *Mission Accomplished*. Enough by anyone's reckoning.

Rezillos: sunglasses after dark.

THE RICH KIDS

In the money London, 1978; went bust in 1979.

Glen Matlock (bass/vocals) must have been in shock when he suddenly found himself an ex-Sex Pistol, because, with all the gutter aristocracy of punk hanging round his knees, he hooked up with a guy from an almost unknown band called PVC2. Granted, they'd had a boy-band hit before then, when they were called Slik, but why pick **Midge Ure** (guitar)? Perhaps he saw something in the lad that the rest of the world had missed.

Matlock and Ure gelled with **Steve New** (guitar) and **Rusty Egan** (drums), a set of reasonable

Glen Matlock leaves Earth.

rock was scribbled down and rehearsed and the guys hit the road as **The Rich Kids**. Mick Ronson was drafted in to produce the experimental – that is, "full of weird, unexpected noises" – *Ghosts Of Princes In Towers* in 1978 (making a mess of their otherwise pristine sound and muddying up their electronica). Nonetheless, they toured and gigged, made some money, mainly on the strength of the curious coming to see the guy who ate the infamous liver paste sandwich made by Steve Jones.

Ure and Egan went on to pose for a while as New Romantics, joining Steve Strange's outfit **Visage** before Ure took over as front man of **Ultravox**. Glen went back to real life for a while, before rejoining the Pistols for the cash-in reunion tour.

◉ **Ghosts Of Princes In Towers (Cherry Red, 2005)**

The one and only Rich Kids full-length has aged terribly and has a pointed anti-punk stance, but remains a reasonably interesting New-Wave-esque album. One to borrow from a friend rather than rushing out to buy.

JONATHAN RICHMAN AND THE MODERN LOVERS

Born in Boston, Massachusetts, May 1951; gonna be rockin' forever.

> "**THE ONLY TIME IT WAS THIS MUCH FUN WAS IN ABOUT 1972, WHEN WE'D JUST STARTED OUT AND NOBODY HAD EVER HEARD OF US.**"
>
> JONATHAN RICHMAN, 1999

Lots of otherwise musically literate individuals have either never heard of **Jonathan Richman** or, almost as bad, know him only as the world's most realistic fluffy puppet and a harmless entertainer of children. So, let's start out by establishing some credentials: according to often-repeated legend, Richman was at more

Velvet Underground shows than Lou himself. One solid fact is that he played his first gig in a support slot for the Velvets – aged just 16 – solo, and playing his own material. Oh, and he had the nerve to ask if he could use their PA … oh, and maybe Sterling Morrison's guitar too, please.

Richman is the guy who wrote "Roadrunner" (attempted by the **Sex Pistols** and successfully covered by thousands of other bands), he wrote a song called "Pablo Picasso" – covered by **John Cale** and featured, in another version by **Burning Sensations**, in über-cult movie *Repo Man* (1984), and he wrote "She Cracked" – covered to blistering effect by **Alternative TV** (at the time, easily the coolest band on the circuit) both on their debut album, *The Image Has Cracked* and, to brain-devastating effect, in their live shows. So, unless you wanna take it outside and duke it out with some of the greatest names in music, we're going to take it as read that Richman is cool. OK?

Head west on Route 9 out of central Boston and after fifteen miles or so, you arrive in beautiful downtown Natick, the Massachusetts suburb where Richman and **John Felice** first met up and formed **The Modern Lovers**. Felice was still in his mid-teens, but already had a couple of years' playing experience under his belt. Richman, however, was a more mature, and well-travelled beast approaching 20, who'd moved up to New York in the early 1970s to hang out with the Velvets like some goofy pet primate. He had met the likes of Andy Warhol and had developed a taste for the devil's music, and after zipping across to Europe to soak up some old-world culture, he returned to New England, called Felice and set about taunting the students, hippies and stoner detritus spread around on the Cambridge Commons in Boston with songs such as "I'm Straight".

Felice had several other commitments (like school, for example) and too much of a mind of his own for the band to gel completely in the early days. He frequently quit the band, staying away as long as he could stand it before showing up again, guitar in hand, like nothing had happened. The rest of the band included **David Robinson** (drums) and his pal **Rolf Andersen** (part-time bass). This line-up attracted the attention of a pair of Harvard film students, **Jerry Harrison** (keyboards) and **Ernie Brooks** (full-time bass), who put down their cameras and followed this gangly, sub-Reed musical messiah to become Modern Lovers.

Richman took the band into the studio in 1972, and with John Cale at the controls, recorded sessions that would eventually appear as *The Modern Lovers* – a set of songs that would make his reputation and put him somewhere near the top of the "people who invented punk rock" pile.

These were the first steps by a shy, stutteringly isolated loner plunged apparently unprepared and unwilling into the role of rock'n'roll front man, and they tragically fell victim to the world vinyl shortage of the early 1970s (a crisis that the record companies also used to downsize their rosters and to punt shockingly bad pressings by major-name artists out to the record-buying public). With Warner scraping together every last smidgeon of plastic to manufacture guaranteed million-sellers, the Modern Lovers' tapes stayed on the shelf until 1977, when Matt Kaufman and Beserkley Records turned Cale's stripped-down production of a man in the grip of a terrible honesty into a European bestseller.

Although Jonathan himself was never totally happy to see what he considered little more than a collection of demos on the market, the album sold bucketloads to an audience of spikyheads across Europe. Crammed with goodies such as Harrison's swirling keyboard magic (calliope-like on "Hospital" for example, and driving like a V8 pumped with nitrous oxide through "Roadrunner"), Jonathan's unbelievably effective lyrics (running the gamut from sub-Ramones-style dumb to Velvet Underground arty intellectual), and bursts of purest exuberance, it was far from mainstream 1-2-3-4 punk rock, but it dripped with emotional intensity.

It also funded *Jonathan Richman & The Modern Lovers*, which is where our tale turns awkward. The new album was recorded by a completely new line-up (Robinson went on to join **DMZ** and then **The Cars**, Harrison of course went on to fame and fortune as a member of **Talking Heads**) and featured songs written five years or more after those on the first release. People buying the album complained of the unjustifiable similarity in titles and the whole thing smacked of rip-off. Tracks such as "Abominable Snowman In The Market" and "Hey There Little Insect" were sweeties for kiddies offered to fans looking for punk-rock protein – satisfying for a while, but bad for the complexion and ultimately nauseating.

Disorientated by the hostility and already pissed off by the oil crisis messing with his career, Richman was by now justifiably sick to the teeth of the music business, although he retained his love of the music world. Shunning his previously staunch rock credibility, he indulged his new taste for whimsical songs of such saccharine tweeness to such an extent that his audience quit him by the busload.

He'd "matured" as a songwriter and found himself most comfortable in a place beyond the art-rock drone, chirping about "Martian Martians", the "Icecream Man" and little dinosaurs. Those in the crowd who followed him to this strange new land were described as "broad-minded" although "brain-wasted" might have been more appropriate.

Eventually, Richman settled down as a musical entertainer – and whether working solo, accom-

---

◉ PLAYLIST: JONATHAN RICHMAN AND THE MODERN LOVERS

1. **ROADRUNNER**
from **The Modern Lovers (Castle 2003)**

2. **ASTRAL PLANE**
from **The Modern Lovers (Castle 2003)**

3. **OLD WORLD**
from **The Modern Lovers (Castle 2003)**

4. **PABLO PICASSO**
from **The Modern Lovers (Castle 2003)**

5. **SHE CRACKED**
from **The Modern Lovers (Castle 2003)**

6. **MODERN WORLD**
from **The Modern Lovers (Castle 2003)**

7. **I'M STRAIGHT**
from **The Modern Lovers (Castle 2003)**

8. **ROADRUNNER (TWICE)** from **23 Great Recordings** by Jonathan Richman (Griffin, 1995)

9. **DODGE VEG O MATIC** from **Rock 'n' Roll With the Modern Lovers (Castle, 2004)**

10. **BACK IN THE USA** from **Jonathan Richman & the Modern Lovers (Castle, 2004)**

panied solely by a drummer, or with a full band, he charmed those who loved him, and irritated the hell out of those who didn't understand, for the next 25 years. Richman's legend now includes love songs of heart-squeezing beauty, albums recorded completely in Spanish, and concerts enlivened by his setting one side of the hall to sing harmony with the other. It's a kind of magic – there can be only one Jonathan Richman, and may he become immortal.

⊚ The Modern Lovers (Castle, 2003)

Now expanded from the original, this is the one all modern lovers of music need to have. Includes "Roadrunner (Twice)" and "Pablo Picasso".

⊚ Jonathan Richman & The Modern Lovers (Castle, 2004)

Oh, if you must. Includes: "Rockin' Shoppin' Center", "Back In The USA" and "Roadrunner (Once)".

⊚ Rock & Roll With The Modern Lovers (Castle, 2004)

Includes "Egyptian Reggae" – allegedly based on "None Shall Escape The Judgement" by kosher Jamaicans Earl Zero and Johnny Clarke – and "Dodge Veg-O-Matic", arguably the last great rock song by the weirdest punk of them all.

TOM ROBINSON

Born Cambridge England 1950

"YEAH, TOM ROBINSON, DON'T FUCKING GIVE UP MATE - DON'T EVER LET 'EM MAKE YOU GIVE UP"

JOHNNY ROTTEN 1978 (JUST BEFORE HE VOMITED OVER TOM'S SHOES)

Songwriter, BBC Radio 6 Music presenter and bisexual activist Tom Robinson was never totally convincing as a punk rocker. Nonetheless, journalistic gurus of the *NME* Burchill and Parsons deemed in "The Boy Looked At Johnny" (their "live from the barricades" report on the state of the New Wave in Britian) that Tom, together with Poly Styrene, was going to be the saviour of punk rock.

Café Society, the acoustic trio he formed at the beginning of the 70s, wasn't about to blow down the walls of Jericho, and it wasn't until seeing The Sex Pistols that Tom moved to a more conventional, electric rock line-up known as the Tom Robinson Band.

At a time when minority groups were under apparently coordinated attack from the state powers that be and boneheads on the street, TRB wore its politics with pride; their logo was a straight copy of the clenched-fist symbol used by the International Socialists (no cheap and easy anarchist solutions for the staunch lefty Tom), their most notorious song was "Glad To Be Gay" when conventional audiences saw homosexuality as little more than a topic for humour, and the band broke speed records in their rush to affiliate with the Rock Against Racism organization.

Ironically, the Tom Robinson Band's greatest hit had nothing to do with politics. "2, 4, 6, 8,Motorway" is a plodding "life on the road" rocker that could have come from any long-haired mid-70s crew of unwashed hippies.

Although the first album, *Power In The Darkness*, went gold, the band had fallen apart by the release of the second, and after a brief fling with a new band called **Sector 27**, Tom quit the UK. With the taxman on his back and a life to reassemble, Tom headed first for Hamburg then to East Berlin where he wrote his big 80s success "War Baby".

With a background of presenting that went well beyond the skills required of a punk rock front man (having spoken and performed for the Secret Policeman's Ball and Amnesty International as well as supporting gay-rights group Outrage!) Tom was immediately at home behind the microphone for his next step. Presenting talk radio on BBC Radio 4 and a stint doing pop DJ routines on BBC Radio 1 has led to his current regular evening slot on BBC 6 Music. He remains intensely dear to the heart of UK punk and his role as one of its midwives cannot be diminished.

⊚ Power In The Darkness (EMI, 2004)

A bruising album of rockers, that also knows when to shift down a gear (for cuts such as "Too Good to Be True"). "2, 4, 6, 8, Motorway" gets a look in too, but it's the political edge that makes this album what it is.

The Roxy, London

"BANNED FROM THE ROXY, OK / I NEVER MUCH LIKED PLAYING THERE ANYWAY"
CRASS, "BANNED FROM THE ROXY"

The most famous of all the British punk venues, **The Roxy**'s heyday was short, overpriced and not tremendously sweet. However, at a time when punk needed a place to play, it served as a focal point (on Neal Street in London's Covent Garden) for the movement. Upstairs, at ground level, the box office staff tried desperately to grab the occasional price of a ticket from the swarms of mohair-clad hooligans crowding downstairs to where the action was. Gigs were intolerably overcrowded, drinks were difficult to obtain, hard to transport and wildly overpriced and all the boys went into the girls' toilets because there was no way to get back to the gents.

Andrew Czezowski, Ralf Jedraszczyk (better known as Jedetcetera) and Barry Jones were the men behind the new club. Previously the home of **Chaguarama's** – possibly the sleaziest gay club in town – it opened its doors as The Roxy on the auspicious date of January 1, 1977, with **The Clash** topping the bill. Public transport in the nation's capital didn't run on public holidays and nobody on the scene was old enough, rich enough or sober enough to drive, so attendance was restricted to those brave souls within walking distance of the venue.

However, the sheer lack of anywhere else to go made the club the capital's punk HQ by default, and within weeks, anyone who was anyone was either on stage, posing on the stairs, queuing outside for entry or bitching about the new exclusivity in vitriolic fanzine rants. Many a romance was consummated on the staircase or in the occasionally clean toilets, and although the number of bands that formed on the premises must go uncounted, it was probably larger than the number of bands that were paid to appear.

The sound was lousy and the acoustics made it easier to hear a conversation from across the room than to make out what the bar staff were trying to shout in your ear. Despite resident DJ **Don Letts** playing a thundering selection of reggae and dub, there was always a 50:50 chance that you would leave having missed the band you had paid to see, or worse, decide you hated them after yet another PA system breakdown.

Although Letts shot The Punk Rock Movie (1978) there, it was the compilation *The Roxy London WC2 (Jan – Apr 77)* that really put the place on the map, conveying an aural snapshot of the UK scene across the Atlantic and spreading the good word outside the capital back at home. Punctuated with snatches of conversation picked up by hidden mics around the club, it remains the greatest live document of the era, despite the aforementioned acoustic mess being a major feature of the album.

Financial acumen was never Andrew Czezowski's strong point and the first Roxy regime was closed down by a posse of landlords, taxmen and local villains who wanted a slice of the action. It reopened almost immediately with a serious box-office team, security guards and even more expensive drinks, but its time as the nursery school was over. The venue kept going under the same name for another year or so, but finally died after months of hosting third- and fourth-generation wannabe punk-rock acts from the sticks and their embarrassingly suburban fans. These days, appropriately enough for the original home of the punk-rock poser, the address is now home to a clothes store.

 PLAYLIST: THE ROXY LONDON WC2 (JAN–APR 77) (EMI, 1977)

Castle have issued a double CD and a 6-CD box set under this title, both obviously with extra material, but this is the track-listing of the original album, the best document of the London scene when it was still comparatively underground.

1. **RUNAWAY**
   Slaughter And The Dogs

2. **BOSTON BABIES**
   Slaughter And The Dogs

3. **FREEDOM**
   The Unwanted

4. **LOWDOWN**
   Wire

5. **1.2.X.U.**
   Wire

6. **BORED TEENAGERS**
   The Adverts

7. **HARD LOVING MAN**
   Johnny Moped

8. **DON'T NEED IT**
   Eater

9. **15**
   Eater

10. **OH BONDAGE UP YOURS**
    X-Ray Spex

11. **BREAKDOWN**
    Buzzcocks

12. **LOVE BATTERY**
    Buzzcocks

THE RUTS

Got into it in Middlesex, England in 1977; out of it by the end of 1980.

> "WE PLAY FAST NUMBERS. WE PLAY SLOW NUMBERS. WE PLAY REGGAE AND WE PLAY GOOD MUSIC AND YEAH, WE'RE VERY PUNK."
>
> DAVE RUFFY, 1979

Formed from the debris of Hit & Run, a going-nowhere-fast pub-rock band, **The Ruts** burst onto the scene in late 1977 flexing their musical muscles and performance-honed tightness as one of the most exciting bands of the era. **Malcolm Owen** accompanied his old school buddy **Paul Fox** (guitar) to a rehearsal down in darkest Rotherhithe with another friend from the days of full-time education and Fox's band-mate from Hit & Run, **Dave Ruffy** (drums) messing around on bass. Never having tried, but always ready to have a go, Owen tried his hand at singing. Several hours later, the guys had beaten four new songs ("Rich Bitch", "Lobotomy", "I Ain't Sofisticated" and "Out Of Order") into submission, and Owen was in the band.

As Ruffy was happiest behind the drums, another friend of the family, **John "Segs" Jennings** (bass) was recruited, and as soon as they had a set scribbled down and rehearsed into acceptability, The Ruts hit the road, making their first appearance playing support to Wayne (now Jayne) County & The Electric Chairs in early 1978 (at the Town Hall, High Wycombe, of all places).

This was a time when a weak, nominally socialist Labour government found itself fighting against the trade unions – the very groups that provided the party's traditional support. In the resulting fallout, politics and pop became enmeshed: the fascists were on the rise, the radicals were being mobilized and there was a definite air of "whose side are you on?" in London's punk scene. The Ruts swiftly became one of the mainstays of the emergent Rock Against Racism movement, a self-explanatory name for an umbrella group of concerned lefties, and embarked upon a gruelling series of benefit gigs and festival appearances around the country, frequently in the company of fellow West Londoners Misty In Roots – crucial reggae band of the time, and conveniently, already involved in the running of a record label.

The band's first single, "In A Rut" / "H-Eyes", on People Unite Records, made its way into the ubiquitous hands of the John Peel team (the band later recorded three sessions for the show) and the increased exposure The Ruts received from radio led to an ugly but pleasantly lucrative bidding war between the larger labels.

Still, it wasn't until early 1979 that they signed up and recorded "Babylon's Burning" / "Society" for Virgin, which made the Top 10 in the UK and led to TV appearances on *Top Of The Pops*. Owen

 **ICONIC SINGLE:
IN A RUT / H-EYES**
(PEOPLE UNITE, 1979)

With both tracks (the B-side a totally unironic diatribe on the evils of smack delivered by a then opiate-free Malcolm Owen) long since available on either The Crack or any of the compilations, the sheer overpowering rush that came on hearing the opening riff of "In A Rut" for the first time is difficult to imagine. It didn't quite stop traffic, but It spread like a nasty rash in a boys' boarding school and remains one of the best punk-rocking "…and this is the name of our band" tunes. Shambling and hesitant at first, menacing, echo-drenched guitar opens the door, then unexpected and spinechilling shards of noise burst out of dark corners; it gets a bit dubby in the middle before culminating in a glorious singalong celebrating the futility of it all.*

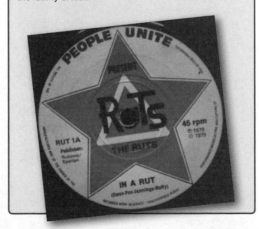

and the band were magnificent and unforgettable live, sweating sincerity, oozing commitment and spitting venom, playing halls packed with steamy, beer-drenched and bouncing punk rockers, and managed to bring some of that excitement to a sterile TV studio filled with ELO fans.

The Crack followed in October 1979 – little more than the band's straight live set with a bunch of sound effects draped artistically over the top, but to an audience already seeing through the lies of the Pistols, The Clash and their contemporaries, it was irresistible. Alongside *Fulham Fallout*, by fellow West Londoners **The Lurkers**, it stood head and shoulders above the mainstream, sanitized New Wave that characterized the industry's first shocked response to the punk explosion. Opening with the blare of a siren and kicking off with "Babylon's Burning", it leapt from thrash to reggae, from celebration through lyrics of dread and warning to the last raucous yell from the crowd at the end of the massively powerful "Human Punk" (recorded live and very loud indeed).

"Something That I Said" / "Give Youth A Chance" performed reasonably well but "Jah War" / "I Ain't Sofisticated" (this latter track inspired by and a tribute to tour-mates **The Damned**) failed to sell, and despite crisscrossing the UK and spending time onstage across the water in continental Europe, The Ruts' progress faltered.

As the decade drew to a close, the "Grin And Bear It" tour turned into the "Back To Blighty" tour, and "Staring At The Rude Boys" / "Love In Vain" took the guys back to the Top 20. From as early as "H-Eyes", Owen's lyrics had revealed an interest in the dark side of the pharmacopoeia, and the love he now sang of was more likely to be found in his veins than in vain. The tour was put on hold while he took time out to recover from a throat infection and make another attempt to get clean. It failed and, with preparations for the recording of the second album under way and Owen's habit spiralling out of control, the rest of the guys sacked him. There was a subsequent reunion, but it ended when, like so many other tragic assholes in this book, he self-medicated himself to death, overdosing on heroin in July 1980.

The Ruts' last single – the prophetically low-key "West One (Shine On Me)" / "The Crack" came out shortly after Owen's death. Although the others carried on as Ruts D.C. (standing for Da Capo), picking up **Gary Barnacle** (sax/keyboards), the fire had gone, the music had changed and Owen's ghost just would not disappear. After an interesting but non-essential dub collaboration with Mad Professor, Ruts D.C. stopped working in 1983.

⊙ **The Crack (Virgin, 1990)**

The "proper" Ruts CD, reissued with the original twelve songs boosted by the addition of three excellent B-sides. Groovy and determined reggae numbers jostle for room with the expected ration of thrash.

⊙ **Bustin' Out – The Essential Ruts Collection (EMI, 2000)**

This collection might have a rotten cover, but there is some very tasty contents, including a enough of Ruts D.C. to give you an idea of what they are about.

THE SAINTS

Formed, Australia, 1974; split 1989, irregular manifestations ever since.

"IF YOU WANT TO BE TRUTHFUL THE EARLY SAINTS WERE PRETTY DREADFUL..."

CHRIS BAILEY, 1998

The Saints started off sounding raw, mean, exciting and dumb, rehearsing in the cheap section of Brisbane and playing loud enough to wake the neighbours several hundred miles down the road in Sydney. The best known of the early Australian punk outfits, they got lucky with a record deal, hit London in 1977, stayed punk for as long as it seemed a good idea, and mutated into styles as diverse as folk and heavy metal over the next decade.

Chris Bailey (vocals/songwriting) was there at the beginning, and the only one of the original line-up to ride the machine till the end. He formed The Saints with **Ed Kuepper** (guitar), **Ivor Hay** (drums) and **Kym Bradshaw** (bass), with a mission to make a disturbing racket and burn off some of their subtropical teenage depression by playing cover versions (there's a CD on sale of the band rehearsing circa 1974 – don't buy it, borrow it from some mug who paid for it) and homebrewed moonshine like "(I'm) Stranded" and "This Perfect Day".

Their take on the ass-kicking, no-nonsense, white-boy rock of the previous decade gave them a growly, over-excited tone like The Kinks, or The Pretty Things after a bunch of multicoloured and heavy-dosage pills. A copy of their self-funded,

extremely limited edition of "(I'm) Stranded" made its way halfway round the globe, and led to a deal with Harvest Records – an EMI subsidiary and home to Pink Floyd, Deep Purple and other hairy dinosaurs. The band followed their single to the UK and set up a base in London, touring to promote the single and recording the follow-up album, also called *(I'm) Stranded* (1977).

The single had been a hit by default, released to a punk audience starving for records: the album came out in less of a vacuum but to rave reviews nonetheless, with Kris Needs of *Zigzag* magazine exclaiming that the album would "sear great holes in the turntable with shards of screaming feedback and guitar walls a hundred miles high... like having your hair burned off with a flame thrower", and was a modest success.

Having stumbled so early onto the perfect punk-rock sound of buzzsaw guitar, throaty vocals and breakneck speed, the guys found room on their second album, *Eternally Yours*, for some slower-paced tunes and even the occasional non-amplified instrument. Deliciously cynical, punch-in-the-face powerful and kitted out with a horn section, the new set included two of the Saints' best tunes – "Know Your Product", a punk take on the "So You Wanna Be A Rock'n'Roll Star" concept, and "This Perfect Day", which went Top 40 in the UK.

By the time the band released *Prehistoric Sounds* they were well on the way to sloughing off the newly unfashionable punk skin. No slouches musically by this time, the lads were ready to expand their range and to let the creative juices flow freely. The album had plenty of musical energy but, as the title hinted, they'd turned for inspiration back to the bluesy horns of 1960s R&B, away from the music of the present and the (no) future.

"Musical differences" between the band members caused a split soon after, with Bailey

Australia's first and best contribution to the late-70s punk-inspired wave of noisy, obstreperous rock'n'roll, this is a big fat slice of robust, turbulent rock cooked up by hairy, snarling Australian blokes.

The moment the needle hits the record, the tune comes roaring in as the guitars work sweat from a riff that's descended, on the evil side of the family, from "Paint It, Black".

The lyrics are stupendously dumb and match the best of Dee Dee Ramone's or The Lurkers' for punk-rock purity. One of the iconic singles of the era it has every erogenous zone of the punk-rock beast engorged and pulsing. Played loud enough at the right time of the evening it is literally breathtaking, it clears the sinuses, obliterates that tense nervous headache and quite possibly lowers cholesterol.

retaining the name and the legacy and Kuepper taking the arty credibility off to his new outfit, **Laughing Clowns**.

Without Kuepper, the Saints were left largely as a Bailey-plus-band act, leaving punk rock behind despite trading under the old brand on and off until the present day. Bailey released regular solo albums under his own name too, but for the pure dyed-in-the-wool punk rocker, nothing post-Kuepper matters very much.

⊚ I'm Stranded (Captain Oi!, 2000)

Easily the best thing the band ever did, almost certainly the best punk album to come out of Australia, and as exciting, tough and reliable today as when it first appeared. Although only the title track was a big hit, the whole record would quite happily kick crap out of anything you cared to stand against it.

⊚ Know Your Product: The Best of The Saints (EMI, 2003)

The best of the compilations currently on offer, this gives you a full-strength shot of pure mood-elevating surge; a shock to the system perhaps, but a necessary one. Featuring "I'm

Stranded", "This Perfect Day", "Lipstick On Your Collar", "River Deep Mountain High", "Demolition Girl", "One Way Street", "No Time" and "Swing For The Crime", this is a marvellous start to any evening out on the town.

SCREAMERS

Formed, Los Angeles, 1975; shut up 1981.

"BE QUIET OR BE KILLED!"

TOMATA DU PLENTY HANDLES THE CROWD JUST RIGHT.

A seminal influence on the minuscule West Coast punk-rock scene, **The Screamers** essentially taught Californians about the new music by using a combination of street politics, camp theatrics and their novel approach to instrumentation. They unfortunately never got around to making a proper record, and live today only in a handful of bootlegs and a ground-breakingly premature VHS video release of a performance for Target Video.

The band was the result of a hectic set of gigs at CBGB's performed by **Tomata du Plenty** (front man/keyboards/percussion/guitar), where the New Wave got under his skin. Heading back west, he hooked up with **Melba Toast** (drag artiste) to appear briefly as The Tupperwares, before Toast switched identities, becoming **Tommy Gear** (keyboards), new recruits **K.K. Barrett** (percussion) and **David Brown** (keyboards) signed on and the band became The Screamers, kicking lumps out of the LA New Wave scene and scaring the living excrement out of the tourists.

The Screamers were on stage before the end of 1977, placing them firmly on the front line alongside The Germs and The Weirdos. As with many such early punkish flowerings, the gigs were as much mixed-media "happening" as full-on rock'n'roll performances, and they had a broad, if suffocatingly local following. Line-up changes and the band's refusal to sign a recording contract meant that they never made an impression outside California, but local success in a state that size meant that they could make a decent living until 1981, when, sick of it all, they stopped screaming and went their separate ways.

SEEDS

First sprouted in Los Angeles, California, in 1965; flourished until 1970.

"SEE, I'M NOT HERE TO DO MUSIC – I'M REALLY HERE TO GIVE GOD'S NAME AND SAVE DOGS..."

SKY SUNLIGHT SAXON

The seminal garage band from the original US punk scene was formed a decade before The Ramones saw the light and on the other side of the continent. **Sky Saxon** (vocals/communication with other planets), a.k.a. Richard Marsh, formed **The Seeds** with **Jan Savage** (guitar) in LA, with **Daryl Hooper** (keyboards) and **Rick Andridge** (drums). Hammering out a set on the fiercely competitive Sunset Strip club scene, the band landed a contract on the strength of their self-penned track "Pushing Too Hard" – a proto-punk classic featuring one of the most inept guitar solos ever committed to vinyl, and *The Seeds*, one of the all-time great garage albums.

Following up with "Mr Farmer" – a Stones/Kinks-tinged rock'n'drone piece that wouldn't embarrass The Fall, and "Can't Seem To Make You Mine" – best described as a tribute to The Troggs, especially the vocal stylings of Reg Presley, The Seeds proved to be a red-hot singles band. On album however, they moved with disturbing speed out of the garage and into the incense-heavy atmosphere of the new psychedelia. *Web Of Sound* (1966) and *Future* were more *Satanic Majesties* than *Sgt Pepper* and the band drifted off into the hallucinogenic fug, knocking out *Raw & Alive: The Seeds In Concert At Merlin's Music Box* (1968)

Safety Pins

Johnny Rotten claims to have worn safety pins to hold his clothes together, forced into this indignity through sheer poverty. However, as he had a couture-trained tailor as his manager, several mums on the scene ready to offer a Sunday dinner and the chance to spruce up, plus as many girly-girl punks who'd swoon at the chance to touch, much less repair his clothing, this can be put down to the gaping holes in his memory.

One of the pillars of the punk aesthetic was to see the beauty in the mass-produced. **Sid Vicious** had his chain and padlock necklace, and the safety pin was just a different expression of the same idea: a shiny, multicoloured, cheap and easily available badge of membership. Tiny pins made a good attachment to earrings or stood in for earrings completely. Kids could wear them to school (and hurriedly cover them up when the jocks stomped past on the corridor), and if you lost one bouncing around like a wild thing in front of a band, it didn't matter. Best of all, you could stick an opened pin into the side of your mouth and make it look like you'd totally perforated your cheek! Great for freaking out the family and other straights who didn't understand.

While every story concerning the **Sex Pistols** has been refracted through the prisms of those involved, most indicators have **Richard Hell** as the original pinned-up poster boy. He and his partner in poetic suffering copped the emaciated street urchin look from band-mate **Richard Lloyd** when as **Television** they first sought fame on the streets of Manhattan. Lots of young men adopted it for various sordid reasons unconnected with rock'n'roll, but mainly because of the effect it had on their clients: the shabby chic stylings of **Dee Dee Ramone** and the rest of the boys working the corner of 53rd and 3rd in the early 70s made it harder for older men to resist. They were street corner hustlers looking down on their luck, sniffing and cold, in ripped T-shirts and junk-store jackets all held together with cheap safety pins; it was good for the corner boys' business and a look just made for late-70s urban rock'n'roll.

Malcolm McLaren saw Television play early on in their career, and again according to some versions of the truth, tried to get Richard to come to London and front a new band he was planning. When that failed he took the look and the expression "Blank Generation" back to London and the rest was soon to become history.

The safety-pin look was much too easy to parody and grew much too widespread. The phenomenon of the safety pin as a serious accessory lasted only a couple of weeks, a month at most, before being picked up by mainstream newspapers and teen magazines. **Patrik Fitzgerald** recorded one of the best punk-rock love songs "Safety Pin Stuck In My Heart" with no apparent irony, but once early-evening TV comedians picked up on the pin as an easy way to a guaranteed laugh, it was dead.

The kind of punks who sit around in tourist spots waiting to be photographed and paid by gullible tourists still wear safety pins, but of course they're no kind of punks at all.

SEX / Seditionaries

SEX was one of the names used by **Malcolm McLaren** for his shop in Chelsea, London, which he shared with **Vivienne Westwood** while punk rock went boom in Britain. The story begins as early as 1971, when the duo set up shop in the back of Paradise Garage, 430 Kings Road. The venture was named Let It Rock, and sold teddy boy fashions and rock'n'roll records to a retro-looking 50s-revival crowd. By 1972 McLaren and Westwood were already trying to push the envelope by spicing up their stock with zips, leather and rubber. In 1974 the famous padded pink "SEX" shop sign was in place, as was shop assistant **Jordan** (see p.178). Not long after that, the young Glen Matlock could be found in-store flogging the sloganeering T-shirts as a Saturday job.

Sex was a great work of art, but hardly the world's most successful fashion outlet. Not only did it take a lot of nerve just to enter the store – when confronted by Jordan in her full dominatrix-from-another-planet regalia, many potential clients turned on their stiletto heels and fled – but it also sold fetish gear: rubber skirts and T-shirts, bondage wear, cuffs, gags, manacles and the like, selling them as fashion items rather than sex-aids for sado-masochists.

It attracted a selective clientele, with a higher proportion than most other shops on the street of drug-crazed club queens, disco weirdoes, dirty rotten scoundrel kids from the bad parts of town and rich suburban teens looking for something stunning to wear. Amphetamines and decadence blended to a **Bowie / Kraftwerk** soundtrack in celebration of the Nazi-chic of Visconti's The Damned and the damaged sexuality of Bogarde's Night Porter. SEX customers were looking to create a buzz, and McLaren was there to sell them something that vibrated in a suitably pleasing way. In 1977 the shop changed it's name to Seditionaries, and slowly drifted away from the rubberier end of fashion to instead concentrate on items that more directly correlated with the music of the scene.

Much of the shop's wittier and more challenging stock is now to be seen in museums, and many of the designs are still either bootlegged or reworked on the high street to this day.

---

and *A Full Spoon Of Seedy Blues* (1969) – the latter credited to the Sky Saxon Blues Band – before splitting up in 1970.

Saxon retired to comparative privacy and seclusion in Hawaii, doing his best to avoid the tag of "godfather" to this or that musical movement. Savage joined the LA Police Department. Go figure.

⊚ **The Seeds / Web Of Sound (Diablo, 2001)**

A flawed masterpiece, but better than no masterpiece at all, this excellent-value compilation of the band's first two albums is (a) widely available and (b) nowhere near as rough-sounding as some online audiophiles would have us believe. It's garage punk rock, recorded some forty years ago by psychedelic musicians who'd never heard the term "quality control" and consequently a bit haphazard but still sounding as raw, mean and malevolent as most of the later punks arriving a decade down the line.

SEX PISTOLS

Formed London, 1975, split 1978, re-formed 1996, rumours of further gunfire 2006.

The opening riff of "Anarchy In The UK" announced the arrival of the Sex Pistols and signalled an end to all the earlier definitions of rock'n'roll. Over night, **Johnny Rotten** (vocals, sneer) became a household name. Less than three years later, with the closing chords of "No Fun" still echoing around the huge Winterland in San Francisco, the band shattered in a mess of self-parody, scandal and sudden death.

To some extent, the Pistols' story followed a template laid down more than a decade previously by The Beatles – there's the rough-diamond band, a bunch of smart but sneaky urchins who'd bite any hand that tried to feed them; the mysterious manager, claiming to know all the scores, pull all the strings and tweak all the media while in fact clinging on for dear life; even the dismissal of one of the original members of the rhythm section; and chasing behind, a thundering herd of beat-crazed teen fans, journalists in pursuit of a headline, and a baggage truck loaded with copycats, fellow-travellers and musical rivals. *A Hard Days Night* indeed.

Before the Sex Pistols however there was The Strand, aka The Swankers, formed by Steve Jones (guitar) with Paul Cook (drums) and Warwick "Wally" Nightingale (vocals, guitar). An everyday West London youth club band with attitude and a novel relationship with the laws of ownership – they'd formed in 1972 and acquired the kind of kit that major acts used, despite playing few gigs and having no fan-base. Through hanging out at SEX – the new name for the old Let It Rock teddy-boy costumiers on the trendy, *World's End* strip of Kings Road – and trying to pilfer the stock, they'd also acquired a manager, Malcolm McLaren.

The complete story of Malcolm's involvement with the band will never be told; his tale, like every other concerning the Sex Pistols, has been retold by too many interested parties for anything resembling total objectivity to have survived, but briefly, his pre-Pistols background combines a talent for selling trousers with a Svengali dream of managing the perfect 70s pop band. His first opportunity came when he talked up a nodding relationship with Syl Sylvain (based on their shared interest in the rag trade) into an unsuccessful stint as manager of The New York Dolls. On a subsequent trip to the city, he tried to recruit Richard Hell, promising to make him a star if he'd agree to front a London band that Malcolm had been nurturing back home. Richard refused, and Malcolm, mut-

tering "Curses! Foiled again!" under his breath, swished back to Chelsea.

The trip hadn't been a total washout however – Malcolm had picked up enough showbiz nous, style tips and musical hints from the New York punk scene to transform his little set of Swankers into the Sex Pistols. He arranged for Wally to leave the band – sacking him for being too musically proficient – and levered one of his shop assistants, Glen Matlock (bass) into the line-up. With a ready-made cadre of style-conscious suburban posers wearing his fashions and aching to be the new band's elite fans, all that McLaren lacked was a charismatic front man.

John Lydon suffered all the usual urban teenage frustrations of life in a dismal mid-70s London, lacking even the comforts of stupidity to deaden the impacts of the life he was trapped in. Born in 1956, he grew, through a haze of illness, house moves and a bitty education, to realize that society offered him no future worth working for. Smart

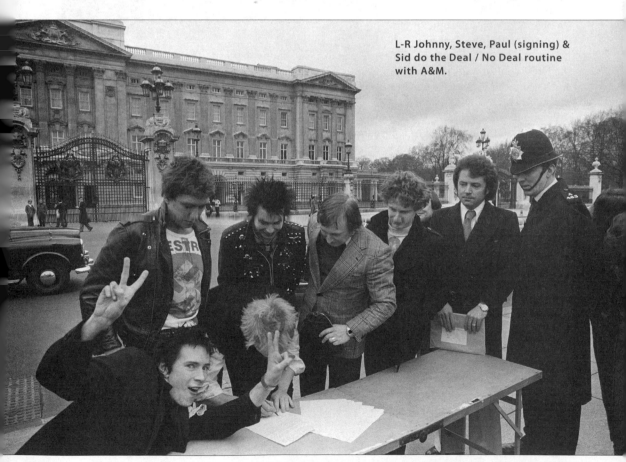

L-R Johnny, Steve, Paul (signing) & Sid do the Deal / No Deal routine with A&M.

enough to see through the hypocrisy and inconsistencies of his Church-dominated secondary education, he turned his back on school and missed most of his qualifications first time around. Hackney Tech accepted him in 1973 to study for a few more pieces of paper and introduced him to John Simon (aka Sime or Sid) Ritchie (alias Beverley, also Vicious). Having had himself thrown out of the parental nest (coming home with cropped bright green hair appears to have been the final straw) John Lydon moved into a squat with John Ritchie and transferred his education to Kingsway College, where a year later he met John Wardle – the man who would be Jah Wobble. Working part-time in various crappy jobs and shar-

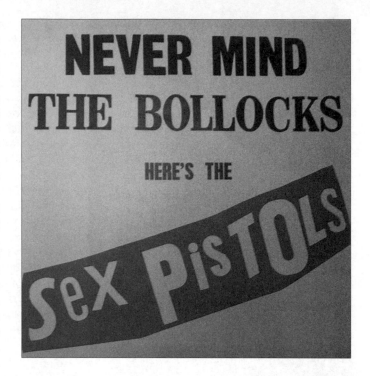

ing an interest in looking good while listening to the latest cool sounds, the three Johns hit it off and began swanning around Chelsea at weekends, inevitably ending up in Sex.

Bernie Rhodes, Malcolm McLaren and Steve Jones all found it impossible to ignore the wild-eyed green-haired yob and finally, in an attempt to stop his sneering at the band and get rid of his obnoxious coterie, Malcolm challenged him to sing. Lydon's abject performance of Alice Cooper's "Eighteen" (a song rewritten a year or so later as "Fifteen" by Eater) combined with his sadly sporadic dental hygiene earned him the nickname Johnny Rotten, and a place in the band.

Malcolm stepped up to bat at this point, paying for rehearsals, encouraging his boys to behave at least semiprofessionally some of the time, and ultimately arranging their first live appearances. Taking his eye off the personnel for a second while he set his plans in train allowed Rotten and Jones to snarl around one another like a brace of alley cats while Cook kept the beat going and everybody learned to hate Matlock. Malcolm thought he was brewing up a boy band that might challenge The Bay City Rollers; Steve and Paul wanted to be either Slade or The Stooges; Matlock had his "wanky Beatles' chords"; and Rotten thought the

sun shone thanks to the genius of Can, Captain Beefheart and Van Der Graaf Generator. There was always going to be a certain amount of tension in the group, with the perennial "musical differences" excuse for once being genuine.

Playing their debut at St Martin's School Of Art (where Glen was a student) in November 1975, the Sex Pistols were terrible. Compensating for lack of technical ability by using volume, aggressive audience baiting, and obnoxious antics on stage, they kept their suburban hangers-on (dismissively referred to as "The Bromley Contingent" by the city-dwelling band-mates) delighted, screaming and scrapping among themselves while bemusing, bewildering and chasing away those audience members not in on the scam.

Although the band never literally burned down a venue, it was rare that they were encouraged to play the same place twice. Rehearsals, travelling to gigs and playing on stage together eventually resulted in a full set list, some increased competence and, despite the constant bickering and lack of genuine friendship, a degree of team spirit – even if this last was most frequently expressed through showers of contempt for one another and verbal abuse of the outside world. Malcolm trotted the boys into studios all over London, arranging for different producers to try a range of sounds, even sneaking old-wave session man Chris Spedding onto the original cuts of a few tracks.

With Vivienne Westwood – Malcolm's partner in crimes against fashion, Jordan (one of the shop's more extrovert staff), Siouxsie's crew and Sid Vicious usually in the audience, early gigs were written up more as a result of drink- and drug-inspired misbehaviour in the crowd rather than on stage, and it wasn't until the 1976 "Punk Festival" held at London's 100 Club that the new music lurched out of the fashionista ghetto and into the mainstream consciousness. The two-day event made the front pages of the music weeklies, saw an upsurge of interest in what till then had been "the cult with no name" in the regular daily press and enabled Malcolm to sell his band and the tapes they'd made first to EMI, then to A&M and ultimately to Virgin, skipping from wave to wave riding the crests of notoriety and cancelled gigs, and pocketing cheques to the value of £100,000 on the way. At the end of 1976, following the band's groundbreaking performance on London Weekend Television's *Today* programme, the show hosted in part by Bill Grundy (see p.29) punk was everywhere, and the Sex Pistols' debut, "Anarchy In The UK", was in every self-respecting record collection in the land.

The New Year saw Matlock replaced by the talentless but better-looking and more easily moulded Sid Vicious. Malcolm was gambling on Steve, Paul and Johnny being able to write the second album while touring to promote the first (the best bits of which usually came from Glen and his magic pen), hoping against the evidence that Sid would find the time to learn the bass on the road.

Malcolm persuaded the record company to fund yet another headline-grabbing promotional gimmick; having released "God Save The Queen" so it would chart in time for Elizabeth II's jubilee festivities, he arranged a Thames riverboat party in June that ended once again, in disaster, even if for once tempered by sympathetic press coverage (see box p.31). The camera crew that was on hand to film the entire mess was part of Malcolm's plan to make a Sex Pistols biopic, a scheme that swallowed up much of the record company largesse he'd picked up the previous year, but such was the whirl of alleged media manipulation surrounding the group by this point that McLaren was rumoured to have orchestrated the whole affair. A swift listen to the police officers' dialogue, or a glance at the dishevelled condition of Malcolm – finally released hours later, having been arrested with eleven others on leaving the vessel – soon dispelled the stories.

A month later the Sex Pistols went top ten again with "Pretty Vacant", following up with "Holidays In The Sun" in October and their only real album, which went straight to the top of the album charts, in November. Virgin's promotion of *Never Mind The Bollocks... Here's The Sex Pistols* saw the company dragged through the courts (and the band once again starring in all the newspapers) to defend the robustness of the title's language (pictured), splattered across its cover in lurid

CELEBRITY PLAYLIST: STEVE JONES

Improbable as it may sound, these days former Sex Pistols guitarist Steve Jones is a DJ running a Los Angeles radio show called *Jonesy's Jukebox* on the Clear Channel-owned station, Indie 103.1. Studio guests on his show have included Brian Wilson, Nancy Sinatra and Courtney Love but he still finds time to play plenty of punk classics and sent us this typical playlist from the West Coast.

1. SPELLBOUND Siouxsie & The Banshees
from **Juju**

2. (I'M) STRANDED The Saints
from **(I'm) Stranded**

3. I DON'T WANNA GROW UP The Ramones
from **Hey Ho Let's Go: The Anthology**

4. TOP OF THE POPS Rezillos
from **Can't Stand The Rezillos**

5. DIRTY PICTURES Radio Stars
from **a 1977 single**

6. PILLS New York Dolls
from **New York Dolls**

7. AMERICAN NIGHTS The Runaways
from **The Runaways**

8. CRUEL TO BE KIND Spacehog
from **Resident Alien**

9. WHAT EVER HAPPENED? The Strokes
from **Room On Fire**

10. NEVER TURN YOUR BACK ON MOTHER EARTH Sparks from **Plagiarism**

black, pink and yellow. With charges dismissed, Glitterbest (Malcolm's promotional company) went into overdrive, signing the band to Warner in the USA and agreeing to perhaps the most ill-advised tour schedule in the history of rock'n'roll. Virtually ignoring the major cities of the industrial northern and Midwestern states where the band would have been, if not understood completely, at least treated to a respectful if rowdy listen, The Pistols were given an itinerary that would have tried the patience of The Osmonds, with hundreds of unnecessary bus miles to cover between shows. As the tour progressed, Sid's condition (exhaustion exacerbated by drug abuse and addiction) worsened while his bass playing stubbornly refused to improve. By the time of the band's final scheduled appearance in San Francisco he'd become a self-destructive hindrance instead of the iconic, pin-up boy that he'd been hired as. Rotten finished the gig, sat on stage asking a question, possibly of the audience, perhaps of himself; his last words as a Sex Pistol were "Ever get the feeling you've been cheated?". Johnny Rotten quit the band that night, Sid headed back to New York and the pharmaceutical caresses of girlfriend Nancy Spungen, while Malcolm, Steve and Paul wondered what to do next.

The answer was Rio! Flying down to Rio de Janeiro wasn't exactly the most rock'n'roll plan, but with Malcolm scraping together every last ounce of Machiavellian persuasiveness at his disposal, the idea of taking a break, getting some sun and

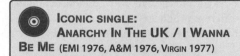

ICONIC SINGLE: ANARCHY IN THE UK / I WANNA BE ME (EMI 1976, A&M 1976, VIRGIN 1977)

Despite *not* being the first punk-rock single, this is the one that scared the daylights out of certain sectors of the establishment and rallied a host of disaffected youth into a proper movement with a style and language of its own. It boasts great lyrics of barely controlled, storm-the-barricades fervour and a guitar riff that still rallies the spikey-heads to the nearest dance floor for a bit of a bounce around. The whole delightful trifle is made even more potent, propelled along by the classic Pistols rhythm section of Matlock and Cook, meshing with precision and apparent bonhomie, before the bitching set in.

hooking up with Ronnie Biggs – an infamous robber on the run from British justice – for a one-off single was sold. Steve and Paul successfully met, recorded with, and taped a video alongside Biggs

Sex Pistols At The Screen On The Green

The Screen On The Green is an independent cinema house in Islington – today one of London's more desirable zones. Back in the late 70s however, when the **Sex Pistols** took it over for the evening, it was a suitably seedy location for the band's still arty-crafty selective appeal.

The band actually appeared at the venue twice, with the first gig on August 29, 1976 set up as a hush-hush semi-secret event attended by the great and good of the music biz, and their hack cohorts from the press. Enough word got out for the Pistols' entourage to make the gig and generate some heat in the 350-capacity venue aided by those few early fans of The Clash and Buzzcocks (who opened up for Johnny Rotten and the lads that evening). Fights predictably broke out, womanly breasts were revealed and pictures snapped for the horrification of the next days' press.

Although the recording isn't of the highest quality, and the musicianship veers between inept and atrocious, the third disc on the Pistols box set carries their entire set from that evening and does a good job of capturing the excitement and buzz of the event, even if the bass and guts of it are missing.

Not much more than six months later, the Sex Pistols returned to The SOTG, playing a showcase first gig to an invited audience with new bass player **Sid Vicious** at the beginning of April 1977. **The Slits** played support, with one of **Don Letts'** first productions – *Sex Pistols No.1* – projected between the girls leaving the stage and the boys taking over. As part of his project on the band, Letts was in the audience that night, filming the Pistols (in a sequence that later featured in his *The Punk Rock Movie*).

(and a local actor dragged up in Nazi uniform doing a Martin Bormann routine).

The footage was incorporated into *The Great Rock & Roll Swindle* – the first Sex Pistols' movie – a horrible mishmash of footage from different sources, recorded by directors of varied ability, that wrote Matlock out of the story almost completely and suffered immensely from Rotten's lack of cooperation. He returned to being Lydon, formed Public Image Limited (see p.252) with Jah Wobble and purged himself of the experience through his new band's music and through his autobiography, *Rotten: No Blacks, No Dogs, No Irish* (1994). Sid killed himself, just 21 (see p.40, Malcolm went on to a solo musical career of sorts while Steve and Paul simply formed another band – The Professionals – which, although short-lived, saw them through the worst of the aftermath. Paul went on to be a much-respected session drummer in Britain, while Steve succumbed to the delights of the LA lifestyle, earning an honest dollar playing sessions and presenting his own radio show.

Re-forming with all the old enmities and rivalries apparently forgotten in 1996 for the 20th anniversary, the Sex Pistols were back on their old venomous form – Rotten threatening to twat a white Rasta who threw a bottle at him during a summer festival. Matlock was back in the squad, with Paul and Steve thwacking competently away like the grizzly old rockers they'd grown up to become. Whether they'll do the same for their 30th anniversary is

---

■ PLAYLIST: SEX PISTOLS

When you absolutely definitely want to knock out the upper register of your hearing, there's no better way than with the noisiest, naughtiest boys ever to swagger out of West London and into the limelight.

1. HOLIDAYS IN THE SUN from **Never Mind The Bollocks Here's The Sex Pistols**
A paramilitary drum beat intro leads into a crashing guitar and a dive bomber riff – sounding just like Slade's angry little brothers, the Pistols released this track at the height of their pomp and never again reached this peak.

2. SATELLITE from **Spunk**
Raw and primitive. Jones and the band have all the equipment set on "SNARL" and Rotten is swigging open a bottle of poison in between lines of lyric, the better to spit it back in the face of the audience.

3. NO FEELINGS from **Never Mind The Bollocks Here's The Sex Pistols**
By the time they got round to recording the final album version, this song had slowed down a little for the lyrics to get through.

4. SEVENTEEN (2ND VERSION) from **Spunk**
Multi-tracked vocals mean Johnny sounds even more rotten, but this is one track that definitely shows the benefits of Malcolm's strong black coffees. Drums raining down like hailstones, sheets of cymbals, guitar trickery – the full English.

5. NEW YORK (LOOKING FOR A KISS) from **Spunk**
Chunkiest guitar line that Jonesy ever conjured and the perfect bass accompaniment – the kind you don't notice – from Matlock provide just the background needed for Rotten to lay into the New York Dolls, safe in the knowledge that David Jo and Johnny Thunders were still hanging out on the other side of the Atlantic.

6. LIAR from **Spunk**
The phased speakers on the guitar and crisp drumming are all very well but what makes this the definitive version of the Pistols' most vitriolic is, of course, Rotten's delivery.

7. SUBMISSION (2ND VERSION) from **Spunk**
Punk's only hymn to the delights of going down Mexico Way, and the only song ever to feature a solo blown on the whistle of an old-fashioned kettle.

8. NO FUTURE (GOD SAVE THE QUEEN) from **Spunk**
The occasional wrong note can be excused as a sign of the artists' desperate sincerity, the lyrics are best described as still to be finalized and it is quite obviously bolted together from two different takes, but this once-bootleg version sparks with more energy than that finally released on the album and as a single.

9. PRETTY VACANT from **Never Mind The Bollocks**
Opening with the most crucial three-note alarm in the history of punk, "Pretty Vacant" hangs the guys out to dry – warts, haemoroids and all – as a dumb but lovely boy band.

10. ANARCHY IN THE UK (1ST VERSION, AKA NOOKIE) from **Spunk**
All guns firing at once, this is the definitive version of the song that made them famous. It bursts with red-faced rage, as Rotten roars like a very pissed-off caged beast, Jones hacks a Dolls-esque path through the chord chart, and Cook beats the fear of gods into his kit.

still undecided at the time of going to press. Like the incarnation of a decade before however, it'll be a spiritless – if tight and professional – rock act, playing greatest hits to a middle-aged audience. Enjoyable enough, but nothing approaching the sheer excitement, amazement and fun of the band that started it all off in the UK.

The role of the Sex Pistols in punk can't be over-emphasized. Despite recording no more than twenty tracks in their high-intensity career, the Pistols were the catalyst that enabled the punk-rock machine to function – where high art and design-conscious couture clothes were fed in at one end, producing powerful music, stunningly new amateur graphics and street fashion at the other.

⊙ Never Mind The Bollocks Here's The Sex Pistols (Virgin, 1993)

Not merely a linguistic shock but also a technical achieve-ment and instant cultural icon, the band's debut album began generating excitement and controversy as soon as the sleeve appeared in shop windows. This ten-track masterwork should of course be in your collection already

⊙ The Sex Pistols Box Set (Virgin, 2002)

Nothing apparently will stem the endless tide of repackaged Pistols product with this three disc monster of a box set just the latest incarnation. If for some reason you're lacking the essential *Bollocks* then this is the perfect alternative. Lots of demo versions, lots of alternate takes and the best of the band's live recordings in one neat set. Not very punk, but a desirable enough little collectable.

SHAM 69

Formed Hersham, Surrey, England, 1975; split 1980. Sporadic reunions ever since.

"MY ATTITUDE MIGHT SEEM THICK TO YOU 'COS I WAS BROUGHT UP TO BE THICK TO KEEP RICH CUNTS IN MONEY."

JIMMY PURSEY, SNIFFIN' GLUE, 1977

When the poseurs of the art/fashion world proclaimed anarchy on the streets of London in 1976, they had little idea of the lumpenprole monster they would unleash. **Sham**

69 are typical of the so-called second wave; taking the do-it-yourself ethic literally, they shot out a wad of loud, raw and aggressively working-class noise, making their name through **Jimmy Pursey** (vocals) yelling his slogans over a sparse, buzzsaw guitar and massive drum sound.

A series of gigs at London's Roxy club gave the band some space to learn a few songs and experience the rush that a crowd can deliver. The band's first EP, *I Don't Wanna/Red London/Ulster Boy*, came with massive street credibility. With its photo cover of six police officers arresting a protester at an anti-Nazi demo, it was released on the ferociously indie Step Forward label with pro-duction by John Cale (ex-Velvet Underground) and beers provided by Mark Perry (of the semi-nal *Sniffin' Glue* fanzine and later of punk band Alternative TV).

Sham's early set of good, sing-along anthems were full of broad-brush generalizations and crude, laddish humour: at some of their early gigs they gave away a live recording, entitled "Song Of The Streets", which relied on a call-and-response of "What've we got?" "FUCK ALL!". Their lowest common denominator approach to music attract-ed the attention of the newly renascent skinheads – lowest brows on the streets and spoiling for a fight most of the time – and with Jimmy's lais-sez-faire approach to crowd control, Sham gigs became events to read and weep about, rather than to attend and be wounded at. By the end of 1977, punks in the know were avoiding events where Sham 69 had been booked to appear, leading to an even higher concentration of crop-headed cock-ney rejects at their gigs.

Not that Jimmy or the rest of the gang – the most stable line-up of which comprised **Dave Parsons** (guitar), **Albie Slider** (bass), and **Mark Cain** (drums) – were in any way racist: you couldn't keep Jimmy away from Rock Against Racism benefits, and he so enjoyed hanging out with the super-lefty and ultra-right-on Clash that they reportedly had to lock him in a cupboard once to prevent him joining them on stage and stealing "White Riot". The problem was with the crowds they pulled.

Sham's response was to sign with Polydor and put out a series of hook-laden singles (includ-ing "Borstal Breakout" / "Hey Little Rich Boy" and "Angels With Dirty Faces" / "The Cockney

Kids Are Innocent" – both 1978) followed by a knockout album. *Tell Us The Truth* (1978) boasted a studio side that verged on concept-album territory with slice-of-punk-life episodes linking the tracks and a few-holds-barred live side (we're talking vinyl here you kids at the back, try and keep up with the retro technology) that captured a good part of the excitement of seeing Sham at their best.

That's Life followed Sham's pattern of boiling down problems to half a dozen monosyllables and shouting equally terse solutions. This album concentrated more on domestic rather than world issues, though, and hit home with a younger generation of punk rockers: kids still living at home with mum and dad but yearning to go out on the streets and make adolescent mistakes.

The sloganizing wore thin pretty quickly though, even in a field that had already started to grow hidebound and proscriptive, and Sham's instant hit appeal wore off just as rapidly as it struck home. Personnel changes soon turned the band into "Pursey and Parsons plus three" and the songwriting descended into the worst kind of soccer hooligan terrace chants. The singles kept coming, but Sham's reputation depended just as much on their concert appearances as on record sales, and with an audience increasingly polarized into grown men with a penchant for violence and pre-teens who really just wanted to bounce around on the sofa, their gigs were becoming ever more farcical.

When *The Adventures Of Hersham Boys* (Note: not "of *the* Hersham Boys") appeared, Pursey and Parsons were backed by a new rhythm section comprising **Dave Tregenna** (bass) and **Rick Goldstein** (drums), and the band appeared on the cover swathed in ponchos and firing revolvers. Pursey's vision of the world as a cowboy movie was given full rein, producer Pete Wilson contributed keyboards and the transformation of Sham from consummate punk-rockers into professional entertainers was complete. Disappointing sales for *The Game* demonstrated that although practice makes for better-quality songwriting, their audience had evaporated. The game was up and Sham split up shortly after its release.

With his audience either growing up into sensible music or disappearing off the radar into a world of Oi!, Jimmy went solo, turning at one point to ballet, at another to releasing songs in favour of cannabis – hippie drug of choice and one a good punk rocker would shun in case it dulled his hatred of the world. Thankfully, sanity returned, and a new version of Sham surfaced in 1987 on the back of interest stirred up by the release of a decent live album.

Given that their best-known single, "Hurry Up Harry", was nothing more than Jimmy yelling at his pal to get a move on so that they could both go to the pub – hardly incisive social commentary – it's hardly surprising that Sham are remembered as a good-time party band. Still, they were the genuine working-class article, unlike so many of their peers, and even today there's little to beat a rousing chorus of "If The Kids Are United" if you're on your way to a demo.

Assorted Shams have been spotted on the punk revival circuit ever since, and now that he doesn't have to worry so much about it being a career, Jimmy seems to have recaptured the "who cares" attitude of his youth. No way is it punk rock, but it's a good gig, and these days, perfectly safe to attend.

PLAYLIST: SHAM 69

1. **ANGELS WITH DIRTY FACES**
   from **The Complete Collection** (Sanctuary, 2004)

2. **BORSTAL BREAKOUT**
   from **The Complete Collection** (Sanctuary, 2004)

3. **GEORGE DAVIS IS INNOCENT**
   from **The Albums: Box Set** (Castle, 2005)

4. **HERSHAM BOYS**
   from **The Complete Collection** (Sanctuary, 2004)

5. **HEY LITTLE RICH BOY**
   from **The Complete Collection** (Sanctuary, 2004)

6. **IF THE KIDS ARE UNITED**
   from **The Complete Collection** (Sanctuary, 2004)

7. **I DON'T WANNA** from **The Punk Singles Collection: 1977-1980** (Captain Oi!, 2005)

8. **RIP OFF**
   from **The Complete Collection** (Sanctuary, 2004)

9. **ULSTER**
   from **The Complete Collection** (Sanctuary, 2004)

10. **WHAT HAVE WE GOT**
    from **The Complete Collection** (Sanctuary, 2004)

From the scarily mad scream of laughter and sound effect of a slamming jail door that open this song, it's a total winner, an effervescent, opportunist, "over the wall and leg it" rock'n'roller with a great punk lyric ("locked in a cell for something I didn't do") and masses of testosterone. The lust-driven, confused protagonist of the song – James Pursey never having been imprisoned, like the hero played by **Johnny Depp** in the very punk rock movie *Cry Baby*, has a love so strong that mere walls and bars will never contain it. The well-bred suits at Polydor must have feared for their pensions whenever "Jimmy Sham" showed up, even if he was carrying a sure-fire hit of teen rebellion like this. So far down the line, Jimmy can't genuinely hack this song any longer but to the current generation of tearaways, this must sound like the beatific chanting of psalms.

◉ **Live And Loud!! (Link, 1987)**
◉ **Live And Loud!! Volume 2 (Link, 1988)**

A brace of fantastic sets capturing the band live at their peak. This is what punk rock is all about.

◉ **Tell Us The Truth/That's Life (Receiver, 1989)**

Worthwhile two-for-the-price-of-one reissue of the group's only essential studio albums.

◉ **Sham 69 – Punk Singles Collection 1977-80 (Captain Oi!)**

Twenty-six slices of three-minute heaven.

SIOUXSIE AND THE BANSHEES

Born 1976; died 1996.

Siouxsie Sioux started out as just a suburban kid growing up right, hosting house parties of speed and sexual experimentation in her parents' absence on the leafy streets of Bromley, Kent in the mid-1970s doldrums. Part of a group of spoilt kids from the sticks, poseurs whose adoration of David Bowie and all his works extended to flirting with the symbolism and ideology of the Third Reich, she became a regular customer for the King's Road designer excesses of Malcolm McLaren and Vivienne Westwood. This bunch, which included Billy Idol and **Steve Severin**, were scorned by the more distinctly urban, culturally aware and gritty Pistols, who dubbed them "The Bromley Contingent" (q.v.).

Siouxsie and Steve first appeared as part of **Siouxsie And The Banshees** at the legendary 1976 punk festival held over a few summer days at the 100 Club on London's Oxford Street. With **Sid Vicious** on drums and **Marco Pirroni** (later of the Ants) playing guitar, this punk supergroup made the mistake of appearing before the movement really kicked off, performing an interminable jam based on the Lord's Prayer (later revived in a more disciplined form at the end of the band's second album).

Canny enough not to jump into the first contract they were offered, Siouxsie worked on her vocal iciness, Steve bought and learned bass, and the S&S axis took their time in recruiting **John McKay** (guitar) and **Kenny Morris** (drums), prompting plaintive "SIGN THE BANSHEES – DO IT NOW!" graffiti to appear on walls around the record company offices of London before Polydor won out and *The Scream* finally took their sound to the rest of the country.

"Hong Kong Garden" hit the streets first. With its distinctly racist lyric, of a "slanted-eyed race of bodies small in size" accustomed to selling its daughters, hidden behind an almost jaunty and upbeat tune, it jarred and shuddered its way into the charts. Analysis in the press and discussion among the crowd led to the image consultants stepping in, and by the time the album came out, the previously racist lyric of "Love In A Void" had been toned down, "too many Jews for my liking" becoming "too many bigots for my liking". The Banshees had learned that their "tomorrow belongs to me" philosophy was unwelcome in the free-for-all of punk on the streets, and Siouxsie quickly ditched her Eagle+Swastika badge.

Those dubious lyrics apart, *The Scream* was one of the great early punk albums. Wildly different from *The Ramones, The Clash, IV Rattus*

Norvegicus and *Never Mind The Bollocks...*, it demonstrated the breadth of experience and musical influences that the movement was able to boast before conformity set in and strangled the scene. Kicking off with the menacing psychedelia of "Mirage", and stomping through familiar punk rock territory with "Carcass" and "Nicotine Stain" the album offered shards of artiness and experiment of a new and less carnal kind.

In "Metal Postcard (*Mittageisen*)", for example, the band produced a song dedicated to renowned anti-fascist artist John Heartfield (born Helmut Herzfeld in 1891), who devoted his politically motivated art – he was a master of the barbed photomontage – to challenging the Weimar Republic and the Nazi regime that followed it. As observed earlier, the Banshees camp learned fast, and Heartfield's image "*Mittageisen*" was co-opted for the single sleeve.

The Banshees' version of "Helter Skelter" owed far more to Charles Manson than Lennon-McCartney, while their explorations of mindlessness and boredom in "Jigsaw Feeling", "Overground", "Switch" and "Suburban Relapse" echoed with the hollowness of the lives they had led back in the 'burbs.

By the time the band entered the studio to record *Join Hands* in 1979, punk's first wave was already retreating. The new bands were inspired by the Pistols and their compadres, but were not personal friends or long-term fans, and they had a new style – a more tribal, oppressive-sounding music better suited to the social and economic turmoil that formed its backdrop. With gloom aplenty and a sour taste in her mouth, Siouxsie took the band deeper into the dark side. Lines such as "Hanging from your climbing frame, swinging from your gallows" (from "Playground Twist") reverberated long after the songs had finished. "Mother/Oh Mein Papa" revisited the early stereo experiments of The Velvet Underground and exposed some parent/child issues within

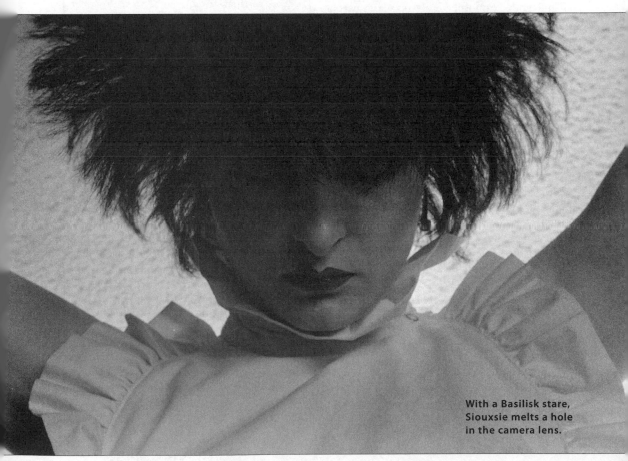

With a Basilisk stare, Siouxsie melts a hole in the camera lens.

the membership. The remaining tracks, such as "Premature Burial", "Icon" and "Poppy Day", qualified it as a proto-goth album, some years before the undead look became popular across the angsty teens of the West.

Siouxsie the SS She-Wolf had become Siouxsie the Ice Queen, dressed in Westwood's finest tartan and professionally styled into a creature beyond recognition. When McKay and Morris quit the band two days into the album's series of promotional gigs, the Banshees had to mutate pretty quickly too. **Robert Smith** was lured from an early mid-life crisis with The Cure (then supporting the Banshees on their tour) into the guitar slot, and **Budgie** (previously with Big In Japan and The Slits) took over the drums.

Although Smith was only a temporary stand-in (he resolved his issues, returned to The Cure and went on to enjoy a very successful Eighties as king of the dark and dismal brigade), his presence tipped the Banshees over the edge from punk rockers into goths. Atmosphere, always a large part of the Banshees appeal, became the most important part of the act, with lyrics becoming little more than a proper rhythmic accompaniment to the bass and drums. Budgie liked what he found in the Banshees (particularly Siouxsie herself) and decided to stay.

Kaleidoscope was recorded with ex-Pistol Steve Jones on half the tracks, and new full-time guitar-slinger **John McGeoch** (ex-Magazine) on the rest. With the album yielding a brace of chart singles ("Christine", a melodramatic tale of a girl with multiple personalities, and "Happy House", disco music for the mental hospital), it was time for the band to conquer the USA.

Although the Banshees were still regularly churning out powerful effective music, they'd left traditional four-to-the-floor punk rock far behind. *Juju* (1981) stayed resolutely at the dark end of the street and the first singles collection, *Once Upon A Time* (1981) merely marked time. However, for *A Kiss In The Dreamhouse* and *Hyaena*, the band grew increasingly fond of lush, extravagant orchestral arrangements and tunes of increasing complexity. *Nocturne* (recorded at the Royal Albert Hall in 1983) appeared between the two studio albums, presenting a warts-and-all document of the Banshees (with McKay off sick and Smith back as temporary guitarist) in concert.

ICONIC SINGLE: METAL POSTCARD / LOVE IN A VOID (POLYDOR, 1979)

Bleak like Ibsen, cold like Bergman and soulless as a wraith, "Metal Postcard" set a new record-low temperature in the field of heartless, emotionally stilted punk rock. With lyrics that evoked the desperate stifling atmosphere of a wholesome 1970s family evening in front of the telly as much as the evil totalitarian machinations of the fascist empires of the 1930s and 40s, Siouxsie lends the doubtful glory of a torchlight procession to the everyday frustrations of a suburbanite teen stuck at home through lack of funds.

The band's fourth single, "Metal Postcard" marked a turning away from the conventional boundaries of punk towards the endless steppes of Siouxsie's ice kingdom. Galloping towards goth, with **The Cure**, **PiL** and **Magazine** in hot pursuit, the track's epic sweeping music and fiercely influential guitar mechanicals – with echoes showing up everywhere from **Joy Division** and the UK's 1980s post-punk gloom to **Interpol** and the doom-struck guitar merchants of today – what makes the single a milestone is its outspoken anti-fascism.

The cover image – a photomontage showing a family tucking into a meal of bicycle frames and domestic hardware was originally known as "Hooray, Butter Is Off" but acquired the title *Mittageisen* (iron meal) after Hermann Goering's statement that "Iron will strengthen a nation, whereas butter and lard only make the people grow fat."

The photomontage they used was the work of famed anti-Nazi artist/activist **John Heartfield**. Born in 1861, he was one of the earliest members of the Dada school and an attendee of the original Zurich Cabaret Voltaire. Noted for the humour and pranksterist approach of his art, his natural rebelliousness made it wise for him to flee the Nazi regime, particularly after the *Mittageisen* image appeared on the cover of the *Arbeiter Illustrierten Zeitung* (Workers Magazine Journal) in December 1935. He survived the war and continued to work as an artist until 1968.

Siouxsie's Nazi armband days were behind her, and the band's choice of this specific image, together with their decision to issue the track in Germany, and with a German-language lyric, before its UK debut, helped – alongside the revised lyrics to "Love In A Void", to lay to rest the gossip about a continuing and more sinister interest in the Third Reich.

⊙ PLAYLIST: SIOUXSIE AND THE BANSHEES

All of these selections can be found on one classic album, which has now been reissued with a ton of extra tracks. Much of the rest of the band's output can be filed under "goth" and probably won't be to your taste.

1. CARCASS
from **The Scream: Deluxe Edition (Polydor, 2005)**

2. HELTER SKELTER
from **The Scream: Deluxe Edition (Polydor, 2005)**

3. HONG KONG GARDEN PEEL SESSION 2)
from **The Scream: Deluxe Edition (Polydor, 2005)**

4. LOVE IN A VOID (PEEL SESSION 1)
from **The Scream: Deluxe Edition (Polydor, 2005)**

5. METAL POSTCARD
from **The Scream: Deluxe Edition (Polydor, 2005)**

6. MIRAGE
from **The Scream: Deluxe Edition (Polydor, 2005)**

7. NICOTINE STAIN
from **The Scream: Deluxe Edition (Polydor, 2005)**

8. STAIRCASE MYSTERY (PATHWAY SESSION)
from **The Scream: Deluxe Edition (Polydor, 2005)**

9. SUBURBAN RELAPSE
from **The Scream: Deluxe Edition (Polydor, 2005)**

10. SWITCH
from **The Scream: Deluxe Edition (Polydor, 2005)**

John Carruthers (ex-ClockDVA) signed up when Smith returned to The Cure, and was just settling in when Siouxsie fell over on stage and shattered her knee. Forced off the road, the Banshees regrouped in the studio and produced *Tinderbox*, their best original work for some years, and *Through The Looking Glass*, an intriguing selection of cover versions ranging from Disney's "Trust In Me" (from *The Jungle Book*) to Iggy Pop's "The Passenger".

Peepshow featured yet another guitarist, Jon Klein, and introduced **Martin McCarrick** (keyboards/cello). Again, it proved to be an interesting, entertaining set, full of challenges to the faithful fan and bursts of sometimes ill-advised stylistic forgery (if you ever craved the sound of The Banshees attempting country music, this is where you'll find it). *Superstition* (1991) was not a remarkably strong or essential album and appeared following the marriage of Siouxsie and Budgie.

The Rapture (1995) had Siouxsie's long-time hero John Cale on board as producer for its best songs, and turned out to be the Banshees' final statement. Citing their disgust at their other old heroes, the Sex Pistols, re-forming for a cash-in reunion tour, the band split up. Since then, Siouxsie and Budgie have continued to work as **The Creatures** (a sporadic side-project they'd begun in the early 1980s), while Severin has turned to writing film scores.

⊙ **The Scream (Polydor/Geffen, 1978)**

Although the music is cold and bracing to the system like the plunge into dark water shown on the cover, the lyrics frequently descend into banality and bad stabs at humour. That said, it still kicks several shades of embarrassment out of their competition, then and now. A fine album, if a bit strict.

⊙ **Kaleidoscope (PVC/Geffen, 1980)**

The Banshees' finest rock album. There's precious little punk here, but it rates a listen and merits a place on the shelf.

⊙ **Once Upon A Time/The Singles (PVC/Geffen, 1981)**

This first volume is essential. The second, *Twice Upon A Time* is, shall we say, for the committed fan and completist only.

⊙ **The Peel Sessions (Strange Fruit/Dutch East India Trading, 1991)**

Two sessions from the beginning of the band's career (1977 and 1978) that go a long way towards explaining their instant appeal.

SKIDS

Started skidding, Dunfermline, Scotland, 1977; on the skids 1982.

"IN THOSE DAYS,...YOU COULD EVOLVE AND BE PRETENTIOUS AND GET AWAY WITH IT."

RICHARD JOBSON, 2004

The Skids rode out of the Scottish countryside into the maelstrom of punk rock with a uniquely inspiring and positive-sounding energy that distinguished them from their more

Ska Punk

Revved up on beer, speed or sheer *joie de vivre*, there's not much to beat the fun of a dance-floor knees-up to something by bands such as **Bad Manners** or **Operation Ivy** – it gets the blood pumping, and is simply the perfect "get the party started" soundtrack, provided you really want the guests to start playfully whacking one another with items of furniture, household pets or the other invitees.

It is powerful stuff, with all the aggression of punk and all the energy of the original Jamaican ska style that inspired it. By blending the essentially upbeat rhythms and melodies of ska with the innate misery and gloom of punk's typical lyrical output, a hybrid developed that stayed angry but lost the irritating whine.

The story of ska punk goes back to **The Clash** and their championing of roots reggae - assisted by film-maker / Roxy Club DJ / renaissance man **Don Letts**. By the end of '78 many otherwise straightforward rock'n'rolling punk bands in Britain included a decent stab at a reggae beat, and there were dozens of respectful cover versions to be heard. When the apocalyptic Rastafarianism of their singles collections had been exhausted, the punk rockers turned to the previous generation of JA music for inspiration and, finding ska to their taste, never looked back.

Looking for a party to call their own as the 70s rolled on into the 80s – and reviving old-school musical styles with a most un-punky sense of reverence – younger kids were looking beyond pure punk in search of something to dance to. Club DJs fed this appetite across the UK, where a strong minority tradition of digging the latest hot sounds from the West Indies had existed since the late 1950s, with new ska bands popping up everywhere – most flourishing briefly on the local circuit before settling for a Friday night residency at the local "Fight Club" bar of ill-repute. These were however, on the whole, purist ska bands, covering **Prince Buster** numbers, **Skatalites** tunes and so forth, with only the bravest attempting their own works on stage.

Whereas most of the Brit bands initially stayed true to the Jamaican template, in the different cultural soil of the USA, the same sort of influences trickling down from older punks led to the creation of ska punk – a flourishing hybrid that shows little sign of dying out anytime soon. Ska-Punk's sheer vitality made it immediately attractive to the party-going generation, with good-times bands such as **The Aquabats**, **Citizen Fish**, **Less Than Jake**, **The Mighty Mighty Bosstones**, **No Doubt**, **NOFX**, **Operation Ivy**, **Rancid** and **Reel Big Fish** dividing up the continental USA between them; while Bad Manners (fronted by **Buster Bloodvessel**, the party-loving, belly-boasting consummate ska-punk front man), **The (English) Beat** and **The Selecter** pretty much took care of Europe.

Although most of the bands mentioned above are still in existence – either working full-time or re-forming for occasional one-offs, the scene is a lot quieter these days, with the current generation of aggravators and upsetters preferring basic ramshackle rock'n'roll to roots riddims.

---

dour and downward-looking peers. **Richard Jobson** (songwriting/vocals/guitar), **Stuart Adamson** (songwriting/guitar/vocals) **Bill Simpson** (bass), **Alastair Moore** (keyboards) and **Tom Kellichan** (drums) teamed up in their home town of Dunfermline in the summer of 1977, forming The Skids from the leftovers of a Bowie-covers and posing glam-rock band called **Tattoo**. Miles off the A&R radar and hidden from most outside influences, the guys were able to indulge in their own fantasy of punk, cooking up a rousing, blood-stirring sound that had much the same effect as the speed their urban counterparts were stuffing up their noses. Richard found a taste for peculiar "art-Caledonian" outfits, Stuart found the "make it sound like bagpipes" setting on his amp and the rest of the lads piled in behind them like they were Robert Burns and Robert The Bruce rousing the clans for the long march south.

The opening skirmish came in April 1978, when their debut, self-released EP Wide Open appeared. A four track 12" slab of now very collectable red vinyl, it introduced "The Saints Are Coming" and "Of One Skin" (later to show up on the first album) alongside "Night And Day" and "Contusion", and led to a contract with Virgin and a huge publicity push for their one true hit single.

"Into The Valley" is now best known as the song nobody knows the second line to. (The lyrics go "Into the valley / betrothed and divine...", but after that, you're on your own.) A combination of Jobson's declamatory style, untidy production and an accent unfamiliar to most who heard it made the words difficult to distinguish, while the sheer energy of the music meant that listeners were too busy dancing to fret about singing along.

From a straightforward punk-rock point of view, the band's contribution to the cause ended with that first hit single. With Jobson at the controls, the band's intriguing and unique, hard-edged but melodic punk was turned into something increasingly glam, arty and pretentious.

Before long, Kellichan left. He was briefly

replaced by musician-at-large **Rusty Egan** (ex-Rich Kids) before **Mike Baillie** stepped in. *Days In Europa*, produced by Be Bop Deluxe's Bill Nelson was a disastrous swerve into prog rock.

The situation worsened – Simpson jumped ship soon afterwards, with **Russell Webb** picking up the bass. When producer Mick Glossop gave Jobson's tendency to turn everything into a torch song free rein for *The Absolute Game*, Adamson finally split and the remaining audience turned off in droves.

By the release of *Joy* (a concept album reflecting the many facets of life north of the border), The Skids had shrunk down to a duo. The end was unavoidable and, despite a last flurry of personnel movements, The Skids ceased to exist in 1982.

Jobson and Webb went on to play in **The Armoury Show**, and released *Waiting For The Floods* in 1984. Since then Jobson has moved through independent television to making films.

◉ **Scared To Dance (Captain Oi!, 2005)**

If "Into The Valley" whetted your desire, then this is the album to buy. Stretched out like a pimped-up limo to a full 20 tracks including live favourites, B-sides and EP rarities, this will answer any questions that might remain as to the influences absorbed by, and now oozing from, bands such as Franz Ferdinand. If nothing else, it comes with a lyric sheet so at last you can singalonga the band's greatest hit.

SKREWDRIVER

Started skrewing in Blackpool, England, 1977; skrewed up by 1978.

Skrewdriver started out as a good old-fashioned punk band and then got into politics. First they turned skinhead, then into a gang of neo-Nazi types.

Ian Stewart's pre-punk band was **Tumblin' Dice**, a standard Stones/Who covers band play-

Skate Punk

In the UK, skateboarders who are old enough legally to drink, vote, and get laid attract the same kind of fascination crossed with repulsion that scoutmasters receive. There's something creepy about grown men with beards and bellies who hang out with adolescent kids, comparing tattoos and grazes. Putting the dubious Peter Pan complexes of the older boarders to one side, there still remain the musicians who feed the insatiable maw that gobbles up the music they call skate punk.

These guys (and it generally IS just guys) see the humble skateboard as a banner of rebellion, with hardcore punk rock the perfect music to accompany it – with both being fast, noisy and difficult to control.

The 80s Southern California skateboard scene captured in the movie *Dogtown and Z-Boys* (directed by Stacy Peralta, 2001), shrugged off any creepiness and a flurry of macho lumberjack shirts, far-from-girly three-quarter length shorts and a set of contusions, cuts and plaster casts to frighten an emergency room full of doctors. They listened to Sk8 punk – also referred to as skate thrash – a particularly abrasive offshoot of hardcore punk, with a hefty dose of heavy-metal techno-flash virtuoso soloing thrown in. The resulting mess is hell on earth to listen to unless accompanied by high-speed video gaming or massively intense thrashing videos, showing teams of suicidal lunatics aiming their boards across pieces of municipal hardware and street furniture.

Looking back for inspiration to early hardcore punk bands including **Black Flag** and **The Circle Jerks**, skate punk relies on the buzzsaw thrash of a Fender guitar's

most treble-heavy setting. Skate punk comes across faster, louder and quite often played more ineptly than any other brand of punk rock.

The music of choice for kids who find **The Dead Kennedys** just a bit too middle-aged, skate punk is for those who overclock computers, shoot speed, mainline espresso and live for the night. Skate punks, through their lifestyle choices (and appalling taste in clothing), came more often than perhaps they deserved to the attention of security guards, cops and "the man" in general. Capable of some righteous self-deprecating humour as well as complaining of how unfair life is and chanting for the downfall of civilization, the music the skaters generate reflects their healthy reluctance to interact with mainstream society.

There has been a degree of crossover between "mainstream" hardcore, the ska punk crews and the skate punks – with **NOFX**, for example, fitting neatly into all three categories – and bands such as **Minor Threat** and **Suicidal Tendencies** being lumped in with the skaters as well as the more traditional hardcore preachers. A new school of more "purist" skate punk bands has grown up specifically to service the requirements of the video game manufacturers, skate movie producers and the teen skaters themselves, with **Big Boys**, **Free Beer** (surely the best band name of its generation), **JFA** and **Los Olvidados** championing the scene and appearing regularly in the skater fanzines. Many 'zines are little more than advertisement features in disguise, however, both *Thrasher* (www.thrashermagazine.com) and *Skate & Annoy* (www.skateandannoy.com) remain recommended titles.

ing gigs for fun and beer money. They mutated into Skrewdriver after Stewart attended the Pistols' Manchester gig, and released "You're So Dumb" in the summer of 1977. Reviewed in *Sniffin' Glue*, the single was slated for sounding dated, and despite the band heading down to London to pick up on the scene and make a little money playing the circuit down south, "Anti-Social" was released at the end of the year to little interest.

The rot began in the New Year with personnel and image changes (even then, a move into the skinhead camp was a blatant play for the racist audience) that left the band as little more than Stewart's playthings, to dress up and position as he pleased.

He and his friends still like to play Nazis on the underground circuit. Stewart has said: "I am not the type of person to creep and crawl to a bunch of weak-kneed, pacifist lefties and two-faced Zionists. One must be honest to people about one's beliefs and especially when the survival of our very race is at stake. I have no doubt that anyone who expounds patriotic beliefs has a little black mark put against his name, and by now I must have a massive black mark near my name. *C'est la guerre*." If this sounds like fun to you, you're reading the wrong book.

SLAUGHTER AND THE DOGS

Whelped in Manchester, 1977; went to the dogs soon after. Still seen at Kennel Club shows in 2005.

"WE'RE SLAUGHTER AND THE DOGS" … "AND WE'RE MURDER AND THE CATS"

ONSTAGE BANTER FROM LIVE AT THE ROXY WC2 ALBUM, 1977

Shambolic, iconic, and so blatantly in the business just for the laughs and the beer, **Slaughter And The Dogs** were one of the first Manchester bands to break through onto the wider UK scene. Lumped together with The

Drones and Buzzcocks, **Mike Rossi** (guitar/songs) and **Wayne Barrett** (vocals/songs) formed the band in the wake of the Pistols' visit to the city with **Howard "Zip" Bates** (bass) and **Brian "Mad Muffet" Grantham** (drums). They took the road down to London as often as possible to play in the cellar clubs of the capital and opened the album *The Roxy London Wc2 Jan-Apr 77* with two of their self-written tracks, "Runaway" and the thrash epic "Boston Babies".

Meanwhile, back home in Lancashire, the kitchen-table record label Rabid Records was looking for acts to sign. A deal was done and "Cranked Up Really High" hit the streets. Monstrously overpowered, with roaring vocals and all instruments set to stun, it mirrored the home-grown Sydney wail of The Saints more than the Slade/glam-rock hybrid seen in London and was early evidence that the Manchester scene was happily independent of influence puffing up from the Smoke.

Putting the traditional Mancunian restraint and good taste to one side, they called their album *Do It Dog Style*, released it (on Decca) in a violently loud fluorescent cover and made sure that it was the loudest record of the month. Sensitive stereo equipment struggled to cope with the volume and interference from kids bouncing round the living room in delirious pogo madness. Sales weren't that encouraging, however, and as punk appeared to be running out of steam, the band took a break.

Rossi and Bates spent the break as **The Studio Sweethearts**, a side project formed with **Billy Duffy** (later Cult member), before getting the old gang back together – minus Barrett (musical differences again) – at the end of 1979. The new singer, **Eddie Garrity**, came with form – he'd previously been Ed Banger, and had committed several musical atrocities with his band The Nosebleeds. The new line-up lasted long enough to record *Bite Back* before falling apart for good-ish, in 1981.

At the time of writing, there's a line-up claiming to be Slaughter And The Dogs gigging in London and on the summer circuit. Apparently they do all the old hits and are a great night out. Nostalgia and punk shouldn't mix, but apparently they do.

⊚ **Do It Dog Style (Captain Oi!, 2000)**

This piece of history is as fresh now as the day they threw it down and beat it up in the studio. It includes the singles – "Dame to Blame", "Quick Joey Small" and "Where Have All The Boot Boys Gone" – and a bunch of high-energy rock'n'roll covers such as The New York Dolls' "Who Are The Mystery Girls".

⊚ **The Punk Singles Collection (Captain Oi!, 2000)**

Just the job! A far better-value purchase, with all the decent singles, and enough of the band's aftermath to put you off their later work.

THE SLITS

Opened up London, 1976; healed over 1981.

"I'VE GOT TO ADMIT THEY SCARED THE SHIT OUT OF ME."

MARK P.

Born of woman in the days before punk had been named as such, The Slits got to choose the best name of all the female punk bands and to make some quite remarkably sophisticated music before the stereotypical punk-rock style became entrenched. The band started out when 14-year-old Arianna Forster and Paloma Romero became, respectively **Ari Upp** (vocals) and **Palmolive** (drums). Together with **Kate Korris** (guitar), ex-member of The Castrators, and **Suzi Gutsy** (bass), this original line-up began like a dozen or so other bands, rehearsing in rented rooms and starting a scene based around their closeness to The Clash, or to the Pistols and McLaren's King's Road nerve centre. Musical differences led to personnel changes before the band

had really begun, with Korris leaving the band to form the Mo-Dettes, while Gutsy took her bass and went to become one of The Flicks. **Viv Albertine** and **Tessa Pollitt** (another ex-Castrator) stepped into their respective breaches, the "classic" line-up was formed, and The Slits played their first gig supporting The Clash during their 1977 White Riot Tour, with Buzzcocks and Subway Sect on the bill at the Harlesden Coliseum in March 1977.

These early gigs were marvellously shambolic affairs, inspired by the "anyone can form a band" ethos and the liberal ingestion of drugs and alcohol by young bodies unaccustomed to them. Women were rarely seen on stage in such active roles, and the sheer unfocused awfulness of their playing helped make them a must-see act. Their appearance in Don Letts' *The Punk Rock Movie* (1978) captures them in their unashamedly amateurish glory. Their aggressive determination to play "come what may and to hell with the sound quality" was very typical of early punk gigs and a refreshing change to the note-perfect technical wizardry of the bands they were slowly replacing in the minds of the capital's bored youth. Still, no matter how strong one's devotion to independent women and their right to be heard on the big rock'n'roll soapbox, a little went a long way, and they stayed unsigned, although a permanent feature of the live circuit, until 1978, when Island Records took them on.

In the meantime, Palmolive had left to join The Raincoats and had been replaced on drums by Budgie (later of The Banshees), who became the band's token male. To make the most of the band's heavy, rhythm-led music, Island co-opted Midas-touch reggae producer **Dennis "Blackbeard" Bovell** to look after things. *Cut*, which appeared in 1979, was a fine, strong album, very dub-reggae in its feel, crammed with ideas and hints of musical directions – notes for expeditions yet to come. However, it was to become infamous for the cover, which showed the girls (Budgie wasn't invited, apparently) covered in mud and very little else. It boosted sales, although according to Albertine: "Nobody could see the strength, the joke, the little twist that we were all a bit fat."

It also demonstrated that, despite themselves, The Slits had grown into inventive, accomplished musicians. The whirl of line-up changes that engulfed British punk as the initial rush wore off

The Slits at the height of their powers.

at the end of the 1970s meant that *Return Of The Giant Slits* didn't show until 1981. Budgie had left in 1979 to be replaced by **Bruce Smith** (ex-Pop Group) who had brought a more African-derived feel to the band's work. Veteran jazzer Don Cherry and reggae master Prince Hammer added their own special spice to the stew, and with a new label (CBS) enthusiastically backing them, The Slits looked set for a more commercial decade.

It wasn't to be, however. The band had run out of juice, and after an indifferent year of lacklustre gigs, they called it quits at the end of 1981. Their legacy is a brilliant debut album and the lasting influence they have had on the subsequent generations of female musicians trying to make it in what is still, mainly, a man's world.

⊚ Cut (Island, 2000)

Dennis Bovell's masterful production carves out a huge hangar of space for the band to weld together their own version of white reggae, one that hopefully reduced The Police to tears of shame.

⊚ Return Of The Giant Slits (Japanese import)

Experimental, forgotten classic that includes some of the band's best work, such as the vocal & dub pairings of "Face Place" / "Face Dub", "Animal Space" / "Spacier" and "Life on Earth" / "Earthbeat". Wearing their reggae influences way up front, *The*

🎵 PLAYLIST: THE SLITS

1. EARTHBEAT
from **Return Of The Giant Slits (Sony, 2004)**

2. I HEARD IT THROUGH THE GRAPEVINE
from **Cut: Remastered (Island, 2000)**

3. IMPROPERLY DRESSED
from **Return Of The Giant Slits (Sony, 2004)**

4. INSTANT HIT
from **Cut: Remastered (Island, 2000)**

5. LOVE UND ROMANCE
from **Cut: Remastered (Island, 2000)**

6. NEWTOWN
from **Cut: Remastered (Island, 2000)**

7. PING PONG AFFAIR
from **Cut: Remastered (Island, 2000)**

8. SHOPLIFTING
from **Cut: Remastered (Island, 2000)**

9. SO TOUGH
from **Cut: Remastered (Island, 2000)**

10. TYPICAL GIRLS
from **Cut: Remastered (Island, 2000)**

Return Of The Giant Slits emphasizes their love and respect for not just Jamaican rhythms but their exploration of the earlier roots music that inspired it. Though veering far away from conventional notions of punk rock (with the exception of the extraordinarily weird vocals), the mere creation of such a powerful statement by a female band was revolutionary enough in itself at the time.

PATTI SMITH

Born Chicago, 1946; still trampin' the long hard path to glory.

"WHEN I WAS YOUNG WHAT WE READ WAS THE BIBLE AND UFO MAGAZINES ... MY DAD WAS EQUAL PARTS GOD AND HAGAR THE SPACEMAN IN MEGA CITY."

PATTI SMITH

Patti Smith single-handedly redefined the role of women in rock'n'roll. She was present at the birth of the new music, moved from hard-edged underground poetry to full on punk racket, broke her damn neck and still came back for more. She dropped a hundred thousand jaws worldwide with her most famous quote "Jesus died for somebody's sins, but not mine", and made a hundred thousand more minds expand into a new and interesting world of punk-poets, question everything they'd been taught and maybe think about joining young Gloria, humpin' on a parkin' meter just waiting for some of that good, sweet, poet meat to sashay by and fall into their clutches.

Born into one of the great dysfunctional families of the USA, Smith threw off the suffocating intensity of her mother's love, religion and a regular career path in a late-adolescent flurry of pregnancy, dropping out and taking a job in a factory, before finally reinventing herself as an underground poet/actor/journalist in New York City. Picking up tips and advice from a series of male muses – beginning with the decadent French poets of the nineteenth century and moving swiftly onto the living flesh of photographer Robert Mapplethorpe and playwright Sam Shepard – she slowly evolved into the most eloquent and fascinating New Wave performer in town, pushed into rock'n'roll by the most enduring of her masculine influences, **Lenny Kaye**.

Kaye's role in the Patti Smith story cannot be overemphasized – he not only pushed her into performing her own material at recitals, but also accompanied her on guitar. As Smith's popularity and stagecraft grew, he helped recruit **Richard Stohl** (keyboards), arranged a recording session and co-founded a label with her to release the end result in 1974 – a waveringly beautiful, poetically

Patti Smith: her neck in a sling, wearing very sweaty trousers and still kicking ass trouper!

embellished version of "Hey Joe" and the self-penned "Piss Factory", which looked back to the worst of her dead-end jobs with a spite and venom undiminished by distance.

A year later Smith was the original pin-up of the New York punk/New Wave scene, surfing along the cutting edge of the avant-garde, talk of the town in New York and across the ocean in London, signed to Arista and peering down in androgynous contempt – in an iconic session and image created by ex-lover Mapplethorpe – from bedroom walls all over the thinking rock'n'roll universe.

Horses appeared at the end of 1975, with Kaye and Stohl joined by **Ivan Kral** (guitar/bass) and **Jay Dee Daugherty** (drums) as The Patti Smith Group. Produced to shiny perfection by John Cale – then at the top of his game and equipped with an instinctive understanding of the spells that Smith and the band wanted to weave – it charted on both sides of the Atlantic and woke the world up to the new New York music scene.

Fast forward to the middle of 1976. Smith and the band are on the permanent touring/promotional treadmill, fed but insulated from the real world by the music industry machine, and gradually being poisoned by the cynicism that accompanies stardom. Old friends were snubbed, and desperately devoted fans were crushed to find a bunch of shallow, show-bizzy entertainers in the dressing rooms, completely unlike the poetic angels they'd imagined.

The machine rolled on, with the band somehow managing to create a second dramatic set of songs during moments snatched away from the noise and glare outside. *Radio Ethiopia* (1976) was already moving them away from the stormy waters of punk rock into the more mature, considered, if still slightly deranged and condescending politics of an obviously deep-thinking US citizen who finds herself suddenly exposed to the rest of the world and its differing points of view after a lifetime in homeland isolation. Smith was part of the intellectual New Wave, more in tune with Tom Verlaine's Television or Richard Hell's well-read Voidoids than with the fun-lovin' Ramones or Heartbreakers, and her connection to the street had snapped. *Radio Ethiopia* was too stately to be filed under "punk", but bulged with inventive New Wave rock'n'roll music and boosted the band's audience up to the next level.

As 1977 kicked off, however, Patti twirled herself off the front of the stage and broke her neck. With the roar of punk's biggest year muffled by hospital windows, Patti spent weeks in recovery, working on her poetry, and with a blinding combination of hope and self-confidence, on the group's third album. In the meantime, Stohl left the band and was replaced by **Bruce Brody**.

Although *Easter*, released in March 1978, would go on to become The Patti Smith Group's best-selling album, it included a song co-written with fellow New Jersey refugee Bruce Springsteen and was, to a large extent, just another straightforward mainstream rock'n'roll LP. "Because The Night" charted round the world and dragged *Easter* into the Top 20 behind it.

By the recording of *Wave* (released in 1979) the band were being produced by Todd Rundgren, performing a Byrds cover ("So You Wanna Be A Rock'N'Roll Star") and Patti was spooning around her latest man – **Fred "Sonic" Smith** of the MC5 (whose head honcho Wayne Kramer was doing federal time for cocaine fun). The album sold well,

🎵 PLAYLIST: PATTI SMITH

1. AIN'T IT STRANGE
from **Land 1975–2002 (Arista, 2004)**

2. BIRDLAND
from **Land 1975–2002 (Arista, 2004)**

3. FREE MONEY
from **Horses: Legacy Edition (BMG, 2005)**

4. GLORIA
from **Horses: Legacy Edition (BMG, 2005)**

5. LAND: HORSES / A THOUSAND DANCES / LA MER(DE) from **Horses: Legacy Edition (BMG, 2005)**

6. MY GENERATION
from **Horses: Legacy Edition (BMG, 2005)**

7. PISS FACTORY
from **Land 1975–2002 (Arista, 2004)**

8. PISSING IN A RIVER
from **Land 1975–2002 (Arista, 2004)**

9. REDONDO BEACH
from **Horses: Legacy Edition (BMG, 2005)**

10. ROCK 'N' ROLL NIGGER
from **Land 1975–2002 (Arista, 2004)**

charted and resulted in the end of the group. Patti and Fred wed and bred, staying out of the music biz for most of the 1980s and raising kids in the Detroit suburbs.

Patti stayed away from music until the workmanlike but uninspiring collection, *Dream Of Life* (1988). With the exception of the frankly weak opening track "People Have The Power", this set of damp soft rock was received by the public and press with massive respect but underwhelming reviews, and prompted her to retreat again.

In 1993 Patti's husband and her brother Todd died within weeks of one another. Fred and Patti had collaborated on a set of songs in the months leading up to his death, but it understandably took some time for her to return to the studio and commit them to tape. *Gone Again* saw Smith reunited with Kaye, Daugherty (who rejoined the band) and John Cale (who guested). In a way, it also handed on her baton to a new generation: saluting Kurt Cobain in "About A Boy", she also made way for a guest appearance by Jeff Buckley, then barely recognized as a rising star. The following year she returned with *Peace And Noise*, hooking up with R.E.M.'s Michael Stipe for vocals on "Last Call". Kaye and Daugherty stayed on board for *Gung Ho* (2000) and Kaye remained in the band for *Trampin'* (2004).

These days, the highlights of a Patti Smith gig will be the greatest hits, but as a consummate professional, she won't go on the road unless there's a new album to promote.

⊚ Horses (Arista, 2005)

New York City rock'n'roll at its finest. Channelling as much of the Velvet Underground's power as he could muster, John Cale wielded his mighty wizardry to make *Horses* timeless; it is just as fresh, occasionally shocking and magnificent today as it was thirty years ago.

⊚ Radio Ethiopia (Arista, 1996)

Featuring Patti on guitar and an industry-approved producer, Jack Douglas, at the controls, this album comes with all the rough edges smoothed away. The set benefits from the vast amount of room that Douglas conjures for them, but it's already sounding too mainstream for the spikyheaded masses.

⊚ Easter (Arista; 1999)

Producer Jimmy Iovine emphasized the band's confident, skilful musicianship, and coaxed career-best vocal performances from Smith herself, but the set stumbles between the mainstream East Coast balladry of the single and the off-the-wall echoes of her visceral clubland poetry performances captured in "Babelogue", without ever regaining its balance.

⊚ Land (1975–2002) (Arista, 2002)

Excellent value, double-disc retrospective.

ICONIC SINGLE:
GLORIA / MY GENERATION
(ARISTA, 1976)

The punch of the growled opening line ("Jesus died for somebody's sins, but not mine") has dissipated a little over the last three decades, but it's still unusual to hear about girl-on-girl love in pop, and virtually sacrilegious for anyone to mess about with a Van Morrison tune to this extent, so the tune stands up to be counted on those grounds alone. Just one song, but it gives you the very essence of Smith.

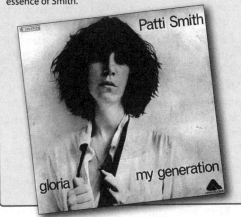

SNATCH : PATTI PALLADIN / JUDY NYLON

Formed London, 1976; disappeared sometime in the 1980s.

"JUDY NYLON'S SEDUCTIVE VOCALS ON 'THE MAN WHO COULDN'T AFFORD TO ORGY' MADE JANE BIRKIN SOUND LIKE HAYLEY MILLS."

JOHN CALE

Snatch had all the ingredients to become one of the most fascinating acts on the New Wave scene, but ended up as just a footnote.

Formed in London by two expatriate Americans, **Patti Palladin** and **Judy Nylon**, they slipped into wonderful, subversive rock'n'roll, worked with Brian Eno on a track that seemed to glorify the urban guerilla activities of the Baader-Meinhof gang and spent a deal of time in the company of Johnny Thunders – which might partially explain the lethargy that also characterizes the band's output.

Although already acquainted with one another by phone, the gals settled in London independently of one another, hooking up later via the expatriate grapevine. Huddled up in Palladin's flat in 1976, they worked up a series of demos, one of which appeared on the B-side of Brian Eno's "King's Lead Hat" single. The unsettling collage "R.A.F." – referring to Andreas Baader and Ulrike Meinhof's Red Army Faction rather than the Royal Air Force – was the result of Nylon latching onto German police tapes released in the aftermath of the gang's murder of former SS officer Dr. Hanns-Martin Schleyer. She played the tapes over an Eno-assisted background of muddy noise and searing guitars, then somehow sneaked the results to Brian.

They next showed up in early 1977 with "IRT"/"Stanley", the official Snatch debut single (they'd played with "cho-cha" as a band name, which would have pre-dated Missie Elliot's use of that particular euphemism by some thirty years). "IRT" grumbled darkly about the condition of the New York subway system and the kind of people that used it, while "Stanley" was a screaming denunciation of dirty boys and the homegrown toys they sometimes feel they need to show to lone women.

Snatch was never intended as a full-time job, and a year passed before product returned to the stores – "All I Want" troubled the lower reaches of the charts in early spring of 1978. In the meantime Palladin worked with Chris Spedding and with Wayne County And The Electric Chairs. An even longer interval kept fans waiting until April 1980 for "Shopping For Clothes" (originally a Leiber/Stoller song, but here distorted into something else entirely) and essentially, that was it.

In the end, Snatch records just stopped appearing, Palladin became ever more closely involved with Johnny Thunders, wrote and sang part of The Flying Lizards' *4th Wall* album and then mutated into a scary vampire/goth/operatic diva creature

imagined more often than seen on the early 1980s black lace'n'velvet scene. Nylon went somewhere more extreme and apart from a collaboration with Adrian Sherwood ("Pal Judy"), hasn't been seen at all for some time.

⊙ **Snatch** (Pandemonium, 1983)

The only album they ever released, cobbled together from the singles, a few odd demos and detritus swept up from Palladin's living-room carpet.

SNFU

Agreed their opinion of society in Edmonton, Canada, 1982; still running and yet to change their minds.

W hen **Mr. Chi Pig** (vocals) hooked up with **Brent Belke** (guitar), his brother **Marc "Muc" Belke** (guitars), **Warren Bidlock** (bass) and **Evan "Tadpole" Jones** (drums), they soon came to decide that "Society's No Fucking Use" and settled on the **SNFU** acronym as their band name. It's no surprise, then, to learn that they played loud, fast, aggressive skate punk with a distinctly political agenda. The fact they're still playing loud, fast, aggressive skate punk more than twenty years later probably merits some kind of award. It makes distinguishing one album from the next kinda hard though.

SNFU started out recording for BYO Records in the mid-1980s, releasing *And No One Else Wanted To Play* and *If You Swear, You'll Catch No Fish* in the same year. By 1988 and *Better Than A Stick In The Eye* they were on Cargo Records, staying there for *The Last Of The Big Time Suspenders* (1992), after which Bidlock and Jones split.

With new recruits **Rob Johnson** (bass) and **Dave Rees** (drums) safely on board, Epitaph Records stepped in to release *Something Green And Leafy This Way Comes* (1993), *The One Voted Most Likely To Succeed* (1995) and *Fyulaba* (1996), the latter produced by Dave Ogilvie of Skinny Puppy. Rees moved on and was replaced by **Sean Stubbs** (drums) but the loss of Brent Belke in 1997 was more significant.

SNFU stumbled a little before continuing as a quartet with *Let's Get It Right The First Time* (1997), still with all the power, noise and emotion, but missing a vital prop. A stopgap release on Alternative Tentacles, *The Ping Pong EP* (2000) kept the pangs at bay for fans starved of loud, fast, aggressive etc. music until the appearance in 2004 of *In The Meantime And In Between Time* on their own label, Rake Records.

⊚ The Last Of The Big Time Suspenders
(Cargo, 1992)

Loud, fast, aggressive, skate punk works best in front of a live audience, and most of this album was recorded in concert.

SNUFF

**Inhaled in London, 1986.
Yet to completely expire.**

"WE DIDN'T EVEN THINK WE WERE A PUNK BAND WHEN WE STARTED...WE THOUGHT PUNK WAS DEAD"

DUNCAN SNUFF

Good time party punks from London's dark and hostile northwestern suburbs, **Snuff** turned a taste for rowdy, boisterous sub-skinhead rave-up tunes into a sporadic sort of cult career, with their first, three-piece line-up doing their best "to make a racket and take the piss out of the charts" from the mid-80s through till 1991. Hosted by irrepressible front man **Duncan Snuff** (drums), supported by **Andy Snuff** (bass) and **Simon Snuff** (guitar) the band released a first EP, recorded a Peel session and two full-length albums in a bid to prop up the sagging remains of the big UK punk rock tent all on their own.

Snuff played everywhere that would have them, from municipal halls in Germany to club gigs in Japan until it all grew to be a bit pointless as the 90s kicked into gear. Simon left the band, which fizzled out as a result, in 1991. Andy and Duncan carried on, showering sparks off into the irresistibly named **Guns'n'Wankers** until a new influx of inspiration passed by in 1994.

Re-formed and boasting a new, richer sound thanks too **Lee Snuff** (keyboards) and **Dave "Redmond" Snuff** (trombone), they picked up where they'd left off, creating a stomping fun'n' games'n'rock'n'roll riot wherever they set up their

stall and putting out Reach (K.Records, 1995) like they'd never been away. Prolific as hellfire ever since, their output swerves from ska punk and thrash versions of popular advertising jingles from the 80s to serious hardcore statements of raw punk integrity.

Fat Mike of **NOFX** was understandably a fan, and signed them up to his Fat Wreck Chords label. With his backing, Snuff punched above their weight in the US and put up a respectable challenge to the home-grown ska-punk / party-punk bands. Similar support from Japan's **Pizza Of Death** label sewed up the Asian market, leaving the band's own **10 past 12** records to deal with domestic demand.

Snuff's maniacal live performances will never be totally pinned down by mere recording technology but if the studio albums intrigue you, then the Kilburn/Caught in Session double album (Golf, 2003) is worth searching out. Catch them next time they decide to sling a set together.

⊚ Demmamussabebonk (Fat Wreck, 1996)

Named in imitation of Duncan's Greek landlord saying "They must be bonkers" (Britspeak for crazy), this is perhaps Snuff's best-intentioned album – that is, all the band showed up at the same time, more or less sober and stayed that way long enough to record it. It's still a lovely, ramshackle, misguided mess of course, but one you could realistically consider playing to the local Women's Institute.

⊚ Six of One and Half a Dozen of the Other: 1986-2002 (10 Past 12, 2005)

Fantastic compilation that compresses their prolific history into a 2-disc set. With fifty tracks spread over the two discs, there's enough here for several sessions of outraged amusement. While the collection includes the band's best original tracks and their more respectful attempts at covering **The Specials'** "You're Wondering Now" and "Do Nothing", listeners are recommended their classic funny cover versions including: "Whatever Happened To The Likely Lads", "I Think We're Alone Now", "Don't Fear The Reaper", "Any Old Iron", "Hokey Cokey" and the unforgettable " Will Survive".

SONIC YOUTH

Formed NYC, 1981; still holding that pose.

Most of the bands in punk-rock history would be happy to confess their indebtedness to the primal stomp of The Stooges and the tainted avant-garde artistry of The Velvet **Underground**, but none have even come close to **Sonic Youth** in triumphantly welding the free-form aesthetics of the former to the gritty urban short stories of the latter. Sonic Youth's studied cool and dedication to substance-over-appearance has made them the NYC band that all others secretly aspire to be, and by keeping up the forced march pressure by continually cutting the mustard as creative, intelligent musicians, they've outpaced, outlasted and outclassed their competition for the past 25 years.

Thurston Moore (guitar) and **Kim Gordon** (bass) were already "an item" when they began hanging out with the noise merchants of Manhattan at the start of the 80s. **Glenn Branca**'s No Wave stylings – an unappetizing mess of jazzy free-noise and pretentious guitar effects – tweaked their antennae and, recruiting **Lee Ranaldo** (guitar) **Anne DeMarinis** (keyboards) and **Richard Edson** (drums) to the team, set up Sonic Youth in 1981.

Ditching the traditional verse-chorus-verse structures of the pop/rock crew, Sonic Youth made their debut at the appropriately named NOISE festival, a summer event organized by Thurston and Kim – whose existing reputation on the city's avant-garde scene helped win the new outfit further gigs and sympathetic press coverage. Influential contacts aside, it was the band's undeniable raw power – boosted further by Lee's habit of using drumsticks to play guitar – their intensity and po-faced seriousness that wowed the crowds and took them, very swiftly, out of the underground and onto the international stage.

A surprisingly instant hit with the NYC elite, and having lost DeMarinis, the remaining four-piece band headed into the studio to lay out their five-track debut – a mini-album simply titled *Sonic Youth* and released on Branca's Neutral Records in 1982.

By the recording of *Confusion Is Sex* in 1983, Sonic Youth had replaced Edson with **Bob Bert** (drums), whose more conventional playing style added some much needed rigour to the sound. He stuck with them through the first European tour later that year where, hooking up with like minds in Germany, they recorded and released the

Sonic Youth, looking quiet and old.

▣ PLAYLIST: SONIC YOUTH

1. **BURNING SPEAR** from **Sonic Youth: Remastered & Expanded (Universal, 2006)**

2. **I DON'T WANT TO PUSH IT** from **Sonic Youth: Remastered & Expanded (Universal, 2006)**

3. **INHUMAN** from **Confusion Is Sex (Geffen, 2005)**

4. **KOOL THING** from **Goo: Deluxe Edition (Polydor, 2005)**

5. **LOUD AND SOFT** from **Sonic Youth: Remastered & Expanded (Universal, 2006)**

6. **SHAKING HELL** from **Confusion Is Sex (Geffen, 2005)**

7. **SHE IS NOT ALONE** from **Sonic Youth: Remastered & Expanded (Universal, 2006)**

8. **SUGAR KANE** from **Dirty (Geffen, 1995)**

9. **TEENAGE RIOT** from **Daydream Nation (Geffen, 1993)**

10. **YOUTH AGAINST FASCISM** from **Dirty (Geffen, 1995)**

Kill Yr Idols EP (1983). Keeping the fans guessing, the band's next project was a tape collage of live concert recordings – *Sonic Death* – released in 1984 on cassette through Thurston's own Ecstatic Peace! label, and not really recommended to anyone except the hardest of hardcore completists.

Sonic Youth went global the next year, with the strength of their material convincing British indie entrepreneur **Paul Smith** (head of DoubleVision records in London) to establish a new label – Blast First Records – to release *Bad Moon Rising* and the *Death Valley '69* EP. Replacing the drummer for the final time (Bert went to join Pussy Galore while new boy **Steve Shelley** – ex Crucifucks – is still with them), Sonic Youth turned their attention to world domination.

Their mid-80s sound had matured beyond the spoiled-brat squawkings of the New York No Wave that had served them well at the outset of their career, with the new stuff giving the band's widened audience a more conventional – if still wilfully underground – rock groove to follow. There were plenty of atonal and indecent assaults on the instruments (Thurston's taste for playing his guitar with a screwdriver had never deserted him), and the tunes still required repeated listenings before they revealed their secrets, but the package was just that little bit easier to swallow.

Capitalizing on their unimpeachable credentials as the grand poobahs of the US underground, they stunned the alt:rock generation with *EVOL* (1986), *Sister* (1987) and *Daydream Nation* (1988), the latter giving them an international hit of sorts with "Teenage Riot". As the 80s petered out, SY moved at last to a " real" major label (Geffen / DGC),

delivering *Goo* (1990) and touring with **Neil Young**. The crossover between these two monsters of rock resulted in a boost to Neil's coolness factor, a new audience of hairy old rockers for The Youth, and a CD of noodling effects and feedback for Young's *Arc:Weld* triple-disc set.

Neil's straightforward rock'n'roll influence coloured *Dirty* (1992), a **Butch Vig** production that also tipped its hat to the grunge drooling down America's musical chops from Seattle, with "Youth Against Fascism" and "Sugar Kane" giving them their first MTV successes, and introducing the couch potato generation to a taste of how exciting it can be out on the edges of rock'n'roll. Moving on from their interesting if doomed **Ciccone Youth** side-outfit – which released *The Whitey Album* (Geffen, 1992) as a big underground joke – Thurston and Lee took a break from SY in 1992 to form, record and release *Dim Stars*, another side project, with **Richard Hell**.

Vig stayed on board throughout *Experimental Jet Set, Trash And No Star* (1994), which charted around the world (going top 10 in the UK) but collected lukewarm reviews, and he was replaced for *Washing Machine* in 1995, a mid-life sea-change album that looked back to the Youth's Lower East-Side past as much as it peered into their more melodic, introspective future; with closing track "The Diamond Sea" stretching effortlessly out to nineteen minutes.

Since headlining the Lollapalooza tour that same year, Sonic Youth have had permanent seats on the music biz gravy train, commanding enough clout to halt it at the most obscure crossings and spend time noodling around in their own noisy experimental filth whenever the fancy takes them. *A Thousand Leaves* (1998; the first set to see new band member **Jim O'Rourke** on board) and *Ghosts & Flowers* (2000) were comparatively mainstream recordings, with *Murray Street* (2002) and *Sonic Nurse* (2004) demonstrating that even this far down the road, there were still worthwhile juices to be squeezed out of the avant garde's husk.

Their most recent outing, *SYR 6* (2005), was a collaboration with **Tim Barnes** (percussionist) and a return to "in concert" material, demonstrating their continuing healthy contempt for melody. Blended with a swaggering, cooler-than-thou, obsessive self-belief, this distaste for taking the easy way out has kept the Youth on top of the tree for more than twenty years. Ditching convention in favour of cacophony and icy cold vocals, de-tuned guitars, performance-art and No Wave noise, they've been the benchmark for the US underground from day one of their career.

⊚ Sonic Youth **(Geffen 2006 reissue)**

The band's debut is still the strongest assertion of their punk-rock credentials, though presented in a distinctly NYC, left-field kinda way. The set has recently been reissued with a bunch of early live recordings that are not to be missed.

⊚ Confusion Is Sex **(Geffen, 2005 reissue)**

Wild, unconfined wandering stoned mess – with standouts "(She's in a) Bad Mood" and a cover of "I Wanna Be Your Dog". It now comes with the *Kill Yr Idols* EP included as bonus tracks.

⊚ EVOL **(Geffen, 2003 reissue)**

The band's most satisfactory full-length recording sees them relaxing a little into the comfy chairs at the front of the avant-garde bus. "Death to Our Freinds" is eye-piercingly intense, leading into the hellfire chiaroscuro of "Expressway To Yr. Skull" and "Shadow of a Doubt".

⊚ Daydream Nation
(Blast First/Enigma/Geffen, 1993)

A double album on original release, and still double the fun of a recording half its length, this shows the band cruising sweetly between the cool beauty of "Teen Age Riot" and "Kissability" and the more robust joys of "Silver Rocket", "Total Trash" and "Eric's Trip".

Speakeasy

(Now Cameo) 48-50 Margaret Street, London W1

Opened in 1966 as a watering hole for the glittering elite of Swinging London, **The Speakeasy** was established in direct competition to the better-known Bag O'Nails, a few hundred metres away, just off Carnaby Street. The Speakeasy's gimmick was its Chicago Gangster / Prohibition Era decor and, assisted by its prime location, the club attracted musicians and scenesters of various persuasions from the clubs, theatres and BBC studios in the vicinity.

When the movers and shakers of London clubland moved on to venues new and more exciting, the Speakeasy lost a lot of its shimmer and glam appeal. **Billy Murcia** (Billy Doll of The New York Dolls) downed his last few drinks in the bar after the band's outstanding success at Wembley in 1972, and **Pete Townshend** practiced the worst public stages of his alcohol problem there (after telling **Steve Jones** and **Paul Cook** of the Pistols that they were the only hope for rock music…and that he loved

them and that they were his best mates…probably).

It was a convenient, late-opening venue for the city's first punk stars, although not always as welcoming or secure as they might have wished: **Joe Strummer** received a kicking from some Teddy Boys in the toilets and a few months later BBC TV and radio presenter **"Whispering Bob" Harris** was given a seeing to by **Sid Vicious**, **Johnny Rotten** and others.

Having been threatened with death for various sins including not featuring The Pistols on his BBC television outlet *The Old Grey Whistle Test*, Harris went to his management for advice. His management also looked after **Peter Frampton** (whose *Comes Alive* album was selling almost as quickly as the pressing plant could turn it out). Frampton's protest, passed to record company A&M by the management team resulted in the Pistols losing their second major label contract.

SPLODGENESS ABOUNDS

Formed London, 1976, and abounding in splodgeness ever since.

"WE'RE WORKING-CLASS TOO, ONLY WHEREAS SOME BANDS SING ABOUT PRISON AND THE DOLE, WE SING ABOUT PILCHARDS AND BUM."

MAX SPLODGE, 1980

Splodgenessabounds started out as a good-time punk-rock band with a taste for bad seaside humour, fart jokes and songs celebrating the ridiculous. Led by madcap vocalist Max Splodge, the band toured the pub/club circuit for a couple of years before striking chart-topping success with "Two Pints Of Lager And A Packet Of Crisps". Record companies began to ply the band (and Max in particular) with ego-boosting chunks of money, ample brown-nosing and the kind of industry-standard persuaders that made the music business the epitome of corruption. Subsequent success came in the shape of a Rolf Harris cover, "Two Little Boys", and appearances on *Top Of The Pops*.

Unsurprisingly, limited success went to Max's head and after he had sacked the whole band a couple of times, Splodgeness's time in the spotlight was over. A bitter man, Max recruited another bunch of Splodgers and ekes out an existence of sorts playing on the revival circuit to audiences consisting mainly of ageing, tattooed drunks.

⊙ **Splodgenessabounds (Captain Oi!, 2001)**

This weighty single-disc compilation of thirty rowdy tracks of riotous nonsense celebrates those bodily functions that others fear to mention, and playing it through from "Malcolm Opera" to "Brown Paper" is way too much for a single sitting. Perhaps not the record to put on unless the party's not being held at your house and you don't have much time for the host – playing it is likely to cause grown adults to bounce around like fools punching one another or knocking over the shelving, a fight may start, someone may even set light to their own farts; it's that kind of a disc.

SQUEEZE

Formed London, 1974; still going

"I'M ACTUALLY QUITE A DECENT CHAP AND THE REST OF THE GROUP ARE WANKERS."

JOOLS HOLLAND

Monstrously successful worldwide and much beloved of middle-aged Americans (who must have enormous difficulties with some of the lyrics), **Squeeze** were the youngest pub-rockers on the circuit when punk happened – skilled musicians with stagecraft galore, a pair of decent songwriters and snappy enough to leap onto the brand-new bandwagon.

The essence of Squeeze has always been **Chris Difford** (guitar/vocals) and **Glenn Tilbrook** (vocals/guitar), who first responded to Difford's shop-window ad for like-minded musicians. Together they put together a band with Tilbrook's old pal from a previous band, **Jools Holland** (keyboards), **Harry Kakoulli** (bass) and **Paul Gunn** (drums), naming themselves after the last, rotten Velvet Underground album.

While gigging around the pubs of South London they replaced Gunn with **Gilson Lavis** (drums), who'd previously worked with Chuck Berry. Kitted out with a fine set of their own compositions, dues paid and settled down as a unit, they signed up with **Miles Copeland** (see The Police) who introduced them to John Cale, who produced their debut *Packet Of Three* EP released on Mark P's label Deptford Fun City in 1977.

The positive response received pushed Squeeze up the ladder from pub-rockers into the sort of act that major labels would sign, and although still recovering from getting their fingers burned by the Sex Pistols, A&M finally made the right offer. Recording the first album, *Squeeze*, however, almost finished their career. The experienced but eccentric Cale was again at the controls, and although he never convinced them to call their first album "Gay Guys", he did talk them into writing a completely new set of material – unrehearsed and unrefined in front of their loyal, but fiercely critical home crowd.

The new songs worked to some extent; they captured some of the essence of life in London, but had more in common with the traditions of British music hall and the comedy ballads of the 1960s than with boredom, anarchy or destroying the establishment by means of swearwords and strange clothes. They fitted perfectly into the quirky British pop world, loved by the mums and dads for their cheeky references to illicit kisses and crafty pints of beer, and produced songs of genuine charm, written with skill and affection for the life they described. Not very punk at all.

They went on to record a swathe of singles that enjoyed immense success. The subsequent recordings, personnel changes and the brouhaha of international pop success are of no interest to us, and we shall, therefore ignore them.

◉ **Squeeze (A&M, 1998)**

Carrying most of the original *Packet Of Three* EP, this is their only genuinely "punk" release.

◉ **Cool For Cats (A&M, 1998)**

Start of the band's endless stream of hits, or anagram thereof, depending on your point of view.

STIFF LITTLE FINGERS

Raised in Belfast, 1977; rigor mortis set in 1982. Revived 1987, but getting limper as the years drift past.

Jake Burns (sore-throat vocals/guitar) had a gig lined up. He'd had to set it up himself because, even as the golden year of 1977 drew to a close, local promoters were still wary of the term "punk rock". But Burns was ready to move, having formed a new group with his pals from **Highway Star** – one of the bands playing well-intentioned cover versions on the Belfast and district circuit – sticking with **Henry Cluney** (vocals/guitar) and **Brian Faloon** (drums), and tracking down **Ali McMordie** (bass/vocals) as replacement after their former bass player left.

The old band name didn't fit the new line-up's punky image. They settled on **The Fast**, only to find out at the last minute that there was already a band in the States working under that name. In desperation, and with the printer on the phone demanding to know what name to put on the bill,

Burns read a song title off the new **Vibrators** album and they became **Stiff Little Fingers** for life. They still needed a little pizzazz, though, to launch them into a crowded UK marketplace. Enter Gordon Ogilvie, the man from the *Daily Express*.

Ogilvie was in the audience for Burns' self-starter of a gig, and stepping in as manager, encouraged the band to do the punk-rock thing of singing about what you know, pointing to the "Troubles" in Belfast as a source of inspiration. Ogilvie stayed with the band until 1983, establishing their own Rigid Digits label and helping with the design of the press kit for their first single, "Suspect Device". Packaging a recording to look like a parcel bomb

Stiff Little Fingers: giving it their all.

was guaranteed to gain publicity and garner a little outrage in the sillier newspapers; fortunately the song itself was fiercely strong, from a band with the talent and dedication to back it up. Jake roared out the lyrics over a storm of guitars, the song had a classic pop structure with a sing-along chorus and hooks galore. John Peel loved it, and with his airplay and support the band landed a deal with Rough Trade.

With Ogilvie established as co-lyricist, "Alternative Ulster", the band's second single, also focused on the Troubles, and reaffirmed Stiff Little Fingers' strictly non-sectarian stance towards them. Their songs turned out to be violent, angry and just as anti-establishment as anything produced by The Clash (the band with which they were most often compared), but unlike their music, SLF's was based upon a genuinely deadly street life, where going for a simple beer in the wrong pub at the wrong time could put you in line for a kicking or being blown up by a nail-bomb.

They linked up with The Tom Robinson Band for a late 1978 tour of the mainland, moving their base to London for the recording of *Inflammable Material* the following year. Faloon stayed in Ireland, giving up his seat to Sheffield's **Jim Reilly** (drums), who pounded forty shades of green out of the kit on the third single, "Gotta Getaway". Still a favourite with the live audience, it strikes a chord on the heartstrings of every expat, Irish or otherwise

Signing to Chrysalis in 1979 gave the band the financial security to put together a searing follow-up to their first album. Typically, they delivered two in short order. With "Straw Dogs" announcing the new, louder, faster, better band, and taking them into the singles charts, *Nobody's Heroes* (1980) continued to shout against the world, banging down fists and kicking over the furniture (but including the tongue-in-cheek beauty of "You Can't Say Crap On The Radio") whereas *Go For It* (1981) was a less strident release that echoed the experience of the diaspora in a London suspicious of anyone with an Irish accent. The anger remained, but the new maturity was beginning to alienate the more hidebound elements of their audience, and new fans were increasingly hard to find.

Hanx! followed towards the end of the year, an exciting document of the guys at the height of their powers, playing to a delirious Christmas crowd and going some way to explaining the wild devotion they attracted. Reilly left the band before the third studio album, *Now Then* (1982), and was replaced by **Brian "Dolphin" Taylor** (drums), ex-Tom Robinson Band, who'd come to know SLF from touring with them. He found himself part of a group that was losing its momentum in the face of a dwindling audience and early 1980s ennui, experimenting with a broader-based, more pop-oriented sound and ready to fall apart. Confronted with lousy sales and almost zero press interest in 1983, Burns announced: "*Now Then* was to my mind the best album we have made. But it is also unfortunately the best I think we will ever make. So I have decided to call it a day."

Re-forming in 1987 the band were able to celebrate their tenth anniversary in style, gigging round the country to heroes' welcomes and easily fulfilling Burns's stated aim of making enough to get back to Ireland for Christmas. Subsequent tours, generally culminating in a hugely inebriated yuletide bash in Glasgow, yielded a series of live albums but little new material. Following the surprise collapse of The Jam, and McMordie's decision to go and find a proper job, **Bruce Foxton** signed on, recording *Flags And Emblems* with the band in 1991.

Soon after this, Burns fell out with Cluney, and Cluney left the band. SLF continue playing the revival circuit, and recorded *Tinderbox* (1997), with Cluney's role being taken by **Dave Sharp** or **Ian McCallum** (both guitar). Taylor eventually left as well, making room for **Steve Grantley** (drums) who had played for Burns' **Big Wheel** side project during the 1980s. *Hope Street* (1999) was something of a return to their old punk form, but was much too little, far too late; *Handheld And Rigidly Digital* (2000), a box set of live recordings, had its moments but was really one for friends and family of the band only.

With McCallum signed on as a permanent part of the team, SLF returned to the studio for *Guitar And Drum* (2003) and the punk-rock bandwagon rolled ever onward. With no reason to give up the ghost, and tickets to Ireland not growing on trees, they'll probably be playing near you next December.

◉ **Inflammable Material (EMI, 2001)**

The most original and powerful album the band ever made. Each song is a tightly focused burst of anger or frustration. The

ICONIC SINGLE:
SUSPECT DEVICE / WASTED LIFE
(RIGID DIGITS / ROUGH TRADE, 1978)

Opening with the solo vocal and best opening lines of the band's career "Inflammable material is planted in my head / It's a suspect device that has left two thousand dead", the drums kick in together with all the guitars at once. Corny as hell, but still delivering as much energy and excitement now as it did back then.

willing but ham-fisted production gets in the way of the tunes here and there, but there's nothing that can't be fixed by turning up the volume. The reissue comes with the original mix of "Suspect Device" and the first part of an interview with Burns from 2001 as bonus tracks.

⊙ Nobody's Heroes (EMI, 2001)

Meatier, beatier, bigger and bouncier in all directions, SLF discover the joys of top-notch kit and a well-equipped studio. Now includes the second part of the interview with Burns.

⊙ Hanx! (EMI, 2001)

One of the best live albums to come out of UK punk. The reissue includes the third part of the Burns interview.

⊙ Go For It (EMI; 2004)

Although some of the fire in their bellies had been quenched, the group's rage continued to smoulder. Recorded by a more mature group of angry young men, the tracks tend to complain rather than demand destruction. The reissue includes the fourth part of the Burns interview, in which Jake talks about the album.

Stiff Record Label

The best-known of the British independents associated with punk, Stiff Records (1979–84) were neither the first nor the most successful. The legend derives from some really lucky signings, the personnel at the top and a talent for some truly awful puns.

Formed in 1976 by a pair of veteran insiders blooded in the pub-rock boom, **David Robinson** and **Jake Rivera** (a suitably shark-like pseudonym adopted by the otherwise harmless Andrew Jakeman), Stiff prided itself on being "The World's Most Flexible Record Label", and found room for the likes of Rachel Sweet and Kirsty MacColl alongside the more predictable angst of **Elvis Costello**, the gruff misanthropy of **Ian Dury** or the noisy energy of **The Damned**.

Rivera's background as manager of Dr. Feelgood (the most unpredictable bunch of guitar-slinging bad boys to escape Essex in years) meshed with Robinson's more laid-back experience working for Brinsley Schwartz, and gave the label a wide and welcoming embrace that appealed to the new punk bands (suspicious as always of "the man") and weirder left-field mob alike. **Nick Lowe** represented a little of both worlds and was the ideal candidate for the label's opening salvo "So It Goes", released as BUY-1.

As the year unrolled and punk picked up speed, Stiff found itself deluged with demos, and new acts were signing up, shooting into the studio and out on tour to promote their new record with bewildering speed. When The Damned and Elvis Costello started bringing in some reasonable revenue, the guys finally found time to sit back and inspect the monstrous thing they'd created.

Whereas the label's earliest releases relied on snappy slogans, cheeky advertising in the music press, and the kind of promotional T-shirt that your mother wouldn't wash for you because of the naughty words printed on it, subsequent flurries of A&R activity meant that the main brains behind the company found less time to devote to the artists and the music they were making.

When Rivera and Costello split off to form Radar Records in 1977 (taking a few other names from the Stiff roster with them) things began to fall apart, but Robinson rallied his forces, signed **Ian Dury** and **Madness**, and took the label to new levels of commercial success, without any need for dubious slogans, hilarious advertising or much wit of any kind. When Dury fell from fashion, and Madness moved elsewhere, the old bandwagon started to look really shabby and, by 1984 Stiff had been absorbed by Island Records.

Though long seen mainly as a punk-rock outlet, first home for The Damned, The Adverts, Richard Hell, Plasmatics and Pogues, as "the world's most flexible label", Stiff had plenty of time for other styles of music, ranging from the horribly saccharine tones of Rachel Sweet to the bitter pop of Jona Lewie. Covering a respectable swathe of "respectable" genres from the plain vanilla R&B of Dave Edmunds, Graham Parker and Any Trouble to the heavier, darker material of Larry Wallis paid the rent and the wages, leaving a little over in the kitty to play with.

Whether they ever broke even on their Lene Lovich, Tracy Ullman or Sean Tyla releases is, unless you were a shareholder, irrelevant. What matters is the degree of risk they were prepared to accept; putting out Devo – four wimps in bathing shorts – in the middle of a storm of punk took some nerve, and who but Stiff would have given Wreckless Eric (still living with his mum, Wreckless Doreen at the time) a chance?

THE STOOGES

Formed Michigan USA 1967, disbanded 1974, re-formed 2003.

"WE HAD... A SWEEPING SOUND, LIKE MONGOLIAN HORSEMEN CHARGING IN, THOUSANDS OF THEM, LITTLE TARTARS WITH SWORDS, FREQUENCIES ONLY A GEEK CAN HEAR"

IGGY TRIES TO DEFINE THE STOOGES IN I NEED MORE

James Osterberg had been **Iggy Pop** for some time when he returned from his *Wanderjahr* soaking up the blues in Chicago. Inspired by Jim Morrisson's shaman-like performance at a Doors' gig, Iggy formed **The Psychedelic Stooges** with his pal **Ron Asheton** (guitar). Recruiting Ron's brother **Scott Asheton** (Drums) and another pal from the neighbourhood, **Dave Alexander** (bass), the new band set off on a blue-collar drug-assisted voyage in search of wild experience, a deeper musical communication with the audience and having a good time all the time.

After a try-out playing a student party on Halloween 1967, they played their first real gig in March 1968, and set about picking up a local fan-base. Detroit and district were famous for the high standards demanded by the locals – reputedly the toughest crowd to please in the whole USA. They found themselves "adopted" by **The MC5**, and through their support, projected too far, too soon onto the music biz treadmill that would ultimately macerate them and spit out the results onto the kerb.

Danny Fields was fascinated by the macho posture and political radicalism of The MC5, and he naturally enough bumped into their "kid brothers" in **The Stooges**; having dropped the "psychedelic" from the name, they played the same venues, frequently on the same bill for the entertainment of the fearsome Motor City audi-ence. Enraptured by the power of their music and the weird, ballet dancer / street hustler antics of Iggy on stage, he took them under his manage-rial wing and signed them, along with their big brother band, to Elektra. Soon **Iggy and The Stooges** (another name they appeared under) had been levered out of the rustbelt and into the pages of teen pin-up magazines.

By the time Danny and the label made their acquaintance, the boys had melded, in the face of hostile reception and shared interest in getting pleasantly wasted, into a rock'n'roll gang, with slang terms, rituals and in-jokes of their own. Proudly certain that theirs was the correct musi-cal direction in which to be headed, the boys took little guidance from their appointed producer John Cale, turning out their self-titled manifesto on the way things were gonna be, despite his input, rather than because of it.

Though *The Stooges* sold relatively few copies on release, in retrospect it has grown to be regarded as the first great American punk album. Hyperbole apart, it does contain some extraordinary music – including "I Wanna Be Your Dog", "No Fun", "1969" and "Not Right" – all quite unlike anything else released in 1969. The album signalled an end to the "peace & love" smoke screen being boosted to the rock audience: the Stooges had outgrown acid and, in the face of rioting on the streets, mass shipments of draftees to Vietnam, unemployment, urban decay and endless interviews with bubbleg-um pop magazines, had turned to drinking spirits and gobbling downers.

In Iggy's own words though, "by 1970 things were going very smoothly". *Fun House*, the band's second full-length recording had sold badly but within record company expectations, bringing the band's live set, as near unchanged as possible, to the studio (including the painful experience of their lengthy free-jazz-noise workout "L.A. Blues" that closed off the show). The Stooges were mak-ing reasonable money – enough for Iggy to hang out in New York, and meet up with Andy Warhol, Lou Reed and **Bowie** – and they appeared to be liv-ing the ideal rock'n'roll life. Iggy's stage act – partly enabled by his taking to the stage incapable of feel-ing pain – had become notorious, involving broken glass, microphones smashed into his teeth, peanut butter smeared all over his torso, nudity and stage diving. They were a big name on the live circuit.

They even had their own equivalent of **The Monkees'** "pad" – the aforementioned *Fun House* – where a caravan of dealers, roadies and deluded young women with romance on their minds trod ruts into the path. In the wake of the second album and the royalties it accrued, somebody introduced heroin into the mixture and instantly, The Stooges' creativity went into deepest cold storage. A few months down the line, the record company sent an executive suit to see how preparations for the third album were progressing. His report to head office led to the band losing their contract forthwith and the end of that particular road.

Two years later, having kicked heroin for a nasty pill problem, mental illness and a cure based apparently on the joys of playing golf, Iggy renewed his relationship with Bowie. Soon it had progressed beyond simple friendship to a shared interest in the same management company, MainMan, which fronted a still drug-dishevelled Stooges – now minus Dave Alexander, who'd retired, but plus **James Williamson** (guitar) – the money to fly to London and make *Raw Power*.

Scrabbling together a set of dark, powerful rockers from recent experience and drug need, the new line-up (Ron now playing bass) tended to show up, play their instruments then head off to Chelsea to find some relief, leaving Bowie in charge of the mix. When it came out – with Bowie's midas touch of a name all over the sleeve and reviews – sales, and content, were better than could have been expected. Bowie's technical skills as a producer, his personal taste in sound and coke-addled sense of proportion however had resulted in a tinny, gutless mix that detracted from the awe-inspiring heights of "Search & Destroy" and the title track – although without ruining them completely.

The band however, was in shambles. Struggling to deal with booze, drugs, egos and financial squabbling finally saw them playing their last gig at Detroit's Michigan Palace in January 1974 to an audience largely comprising the hefty brigade from a local biker gang. They'd decided, in the face of a degree of provocation from a big-mouthed Iggy interviewed on local radio, to initiate new members by setting them loose on the band. The gig was taped and released a few years later, with excerpts from a similar performance of the same period, as *Metallic K.O.* – the only live album where the sound of missiles whistling past the

singer's ear has been recorded. It showcases a band going through the motions – magnificently, but without the inspiration or deadly beauty that had inspired their teen fans, and without the intestinal fortitude to go and round up an older audience more in tune with their own new interests.

Iggy's solo career took off and flew for a few short years before he plunged to earth again, clean and sober but uninspired and delivering a set of average middle-of-the-road (by his standards) releases that occupied much of the 80s and 90s (see p.241). The Ashetons went on to form **Destroy All Monsters** – a band with a far better name than reputation or set list, and James Williamson sporadically showed up to hang onto Iggy's coat tails for a few months before slipping off again into the dark and night-time he preferred.

The story could have ended there, but what a bummer that would have been. Fortunately, we can for once relish a happy-ish ending for, in 2003, Iggy re-formed The Stooges, pulling Ron and Scott off their mum's couch and back, first, into the studio to perform on his *Skull Ring* album, then onto the road for a Stooges world tour that saw the Asheton brothers (accompanied by **Mike Watt**, ex-Minutemen on bass, in place of Dave, deceased) finally relishing the kind of applause the audience who'd grown to love them thought they deserved. Playing *Fun House* from beginning to end (with the brilliant tweak of bringing on **Steven Mackay** to re-create his ear-splitting tenor sax jazznoise that closes "L.A. Blues"), followed by a greatest hits set, and fronted by the whip-like, uber-supple, strangely ageless beauty of the Ig, The Stooges were an inspiration to all who saw them.

Their legacy includes a raft of "rarities" albums of dubious worth, and live recordings some of appalling quality. Apart from the three studio albums below, the DVD *Live In Detroit* is the only recommended extra.

◉ **The Stooges (Warner, 2005)**

Remastered and expanded to two discs' worth of highly enthusiastic, fiercely aggressive Detroit rock, The Stooges' first recording glistens and sparkles with great music including "1969", "No Fun", "Real Cool Time", "Little Doll".

◉ **Fun House (Warner, 2005)**

Having had the same treatment as the first album, *Fun House* is now an even more startling set. "Down On The Street", "Loose", "T.V. Eye", "Dirt", "1970" and "Fun House / L.A. Blues" are joined by a complete disc of alternate takes and otherwise unheard items including "Slide" and take #2 and #22 of "Loose".

⦿ Raw Power (Sony 1997)

No extras, not remastered, but just look at the tracks it does contain, then run to the record store to pick up "Search and Destroy", "Gimme Danger", "Your Pretty Face Is Going To Hell", "Penetration", "Raw Power", "I Need Somebody", "Shake Appeal" and "Death Trip"

THE STRANGLERS

Went full throttle in Chiddington, Sussex, 1974. Still hanging around.

"...SOMETIMES THEY SOUND LIKE THE DOORS, OTHER TIMES LIKE TELEVISION, BUT THEY'VE GOT AN ID OF THEIR OWN."

MARK P, SNIFFIN' GLUE

When punk kicked off in the UK, **The Stranglers** were ready. Older than the competition, they had songwriting and gigging experience to spare, a pre-formed image and a ready-formed taste for the dark side of life that endeared them to their new audience of bored teenagers and wild, wild youth.

Hugh Cornwell (guitar/vocals), **Jean-Jacques Burnel** (bass/vocals), **Dave Greenfield** (keyboards) and **Jet Black** (drums) first worked together pre-punk as The Guildford Stranglers (named for the nearest town of any size to their village base), lurking from pub to pub on the local circuit, scaring the drinkers with their intricate Doors-like keyboard trills, butch backing vocals and psychedelic imagery. When punk showed up, The Stranglers were co-opted onto a bandwagon that would otherwise have appeared virtually empty.

Audiences took to The Stranglers as soon as they made the move up to London's new clubs, and were prepared to excuse the long hair, guitar solos and extreme age of the band members (some of whom were approaching 40) in exchange for evenings of visceral grinding bass, caveman grunts, clever guitar work and some great sing-along lyrics. The guys fell out with the music press early

on, however, and their material never achieved the appreciation or reviews that it deserved.

United Artists were easier to convince, and signed the band at the end of 1976 on the strength of their early demos and rapidly growing fan-base (boosted by The Stranglers' first major-league gigs, supporting The Ramones, and later Patti Smith), and putting them into a proper studio with producer **Martin Rushent** to record "London Lady" / "(Get A) Grip (On Yourself)". Released at the end of January 1977, the two tracks neatly summed up the band's dubious attitude to the liberated female and their perennial complaining about "the biz". *IV Rattus Norvegicus* hit the stores in April, but it was the release of "Peaches" / "Go Buddy Go" that launched the controversy that surrounded them for the remainder of their earliest career.

The original version of the A-side featured the words "shit" and "clitoris", while the B-side was a cheerful ode to drug abuse and cheap meaningless sex. Although a more radio-friendly mix was rushed to the broadcasters in time for the single to make it into the charts, by the time it arrived, everyone who cared knew The Stranglers were on the right side, and only those who'd never understand were taking them seriously. "Bring On The Nubiles" and "Choosey Suzie", for example, also contained some outrageous ideas expressed in very dodgy language, but they showed only one facet of the lads' all-round evil personae – this band dressed all in black from almost the very beginning, selected a rat as their logo, sang about life "down in the sewer", did that awful jokey line about Christ on the cross "just hangin' around"... It was hard to join in the vocals without wearing a silly grin.

Despite having the reputation of being the most evil band on the scene, there was a distinctly camp side to The Stranglers too: providing the backing for a very posh vocalist was just one of their little jokes. "Mony Mony" / "Mean To Me", a quickie single by the band's "secret" side project **Celia And The Mutations**, appeared in July and sold to the curious. **Celia Gollin** and Burnel recorded a follow-up later in the year ("You Better Believe Me" / "Round And Round"), which performed even worse and sold only to the easily persuaded. *No More Heroes* stomped up the charts on release in July, mixing old live favourites such as "I Feel Like A Wog" and "Peasant In The Big Shitty" with new material that included their tribute to their arch-fan "Dagenham Dave".

"Straighten Out"/"Something Better Change" took the band into the charts again towards the end of the year, giving them a top-ten position during the highly profitable Christmas period. However, it was the sex and violence stories that they accumulated in 1977 that made them into one of the tabloids' most hated acts. Camp or not, the appearance on stage of topless dancing girls was generally frowned upon, especially at an open-air gig in Battersea Park. At about the same time, Cornwell was busted for a T-shirt logo spoofing the Ford Motor Company's intellectual property with another four-letter F-word, and they fell out big time with the Raggere (Swedish hooligans with a taste for British punk blood).

When "Five Minutes" cruised coolly out of the studio in early 1978, it sounded like a plea for respite, and when *Black And White* appeared in May that year, despite its excellent quality production, skilled songwriting and note-perfect musicianship,

The Stranglers were no longer a punk band. "Nice And Sleazy" / "Shut Up" pressed a few of the right buttons, but the rest of the new set saw the band returning to their soft-rock roots. Bacharach and David's "Walk On By" never sounded as opiatedly uncaring as it did in The Stranglers' version, but young spikyheads were confused as to why their favourites should be recording that aged crap in the first place.

A stopgap live album, *Live (X-Cert)*, released in February 1979 and partly recorded at the controversial Battersea Park open-air gig mentioned above, kept the old-school fans satisfied, but by September and the release of *The Raven*, it was clear that the lads had interests beyond the parameters of punk.

The Stranglers worked the music business treadmill without a break throughout the eighties, even finding time for a few solo albums, knocking out the product and touring in the face of narcotics busts (Cornwell, 1980), inciting riots (the whole band, Nice, France, 1980), equipment theft (US,

Stranglers; in black, natch.

🎵 PLAYLIST: THE STRANGLERS

1. FIVE MINUTES from **Peaches: the Very Best of the Stranglers (Liberty, 2002)**

2. GOLDEN BROWN from **Peaches: the Very Best of the Stranglers (Liberty, 2002)**

3. (GET A) GRIP (ON YOURSELF) from **Peaches: the Very Best of the Stranglers (Liberty, 2002)**

4. HANGING AROUND from **IV Rattus Norvegicus (EMI, 2001)**

5. LONDON LADY from **IV Rattus Norvegicus (EMI, 2001)**

6. NICE 'N' SLEAZY from **Peaches: the Very Best of the Stranglers (Liberty, 2002)**

7. NO MORE HEROES from **Peaches: the Very Best of the Stranglers (Liberty, 2002)**

8. SOMETHING BETTER CHANGE from **Peaches: the Very Best of the Stranglers (Liberty, 2002)**

9. SOMETIMES from **IV Rattus Norvegicus (EMI, 2001)**

10. STRAIGHTEN OUT from **Peaches: the Very Best of the Stranglers (Liberty, 2002)**

1980) and change of manager. *The Men-In-Black* (1981) saw them trapped in the image they'd built for themselves, *La Folie* (1981) gave them a subversive hit with "Golden Brown", and they forced EMI to accept "Strange Little Girl", a spooky little number written back in 1975 – and which the label had at that time refused – as their parting shot before moving to Epic.

The group's new label put out *Feline* (1983) and *Aural Sculpture* (1984), *Dreamtime* (1984), *All Live And All Of The Night* and *Ten* before Cornwell finally jumped, deserting a ship of blandness he'd grown to detest.

Burnel stepped into the breach and recruited **Paul Roberts** (ex-Sniff 'n' The Tears) after Roberts arrived at his audition announcing "I'm your new singer". Since then, The Stranglers have continued to record and release top-quality albums for an ever-dwindling band of devoted followers, but have produced nothing to interest seekers of the punk-rock truth. As usual, the group's early stuff is their best: it might have been crude, rude and outrageous, but it was immense fun.

◉ IV Rattus Norvegicus (EMI, 2001)

Though rushed and occasionally patchy, this is still prime source material. An album not to be missed.

◉ No More Heroes (EMI, 2001)

More good stuff, raised and bottled before the well ran dry.

◉ Live (X Cert) (EMI, 2001)

Capturing the band at their peak, this is easily the best of the many Stranglers compilations on the market.

Straight Edge

It's difficult at first to see the connection between the libertarian ideals of punk rock and the self-denying spartans of the straight edge movement launched by **Minor Threat's Ian Mackaye**. By denying the pleasures of booze, drugs, promiscuous sex and general good times, straight edge philosophy smacks of the envy of those who ain't getting any, and investigation proves it to be most popular amongst regimented teens still living under the parental roof. (It must be really irritating to the parents too – how are they gonna bust kids who already go out of their way to avoid a good time?)

SXE, as it's also known, developed in the clubs of Washington, DC, especially those catering to the underage thrash/hardcore crowd. Its central message of "don't drink/don't smoke/don't fuck" was forced on the poor little mites, but they expanded it into more positive lifestyle choices – moving into vegetarianism or veganism, adopting a low-impact approach to the environment and an admirable awareness of political issues. With local band **The Teen Idles** generally considered to be the first straight edge band and Minor Threat further linking the movement to the nation's capital, it was safe for offshoots to bud off and root themselves into the ground elsewhere. New York City, that cesspool and world-famous den of iniquity, had a flourishing SXE scene with Gorilla Biscuits, Bold, Wide Awake and Youth Of Today setting the rules and making sure nobody broke 'em.

Straight edge led naturally to an intolerance of those who dared to disagree, which again contributed to the anti-punk feeling of the whole scene. While there's no denying the benefits of a drug-free lifestyle, the benefit of a movement that concentrates so much of its attention on just saying no has to be debatable.

STUPIDS

Hurtled straight outta the mean streets of Ipswich, 1984/5.

"WHAT WE WERE LOOKING FOR WAS A BAND THAT, METAPHORICALLY AT LEAST, LIT THEIR FARTS ON STAGE. THE STUPIDS WERE THAT BAND."

JOHN PEEL, 1986

U K hardcore musical nutcases based around **Tommy Stupid** (vocals/guitar/drums), **The Stupids** were a rousing reminder in an otherwise depressingly dour 1980s scene that it was all supposed to be about having a laugh, enjoying yourself and bringing about the collapse of society as we know it at the same time – with guitars. Tommy initially lined up with **Wolfie Retard** (bass/vocals), **Ziggy** (drums) and **Marty Tuff** (guitar), although the revolving Stupids membership has also included vocalists **Ed Shred** and **Dave Dissident**, alongside bassmen **Pauly Pizza**, **Stewie Q**, **Stevie Snax** and **Nick Schnozza**.

Tommy was a firm believer in the maxim Faster=Better and burned the fingers off most guitarists trying to keep pace with his madcap drummery. When he finally found a studio that would let him and his friends come round to play and make noise, he set about recording a swathe of tracks, the best of which would ultimately appear on the so-called *Violent Nun* EP (named for its cover picture of a sister involved in a scuffle with a cop) and, adding personnel and instruments at whim, their first full-length outing, *Peruvian Vacation*.

John Peel loved the band, had them in for a session and played their material regularly, probably encouraging them to return to the same home studio to put together *Retard Picnic* (1986) in a mind-threshing session that resulted in 24 tracks being finished in a twelve-hour stretch.

Quality and production values of this standard couldn't be maintained for long, and, after a few final sputtering bursts of sound, impossible to find except by chance even on release, The Stupids went their separate ways.

⊚ Peruvian Vacation/Violent Nun (Clay, 1993)

"The best track on the album for me is 'Always Never Fun' which uses an electric drill instead of a lead guitar solo." Andrew Fryer, 1993.

⊚ Retard Picnic, Feedback Session & Stupids Flexi CD (Clay, 1993)

Sounds gave *Retard Picnic* a four-star review and called it "a smouldering bomb-fire of white noise!" You don't want to argue with *Sounds*, now do ya?

⊚ Stupid Is As Stupid Does – The Stupids Collection (Castle, 2002)

As fine a collection of dumb-ass Britcore noise as you could hope to find, this has the additional benefit of being widely available. Two discs with 67 delirious tracks.

SUBURBAN STUDS

Stud muffins from Birmingham in 1976, cold meat pies by 1978.

I n the mid-1970s, **Gnasher** were an unappealing glam-rock band on the Midlands' disco/nitespot scene. Changing their name in 1976 to **The Suburban Studs** and buying up a truckload of stage gear and bad face paint did nothing to improve their sound, and in a refreshing demonstration of punks' inability to be led around permanently by the nose, they failed spectacularly.

But they tried so hard: the front man's stage name changed to **Eddy Zipps** (vocals/guitar), who together with **Steve Heart** (sax), **Keith Owen** (guitar), **Paul Morton** (bass) and **Steve Pool** (drums), assembled a set of unconvincing "punk-by-numbers" tunes, which rarely managed to catch the urgency or vibrant joy that they needed, but which landed them a deal with Pogo Records and distribution through WEA.

They had all the necessary street cred, appearing at the 100 Club's August 1976 punk festival supporting The Clash and the Sex Pistols, and headlining (with The Clash as support!) back home in Birmingham's Barbarellas later in the year. They'd worked on their image too. John Ingham reviewed their London appearance as "a laughable mixture of tacky jumpsuits, tacky make-up, tacky props and tacky music". By the time they played Barbarellas, however, they all had the proper haircuts, the slap had been replaced by authentic-looking sneers, and they were well on the way to ditching the saxophonist (he went on to form the more mod-oriented **Neon Hearts**).

But nothing worked, and the audience still saw them as a bunch of chancers hopping unsuccessfully along behind the bandwagon. They put out a couple of singles – "Questions"/"No Faith" in 1977 and "I Hate School"/"Young Power" in 1978 (now extremely collectable simply because of their rarity) – and an album, now rereleased as a complete collection, but still not selling any copies.

◉ **Slam – The Complete Studs Collection**
(Anagram, 2000)

If you must, then this is the easiest to find. It carries the full original track listing and a mammoth eleven bonus tracks, none of which you'll want to hear twice.

SUICIDAL
TENDENCIES

Formed in Venice, California; threatening suicide since the 1980s.

There's an extremely thin line dividing genuine hardcore punk-rockers from lame-ass tattooed heavy-metal losers, and the jury has yet to decide which side **Suicidal Tendencies** should fall on. Moulding the West Coast skate punk scene almost single-handedly in their earliest efforts certainly places them among the elect; checking out their recent output, on the other hand, sends them on the express down elevator to the other place. Still, they've never shied away from controversy, and probably couldn't care less about what anybody this side of the Atlantic has to say about them anyhow.

Mike Muir (godzilla vocals) certainly has the air of a man certain of his own righteousness, and his jet-engine roar definitely won him a huge and dedicated following amongst skateboarders – young punks with a taste for rowdiness – when he got together with **Grant Estes** (guitar), **Louiche Mayorga** (bass) and **Amery Smith** (drums) to make an immense racket in the name of hardcore.

Despite finding it difficult to pin down a regular gig (fans kept trashing the venues, and eventually ST were banned from playing anywhere

in LA), the band built up an audience sufficient for local indie label Frontier to risk issuing their stuff. "Institutionalized", the most powerful cut on *Suicidal Tendencies* (1983), took the band nationwide when the video won repeated plays on MTV, showing up later in the film *Repo Man* (1984) and in an episode of *Miami Vice*. But deprived of a home base and major-label deal through the actions of their naughty audience – bolstered by rumours linking the group to one or other of the mean-hombre street gangs of Los Angeles – the original band fizzled out and disappeared until 1987.

The new line-up comprised Muir and Mayorga plus **Rocky George** (guitar) and **R.J. Herrera** (drums), and turned up trumps again with their second album, *Join The Army* (1987), winning a new generation of fans to their cause with "Possessed To Skate". This time round a major label was prepared to take the bait, and Epic signed them up.

By the time the band made it to the new label's facilities, however, Mayorga had quit. Muir replaced him with **Bob Heathcote** (bass)

Suicidal Tendencies' Mike.

PLAYLIST: SUICIDAL TENDENCIES

1. BERSERK! from **Prime Cuts: The Best of Suicidal Tendencies (Epic, 1997)**

2. FASCIST PIG from **Suicidal Tendencies (Frontier, 2002)**

3. FEEDING THE ADDICTION from **Prime Cuts: The Best of Suicidal Tendencies (Epic, 1997)**

4. GO SKATE! (POSSESSED TO SKATE '97) from **Prime Cuts: The Best of... (Epic, 1997)**

5. I SHOT THE DEVIL from **Suicidal Tendencies (Frontier, 2002)**

6. INSTITUTIONALIZED from **Suicidal Tendencies (Frontier, 2002)**

7. NO FUCK'N PROBLEM from **Prime Cuts: The Best of Suicidal Tendencies (Epic, 1997)**

8. NOBODY HEARS from **Prime Cuts: The Best of Suicidal Tendencies (Epic, 1997)**

9. POSSESSED from **Suicidal Tendencies (Frontier, 2002)**

10. TRIP AT THE BRAIN from **How Will I Laugh Tomorrow... (Virgin, 1988)**

and brought in additional guitarist **Mike Clark**, redrafting the band's blueprint to craft a dark and rusty heavy metal beast from the original shiny hardcore songbird.

How Will I Laugh Tomorrow When I Can't Even Smile Today (1988) sounded like the work of a completely different band. Grunge was just around the corner and ST were already leaning in to take the curve. *Lights, Camera, Revolution* (1990) showed the band's flirtation with heavy metal had turned into something permanent and substantial. Despite another hiatus in the mid-1990s, wooing a new audience seemed to work for them, as they're still belting out noise at ear-bleeding volume in a West Coast town tonight.

⊙ **Suicidal Tendencies** (Virgin; reissued 1988)

As well as the epic "Institutionalized", Mike Muir and friends also present worthy cuts in the form of "Fascist Pig" and "Possessed". This set was a powerful beginning for a powerful band.

SUICIDE

Kicked off 1970; kicked the bucket 1981, with occasional reunions.

Lumped in with the rest of the New York punks by virtue of their sheer oddity and incompatibility with any other available pigeonhole, **Suicide** were the template electro-weirdness band that Throbbing Gristle, Cabaret Voltaire, Soft Cell, Depeche Mode and a whole genre of later synthesizer acts used as the basis for their own stabs at futuristic nonsense. By the time the New Wave came around, **Alan Vega** (voice) and **Martin Rev** (instruments) had been lurking on the outskirts of the city's art-rock scene for some time: Vega had

previous form as a sculptor, while Rev's taste for free-form jazz noize predated the city's No-Wave soundmonsters by a good decade.

As ruggedly confrontational as The Stooges had been, they started out as a trio but ditched the guitar player for a more focused two-pronged assault, developing a heinous reputation for playing music to scare the crap out of the audience. Over swathes of tormented circuitry – Rev started out with a beaten-up Farfisa organ held together with duct tape and prayers to the gods of electronica, Vega moaned the hellish fate of those who murder or take their own life, with music and vocals meshed together and amplified beyond legal limits. Sounds good, huh? Sounds meaty, tasty and fried?

Stir in Vega's leather-boy tactics of insulting the audience, whacking at the walls with a bike chain, challenging preconceptions and giving Performance Art the beginnings of its bad name, and it's easy to see them fitting right in with an excitable punk crowd that had yet to find a stereotype to follow. When Suicide brought their crowd-baiting routine across the Atlantic to cash in on the blossoming punk scene, they found it worked all too well, and Vega often found himself pummelled senseless on his own stage after abusing the wrong section of the audience one time too many.

Supporting The Clash or on tour with Elvis Costello, Vega was covered in spittle every night, had his nose broken on one occasion and provoked a full-scale riot in Belgium. When *Suicide* was released in 1977 (on ex-New York Dolls manager Marty Thau's Red Star label), listeners were polarized by its dark subject matter, ghostly vocals and relentless electronic grind. But Rev's knack of conjuring up the right minimalist racket to back up Vega's latter-day beatnik poetry made extended pieces such as "Frankie Teardrop" essential listening, even to a crowd more accustomed to three-minute heroics driven by buzzsaw guitars.

"Cheree" was released as a single (and swallowed whole by The Jesus & Mary Chain for later regurgitation), but preferring to tour rather than return to the studio, Suicide lost momentum. Although *Alan Vega / Martin Rev – Suicide* followed pretty much the same path as their first album, handing production over to Ric Ocasek let the pop outweigh the weird, and despite the enduring beauty of Ocasek-led tracks such as "Dream Baby Dream", the album disappeared into the gap between subcultures. With sales insufficient to make it worthwhile keeping on, Suicide dissolved, leaving the way clear for Ministry, Sisters Of Mercy, Spiritualized and the gang to carry the torch forward.

Meantime, the guys went on to solo careers with varying degrees of success and of limited interest to us punk-rock adventurers. They re-formed on a wave of nostalgia in 1998, releasing an album of new material, *American Supreme*, in 2002. While it captured some of the old excitement, it lit few real flames.

⊚ Suicide (Mute, reissued 2000)

Includes Bruce Springsteen's favourite Vietnam vet murder/suicide epic, "Frankie Teardrop", and comes with a second disc comprising a live set recorded at CBGB's in 1977, plus the marvellous chaos of "23 Minutes Over Brussels".

⊚ Ghost Riders (ROIR, reissued 1998)

Fine document of the duo's 1981 tenth anniversary performance in Minneapolis.

SUM 41

Started working it out in Toronto, Canada, 1996; gonna stay with us until it all adds up.

All the moves, all the right haircuts, sporting beaten-up T-shirts and poses of pure Johnny Rotten-style aggression, **Sum 41** are a fourth-generation version of the local rock group down the street parodied back in the 1960s by The Monkees in "Pleasant Valley Sunday" – bogus as the meat and ketchup in your local Texican Fried Chicken outlet and, to kids of a certain age, just as tasty and irresistible.

Sum 41's Bizzy D does the business.

Suburban kids of the worst kind, **Deryck "Bizzy D" Whibley** (vocals/guitar) and **Steve "Stevo32" Jocz** (drums) grew up seeing Beavis and Butthead as lifestyle gurus, on a diet of bad metal videos and second-rate punk pre-selected, judged and filtered by the machinery at MTV. Together with **Jay "Cone" McCaslin** (bass) and **Dave "Brownsound" Baksh** (guitar), they became Sum 41 and bashed out a set of bright and shiny pop songs, each with a punky twist. *Half Hour Of Power* (2000) was one of a series of interchangeable, punk-by-numbers albums churned out by major labels at the time, all desperately treading water and staying afloat by means of apparently safe options like Sum 41, bands of persuadable kids with stars in their eyes.

All Killer No Filler (2001) fine-tuned their sound to the marketplace by enlisting producer **Jerry Finn** (the man in charge of studio details for Green Day and Blink 182) to sprinkle magic over their sugary teen-punk melodies. It sold a truckload and led, naturally, to a swift follow-up, *Does This Look Infected?* (2002). Relentless touring – even though the guys are still in their early twenties, their schedule of three-hundred-plus gigs a year would get anyone down – meant a slightly longer interval before *Chunk* appeared in 2004.

As the guys have matured, their song titles have moved from the puerile ("Grab The Devil By The Horns And Fuck Him Up The Ass") to the adolescent ("Four Floors Of Whores") but why should they mess with such an obviously powerful and successful formula? It has absolutely nothing to do with real punk rock of course, but why should they or their audience care what a bunch of old guys think about it?

⊙ Chuck (Mercury, 2004)

If you must, then this is your best bet.

SWELL MAPS

Formed Leamington Spa, England, 1972; off the map 1980

Swell Maps are charts used by surfers on shore to measure the intensity of the waves they hope to ride. How it also became chosen as the name of the most enigmatic band in British punk remains something of a mystery. This much, however is clear...

Tiring of the usual adolescent routine of knocking the crap out of one another, Nicholas Godfrey became **Nikki Sudden** or **Nikki Mattress** (vocals/guitar) and his brother Kevin became **Epic Soundtracks** (keyboards/drums). Hooking up with school pals Richard Earl (who chose to be **Dikki Mint** or **Biggles Books**) on guitar and **Jowe Head** (which might be his real name) on bass and vocals, they became Swell Maps.

They passed the early 1970s cooped up in crowded bedrooms, producing interminable do-it-yourself cassettes of increasingly unsettling music before latching on to punk and its ethos of getting in front of an audience to play. Setting out their stall with "Read About Seymour" on their own label (Rather, 1978), they spent the next few years perplexing and challenging as many folk as they entertained with their cheerfully noisy and relentlessly experimental music.

"Dresden Style" led to a deal with Rough Trade and *A Trip To Marineville* (Rather, 1979) which took their infuriatingly off-kilter punk sound to a wider audience. John Peel adored it, and the more cerebral end of the punk-rock journalistic world was thrilled, but it left a public more used to back-to-basics rock'n'roll confused and unmoved, especially in the direction of the record shops. *Jane From Occupied Europe* was equally stuffed plump with ideas, but descended at times into stoner-oriented humour and misguided musical experimentation.

Listening to later albums such as *Whatever Happens Next* and *Collision Time* is like watching footage of a fatally damaged aircraft spiralling a trail of smoke down to its doom as the music disappears increasingly up its own fundament, and the band split up in 1980. Although Nikki Sudden died unexpectedly (he'll be missed) in March 2006, Head and Soundtracks still show up on the indie scene, and with high-profile fans including Thurston Moore of Sonic Youth and everyone in Pavement, the legacy of Swell Maps is unlikely to disappear anytime soon. Definitely a band to listen to and consider rather than scream out loud and dance to.

⊙ international Rescue (Alive, 2004)

Compilation/greatest hits album that's perhaps the best entry point for beginners. The band's most acceptably "punk rock" period is covered in depth with "International Rescue", "Let's Build A Car", "Secret Island", "Read About Seymour" sitting comfortably alongside their raucously brilliant cover version of "Get Down and Get With It".

TALKING HEADS

Started talking New York City, 1975; went quiet 1991.

The epitome of art-school New-Wavers, **Talking Heads** were, for a few years, the most exciting and inventive of the New York crew. Steered carefully away from the dead end of four-to-the-floor punk thrashing and too smart to be pigeonholed, the band kept apart from the comings and goings of various musical fashions and for a decade were the most inspirational rock band on the planet.

David Byrne (highly strung vocals/erratic guitar/bundle of nerves) and **Chris Frantz** (drums) had been in a band together at the Rhode Island School of Design (Talking Heads were never gritty street punks) in the early 1970s. **Tina Weymouth** (bass) started out as a fan of the band, but fell into a relationship with Frantz and was co-opted into

picking up the bass after graduation, when the trio moved to the big city to try their hands at showbiz before getting into serious careers. Learning their chops on 1960s pop hits and garage band classics, by the summer of 1975 they were ready for their first gig, supporting The Ramones at CBGB's.

Talking Heads came to the New Wave party with a unique vision and a sure-fire hit ready to go. Their jerky and unsettling "Psycho Killer" had been part of Byrne and Frantz's life since their days as The Artistics back in Rhode island, and stood proudly alongside Patti Smith's deconstructions of New Jersey life among the aliens, and Television's crystalline guitar-led spiral staircases of nonsense, as an example of just how New and powerful a Wave could be when it hit the right spot at the right time. Byrne cultivated a geek-on-drugs persona on stage and in interviews that rendered him utterly compelling, whether discussing the influence of minimalism on his music or his preference in pizza toppings

PLAYLIST: TALKING HEADS

Starting out making music that sounded as if the band was afraid of its own shadow, NYC's Talking Heads championed the nerdy, well-informed, polite but weird end of the punk spectrum, with these classic cuts illustrating just how strange you can get down on the Lower East Side.

1. **AIR** from **FEAR OF MUSIC** remastered and expanded (2006, WEA)

2. **CITIES** from **FEAR OF MUSIC** remastered and expanded (2006, WEA)

3. **FOUND A JOB** from **MORE SONGS ABOUT BUILDINGS AND FOOD** (1987, Sire)

4. **NEW FEELING** from **TALKING HEADS: 77** remastered and expanded (2006, WEA)

5. **PSYCHO KILLER** from **TALKING HEADS: 77** remastered and expanded (2006, WEA)

6. **PULLED UP** from **TALKING HEADS: 77** remastered and expanded (2006, WEA)

7. **STAY HUNGRY** from **MORE SONGS ABOUT BUILDINGS AND FOOD** (1987, Sire)

8. **TENTATIVE DECISIONS** from **TALKING HEADS: 77** remastered and expanded (2006, WEA)

9. **WARNING SIGN** from **MORE SONGS ABOUT BUILDINGS AND FOOD** (1987, Sire)

10. **WHO IS IT?** from **TALKING HEADS: 77** remastered and expanded (2006, WEA)

By the end of the year they were an essential in any article celebrating the scene – the "intellectual" balance to the obligatory picture of saucepot Debbie Harry of Blondie and The Ramones – looking like the bastard offspring of a Viking raid on Herman's Hermits. They spent the next year building on their local reputation, signing **Jerry Harrison** (keyboards and ex-Modern Lovers), flirting with different labels and recording demos (notably for Beserkely in California) before signing to Sire and finishing December 1976 with the release of "Love => Building On Fire" ("love goes to a building on fire").

Storming ahead into punk's year zero with New York hanging off their every sly, enigmatic, disjointed comment, Talking Heads plotted their invasion of Europe, heading over in April to an ecstatic welcome from the British end of the New Wave and touring to sell-out crowds up and down the country. The group looked more like accountants on a binge than desperate anarchists about to break down the walls of heartache and late-period capitalism, but despite superficially having absolutely zero in common with the spikyheaded crews who showed up mob-handed at their gigs to welcome them, they found a depth of understanding and fellow feeling in Europe that contrasted with the incomprehension that greeted them outside their home town back in the USA. The band backed up the intense live work with *Talking Heads 77* – produced to shiny steel perfection by pop master Tony Bongiovi, dripping with edgy urban paranoia and lyrically bursting out with terrors. Production, musicianship and elegant, clipped diction combined to make the Heads' neurotic yet perceptive message that all hope is effort wasted stand out loud and clear. "Psycho Killer" became a must-play at all the best parties, John Peel jumped on board immediately and their reputation was made.

Hooking up with Brian Eno was their smartest move, however; he saw the band on their first London appearance at The Rock Garden and got in touch. He was uniquely positioned in terms of self-confidence and industry backing to give Talking Heads room to move out of the constrictions of the New Wave. Starting with *More Songs About Music And Food* (1978), Eno wormed his way to the heart of the band, "treating" instruments, producing by the seat of his frilly bloomers

and throwing in the odd bit of advice suggested by his Oblique Strategies cards. It could have been a disaster – instead, luck and Eno's magic created the New Wave album of the year and took the band into the US charts with their bold reinterpretation of Al Green's otherwise untouchable classic "Take Me To The River".

Fear Of Music (1979) saw Talking Heads zoom way beyond the New Wave and into a higher orbit – one occupied exclusively by global acts of the Bowie/Stones/Queen crowd, where all contact with the nourishing reality of everyday life has given way to an air-conditioned superstar cocoon. The band stayed at the top of their profession for the rest of the decade without once running out of ideas or losing the will to take risks with their sound, but despite critical success, creating a large chunk of the decade's best music and charting all around the world, they could never return to their quirky New Wave roots.

Still without question the consummate artschool New Wavers, they sometimes wandered off down experimental dead ends, but never mistook the direction they were headed in.

ICONIC SINGLE:
PSYCHO KILLER / PULLED UP
(SIRE, 1977)

Talking Heads' signature tune, the one used to open their magnificent in-concert movie and still the only track on Norman Bates's iPod, "Psycho Killer" is a foretaste of the "preppy gone mad" protagonist of Brett Easton Ellis's American Psycho (who, strangely, preferred Blondie and Phil Collins). Tense, nervous, can't relax? Call David for immediate treatment and a guaranteed cure. Heh heh heh...

Talking Heads: 77 (Sire, 1977)

An outstanding debut, even in a year crammed with exceptional first albums. Full of fizzing, popping, catchy tunes, charmingly upsetting lyrics and musical twists.

More Songs About Buildings And Food (Sire, 1978)

Talking Heads were so worshipped by The Undertones that they stole the title structure for their own More Songs About Chocolate And Girls, and this is the album that introduced the fearsome five-brained chimera that formed when the Heads began working with Eno. Over the next few years, the band recorded several sets of carefully constructed arty pop songs with Eno, this being the first and most extensively experimental, featuring novel combinations of acoustic and electronic instruments and several well-intentioned stabs at some credible funk.

Fear Of Music (Warner, 1984)

Another Eno production. The band started building complex rhythms from around the world into their songs, especially on the opener "I Zimbra", thus reducing the emphasis on lyrical precision and leaning more to the funk that was to carry them on to the next stage of their journey.

Remain In Light (Sire, 1980)

Again produced by Eno, but using the best session musicians available. With a horn section, numerous people hitting unnameable instruments and the funkiest bass ever heard on an album by honkies, this is the band's most complete statement and their most accomplished.

TEENAGE JESUS AND THE JERKS

Formed New York City, 1977; split into a million artistic fragments 1979.

Opinion is still divided over the contribution made by **Lydia Lunch** to New Wave music and to the joy of nations in general. The laughter of her genius can so easily be misconstrued as the "look at me!" whine of an overindulged brat, disastrously encouraged in the belief that her outpourings were art.

Consider her first band, **Teenage Jesus And The Jerks**. Assembled haphazardly into an atonal, confrontational "No Wave" band, they played guerrilla-like gigs, more cacophonous assault than entertainment, that rarely lasted more than fifteen minutes. **Lydia Koch** came from Kentucky and was just 16 when she discovered her inner Lunch persona. She initially shared the stage with fellow No-Wave bandwaggoner **James Chance** (saxophone), **Reck** (bass) and **Bradley Field** (drums). Replacing Reck with **Gordon Stevenson** (bass) and ditching

Chance (who went on to form his own act, The Contortions) did nothing to increase their accessibility, but they charmed Eno sufficiently for him to record three of their efforts for his *No New York* compilation. A flurry of last-minute personnel changes in 1979 did even less to cement the band's relationship with its audience and, by the end of the year, Lydia had fluttered away in search of her next fix of the muse.

Teenage Jesus & The Jerks (Atavistic, 2001)

Credited to Lydia Lunch (although "Blamed on Lydia Lunch" is perhaps a better opening phrase), this is the real deal straight from the gates of the No Wave. Sad, ugly lyrics of deprivation, abuse and pain swoop and caw like carrion-feeding fits of depression made flesh. Not by any means one of the all-time great feel-good recordings, the album has just as many pretentious, noisy and foul moments as it boasts episodes of glittering fiery beauty.

TELEVISION

Tuned in New York City, 1973; turned off 1978. Re-tuned briefly in 1993 and sporadically since then.

A band formed exclusively from such fascinatingly clever, creative types, each with a yen for the limelight, was never going to hang together for long. That **Television** endured sufficiently to develop their still resounding legend is something for which the gods who care for us music fiends should all be thanked. **Tom Verlaine** (vocals/endless guitar lines of searing beauty) and **Richard Hell** (reluctant and amateur bass/bitter vocals) had been bad boys at school together, taking the "total derangement of the senses" route in search of the eternal truths and beauties of poetry. It led them instead to cold street corners in New York City, where young men hustled to keep their habits at bay. By the early 1970s, Verlaine and Hell had made a few friends (including Patti Smith – Tom later played on her debut single), assimilated somewhat into city life, and had formed a band – **The Neon Boys** – with **Billy Ficca** (drums). Adding **Richard Lloyd** as sparring partner for Verlaine on guitar and changing the name to Television, they created a whole new style of improvised music, shying away from the overused paths of rock and leaping instead from crag to boulder in a wild exploratory, celebratory whirlwind of chiming guitar lines and incomprehensible touches of lyrical genius. In short, they rocked, even though Hell's contribution seems to have been more decorative than musical.

Hell helped define the template for dumb-ass bass players that still threatens to dislodge that of the depraved drummer from the top of the popular stereotype rocker charts. By gleefully pogoing round the stage, abusing the audience and resolutely refusing to improve his acquaintanceship with his instrument, he set out an early draft of the rules of punk-rocker misbehaviour, but he must have driven Verlaine and the others, heading fast in the direction of professional musicianship, mad with frustration. His inability or unwillingness to keep up and follow his band-mates through their by now almost telepathic jam sessions on stage made him a liability. Island Records funded Eno to produce half a dozen demo tracks in 1975, but on hearing of Hell's continuing trouble with the intricacies of the band's signature tune "Marquee Moon", decided against releasing any of them.

Hell couldn't be ignored – his songwriting was too good and he was too vital a part of the band – but he could be squeezed, and as Television's reputation on the club scene grew, his contribution to the set was reduced to that of side-man as, one by one, his great songs were dropped from the set. When, towards the end of the band's legendary residency at CBGB's, the last one fell off the list, he stopped coming along to gigs. **Fred Smith** (bass) was recruited from **Blondie** on the brink of their commercial breakthrough, trading financial success for a career on the underside of rock'n'roll (and that's what happens if you leave your bandmates in the lurch, punk rockers).

Hell took his songs (including "Blank Generation", "Betrayal Takes Two", "Love Comes In Spurts" and the best scotch and soda song ever, "Down At The Rock And Roll Club") and quit in early 1975. After a soul-sapping episode with **Johnny Thunders** and the rest of **The Heartbreakers**, he went on to experience the joys of life as a front man with his own band, **The Voidoids**, and had a taste of the fame and some of

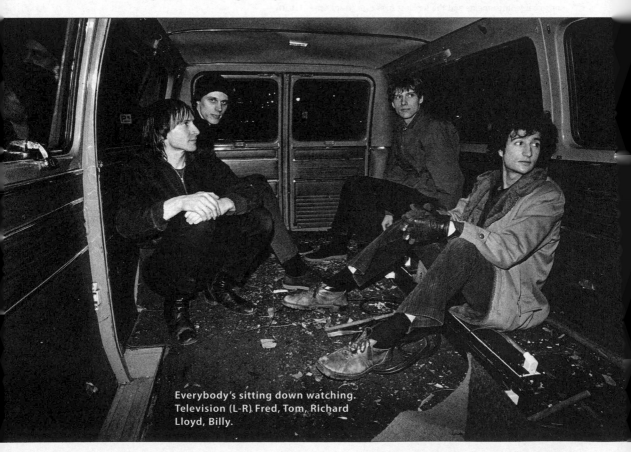

Everybody's sitting down watching.
Television (L-R) Fred, Tom, Richard
Lloyd, Billy.

🎵 PLAYLIST: TELEVISION

One masterful album and a far-from-faultless live recording of the band were Television's sole worthwhile legacy. You really should have both of them, but here's our pick of the bunch.

1. ELEVATION from **MARQUEE MOON: REMASTERED & EXPANDED (Rhino, 2003)**

2. FOXHOLE from **BLOW UP; LIVE (1999, ROIR)**

3. FRICTION from **MARQUEE MOON: REMASTERED & EXPANDED (Rhino, 2003)**

4. LITTLE JOHNNY JEWEL from **BLOW UP; LIVE (1999, ROIR)**

5. MARQUEE MOON from **BLOW UP; LIVE (1999, ROIR)**

6. PROVE IT from **MARQUEE MOON: REMASTERED & EXPANDED (Rhino, 2003)**

7. SATISFACTION from **BLOW UP; LIVE (1999, ROIR)**

8. SEE NO EVIL from **MARQUEE MOON: REMASTERED & EXPANDED (Rhino, 2003)**

9. TORN CURTAIN from **MARQUEE MOON: REMASTERED & EXPANDED (Rhino, 2003)**

10. VENUS DE MILO from **BLOW UP; LIVE (1999, ROIR)**

---

the commercial success he thought he deserved.

With Island now looking elsewhere for the next big thing, Television went back to Uncle Billy - **William Ork**, a face from the Max's Kansas City/ Warhol/Velvets era of the New York underground scene. He'd already stepped in to lend the Neon Boys a hand, providing rehearsal space and encouragement as well as promoting the renamed band's first gig at the Townhouse Theater on West 44th Street in March 1974. Ork's under-celebrated role as conduit between the old guard and the avant-garde now extended to forming his own label, Ork Records, to release Television's debut recording.

"Little Johnny Jewel" was a two-part marathon introduction to everything the band believed in – demon-driven wild rides up and down the guitar neck with everyone happy if most of the notes showed up in the right place, sensitive interpretative drumming and a bass line that not even Hell could have messed up. When Lloyd heard the rest of the band discussing releasing an eight-minute commercial suicide note as the band's debut single, he grabbed his guitar and split. Art for art's sake was all very well, but he had rent to pay; one has to see his point. **Peter Laughner** from Rocket From The Tombs stepped in, but rent paid, Lloyd was soon back in the band, and after knocking out a swift and exceedingly collectable EP for Stiff in the UK, the band holed up in the well-furnished studios of Elektra Records to work on *Marquee Moon* (1976).

Hearing the album for the first time stopped the world – it froze everything outside the room you were in. Long guitar solos weren't meant to be exciting, but these guys sounded like they were using their guitars to fight one another. The *NME* called it a "24-carat inspired work of genius" and it went into the Top 30 in the UK (opening the floodgates for the rest of the New York New Wave, most of whom were already queuing for tickets across the Atlantic). "Marquee Moon" and "Prove It" both charted as singles in the UK.

It was never punk rock though: Television were by this point one hundred percent defiantly New Wave, in fact arguably the first New Wave band in the world. However, despite inventing the look (Verlaine and Hell still argue about precisely whose look Malcolm McLaren stole for the Sex Pistols), cultivating all the snotty-nosed streethood junkie moves, and writing some of the era's most brutal, slice-of-life lyrics (when they touched down from their searingly beautiful etc. guitar journeys), they looked back to the extended jams of San Francisco's acid-rocking impro-renaissance of the late 1960s as much as they looked forward to the freedom and experimentalism of the 1980s. The band had spent a good four years honing the *Marquee Moon* set to perfection. Now, having finished it and watched it leave the studio, they became aware of record company pressure to come up with something new.

Adventure (1978) reeked of the hurry in which it was recorded. "Dream's Dream", "Foxhole", "Carried Away" and "Glory" stood out, and any given track can still punch above its weight when matched with the formulaic ramalama being churned out by bands all around them, but it wasn't *Marquee Moon* Part Two and the buyers stayed away, put off by some vicious reviews.

None of this helped smooth egos, especially on the tour bus, and in July 1978 Lloyd grabbed his guitar and split again. This time the band stayed folded until 1993, by which time all that New Wave/old wave stuff had been forgotten about. The reunion didn't last, and even though the band put out a balls-nailed-to-the-mast album to go with it, nobody was that excited, and everybody had moved on to something new long ago. A repeat performance in 2001 attracted much the same ripple of interest but it was a case of too little, much too late.

⊚ Marquee Moon (Rhino, reissued 2003)

One of the classic, seminal New Wave recordings, and the one that took the New York scene to a worldwide audience, there's not a single piece of "punk rock" on the album, even in its current remastered and expanded format. This remains however, the essential Television purchase; the best thing they ever did, still influencing bands forming today.

⊚ The Blow-Up (ROIR, reissued 1999)

The other essential Television recording, captured live in concert and with the guys absolutely bouncing off the ceiling. The selection of covers – the opening "Blow Up" is a rebranded version of the 13th Floor Elevators' "Fire Engine" – is patchy, but overall this is scarily good.

TELEVISION PERSONALITIES

Formed London, 1977; retired 1998.

"THEY SHOULD HAVE BEEN BIGGER THAN THE BEATLES."

ALAN MCGEE OF CREATION RECORDS, 1998

It's all the fault of **Dan Treacy** (vocals/songwriting/guitar). If he hadn't formed **Television Personalities** and kept them going in one form or another for twenty years, we could have closed the chapter on punk long ago, having written it off as just another dour rock'n'roll fad stamped into the dust by the depression of the 1980s. As it is, he's continually reminded us that punk-rocking is largely about having fun, recalling the slapdash thrills of getting it near as possibly right first time, then moving on to the next burst of joy

before it gets booooooooooooring. And he knows where Syd Barrett lives.

Nobody should be surprised to hear that such a national treasure first came to public attention through the John Peel show. Nor that Peelie invited the band back repeatedly to shower their own particular strain of shite over the high, the mighty and the irritatingly popular. To hear them name-checked by later, arguably greater bands including Pavement, The Jesus & Mary Chain and even The Pastels (a band even more twee than their name suggests), however, is little short of amazing.

The legend of Television Personalities goes back to the King's Road in London, to a dry-cleaners' shop opposite Malcolm McLaren and Vivienne Westwood's boutique, Sex. Mrs Treacy, Dan's mum, had the unenviable task of rinsing the spittle off the Pistols' costumes and carrying out the running repairs necessary when the band were falling off stages and bar stools every night. Eyes widened by such glamour, Treacy and his mates – including **Edward Ball** (vocals/ keyboards/part-time member of **The Times**) and **Joe Foster** (guitar) became **O Level** for a while (they also appeared as **Teenage Filmstars** or **Missing Scientists**, if the fancy took them) and recorded "14th Floor" - a spoof punk-rock track that parodied the scene's high-rise alienation fascination before most people who heard it had realized there was a scene to be spoofed. A copy made its way by devious methods to the BBC, where Peel's reaction was enough to convince the band to become Television Personalities, and their families to fork out for a single, "Posing At The Roundhouse", and the *Where's Bill Grundy Now?* EP (1978) – containing the New Wave's most enduring tribute to the TV man who got drunk, flirted with Siouxsie and flushed his career down the pan by allowing the Pistols to speak their dirty minds on camera.

"Part-Time Punks", a typically wistful sneer at... well, you can imagine... was the EP's standout track. It went to the top of the era's admittedly sparsely populated indie charts (proving popular enough to appear on the *NME*'s celebratory *Pogo A Go Go* cassette a few years later) and was the band's greatest hit.

And Don't The Kids Just Love It (1981) saw TVP move away from their juvenile punk posing towards the celebration of a pop-art/mod/Carnaby Street 1960s England that never really existed outside of Treacy's head. His unique way of blending whimsical lyrics (tinged always with menace) and dry, ramshackle guitar of the most pleasingly amateurish kind drew a nationwide audience of late-night stoners, students and connoisseurs of the weird.

Mummy Your [sic] Not Watching Me followed a year later on the band's own label Whaam! and spearheaded the great psychedelic revival of the 1980s (prompted by a widespread resurgence of interest in the original garage-punk rockers of the 1960s on both sides of the Atlantic). It continued to showcase Treacy's fascination with famous names - "David Hockney's Diaries" and "Lichtenstein Painting" - and featured a new and more poignant music in tracks such as "Adventure Playground", "Where the Rainbow Ends", "Magnificent Dreams" and the superbly, swooningly gorgeous "If I Could Write Poetry".

Whaam! changed its name to Dreamworld shortly afterwards in exchange for a substantial chunk of money offered by Simon Napier-Bell (Wham's manager) or under duress when threatened by Simon Napier-Bell's lawyers (depending which legend you choose to believe). Whatever the truth, TVP found themselves with ample studio time to record *The Painted World*, a moodier collection of songs ideally suited to the prevalent gloom in the world outside (for various financial reasons, the album remained unreleased until 1985). In the meantime, *They Could Have Been Bigger Than The Beatles* (1982) – a stopgap set of demos, outtakes and loose stabs at cover versions – appeared, keeping the band alive and their material on the radio.

Things went quiet for a while, *Chocolat-Art* (1985) a live recording sneaked out in Germany, Ball left the band and a new line-up coalesced around a bitterly disillusioned Treacy, plus ex-Swell Maps **Jowe Head** (bass) and **Jeff Bloom** (drums). Treacy had spent his time away from the limelight writing songs, and by now without a deal, his only outlet was the odd live appearance. It wasn't until 1990 that TVP returned to the record shops with the *Salvador Dali's Garden Party* EP, followed in 1990 by *Privilege*, their best work for almost a decade. Quality notwithstanding, the album sold appallingly. *Closer To God* (Fire/Seed, 1992) was a harrowing insight into a descent into drugs hell, and performed badly in terms of sales.

While another compilation of early singles and rarities, *Yes Darling, But Is It Art?* (1995), caused a predictably brief flurry of interest, the virtual solo album *I Was A Mod Before You Was A Mod* (1995, reissued Overground, 2005) and swansong *Don't Cry Baby... It's Only A Movie* (1998) failed to perform at all, despite the inclusion of inspired cover versions of songs such as Jonathan Richman's "Pablo Picasso" and Psychic TV's "Godstar".

Treacy has retreated from the pop scene – understandably given his experiences and increasingly troublesome medical problems. While the albums require a little extra dedication to the delicious subtleties of English as she is lived and spoke, Television Personalities' most accessible work is always available in compilation form – with *Part-Time Punks* (1999) as the best of the current bunch.

⊚ Privilege (Fire, 1990)

It's virtually impossible to inject humour into sad songs, and just as hard to fit gloom into funny tunes. Dan and the boys succeed magnificently on both counts here, and manage to give it all a groovy mod twist. Remarkable stuff.

⊚ Part-Time Punks: The Very Best Of Television Personalities (Cherry Red, 2001)

Not quite the full definitive anthology of the band, but easily enough for beginners, this 22-track compilation is an excellent mix of the "hits" (such as they were), interspersed with otherwise impossible to locate B-sides, rarities and the like, covering 1977-1989.

TENPOLE TUDOR

Camped up, London 1974.
Upped tents and departed 1982.

Close-eyed viewers of the opening sequence of *The Great Rock'n'Roll Swindle* would have noticed that one of the more outrageous performers ostensibly auditioning to replace Johnny Rotten at the tail end of **The Sex Pistols'** career showed up a little later in the film, playing opposite Irene Handl's ice-cream vendor as the world's most gangly cinema usher. He stole the entire section, rendering the plot even more difficult to follow, and warbled his way to fame with an unforgettable performance of "Who Killed Bambi?" – a song based on the earlier working title for the film project – singing with rowdy glee and popping eyes into the outstretched tube of the vacuum cleaner he'd just been using on the foyer's plush carpeting.

This was the world's first encounter with **Eddie Tudorpole** (aka Eddie Tudor, aka Tentpole Tudor; actor, musician, whatever) and the world recoiled with a mixture of amusement, bemusement and horror. Eddie put the band together way before punk showed up, with **Bob Kingston** (guitar), **Dick Crippen** (bass), and **Gary Long** (drums).

Eddie used the fame that stuck to him as a result of this appearance as leverage with Stiff Records, who fronted him the money to record *Eddie, Old Bob, Dick and Gary* (1981). Springing "3 Bells In A Row", "Wunderbar" and "Swords Of A Thousand Men" onto the public could have been considered felonious assault but instead it won the band chart success, a few stunning appearances on mainstream TV (BBC's *Top Of The Pops* never really recovered from the band waving round musical instruments as if they were broadswords and bucklers), and a few quid in the pension fund for when the spotlight moved on.

Cashing in while they were able to, Tenpole Tudor rushed out *Let the Four Winds Blow* later in the year but, sensing a change in the weather, Eddie left the band (which continued briefly under the name The Tudors) for a solo career as a Cajun-style singer, fronting a competent if uninspired new group, also known as Tenpole Tudor. This was far too many tudors for the British public and, in a burst of revolutionary torpor, both bands were largely ignored. Eddie moved away from music during the 80s in favour of a series of decent movie cameos – chewing up the scenery as a hotel clerk in *Sid & Nancy*, Ed The Ted in *Absolute Beginners* and Rusty Zimmerman in *Straight to Hell*. He took over from Richard O'Brien in 1994 as presenter of TV's *The Crystal Maze* (an inspired choice) and has continued work as a jobbing actor ever since with his most notable recent appearance being as Spike Milligan in the biopic *The Life And Death Of Peter Sellers* (2004).

⊙ **Swords of a Thousand Men: The Very Best of Tenpole Tudor** (Metro, 2001)

This compilation will answer all your questions about the silliest band to make it onto vinyl as a result of punk rock. It boasts all the best singles and enough of the better album tracks to get your party started, with standouts "Swords Of A Thousand Men", "Let The Four Winds Blow", "Conga Tribe", "Wunderbar", "Throwing My Baby Out With The Bathwater", "Tell Me More" and "Three Bells In A Row" appearing.

THIS HEAT

Hotted up in London, 1975; dissipated 1982.

Happily hidden away at the unlistenable end of the industrial scale and providing a fair definition of "confrontational" from before the outset of punk, this outfit skated round the experimental outskirts of the New Wave, developed a dub-reggae habit and caved in under the pressure of divergent musical and social interests before they had time to put a foot wrong. Cerebral art-rockers with such blatant jazz interests were never going to fit in as punks, but the band's monstrously overpowering music was definitely a facet of that period's explosion of creativity, running parallel to Alternative TV, Wire, Public Image Ltd, Throbbing Gristle and Cabaret Voltaire in the scary noises and unpredictability stakes.

The core of the band comprised **Charles Bullen** (vocals/multi-instrumentals) and **Charles Hayward** (vocals/multi-instrumentals, ex-Gong/Quiet Sun) – committed musical experimentalists who had worked together in the early 1970s as **Dolphin Logic**. Adding **Gareth Williams** (vocals/multi-instrumentals) and **Chris Blake** (technical wizardry/tape loops), the pair of Charlies ventured in from the dawn of the New Wave under the new name **This Heat**, holing up in a studio of their own below ground in a disused meat freezer in London's trendy but desperate Brixton and peppering John Peel with tapes of their own peculiar take on "pure pop for now people".

Peel let them into the BBC for a brace of sessions, the like of which had rarely been broadcast on mainstream radio. Constant gigging and "outreach work" with filmmakers, dance troupes and a whole bunch of what would later be conveniently bundled together as "world musicians" led the band to a densely blended stew of sounds, rhythms and percussion from around the globe, overly rich for most tastes and strong enough to force many listeners who couldn't stand This Heat to get out of their kitchen.

When the coterie of wild men from the butcher's warehouse began to work with a pair of madcap free jazzers who had previous convictions for prog rock, however, nothing good could come of it. **David Cunningham** and **Anthony Moore** (ex-Slapp Happy) co-produced *This Heat* in 1979, throwing their own taste for difficult music into the already stiflingly overcrowded sound, and made it available through David's own label, Piano. Bringing *musique concrète* to the masses was largely wasted effort, but nonetheless, the album stood out – even in a year of phenomenal creative work from all ends of the New Wave – for its disturbingly aimless explorations, the unsettling prediction of No Wave, and for simultaneously looking back to the golden age of Faust, Neu!, Can and the rest of the cosmic crew of early 1970s Germanic prog rock.

Curiously under-appreciated at home in the UK, the album began This Heat's international success and saw the band's name become one to drop in Germany, Japan and in the more thoughtful corners of the USA. Touring Europe in 1980, they stunned audiences with a custom-built sound rig of their own design (operated by **Jack Balchin**, ex-Henry Cow), and by adding layer upon layer of complexity thanks to **Pete Bullen** (additional tape-loop manipulation and sound bending).

Returning to the studio, the band first put out "Health And Efficiency", a single named after the UK's premier naturist publication, then gave us *Deceit* (humour was never their selling point) in 1981. **Martin Frederick** (who went on to become part of the On-U Anglo-dub sound system collective) mixed the second album and folded unfeasible amounts of reggae-based fruit, sparklers and mini-umbrellas into This Heat's explosively crowded cocktail glass. By creating an even more challenging cacophony for the ears to take in, both in the studio and live, Frederick ensured that the band's fans remained selective, few in number and recognizable by their inability to stop twitching, staring with paranoid eyes and muttering to themselves in the days following a gig.

In 1981 it all grew too much for Williams. He left the others and headed off to study Indian dance. His premature death in 2001 deprived the world of one of the great musical polymaths, a true innovator, all-round nice guy and friend of Rough Guides.

Trefor Goronwy (bass), **Ian Hill** (keyboards) and **Steve Rickard** (engineer de luxe) joined the rest of This Heat for a last European tour before the band finally folded in 1982. Charles Hayward, Goronwy and Rickard reappeared as **Camberwell Now** later in the decade, releasing a

number of singles and *All's Well*, a compilation of all their material, on the Swiss-based experimental Recommended Records in 1992.

Repeat (1993) and *Made Available* (1996, ironically currently unavailable), the latter a collection of tracks recorded for the John Peel show, mopped up the rest of the mess, appearing and disappearing from view fairly quickly. All This Heat material is worth a listen, and if you can find it at all, you might just find it entertaining.

⦾ **Out Of Cold Storage (RER, 2006)**

At last, the career-spanning retrospective that a generation of avant-garde noise fans have been waiting for has arrived. six full discs of wild, free-form explorations ranging from the tense, tight-knit claustrophobia of the band's first studio work, to the deafening bombastics of their live appearance, calling in at all points – world musical, dub-mental and more – en route.

⦾ **This Heat: Remastered (RER, 2006)**

First in what one assumes will turn out to be a continuing series of cleaned up masterpieces by this great lost band, this is the one to buy as a taster before splashing out your dough on the 6-disc set.

THREE COLOURS RED

Formed London, 1994; bled to death 1999, resuscitated 2000.

Short-lived but extremely loud, Three Colours Red was put together by **Pete Vukovic** (vocals/bass) with **Chris McCormack** (guitar), **Ben Harding** (more guitar) and **Keith Baxter** (drums), and named after the film by Krzysztof Kieslowski. They rocked their hearts out with a few short sets of heartfelt punk music, then split up and went on to better things elsewhere when the fun wore off.

Picking up a select but dedicated audience through live gigs, they released a fine single "This Is My Hollywood" on the none-more-indie Fierce Panda label, parlaying its success into a deal with almost-as-indie but bigger Creation Records.

Label boss Alan McGee fell in love with 3CR's raw energy, and captured it on their next single, "Nuclear Holiday", punting it out to radio stations with the enthusiasm of a true fan and believer. Another two singles preceded their 1997 debut album *Pure*, which won a wider audience through its perfect blending of punk with just a touch of metal. "Love's Cradle" and "Copper Girl" stand out, and echo the band's appreciation of Bob Mould's work with **Sugar**.

Revolt came out in 1999, bringing more of the same (standouts include "Beautiful Day", "Paralyse", "Paranoid People" and "This Is My Time"), but after a brace of exceptionally intense festival appearances later that year, egos intervened and 3CR went in four different directions. They've re-formed on several occasions since then and released a further single "Repeat To Fade" in 2003, but have yet to get back together sufficiently for a convincing or creative revival to be announced.

⊙ **Pure (Creation, 1997)**

Cracking debut, with nary a duff track among the thirteen it contains, this remains the band's most impressive, confident and, yes, purest piece of work. Standout tracks are hard to pick, but "This Is My Hollywood", "Nuclear Holiday" and "Copper Girl" are hard to beat.

THREE JOHNS

Born Leeds, 1982; split up 1988.

"... pure pop for now people, especially those who hated Thatcher."

John Dougan, All Music Guide

Jon Langford was a busy chap: one of the main driving forces of **The Mekons**, and a sought-after producer, the last thing he needed was a side-project agit-prop band. Still, he kept potential problems to a minimum by recruiting only like-minded chaps who all answered to the same name, and by insisting the band use a drum machine instead of a human percussionist (as the old joke says, you only need to punch the instructions in once). Jon (mad guitar/vocals) linked up with **John Hyatt** (more guitar/nutty vocals), **John "Philip" Brennan** (bass) and the above-mentioned rhythm box to become **The Three Johns**, bold thorn in the side of the fascists.

Politically-led post-punk art-rock with a dance beat was a peculiarly 1980s phenomenon and surprisingly widespread. Fiercely popular among the majority of young voters who were embarrassed by the excesses of Thatcherism and needed "right-on" tunes to get drunk and flirt to, The Three Johns were only one of the bands aiming to get on any blacklists being compiled. Gigging and working alongside The Gang Of Four, The Redskins, Billy Bragg and any number of ranting poets, The Three Johns brought humour, impressive Marxmanship and talent to a scene otherwise dominated by worthy but uninspired makeweights. Their sharp fingers pointed out the transatlantic folly of the Thatcher/Reagan political axis of evil, stabbed accusingly into the chests of home-grown boneheads, and made amusingly vulgar gestures at the same time.

The band bolted neatly onto the zeitgeist, kicking off with a deft two-chord knife-thrust into the heart of the South African apartheid regime. "English White Boy Engineer" (a Mekons cover) was released in 1982 on Leeds' own little hotbed of revolution, the CNT label. "Men Like Monkeys" followed the next year, but the full-length *Atom Drum Bop* (1984) almost derailed the great leap forward by diluting their lively, spirited and humorous calls to rebellion with ill-conceived, directionless and miserable blues riffs. Fortunately, the band were best known for their alcohol-fuelled, often shambolic but never dull live appearances, where the prevailing mood was one of "the revolution starts as soon as the bar closes". *Live In Chicago* (1986), one of the most exciting in-concert recordings of the decade, has the band in the most radical town in the US playing to a crowd who knows and loves them for their naughty leftie stance.

The World By Storm (1986) was a studio album that saw the lads reverting in part to the noodling of their debut. Its reputation, however, was saved by a blistering set of hard-hitting lyrics, delivered with distilled venom by Hyatt, who was approaching the peak of his powers as a vocalist.

This was, unfortunately, the end of the band's best period. They continued touring for another couple of years before falling apart, with their last recorded outing, *Death Of Everything And More* (1988), appearing at the end of their final US tour. Langford went back to being a Mekon and producer, Hyatt lectures in art, Brennan keeps his hand in with production, engineering and management, and the drum machine retired when the batteries went flat.

⊙ **The Best of the Three Johns** (Dojo, 1996)

Not easy to find, but more readily available than anything else they recorded, this 16-track compilation touches all the band's important bases. If you see anything else by The Three Johns, buy it immediately.

JOHNNY THUNDERS

Born John Anthony Genzale, Jr, became Johnny Volume in high school and Johnny Thunders in 1971; died 1991.

Johnny Thunders was the American antithesis of Johnny Rotten, and despite dying for his habit, was rock'n'roll's heroin poster-boy until Kurt Cobain of Nirvana left his brains all over the wall a decade later. Where Rotten's English scheme was all about shouting until the system collapsed under the browbeating, Thunders' route was to turn his back on what he didn't like and couldn't change, and numb his brain until it could cope with the pain.

Thunders' uniquely sleazy way with a guitar, lasciviously bending a misplaced note until it screamed for release, had been developed during his time as a lipstick killer with the **New York Dolls** (see p.212), and perfected in any number of big-city shooting-gallery studios. When Johnny staggered away from the wreckage of the Heartbreakers, it was as a fatally damaged solo artist. For the rest of his life, Johnny's talent was squandered paying for the drugs that would eventually kill him.

Thunders had a rock'n'roll heart and had paid his dues since high school days, fronting Johnny And The Jaywalkers, breaking hearts and getting a taste for applause. The glam-rock era led him to a band called Actress, where he met up with **Arthur Kane** and **Billy Murcia**. Together with **Syl Sylvain** and **David Johansen**, the threesome would become The New York Dolls, stars of the teen mags with an absolutely voracious appetite for booze, drugs and girls.

After three years of high-pressure rock'n'roll lifestyling around the world, the Dolls, like most teeny pop bands, imploded. Their original audience had grown up, they were seen as déclassé by the new generation, and they were getting to be skanky old men in their twenties with beards and bad habits. The difficulties of locating heroin in the backwoods of Florida on their 1975 tour (combined with the intolerable pressure of having Malcolm McLaren trying to be the band's manager) led to the unplanned end of the Dolls.

Once the boys felt well enough to continue, they recruited disaffected Television man **Richard Hell** as bassist and have-guitar-will-travel dude, **Walter "Waldo" Lure**, and knocked out a fast-paced, hard-hitting, down in the very gutter of the streets rock'n'roll set as **The Heartbreakers**, booting lumps off the local competition on stage, out-thugging The Ramones and tearing up the UK and American scene for one essential album, *L.A.M.F,* before musical differences led to a split in 1978.

🔊 PLAYLIST: HEARTBREAKERS

The Heartbreakers live and on form were the best band to hit London in the late 70s. In concert but incapable through booze and drugs they were unlistenable. Their playlist combines the best of their studio tracks with selections from their finest live recording.

1. ALL BY MYSELF
from **L.A.M.F.: ENHANCED** (Rhino, 2000)

2. BORN TO LOSE from **LIVE AT THE LYCEUM BALLROOM, LONDON 1984** (Receiver, 1999)

3. CHINESE ROCKS
from **L.A.M.F.: ENHANCED** (Rhino, 2000)

4. GET OFF THE PHONE
from **L.A.M.F.: ENHANCED** (Rhino, 2000)

5. I WANNA BE LOVED
from **L.A.M.F.: ENHANCED** (Rhino, 2000)

6. IT'S NOT ENOUGH
from **L.A.M.F.: ENHANCED** (Rhino, 2000)

7. LET GO
from **L.A.M.F.: ENHANCED** (Rhino, 2000)

8. ONE TRACK MIND from **LIVE AT THE LYCEUM BALLROOM, LONDON 1984** (Receiver, 1999)

9. PIRATE LOVE
from **L.A.M.F.: ENHANCED** (Rhino, 2000)

10. TOO MUCH JUNKIE BUSINESS from **LIVE AT THE LYCEUM BALLROOM...** (Receiver, 1999)

L-R: Waldo, Billy, Johnny. Jerry's just popped out, he'll be right back.

🎵 PLAYLIST: JOHNNY THUNDERS

With so many posthumous releases recorded live under appalling conditions on substandard equipment, Johnny's playlist comes mainly from his best solo album, with additional tracks from the best of the compilations.

1. DEAD OR ALIVE
from SO ALONE (Warner, 2005)

2. DOWNTOWN
from SO ALONE (Warner, 2005)

3. HURT ME
from BORN TO LOSE (Jungle, 1999)

4. LITTLE BIT OF WHORE
from BORN TO LOSE (Jungle, 1999)

5. LONDON BOYS
from SO ALONE (Warner, 2005)

6. M.I.A.
from BORN TO LOSE (Jungle, 1999)

7. SHE'S SO UNTOUCHABLE
from SO ALONE (Warner, 2005)

8. SO ALONE
from SO ALONE (Warner, 2005)

9. TOO MUCH JUNKIE BUSINESS/PILLS
from BORN TO LOSE (Jungle, 1999)

10. YOU CAN'T PUT YOUR ARMS ROUND A
MEMORY from SO ALONE (Warner, 2005)

Thunders put together *So Alone* (1978), nominally a solo outing, with a little help from his friends. "London Boys" – a pointed dig at Johnny Rotten – was recorded in association with Steve Jones and Paul Cook from the Pistols. Various other badly behaved luminaries of the London rock'n'roll establishment were roped in to produce the punk-rock equivalent of one of those tedious gigs where the star's celebrity pals appear for a verse, a chorus and a round of applause. Except of course, it was anything but tedious – Thunders could call on Paul Gray (Eddie & The Hot Rods/The Damned), Phil Lynott (Thin Lizzy), Steve Marriott (Small Faces/ Humble Pie), Patti Palladin (Snatch) and Peter Perrett (The

Only Ones), and he made sure there was enough of anything that anyone might feel the need of, just to make the sessions go with a swing. The album swaggered into the shops with a lopsided grin and wearing a pirate hat, and still sounds like the best party you never went to. Thunders even shared the stage with Sid Vicious for a brief period, when, post-Pistols, the two of them dreamed up an idea for a band called The Living Dead (basically Johnny and Sid, most of the *So Alone* crowd, and whichever of their more degenerate pals could be bothered to show up and was capable of performing at the gig).

Moving back to the USA, Thunders continued to trade his good looks, bubbly personality and blisteringly intense performances for bag after bag of powdered fun, surfacing throughout the 1980s either solo or with scratch bands of pick-up musicians keen to say they had played with a legend. The star himself often took part of his fee up front, in the arm. There are dozens of live recordings taken from this period on the market, with many being bootleg recordings of very dubious quality. Thunders was well aware that a large, slimy swathe of these late-period fans showed up at least partly to see if he'd make it through the gig without collapsing and turning blue right there on stage, but by this time he rarely seemed to care. Despite pulling himself together in 1985 for *Que Sera Sera*, a solid set of originals, he grew infamous for showing up drunk and with horrific cigarette burns – on his clothes and on the skin underneath – leading many to debate whether his eventual demise would come through an overdose or exploding into flame.

Thunders next recorded seriously towards the end of the decade, first on a weird retro-looking doo-woppy covers album with Patti Palladin called *Copy Cats* (1988), then with **Wayne Kramer** – another role model for the spikyhead nutcase generation, with a pedigree that included the MC5 and federal time served for dealing coke – as part of **Gang War**. This band had a name so terrible that even a pair of drug fiends like Thunders and Kramer found it hard to take seriously, and after just the one album in 1990, the band split up.

Thunders ended up playing with a group happy to be called **The Oddballs**. Packing up and doing one last interview at the end of a tour with them, he declared his intention to blend trad jazz from the roots with his own freebooting style of rock and head off south to the Big Easy. Moving away from his home city of sin and degradation was a good idea; moving to New Orleans, another town where it's easy to get any damn thing you might desire, 24 hours a day, every day, wasn't so smart. Though he had been diagnosed with lymphatic cancer and was refusing to be treated for it, when Thunders showed up dead in a hotel room in April 1991, reportedly with cocaine and methadone in his bloodstream, all the obvious conclusions were drawn. His fans refused to let him go quietly, though, and conspiracy theories about who wanted him dead were circulating before the autopsy results were out.

King Outlaw (also known as *Born To Lose* and *The Last Rock'n'roll Film*) – a dark-side gloomy biopic by Lech Kowalski, the man who filmed *D.O.A.* (1980), appeared towards the end of 1997. There's a fine DVD available of Johnny And The Heartbreakers on their 1984 reunion tour, called *Dead Or Alive*; it's only 90 minutes long and most of the interviews descend into drugged silence, but the live footage is lovely to behold.

⊙ So Alone (Warner, reissued 2005)

Thunders' best solo album and the only really essential item from his post-Heartbreakers career. The reissue adds "So Alone" (inexplicably omitted from the original) and "The Wizard" as bonus cuts.

TOWERS OF LONDON

Formed in Wolverhampton, England, 2005.

When **Dirk Tourette** (guitar) and his bro' **Donny Tourette** (vocals) teamed up to make a rock'n'roll noise, there were bound to be sparks and four-letter words aplenty. Their first line-up was called The Tourettes and boasted some of the ugliest haircuts ever allowed on the British punk scene. When they signed **Tommy Brunette** (bass) and **Snell** (drums), they were buying themselves a one-way ticket to the slammer. Luckily, they found **The Rev** (guitar) whose spiritual guidance and pastoral care have kept them out of jail, so far, and adopted the new **Towers Of London** name.

The Tourette brothers are proudly descended from the punk-rock traditionals such as The Sex Pistols, whereas The Rev contributes a more Guns'n'Roses vibe – just as debauched but with a little more grease added to the sleaze.

Swaggering around like they were the privileged and spoilt offspring of the Sex Pistols with tracks such as "Beaujolais", "I'm A Rat", "I Lose It", "How Rude She Was", "Fuck It Up", "On A Noose" and "Kill The Pop Scene" they are the consummate neo-punk band for the new century. They bring the steaming arrogance of Zigue Zigue Sputnik to a scene that had become contended, self-satisfied and too bloody quiet, delivering body-shuddering punches of tightly concentrated devilish punk energy with every one of their songs. They fight one another, they scrap with the audience, they're convinced of their own invincibility and take a shitload of drugs. Ladies and gentlemen, it's the return of The Motley New Velvet Stooges Dolls Crue Underground!

◉ **Blood Sweat And Towers** (TVT, 2006)

A fine, eleven-track introduction to the wonderful and frightening world of ToL, a set of initials that one hopes will be as successful as PiL. All the singles, all the outrage, all the tight-white trousers and hairspray you could want.

TRUE SOUNDS OF LIBERTY (TSOL)

First rang true in Huntington Beach, California, 1979; stayed free till 1986, then went glam/ metal. Oh dear.

Orange County, California must have been the noisiest parish in the union back in the late 1970s when tons of kids, well off by European standards, got into punk rock and expensively loud amplification all at once. **True Sounds Of Liberty** combined the energy and intensity of punk with the raw power and attack of good-quality equipment, plus the firm belief that more volume is more fun. They were an impressive-looking bunch too – compared to the malnourished urchins of London and New York, these were corn-fed giants (the white face paint was a mistake, though – it always is).

In their previous incarnation, **Vicious Circle**, the guys had been known for the enthusiasm of their audience, and had a rotten reputation for provoking their fans into riot and mayhem. **Jack Greggors** (vocals) took the wise precaution of changing his last name for every new album, whereas **Ron Emory** (guitar), **Mike Roche** (bass) and **Todd Barnes** (drums) relied on the fact that they looked as if they'd like nothing better than to finish off a gig by punching the lights out of the promoter or venue owner. Still, to avoid trouble and the numerous bans they accumulated, a change of band name was required – and so **TSOL** appeared on the scene, tearing the ass out of South Bay and Orange Co. venues much as before, but with a new focus on the cool new noise of hardcore music. They already knew their chops as musicians, and when the *True Sounds Of Liberty* EP came out (on the magnificently named Posh Boy label), new fans up and down the West Coast signed up for the ride.

The band, meanwhile, signed up for some top-notch gigs, kicking off 1981 by supporting big names – such as The Damned and Dead Kennedys – in big venues in big cities including San Francisco and Los Angeles, and recording their debut full-length recording, *Dance With Me*. The album blended raw'n'political hardcore and cheap'n'nasty horror-comic material (very similar to the vein being mined on the East Coast at the same time by The Misfits), sold in enormous quantities and put TSOL into a new and higher orbit where they were the headline act. This new goth-pop life of financial security in the music-biz cocoon naturally began to eat away at the band's ability to keep in touch with their roots, and as always in this story, increased popularity led inevitably to a drop in punk-rock appeal.

Beneath The Shadows (1981) saw them signed to the bigger and better Alternative Tentacles label, but sounding pompous and bloated. The line-up was boosted by the addition of **Bob Kuehn** (keyboards) who filled in a lot of the spaces in the band's previous sound and made for some dense, uneasy listening. Despite the debut containing songs about necrophilia and other gothic fascinations, there was even more emphasis on the ghoulish and gruesome, far less attention to punk-rock concerns and a disturbing new tendency for the band to dress up like movie monsters for live appearances. When Greggors quit in 1984 for new and different names in new and different groups, followed swiftly by Barnes, the rot set in and was soon irreversible. **Joe Wood** (vocal, guitar) and **Mitch Dean** (drums) were recruited to take on the newly available roles and *Change Today* (1984) was rush-released to keep the fans on board. It didn't do the trick, and neither did *Revenge* (1986).

TSOL pushed on regardless, hanging on to life in the music-biz intensive care ward for the rest of the 1980s and into the next decade, despite haemorrhaging their audience and replacing the members that quit like so many blood-soaked bandages. By 1990 all the original members had left the group and the new lot were a standard hair-metal band, MTV-friendly and safe as milk.

Finally, though, the torment ended. Falling apart in as many different directions as possible, almost everyone who had ever been in the band decided independently to carry the torch and name of

TSOL forward, and for a while there were several "original" TSOL line-ups on the scene. Lawsuits intervened and the situation was eventually clarified. By this stage, however, few people really cared, and although there are still the occasional TSOLs to be seen here and there, it all went sour many years ago.

⊙ TSOL/Weathered Statues (Nitro, 1999)

Excellent collection of pretty much everything TSOL ever did that was worth hearing. With "Weathered Statues" and the whole of their first EP included, this is good old-school hardcore from the place they invented it.

TUBES

Formed San Francisco, 1972; still riding the underground.

The group that gave the world's snot-nosed spoilt brats their own anthem, "White Punks On Dope", were never a punk band. In fact, given that their roots go back to the late 1960s, they weren't even a New Wave act. Whatever, they were slack, occasionally hilarious, and did give us all a big old song to chant along with. Bands that try to be funny rarely manage to keep it up for long, and The Tubes' satire was written in a very broad brush, but for a band aiming at stadium-sized crowds and multi-platinum albums, subtlety was never an option.

Still, once upon a time in Arizona towards the end of the 1960s, there was a band called **The Beans**, which included **Bill Spooner** (guitar), **Vince Welnick** (keyboards) and **Rick Anderson** (bass) in its line-up. An early taste for the outrageous caused them to do occasional shows as The Radar Men From Uranus. When The Beans moved north to San Francisco in 1972, they hooked up with **Michael Cotten** (keyboards), **Prairie Prince** (drums), **Roger Steen** (guitar) and former roadie and born front man **Fee Waybill** (vocals). Together, they were **The Tubes**, a proper rock band with an agenda to make millions of people laugh (well, to make millions, at least). Fee charged body and soul into his new role – he once broke his leg on stage and finished the gig regardless – embracing a whole slew of characters ranging from the crippled Nazi Dr Strangekiss and the ultimately debauched rockstar Quay Lude, to Johnny Bugger, an easily digested punk-rocker composite persona. Before too long, the band had a huge live reputation and were ripe for a record deal. A&M gave them the nod in 1975, with *The Tubes* appearing later that year.

Pre-DVD, any recording of a band that relied solely upon bad puns and a tightly choreographed stage act was pretty much doomed. Funkadelic/ Parliament did shows just as weird, and Pink Floyd did shows even bigger, but those bands had talent to spare as musicians and songwriters. The Tubes had little more than huge fake plastic tits and neon-bright feather boas to fall back on. The soft-porn section of their shows helped to get them banned here and there in the UK, and drummed up a little controversy, but it was all very tacky.

The album included "White Punks On Dope", which became a counter-culture hit in the UK after the band's widely trailed European tour introduced their shtick to an audience more used to denim-clad hairies. When some clever marketing bod introduced very collectable badges enigmatically saying "WPOD", the band found themselves immensely popular with white punks (whether on dope or not). "Don't Touch Me There", the album's only other standout track, sounded like it came straight from *The Rocky Horror Picture Show* soundtrack recording and is still a pretty funny tune about sweat-smeared adolescent yes/no, stop it/do it again conversations.

Subsequent albums failed to perform anywhere near as well, being hampered by the obvious lack of visuals, and although *Young And Rich* (1976), *The Tubes Now* (1977) and *What Do You Want From Live* [sic] (1978) all had their moments, none of them approached the excitement of the full on Tubes experience. By 1979 and *Remote Control*, the band had moved away from punk and New Wave concerns, and had taken their music back to the genial soft rock they found most comfortable. Since then, although they continue to stomp the halls like the rock'n'roll dinosaurs they undoubtedly are, The Tubes have become a parody of a parody, and these days, even live, they lack the punch to make them a worthwhile evening out.

⊙ White Punks On Dope (Acadia, 2003)

Most recent of the zillions of compilations available, with the title cut and "Don't Touch Me There" the only tracks you'll ever want to hear twice. You'd be better off buying a cheapo punk compilation with a richer and more interesting mix of artists.

U.K. SUBS

Formed in a hairdresser's in Tooting, London, in 1976. Probably gonna dance on your grave, chum.

Legend has it that hairdresser-turned-punk-rock-fixture **Charlie Harper** (gravel-gargling vocals) was converted into one of the scene's first punk rockers after a Damascene conversion courtesy of The Damned back in 1976. Whether this is true or whether he merely leapt onto a passing bandwagon when in need of a lift home is beside the point; what matters is that the band he leads, **U.K. Subs**, never sold out, never compromised (much) and never quit.

At 32 years old, he was also one of the scene's oldest characters, with some serious background to draw on, and the stamina to throw himself around like an Iggy Pop with new batteries. Before he formed the **U.K. Subversives** (instantly shortened to "Subs" by band and fans alike), Charlie

had been David Charles Perez, and the front man for Marauder, one of the many bands dedicated to preaching the raw truth of vintage R&B to a pub-rock audience of the largely already converted and generally drunk. After hearing the siren call from Dave Vanian and the gang, he found himself a band – **Paul/Steve Slack** (bass), **Richard Anderson** (guitar) and short-term sticksman **Robbie Harper** (drums) and set about rehearsing back in his South London salon. From the start, the Subs championed a blend of muscular punk rock grown from Charlie's R&B roots, but played much louder and far faster. Finding a drummer who would stay long enough to get a mention here was more of a problem, but after every wannabe musician within a four-mile radius of Charlie's base had been tried and found wanting, **Pete Davis** (drums) finally agreed and became the Subs' semi-detached percussion man. Anderson made a wrong move and **Nicky Garrett** (guitar) shoved his way into the band.

A U.K. Subs Alphabet

As the years have passed, U.K. Subs have slowly filled the gaps in their ABC of album titles. What they'll do when they run out of available letters is anyone's guess, but it's unlikely to involve the "splitting up and retiring" option

Another Kind of Blues (1979)
Brand New Age (1980)
Crash Course (1980)
Diminished Responsibility (1981)
Endangered Species (1982)
Flood of Lies (1983)
Gross-Out USA (1985)
Huntington Beach (UK Subs) (1986)
In Action — Tenth Anniversary (1986)
Japan Today (1988)
Killing Time (1989)
Left For Dead (2003)

Mad Cow Fever (2001)
Normal Service Resumed (2003)
Occupied (1996)
Punk Can Take It (2001)
Quintessentials (2002)
Riot (1997)
Self Destruct: Punk Can Take It Vol.2 (2001)
Time Warp (2001)
Universal (2002)
Violent State (2005)
World War (2003)

Charlie's gang: U.K. Subs.

This line-up stayed together long enough to land the first of several John Peel sessions, and a recording contract leading to their full-length debut *Another Kind Of Blues* in 1979. They'd been recorded before, however, on a night when Davis's place was taken by the happily named **Rory Lyons** (drums), at the Roxy Club in London (just before it changed hands and reopened as a parody of itself). This performance was later released as *Live Kicks*.

"Another Kind Of Blues" was a knowing reference to the pills of choice back then in London, a barbaric amphetamine-like combination of chalk and rat poison known as "speckled blues". Charlie then titled the Subs' first album with the first letter of the alphabet, beginning a series that's yet to finish (see box opposite).

For a punk band, the group had enjoyed considerable success with their singles, and had been the subject of a well-received Julien Temple documentary film, *Punk Can Take It* (1979). A spirited parody of 1940s Ministry of Information propaganda films, this followed the Subs around a 1970s Britain looking as gritty and dated as the era it spoofed, and delivered some classic footage of the band and their fans. By the time *Another Kind Of Blues* reached the stores in 1979, however,

the audience for good old-fashioned politically inclined rock'n'roll had moved on. That year in the UK, the kids were getting it on to scary electronic experimental music, crazed "global" drum beats and echo-drenched vocals from skinny white boys wearing even whiter make-up. This was the dawn of the goth, and spikyheads were wildly out of fashion.

The band tried, and failed to make it in the USA, tagging along on the 1980 Police tour, and reverting to plans B and C (*Brand New Age* and *Crash Course*) back home to try and shore up their disappearing audience. Most bands would quit after plans D and E also came to nothing, and to be fair but brutal, there was little punk in either *Diminished Responsibility* (1981) or 1982's metallic *Endangered Species*. But all the personnel changes (replacement drummer **Steve Roberts** took Davis's seat, and new bassist **Alvin Gibbs** came in for a while before going on to work with Iggy Pop – his book *Neighbourhood Threat* is a recommended read for all you punks and aspiring musicians), and genre swapping eventually came to nothing. After spending a gruelling 1980s without Garrett, working their way onward through the alphabet, the Subs went back to what they knew best: punk rock.

PLAYLIST: UK SUBS

Proudly resistant to any musical progress, the Subs remain essentially a "3 minutes and out" singles band. Their greatest hits, and most of the titles listed below, come on the *Punk Singles Collection* (Anagram, 2004), but full album release details are included for your punk-rockin' convenience.

1. B1C
from **Another Kind Of Blues (Captain Oi!, 2000)**

2. BARMY LONDON ARMY from **Diminished Responsibility (Captain Oi!, 2000)**

3. C.I.D.
from **Another Kind Of Blues (Captain Oi!, 2000)**

4. DF118
from **Occupied (Fall Out, 1996)**

5. I LIVE IN A CAR
from **Another Kind Of Blues (Captain Oi!, 2000)**

6. PARTY IN PARIS
from **Universal (Captain Oi!, 2002)**

7. TEENAGE
from **Brand New Age(Captain Oi!, 2000)**

8. THIS GUN SAYS
from **Huntington Beach (Captain Oi!, 1999)**

9. TOMORROW'S GIRLS
from **Another Kind Of Blues (Captain Oi!, 2000)**

10. WARHEAD
from **Violent State (Combat Rock, 2005)**

Ultimately, the revival scene caught up with them and they enjoyed a return to fame – if on an even smaller scale – on the punk memorabilia / revival circuit. The same mid-1990s mini-boom that inspired the Pistols to get back together resulted in the release of a bunch of greatest hits collections – many of them unofficial. Spending more time in court than on stage for a while, Harper and the band wrestled back control of their catalogue, and most collections on sale today come with the band's blessing. To this day the Subs play rockin', high-energy, fast-paced social conscience music, and they remain one of the country's best-loved and most successful punk outfits.

⊙ **Another Kind of Blues** (Captain Oi!, 2000)

If the phrase "Next Please, B1C" means anything to you at all, then you need this album. Even if you've never had the personal pleasure of registering for state benefits in the UK, you should find plenty of emotional resonance in the rest of this blunderbuss of a debut. It's a joyous maelstrom of apocalyptic nuclear fear, speed anthems and the finest punk-rockery.

⊙ **Gross Out USA** (Fall Out, 1995)

The band's third live album (recorded after *Live Kicks* and *Crash Course*), knocks out sixteen stunning songs and is the most satisfying record available of the U.K. Subs' tremendous live performances.

⊙ **The Punk Singles Collection** (Anagram, 2004)

The best of the compilations available at the time of writing.

**ICONIC SINGLE:
C.I.D.** (PINNACLE, 1978)

"He's an underground undercover agent for the C.I.D., C.I.D., C.I.D. / Got a loaded .44 / Walking armoury store." Despite the track's fairly lame lyrics (undercover CID officers weren't that menacing, and so easy to spot – whenever they turned up at punk gigs they were the only ones in plain clothes), it was a commercial success and went into multiple pressings – almost all on brightly coloured vintage punk-style vinyl. A damn fine slice of punk rock from the unpolluted source.

THE UNDERTONES

Surfaced in Derry, Northern Ireland, 1975; sank 1983. Bobbed back up and still treading water.

Amidst the petrol bombings, punishment beatings and sniper alleys of Northern Ireland in the 1970s, a military regime was trying to keep the peace. Once the kids there got their hot little hands on the first Ramones album however, the battle was lost; there was just no stopping them from bopping. Hidden away on a Derry housing estate, **Feargal Sharkey** (ex-choirboy and purveyor of "distinctive" vocals), **John O'Neill** (guitar) and his brother **Damian O'Neill** (also guitar), **Michael Bradley** (bass), and **Billy Doherty** (drums) took apart da brudders' bubblegum nihilism and built their own version, stripped down even beyond the minimalism of the original, and resolutely taking absolutely no notice of the internecine strife on the streets outside.

As **The Undertones**, they produced a rare, exhilarating punked-up pop, identifiable as soon as Sharkey opened his mouth. The Undertones wrote carefully crafted pop tunes that broke out of the New Wave ghetto and hit the charts.

Just like in the movies, our discouraged heroes were on the brink of splitting up before they really got started. As The Boomtown Rats and Stiff Little Fingers were finding, it didn't matter where in the island of Ireland you based yourself, neither did it matter which side you followed in football, politics or religion. What mattered most was – "Are you a showband? If not, at least, say you're a country and western act? No? You're what? Punk rock? Oh, then I'm sorry son ... I'm sure you understand."

Enter stage left, Belfast record-shop boss, the magical Terry Hooley. A true believer in the band's power and scope, he helped out with their first recordings, and released the *Teenage Kicks* EP on his own Good Vibrations label in September 1978. Gambling their future on the price of a stamp, the guys sent a copy to the BBC in London and bam!, The Undertones had a hit, on John Peel's show at least, and Damian found himself being asked for autographs by colleagues at work.

> ## "Our only hope was John Peel, and we sent him a copy – that was the only copy we sent anyone."
>
> ### Feargal Sharkey

Peel famously stated his love of the track "Teenage Kicks" dozens of times – he played it twice in succession on his show, a small-sounding innovation but something that had never been done before, and he confessed that every time he played it, he welled up with tears, choked on the lump in his throat and had to segue into the next track until he recovered his composure. This now extraordinarily collectable disc included "Smarter Than You", "True Confessions" and "Emergency Cases" alongside the title cut, and Peel turned every one of them into an instantly recognizable hit.

Sire stepped in to do its major-label thing, rushing the guys into the studio and squeezing *The Undertones* out of them – presumably by some industrial / mechanical process – in 1979. The lads blew some of their £60,000 advance on a slap-up feed at a *McDonald's* in London. The rough edges that remained on the recording merely added to the charm of the whole, and seemed to reinforce the lads' experience of Northern Ireland's genuine "no future" atmosphere – forcing politically charged but essentially middle-class bands on the mainland (hello there to The Clash, the Pistols and Sham 69) to indulge in a certain amount of uncomfortable self-analysis.

The Undertones joined The Clash's tour of the USA later that year, picking up a respectably sized American fan-base and ignoring the enticements of the evil empire so totally that it almost seemed a calculated pose intended to shame the headline act into dropping "I'm So Bored With The USA" from their set.

Undertones: (L-R) Feargal, Michael, John, Damian and Billy.

PLAYLIST: UNDERTONES

Stuffed so full of talent that the limited technicalities and amateur musicianship of punk would never hold them for long, The Undertones produced a set of miniature epics, each illustrating a perfect slice of adolescent life.

1. CRISIS OF MINE
from **POSITIVE TOUCH** (Sanctuary, 2006)

2. EMERGENCY CASES
from **THE UNDERTONES** (Sanctuary, 2004)

3. GET OVER YOU
from **THE UNDERTONES** (Sanctuary, 2004)

4. I GOTTA GETTA
from **THE UNDERTONES** (Sanctuary, 2004)

5. I TOLD YOU SO
from **HYPNOTISED** (Sanctuary, 2005)

6. IT'S GOING TO HAPPEN
from **POSITIVE TOUCH** (Sanctuary, 2006)

7. MY PERFECT COUSIN
from **HYPNOTISED** (Sanctuary, 2005)

8. SMARTER THAN YOU
from **THE UNDERTONES** (Sanctuary, 2004)

9. TEENAGE KICKS
from **THE UNDERTONES** (Sanctuary, 2004)

10. YOU'VE GOT MY NUMBER (WHY DON'T YOU USE IT) from **THE UNDERTONES** (Sanctuary, 2004)

Rocking into the new year with *Hypnotised* (1980), the Undertones continued to cheerily confess to their teenage fixations with chocolate, schooldays and the holy grail – girls, in all their unapproachable glory. "Wednesday Week" and "My Perfect Cousin" charted impressively but it wasn't until *Positive Touch* (1981) that the guys began to broaden their range and to address their subjects with any kind of professional-musicianly maturity. They bolted on horn sections, a piano player and all kinds of unnecessaries, creating an unwieldy composite beast – punk rock, but with an orchestral, widescreen vision – that was awkward, scratchy and uncomfortable as a well-meaning auntie's first attempt at knitting a pullover. "It's Gonna Happen" sounded both strange and lovely, went into the charts and split the fan-base in two. The Undertones weren't a punk band any more.

Beautifully naïve at the outset of their career, the band had an equally impressive indifference to commercial success, refusing to become "stars" or act like conventional rock-biz assholes. However, they committed the one unforgivable sin in pop – they grew up. When *The Sin Of Pride* appeared in 1983 (following ominous disagreements and a dodgy single, "The Love Parade"), the guys had dislodged the fairy dust, and were no longer able magically to conjure top pop tunes out of thin air. After a summertime flurry of farewell gigs and festival appearances, The Undertones split up.

Sharkey went on to a weird solo career as a warbling soul man, picking up some chart success but never looking back to the New Wave. The brothers O'Neill formed **That Petrol Emotion** and had a stab

ICONIC SINGLE:
TEENAGE KICKS (LABEL, DATE)

With a clanging guitar intro that's as recognizable as the opening bars to the National Anthem (and far more popular), "Teenage Kicks" stands as an unstained icon of pure pop beauty, with an appeal that's spread since its release far beyond any narrow punk / New Wave ghetto, into the consciousness of the whole music-loving world.

This song, so dear to John Peel that he specified its opening lines be engraved on his tombstone, managed to capture all the delicious, hot sweat-tainted frustration of adolescent desire in a manner unmatched since the glory days of The Shangri-Las in a couple of tersely phrased verses and a chorus of crescendo anticipation. Feargal's vocals never sounded more strangulated, the O'Neill brothers and their guitars chime with a tear-jerking loveliness of their own while the rhythm section of Michael and Billy flail away as if their future sex lives depended upon it. In the Jungle Book of punk, this roars triumphant with sheer, carnal delight.

at more hard-hitting political punk rock, with success taking them through a hard decade. Undertones reunion plans came and went, usually falling apart at the last minute due to ego problems, until in 1999 the O'Neills recruited **Paul McLoone** (vocals) and got the rest of the band back together without troubling Sharkey.

In 2001, a marvellous documentary showed members of the band recalling their early days to none other than John Peel. The interviews – all but Sharkey's conducted in Derry – were interspersed with archive footage of a Northern Ireland that thankfully no longer exists. An expanded DVD version, *The Story Of The Undertones: Teenage Kicks* (Sanctuary, 2003), also contains the promo videos for all the band's best singles, making it an essential purchase. Meanwhile the McLoone-led Undertones are regularly seen beaming grins from stages up and down the country, giving the group more sales success than at any time in the previous twenty years. *Get What You Need* (2003) received a unanimously warm welcome from the music press and diehard fans alike, appealing equally to a new audience who had been dragged along to gigs by nostalgic parents.

⊚ **Undertones (Sanctuary, 2003)**

As the consummate singles band of the era, it seems strange to recommend the Undertones' debut studio set over a greatest hits collection. But the boys from downtown Derry never recorded anything that came close to this masterful first full-lengther.

UT

Formed NYC, US, 1978; disbanded 1990.

Forming toward the end of the 1970s, Ut was a three piece outfit – Nina Canal (ex-Dark Days), **Sally Young** and **Jacqui Ham** – that started scaring the bejaysus out of anyone within earshot with their distinctly noisy and "free" take on the New Wave groove. Finding themselves lumped in with the rag, tag and bobtail detritus of the Big Apple's No Wave scene (essentially a bunch of art-rock poseurs who fancied the chance of working with Brian Eno), Ut tried hard to prove themselves to be among the more interesting groups on the scene, but found little recognition among their peers.

Their material has been described as anti-rock – Ut were wilder than The Slits, more committed to the struggle than The Au Pairs and far more nerve-jangling than Liliput. Remaining too extreme even for the pretentious dissonance fans of the No Wave, they upped sticks and hit the UK, where they landed a deal with Blast First and released the *Ut* EP (1984), *Early Live Life (1987)* and *In Gut's House* (1987); the latter featured the band's finest moment, "Evangelist".

Ut began to lean on the beat a little at this point, and picked up some sympathetic press coverage, but their sound still had nothing to dance to. Free music had its place in the later days of the New Wave but its place was already filled by groups such as Test Department, This Heat and, at the poppier end of the market, label-mates Sonic Youth – Ut were surplus to requirements.

Eventually in 1989, Ut took the opportunity to record *Griller* (Blast First, 1989) with rising-star producer **Steve Albini**. When it sold in the dozens rather than thousands, Canal and the gals finally came to accept that the world wasn't ready for Ut and split up. Ut's influence has been detected in the work of later bands including Bikini Kill, Veruca Salt and Sonic Youth, while the girls themselves have cropped up in numerous other projects, most notably Jacqui Ham's **Dial** project.

⊚ **In Gut's House (Blast First/Mute; 1987)**

This band have always been an acquired taste, but their records are worth tracking down nonetheless. This is probably the neatest place to start.

THE VELVET UNDERGROUND

Formed New York, 1965; disbanded 1971.
Re-formed 1992; disbanded 1995.

"The only reason we wore sunglasses on stage was because we couldn't stand the sight of the audience."

JOHN CALE

Experts, especially musicologists and heavy-duty rock journalists, can easily zoom in so close to their subject that they lose sight of why it entranced them in the first place. In the same way that a dog-show judge will ignore the joy of a puppy sitting on their lap and licking their face, people who write about **The Velvet Underground** often forget the peculiar thrill they bring – more akin to having someone sit on your face to lick your lap – in their earnest, well-researched and mindlessly detailed archaeological analysis of the band's immense importance and weighty influence on anyone who's been anyone in the song'n'dance biz since then.

Nevertheless, The Velvet Underground are unique in rock history. No other band ever achieved so little during its lifespan and had such a vast influence on the generation that followed. And all **Lou Reed** (guitar/vocals) ever wanted was to be a rock'n'roll star. Starting out as a doo-wopper in The Shades back in the 1950s, Lou felt the three-chord trick deep down in his rock and roll heart.

The band first brewed up a storm on the US East Coast around 1966, building up a dour menacing cold front in direct opposition to the peace'n'love vibes radiating their way from the San Francisco acid rock scene. Lou and his trusty sidekick **Sterling Morrison** (guitar) had met up earlier in the decade at Syracuse University NY, sharing a taste for wildly cool music played at extreme volume. They briefly parted company on leaving the world of academia – Lou shortly surfacing in a tunes-by-the-yard song factory on Mahattan's tin-pan alley – but when Lou found there was another like-minded soul in the shape of **John Cale** (bass, viola, organ, vocals) working down the hall at the same crappy music publishers, he rushed to the phone, called Sterl and set up a rehearsal.

Lou had written a song, "(Do) The Ostrich", a strictly for kids dumb-ass pop song based on a spurious new dance routine, and with John and Sterling, set about recording and releasing it under the name of The Primitives. Slapping on some cheap and nasty "party" sound effects added little to the mood and made the final mix so muddy that the radio stations wouldn't touch it. However, it indicated that the guys shared a vision in which rock music was stripped of all its unnecessary fripperies, tuned up high, chromed, polished and revealed as a sleek, overpowered, chopped hog that you'd just die for a chance to ride.

Picking up a temporary drummer (**Angus MacLise** – who quit the band before their first appearance as he didn't dig being paid to gig), the triumvirate set about their task to reveal and work on the basic heart that made the rock beast tick. John and Lou set about recording some demos (included as disc no.1 of the *Peel Slowly And See* box set) showing influences that ranged between a troubadour-style "Venus In Furs" to a shit-kickin' country'n'western version of "Heroin". Luckily, before any of that old rubbish made it to vinyl, the guys replaced Angus with Saint **Moe Tucker**, found the world's coolest band name on the title of a pulp S&M novel, and hooked up with **Andy Warhol**.

Warhol's influence on the band brought as many benefits in the way of opened doors, album artwork, publicity and finance as it did disadvantages (his picky interference, protectiveness, assumption of ownership and introducing **Nico**), but he never managed to boost the band out of its underground niche and onto the world stage in the same way The Doors or the rest of the L.A. stoners had been. Forced to remain in their comfortable East Coast sewer, and stuck with a one-time model as part-time chanteuse, the band assembled a stunning, soul-wrenching set of songs, rehearsed them to brittle, sharp perfection and recorded them for prestigious "freak" label Verve as *The Velvet Underground And Nico* (1967).

An ex-Warhol Superstar, turned gloomy junkie, Nico had materialized, vampire-like, on the NYC art scene having fled her haunted castle in Europe. Passing her on to the Velvets was the only way Andy could be rid of her, but it was to a group already overstuffed with ego, and despite making some of the set forever her own, there was no way Lou would share the front man role with someone taller, better-looking and so anti-Semitic.

Backstage music biz chicanery held up the release of their album so that Jim Morrison and *The Doors* could reap the press benefits of being the first "freak" record on the streets but theirs was in the stores just a week later. Unfortunately it peaked at #171 in the US album charts, and never even beeped onto the radar screens in Europe or the rest of the world.

The first "popular music" recording to address opiate addiction, "Heroin" was the album's most immediately attractive and shocking cut. Any attempt to deal with the joys of the white horse was bound to attract criticism, particularly in such a fine piece of music and, despite the song ultimately coming down on the anti side of the argument, it made the band notorious. With the album's other prime cuts looking at the lighter side of sado-masochism, scoring smack up in Harlem, the blank-eyed stares of the amphetamined debutantes surrounding Andy, and exploring the John Cale school of droner rock, it was unclassifiable and like nothing else on the market. Extended feedback, noise confusion and industrial-strength machine rhythms were interspersed with tinkling examinations of shabby socialites and preening, drug-addicted drag queens. It grew to become arguably the most influential album in rock, and one of the best loved if slowest-selling gold albums in history however, and by increasing the pressure on the band to perform – especially in the wake of dismissing Andy Warhol from his management function – it merely stimulated them to do better.

Stimulating themselves in slightly less legally acceptable ways too, the Velvets descended to a subterranean studio and produced a dark, thundering masterpiece – *White Light / White Heat*. Released in December 1967, it slammed a heavy metal door shut on the Summer of Love, setting off the booming clanging reverberations that make the second album such a beautiful noise.

Dirty and sweet, clad in black, the album showed a grainy image of the band, frozen in a squalid room somewhere in a squalid apartment, and appeared as the stark opposite of the hippy-dippy candypop output of the bongo-playing punks in Frisco. While California's flower children blew bubbles and danced in the park, Lou's inspirational angels flicked bubbles clear of their works before setting their fingers dancing up their arms looking for a vein. *White Light / White Heat* was, if anything, even less compromising in content than the first album had been: the title track celebrated banging up crystal meth, "The Gift" had its hero stabbed in the head, and "I Heard Her Call My Name" starts mid-song with a wail of feedback and Lou gibbering lyrics like a teletype spitting the football results. The set's absolute standout however was "Sister Ray". Clocking in at exactly the amount of time it takes to shower, shave and cook up a shot, the track is a seventeen-minute-thirty-seven-second battle between Lou's guitar and John's amplified electric organ. Lyrically just another slice of life from the Lou Reed scrapbook, the song blossoms like one of **William Burroughs'** more traditionally literate passages – transsexual prostitute intravenous drug orgies that ended in accidental homicide were probably a fairly everyday occurrence chez Velvets at that time – but it's the battle of wills and wattage that draws the listener in. By the end of the song, recorded in "one last take" before the band went home to kill one another at the end of the planned sessions,

Lou's screaming the words as loudly as his little throat will stretch to, John's trampling the keyboard, with a viola gripped in his teeth, Moe's in tears and Sterling's already packed up to leave. If the track had ended in a burst of gunfire nobody would have been surprised.

Something had to change, and John decided it should be him. He quit the band, going onto a hugely impressive solo career as musician, producer, shaman and wise guide to subsequent generations of mad-eyed musicians. He was replaced, musically at least by **Doug Yule**, who would pick up and play anything with strings from a mandolin to a harp (though he specialized in the electric guitar side of things), but The Velvet Underground was now Lou's band, and it followed his lead.

The Velvet Underground, album no.3, appeared in 1969, and with the exception of the now dated-sounding stereo experiments of "The Murder Mystery", a lot of the madness and tension had left the band. What remained was still thought-provoking, challenging stuff – though Moe's comedy "After Hours" smacked a little of the obligatory Ringo track on a Beatles album – with "I'm Set Free" and "Jesus" looking at the ecstatic release offered by a chemical or spiritual saviour, "Candy Says" an enthralling meditation on gender realignment and "Pale Blue Eyes" simply the best love song ever written.

An oil crisis put the price of vinyl up through the roof soon after the album's release, and nasty capitalist economics intervened malevolently on record company budgets. With not enough plastic to go around, the fat cats wanted to be certain every sliver they held would be snapped up. Soon, across the board, the wilder excesses of rock'n'roll were being sliced away. The Velvets realized that life was easier in the middle of the road and turned out *Loaded* (1971). Luckily it became their last "real" album, as the musical direction it indicated Lou was taking would have veered pretty unpleasantly close to the mainstream. Apart from "Sweet Jane" (the other best love song in the world), "Train Round The Bend" (the anti-country song *par excellence*) and Lou's thinly disguised autobiography "Rock'n'Roll", it was a standard, done-by-the-book rock album, that could have been written anywhere in the USA: no more junkies, no more transsexual prostitutes, no more lost party girls with nine-days-awake eyes.

Presumably driven mad by self-disgust, Lou had quit the band by the time *Loaded* hit the shops. Paying penance through the medium of Metal Machine Music, fearsome amphetamine abuse and some diabolically bad covers of his own great tunes, he stumbled through the rest of the 70s and into the 80s before recovering his composure and dignity, reinventing himself as one of rock's elder statesmen and many godfathers of punk. Without Lou, the Velvet Underground's time was predictably limited and, in a flurry of personnel changes, the rump of the band released *Squeeze* (featuring none of the original members). Moe went on to a solo career as mother of five, and drummer for hire (check *Life In Exile After Abdication*, 1989, for her retrospective "best of"), Sterling went back to college, took a doctorate in English then became a ferryboat captain (hoorah!)

Bowie famously claims to have been the first to perform a Velvets cover version, his stab at "White Light / White Heat" inspired by a demo smuggled back from the US before the album came out officially, but when punk happened in London then EVERYBODY had at least one of Lou's tunes in their set. He punched all the buttons on punk's check list – drugs, realism, feedback, rock'n'roll with a two-drink minimum and a three-chord maximum – and if you couldn't hack your way through "Waiting For The Man", then a career in entertainment was looking unlikely. With hugely increased popularity coming as a new generation discovered the back catalogue, Verve / MGM cashed in with a couple of outtakes and rarities collections – *V.U. Rare Recordings 68-69* and *Another View* – and a live album at last - *1969 Vols 1 & 2*; originally a mid-priced double album on vinyl, this is now only available as two full-priced separate CDs. Shameful.

Lou and John had long since grown up sufficiently that they could be in the same room simultaneously but it took the death of Andy Warhol and their co-authoring of *Songs For Drella* in tribute to him to set them working together again. Taking a collective deep breath, the original quartet reunited in late 1992 and toured, first in Europe – which had always loved them more than their home crowd, then in stadiums across the USA in support of U2, ultimately releasing *Live MCMXCII* before splitting up again.

When Sterling Morrison died unexpectedly in 1995, Lou announced there could be no more

Velvet Underground. He was right to draw matters to a close with the band's reputation intact and dignity restored.

⊙ The Velvet Underground And Nico
(Polydor, 1996)

This is the Velvets making their first, and biggest, splash. The most essential purchase of them all.

⊙ White Light / White Heat (Polydor, 1996)

The world's most telling drug album. For full effect, listen to it in a dark room, alone, when the rest of the world is asleep.

⊙ Velvet Underground – Peel Slowly And See
(Polydor, 1995)

A lovingly remastered boxed collection of the four studio albums, plus demos, singles, live tracks and other stuff, including an entire six-track CD of previously unreleased recordings.

VERUCA SALT

Formed Chicago, 1993; dissolved 1998; reformed 2000.

■oo pop, and boasting too obvious a sense of humour for the doctrinaire indie scene of the 1990s, but simultaneously way too raw for the mainstream, **Veruca Salt** (named after one of the less appealing little girls in Roald Dahl's Charlie And The Chocolate Factory) were ignored by one side and abused by the other. No wonder they ended up as one of the angriest punk bands of their era. With product appearing on the acceptably left-field Minty Fresh label and boasting two front women, everything should have been in place for instant commercial success. **Louise Post** (guitar/vocals), **Nina Gordon** (vocals/guitar), **Steve Lack** (bass) and Nina's brother **Jim Shapiro** (drums) started off well enough – they showed up out of nowhere in 1994 on the magnificently named Scared Hitless label, with a killer single "Seether" / "All Hail Me" that burned its way onto the playlists of alternative, indie and cerebral college radio stations alike, and prepared the way for their debut full-lengther *American Thighs*.

The album boiled over with great power-pop tunes that owed as much to The Flamin' Groovies as to Nirvana or The Breeders, and for a while it was difficult to distinguish the band members from one another due to the density of the crowd around them – major label dudes and dudettes were in a corporate blood feast, a feeding frenzy

ugly to behold. Signing to one or another of the big beasts was inevitable, but when Veruca Salt finally did the deed with Geffen Records, the cries of "sell-out" could be heard coast to coast. For the sin of making a deal worth a few dollars (and this is America ferchrissakes!) reason, the band lost its precious street-cred, and mocking the Salt became an easy pastime for the lazier indie journalist and fanzine hack alike.

Moving to the major-label world of corporate monolith and product placement was the left-field scene's equivalent of peddling your kid sister's ass in a back alley – blatantly unforgivable behaviour and quite beyond the pale.

VS, one hopes, laughed all the way to the bank as the album (rereleased with professional full-scale marketing behind it) went gold, and MTV picked up on "Seether". They lured Steve Albini in to produce the magnificently titled EP *Blow It Out Your Ass It's Veruca Salt* in 1996 before heading back into the studio, surfacing in 1997 with *Eight Arms To Hold You*.

Even the band's uncoolest and most devoted fans found *Eight Arms* hard to handle. Inexplicably, the band had allowed their sound to drift across into hairy metal territory, shedding strips of the fanbase off the car without picking up even a touch-up spray can's worth of new supporters. It sold well enough, but to the delight of the meanies who continued to flood the fanzines with anti-Salt hate mail, critical opinion was best described as "mixed" and Shapiro jumped ship, followed in short order by Gordon, who had plans of her own.

Stacy Jones (drums) took Shapiro's place for a while, but in the end Post found it easier to replace everyone in the band except herself, and keep the Veruca Salt brand going with a completely new team comprising Post plus **Stephen Fitzpatrick** (guitar), **Suzanne Sokol** (bass) and **Jimmy Madla** (drums). She quit Geffen and moved onto a more human-scale label more in line with her vision. She may have had enough of corporate hell but she has stayed true to the noisy well-crafted songwriting that characterizes her work, with *Resolver* appearing on her new home, Beyond, in 2000.

⊙ American Thighs
(Minty Fresh / DGC / Geffen, 1994)

With songwriting divvied up between Gordon and Post, the album judders and veers in an attempt to head in two directions at once, lurching between the off-kilter rhythms of "Seether" to the downright unusual melodies of "Celebrate You".

THE VIBRATORS

Started to vibrate London, 1976; batteries ran down in 1978. Now fitted with a mains adaptor and offering permanent pleasure.

Hurtling out of the traps at the very dawn of punk like a gingered-up greyhound, **The Vibrators** – **Ian "Knox" Carnochan** (vocals/guitar), **Pat Collier** (bass), **John Ellis** (guitar), and **Eddie The Drummer** (yes... drums) – were cheerfully second-rate but always available on nights when you couldn't get a date; they played everywhere and were always on the bill. Thirty years down the line, they are still happy no-hopers who'll play anywhere, and they're still on the bill, about halfway down the poster in medium-sized print, listed below the headliners but above the unknown Belgian act that usually opens the day's fun and games.

Collier and Ellis came with form – they'd been part of Bazooka Joe, the plodding pub band that Adam Ant left on seeing the Pistols for the first time. London's streetwise punk kids recognized the new band as a gang of charlatans who would do anything for a hit, and they took a lot of incoherent drunken abuse from the audience for "breaking the rules". Not only did they record with a session musician (a job title used as a term of abuse amongst the true-believer, "keep it real" crowd that supported punk's DIY ethos), but they did a deal with pop Svengali Mickie Most, producer and label owner best known for acts such as The Sweet, Smokey, Mud and Suzi Quatro. With their credibility blown out of the water before it had a chance to settle, The Vibrators settled down to a

Vibrators: Always a big hit with the girls.

🎵 PLAYLIST: THE VIBRATORS

Though they're still among us, The Vibrators' small number of essential cuts were all recorded by the end of the 1970s. Try these recently reissued cuts for size:

1. 24 HOUR PEOPLE
from **V2 (Captain Oi!, 2000)**

2. AUTOMATIC LOVER
from **V2 (Captain Oi!, 2000)**

3. FEEL ALRIGHT
from **V2 (Captain Oi!, 2000)**

4. FLYING DUCK THEORY
from **V2 (Captain Oi!, 2000)**

5. I NEED A SLAVE
from **PURE MANIA (Columbia, 1999)**

6. NAZI BABY
from **V2 (Captain Oi!, 2000)**

7. PURE MANIA
from **V2 (Captain Oi!, 2000)**

8. STIFF LITTLE FINGERS
from **PURE MANIA (Columbia, 1999)**

9. SULPHATE
from **V2 (Captain Oi!, 2000)**

10. WHIPS AND FURS
from **PURE MANIA (Columbia, 1999)**

career as the band every little punk loved to hate.

Still, in the absence of much else for music-starved punklings up and down the country to buy, The Vibrators scored a couple of minor hits with their earliest singles, both in 1976. After "We Vibrate" / "Whips And Furs" came another pair of punk-by-numbers tunes, dropping buzzwords from the London scene for the edification of the provincials. "Pogo Dancing" / "Pose" was recorded with Chris Spedding – the good-natured and highly skilled session man mentioned above, who had added some professional guitar polish to early Sex Pistols recordings. By the end of the year they had opened for Iggy Pop and for The Stranglers, shared a stage with the Sex Pistols and were a name to be dropped by sniggering music press journos on the look out for any hint of sex, drugs or punk-related outrage.

Wresting some control of their destiny, The Vibrators cut a new deal with Epic and started knocking out some more credible material. January 1977 saw "Baby Baby" / "Into The Future" hit the shops, with *Pure Mania* following a few months later in July.

Pat left later that year, going on to immense success as a producer and making room for **Gary Tibbs** (bass), recruited – in fine punk-rock style – from the audience. He toughened up the band's sound in time for the recording of their second album, *V2* (1978), but the album bombed so badly it was said to be in danger of causing more damage than the Nazi secret weapon it name-checked. Gary went off to improve his chops and pay his dues as one of the Ants (and later as part of Roxy Music) before returning to the band.

By 1978 and two years of relatively unrewarding struggle, everybody had had enough and a move to Berlin intervened while everyone regained their breath and sense of proportion. The original four-piece line-up re-formed in 1982 to release *Guilty* and *Alaska 127* (named for the address of Collier's rehearsal rooms in Waterloo, London) and waded knee-deep through personnel changes through the dark days of the 1980s and 1990s, firing out the odd album like a distress flare in the vain hope of rescue.

Finally, of course, the revival circuit caught up with them and even now they're playing most weekends somewhere in Europe, where their popularity – particularly in those countries not renowned for their national sense of humour – remains undiminished, even though these days Knox qualifies for free travel on the buses (he joined his first band in 1959 and has been bashing out the meaty three-chord wonders – call it R&B, call it rock'n'roll, add some slap and it's glam, mess up your hair and it's punk – ever since.

⊚ Pure Mania/V2 (Track, 2004)

Lovely raw material from the very earliest days of punk rock, most of these sound like the band had been listening more to Mud and The Sweet than the recommended course of MC5 and Stooges riffs, with most tunes squealingly innocent when compared to the sleaze of New York's then current output. Chirpy and cheap, but even so, there's no excuse for "Whips and Furs" or "Pogo Dancing". The CD comes with the more pompous and less successful *V2* bundled in as part of the deal, and it seems a shame to turn down an album that's not entirely without merit.

⊚ The Best Of (Columbia, 2001)

Superlative value collection, with all the studio stuff you might need and a fantastic set of live tracks to boot.

Sid Vicious

Born London, 1957; died New York, 1979.

"This is just a rough patch. Things'll be much better when we get to America, I promise."

Sid in Sid & Nancy (Alex Cox; 1986)

Sid Vicious: Nice trousers, great pose.

ar more valuable to the history of punk rock as an icon and antihero than he ever was as a musician, **Sid Vicious** – like Hendrix, Jim Morrison and all those other poor saps who did too much, much too young – has made more money, and grown even more famous dead than when alive. He has grown to represent the stereotypical punk rocker in the public mind, which is a shame: most punk kids just wanted to dress weird and bounce around on the dance floor, whereas people like Sid made it dangerous to go out for a fun night at the Roxy, The Vortex or even the local pub. Despite the facts – nobody forced him to whack a journalist with a bike chain, to become a junkie, to get involved with **Nancy Spungen** (punk's own Cruella De Ville), or end up facing prosecution for her murder, he started out as a nice enough, fun-loving guy, maybe not as smart or sarcastic as his schoolmate John Lydon, but game for a laugh, ready to gurn for his pals' camera snapshots and reluctant to say no to any kind of amusing or outlandish challenge.

More than most of his contemporaries, particularly on the generally well-fed and looked-after British scene, **John Simon Beverley** (also known as **Simon John Ritchie** and likely to give whichever name he thought would get him into the least trouble when asked) came from the kind of background that would have made Charles Dickens salivate in anticipation of the royalty cheques he could expect for writing it up. His mum, Anne, brought him up as a single parent in an era when society still looked askance at a broken home, and as the scandals surrounding her son grew towards the end of his life, she saw herself variously described in the press as a hooker and a junkie.

Nevertheless, her son stayed in education well beyond the age at which most promising tearaways kiss goodbye to the head teacher, forming a friendship with Mrs Lydon's little boy Johnny that lasted past school days, taking them both into London's jumping livewire squat, rock and amphetamines scene. (You can forget Malcolm McLaren and his manipulations, forget The Clash, Patti Smith and The Ramones: if there hadn't been such a huge amount of cheap but potent speed on the streets in London in the mid-1970s, nothing in this book would have happened.) Sid had already done some sub-amateurish busking at Underground stations with his mate, but found there was no place for him when Lydon turned Rotten and joined a band. Johnny renamed his pal Sid Vicious, partly because there were already too many Johns on the scene and partly because of the legendary anti-social behaviour of a pet hamster, which took a chunk out of Rotten's dad's hand. Although Sid loyally became Rotten's biggest fan, he never took to his new nickname, claiming that it made him sound thick and stupid (which usually prompted the reply "but you ARE, Sid" from whichever bandmate was within earshot). However, he grew to fit it.

Sid soon took with relish to the life of booze, pills and powders associated with nights out on the town with rock stars. Drugs made it easier for him to associate with those around him, and he found the booze helped his first appearance on stage, drumming for The Flowers Of Romance behind Ms Sioux and Marco Pirroni.

However, musical skills – even those basics needed to keep time with Siouxsie's gothic stomps – were beyond him, and The Flowers dissolved, leaving Sid as just a member of the audience again. John Ritchie had been known for his sweet nature, but Sid Vicious, cranked up on lager and speed, appointed himself as Defender of the Sex Pistols, überfan and Master Of Revels. He's alleged to have invented the pogo (as if the only dance move possible on a crowded floor needed inventing) and was certainly on the list of suspects as the guy who threw a glass during a Damned gig, hitting a kid in the crowd, and definitely the guy who wrapped a bike chain round his fist to clobber Nick Kent of the *NME* in June 1976. He hung out with the Pistols as much as he could, and charmed Malcolm into believing in him sufficiently to give him the job as Glen Matlock's replacement, despite his continued and obvious inability to play the

bass, write a song or devote himself to anything he wasn't able to master within his three-minute concentration span.

Nonetheless, he tried. He certainly threw himself body and soul into the superficial bits of rock'n'roll rebellion, cultivating his "wild man" image to the maximum with a series of well-publicized incidents of increasingly nihilistic behaviour. Less well covered at the time was the arrival of some major league bad influences from across the Atlantic [cue sound effects of violent thunder storm]...

The **Heartbreakers** jumped right onto the first plane at the chance to play a tour in the UK, despite two of the band having walked out on **Malcolm McLaren** in his former guise as **New York Dolls** manager a few years previously. Malcolm, for his part, was well aware that Johnny Thunders and Jerry Nolan sported sleek, well-formed heroin habits, that the rest of the band were said to at least dabble, and that, all things considered, they were more trouble than they were worth. When Nolan's ex-girlfriend Nancy Spungen (bad-news drug-loving rock chick *par excellence*) staggered off the plane in London a couple of days after The Heartbreakers, drunk to the gills and – in the words of one of Johnny Thunders' earlier hits, "lookin' for a kiss" – the characters were assembled for the next act of the tragedy.

> # "You see, Sid decided quite some time ago that he was going to become an arsehole, and he did."
> ## John Lydon, Melody Maker, October 20, 1978

Malcolm was up to his ears in the arrangements for the forthcoming Anarchy In The UK tour and was at first pleased to hear that Nancy's torch for Nolan had gone out, but when he saw her demon eyes wandering up and down Sid's lithe frame he arranged to have her bundled into a cab and shipped back out to the airport. Sid intervened, became her knight in shining dog-chain collar and fell into the punk scene's most heart-wrenching heroin habit, seemingly overnight.

With Sid letting Nancy take control of the life he had already begun to lose interest in, the effects on his health and relationship with the band were disastrous. Even when Rotten, his best mate, pleaded with him to ditch the drugs and the girl, Sid ignored him. Nils Stevenson, the Pistols' tour manager, said that Sid grew to "dislike everything – except heroin and Nancy". Throughout rehearsals, the band's rare UK live appearances and the Pistols' disastrous tour of the USA, Sid resolutely refused to improve his playing, dedicating his every spare moment to tracking down a fix, even if it meant taking a beating from the security guys appointed by the record company to "look after" him.

"He couldn't play the bass and it made doing gigs just a waste of time, 'cos I had no idea what was going on behind me. There was no tune that I could pick out on."

John Lydon

With the Pistols now off Sid's agenda, he moved with Nancy and Socks (a kitten that would probably have preferred to have stayed in the pet store) to New York's most infamous lodgings, the Chelsea hotel (once the haunt of the city's bohemian cultural elite, now little more than a flop house for dealers and their clients).

Their time at the Chelsea was a mess. After burning themselves out of the first room they took when one of them (probably not Socks) fell asleep on the bed with a lit cigarette, they kept all their possessions strewn around their new home, Room 100, in countless carrier bags from Harrods. Nancy was wandering round the big bad city with $10,000 in her handbag, picking up heroin with Tuinal and Dilaudid chasers. Somehow through the fog of cigarette smoke and opiates, Nancy decided that she was Sid's new manager and even managed to score him a few gigs on notoriety value, if not on grounds of talent, down at Max's Kansas City (recordings made of his time

here should be avoided at all costs). In his book *El Sid: Saint Vicious*, David Dalton wrote that Nancy needed to "yank [Sid] back up onto his feet" every time he keeled over, and fans expecting to experience the wiry young ex-Pistol found themselves faced with someone looking more like William Burroughs. It was embarrassing.

In a feeble attempt to kick their habit, Sid and Nancy went down to the Spring Street methadone clinic, but it didn't last. Claiming more beatings, this time from other addicts, Sid dropped out, and with Nancy for company he started taking methadone on top of everything else. Nancy was the first to fall ill as a result of their regime, and her already volatile temper worsened. Sid was alleged to have hit Nancy with his bass on more than one occasion, but they both carried bruises and cigarette burns and, when in the right mood, she was strong enough to whack him back with a wardrobe.

Nancy died sometime in the early hours of Thursday October 12, 1978, in a whirl of booze, drugs, knives, mysterious visitors, missing dollars and another beating for Sid (he got racist at the bellhop, who in turn got stomping on his ass). At 10.30 am, Sid was observed heading toward his room. Fifteen minutes later the paramedics and police arrived. They found Nancy's body in the bathroom and called homicide. Sid was arrested, taken downtown and interrogated. He confessed, and unable to raise the $50,000 bail, went into forced detox at New York's notorious Riker's Island prison (where he took a further beating). Malcolm McLaren went to the record company for the money, but it took a couple of days for everything to come together and for Sid to be back on the streets.

By the time he had showered, shaved and scored, Nancy's funeral had taken place without him, and his mum was in town staying on Madison Avenue at the Seville. Within a week, Sid was back in hospital after a methadone overdose and trying to cut his wrists open. Mum called round on a visit just in time to summon the medics and save him. Another attempt to withdraw and get clean collapsed when he glugged down his methadone too quickly for his schedule and was refused additional supplies. He cut himself badly with a razor blade on October 28, and unable to throw himself out of the window, found himself shut up in Bellevue mental hospital after Malcolm called in the paramedics. He was detoxed against his will again before being released into the dubious care of his mother.

Sid stumbled from club to bar to shooting gallery until December, when he got into a fight with Todd, Patti Smith's brother, taking yet another beating in the process and ending up spending another seven weeks in Riker's Island prison detox unit.

And then, his system clean, his body still weak and his brain addled with the sickness in his heart, Sid was released. On February 1, 1979, his mum bought him some heroin to save him from getting beaten up yet again on the street in some deal gone wrong. He shot it up, took some more and then he died.

The next morning, when his mum brought him a cup of tea, "he was lying there quite peacefully. I shook him until I realized he was very cold and very dead."

◉ **Sid Sings (Virgin, 1994)**

Alongside Sid's version of the Sex Pistols' "Belsen", dig in and sample 10 other covers, including Iggy's "Search And Destroy" and "I Wanna Be Your Dog", that old favourite "Stepping Stone", and "Take A Chance On Me", among others.

THE VON BONDIES

Roared out of their Detroit garage in 2000 like the petrol crisis never happened; still running.

F ormed when **Jason Stollsteimer** (vocals/guitar) hooked up with **Marcie Bolen** (more guitar), **Carrie Smith** (bass), and **Don Blum** (drums), **The Von Bondies** make a righteous noise in a style that owes as much to the **Stooges** and MC5 of their hometown as it does to Nirvana and the late period punk/grunge kids of the 1990s. The extent of their debt to Detroit rivals The White Stripes is still to be determined, and won't be finally decided till everyone's split lips have healed and the dust kicked up by their scuffle has settled. Still, dispensing with the testosterone driven ego-madness associated with both camps and returning purely to the music, The Von Bondies kick ass.

They had luck, sure, but they also had a fistful of righteous tunes to back it up. When they finally got loud and confident enough to blow the doors off the garage they'd been rehearsing in, they kicked around the Michigan club scene, making waves, putting noses out of joint, sneering lots and generally having all that rock'n'roll fun that makes punk rockin' such a valid career choice for today's young people.

With a growing local audience and reputation for tearing the roof off whichever sucka they were playing, they went nationwide with their first single – "It Came From Japan" / "My Baby's Cryin'" was released in 2000, with production shared by Jim Diamond of The Dirtbombs and golden boy Jack White of The White Stripes. White liked the cut of their jib and invited the VBs to record a track for his *Sympathetic Sounds Of Detroit* compilation. Wheels began to turn, and with Jack again serving as producer, their first album, *Lack Of Communication*, appeared to standing ovations in the late summer of 2001. An instant classic of

🔊 **JASON STOLLSTEIMER'S CELEBRITY PLAYLIST**

In the great tradition of Detroit garage bands dating back to the Stooges and the MC5, Jason Stollsteimer and The Von Bondies make ferociously gritty punk music with a raucous intensity. He sent us this playlist from a studio in the Motor City, while working on the follow-up to Pawn Shoppe Heart...

1. I PUT A SPELL ON YOU Screamin' Jay Hawkins
   from **Voodoo Jive : The Best of Screamin' Jay Hawkins**

2. I DON'T WANNA HEAR IT Minor Threat
   from **Complete Discography**

3. COMPLICATION The Monks
   from **Black Monk Time**

4. N-SUB ULYSSES Nation Of Ulysses
   from **Plays Pretty for Babies**

5. HEROIN Velvet Underground
   from **The Velvet Underground and Nico**

6. I WANNA BE YOUR DOG The Stooges
   from **The Stooges**

7. UNITY Operation Ivy
   from **Operation Ivy (Energy)**

8. SHE'S LIKE HEROIN TO ME The Gun Club
   from **Fire of Love**

9. RELEASE THE BATS The Birthday Party
   from **Junkyard**

10. WHERE WERE YOU The Mekons
   from **Heaven and Hell**

21st century punk rock, it crammed an awful lot of energy into each of the tracks and brought a warm glow to all the valve-amplifier freaks who caught an earful. White was still more of a performer and fan than professional producer and the sound was sometimes a bit muddy but it gave the whole album a feeling of being "real" music, written and performed by people who loved and cared about what they were doing, in an offhand punk-rock kind of way.

Touring with Jack and Meg's **White Stripes** gave the Von Bondies an international profile and led to the music industry moguls sending their goons to sniff round Motor City in search of the new Detroit garage-rock movement they'd convinced themselves must exist. The Von Bondies took Warner's bait and set to work on a new set. To keep the fans happy and the band fed, *Raw And Rare* came out in 2003, a compilation of sessions taped for the BBC in 2001 and 2002, plus live numbers recorded in concert at The Lager House in Corktown, Detroit.

With their live act honed by some high-pressure touring, and selected to open for Detroit's finest – **Iggy And The Stooges**, when the latter re-formed in 2003, the band were in excellent shape and they returned to the studio with bright eyes, shiny coats and their tails held high. *Pawn Shoppe Heart* was produced by Jerry Harrison (ex-**Talking Heads**), with Diamond once again sitting in to make sure things didn't get too cleaned up. Although its title nodded towards prog rockers Van Der Graaf Generator and their 1970s epics, the music had none of the Brits' pomposity or melodrama – instead it burned like some illegal fuel composed of nitrous and gasoline, giving a whole new meaning to white light/white heat.

Smith dropped out of the band towards the end of 2004, and was replaced by **Yasmine Smith** (bass, no relation).

The differences of opinion between the various bands currently on the Detroit scene has served to show them as completely distinct entities sharing little more than geography and passion. That town is certainly big enough for all concerned and a good deal more. Let's hope that the Detroit rock mine never runs out of ore.

◉ Lack Of Communication (Sympathy For The Record Industry, 2001)

Jason Stollsteimer sings his own songs with a dirtied-up voice of some scary intensity. Jim Diamond's production scratches and distorts the rest of the band to match Stollsteimer's wailing, and by the gods below, it works!

◉ Pawn Shoppe Heart (Sire/Reprise, 2004)

A fine example of what punk rock means in the twenty-first century. It's loud, brash, glammed up and sweetly raw, all at once. It's a sexy, down'n'dirty affair (hold on for their version of "Try A Little Tenderness" – you'll be moist by the end of it), where everybody gets to join in on backing vocals and everyone sounds like they're having fun.

ANDY WARHOL

Born Pennsylvania, 1928; died 1987.

Warhol may not have been a punk as such, but he has a place in the story, so please allow us the indulgence of this A-Z entry before we return to the next injection of thundering guitar music.

Andy Warhol was born in 1928 and, despite living the whole of his life in the USA, never felt entirely at home. Arguably the most important American artist of the 20th century, his work pales when compared to his role as catalyst and influence to the most important artists and musicians of the 60s and 70s.

Andrew Warhola stuck out in all the wrong ways when growing up – the gay, albino, first-generation Slovak immigrant artist was a species otherwise completely unknown in the great state of Pennsylvania – and as soon as he was able, he headed to the bright lights of New York where he landed rent-paying work as a commercial artist.

"BEING BORN IS LIKE BEING KIDNAPPED. AND THEN SOLD INTO SLAVERY."

The money it brought in paid for materials and studio space and with a new name, and an exhibition or two under his belt, Andy Warhol found inspirational, artsy people were beginning to flutter toward his pallid flame.

Andy was already well known as a leading light of the Pop Art movement (even Joe Public was aware of "the guy who does the soup cans / Coca Cola cans / Marilyn Monroes" etc) when he met **The Velvet Underground** (see p.338).

He put together a multimedia spectacular show based on his own movies, the acid-test culture springing up across the country in California and the music of **Lou Reed**, **John Cale** and the others. Although the tour grew into a legend of its own and despite Andy signing up sure-fire crowd pleaser Nico as co-singer, The Velvets were too cool, urban and hip in an East Coast way to ever nurture a love+peace culture in New York City. The experimental exploding plastic inevitable tour ground to a halt, **Nico** was shunted out of the band and Lou sundered his friendship with Andy by telling him his services as manager / producer would no longer be required.

Warhol's long nights hidden away in the VIP area of Max's Kansas City helped put the club on the map for all the hip young acts in town, with Iggy and The New York Dolls falling under his spell for a short while. When punk took off in town, of course Andy had to be there to observe it, and he was soon being spotted at Blondie gigs.

Andy's relevance to punk comes from more than his early championing of Lou and the gang – his desire to make art from the mass-produced detritus of modern America was echoed by punk's adoption of unexpectedly beautiful urban *objets trouvés* such as Sid Vicious's padlock/chain necklace and the movement's subversion of images ripped from advertisements and forced into anti-commercial cut'n'paste propaganda. Warhol wanted to work like a robot – Devo, Gary Numan and Kraftwerk (this last band itself an influence on the punk rockers) took him literally and appeared on stage done up like cyborgs going out on a hot date. His reinvention of the Renaissance artist's apprentice – hiring artworkers to do the manual work while he got on with the conceptual stuff – led circuitously to PiL's sitting out the gig behind a screen while a tape played out to the audience.

Warhol's intense focus on some of the more repellent aspects of Western culture (his *Electric Chair* series in particular, but also his fixation with one single snapshot of Marilyn and his nit-picking analyses of the mighty dollar bill) of course highlights one of the main themes behind punk rock. The Dead Kennedys owe much to Warhol's peculiar sideways squint at americana.

He is best known for his notion that "In the future, everyone will be world famous for 15 minutes", which concept is echoed in Buzzcock's "We just came up from nowhere and we're going straight back there". His films varied from the very quintessence of boredom (24 hours of the Empire State Building for example) to the height of camp (*Flesh*), both areas richly mined by the spikeyheads.

Warhol died in New York City following routine surgery at the age of 58. He left a small fortune, exhibits in museums around the world and a reputation for a canny crossbreed of art and commercialism that punk rock, and every movement with a hint of sincerity since then, has adopted as its own.

WEEZER

Formed in Los Angeles, 1993; still weezing away like they've been breathing the local air.

Weezer are a band who play a kind of ironic New Wavey music and who, despite knocking around the scene for more than a decade, somehow retain sight of their charmingly geeky, quirky roots.

The guys who make up the band are consummate bedroom rockers – too weedy, socially awkward or bone idle to clean out the garage, and reluctant to invite pals round to "jam" just in case nobody turns up. In the wrong hands, this could have led to the sub-Morrissey self-pity of Emo (a kind of grunge-lite for a new generation), but with **Rivers Cuomo** (vocals/guitar) – surely a man named for stardom – at the controls, and trusty henchmen **Matt Sharp** (bass) and **Patrick Wilson** (drums) by his side, Weezer have steered a swift

but sure course through the rocks that have sunk so many other previous bands.

Weezer formed when Cuomo got out of college in California during the early 1990s, and the band began the weary process of playing up and down the club circuit in LA, honing skills, learning chops, paying dues and schmoozing their way into a decent deal with a major label. Producer Ric Ocasek, whose background in The Cars gave him a feel for the band's dry humour and "indie" mood, added more depth to their sound and kept it raw, rough 'n' street by roping in **Brian Bell** (guitar) just three days before they went into the studio to record their debut.

With *Weezer* recorded, mixed and sent off to the factory, Cuomo headed back to his home state to complete his education, leaving the marketing wizards at DGC to arrange the next steps. (He'd had an offer from Harvard – no, it ain't punk rock, but you can see the guy's point of view.) First up came "Undone (The Sweater Song)", a minor hit in 1994, but it was the double whammy of "Buddy Holly" – a brilliant song backed with a superb promo video – that turned them from local heroes into international supergeeks. Though the follow-up, "Say It Ain't So", did pretty well in 1995, it never matched the success generated by promo director Spike Jonze's groundbreaking technique, which spliced nostalgia-rich footage from the TV sitcom *Happy Days* with seamlessly matched shots of the band doing their stuff.

Cuomo returned to Harvard and his studies, shunning the attention of his music biz contacts and pals in the band, and ultimately dropping completely out of sight for a while. Unaware that he'd gone missing, Sharp and Wilson formed **The Rentals**, a sparking, punchy New Wave revival band with a good heart, and went into the charts towards the end of 1995 with a single, "Friends of P".

When Cuomo finally came staggering out of the Massachusetts woods in early 1996, he had already completed the bulk of the songs that would become *Pinkerton*. Weezer's second full-length offering had elements of the concept album about it, but with the band working as one (albeit somewhat grudgingly – after all, even if Cuomo did write the bulk of the songs, who had died and made him king of the band?), it came out to relatively good reviews – even if it stayed resolutely away from the charts, in accordance with Rivers' reluctance to see the band pigeonholed as a novelty act that relied on clever video tricks to boost sales.

On record, nothing matched their hook-laden mix of pointless pop and social comment, but live in concert, their reputation as a good night out began to plummet as Cuomo descended into a private mental hell of stage fright and disappearing confidence.

Sharp returned to The Rentals, making space for **Mikey Welsh** (bass) to sit in and learn the new material that would make up another eponymous album: *Weezer* (2001), usually referred to as *The Green Album* and also produced by Ric Ocasek. This not only returned them to the album charts, but also gave them another couple of single hits. "Hash Pipe", a track that showed a more downbeat side to a band that was growing up, was the more successful and intriguing of the two, but "Island In The Sun" also did well.

Just as Weezer were getting back on form, Welsh got sick and had to leave the band. Scott Shriner (bass) took his place for *Maladroit* (2002). A flurry of legal problems kept the band busy for a while, and they worked almost exclusively on their various side projects until the end of 2003. When the dust settled, the band went back to the studio with Rick Rubin to record *Make Believe* (2005), which has sent them back into the public arena again with "Beverly Hills", (a massive TV hit around the world) and most recently "We Are All On Drugs", demonstrating there's some world-weary but still snot-nosed life in the band.

⦿ Weezer (Geffen, 1995)

The deluxe reissued edition of the band's first and best recording includes a second disc of live tracks, outtakes and demos, making it the essential Weezer album to have. Proudly not making a single step forward in musical complexity or lyrical profundity throughout their career, this is the pure uncut source material from which the rest descended.

THE WEIRDOS

Got weird in 1976, Los Angeles; went underground in the 1980s. Still weird now and then.

The Weirdos were the first band on the West Coast to really understand the new and exciting world of punk rock, and it's all thanks to the Denney brothers. **John Denney** (vocals) and his bro **Dix Denney** (guitar) were at the core of the band in the beginning, and have stayed in there swinging ever since; talk to the Denneys and you talk to the soul of Los Angeles punk. The original Weirdos comprised John and Dix plus **Cliff Roman** (guitar) and **Dave Trout** (bass). There was no drummer.

Finally the guys burnt the long hippy hair off the otherwise acceptable **Nickey Beat** (drums) and put out a couple of fine genre-defining singles – "Destroy All Music" (b/w "A Life of Crime" and "Why Do You Exist") and "(We Got the) Neutron Bomb" (b/w "Solitary Confinement"). In 1979 they released a six-track EP, *Who? What? When? Where? Why?*, which included a rather fetching cover of the old Hank Mizell number and UK chart hit "Jungle Rock". By this time, however, **Danny Benair** (drums) had taken Beat's place, and although another EP, *Action Design*, followed in 1980 – with the cover version this time being The Doors' "Break On Through" – the band then split up.

Keeping the brothers Denney apart was a different proposition, however, and although The Weirdos didn't release another record until 1990, John and Dix would re-form the band occasionally for incendiary live shows at which they showcased tunes that otherwise they alone would have heard. By 1988 they were back working with Roman (sharing bass duties with high-profile fan **Flea**, taking a break from The Red Hot Chili Peppers) and Beat, picking up their unfortunately interrupted career where they'd dropped it and finally putting out some serious full-length recordings. *Condor* (1990) was followed swiftly by the release of *Weird World*, a 1991 compilation of some of the guys' archive of a zillion home recordings, but then, frustratingly for their growing international audience, they split up again.

These days, whenever the guys can get the time off from their day jobs, they're seen on sporadic, short-lived "tourettes", with **Zander Schloss** – ex-Circle Jerk and the guy who played Kevin in the fine movie *Repo Man* (1984), on bass, and with **Shawn Antium** drumming.

⦿ Who? What? When? Where? Why? EP (Bomp!, 1979)

If you've a taste for late-1970s hardcore, then you have to buy all The Weirdos' early stuff. If you like the early stuff then you have to buy the rest. Go on, there aren't that many of them.

WIPERS

Wiped out all comers in Portland, Oregon, 1976 and punkier than you ever since.

"My goal was, originally, to do fifteen albums in ten years, never do interviews, never release photographs, have absolutely no information about us at all, and never tour."

GREG SAGE

Led by **Greg Sage** (vocals/guitar), punk rock's very own mountain man, **The Wipers** were early converts to the sheer delirious delight of playing as loud and as fast as possible. Alongside **Doug Koupal** (bass) and **Sam Henry** (drums), Sage redefined the term power trio, creating a helluva racket in the wild Northwest that was, unfortunately, never loud enough to attract the following the band deserved. Despite losing his way a little, and heading into noodling guitar solo territory in the 1980s and 1990s, Sage has kept his independence and pioneer noise-merchant spirit burning through almost three decades of rip-offs, disillusionment and itchy flannel shirts.

The Wipers surged out of the hills like a storm-driven avalanche, booting the singer-songwriters off their stools through sheer volume and attitude, and soaking up a beer-swilling audience ready at a moment's notice to yell "rebellion!" and march on the nearest seat of government. Cooking up a fervid audience with intense live performances soon led them to the studio; early recordings were paint-blisteringly hot, packed full of hooks and rehearsed to military-band precision tightness. *Is This Real?* (1980), the band's debut album, was as ferociously independent as a junkyard cat with

an ear missing, coming out on Sage's own Trap label and distributed mainly by word of mouth and runners carrying individual copies in cleft sticks. It broke out of Portland and word began to spread across the underground of this delicious new secret. In Europe, particularly in Britain, The Wipers were picked up and quietly cherished by an audience of aficionados; at home, they couldn't get arrested.

Greg and the guys did their best to bury the acutely painful and personal lyrics of pain and the ugliness of life beneath multi-layered stacks of distortion and overdrive, but those listeners who brushed their way through the rubble and detritus of tortured sound found nuggets of pure tragic gold. These guys sounded more alienated than a redneck recovering from an anal probe carried out in a spaceship laboratory. Sage's acute ear for overheard angst took inspiration from walking the mean streets of Portland, giving him a unique insight into the quiet desperation flooding the human condition.

Sage had his first brush with "success" when Nirvana covered a couple of tracks from *Is This Real?*, although for twenty years Sage didn't see a dime from his own recording of the album. Copycat bands from across the grunge scene picked up the trail, and before long, Sage found himself hemmed in by words that included "seminal", "influential", "prophetic" and the like. Faced with an invasion from the direction of Seattle, Sage headed back to the hills to work in peace and seclusion on his catalogue of desperate loneliness.

Over the years and through a series of soul-munching body punches from the industry, The Wipers mutated from a genuine band of collaborators into a "Sage +friends" outfit, stabilizing for a while with **Brad Davidson** (bass) and **Brad Naish** (drums), and later with **Steve Plouf** (drums). Dennis Hopper used a Wipers track on the *River's Edge* (1986) movie soundtrack, and in 1992, Kurt Cobain produced an interesting tribute album, *Fourteen Songs For Greg Sage And The Wipers*, which included Wipers covers by **Nirvana**, **Hole** and a host of local heroes including M99, Crakerbash, Poison Idea, The Whirlees, Hazel, Calamity Jane, Saliva Tree, Honey, Nation Of Ulysses, Thurston Moore (with Keith Nealy), and Napalm Beach.

Sage is just as grimly uncompromising these days as he was when he turned down Kurt Cobain (who wanted The Wipers to open for Nirvana). Inspired to create despite his enduring and justified disgust with the music biz, Sage further asserts his independence through Zenorecords – a one-stop shop for all your Wipers needs – where recordings are created, produced and mastered. It also holds Greg's sonic workshop, where he builds one-off pieces of equipment to create and capture unique sounds.

⦿ Wipers Box Set: Is This Real/Youth Of America/Over The Edge (Zeno, 2001)

Covering Sage's major creative period and containing his best-known material, this three-disc set is your ideal way into the dark disturbing underbrush of his mind. Bitter as wormwood, sour as tamarind and dark as the face of an artist robbed of his royalties, this is hard work, but very worthwhile.

WIRE

Connected Watford, England, 1976; shorted out 1980, sparking intermittently ever since.

S tanding way over on the far-out art-school side of punk, but dressed to impress, lit beautifully and sporting a selection of wry, knowing smiles, **Wire** are nowadays as respectable, enduring and radical as Her Majesty the Queen (Gor'bless'er!). It wasn't always thus though – the band showed up on the seminal *Live At The Roxy Club, London Wc2*, performing "Lowdown" and "1-2-X-U", and although they kept a sensible distance from the formulaic mob already engaged in dictating a uniform for "punks" to wear, they came from the same fashion/anti art sources as all the other first-wave London bands, and were just as happy to entertain hugely enthusiastic spikyhead audiences as they were to impress the grey-rain-coated intelligentsia with their haiku-like lyrics, intriguing titles and enigmatic pronouncements on their own work.

Whether the art school in distinctly unglamorous Watford had the prestige of those in central London is debatable, but when students **Colin Newman** (vocals/ guitar) and **George Gill** (guitar/vocals) formed a band, they certainly found as much freedom and time to work on their music as did their peers in the capital. **Bruce Gilbert** (more guitar) actually had a job at the college before joining in. At this stage the band was known as **Overload** – a rotten name by the standards of any era – and even in the white-hot creativity of punk, a three-guitar line-up was going nowhere. Overload became Wire when **Graham Lewis** (bass) and **Robert Gotobed** (a.k.a. Robert Grey, drums) signed up, Gill was persuaded to go and the three-piece abomination became a more regular quartet of power, wit and creative destruction.

Wire set out to be challenging, interesting and involving in a way that the bulk of the new bands patently were not – sufficiently so to convince Mike Thorne of EMI's Harvest label (then in the process of recording bands for *The Roxy* album) to sign them up and drag them into a real studio to capture the magic. Together, he and the band laid down 21 tracks, which appeared towards the end of 1977 on *Pink Flag*.

Chairs Missing (1978) offered a distinct progression, musically and otherwise, in the band's output. To fight the chill of the cold dawn of post-punk, Wire layered sound on sound, weaving the proverbial rich tapestry and resorting to all kinds of tricks in the studio that would make the new material difficult to re-create in front of a live audience. This led the guys out of punk rock's barn dance and into a New Wave gavotte, where they could indulge themselves in brainy creativity without being chased off stage by the pretentiousness police.

Wire managed to stick to punk's white-hot pace of creation, though, writing reams of new material, testing the most promising songs out in front of a live audience and mercilessly throwing out any that

didn't melt the mascara off the front three rows. They even found time to tour the USA. Released in 1979, *154* was the band's third album in less than two years and continued their frenzied hurtle through rock's back pages. This time we all got off the bus at psychedelia station, and walked around giggling at the furniture for a while. Another overseas tour (this time of Europe, with Roxy Music) kept the guys in each other's faces, huddled together in the fetid familial stink of a tour bus full of egos. It was all ultimately far too much, taken too quickly all at one sitting, and like overindulged toddlers, the boys in the band began to feel bloated. After a row with the record company that terminated their business relationship and a short set of gigs in 1980 that revealed a group in decay, Wire split up.

Half a decade of solo projects (of varying degrees of interest, but not to us) intervened, tempered by rumours of reunion in the music press. Meetings in 1985 led to rehearsals (with the band referring to itself as a "beat combo" in press releases) and studio time being booked, the release of the *Snakedrill* EP in 1986 and the return to full-length releases a year later, when *The Ideal Copy* showed up.

Although the 1987 incarnation was identical in personnel, everyone involved in it was older and wiser after fiddling about with their individual musical endeavours for five years. The guys' tastes had changed, maturing and widening in the time out of the spotlights. Old fans flocked to buy the new material, though some were foxed to see Wire's music yelping happily forward into the newly planted forest of electronic equipment and computer-controlled precision recordings. Word spread to kid siblings, with first-generation fans

boasting how the old guys had more of a grip on the sample'n'sequencer technology than new bands that grew up playing around with it.

A bell is a cup...until it is struck (1988) came from even deeper in the jungle of chips, diodes and transistors the guys had occupied, signalling the direction they would follow with *It's Beginning To And Back Again* in 1989, the album that triggered Wire's second split. As the music had grown increasingly complex, Gotobed had seen his role as drummer mutate into that of percussionist. When he saw it beginning to change even further – making him into some kind of punk-rock computer programmer – he jumped over the side and started swimming. The others continued as **Wir** for a year or so before giving it up again.

Cover versions recorded or stolen outright by the indie crew in the 1990s kept the band in the public mind, and reunions here and there in the years since then have been rapturously received by ageing crowds of ex-punks and old New Wavers, particularly since they stopped messing with everyone's head and started playing the old stuff again. Even now a Wire gig is always an event – with rarely a dull moment.

⊙ Pink Flag (Pink Flag, 2006)

Newly reissued in a pristine remastered state – with everything carried out under supervision of the band members – the first Wire album is an even more remarkable historical artefact. If brevity be truly the soul of wit, this album has the funniest songs of the 70s.

⊙ Chairs Missing (Pink Flag, 2006)

Typically swimming against the prevailing stream of serious, post-punk, chin-stroking chilliness, Wire add a warm, valve-amp and buttered-scone vibe to their music. Yummy.

🎵 PLAYLIST: WIRE

Far too brainy to fit the punk-rock stereotype, Wire were consummate art-punks whose two-minute masterpieces resulted in hours of chin-stroking deliberations among the fans.

1. 12XU
from **PINK FLAG (Pink Flag Records, 2006)**

2. FEELING CALLED LOVE
from **PINK FLAG (Pink Flag Records, 2006)**

3. I AM THE FLY
from **CHAIRS MISSING (Pink Flag Records, 2006)**

4. I FEEL MYSTERIOUS TODAY
from **CHAIRS MISSING (Pink Flag Records, 2006)**

5. LOWDOWN
from **PINK FLAG (Pink Flag Records, 2006)**

6. BEING SUCKED IN AGAIN
from **CHAIRS MISSING (Pink Flag Records, 2006)**

7. PINK FLAG
from **PINK FLAG (Pink Flag Records, 2006)**9.

8. THREE GIRL RHUMBA
from **PINK FLAG (Pink Flag Records, 2006)**

9. ONCE IS ENOUGH
from **154 (Pink Flag Records, 2006)**

10. TWO PEOPLE IN A ROOM
from **154 (Pink Flag Records, 2006)**

Named for the number of gigs they'd played at time, you get fourteen tracks for your money, but one of them glows with pride under the title "Map Ref 41 Degrees N 93 Degrees W".

JAH WOBBLE

Born Whitechapel, London, 1957; still wobbling.

"The gunslinger with the fastest, meanest bass on the block."

Sounds

John Wardle (bass/vocals/loads of other instruments) knew John Lydon and John Ritchie from way back before punk. A whirlpool of nicknaming based on personality, character traits and tastes both musical and pharmaceutical gave the world **Jah Wobble**, Johnny Rotten and Sid Vicious respectively, three pseudonymous musketeers on London's early punk scene. Wob picked up the bass that had been purchased for Sid, learned the basics like everyone else – by jamming along with his favourite records – and despite losing out on a chance to replace Glen Matlock when he was squeezed out of the Sex Pistols, he found himself very conveniently placed and skilled enough to be part of the gang when Rotten switched back to Lydon and formed **Public Image Ltd.**

Wob's nickname was very obviously based partly on his taste for the rawest dub reggae that he could lay his hands on: other bands on the scene claimed to love the rebel music, but nobody had vinyl like he did. The "Wobble" came apparently from the trouble he had staying upright during his earliest, chemically assisted attempts to master the bass, but despite playing propped up in a comfy armchair for the first **PiL** TV appearance (on BBC's *Old Grey Whistle Test*), there was no one on the scene to match him for skill, precision and that elusive but instinctive and vital understanding of what bass means to a rock'n'roll band.

His contribution to the initial ethos of PiL and to the band's first two albums was immeasurable. Learning fast, he scared the pose out of his bandmates by using a particularly menacing stare, and

progressed from simply following Keith Levene's guitar lines on *Pil: First Edition* to completely dominating the rhythmic message of *Metal Box: Second Edition*. In the space of a few months he turned from disciple to maestro, giving the punk genre some "serious" musical credibility when, post-Pistols, it was in danger of becoming nothing more than a series of novelty records. As part of the all-for-one creative team, Wobble was instrumental in laying out the boundaries of what would later be called "post-punk", setting the template for experimentation and drawing up the guidelines for the festival of neo-sonic extreme music that characterized the 1980s.

Wobble quit PiL in 1980 after musical differences with both Lydon and Levene, and began a jagged solo career of records best described as "challenging" or "interesting". The prevailing gloom of his outlook and undeniably awful singing voice was punctuated by sporadic bursts of incredible brilliance and his ever-present unbelievable bass work. High points include his work with Can's Holger Czukay and Jaki Liebezeit, some of his excursions into "world music" and his remarkable decision to take a regular job on the London Underground and drop completely out of sight.

It took a few years of regular pay cheques and irregular shift work before he was ready to get back to music (he still works on the Tube when he's not on tour or in the studio). *Without Judgement,* the first recording by **Jah Wobble's Invaders Of The Heart** (mainly the work of JW plus guitarist **Justin Adams**) didn't appear until 1989. Warner grew interested enough to offer a deal, with *Rising Above Bedlam* appearing in 1991. The critics lapped it up, with the serious newspapers struggling to outdo one another with the plaudits: when *The Guardian* called his work "a great example of exceptionally creative music that can stand on its own feet without the aid of fancy clothes", *The Daily Telegraph* escalated and hit back with: "Amid this catalogue of decline and decay in modern music, Jah Wobble shines like a beacon of integrity and hope." Only a fool would argue with such heavy-hitting publications, and the music that so entranced them was undeniably great stuff. However, nobody could claim it was punk rock.

JW's financial career highlight was probably the "Visions of You" single, which took him and Sinead O'Connor into the charts in 1991; his artistic zenith, perhaps *The Inspiration Of William*

Part II.

Blake (1996). Since 1997, he has released all his work on his own label, 30 Hertz.

Wobble's collaborations continue to be riveting, juxtaposing musicians, genres and styles with the gleeful abandon of a Dadaist arranging for an umbrella to encounter a sewing machine on an operating table, but once a musician has been called "avant-garde" and turned up in the same sentence as Stockhausen, it's difficult to retain any kind of punk veneer. To his credit however, Jah Wobble has been cheerily indifferent to any of the labels hung around his neck since he left PiL, and just gets on with his own thing, staying true to punk's DIY ethos and to its spirit of "if you don't like it, then fuck off".

⊙ **I Could Have Been A Contender** (Trojan, 2004)

Marvellous three-CD box set all about the greatest living Englishman. A bargain at twice the price. Includes enough jet-engine bass frequencies to shake your teeth loose, blow speakers and possibly demolish nearby sheds. Beware of turning it up too loud.

WRECKLESS ERIC

Born Eric Goulden in Newhaven, England; wreckless since 1976.

It took the combined magic of Stiff Records' A&R people and the punk scene's willingness to accept the "differently talented" to make a star

Wreckless Doreen's boy Eric (born Goulden).

of **Wreckless Eric**, a frequently inebriated unpredictable curmudgeon of a man who couldn't sing, didn't care, and would have gleefully abused your stupidity in buying a ticket if you'd been rash enough to offer criticism from the crowd.

Eric's yearning for the stage was no doubt born before he began clambering unannounced to the microphone at the early punk gigs he attended, but it was there, in the fierce arena of beer-fuelled quips and outright insult, that he learned his craft. To preserve his skin and in tribute to his sheer drunken bravado, Nick "Basher" Lowe and Stiff came to his rescue, recording "Whole Wide World" b/w "Semaphore Signals" (with Lowe playing most of the instruments in his usual desire to "bash this one out and get on" to the next slice of amusement) and sending him out on tour as part of the Live Stiffs package. "Whole Wide World" was based on a riff of such Troggs-like simplicity that Eric should, if there were any justice, have been granted an annual stipend from the Musicians Union as its creator.

Alcohol had already revealed Eric's inner artiste, now it ripped the mask off Eric the tour-bus entertainer; legends of unbridled weirdness on the road and life-threatening stupidity backstage threatened to drown out the reportage of the music. Forgetting most of the actual performances while or immediately after they happened, Eric loved touring and couldn't wait to get back on the bus for the second label tour later that year.

"Take the Cash (K.A.S.H.)" kept the Wreckless brand in the public eye but it was the joyous amateurism and surprisingly well-constructed songs that propelled him through *Wreckless Eric* (1978) and into *The Wonderful World Of...* (1979). Usually comprising little more than three chords and a winning smile, Eric's tunes had an unmistakeable shambolic glory and instant appeal: no matter how many times you heard him strain for a high note, you never stopped willing him to make it.

He had an appalling 1980s and 1990s – when his career hit the skids, he hit the bottle, fell out of love with Stiff and for a while, quit music entirely. His mid-1980s mob, **Captains Of Industry**, were entertaining enough, but the people came to see Wreckless, and after a while as **The Len Bright Combo**, the old persona was revived and rehearsed. After successful flight trials in France (where the Goulden household had relocated), Wreckless took to the skies again, issuing a suitably ramshackle autobiography, *A Dysfunctional Success* in 2003. Still touring and recording – Wreckless Eric's most notable recent outing was performing "Clever Trevor", a song generally accepted to have been written with him in mind, on the album of tributes *Brand New Boots And Panties* (Gold Circle, 2001), which – with the exception of Robbie Williams' version of "Sweet Gene Vincent" adding insult to Ian Dury – was a worthwhile compilation.

⊙ Greatest Stiffs (Metro, 2001)

If you really feel you need an entire album's worth of Wreckless, then this is the current best-selling compilation. As the title says, it has all the greatest stiffs you'd be looking for, sung badly but with an amazing backing band of otherwise respectable fans of our greatest eccentric.

X Y Z

X

Formed Los Angeles, 1977; still around.

Punk rock rolled across the USA and finally bounced off the West Coast, having picked up some dents and bruises on the way. The beaten-up version that ended up in LA gave us X, the only punk band with its roots in a poetry workshop.

Exene Cervenka (vocals) had originally rolled in from Florida. She met Baltimore native **John Doe** (bass/vocals) under the strip-light intensity of a Venice reading; love burst through the door and the sonnets went out of the window. Realizing there was way more fun to be had thrashing around on stage, screaming out your heart, soul and spleen, than there was in reciting tales of child abuse or the glory of the working man to an audience wearing shades, accompanied by a beret-wearing bongo player, they decided their own late-period bohemian decadence was just punk-rock nihilism under a new and different label, and hurled themselves headlong onto the bandwagon. The couple were fortunate enough to locate **D.J. Bonebrake** (drums) before anyone else snapped him up, and leased a lifetime's worth of street credibility in **Billy Zoom** (guitar) – a vintage rockabilly rebel, part wildman, seven-tenths outlaw and probably with hoodlum tendencies too – and X was born.

By the time Ray Manzarek (ex-Doors) roped them together and herded their collectively nihilistic asses into the studio, they had matured into a razor-sharp, crowd-baiting snakepit of venomous attitude, seasoned by years of working the clubs and living the late-night life of the professional rocker. They were hardcore to the bone and able to shake off any sneers they might have attracted for hooking up with such a prime old hippy as Manzarek, particularly when *Los Angeles* (1980) hit the streets. The album roared out of the stores, painting an accurate if unpleasantly detailed portrait of what the band had been doing, how they felt about it afterwards and the long-term side effects, if any. Standout tracks such as "Sex And Dying In High Society", "The World's A Mess; It's In My Kiss" and the nasty tale of sex crime "Johnny Hit And Run Pauline" illuminated the hidden underbelly of the city of fun, and shone a torch on all the dirty little angels that end up there.

Manzarek was at the controls again for *Wild Gift* (1981) – another slice of artsy hardcore – and managed to stay on board for *Under The Big Black Sun*, the 1982 release that saw Doe and Exene unleashing their inner beatnik and writing a set that strained to go in too many directions at once. With influences as diverse as high-plains country whining and the most poisonous of heavy metal glaring out of the music – often uncomfortably piled on top of one another in the same song – the set bizarrely attracted a wider audience, and set X on the path to more mainstream rock'n'roll success. Who would have thought it, eh?

As time passed, fashions changed, and X moved away from beating on their sociopolitical soapbox. Doe and Cervenka got married and worked on side projects outside the band (Cervenka hooked up with Lydia Lunch at one point – truly a meeting of great minds, though probably a bit noisy) before returning with *More Fun In The New World* (1983), an album that saw X jump two-footed into the folk camp. Despite such fantastic songs as "Make The Music Go Bang" and "I Must Not Think Bad Thoughts", the band were already orbiting planet bland. When *Ain't Love Grand* (1986) turned out to be a straightforward rock album, Zoom quit, and few would blame him.

Bonebrake, Doe and Cervenka continued for a while, and in fact X has never officially disbanded. Since the demise of the original line-up however, none of the numerous individual or group projects has been of any punk-rock interest, even the 1998 reunion which saw Zoom back in the band.

⦿ Los Angeles (Rhino, 2001)

Easily the band's best, this album boasts "Johnny Hit And Run Pauline", "Nausea" and "The Unheard Music", among others. This Rhino reissue comes with a fistfull of early demos, which should keep the completists in the audience happy.

X-RAY SPEX
Radiated the London scene 1977–79

"SOME PEOPLE THINK LITTLE GIRLS SHOULD BE SEEN AND NOT HEARD...BUT I THINK 'OH BONDAGE! UP YOURS!'...1-2-3-4!"

With that magnificent, instantly iconic opening line, **Poly Styrene** (vocals, born Marion Elliot) led **X-Ray Spex** from nowhere straight up to the front of the punk rock pack; boasting a "fuck you!" rebellious attitude, a hint of sexual perviness, and some fine high toned feminism, all it lacked was a cuss word to be the perfect encapsulation of everything punk originally stood for.

Still, appearing for the first time on the *Live At The Roxy London WC2* compilation showed that the band was on the scene early enough to help shape it, and before it had even thought about congealing into uniformity. Together with **Lora Logic** (saxophone, and previously known as Susan Whitby, Marion's mate from school), she placed an ad in the *NME* and *Melody Maker* crying out for "Young Punx Who Want To Stick It Together". Hiring **Jak Airport** (easy guitar, otherwise Jack Stafford), **Paul Dean** (bass, confidence boost-

ing influence) and **B.P. Hurding** (dreadnought drummer) on the grounds they were "talented and cute", Poly introduced the band to her candy-coloured, twisted visions of an ersatz, fluorescent world, herding them through a good half-dozen rehearsals before letting them loose on a paying audience.

The band's debut – at The Roxy – came just weeks after Poly's illumination at a **Sex Pistols** gig. Marion's alter ego had dealt for as long as she could remember with bone-headed comments on her mixed-race ancestry (dad was displaced, by some considerable distance, from his home in Somalia, Mum was from Hastings, England); she'd also sold her own designs from the Poly Styrene stall in London's Beaufort Market to a trend-obsessed public and had before that served time behind the counter in Woolworths, so appearing at London's most fashionable venue, in front of a bunch of rowdy, aggressive kids, wired to the gills on speed and cans of warm Breaker Malt Liquor, was a stroll in the park by comparison. The appearance led first to a residency at *The Man In The Moon* – a pub on the Kings Road in Chelsea, a few doors away from the market and Malcolm McLaren's den, Seditionaries, then to a UK tour. Being so close to the centre of the maelstrom helped the band return to the Roxy, sign to EMI and appear on TV – though having two young women sing about the joys of bondage, wearing tight plastic clothing (as the rumours and cloth-eared older generation of journalists would have it) didn't do the band much harm either.

For a while, X-Ray Spex could do nothing wrong: a set of blistering, loveable, funny, positive and dance-tastic singles – "Oh Bondage! Up Yours!", "The Day The World Turned Day-Glo", "Identity" and "Germfree Adolescents" – took the band through till 1978, picking up fans like a nylon shirt collects dandruff. Poly's songs were clever, cheery, inspirational chips of boiled-sweet sparkle, bellowed out with little regard for melody, above the delicious thrash of the London scene's most enthusiastic musical gang. Even though Lora quit the band before the album appeared (returning to the real world for a while to finish school, then forming her own outfit **Essential Logic**), her replacement **Rudi Thompson** (Sax appeal and Bubble gum fun according to Poly's site, also known as Steve Thompson) fitted right in, and had a few more technical chops to contribute. The recording of the album was progressing without

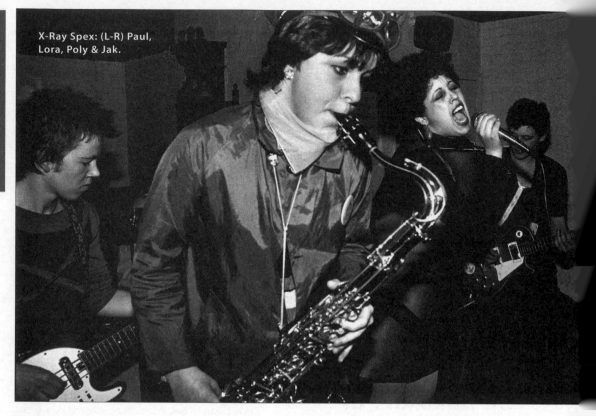

X-Ray Spex: (L-R) Paul, Lora, Poly & Jak.

any major hitches and things were looking good.

Dancing, yelping, squealing and having to hold on her hat with both hands to prevent sheer *joie de vivre* blowing it off her head and through the roof, Poly Styrene's live performances were inspired and inspirational, convincing a swathe of the audience to change from girl-consumers into empowered-female-producers, making a riotous noise of their own. Off stage however, Poly was a reluctant star. Deeply shy, she found that the band gave her support, and somewhere to hide when tired of confronting her demons but, like Lora had, she found some aspects of stardom intolerable. Songs such as "I Can't Do Anything" and "I Live Off You" might not have been autobiographical, but they revealed a sensitive, thoughtful side and hinted at the vulnerability any new band will feel when fired like a flashbulb into the public's face.

X-Ray Spex stole the show at London's famous Victoria Park Concert in 1978, doing more for the cause of Rock Against Racism in a 30-minute celebration of the punk-rock ethos than any number of highbrow lectures or lowbrow pamphlets could ever dream of achieving. As the year came to an end, *Germfree Adolescents* appeared in the shops, selling well in the run up to Christmas, ecstatically received by the music press, and receiving sufficient promotional push from the label to make it to the mainstream papers.

Early in the new year however, the wheels came off and the band crashed in a cloud of dust. "Age" did well enough on release but management shenanigans (as detailed in Poly's website biography), personnel changes (in the shape of **John Gun** – who appeared when B.P. left unexpectedly), road-weariness and an increasing disgust with the whole goddamn business (which had left her broke after so much hard work) were enough, when placed alongside her increasing spiritual interests, to convince Poly to put the band on hold.

John formed **The Living Legend**, B.P. was already part of **Classix Nouveau**, and the other two gigged for a while as **Airport & Dean**. Poly couldn't keep away from music completely either, and started the eighties by issuing *Translucence* (Reissued by Receiver, 1990) – a nu-jazz / electronic meditation of an album with a beauty that however has nothing to do with punk rock. She stayed away then until 1986's *God's And Goddesses* EP, disappearing again until a short and under-publicized stint spent in **The Dream Academy**.

The original line-up of X-Ray Spex re-formed for a moment in the mid 90s, releasing *Conscious Consumer* (1995) to enthusiastic reviews and appearing for one momentous night at London's Brixton Academy. Enter the London emergency services, stage left, in the shape of a fire engine that went unnoticed as Poly crossed the road. In the collision she broke her pelvis and all plans were put on hold until she recovered. Although Poly's now back on her feet, there has been no further mention of putting the band back on the road.

⊚ Germfree Adolescents (Castle, 2005)

Crammed from beginning to end with a wild, soap-scented, glee that celebrates the pure weirdness of a society that could think up plastic flowers, and now expanded to a massively welcome 23 tracks in length, there is still not a single bad tune on the album – tackling subjects from male oppression to the bizarre repulsive attractions to be found at the fringes of western civilization.

ICONIC SINGLE:
OH BONDAGE! UP YOURS!
(VIRGIN, 1978)

Iconic single from the dawn of Britpunk. A live version appeared on the seminal *Live At The Roxy London WC2* album, which – bolstered by the band's incendiary appearance on Sunday lunchtime I V – won them the deal with Virgin. X-Ray Spex were among the sharpest knives in punk's kitchen drawer, and knew exactly what they were doing when aiming this poison dart at the top of the charts. Chunky guitar, a sax blown so hard it had to be full of lung fragments by the end of the take and the divine Poly doing her full-throttle vocal roar, pipes and valves all wide open. Beautiful

XTC
Formed Swindon, England, 1975; still spotted thirty ecstatic years later.

Roped into the New Wave rush when their *3D EP* – a four-track sampler released in late 1977 with a migraine-inducing colour-separated 3D cover – was picked up by John Peel and DJs in the punk clubs, XTC must have looked back wistfully to their Wiltshire homes and wondered what was happening to them.

Andy Partridge (vocals/guitar) and **Colin Moulding** (bass/vocals) had been **Star Park**, writing songs since 1975, when news of New York's New Wave explosion first troubled the rural idyll. Together with **Barry Andrews** (keyboards) and **Terry Chambers** (drums), they renamed themselves as **The Helium Kidz**, a tribute to the early Tom Verlaine/Richard Hell outfit **The Neon Boys**) and a vehicle for the unusually spiky, angular guitar pop they found themselves creating.

The guys' first full-length album *White Music* (1978) was crammed with prime cuts of inquisitive, self-conscious classic pop, too dense to be fully appreciated in a single sitting. Twitching like the tortured pop of Talking Heads but as serenely English as spinsters playing cricket while sipping pints of warm beer on their bicycles, XTC's first set had a mixed reception from critics and record buyers alike. While the music was undoubtedly of the New Wave and certainly pushed out the boundaries, it dealt with subjects that never occurred to the hard-edged urban street-rockers.

XTC could write sensitive lyrics about sensible themes, and were equally comfortable producing psychedelia – either was sufficient to attract the odd glance from the purists, and both together drove some of the pinheads into a frenzy. Apart from receiving the odd unprovoked punch on the streets of his hometown, Partridge, who as front man took most of the flak, pressed on regardless down the path he had chosen and defied anyone to knock him off course – paradoxically, a classic punk attitude. *White Music* took the band to the lower reaches of the Top 40 and saw them on their way to the toppermost of the poppermost.

Go2 (1978) laid off the jerkiness and leant back into both groove and melody. The set still bubbled and rippled with sheer musical delight, and the tunes simply glistened with unique pop hooks.

▣ PLAYLIST: XTC

XTC progressed rapidly away from the basic, spiky and angular punk after their first albums but, full of vim and vinegar at the start of their career, they were deliciously abrasive.

1. COMPILCATED GAME
from **DRUMS AND WIRES (Virgin, 2001)**

2. CROSSWIRES
from **WHITE MUSIC (Virgin, 2001)**

3. DAY IN DAY OUT
from **DRUMS AND WIRES (VIrgin, 2001)**

4. I'M BUGGED
from **WHITE MUSIC (Virgin, 2001)**

5. MAKING PLANS FOR NIGEL
from **DRUMS AND WIRES (Virgin, 2001)**

6. NEON SHUFFLE
from **WHITE MUSIC (Virgin, 2001)**

7. RADIOS IN MOTION
from **WHITE MUSIC (Virgin, 2001)**

8. SCIENCE FRICTION
from **WHITE MUSIC (Virgin, 2001)**

9. STATUE OF LIBERTY
from **WHITE MUSIC (Virgin, 2001)**

10. THIS IS POP
from **WHITE MUSIC (Virgin, 2001)**

The press signed up in support, and with new renaissance man **Dave Gregory** (guitar/keyboards/vocals) replacing Andrews, it was a primrose path they followed into the studio, where superproducer Steve Lillywhite helped them mould *Drums And Wires* (1979). Despite giving the band its first mainstream chart success ("Making Plans For Nigel"), it saw them wave goodbye to the New Wave and return to creating the classic,

gently ironic, witty pop they had always been best at. By comparison with the earlier stuff, *Black Sea* (1980) was a package of hits, yielding "Generals And Majors" and "Sgt. Rock (Is Going To Help Me)" as well as less military items.

Things couldn't have been more promising for the band, but they threw it all away. A lengthy world tour led to musical differences of epic proportions, with Partridge losing the plot big time in 1982 and picking up the world's nastiest case of stage fright. The tour collapsed and momentum fell away. XTC have been with us in one form or another ever since, with Partridge, usually with Moulding (and whoever else happens to be around) issuing some excellent and interesting recordings. Always worth a listen, and meriting the band's enduring cult following, but nothing like their first and best work.

◉ ICONIC SINGLE:
3D EP (VIRGIN, 1977)

One of the most blistering of all the skin-bubbling New Wave debut recordings, the 3D EP blasted out of the mean streets of Swindon and into the hearts of anyone with an ear for the quirkily magnificent, the delightfully off-centre and the joyously twisted left-field. Featuring "Science Friction", "Radios in Motion" and their very first jaw-dropping epic, "This Is Pop", this was an essential purchase on release. All three tracks are now included in the *White Music* reissue.

◉ White Music (Virgin, 2001)

Ultimately a fierce, even anthemic album, *White Music* creates a first impression that's all adolescent bluster. Jerky half-ashamed solos and stuttering rhythms kick off most of the songs, and the production reeks of half-empty youth-club rehearsals performed in red-faced embarrassment for a sniggering crowd of unapproachably cool kids. Andy's voice is lent a stadium-filling boom through studio wizardry and several strong cups of hot tea however, and taken as a complete set, it remains one of the most important albums of the early UK scene.

◉ Drums & Wires (Virgin, 2001)

Remastered and expanded by three tracks from the twelve that made up the original, *Drums And Wires* was XTC's farewell to punk. Its maturity encapsulated in the highlight "Making Plans For Nigel", it points out the witty, eccentric best-of-British direction that Andy would take in future. His wistful, pointy-sharp lyrics – that sum up the New Wave's no-nonsense approach to life – would in future be wrapped in more delicate, cleverly constructed tunes.

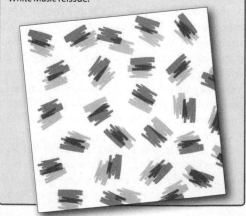

YEAH YEAH YEAHS

Formed New York City, 2000.

In the same way that **Blondie**'s magic came not exclusively from the photogenic soft-focus charms of Debbie Harry, there's more to **The Yeah Yeah Yeahs** than **Karen O** (vocals) and a great band name. Karen was originally from New Jersey but studying out of state in Ohio. She met **Nicolas Zinner** (guitar) when she left her college for the big bad city. In need of somebody to beat the skins, she phoned back to Ohio (the geography lesson ends here) for an old college buddy, **Brian Chase** (drums), and set about reinventing punk rock for the twenty-first century.

They were perfectly placed for the NYC scene's rediscovery of skinny-tied white-boy guitar rock, and wowed their way into support slots for The Strokes and Detroit's White Stripes on the strength of the fierce wild fan-base they were collecting. By the end of 2001 they'd formed a label, Shifty, and released the *Yeah Yeah Yeahs* EP.

Apparently incapable of putting a foot wrong, the band sold their souls to the hype machine, gritted their teeth and held on. In a few short months they went from local heroes to nationwide talking point, touring the States with Girls Vs Boys, and internationally (with the Jon Spencer Blues Explosion) after killing the competition stone dead at the 2002 South By South West festival.

When they finally came to the UK to headline, the music journalists were a slavering mass, barely staying ahead of Karen's audience of fetishistic and googly-eyed grrrl devotees. It's amazing the frenzy that a few months of eyeliner and knicker-flashing, spiced up with some shock-tactic vocabulary, can whip up.

The Pretenders' Chrissie Hynde never sang anything as direct as "As a fuck, son, you suck!" perhaps, but that isn't to say she never thought it. Hole's Courtney Love was just as fierce as Karen but just too Hollywood to take seriously, Polly Harvey had the vocabulary but just seemed too opposed to any

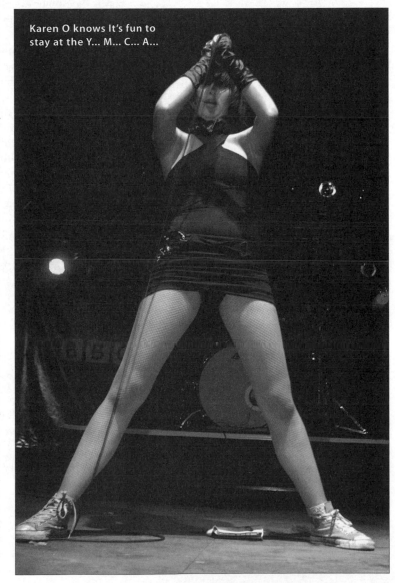

Karen O knows It's fun to stay at the Y... M... C... A...

kind of good times. For a generation starving for heroines, Karen O was a three-course meal in herself and when *Fever To Tell* appeared in the spring of 2003, it drew favourable comparisons with all those early girl-fronted New Wave acts.

It helps of course that the music they make is good honest rock'n'roll delivered with a perfectly manufactured sneer, but only time will decide if they're the next real big thing or just another falsely messianic flash in the pan.

⊚ Yeah Yeah Yeahs EP (Wichita, 2005)

The band's stunning 2001 debut release is still available and an essential for anybody who loves kick-ass girl-fronted punk-rock noise. With "Bang" and "Mystery Girl" backed up with "Art Star", "Miles Away" and "Our Time", this is a five-card trick that beats any other hand.

⊚ Fever To Tell (Polydor, 2003)

Hyped to the max by the label, the band's first album hurtled up the charts. For once however, the promo machine was boosting a product worth the repeated attention of those who blindly bought it. Highlights such as "Date With The Night" and "Y Control" were set out as singles so full of hooks it's no surprise they captured such a wide-ranging fan-base.

ZOUNDS

Formed, begad, in Oxford, England, 1977; endured, gadzooks, until 1983.

Steve Lake (bass/vocals) was an establishment-quelling anarcho-punk of the old school who had already skinned up in more squats than you've had hot dinners by 1977. Not that it seemed to lighten his mood at all: **Zounds**, the band he founded with **Steve Burch** (guitar), and **Jimmy Lacey** (drums) had an even more pessimistic outlook than their label mates and anarcho-syndicalist fellow travellers **Crass**. Adding **Nick Godwin** (more guitar) turned them into the most doom-drenched quartet on the mud-bedraggled free-festival circuit but it was all too much fun for Burch, and he headed for somewhere darker, replaced as main six-stringer-slinger by **Lawrence Wood** (guitar). Lacey also went missing and was replaced by **Josef Porter**.

Far too steeped in the ethics of punk and given to messing with people's heads as a matter of course, Zounds mixed up their four-to-the-floor basic punk business with hints of ragged *kosmische* music from the back-end cities of industrial Germany, and inevitably, eventually hooked up with Crass, the superstars of anarcho-punk, who had money to burn and commitment to spare.

Crass offered these new "discoveries" the opportunity to record, and provided Penny Rimbaud to produce their debut release "Can't Cheat Karma" b/w "War Subvert". The Crass brand helped the single sell, as did some very circumspect radio airplay by late-night establishment DJs, and Rough Trade were brought in to handle "Demystification" on its release in 1981.

The band stayed with Britain's indiest recording company for *Curse Of The Zounds*, in 1982. Although jammed to the gunnels with portentous threats of nuclear doom, police brutality and worse, it came stained with the label "anarcho-punk" which meant that only the most unapproachable and unappealing of punk audiences ever took the time to listen to it. Calling on Clash-collaborator Mikey Dread to inject some roots credibility and even perhaps a trace of fun into the mix, Zounds released "Dancin'" b/w "More Trouble Coming Every Day" before sinking back into the now floundering free-festival circuit in a confusion of last-minute personnel changes.

La Vache Qui Rit, a 1983 EP, was Zounds' swansong. In 1998, Steve Lake put together a kind of Zounds for a one-off event, and cut a benefit single, "This Land", in support of the McLibel Defence Fund with bassist Protag (bass, ex-Blyth Power) and Stick (drums, also of Extreme Noise Terror). It sold half a dozen copies to friends and family, and then he went back to his day job, applying termites to the foundations of society.

⊚ The Curse Of Zounds (Broken Rekids, 2001)

The band's only full-length recording and something akin to the Dead Sea Scrolls of anarchist/punk rock. Not afraid to put a little theory in among the slogans, this is intelligent music with lyrics worth a listen and a moment or two's consideration. Oh yeah, and it rocks like a motherfucker.

Part Three

Punkology

Part Three
Punkology

Punk's not dead – though it has largely returned to the underground lair it sprang from briefly in the late 70s. As for the mainstream, the internationally branded, so-called punk bands that clutter the charts today may have been blanded-out by the marketing departments but they receive so much of the limited media attention devoted to punk that the real deal is more difficult to track down.

Yet there is a growing archive of practical information and musical inspiration to refer to – band films, documentaries, TV biographies have been re-issued as DVDs, accompanied by uncountable official and unauthorised websites where facts, advice and help are shuffling up alongside gossip, rumours and lies. Add in this the hundreds of books and websites to be tracked down and you have a formidable set of resources to hand. This section will help you find what you need.

Punk Transmissions

TV Punk

TV's taste for the current (despite its reputation for showing little except repeats) means there's no regular slot featuring spiky-headed ravers of the original punk years on the broadcast networks in Europe or the USA, although **Johnny Rotten**'s recent reinvention as "game for a laugh" Uncle Punky in *I'm A Celebrity Get Me Out Of Here* sent a shiver down many spines. Fortunately Johnny proved far too reluctant to play ball to be offered a series of his own.

Punks on your screens these days are more likely to be animated airheads such as the odious **Bratz** – a tribe of animated youngsters whose lives revolve around shopping in the malls, fashion-slamming those less cool than themselves and consuming, consuming, consuming. A fine example to set our pop kids. As another co-opting of a youth movement by the forces of darkness and global capitalism, its unsurprising, but sad nevertheless.

Public Access Punk

In the US, public access TV and the widespread availability of low-budget, free-to-view cable stations have allowed programmes such as Massachusetts' best-kept secret, *The Life We Lead* to blossom as an updated equivalent to the vintage fanzines of the 70s. The show is hosted by **Sean Huck** on BNN (Tuesdays at Midnight).

An ex-Kentuckian punk himself, Sean washed up in Boston, landing in the middle of the East Coast's liveliest scene where he found a ready-made network of dedicated kids keeping the ethos alive – supporting the local gig circuit, buying the T-shirts as well as the records and, of course, forming bands. Noting the lack of any decent TV coverage, Sean contacted BNN and talked himself into the job of punk reporter at large.

Sean's pro-quality equipment was generously and unwittingly loaned to him by the company where he worked by day, which meant he was capable of putting out shows with real production values. This show is well worth catching if you can.

The Young Ones

The Young Ones (1982–84) revolved around a student house from hell and remains a much missed BBC sitcom; the show also acted as a springboard for several comedians who were soon-to-become household names. Among those names was **Rik Mayall**, who played Rick – an idealist wannabe revolutionary, who'd have his mother prepare a packed lunch for him to take to the barricades should the glorious day ever come.

Mayall's comedy partner was **Adrian Edmondson**, who played Vyvyan, a more traditional punk stereotype – dumb to the point of being fearless and prepared to hammer metal studs into his forehead. Together, these two squabbled over and misruled the house they shared with **Nigel Planer** (Neil – token hippy and target of the entire household's venom), and **Christopher Ryan** (Mike – perma-student of nobody was ever sure which subject).

Alongside each episode's story, the quartet hosted exciting and unexpected punk bands as guests on the show, ranging from **Motorhead** and **The Damned**, through **John Otway** and **Madness**, to **Amazulu, Rip, Rig & Panic** and **Dexy's Midnight Runners** (who appeared in the bathroom performing "Jackie Wilson Said"). No attempt was ever made to explain the bands' showing up unannounced, mid-story, but with plots that included Vyvyan strik-

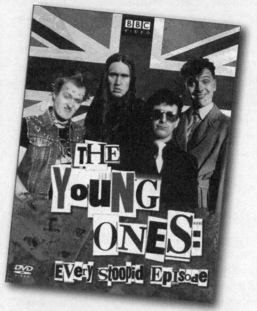

ing oil in the cellar, an atom bomb hitting the house, and Neil being forced to act as a human vacuum cleaner, nobody really cared or even noticed.

The Young Ones: Every Stoopid Episode is available on DVD from BBC VIDEO almost everywhere.

Even at the height of the punk craze at the end of the 1970s and through the 1980s, TV in Britain found it easier to make fun of the scene's fashion and idealism (see *The Young Ones* box above) or to pander to prevailing beliefs (a good example being Mary the Scottish punk from *Eastenders* – who squatted, boozed, prostituted and heroined her way to the nation's hearts) than to give it serious attention. There was the occasional oasis of hope, such as *Revolver*, with **Peter Cook** (see below), but they were few and far between.

⊞ Revolver Granada International, 1978,
Dir Chris Tookey, 7 x 30 min editions plus pilot

The only reason the average British punk left the pub before closing time on summer Fridays in 1978, this short-lived work of beauty was hosted by Peter Cook – playing essentially himself but supposedly portraying the embittered owner of a down-at-heel nightclub, scraping by with a roster of punk acts and an audience that should have shown more respect.

Across in the States, where the first flowerings of punk died out before they could take root in the public consciousness things were worse; aside from **Adam Ant**'s attempts to build an acting career for himself (he showed up in *The Equalizer* on US TV), the scene's only tribute came from the 1998 movie *SLC Punk!* (directed by **James Merendino**) – a dreadful production that follows the lives of two Salt Lake City punks.

TV coverage of punk music in the UK was pushed into the late night slots, and bands initially had to slip in between the dinosaur rockers customarily shown on old wave programmes, such as *The Old Grey Whistle Test* (BBC; 1971–87). When *The Tube* (Channel 4; 1982–87) and *SnubTV* (BBC 2; 1989–92) appeared in the 80s, the volume of alternative music coverage increased but the moment had undoubtedly passed.

Still, as network broadcasters have little time for punk rock, we should be thankful that the DVD never forgets. Live 'in concert' footage, documentaries, feature films and promo-video collections abound. But be careful; products on sale vary enormously in quality – from broadcast-standard to blatantly amateur concert clips.

The very few contemporary punk shows on the air concentrate, understandably, more on today's scene than on the past. Based almost exclusively in the USA on regional cable channels, until recently they could only reach a local audience. Thanks to the Web, however, punks worldwide can tune in and pick up on the newest bands and hear their hottest waxings at any time. Check *The Punk Show* out online:

⊡ **The Punk Show**
www.muchmusic.com/tv/thepunkshow

Shown live at 11pm US Eastern Time on Saturday nights and battering the eyes and ears for a full half hour, *The Punk Show* manages to squeeze in loads of ska, Oi! and hardcore alongside the best of the straight-ahead punk scene.

Internet Radio

Perhaps even more important, has been the growth of Internet radio stations and, more recently, Podcasting (where you subscribe to regular downloadable shows via an "aggregator" program such as iTunes). Here's a few Internet radio stations worth checking out online:

⊡ **Punk Radiocast www.punkradiocast.com**

Claiming to be "DJing the revolution" from Canada and playing a scintillating mix of old and new school punk from round the world.

⊡ **HussieSkunk www.hussieskunk.com**

If your boat gets floated by Bad Religion, At The Drive-In, Dropkick Murphys or D.O.A., then you need some *HussieSkunk* in your life.

⊡ **Punk FM UK www.punkfm.co.uk**

Dedicated to the music of 1976–79, live and updated regularly and an extremely useful resource for music hunters.

⊡ **TrashSurfinInternetRadio radio.trashsurfin.de**

Original punk, rock'n'roll, glam and garage coming to you from Germany playing stuff from the 60s up to today's stuff. "Our faves are artists like the Ramones, Dead Boys, Johnny Thunders, New York Dolls, Saints, Stooges etc. and bands that sound like them! So be prepared for the rock'n'roll fix of your life..."

Documentaries

TV's discovery of nostalgia as yet another way of force-feeding repackaged material to the audience has led to a bunch of more or less informative and exciting punk documentaries appearing on our screens and in stores. Here's our pick of the crop. Some of these will be available to track down on DVD, though many you are more-likely just to stumble across on terrestrial or cable channels at some silly time in the early hours.

⊡ **So It Goes ITV, 1976–77**

Hosted by Manchester's Machiavelli, Tony Wilson, *So It Goes* concentrated on new music, not all of it punk, and featured bands recorded without the distractions of an audience. Best remembered for the astounding and electric performance delivered by the Sex Pistols.

⊡ **TV Party Dir Danny Vinik, 2005, 91m**

A documentary about Glenn O'Brien's *TV Party*, the US public access TV show that ran from 1978-82. Applying punk rock's DIY ethos to the new medium of amateur telly, and hosting some of the great bands of the era, O'Brien's show – co-hosted by Chris Stein from Blondie – rapidly became the subject of legend. Vinik's documentary features some classic in-concert clips alongside some of the funniest punk interviews to make it through to the 21st century. On sale as a three-disc set (comprising the documentary and two episodes from the series) including interviews with Glenn O'Brien, Debbie Harry, Chris Stein and Arto Lindsay plus footage from the original show. Also featuring: David Byrne, James Chance, Mick Jones and Andy Warhol.

⊡ **The Punk Years Dir John Robb, 2002, 25 min**

Robb's well-intentioned documentary tries to compress everyone important into far too short a time. Currently unavailable to buy but appearing regularly on UK cable stations, it covers the MC5/Stooges era, through "Anarchy In The UK" and on to deal with the punks of today. Alongside the usual musical history section it includes some fascinating interview snippets, touching on the fanzine and fashion aspects of the movement although looking mainly at the music. Robb's accompanying book *Punk Rock: An Oral History* (Ebury, 2006) fleshes out the missing details.

⊡ **Punk: Attitude Dir Don Letts, 2005, 90 min**

Don Letts' career as a director owes much to his being on the scene right from the start. This movie trumped his earliest work – *The Punk Rock Movie* (1978) – and benefited from being produced after all the fuss had died down and by including more comment from the US punk crew. It pushes Letts' theory that punk has, to some extent, been a part of society forever, and a vital part of rock'n'roll for more than 50 years. The interview footage is worth the price of purchase; the live footage makes it an absolutely essential buy.

⊡ **The Decline Of Western Civilization**
Dir Penelope Spheeris, 1981, 100 min

Semi-verité documentary (post-production shenanigans regarding audience footage, nothing serious you Dogme freaks) on the LA scene at the start of the 80s. Includes prime performances by Black Flag, The Germs, X, Alice Bag Band, Circle Jerks, Catholic Discipline, and Fear.

⊡ **Urgh! A Music War**
Dir Derek Burbidge, 1981, 96 min

Hard to find and only sporadically in print, this movie looks at the punk / new wave scene, touching on both sides of the Atlantic. Almost forty tracks are featured, by artists including 999, Athletico Spizz 80, Au Pairs, Chelsea, John Cooper Clarke, The Cramps, Dead Kennedys, Devo, Echo & the Bunnymen, Gang of Four, Joan Jett and the Blackhearts, Magazine, The Members, Gary Numan, Oingo Boingo, John Otway, Pere Ubu, The Police, Splodgenessabounds, Steel Pulse, X and XTC.

Punk Movies

You can't beat a good rock'n'roll band movie; and if The Beatles could do it, why couldn't punk rockers? Well they did. All of these flicks should be very easy to find on both DVD and VHS; most also saw the release of accompanying soundtrack CDs that are also worth getting your hands on.

☑ Rock 'n' Roll High School
Dir Allan Arkush, 1979, 93 min

The Ramones movie. Though their acting is more wooden than anyone could imagine, and the plot that was already corny in the 1950s, it will take more than this (even with a cast of stereotypical jocks, nerds and babes) to detract from the band's blistering live stuff.

☑ Breaking Glass Dir Brian Gibson, 1980, 104 min

The Hazel O'Connor movie. This was an awful British attempt to do the "a star is born" plot in a punk rock setting. That said, with suitable lubrication, this is almost funny and has some very nostalgic "fashion" moments. File at the "New Romantic" end of punk.

☑ Rude Boy
Dir Jack Hazan & David Mingay, 1980, 133 min

The Clash movie. Badly acted by The Clash, with unconvincing performances from the remainder of the cast, this attempts to tell the story of a band moving into the big time. It portrays the troubles of one of their entourage and illustrates the great British decline all in one small film. The "in concert" footage, however, makes up for any amount of mock-cockney posing.

Sid & Nancy Flicks

☑ Sid And Nancy Dir Alex Cox, 1986

Director Cox does an interesting job of the Sid and Nancy "love story". Vicious is played by Gary Oldman who, as usual, steals the show (though it's hard not be distracted by the fact the actor has managed to reach an age that Sid never even came close to). Chloe Webb is Nancy Spungen and David Hayman pops up as Malcolm McLaren.

☑ D.O.A. Dir Lech Kowalski 1981

Hard-hitting documentary on the Sid Vicious & Nancy Spungen story with interesting if slurred comments from people on the scene at the time, such as Stiv Bators, Terry "tory crimes" Chimes and Paul Cook, plus tons of live performances from the London crew – including the Sex Pistols, the Rich Kids, X-Ray Spex, Sham 69 and Generation X.

☑ The Great Rock 'n' Roll Swindle
Dir Julien Temple, 1980, 103 min

The original Sex Pistols movie. With Glen Matlock airbrushed out of the story entirely and Johnny Rotten's contribution limited to concert footage and animated sequences, it's far from definitive, with accuracy even further out of sight. It's an interesting movie though, and gives an insight into the machinations of McLaren.

☑ The Filth And The Fury
Dir Julien Temple, 2000, 108 min

Again directed by Julien Temple, this is the other Sex Pistols movie. Rotten's side of the story muddies as many waters as it filters through – a great little flick nonetheless. As well as the expected interviews and gig clips, there are some fascinating rehearsal and recording studio scenes.

☑ 1991: The Year Punk Broke
Dir Dave Markey, 1992 , 99 min

The Sonic Youth movie, kinda, but it also boasts live performances and footage from the whole NYC/Seattle scene during the year prior to the release of *Nevermind*, when everything changed for one notable band featured in this ninety-minute film. Thurston Moore is frequently the centre of attention, however, and is clearly loving out, though the finest moments come when the Youth take to the stage.

Punk Websites

Broadband access and the affinity that rebellious spikey heads have with our silicon superiors have turned the Web into punk heaven.

As all you twenty-first-century cyberpunks are already more than likely aware, you can find official, semi-official, and downright hostile, copyright-ignoring amateurish tribute sites to all the bands and record labels we talk about out there on the Web simply by typing www.band-name.com into your browser or by Googling their skanky old asses. What you might not stumble across so easily though are excellent genre sites, such as Rockin' Rina's *Women of 70s Punk* (www.comnet.ca/~rina/) and superb online fanzines such as *Perfect Sound Forever* (www.furious.com/Perfect).

Music Sites

⊡ Blanktv www.blanktv.com

Blanktv hosts hundreds of online music videos, many of them of major interest to the punk-hungry web surfer. There's mayhem and mindless violence covering the whole punk epoch. Be warned however, this site does like its bad language and gratuitous sexual content, so don't cross the threshold if you are likely to be offended. As the site's own disclaimer says "If you're a right inconsiderate bastard and don't mind breaking your poor mother's heart, you should be at least eighteen years of age before entering such a den of iniquity".

⊡ InterPunk www.interpunk.com

Billing itself as "The Ultimate Punk Music Store", this is the place to go to find the music you love, whether that be punk, ska, hardcore or emo. As well as sounds you can loud up on badges, T-shirts, fanzines and DVDs.

⊡ MySpace www.myspace.com

You'll find musicians ancient and modern here, posting up their personal blogs as well as their newest musical works for public criticism (be nice to 'em). It's an amazing place to stumble across new sounds as you skip from artist to artist via the "Friends" network lists.

⊡ Punk Rock Videos www.punkrockvideos.com

A great source for live videos of punk bands. All the shows here can be ordered for $15.00 for 2 full hours of material – this means you can order up their entire catalogue of your favourite band and bolt on some material by complete unknowns at the end to fill up the space. In short, you pay by the hour, not per show. Everything here was shot in clubs around the world by fans, so quality can get dodgy at times but, hey, it beats MTV. They ship VHS tapes and DVDs to anywhere on the planet and take PayPal.

News Sites

⊡ PunkMusic Community www.punkmusic.com

Once you've battled your way past the confusing home page, this punk portal has some great content on offer. The list of bands covered is bewildering, with truck loads of biographies, gig listings and news. This is a great place to find links to the specific artist websites that don't always pop up with Google.

⊡ PunkNews.org www.punknews.org

This splendid site carries its own, bespoke-written content and with Earth-shattering stories covering both new releases by major artists, and personnel changes in the minor leagues. There are several sites like this out there,

and they all merit individual perusal for the local colour they offer. Also check out www.punknews.co.uk and www.punknews.com.

⊡ TruePunk www.truepunk.com

Chat, message boards, interviews, articles, reviews, contests, photos, news ... what more could you want from a kick ass punk rock website.

⊡ Wreck The Place www.wrecktheplace.com

Another solid news portal, bursting with reviews, gossip and the like. There's a worthwhile "Mixtape" section where you can sample some pretty obscure sounds via streaming MP3s, and click the "International" link for the low down on punk around the Globe ... Peruvian punk anyone?

History & Commentary

⊡ We Created It; Let's Take It Over!
www.inch.com/~jessamin

Jessamin Swearingen's excellently-crafted essays on the emergence of punk in the USA fill in many of the gaps still widespread in the accepted general history of the movement.

⊡ Punk 77 www.punk77.co.uk

This UK site features some great "punk explosion" interviews, pictures, essays and an in-depth potted history. There are loads of biographies, for acts from both sides of the Atlantic, and the site is regularly updated.

Punk Publishing

Youth cults, even noisy, raucous, boisterous ones such as punk rock, can be delicate and a bit like butterflies – wonderful to experience in their wild, natural state but of only morbid interest once gassed, pinned and mounted in a glass case. Punk in particular has been the subject of way too many academic studies, and university bookshelves drip with unwanted, unreadable analyses.

We've cut the academic bullshit to the bare minimum, while the tomes listed below all help in some way to convey the joyous, all-is-possible spirit of the punk age. Nothing beats having actually been there, back in the day, but the *New Musical Express* reprint of its classic punk coverage (*NME Originals, Volume 1 Issue 2*) does a pretty good job of summarizing the sordid, back stabbing, bitchy delights of the original UK scene, while *Please Kill Me* and the reprinted *Sniffin' Glue*, *Search And Destroy* and *PUNK* fanzines fill in a lot of the gaps.

The titles below are all worth attention but invest wisely – and remember, punk is something you do, not read about.

Essential History

England's Dreaming: Anarchy, Sex Pistols, Punk Rock, And Beyond
Jon Savage (Faber & Faber, 2005)

Volume One of the absolute must-have history books for anyone with an interest in the nuts and bolts of what happened and when. Refreshingly one-sided at times and concentrating on the Sex Pistols as icons symbolic of the whole punk movement, it nevertheless digresses enough to provide a fine wide-ranging overview.

Please Kill Me: The Uncensored Oral History of Punk Legs McNeil, Gillian McCain (Abacus, 1997)

Volume Two of punk's rise, decline and eventual fall comes from the sordid streets of 70s New York City. Legs and his tape machine crawled into a number of sewers, dive bars and sleazy record company offices to record this very funny, and remarkably detailed oral history.

The Boy Looked At Johnny: Obituary Of Rock and Roll Julie Burchill, Tony Parsons
(Pluto Press, 1977, reprinted Faber & Faber, 1987)

Third and final volume in the punk archive. This is a witty, biased, cutting, enthusiastic, soaking up some of the bullshit whilst never believing the hype, delightfully self-contradictory and very wrong here and there book, but still hands down the best punk read written by kids who were there at the time.

It Makes You Want To Spit: The Definitive Guide To Punk In Northern Ireland
Sean O'Neill (Reekus Music, 2003)

A well-observed and finely detailed focus on the one UK scene where the kids really had something to worry about.

Lipstick Traces: A Secret History Of The 20th Century Greil Marcus
(Faber & Faber, 2006)

Anything by Greil is worth reading (see below also) for the sheer quality of his prose. His successful blending of detail with anecdote means there's a rich, satisfying helping of information in every bite.

In The Fascist Bathroom: Punk In Pop Music, 1977–1992 Greil Marcus
(Thunder's Mouth Press, 2004)

Greil's sociological and political ruminations are as riveting as the musical journalism he wraps them in, and with this collection of re-worked pieces previously published in various US mags he gets to grips with the style, lyrics, tunes and cultural significance of the late 70s British invasion – looking at, among others, the Sex Pistols, The Clash, Elvis Costello, Gang Of Four, and The Mekons.

Make The Music Go Bang: The Early LA Punk Scene Don Snowden (Editor), Gary Leonard
(Saint Martin's Press, 1997)

Collected despatches from the extreme Western Front. As usual in US culture, everything loose in punk tended to roll down into Los Angeles sooner or later. This tells some of the more believable tales and a few that make the blood run backwards.

Psychotic Reactions And Carburetor Dung: The Work Of A Legendary Critic: Rock'n'roll As Literature And Literature As Rock'n'roll
Lester Bangs (Serpent's Tail, 2001)

If you've any interest in becoming a music journalist, philosopher or speed freak, you should start here. Lester swiped gonzo journalism from Hunter S. Thompson and applied it, magnificently, to music writing. From his mushy pen descended all the greatest 70s inky press hacks who made the *NME*, *Melody Maker* and the rest of them such essential reading.

Rip It Up And Start Again
Simon Reynolds (Faber & Faber, 2006)

Best of the recent essay-memoir collections to appear in the UK; it rounds up all the usual subjects and extending their tales into the dark British 80s. It's chock full o'nuts, but thanks to Simon, they've usually got something interesting to say.

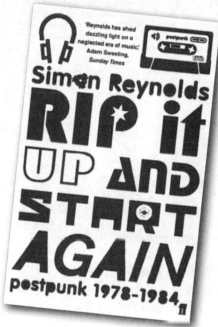

Sound Of The City
Charlie Gillett (Souvenir Press 1983)

Charlie's the godfather of so many new musical genres to achieve success in the UK that there should be a statue of him in the park and marches in his honour. As the world has yet to treat him as he deserves, we must rely instead on his incisive, fair-minded, warm-hearted intelligent criticism and commentary. This volume deals with punk, amongst other topics, and is a very highly recommended read.

From The Velvets To The Voidoids: A Pre-punk History For A Post-punk World (now re-subtitled "The Birth Of American Punk Rock") Clinton Heylin (Helter Skelter Publishing, 2005)

Clinton's another author yet to craft a rotten phrase and his skills at poking through the ordure to reveal the truffles deep inside goes unchallenged. This is a fine book of seedy content, based in NYC.

Punk: Loud, Young And Snotty – The Story Behind The Songs Steven Wells (Thunder's Mouth, 2004)

Anecdotes-a-go-go from "Swells" – UK punk's most consistently provocative writer. Boosted to epic status through the inclusion of Wells' own intelligent (and very funny) theorizing, this tome throws open doors, pulls back curtains and shines bright lights into dark corners of punk's best songs and most interesting characters.

We Owe You Nothing – Punk Planet: The Collected Interviews Daniel Sinker (Akashic, 2001)

Punk Planet was founded in 1994 and is still a major part of the new-school scene. Ready when necessary to refer to grizzled old heroes from back in the day, they manage to celebrate the past without adding so much nostalgia that the brew becomes undrinkable. With contributions from artists ranging from Sleater-Kinney and Kathleen Hanna to Jello Biafra, Noam Chomsky and Henry Rollins, it looks at punk rock as part of the broader punk / subversive / prankster underground.

Search and Destroy: Authoritative Guide To Punk Culture Vols. I & II
V. Vale (V/Search, 1996–1997)

Vicky's stuff was just perfect, and the reprinted memories here still jump out and grab you.

Sniffin' Glue: The Essential Punk Accessory
Mark Perry, et al (Sanctuary Publishing, 2000)

Not exactly piled high in the shops, even the largest bookselling river on the Internet takes 6 weeks or more to track this down, but for such a great read it's worth the wait. It represents the very beginning of punk rock journalism – kids writing about music made by kids for other kids on badly mimeographed, typewritten scraps of paper. Standing alongside the reprinted *Glues* – each presented on delightfully accurate lavatory-quality paper – Mark's reminiscences fill in a lot of behind-the-scenes details, dropping hints of gossip and shenanigans. Punk's amphetamine-powered, cranked up self-belief was never better represented than by these defiant pages.

Picture Books

Rock photography is always a pleasure, doubly so with punk; here's a selection of some of the best eye candy in the shop window.

Fanzine Reprints

The fanzine scene crystallizes the difference between early New York punk and the UK scene – NYC's *PUNK* magazine was packed with paid-for advertising from issue #1 and clung grimly onto its place at the newsstands until the punk crowd had disappeared, whereas *Sniffin' Glue* fretted about the morality of taking money from the establishment until the day it closed, after just 12 issues.

PUNK: The Original. A Collection Of Material From The First, Best, And Greatest Punk Zine Of All Time John Holmstrom, Editor (High Times Press, 1998)

PUNK was never frightened of sounding off about how great it was (in its own opinion) and, by hitching a ride on the spirit of the age as she fluttered by, the team involved had fun, got high, saw a shed-load of bands come and go and got paid for the experience.

And God Created Punk
Erica Echenberg, Mark P (Andre Deutsch, 1996)

With Erica on the photomachine and Mark supplying the words, this collection provides a fascinating mix of nostalgia, "oh-my-god!" fashion shots and head-spinning portraits of a bunch of today's heroes, back when they were younger and sillier.

Banned In D C: Photos And Anecdotes From The DC Punk Underground Cynthia Connolly, Leslie Clague (Sun Dog Propaganda, 1988)

Much the same as Mark 'n' Erica's book in its intent but with more tattoos on view, and covering the 1979–85 US east coast circuit.

Fuck You Heroes: Photographs, 1976–1991
Glen E. Friedman, et al
(Consafos Press, 1998)

The "Fuck You Heroes" title is a quote from one of Iggy's wilder on-stage declamations captured on tape and later released as the *Live At The Paris Hippodrome 1977* CD. Glenn was there. In fact, Glenn was pretty much everywhere with his camera and a pocket full of film. Magnificent, touching and revealing photography of a classy set of rock'n'punk icons.

Punk Girls

⊞ Cinderella's Big Score: Women Of The Punk And Indie Underground (Live Girls)
Maria Raha, Kim Gordon (Seal Press, 2004)

Top notch set of articles by and about the hardest-rocking women in showbiz.

⊞ Pretty In Punk: Girls' Gender Resistance In A Boys' Subculture
Lauraine Leblanc
(Rutgers University Press, 1999)

Expensive but intriguing, this book covers the female side of punk rock history and sets out ways to better living through punk rock and its attitude. Heavy and sociologically oriented, this is no bedside read.

⊞ Legends Of Punk: Photos From The Vault
Rikki Ercoli (Manic D Press, 2003)

Very good looking set of snaps, showing Sid Vicious, Johnny Rotten, Patti Smith, Blondie, The Ramones, The Clash, Misfits and Richard Hell (among others) hanging out in NYC, looking much too young to know about the subjects they dealt with in song.

⊞ Shockwave ("Punk Rock" in US edition)
Virginia Boston (Plexus, 1978)

A collection of more than 200 shots of the bands and audiences that made the earliest days of punk such a shock to the straight world and such a laugh to be part of. Collected and illustrated with fanzine clippings and quotes from those on the scene.

Arty Stuff

Graphic design and fashion have always been an important part of punk, not only because records need covers and the kids need T-shirts, badges and posters, but also as a powerful form of subversion and self-expression.

⊞ Up They Rise – The Incomplete Works Of Jamie Reid
Jamie Reid and Jon Savage
(Faber and Faber, 1987)

Hard to find "art book" for the coffee table with excellent prints padded out with incomprehensible text bashing out the theory behind the safety-pinnery.

⊞ Fucked Up + Photocopied: Instant Art of the Punk Rock Movement
Bryan Ray Turcotte (Editor), et al (Gingko Press, 2002)

Excellent compilation of the new school's take on the old-school punk style of photomontage. Heavily tilted towards our skateboarding brethren, it nonetheless shows that the inspiration and style hasn't been beaten out of them entirely, despite their repeatedly hitting their heads on the concrete.

⊞ Vivienne Westwood
Claire Wilcox (V&A Publications, 2005)

Originally published to coincide with a fab exhibition dedicated to the godmother of punk fashion, it was written with the co-operation of the lady herself. Covers the whole of her, still subversive, career.

⊞ Beneath The Paving Stones: Situationists And The Beach, May 1968
(AK Press, 2001)

The Situ link to Punk is well covered in *England's Dreaming*, but if you want a taste of the real thing check out these three influential Situationist pamphlets from the 60s. Still inspiring after all these years.

⊞ Dada: Art and Anti-Art
Hans Richter
(Thames & Hudson, 1966)

Some of the essays are heavy going, containing lethal levels of theoretical art-talk, but the history's done well, and the picture section is of the usual high-quality T&H standard; it falls out of the book when you open it, but that's Dada for you.

Biographies

⊞ New York Dolls: Too Much Too Soon
Nina Antonia (Omnibus, 2003)

Antonia has the Dolls / Thunders market pretty much sewn up for her exclusive use and can at least boast genuine friendly time spent with the characters she unveils for us in this sad and depressing biography. The boys had good times but they were much too short.

⊞ Poison Heart: Surviving The Ramones
Dee Dee Ramone, Veronica Kofman (Omnibus, 1997)

Although Dee Dee's sheer goofiness and stock of on-the-road / on-the-game / on-the-drugs anecdotes means there's a laugh on every page, it leaves an ultimately sad memory of a band that hated one another's guts but still played at being brudders for twenty years.

⊞ Sex Pistols
Fred and Judy Vermorel
(Omnibus 1987, Star Universal 1978)

Fascinating for having been written and published before the blood was dry on the band's final contract, Fred and Judy hung around the group and apparently got on everyone's nerves for months, researching the book they'd agreed with Malcolm. When they were finally ejected from the entourage there was no further reason to hide all the backstage filth and on the road bad behaviour.

⊞ Dead Kennedys: The Unauthorized Version
Marian Kester, F-Stop Fitzgerald (Last Gasp, 2004)

The actual biographical info isn't all that, but the fantastic photographic history included more than makes up for it.

⊞ Get In The Van: On The Road With Black Flag
Henry Rollins (2.13.61, 1996)

Funny, and at times scary, Rollins here proves to be a very accomplished writer and paints an unmissable picture of life on the road in an 80s hardcore outfit.

🔲 I, Shithead: A Life In Punk
Joey Keithley (Arsenal Pulp Press, 2003)

Also known as Joey Shithead, he founded legendary punk pioneers D.O.A. in 1978. Shouting out loud about his punk credentials and bringing in his own political point of view this is about as mean and snot-nosed an autobiography as you'll get.

🔲 Neighbourhood Threat: On Tour With Iggy Pop Alvin Gibbs (Codex, 2000)

Alvin's on-the-road memoir is a great, detailed and instructive account of life with the more modern, slightly more restrained Mr. Pop.

🔲 Iggy Pop: I Need More Iggy Pop (2.13.61, 1997)

Iggy's oral history is the best solo-artist work on the shelves simply because he has more incredible stories than anybody else in the music biz.

Reference Books

🔲 Punk Diary: 1970–1979
George Gimarc (St. Martin's Press, 1994)

🔲 Post Punk Diary: 1980–1982
George Gimarc (St. Martin's Press, 1997)

These two volumes each come with a CD of the tunes that were rocking America during the periods covered but, apart from that and the inclusion of some interesting newspaper clippings, they're for those whose interest extends beyond obsession and into compulsion, with day-by-day detail of who played where and which records came out when.

🔲 Up Yours!: A Guide To UK Punk, New Wave And Early Post Punk
Vernon Joynson (Borderline Productions, 2001)

Painfully and obsessively detailed, and beautifully printed on heavyweight shiny paper, this is a wrist-breaking read of interest mainly to the vinyl-collecting element of our readership.

Books About Sid

Kurt Cobain's posthumous publishing career of course dwarfs that of the greatest dumb'n'dead rock'n'roller of them all. Still, he was a good-looking cuss, and punk's first real icon.

🔲 The Sid Vicious Family Album
Anne Beverley (Virgin Books, 1980)

The best of the picture books.

🔲 And I Don't Want To Live This Life
Deborah Spungen (Corgi, 1984)

Interesting take on the whole sorry mess from Nancy's family's point of view

🔲 Sid And Nancy Alex Cox and Abbe Wool (Faber and Faber, 1986)

The book of the film of the life and death. Could this be considered as cashing in?

🔲 Sid's Way Keith Bateson and Alan Parker (Omnibus Press, 1998)

A good read, falling somewhere between biography and picture book.

🔲 Sid: Sid Vicious Rock'n'Roll Star
Malcolm Butt (Plexus, 1997)

All the filth and fury of Sid's early life presented in a way that suggests it might explain his descent into drugs and early death.

🔲 Vicious – Too Fast To Live...
Alan Parker (Creation Books, 2004)

Written in collaboration with Sid's mum, there's probably a word or two of truth in here somewhere.

Index

Welcome to the Index. As well as all the bands and key players, we've highlighted which entries have an accompanying playlist, while *Celebrity Playlists* are styled thus.